OXFORD COMMENTARIES ON INTERNATIONAL LAW

General Editors: *Professor Philip Alston*, Professor of International Law at New York University, and *Laurence Boisson de Chazournes*, Professor of Law at the University of Geneva

The United Nations Principles to Combat Impunity

The United Nations Principles to Combat Impunity

A Commentary

Edited by

FRANK HALDEMANN AND
THOMAS UNGER

Assistant Editor

VALENTINA CADELO

GENEVA ACADEMY
Académie de droit international humanitaire et de droits humains
Academy of International Humanitarian Law and Human Rights

OXFORD
UNIVERSITY PRESS

OXFORD
UNIVERSITY PRESS
Great Clarendon Street, Oxford, OX2 6DP,
United Kingdom

Oxford University Press is a department of the University of Oxford.
It furthers the University's objective of excellence in research, scholarship,
and education by publishing worldwide. Oxford is a registered trade mark of
Oxford University Press in the UK and in certain other countries

First Edition published in 2018

Impression: 1

Published in the United States of America by Oxford University Press
198 Madison Avenue, New York, NY 10016, United States of America

British Library Cataloguing in Publication Data
Data available

Library of Congress Control Number: Data Available

ISBN 978–0–19–874360–6

Printed and bound by
CPI Group (UK) Ltd, Croydon, CR0 4YY

Acknowledgements

The idea of this Commentary goes back several years. Its publication would not have been possible without the continuous commitment and help of many. Warm thanks are owed in particular to Paola Gaeta, Professor at the Graduate Institute of International and Development Studies, for her generous help and advice. Paola was fundamentally involved in launching, guiding and supporting the project along the way. Our heartfelt thanks go also to Valentina Cadelo, our assistant editor to this volume. Displaying a great sense of commitment, Valentina carried out her responsibilities with great efficiency, humor and diplomacy, thus making a critical contribution to the project.

We thank the contributors to this volume for their hard work, patience and dedication to this project. It has been a privilege to work with such a distinguished group of scholars and practitioners. We particularly thank Diane Orentlicher, Professor at the American University Washington College of Law, for responding so positively to this project, for reading carefully the draft version of our introduction and for writing a deeply insightful prologue that offers an insider-view of the processes and reflections leading to the current, 'updated' version of the UN set of Principles to combat impunity.

We also thank the advisory board members of this project. We have been fortunate to be able to count on the support and encouragement of a remarkable group of leading experts in the fields of human rights and transitional justice: Prof. Juan E. Méndez, Prof. Paola Gaeta, Prof. Christof Heyns, Prof. Asma Khader, Dr. Fatsah Ouguergouz, Prof. Naomi Roht-Arriaza, Prof. Ruti G. Teitel and Prof. Theo Van Boven. We particularly thank Prof. Heyns for his careful comments on a previous version of the introduction to this volume.

Our warm thanks go also to the various interns who became involved in this project throughout the years. Elena Carpanelli, Ilya Nuzov, Claudia Maritano, Francesca Pastore, and Michael Mazliah provided each valuable support to the project through various research activities.

We had the chance to carry out this project with the support of our academic home institution, the Geneva Academy of International Humanitarian Law and Human Rights. The Geneva Academy provided, and continues to provide, a stimulating environment for thinking about the role of human rights in fighting impunity. Special thanks go to the Director of the Geneva Academy, Professor Robert Roth, as well as to the Academy's Executive Manager, Kamelia Kemileva, for their support throughout the project.

It has been a pleasure to work with Oxford University Press and the editors who accompanied this project, particularly Merel Alstein, Natasha Flemming and James Baird. We especially thank Catherine Minahan for her outstanding and painstaking copy-editing and proofing work.

We dedicate this volume to the past, current and future students of the Geneva Academy Master in Transitional Justice, Human Rights and the Rule of Law. As co-directors of this programme, we had the privilege to teach an amazingly vibrant and intellectually curious student community. We hope that the present volume will stimulate their thinking and work in relation to transitional justice and the fight against impunity.

A very warm thank you finally goes to our partners, Graziella and Nadine, for bearing with us throughout the highs and lows of undertaking this project.

Frank Haldemann and Thomas Unger
Geneva, 18th December 2017

Contents

Table of Cases xi
Table of Legislation xxi
List of Contributors xxxi

Prologue (Diane Orentlicher) 1
Introduction (Frank Haldemann and Thomas Unger) 4
Preamble (Theo van Boven) 26
Definitions (Sandra Krähenmann) 34

PART I COMBATING IMPUNITY: GENERAL OBLIGATIONS

Principle 1. General Obligations of States to Take Effective Action to Combat Impunity (Naomi Roht-Arriaza) 47

PART II THE RIGHT TO KNOW

A. GENERAL PRINCIPLES

Principle 2. The Inalienable Right to the Truth (Dermot Groome) 59
Principle 3. The Duty to Preserve Memory (Julia Viebach) 71
Principle 4. The Victims' Right to Know (Dermot Groome) 79
Principle 5. Guarantees to Give Effect to the Right to Know (Thomas Unger) 87

B. COMMISSIONS OF INQUIRY

Principle 6. The Establishment and Role of Truth Commissions (Ilya Nuzov and Mark Freeman) 97
Principle 7. Guarantees of Independence, Impartiality, and Competence (Ilya Nuzov and Mark Freeman) 107
Principle 8. Definition of a Commission's Terms of Reference (Alison Bisset) 116
Principle 9. Guarantees for Persons Implicated (Alison Bisset) 123
Principle 10. Guarantees for Victims and Witnesses Testifying on Their Behalf (Alison Bisset) 129
Principle 11. Adequate Resources for Commissions (Howard Varney) 136
Principle 12. Advisory Functions of the Commissions (Isabel Robinson and Howard Varney) 144
Principle 13. Publicizing the Commission's Reports (Catherine Harwood and Carsten Stahn) 152

C. PRESERVATION OF AND ACCESS TO ARCHIVES BEARING WITNESS TO VIOLATIONS

Principle 14. Measures for the Preservation of Archives (Valentina Cadelo and Trudy Huskamp Peterson) 163
Principle 15. Measures for Facilitating Access to Archives (Valentina Cadelo and Trudy Huskamp Peterson) 172
Principle 16. Cooperation Between Archive Departments and the Courts and Non-Judicial Commissions of Inquiry (John D Ciorciari) 181
Principle 17. Specific Measures Relating to Archives Containing Names (Valentina Cadelo and Trudy Huskamp Peterson) 188
Principle 18. Specific Measures Related to the Restoration of or Transition to Democracy and/or Peace (John D Ciorciari) 196

PART III THE RIGHT TO JUSTICE

A. GENERAL PRINCIPLES

Principle 19. Duties of States with Regard to the Administration of Justice (Kai Ambos) 205

B. DISTRIBUTION OF JURISDICTION BETWEEN NATIONAL, FOREIGN, INTERNATIONAL, AND INTERNATIONALIZED COURTS

Principle 20. Jurisdiction of International and Internationalized Criminal Tribunals (William A Schabas) 219
Principle 21. Measures for Strengthening the Effectiveness of International Legal Principles Concerning Universal and International Jurisdiction (Paola Gaeta) 226

C. RESTRICTIONS ON RULES OF LAW JUSTIFIED BY ACTION TO COMBAT IMPUNITY

Principle 22. Nature of Restrictive Measures (Giulia Pinzauti) 245
Principle 23. Restrictions on Prescription (Giulia Pinzauti) 250
Principle 24. Restrictions and Other Measures Relating to Amnesty (Ilia Maria Siatitsa and Marieke Wierda) 258
Principle 25. Restrictions on the Right of Asylum (Colin Harvey) 270
Principle 26. Restrictions on Extradition/*Non Bis in Idem* (Robert Roth) 281
Principle 27. Restrictions on Justifications Related to Due Obedience, Superior Responsibility, and Official Status (Max du Plessis) 291
Principle 28. Restrictions on the Effects of Legislation on Disclosure or Repentance (Christopher Gosnell) 305
Principle 29. Restrictions on the Jurisdiction of Military Courts (Fionnuala Ní Aoláin) 315

Principle 30. Restrictions on the Principle of the Irremovability of Judges (Christopher Gosnell) 324

PART IV THE RIGHT TO REPARATION/GUARANTEES OF NON-RECURRENCE

A. THE RIGHT TO REPARATION

Principle 31. Rights and Duties Arising Out of the Obligation to Make Reparation (Frank Haldemann) 335

Principle 32. Reparation Procedures (Pierre d'Argent and Isabelle de Ghellinck) 349

Principle 33. Publicizing Reparation Procedures (Lisa J Laplante) 361

Principle 34. Scope of the Right to Reparation (Lucas S Grosman) 369

B. GUARANTEES OF NON-RECURRENCE OF VIOLATIONS

Principle 35. General Principles (Alexander Mayer-Rieckh and Roger Duthie) 383

Principle 36. Reform of State Institutions (Alexander Mayer-Rieckh and Roger Duthie) 392

Principle 37. Disbandment of Parastatal Armed Forces/Demobilization and Social Reintegration of Children (Roger Duthie and Alexander Mayer-Rieckh) 399

Principle 38. Reform of Laws and Institutions Contributing to Impunity (Roger Duthie and Alexander Mayer-Rieckh) 406

Index 413

Table of Cases

AFRICAN COMMISSION ON HUMAN AND PEOPLES' RIGHTS (AComHPR)

Amnesty International and Others v Sudan, Communications nos 48/90 et al (AComHPR, 15 November 1999) 67, 68, 83
Annette Pagnoulle (on behalf of Abdoulaye Mazou) v Cameroon, report no 39/90 (AComHPR, 24 April 1997) 318
Article 19 v Eritrea, Communication no 275/2003 (ACHPR, 30 May 2007) 67–8, 83–4, 373–5
Civil Liberties Organisation, Legal Defence Centre, Legal Defence and Assistance Project v Nigeria, report no 218/98 (AComHPR, 7 May 2001) 318
Constitutional Rights Project v Nigeria (in respect of Wahab Akamu and Others), report no 60/91 (AComHPR, 22 March 1995) 318
Constitutional Rights Project v Nigeria, Communication nos 143/95 and 150/96 (AComHPR, 5 November 1999) 68, 84
Forums of Conscience v Sierra Leone, report no 223/98 (AComHPR, 6 November 2000) 318
Mouvement Burkinabe des Droits de l'Homme et des Peuples v Burkina Faso, Communication no 204/97 (AComHPR, 7 May 2001) 263
Social and Economic Action Center et al v Nigeria, Communication no 155/96 (AComHPR, 27 May 2002) 263
Zimbabwe Human Rights Forum NGO v Zimbabwe (Case no 245/02) (AComHPR, 15 May 2006) 17, 48, 52, 263

BELGIUM

HSA et al v SA, Cass 2e civ, 12 February 2003, no P.02.1139.F (Belgium), translated in (2003) 42 ILM 596 300

CANADA

Ezokola v Canada (Citizenship and Immigration) 2013 SCC 40; [2013] 2 SCR 678 276
Pushpanathan v Canada (Citizenship and Immigration) [1998] 1 SCR 982 276
R v Finta [1994] 1 SCR 701 298
R v Latimer [2001] 1 SCR 3 286

CHILE

Miguel Angel Sandoval, Rol no 517-04, Penal Chamber (17 November 2004) 50

COMMITTEE AGAINST TORTURE (CAT)

AS v Sweden, Communication no 149/1999 (2000) CAT/C/25/D/149/1999 286
FB v The Netherlands Communication no 613/2014 (2015) CAT/C/56/D/613/2014 275
Jahani v Switzerland, Communication no 357/08 (2011) CAT/C/46/D/357/2008 275
NTW v Switzerland, Communication no 414/2007 (2012) CAT/C/48/D/414/2010 275
PSB and TK v Canada, Communication no 505/2012 (2015) CAT/C/55/D/505/2012 275

COURT OF JUSTICE OF THE EUROPEAN UNION (CJEU)

C-57/09 and C-101/09 Bundesrepublik Deutschland v B and D [2010] ECR I-10979 277
C-131/12 Google Spain SL, Google Inc v Agencia Española de Protección de Datos, Mario Costeja González (Judgment) (CJEU, Grand Chamber, 13 May 2014) 193
C-373/13 HT v Land Baden-Württemberg [2016] 1 CMLR 6 277

EUROPEAN COURT OF HUMAN RIGHTS (ECTHR)

Abakarova v Russia (Judgment) (ECtHR, 15 October 2015) 214
Ahorugeze v Sweden (2012) 55 EHRR 2 . . . . 278, 285
Ahmad and Others v UK (2013) 56 EHRR 1 278
Aksoy v Turkey (Judgment) (ECtHR, 26 November 1996) 375
Aksoy v Turkey App no 21987/93 (Judgment) (ECtHR, 18 December 1996) 124, 263
Al-Adsani v the United Kingdom App no 35763/97 (ECtHR Grand Chamber, 21 November 2001) 353
Al Nashiri v Poland, App no 28761/11 (Judgment) (ECtHR, 24 July 2014) 99
Al Saadoon and Mufdih v United Kingdom App no 61498/08 (Judgment) (ECtHR, 2 March 2010) 286
Antonieta Tudor v Romania (Judgment) (ECtHR, 24 September 2013) 175, 192
Armani da Silva v the United Kingdom (Judgment) (ECtHR, 30 March 2016) 213–14
Ärtze für das Leben v Austria App no 10126/82 (ECtHR, 21 June 1988) 355
Asiye Genç v Turkey (Judgment) (ECtHR, 27 January 2015) 214
Association for European Integration and Human Rights and Ekimdzhiev v Bulgaria App no 62540/00 (ECtHR, 28 June 2007) 366
Association for the Defence of Human Rights in Romania– Helsinki Committee on behalf of Ionel Garcea v Romania (Judgment) (ECtHR, 24 March 2015) 214
Aswat v United Kingdom App no 17299/12 (Judgment) (ECtHR, 16 April 2013) 286
Aswat v UK App no 62176/14 (inadmissible) (ECtHR, 29 January 2015) 278
Babar Ahmad v United Kingdom App nos 24027/07 and others (Judgment) (ECtHR, 10 April 2012) 287
Benzer v Turkey App no 23502/06 (ECtHR, 24 March 2014) 48
Bouyid v Belgium (Judgment) (ECtHR, 28 September 2015) 213
Broniowski v Poland App no 31443/96 (Judgment) (ECtHR, 28 September 2005) 345
Çakici v Turkey App no 23657/94 (Judgment) (ECtHR, 8 July 1999) 344
Cangöz and others v Turkey (Judgment) (ECtHR, 26 April 2016) 214
Ceesay v Austria (Judgment) (ECtHR, 16 November 2017) 213–14
Chahal v UK (1997) 23 EHRR 413 277
Ciraklar v Turkey (Judgment) (ECtHR, 28 October 1998) 318
Coëme and others v Belgium (Judgment) (ECtHR, 22 June 2000) 254
De Souza Ribeiro v France App no 22689/07 (ECtHR Grand Chamber, 13 December 2012) 353
Cyprus v Turkey App no 25781/94 (Judgment) [2001] ECHR 1 . . . . 67–8, 81, 83, 99, 342
El-Masri v Former Yugoslav Republic of Macedonia App no 39630/09 (Judgment) (ECtHR, 13 December 2012) 156, 213, 377
Ergin v Turkey (No 6) App no 47533/99 (ECtHR, 4 May 2006) 319–20
Findlay v United Kingdom (Judgment) (ECtHR, 25 February 1997) 109
Gerger v Turkey (Judgment) (ECtHR, 8 July 1999) 318
Giuliani and Gaggio v Italy (Judgment) (ECtHR, 24 March 2011) 214
Golder v United Kingdom App no 4451/70 (Judgment) (ECtHR, 21 February 1975) 342
Haralambie v Romania (Judgment) (ECtHR, 27 October 2009) 175, 192
Harkins and Edwards v UK App nos 9146/07 and 3326507 (Judgment) (ECtHR, 17 January 2012) 286
Hirsi Jamaa and others v Italy (2012) 55 EHRR 21 275
Husayn (Abu Zubaydah) v Poland (Judgment) (ECtHR, 24 July 2014) 176, 213

Hutten-Czapska v Poland App no 35014/97 (Judgment) (ECtHR, 19 June 2006). 345
Incal v Turkey (Judgment) (ECtHR, 9 June 1998) 109, 318, 321
Janowiec and others v Russia (Judgment) (ECtHR, 16 April 2012) 176, 344
Janowiec v Russia (Judgment) (ECtHR Grand Chamber, 21 October 2013. . . . . 176, 183
Jeronovics v Latvia (Judgment) (ECtHR, 5 July 2016) 213
Joanna Szulc v Poland (Judgment) (ECtHR, 13 November 2012) 175, 192
Kamburov v Bulgaria App no 14336/05 (Decision) (ECtHR, 6 January 2011) 166, 192
Karatas v Turkey (Judgment) (ECtHR, 8 July 1999) 318
Kaya v Turkey (Judgment) (ECtHR, 19 February 1998) 213
Kenedi v Hungary (Judgment) (ECtHR, 26 May 2009) 176
Kolk and Kislyiy v Estonia (Decision) (Admissibility) (ECtHR, 17 January 2006). 254
Kolyadenko and others v Russia (Judgment) Application nos 17423/05, 20534/05, 20678/05, 23263/05, 24283/05, and 35673/05 (ECtHR, 28 February 2012) 366
Krombach v France App no 29731/96 (Judgment) (ECtHR, 13 February 2001). 289
Kudła v Poland App no 30210/96 (ECtHR Grand Chamber, 26 October 2000) 352
Kurić and others v Slovenia (ECtHR Grand Chamber 26 June 2012) 357
Kurt v Turkey (Judgment) (ECtHR, 25 May 1998) 166
McCann and others v the United Kingdom (App no 18984/91) (ECHR, 27 September 1995) 16, 213, 222
Marguš v Croatia App no 4455/10 (Judgment) (27 May 2014) 16, 213, 263–4, 266, 268, 287–8
Maria Atanasiu and others v Romania (Judgment) (ECtHR,12 October 2010) 175, 345
Martin v United Kingdom (Judgment) (ECtHR, 24 January 2007). 320
Mikheyev v Russia (Judgment) (ECtHR, 26 January 2006) 375
M Özel and others v Turkey (Judgment) (ECtHR, 17 November 2015). 214
MSS v Belgium and Greece (2011) 53 EHRR 2. 275
Musikhanova and Others v Russia (Judgment) (ECtHR, 4 December 2008) 184
Mustafa Tunç and Fecire Tunç v Turkey (Judgment) (ECtHR, 14 April 2015). 214
Opuz v Turkey (Judgment) (ECtHR, 9 June 2009) 39
Othman (Abu Qatada) v UK (2012) 55 EHRR 1 . . . . 275, 278, 285
Oyal v Turkey App no 4864/05 (ECtHR, 23 March 2010) 342
Papon v France (Decision) (Admissibility) (ECtHR, 15 November 2001) 254
Pereira Henriques v Luxembourg [2006] ECHR 60255/00 (Fourth Section, 9 May 2006) 366
Rad v Romania App no 9742/04 (Decision) (ECtHR, 9 June 2009) 166
Ribitsch v Austria (Judgment) (ECtHR, 4 December 1995). 375
Roche v United Kingdom (2006) 42 EHRR 30 366
Rotaru v Romania (Judgment) (ECtHR, 4 May 2000). 192
Saadi v Italy (2009) 49 EHRR 30 277
Salah v the Netherlands App no 8196/02 (Judgment) (ECtHR, 6 July 2006) 343
Sasita Israilova and Others v Russia (Judgment) (ECtHR, 28 October 2010). 184
Scordino v Italy (No 1) App no 36813/97 (Judgment) (ECtHR, 29 March 2006). 342, 352
Selmouni v France App no 25803/94 (Judgment) (ECtHR, 28 July 1999) 342
Siliadin v France (Judgment) (ECtHR, 26 July 2005) 40
Šilih v Slovenia App no 71463/01 (ECtHR, Grand Chamber, 9 April 2009) 222
Soering v UK (1989) 11 EHRR 439 . . . . 275, 286
Suprun v Russia App no 58029/12. 178
Tarakhel v Switzerland (2015) 60 EHRR 28 275
Tarbuk v Croatia (Judgment) (ECtHR, 11 December 2012) 268
Touvier v France (Decision) (Admissibility) (ECommHR, 13 January 1997). 254
Trabelsi v Belgium, App no 140/10 (Judgment) (ECtHR, 7 October 2014). 286
Tyrer v the United Kingdom App no 5856/72 (ECtHR, 25 April 1978) 25
Waite and Kennedy v Germany App no 26083/94 (ECtHR Grand Chamber, 18 February 1999) . . . 353
X v Germany (Decision) (Admissibility) ECommHR, (6 July 1976) 254
X and Y v the Netherlands App no 8978/80 (ECtHR, 26 March 1985) 48
Yeter v Turkey App no 33750/03 (Judgment) (ECtHR, 13 January 2009). 52
Zoltai v Hungary and Ireland (Decision) (ECtHR, 29 September 2015) 214

EXTRAORDINARY CHAMBERS IN THE COURTS OF CAMBODIA (ECCC)

Prosecutor v Ieng Sary, Case File No 002/19-09-2007/ECCC/TC 262, 264, 312

FRANCE

Fédération Nationale des Déportés et Internés Résistants et Patriotes and Others v Barbie, Court of Cassation, Barbie (Decision) (26 January 1984) 255

GUATEMALA

Prosecution in the Trial of Rios Montt v Ministry of National Defence (5 March 2008) 177

HUMAN RIGHTS CHAMBER FOR BOSNIA AND HERZEGOVINA (HRCBiH)

Srebrenica Cases, Case no CH/01/8365 (Decision on admissibility and merits) (7 March 2003) 67–8
Unković v Bosnia and Herzegovina, Case no CH/99/2150 (Decision on review) (10 May 2002) 67–8, 81

INTER-AMERICAN COURT OF HUMAN RIGHTS (IACtHR)

Afro Descendant Communities Displaced from the Carica River Bassin (Operation Genesis) v Colombia (Judgment) (Preliminary objections, merits, reparations and costs), IACtHR Series C no 270 (20 November 2013) 343
Almancid-Arellano v Chile (Judgment), IACtHR Series C no 154 (26 September 2006) 288
Almonacid Arellano et al v Chile (Judgment) IACtHR Series C no 154 (26 September 2006) 48, 213, 263
Aloeboetoe v Suriname (Reparations and Costs) (Judgment) IACtHR (10 September 1993) . . . 357, 375
Anzualdo Castro v Peru (Preliminary objection, merits, reparations and costs) (Judgment) IACtHR Series C no 202 (22 September 2009) 67, 213
Baena et al v Panama (Judgment) IACtHR Series C no 72 (2 February 2001) 374
Baldeón-Garcia v Peru IACtHR Series C no 147 (6 April 2006) 67
Bámaca-Velásquez v Guatemala (Order of the Court) IACtHR Series C no 70 (25 November 2000) 65, 67–8, 99, 176, 213
Barrios Altos v Peru (Judgment) IACtHR Series C no 87 (30 November 2001) 48, 52, 67, 212, 254, 263, 311, 376–7
Benavides Cevallos v Ecuador (Merits, Reparations and Costs) (Judgment) IACtHR Series C no 38 (19 June 1998) 376
Blake v Guatemala IACtHR Series C no 36 (24 January 1998) 66–7, 254, 346
Blanco-Romero v Venezuela (Judgment) IACtHR Series C no 138 (28 November 2005) 64
Castillo-Páez v Peru (Judgment) IACtHR Series C no 34 (3 November 1997) 64
Castillo Petruzzi v Peru (Judgment) IACtHR Series C no 52 (30 May 1999) 321, 357
Castro-Castro Prison v Peru (Merits, Reparations and Costs) (Judgment) IACtHR Series C no 160 (25 November 2006) 377
Chitay Nech et al v Guatemala, IACtHR Series C no 212 (25 May 2010) 67
Chumbipuma Aguirre and others v Peru (Judgment) (Merits) IACtHR Series C no 75 (14 March 2001) 254
Claude Reyes et al v Chile (Judgment) (Merits, Reparations and Costs) IACtHR Series C no 151 (19 September 2006) 365
Comunidad Mayagna (Sumo) Awas Tingni v Nicaragua (Merits, Reparations and Costs) IACtHR Series C no 79 (31 August 2001) 376
Contreras et al v El Salvador (Judgment) IACtHR Series C no 232 (31 August 2011) 65, 176, 213

El Mozote and Nearby Places v El Salvador (Merits, Reparations and Costs) IACtHR Series C no 252 (25 October 2012) 17
Gelman v Uruguay (Judgment) IACtHR Series C no 221 (24 February 2011). 48, 213, 263, 267
Girls Yean and Bosico v The Dominican Republic (Preliminary Objections, Merits, Reparations and Costs) (Judgment) IACtHR Series C no 130 (8 September 2005). 376
Goibúru et al v Paraguay (Judgment) IACtHR Series C no 153 (22 September 2006) 37, 67, 165
Gomes Lund et al ('Guerrilha do Araguaia') v Brazil (Judgment) IACtHR Series C no 219 (24 November 2010) 48, 174, 176, 182–3, 263
González et al ('Cotton Field') v Mexico (Preliminary objection, merits, reparations and costs) IACtHR Series C no 205 (16 November 2009). 23, 39, 222
Gonzales Lluy et al v Ecuador (Judgment) (Preliminary objections, merits, reparations, and costs) IACtHR Series C no 298 (1 September 2015). 343
García Prieto et al v El Salvador (Judgment) IACtHR Series C no 168 (20 November 2007). 213
Gutiérrez Soler v Colombia (Judgment) IACtHR Series C no 132 (12 September 2005) 37
Heliodoro Portugal v Panama (Judgment) IACtHR Series C no 186 (12 August 2008) 212–13
Jose Miguel Gudiel Alvarez and others v Guatemala (Diario Militar case) IACtHR Series C no 253 (20 November 2012). 176
Juan Humberto Sanchez v Honduras (Preliminary Objections, Merits, Reparations and Costs) IACtHR Series C no 99 (7 June 2003) 344, 377
Kawas-Fernández v Honduras (Merits, Reparations and Costs) (Judgment) IACtHR (3 April 2009) 376
La Cantuta v Peru (Judgment) IACtHR Series C no 162 (29 November 2006. . . . . . 52, 67–8, 213, 288
La Rochela Massacre v Colombia (Judgment) IACtHR Series C no 163 (11 May 2007) 52
Las Dos Erres Massacre v Guatemala (Preliminary objections, merits, reparations and costs) IACtHR Series C no 211 (24 November 2009) 67–9
Loayza-Tamayo v Peru (Merits) (Judgment) IACtHR Series C no 33 (17 September 1997). 374, 377
Lori Berenson Mejía v Peru (Judgment on the Merits, Reparations and Costs) IACtHR Series C no 119 (25 November 2004). 374
Manuel Cepeda Vargas v Colombia, IACtHR Series C no 213 (26 May 2010) 67, 212–13, 376
Mapiripán Massacre v Columbia IACtHR Series C no 134 (15 September 2005) 67, 74–5
Massacre v Colombia (Judgment) (Merits, Reparations and Costs) IACtHR Series C no 163 (11 May 2007) 346
Massacres of El Mozote and neighboring locations v El Salvador (Judgment) IACtHR Series C no 252 (25 October 2012) 48, 212, 263, 268
Mendoza et al v Argentina (Judgment) (Preliminary objections, merits, and reparations) IACtHR Series C no 247 (14 May 2013) 343
Miguel Castro-Castro Prison v Peru (Judgment) IACtHR Series C no 160 (25 November 2006). 213
Moiwana Community v Suriname (Merits) IACtHR Series C no 124 (15 June 2005) 50, 213
Molina-Theissen v Guatemala (Reparations and Costs) (Judgment) IACtHR Series C no 108 (3 July 2004) 376
Monseñor Oscar Arnulfo Romero and Galdamez v El Salvador, Case 11.481, Report N° 37/00, OEA/Ser.L/V/II.106 Doc 3 rev at 671 (1999). 124
Montero-Aranguren et al v Venezuela (Detention Center of Catia) (Judgment) IACtHR Series C no 150 (5 July 2006) 67
Myrna Mack-Chang v Guatemala (Merits, reparations and costs) (Judgment) IACtHR Series C no 101 (25 November 2003), ... 74, 99, 156, 174, 176, 263
19 Merchants v Colombia (Merits, Reparations and Costs) (Judgment) IACtHR Series C no 109 (5 July 2004). 376
Osorio Rivera y Familiares v Perú (Judgment) IACtHR Series C no 274 (26 November 2013) 212
Paniagua Morales et al v Guatemala (The White Van Case) (Judgment) IACtHR Series C no 37 (8 March 1998) 37
Paniagua Morales et al v Guatemala (The White Van Case) (Judgment) (Reparations) IACtHR Series C no 37 (25 May 2001) 365
Plan de Sanchez Massacre v Guatemala (Merits, reparations and costs) (Judgment) IACtHR Series C no 116 (19 November 2004). 74–5, 346, 356–7
Pueblo Bello Massacre v Columbia, IACtHR Series C no 140 (31 January 2006) 67

Radilla Pacheco v Mexico (Judgment) IACtHR Series C no 209 (23 November 2009) 213
Reggiardo Tolosa v Argentina (Provisional Measures) 374
Rochela Massacre v Colombia (Merits, Reparations and Costs) IACtHR Series C no 163 (11 May 2007) 269
Rodríguez Vera et al (the disappeared from the Palace of Justice) v Colombia (Judgment) IACtHR Series C no 287 (14 November 2014) 212
Rosendo Radilla Pacheco v Mexico (Judgment) IACtHR Series C no 209 (23 November 2009) 318
Trujillo Oraza v Bolivia (Reparations and Costs) IACtHR Series C no 92 (27 February 2002) . . . 344, 377
Valle Jaramillo et al v Colombia (Judgment) IACtHR Series C no 192 (27 November 2008). 213
Velásquez-Rodríguez v Honduras (Merits) IACtHR Series C no 4 (29 July 1988) 13, 16, 39, 48–9, 99, 124, 212, 222, 263, 339, 343, 384, 408
Vélez Restrepo and Family v Columbia (Preliminary Objections, Merits, Reparations and Costs) IACtHR Series C no 248 (3 September 2012) 68
Veliz Franco y otros v Guatemala (Judgment) IACtHR Series C no 277 (19 May 2014) 212
Villagran-Morales et al IACtHR Series C no 63 (19 November 1999) 66, 83
Villagrán Morales et al v Guatemala (The Street Children Case) (Judgment) IACtHR Series C no 77 (26 May 2001) 365
Wong Ho Wing v Peru (Judgment) IACtHR Series C no 297 (30 June 2015) 285
Ximenes-Lopes v Brazil IACtHR Series C no 149 (4 July 2006). 67–8, 83

INTERNATIONAL COURT OF JUSTICE (ICJ)

Belgium v Senegal (Questions relating to the Obligation to Prosecute or Extradite), (20 July 2012) 50, 209, 233, 284
Democratic Republic of the Congo v Belgium (Judgment) (14 February 2002). 228, 230–1, 237–8, 246, 298–300, 303
Democratic Republic of the Congo v Uganda (Judgment) [2005] ICJ Rep 168 370
Germany v Italy: Greece Intervening, (Judgment) [2012] ICJ Rep 99 297
Germany v United States [2001] ICJ Rep 466 346
Legal Consequences of the Construction of a Wall in the Occupied Palestinian Territory (Advisory Opinion) [2004] ICJ Rep 136 370
Nicaragua v United States of America (Judgment) [1986] ICJ Rep 14 14

INTERNATIONAL CRIMINAL COURT (ICC)

Prosecutor v Al Bashir (Decision on the Cooperation of the Democratic Republic of the Congo Regarding Omar Al Bashir's Arrest and Surrender to the Court) ICC-02/05-01/09-195 (9 April 2014) 300
Prosecutor v Bemba Gombo, ICC-01/05-01/08-2140 (23 February 2012) 215
Prosecutor v Gaddafi et al (Judgment on the appeal of Mr Abdullah Al-Senussi against the decision of Pre-Trial Chamber I of 11 October 2013 entitled 'Decision on the admissibility of the case against Abdullah Al-Senussi') ICC-01/11-01/11 OA 4. . . . . .224, 300
Prosecutor v Lubanga (Decision on Victims' Participation) ICC-01/04-01/06-1119 (18 January 2008) 211
Prosecutor v Lubanga (Judgment on the Appeals of the Prosecutor and the Defence against Trial Chamber I's Decision on Victims' Participation of 18 January 2008) ICC-01/04-01/06OA9OA10 (11 July 2008) 69, 211
Prosecutor v Lubanga (Scheduling Order Concerning Timetable for Sentencing and Reparations) ICC-01/04-01/06-2844 (14 March 2012). 211
Prosecutor v Lubanga (Decision establishing the principles and procedures to be applied to reparations) ICC-01/04-01/06 (7 August 2012) 353, 365
Prosecutor v Lubanga (Order for Reparations) ICC-01/04-01/06 A A 2 A 3 (3 March 2015) 344
*Pro*secutor v Lubanga (Judgment on the appeals against the 'Decision establishing the principles and procedures to be applied to reparations' of 7 August 2012) ICC-01/04-01/06 (3 March 2015) 353, 357

Prosecutor v William Samoei Ruto and others, Appeals Chamber Judgment on the appeal of the republic of Kenya against the decision of Pre-Trial Chamber II of 30 May 2011 (30 August 2011) 287

INTERNATIONAL CRIMINAL TRIBUNAL FOR RWANDA (ICTR)

Prosecutor v Akayesu (Judgment) ICTR-96-4-T (2 September 1998) 62
Prosecutor v Bagaragaza (Decision on Rule 11bis Appeal) ICTR-05-86-AR11 (30 August 2006) 223
Prosecutor v Bizimungu, Decision on Prosper Mugiraneza's Motion Regarding Cooperation with the Republic of Burundi ICTR-99-50-T (30 October 2008). 184
Posecutor v Kamuhanda (Trial Chamber Judgment) ICTR-99-54A (22 January 2004) 296
Prosecutor v Kayishema & Ruzindana (Judgment) ICTR 95-1-T (21 May 1999) 298

INTERNATIONAL CRIMINAL TRIBUNAL FOR THE FORMER YUGOSLAVIA (ICTY)

Prosecutor v Anto Furundžija (Trial Chamber) IT-95-17/1-T (10 December 1998). 256, 264
Prosecutor v Blaškić (Order to the Republic of Croatia for the Production of Documents) IT-95-14 (21 July 1998) 184, 223, 297
Prosecutor v Delalić et al ('Celebici') (Trial Chamber Judgment) ICTY-96-21-T (16 November 1998). 293, 302
Prosecutor v Dusko Tadić (Decision on the Defence Motion for Interlocutory Appeal on Jurisdiction) IT-94-1-AR72 (2 October 1995). 13, 40, 284
Prosecutor v Erdemović (Appeals Chamber) (Judgment) ICTY IT-96-22-A (7 October 1997) 294–5
Prosecutor v Furundžjia (Judgment) IT-95-17/1-T (10 December 1998). 62
Prosecutor v Furundzija (Judgment) (Appeals Chamber) IT-95-17/1-A (21 July 2000) 325
Prosecutor v Kamuhanda (Trial Chamber Judgment) ICTR-99-54A (22 January 2004) 296
Prosecutor v Karadžić and Mladić (Review of the Indictments Pursuant to Rule 61 of the Rules of Procedure and Evidence), ICTY, IT-95-5-R6 and IT-95-18-R61 (11 July 1996) 69
Prosecutor v Karadžić (Decision on the Accused's Holbrooke Agreement Motion) (Trial Chamber) IT-95-5/18-PT (8 July 2009). 312
Prosecutor v Karadžić (Decision on Karadžić's appeal of Trial Chamber's decision on alleged Holbrooke Agreement) (Appeals Chamber) IT-95-5/18-AR73.4 (12 October 2009) 312
Prosecutor v Kayishema & Ruzindana (Judgment) ICTR 95-1-T (21 May 1999) 298
Prosecutor v Kordic & Cerkez (Judgment) IT-95-14/2-T (26 February 2001) 298
Prosecutor v Krstic (Judgment) IT-98-33/T (2 August 2001). 298
Prosecutor v Kunarac (Judgment) IT-96-23-T (2 February 2001) 62
Prosecutor v Mucić et al (Trial Chamber Judgment) ICTY-96-21 (16 November 1998). 295–6
Prosecutor v Orić (Trial Chamber Judgment) ICTY-03-68 (30 June 2006) 295–6, 302
Prosecutor v Popović (Appeals Judgment) IT-05-88 (30 January 2015) 83, 85
Prosecutor v Tadić (Decision on the Defence Motion for Interlocutory Appeal on Jurisdiction) IT-94-1-AR72 (2 October 1995) 222
Prosecutor v Tihomar Blaskic (Judgment on the Request of the Republic of Croatia for Review of the Decision of Trial Chamber II of 18 July 1997) IT-95-14 (28 October 1997) 184

INTERNATIONAL MILITARY TRIBUNAL AT NUREMBERG (IMT)

France and ors v Göring (Hermann) and ors (Judgment and Sentence) [1946] 22 IMT 203, (1946) 41 AJIL 172, (1946) 13 ILR 203, ICL 243 (IMTN 1946), 1st October 1946, International Military Tribunal [IMT] 297–298

JERUSALEM

Israel v Eichmann (District Court, 12 December 1961) 302

PERMANENT COURT OF INTERNATIONAL JUSTICE (PCIJ)

Factory at Chorzów, Germany v Poland, PCIJ Series A no 9 (1927) 336, 370–1
Greece v Britain Mavrommatis Palestine Concessions, PCIJ Series A no 2 (1924) 13

REPUBLIC OF LIBERIA

Williams v Minister of Justice, Attorney General, Independent National Human Rights Commission and Government of Liberia, Supreme Court of the Republic of Liberia, 21 January 2011 145

RUSSIA

International Memorial Society v Russian Minister of Interior, decision of the Cassation Chamber of the Supreme Court (24 March 2011) 176

SOUTH AFRICA

Azanian Peoples Organization (AZAPO) and Others v President of the Republic of South Africa and Others (CCT17/96), 25 July 1996 . . . . 267, 310, 359
Du Preez and Van Rensburg v Chairman, South African Truth and Reconciliation Commission, Case no 4443/ 96 (Cape of Good Hope Provisional Division, 30 April 1996), 1996 (3) SA 997 (C) 126
Magidiwana and Another v President of the Republic of South Africa and Others (37904/2013) [2013] ZAGPPHC 292, [2014] 1 All SA 76 (GNP) (14 October 2013) 140
Minister of Justice and Constitutional Development and Others v Southern African Litigation Centre and Others (867/15) [2016] ZASCA 17, 2016 (4) BCLR 487 (SCA) 301
Nieuwoudt v Chairman, South African Truth and Reconciliation Commission (1996) 2 All SA 660 (SE) 126
Nkadimeng v National Director of Public Prosecutions and Others, Case no 35554/2015 149
Richtersveld Community and Others v Alexkor Ltd and Another 2001 (3) SA 1293 (LCC) 347
Southern Africa Litigation Centre v Minister of Justice And Constitutional Development and Others (27740/2015) [2015] ZAGPPHC 402 (24 June 2015) 301

SPAIN

Fidel Castro case, no 1999/ 2723, Order (Audiencia nacional 4 March 1999) (Spain) 300
Menchú Tumn (Rigoberta) and ors v Two Guatemalan Government Officials and Six members of the Guatemalan Military, Constitutional Tribunal, (26 September 2005) 238

SPECIAL COURT FOR SIERRA LEONE (SCSL)

Prosecutor v Charles Ghankay Taylor (Decision on Immunity from Jurisdiction) (Appeals Chamber) SCSL-2003-01-1 (31 May 2004) 299
Prosecutor v Charles Ghakay Taylor (Trial Chamber) (Decision on prosecution motion for admission of extracts of the report of the Truth and Reconciliation Commission of Sierra Leone) SCSL-03-1-T (19 February 2009) 119

Prosecutor v Kallon and Kamara (Decision on Challenge to Jurisdiction: Lomé Accord Amnesty) SCSL-2004-15-AR72(E) (13 March 2004) 262, 264
Prosecutor v Samuel Hinga Norman (Pre-Trial Chamber) (Decision on the Request by the Truth and Reconciliation Commission of Sierra Leone to Conduct a Public Hearing with Samuel Hinga Norman) SCSL-03-08-PT-101 (29 October 2003). 120
Prosecutor v Samuel Hinga Norman (Appeals Chamber Decision on Appeal by the Truth and Reconciliation Commission for Sierra Leone and Chief Samuel Hinga Norman JP) SCSL-03-08-PT-122-I and II (28 November 2003) 120, 132

UGANDA

Thomas Kwoyelo Alias Latoni v Uganda, HCT-00-ICD-Case no 20/10, Constitutional Petition no 036/11 (22 September 2011) 266–7

UN HUMAN RIGHTS COMMITTEE (UNHRC)

Ahani v Canada, Communication no 1051/2002 (2004), UN Doc CCPR/C/80/D/1051/2002. 275
Bautista de Arellana v Colombia, Communication no 563/1993, UN Doc CCPR/C/55/D/563/1993 . . . . . 214, 352
Bousroual v Algeria, UN Doc CCPR/C/86/D/1085/2002 (15 March 2006) 67, 68, 83
Burkino Faso Miriam Sankara et al Communication no 1159/2003, UN Doc CCPR/C/86/D/1159/2003 (11 April 2006) 67, 68
Coronel et al v Colombia, Communication no 778/1997, UN Doc CCPR/C/76/D/778/1997 214
Dalisa Dovadzija and Sakiba Dovdzija v Bosnia and Herzegovina, Communication no 2143/2012, UN Doc CCPR/C/114/D/2143/2012 214
Dmitry Tyan v Kazakhstan, Communication no 2125/2011, UN Doc CCPR/C/119/D/2125/2011 214
Ernesto Benitez Gamarra v Paraguay, Communication no 1829/2008, UN Doc CCPR/C/104/D/1829/2008 214
González v Argentina, UN Doc CCPR/C/101/D/1458/2006 222
HEAK v Denmark, Communication no 2343/2014, UN Doc CCPR/C/114/D/2343/2014. 275
Hamida v Canada, Communication no 1544/2007 (2010), UN Doc CCPR/C/98/D/1544/2007 . . . . . 275, 278
MacCallum v South Africa, Communication no 1818/2008, UN Doc CCPR/C/100/D/1818/2008 214
Mamatkarim Ernazarov v Kyrgyzstan, Communication no 2054/2011, UN Doc CCPR/C/113/D/2054/2011 214
María del Carmen Almeida de Quinteros et al v Uruguay, Communication no 107/1981, UN Doc CCPR/C/OP/2 (1990) 67, 83
MI v Sweden, Communication no 2149/2012, UN Doc CCPR/C/108/D/2149/2012 275
Nijaru v Cameroon, Communication no 1353/2005, UN Doc CCPR/C/89/D/1353/2005 214
Pestaño et al v Philippines, UN Doc CCPR/C/98/D/1619/2007 222
Purna Maya v Nepal, Communication no 2245/2013, UN Doc CCPR/C/119/D/2245/2013 214
Quinteros v Uruguay, Communication no 107/1981 48
Rafik Belamrania v Algeria, Communication no 2157/2012, UN Doc CCPR/C/118/D/2157/2012 214
Rodríguez v Uruguay, Communication no 322/1988, UN Doc CCPR/C/51/D/322/1988 (1994) 124
Sathasivam/Saraswathi v Sri Lanka, Communication no 1436/2005, UN Doc CCPR/C/93/D/1436/2005 214
Saker v Algeria, Communication no 992/2001, UN Doc CCPR/C/86/D/992/2001 214
II Khwildy v Libya, case 1804/2008 (1 November 2012) 338

Titiahonjo v Cameroon, UN Doc CCPR/C/91/D/1186/2003 (26 October 2007) 67, 83
Toktakunov v Kyrgyzstan App no 1470/2006 (Merits) UN Doc CCPR/C/101/D/1470/2006 (21 April 2011) 365
Urtmatbek Akunov v Kyrgyzstan, Communication no 2127/2011, UN Doc CCPR/C/118/D/2127/2011 214
X v Denmark, Communication no 2007/2010 (2014), UN Doc CCPR/C/110/D/2007/2012. 275
Zohra Madoui v Algeria, UN Doc CCPR/C/94/D/1495/2006 (1 December 2008) 67, 68, 83
Zyuskin v Russian Federation, Communication no 1605/2007, UN Doc CCPR/C/102/D/1605/2007 214

UNITED KINGDOM

Al-Sirri v Secretary of State for the Home Department; DD (Afghanistan) v Secretary of State for the Home Department [2012] UKSC 54 276
Bo Xilai, Re(2005) 128 ILR 713 303
Othman v Secretary of State for the Home Department [2013] EWCA Civ 277 275
R (JS (Sri Lanka)) v Secretary of State for the Home Department [2010] UKSC 15 277
R v Bow Street Metropolitan Stipendiary Magistrate and others, ex p Pinochet Ugarte (No 3) [1999] 2 All ER 97. 299–300
R v Secretary of State for the Home Department, ex p Bentley [1994] QB 349 249

UNITED STATES OF AMERICA

Abdullahi v Pfizer, Inc, 562 F 3d 163 (2nd Cir 2009) 345
Baker v Carr, 369 US 186 (1962). 249
Esther Kiobel, et al v Royal Dutch Petroleum Co, et al, Brief of the Governments of the Kingdom of the Netherlands and the United Kingdom of Great Britain and Northern Ireland as Amicus Curaie in support of Neither Party, No 10-1491 149
Filártiga v Peña-Irala, 630 F 2d 876 (2d Cir 1980). 345
Kadic v Karadžić, 70 F 3d 232, 244 (2d Cir 1995) 228
Khulumani v Barclay National Bank Ltd, 509 F 3d 148 (2nd Cir 2007) 345
Kiobel v Royal Dutch Petroleum Co, 133 S Ct 1659 (2013) 345
Marbury v Madison, 5 US 137 (1803). 249
Ortiz v Fibreboard Corp, 527 US 818 (1999) 345
Plaintiffs A, B, C, D, E, F v Jiang Zemin, 282 F Supp.2d. 300
Tachiona v Mugabe, 169 F Supp.2d 259 (SDNY 2001). 300
United States of America vs Otto Ohlendorf, et al ('Einsatzgruppen' case) 294
Yamashita, Re no 61, Misc,, 327 US 1; 66 S Ct 340; 90 L Ed 499; 1946 US LEXIS 3090 293
Zivotofsky v Clinton, 123 SCt 1421 (2012). 249

Table of Legislation

NATIONAL INSTRUMENTS

Algeria

Algerian Charter for Peace and National Reconciliation, 2006 267

Australia

War Crimes Act, 1945
- Preamble 231
- Section 11 231

Bosnia and Herzegovina

Law on the Human Rights Ombudsman of Bosnia and Herzegovina, Dayton Accords, 1995
- Art 28 184
- Annex VI 184

Brazil

Law on Access to Public Information, Law no 12.527, 2011
- Art 21 184

Lei da Comissão da Verdade, Ley no 12528/201, 2011
- Art 4(II) 185

Canada

Maher Arar Rules of Procedure and Practice, 2004
- r 43–56 156

Colombia

Final Agreement to End the Armed Conflict and Build a Stable and Lasting Peace, 2016 308

Justice and Peace Law (Law 975), 2005 269

Legal Framework for Peace (Legislative Act 1/2012), 2012 269

Victims and Land Restitution Law (Law 1448), 2011
- Art 3(4) 356

Germany

Act Regarding the Records of the State Security Service of the Former German Democratic Republic (Stasi Records Act), 1991 168
- Art 13 190
- Art 35–38 199

Code of Crimes against International Law, 2002 238

German Judiciary Act, 1972 (as amended 8 June 2017)
- Art 61 327
- Art 62 327

Ghana

National Reconciliation Commission Act, 2002
- s 8(1)(a) 112
- Art 6(5) 113

Guatemala

Law on Access to Public Information, Decree no 57/2008, 2008
- Art 24 184

Ireland

Irish Constitution 320

Kenya

Truth, Justice and Reconciliation Act, 2008
- s 5(g) 130
- s 5(h) 130
- s 6(n) 118
- s 6(o) 118
- s 25(2) 132
- s 25(4) 132
- s 52(2) 133

Truth, Justice and Reconciliation Commission Bill, 2008
- cl 10 113–14
- cl 14 113
- cl 21(2) 112

Latvia

Archives Law, 2011
Art 4 200
Art 6–11 200

Liberia

Act to Establish the Truth and Reconciliation Commission, 2005
s 4(a) 118
s 4(b) 130
s 7 102
s 23 113
s 26(n) 131
s 39(a) 112
Truth and Reconciliation Commission of Liberia Mandate
s 26(m) 155

Libya

Law 38 on Some Procedures Concerning the Transitional Phase, 2012
Art 4 266

Mauritius

Truth and Justice Commission Act, 2008
s 3 113
s 3(1) 113
s 3(4) 112
s 3(5) 113
s 14(1) 114

Mexico

Ley Federal de Archivos, 2012
Art 14–17 200

Netherlands

Dutch Implementation Act, 1988 228

Peru

Institutional Cooperation Agreement between the Prosecutor's Office and the Truth and Reconciliation Commission, 2002 119
s II 132
Ley de Transparencia y Accesso a la Información Pública, Ley no 27806, 2003
Art 15(C) 184

Sierra Leone

Peace Agreement between the Government of Sierra Leone and the Revolutionary United Front of Sierra Leone (Lomé Peace Agreement), 1999
Art 16 211
Sierra Leone Citizenship Act, 1973 410
Truth and Reconciliation Commission Act, 2000 155
s 6(2) 130
s 7(3) 132
s 8(1)(a) 158
s 19(2)(a)(ii) 133

Slovenia

Classified Information Act, Law no 50/06, 2006
Art 3 184

Solomon Islands

Truth and Reconciliation Commission Act, 2008 155
Art 12 112

South Africa

Promotion of National Unity and Reconciliation Act, 1995 . . . . . . 259, 308
s 11 . . . . 186, 200
s 29 . . . . 120, 185
s 30 120
s 30(1) 126
s 31 120
s 31(3) 120
s 32 120
s 34(1) 140
s 35 131
s 41(2) 110
s 46(5) 139
South African Promotion of Access to Information Act, Act no 2, 2000 133

South Korea

Framework Act on Clearing Up Past Incidents for Truth and Reconciliation by Law No 7542, 2005
Art 3 112
Art 8 112
Art 11 113
Art 12 113

Spain

Organic Act no 6/ 1985
Art 23(4) 238

Sweden

Freedom of the Press Act, 1766 172

Switzerland

Swiss Criminal Code
Art 7, s 4 287

Tunisia

Loi organique n° 2013-53 du 24 Décembre 2013 relative à l'attribution et l'organisation de la justice transitionnelle
Art 20 114
Art 21 112

Uganda

Ugandan Amnesty Act, 2000 267

United Kingdom

Freedom of Information Act, 2000 . . . . . . 64, 133
Inquiries Act, 2005
s 8(1)(a) 114
s 9(1) 113
Protocol Between the Iraq Inquiry and Her Majesty's Government regarding Documents and Other Written and Electronic Information, 2009
s 7 156
War Crimes Act, 1991
s 1 231

United States

Alien Tort Statute, 1789, 28 USC 228, 341
§ 1350 341
Freedom of Information Act, 1966
§ USC para 552 64
Military Commissions Act, 2009
Title XVIII, HR 2647— 385 §948b 317
Uniform Code of Military Justice, 816.30, 822.22 317
United States of America Freedom of Information Act (FOIA), 1967 133

Uruguay

Law on Access to Public Information, Law no 18381, 2009
Art 12 184

INTERNATIONAL INSTRUMENTS

1899 and 1907 Hague Conventions for the Pacific Settlement of International Disputes
Art 9 111
1906 Convention (I) for the Amelioration of the Condition of the Wounded and Sick in Armies in the Field
Art 4 79
1907 Convention (IV) respecting the Laws and Customs of War on Land and its annex: Regulations concerning the Laws and Customs of War on Land
Art 14 79
Art 16 79
Art 23 199
Art 43 199
Art 53 199
Annex 199
1907 Hague Conventions for the Pacific Settlement of International Disputes . 111
Art 5 111
Art 9 111
1919 Treaty of Peace between the Allied and Associated Powers and Germany (Treaty of Versailles)
Art 227 306
1929 Convention Relative to the Treatment of Prisoners of War
Art 8 79
Art 36 79
Art 38 79
Art 41 79
1929 International Convention for the Suppression of Counterfeiting of Currency
Art 9 240
Art 9(2) 233
1936 Convention for the Suppression of the Illicit Traffic in Dangerous Drugs
Art 8 240
1945 Charter of the United Nations (UN Charter) 29
Preamble 274
Ch I
Art 1 . . . . 29, 274
Art 2 274
Ch VII 299

Ch IX
Art 55 26
Art 56 . . . . 26, 29
Ch XVI
Art 103 236
1945 Statute of the International Court of Justice (ICJ)
Art 38 . . . . 14, 62
Art 38(1) 13
Art 38(1)(a) 207
Art 38(1)(c) 62, 209
Art 38(1)(b) 62
1945 United Nations Charter of the International Military Tribunal—Annex to the Agreement for the prosecution and punishment of the major war criminals of the European Axis ('London Agreement')
Art 6 299
Art 8 292
1946 Constitution of the International Refugee Organization
Annex
Pt II. 273
1946 International Military Tribunal for the Far East – Special proclamation by the Supreme Commander for the Allied Powers at Tokyo
Art 6 292
1948 American Declaration of the Rights and Duties of Man
Art 18 109
Art 26 109
1948 Convention on the Prevention and Punishment for the Crime of Genocide (Genocide Convention) 220, 223, 254
Art IV 208
Art V 208, 221, 261
1948 Universal Declaration of Human Rights (UDHR) 272, 315, 406, 407
Preamble 26
Art 2(3)(a) 315
Art 8 . . . . 137, 315, 352
Art 10 . . . . 109, 258, 315, 319
Art 11 258
Art 12 . . . . .118, 124
Art 14(1) 272
Art 14(2) 273
Art 18–20 258
1949 Geneva Convention for the Amelioration of the Condition of the Wounded and Sick in Armed Forces in Field (GC I) 208, 229, 233–6, 254, 261
Art 4 79
Art 15 79
Art 16 79
Art 49 . . . . 99, 221, 233
Art 50 . . . . 221, 233
Art 51 221
Art 129 . . . . 221, 233
Art 130 221
Art 146 . . . . 221, 233
Art 147 221
1949 Geneva Convention for the Amelioration of the Condition of Wounded, Sick and Shipwrecked Members of Armed Forces at Sea (GC II) 208, 229, 233–6, 254, 261
Art 16 79
Art 49 . . . . 221, 233
Art 50 . . . . 99, 221, 233
Art 51 221
Art 129 . . . . 221, 233
Art 130 221
Art 146 . . . . 221, 233
Art 147 221
1949 Geneva Convention Relative to the Protection of Civilian Persons in Time of War (GC IV) 208, 229, 233–6, 254, 261
Art 14 99
Art 25 79
Art 26 . . . . 79, 82
Art 49 . . . . 221, 233
Art 50 . . . . 221, 233
Art 51 221
Art 106 79
Art 107 79
Art 129 . . . . 79, 221, 233
Art 130 . . . . 79–80, 221
Art 138 79–80
Art 146 . . . . 221, 233
Art 147 221
1949 Geneva Convention Relative to the Treatment of Prisoners of War (GC III) 208, 229, 233–6, 254, 261
Art 3 319
Art 49 . . . . 221, 233
Art 50 . . . . 221, 233
Art 70 79
Art 71 79
Art 122 79
Art 129 . . . . 99, 221, 233

Art 130 221
Art 146 . . . . 221, 233
Art 147 221
1950 Convention for the Protection of Human Rights and Fundamental Freedoms (ECHR) 175–6, 192, 213, 254, 264, 268, 275, 278, 321, 338, 342–3, 366
Art 1 . . . . 212, 339
Art 2 . . . . 48, 366
Art 3 . . . . 67, 81, 83, 174, 176, 277–8, 286, 353
Art 6 . . . . 275, 277–8, 320, 353
Art 6(1) 109
Art 8 . . . . 68, 119, 125,193
Art 8(1) 174
Art 10 . . . . 174, 366
Art 10(2) 181
Art 13 . . . . . . 68, 83, 174, 212, 352, 355, 366
Art 38 . . . . 176, 184
Art 41 . . . . 338, 342–3, 375
Protocol 1
Art 1 68
Protocol 7
Art 4 222
Art 4(2) 283, 288
Protocol 11 264
Protocol 14 . . . . 264, 344
Art 12 344
1951 Convention relating to the Status of Refugees 270-1, 273–4, 276, 278
Art 1(2) 273
Art 1(A)(2) 273
Art 1F 270–1, 276, 278, 309
Art 1F(a) 276–7
Art 1F(c) 276
Art 2 273
Art 32 . . . . 274, 278
Art 33 . . . . 271, 273–4, 278
Art 33(1) 273
Art 33(2) 273
1954 Convention for the Protection of Cultural Property in the Event of Armed Conflict 198
Art 1 199
Art 5(2) 199
1956 Supplementary Convention on the Abolition of Slavery, the Slave Trade, and Institutions and Practices Similar to Slavery
Art 4 208
Art 6 208
1957 European Convention on Extradition CETS no 024
Art 9 283
1959 European Convention on Mutual Assistance in Criminal Matters 133
1966 International Covenant on Civil and Political Rights (ICCPR) 64, 66–8, 181, 183, 222, 254, 263, 285, 309, 315, 362, 406–7
Art 2 365
Art 2(1) 212, 384
Art 2(3) 68, 137, 212, 339, 342
Art 2(3)(a) 315, 338
Art 2(3)(b) 137
Art 3 352
Art 3(a) 355
Art 7 . . . . 67, 83, 174, 278, 285–6
Art 8 315
Art 9(1) 319
Art 9(5) 338
Art 10 315
Art 13 355
Art 14 . . . . 309, 315
Art 14(1) 324
Art 14(6) 338
Art 14(7) 222
Art 17 . . . . 118, 124, 174
Art 18 258
Art 19 . . . . 174, 258, 362
Art 21 258
Art 22 258
1966 International Covenant on Economic, Social and Cultural Rights 66
1967 Declaration on Territorial Asylum . 273, 309
Art 1(2) 270, 309
1967 Protocol relating to the Status of Refugees 273
1968 UN Convention on the Non-Applicability of Statutory Limitations to War Crimes and Crimes against Humanity 251–2, 261
1969 American Convention on Human Rights (ACHR) 37, 39, 64, 66, 176, 254, 283, 322, 338, 344, 352, 362, 377, 408
Art 1(1) 64, 83, 212, 339
Art 2 212
Art 5 67
Art 8 . . . . 64, 68, 83, 365
Art 8(1) 109
Art 8(4) 288
Art 8(5) 109
Art 11 . . . . 119, 125
Art 13 . . . . 64, 365
Art 13(2) 181
Art 14 . . . . 119, 125
Art 22(7) 272
Art 22(8) 275

Art 25 .... 64, 68, 212, 352, 365
Art 25(1) 83, 356
Art 63(1) 338, 343
Art 64(1) 343
1969 Convention on the Specific Aspects of Refugee Problems in Africa 274
Art 1(5) 274
Art 11(3) 274
1970 Convention on the Means of Prohibiting and Preventing the Illicit Import, Export and Transfer of Ownership of Cultural Property 198
Art 1 199
1970 Hague Convention for the Suppression of Unlawful Seizure of Aircraft
Art 4(2) 232
1971 Convention for the Suppression of Unlawful Acts against the Safety of Civil Aviation
Art 5(2) 232
1975 Additional Protocol to the European Convention on Extradition CETS no 086
Art 2 283
1977 Protocol Additional to the Geneva Conventions of 12 August 1949, and relating to the Protection of Victims of International Armed Conflicts (Protocol I) 34, 39, 59, 63, 79, 91, 99, 111, 293
Art 11 221
Art 12 111
Art 32 79–81
Art 33 80
Art 33(3) 82
Art 34 80
Art 85 208
Art 87 293
Art 90 111
1977 Protocol Additional to the Geneva Conventions of 12 August 1949, and relating to the Protection of Victims of Non-International Armed Conflicts (Protocol II) 210, 261, 310
Art 5(2)(b) 79
Art 6(5) 210, 261, 310
Art 8 79
1978 Second Protocol to the European Convention on Extradition
Art 3 288
1979 International Convention against the Taking of Hostages
Art 5(3) 232
1980 Belgrade Minimum Rules of Procedure for International Human Rights Fact-Finding Missions ('Belgrade Rules') 111–12
Section II, Rule 4 111
Section II, Rule 6 112
1981 African Charter on Human and Peoples' Rights (ACHPR) 64, 263, 272, 274
Art 5 .... 67, 83
Art 7 83
Art 7(1) 109, 321
Art 7(1)(a) 356
Art 12(3) 272, 274
Art 18 .... 68, 84
Art 23(2) 274
Art 26 .... 83, 109
1982 UN Convention on the Law of the Sea
Art 102 240
1984 Convention Against Torture and Other Cruel, Inhuman or Degrading Treatment or Punishment 228, 237, 254, 261, 275, 376
Art 2 386
Art 3 275
Art 4 208
Art 5(2) 232
Art 7(1) 233
Art 7(2) 261
Art 12 .... 99, 111, 233
Art 14(1) 338
1985 Declaration of Basic Principles of Justice for Victims of Crime and Abuse of Power
Art 7 352
Annex
para 1 340
para 2 340
1985 Inter-American Convention to Prevent and Punish Torture
Art 13(4) 275
1985 UN Basic Principles on the Independence of the Judiciary 325, 330
Preamble 325
Principles 18–20 112
Art 1 327
Art 4 327
Art 5 330
Art 10 326
Art 11 326
Art 12 326–7
Art 17–19 327
1988 Rome Convention for the Suppression of Unlawful Acts against the Safety of Maritime Navigation
Art 6(4) 232
1989 Convention on the Rights of the Child 124, 403
Art 7 85
Art 8 85

Art 16 . . . . 119, 125
Art 40(2)(b)(iii) 109
1989 UN Principles on the Effective Prevention and Investigation of Extra-Legal, Arbitrary and Summary Executions. 111
Principle 10 111
Principle 11 111
1990 African Charter on the Rights and Welfare of the Child
Art 19 . . . . 68, 84
Art 19(3) 68, 81, 84
Art 19(4) 84
1991 UN Declaration on Fact-Finding in the Field of Maintenance of International Peace and Security 111
Art 26 154
Annex 111
para 3. 111
para 23. 111
1992 Declaration on the Protection of All Persons from Enforced Disappearance 137
Art 13(1) 64
Art 13(2) 137
Art 20 371
1992 Inter-American Convention on Mutual Assistance in Criminal Matters 133
1992 Peace Agreement signed at Mexico City on 16 January 1992 between the Government of El Salvador and the Frente Farabundo Martí para la Liberación Nacional ('Chapultepec Peace Agreement')
s I.3.A 393
1993 Statute of the International Tribunal for the Prosecution of Persons Responsible for Serious Violations of International Humanitarian Law Committed in the Territory of the Former Yugoslavia since 1991 (ICTY Statute) 62, 246, 292
Art 6(3) 293
Art 7(2) 298
Art 7(3) 293
Art 7(4) 292
Art 10 246
Art 22 131
1993 Vienna Declaration and Programme of Action 37
Part II
para 60 . . . . 48, 407
para 91 . . . . 26, 48
1994 Convention on the Safety of United Nations and Associated Personnel
Art 3(2) 232
1994 Inter-American Convention on Forced Disappearance of Persons. 316
Art VII. 253
1994 Statute of the International Criminal Tribunal for Rwanda (ICTR Statute) 62
Art 6(2) 298
Art 6(4) 292
Art 9 246
Art 21 131
1997 International Convention for the Suppression of Terrorist Bombings
Art 6(4) 232
1997 Permanent Court of Arbitration Optional Rules for Fact-finding Commissions of Inquiry
Art 4(2) 111
Art 5 111
1998 Rome Statute of the International Criminal Court (ICC). 40, 88, 206, 215, 219–20, 253, 255–6, 265, 301, 303, 313, 336
Preamble 206, 264
para 2 12
para 4 12
para 6 . . . . 208, 221
para 10 206
Art 1 206
Art 5 206–7
Art 6 207
Art 7 . . . . 207, 253
Art 8 . . . . 40, 207
Art 13(b) 223
Art 13(c) 210
Art 15 210
Art 15(2) 210
Art 15(3) 210
Art 16 223
Art 17 . . . . 206–7, 222, 281, 313
Art 17(2)(a) 287
Art 19(2) 210
Art 19(3) 210
Art 20 281
Art 20(3) 246
Art 27(2) 298
Art 28 . . . . 293, 295, 302
Art 28(a)(ii) 296
Art 28(b) 296
Art 29 253
Art 33(1) 293
Art 33(2) 293, 294
Art 43(6) 131
Art 53 265
Art 68 131
Art 68(3) 85, 210–11

Art 72(7)(a)(i) . . . 184
Art 72(7)(a)(ii) . . . 184
Art 75 . . . 371
Art 75(2) . . . 341
Art 79 . . . 341
Art 87(7) . . . 184
Art 90(4) . . . 235
Art 98(1) . . . 300
Pt 9 . . . 223
2000 Charter of Fundamental Rights of the European Union
Art 18 . . . 272
Art 19(2) . . . 275
Art 42 . . . 64
Art 47 . . . 352
2000 EU Convention on Mutual Assistance on Criminal Matters . . . 133
2000 Optional Protocol to the Convention on the Rights of the Child on the Involvement of Children in Armed Conflict . . . 400
2000 UNTAET Regulation 2000/15 . . . 256
s 21 . . . 292
2001 ILC, Articles on Responsibility of States for Internationally Wrongful Acts . . . 48, 385, 401
Art 31 . . . 48
Art 31(1) . . . 339
Art 33(2) . . . 339
Art 37 . . . 48
Art 41 . . . 48
Art 58(3) . . . 48
2001 UN Transitional Administration in East Timor (UNTAET) Regulation 2001/10 . . . 155
s 4.1 . . . 113
s 17.1 . . . 120
s 17.2 . . . 120
s 36.1 . . . 131
2002 ICC Rules of Procedure and Evidence (RPE) . . . 206
r 72(4)–(5) . . . 184
r 89 210
r 90(2) . . . 211
r 93(4) . . . 184
2002 Statute of the Special Court for Sierra Leone, Annex to the Agreement between the United Nations and the Government of Sierra Leone on the Establishment of a Special Court for Sierra Leone
Art 9 . . . 246
2003 Principles and Guidelines on the Right to a Fair Trial and Legal Assistance in Africa . . . 326
2003 UNGA, United Nations Convention against Corruption
Art 6(2) . . . 138
2004 Arab Charter on Human Rights
Art 28 . . . 275
2005 Regulations of the Trust Fund for Victims
r 98(5) . . . 341
2006 ICC, Regulations of the Registry
r 103 . . . 364
2006 International Convention for the Protection of All Persons from Enforced Disappearance (ICED) . . . 59, 63–4, 89, 99, 137, 183, 261–2
Art 3 . . . 99, 208
Art 6 . . . 89, 99
Art 7 . . . 208
Art 9 . . . 208
Art 9(2) . . . 221, 232
Art 11(1) . . . 135
Art 11(2) . . . 261
Art 12 . . . 137, 183
Art 13(1) . . . 64
Art 15 . . . 373
Art 16 . . . 275
Art 17 . . . 137
Art 17(3) . . . 373
Art 18 . . . 373
Art 18(1) . . . 81
Art 24 . . . 89, 385
Art 24(2) . . . 63, 99
Art 24(4) . . . 338
Art 24(5) . . . 338
2006 United Nations Basic Principles and Guidelines on the Right to a Remedy and Reparation for Victims of Gross Violations of International Human Rights Law and Serious Violations of International Humanitarian Law
Art 11(c) . . . 99
Art 12(b) . . . 353
Art 18 . . . 372
Art 24 . . . 99
2007 Statute of the Special Tribunal for Lebanon
Art 3(2) . . . 293
2008 Optional Protocol to the International Covenant on Economic, Social and Cultural Rights . . . 8
2011 EU Directive 2011/95/EU of 13 December 2011 on standards for the qualification of third-country nationals or stateless persons as beneficiaries of international protection, for a uniform status for

refugees or for persons eligible for subsidiary protection, and for the content of the protection granted (recast) [2011] OJ L337/9 (European Union Qualification Directive) 274
Art 12 274
Art 12(2)(b) 274
Art 12(2)(c) 274
Art 12(3) 274
Art 17 274
Art 17(1)(d) 274
Art 17(3) 274
2011 Universal Declaration on Archives, adopted by UNESCO 164
2012 Declaration of Human Rights of the Association of Southeast Asian Nations (ASEAN)
Principle 3 68
Principle 5 68
Principle 14 67
2012 Directive 2012/29/EU of the European Parliament and of the Council of 25 October 2012 Establishing Minimum Standards on the Rights, Support and Protection of Victims of Crime, and Replacing Council Framework Decision 2001/220/JHA, [2012] OJ L315/57 211
Art 10 212
Art 11 212
Art 16 212
2012 Special Court for Sierra Leone, Rules of Evidence and Procedure, (as amended 31 May 2012)
r 8 185
2013 IACtHR, Rules of Procedure
r 25 185
2013 Treaty on Mutual Assistance on Criminal Matters between UK and Jordan 275
2014 Statute of the African Court of Justice and Human and Peoples' Rights, Annex to the Protocol on Amendments to the Protocol on the Statute of the African Court of Justice and Human Rights, adopted at the Malabo summit
Art 6 206
2015 Extraordinary Chambers in the Courts of Cambodia, Internal Rules (rev 9)
r 5 185
2015 ICTY Rules of Procedure and Evidence (rev 50),
r 54 bis (A) 184
r 54 (E) 184
r 54 (F) 184
2016 European Court of Human Rights, Rules of Court
r 61 346
2017 Documentary Management Protocol of the files referring to grave and overt violations of Human Rights and violations of International Humanitarian Law 169

List of Contributors

Kai Ambos is the Chair of Criminal Law, Criminal Procedure, Comparative Law and International Criminal Law at the Georg-August-University Göttingen and Director of the Centre for Latinamerican Criminal Law and Justice (CEDPAL) at the same university. He is also judge at the Kosovo Specialist Chambers, The Hague, and *amicus curiae* of the Colombian Special Jurisdiction for Peace, Bogota, Colombia.

Alison Bisset is Associate Professor in International Human Rights Law at the University of Reading.

Valentina Cadelo is Associate Legal Adviser, International Commission of Jurists, Middle East & North Africa Programme.

John D Ciorciari is Associate Professor of Public Policy at the University of Michigan's Gerald R. Ford School of Public Policy, where he also directs the International Policy Centre.

Pierre d'Argent is a full professor at the Université de Louvain, associate member of the Institute of International Law and member of the Brussels Bar.

Isabelle de Ghellinck is a member of the Brussels Bar.

Max du Plessis is a Barrister in South Africa and Associate Tenant at Doughty Street Chambers, London. He is also an Honorary Research Associate at the University of KwaZulu-Natal.

Roger Duthie is Director of Research at the International Center for Transitional Justice.

Mark Freeman is the founder and Executive Director of the Institute for Integrated Transitions.

Paola Gaeta Professor of International Law at the Graduate Institute of International and Development Studies (Geneva) and Adjunct Professor at the Law Department of Bocconi University, Milan.

Christopher Gosnell is a counsel in private practice who has represented defendants before the ICTY, SCSL and ICTR.

Dermot Groome is a Professor of International Criminal Law at Penn State's Dickinson Law.

Lucas S Grosman is the President of Universidad de San Andrés, Argentina.

Frank Haldemann is the Co-Director of the Master of Advanced Studies (MAS) in Transitional Justice, Human Rights and the Rule of law at the Geneva Academy of International Humanitarian Law and Human Rights

Colin Harvey is Professor of Human Rights Law at Queen's University Belfast School of Law.

Catherine Harwood is a PhD Candidate at the Grotius Centre for International Legal Studies at Leiden University.

Sandra Krähenmann is Research Fellow at the Geneva Academy of International Humanitarian Law and Human Rights.

Lisa J Laplante is an Associate Professor at New England Law/Boston, where she also directs the Center for International Law and Policy.

Alexander Mayer-Rieckh is a human rights, transitional justice and security sector reform expert with over 20 years of advisory and management experience in transitional contexts.

Fionnuala Ní Aoláin is concurrently the Dorsey and Whitney Chair in Law at the University of Minnesota Law School and a professor of law at the University of Ulster's Transitional Justice Institute in Belfast, Northern Ireland.

Ilya Nuzov is a former Teaching Assistant at the Geneva Academy of International Humanitarian Law and Human Rights and has worked as a legal advisor at the International Center for Transitional Justice.

Diane Orentlicher is a Professor of International Law at American University Washington College of Law.

Trudy Huskamp Peterson is an archival consultant and certified archivist, who spent twenty-four years with the US National Archives.

Giulia Pinzauti is an Assistant Professor of Public International Law at the Grotius Centre for International Legal Studies, Leiden University.

Isabel Robinson is a legal advisor to the Australian Red Cross, Humanitarian and Medical sectors.

Naomi Roht-Arriaza is a Distinguished Professor of Law at the University of California, Hastings College of Law in San Francisco.

Robert Roth is Professor of International Criminal Law at the Geneva Faculty of Law and the Director of the Geneva Academy of International Humanitarian Law and Human Rights.

William A Schabas is Professor of International Law at Middlesex University, London, and Professor of International Law and Human Rights at Leiden University.

Ilia Maria Siatitsa is a Researcher at the Geneva Academy of International Humanitarian Law and Human Rights.

Carsten Stahn is a Professor of International Criminal Law and Global Justice at Leiden University Law School, and Programme Director at the Grotius Centre for International Legal Studies.

Thomas Unger is Co-Director of the Master of Advanced Studies (MAS) in Transitional Justice, Human Rights and the Rule of law at the Geneva Academy of International Humanitarian Law and Human Rights Geneva Academy of International Humanitarian Law and Human Rights.

Theo van Boven is Emeritus Professor of International Law at the University of Maastricht.

Howard Varney is a Senior Program Advisor with the International Center for Transitional Justice.

Julia Viebach is a Leverhulme Trust Early Career Fellow at the University of Oxford, Faculty of Law.

Marieke Wierda is the Rule of Law Coordinator for the Dutch Ministry of Foreign Affairs. Her contribution to this Commentary has been written in her personal capacity and does not necessarily reflect the position of the Dutch Ministry of Foreign Affairs.

Prologue

Diane Orentlicher

As I wrapped up my work updating the United Nations (UN) Set of Principles to Combat Impunity in 2005,[1] the value of a detailed commentary was already clear. The UN's merciless word limits meant that the report I drafted to accompany the Updated Principles could provide only the most laconic treatment of issues so complex as to warrant a nuanced, in-depth treatment. And so I could not have been more pleased to learn that leading experts had been engaged to produce this Commentary. I was delighted, as well, to accept the editors' invitation to offer reflections on the process of updating the Principles.

By their nature, the Principles presented distinct challenges for someone tasked, as I was, to update their text. To begin, the Principles serve two fundamentally different functions, whose harmonious integration in a single instrument called for careful calibration.

On the one hand, the Principles function as a classic soft law instrument: rooted in the bedrock obligation of states to ensure protection of individuals from grievous harm, they reflect established principles of international law, while in some respects affirming nascent developments. Precisely because they were considered a reliable distillation of established law and emerging practice, the Principles had a profound impact soon after Louis Joinet completed their original text.[2] As I approached the task of updating them, preserving the authority of Joinet's masterful text was of paramount importance. Thus I have been gratified to learn that, in myriad countries that have made hard-won gains against deeply entrenched impunity, the Updated Principles have provided a key source of support and inspiration since their endorsement by the UN Commission on Human Rights.[3]

On the other hand, alongside their codification function, the Principles were, in Mr Joinet's conception, 'standards drawn from experience'[4] that could serve 'as a broad strategic framework for action against impunity'.[5] The Resolution calling for their revision affirmed their dual nature: the 1997 text was to be updated not only 'to reflect recent developments in international law and practice', but also to take account of best practices

[1] The Updated Set of Principles for the protection and promotion of human rights through action to combat impunity was published in an addendum to the *Report of the independent expert to update the Set of Principles to Combat Impunity*, UN (Document) Doc E/CN.4/2005/102 (18 February 2005) (hereinafter '*Report of the independent expert*').

[2] In a 2004 study, I noted the Principles had, since their presentation by Mr Joinet in 1997, 'already had a profound impact on efforts to combat impunity', and continued: 'They have become a key reference in decisions by the supervisory bodies for the American Convention on Human Rights, which, in turn, have prompted national Governments to dismantle seemingly impregnable barriers to justice. The Principles have also been cited directly by national authorities in support of measures to combat impunity.' *Independent Study on best practices, including recommendations, to assist states in strengthening their domestic capacity to combat all aspects of impunity, by Professor Diane Orentlicher*, UN Doc E/CN.4/2004/88 (27 February 2004), para 8 (hereinafter '*Independent study on best practices*').

[3] UN Commission on Human Rights (UNComHR) (Resolution) Res 2005/81, paras 20–23.

[4] *Revised final report prepared by Mr Joinet pursuant to Sub-Commission decision 1996/119*, UN Doc E/CN.4/Sub.2/1997/20/Rev.1 (2 October 1997), para 45 (hereinafter '*Revised final report prepared by Mr Joinet*').

[5] Ibid, para 46(1).

in combating impunity as elaborated in an independent study I had been tasked to prepare the previous year and other sources.[6] As a source of practical guidance derived from 'best practices', the Principles reflect a core premise: the accrued experience of countries that have endured the wholesale collapse of legal protection is a precious resource for societies confronting their own legacies of impunity.

Distilling that experience to provide useful guidance in a broad range of settings presented challenges of another kind. Most obviously, the lived experiences that inform the Principles are astonishingly complex, constantly evolving (sometimes, it seems, at warp speed) and infinitely diverse. Indeed, each society's experience in confronting the crushing costs of impunity is singular.[7] Several issues addressed in the Principles are, moreover, among the most intensely debated in the field of human rights. Particularly in light of these challenges, I was extremely fortunate to be able to mine the insights of individuals possessing exceptional expertise, among whom I owe a special debt to Pablo de Greiff and Priscilla Hayner, governments, and a global corps of domestic human rights advocates, survivors, and non-governmental organizations, who generously shared their knowledge, perspectives, and wisdom.

Another consideration loomed large in my work. When a country has descended into the darkest abyss of human degradation, it matters deeply that its citizens deliberate together, in an inclusive way, about how to confront their legacy of impunity. No set of principles could or should displace the quintessentially local project of communal reckoning. Accordingly, I approached the task of updating the Principles determined to honour the unique experience and agency of each society that might benefit from their guidance, even as I sought to clarify the contours of legal obligation.

The Updated Principles reflect this commitment in various ways. First, they repeatedly affirm the importance of broad public engagement, 'in which the views of victims and survivors especially are sought', in a society's deliberations about programmes to combat impunity.[8] Second, where appropriate, the Updated Principles use such words as 'may' or 'should'[9] instead of 'shall', with a view to leaving suitable latitude to adapt broad principles, ideally through an inclusive deliberate process, to diverse contexts. Third, and for much the same reason, a few passages retain a certain measure of ambiguity (or, perhaps more precisely, flexibility).[10]

The last of these would serve another purpose, as well—or at any rate that was and remains my hope. I was keenly aware that our appreciation of the complexities and challenges bound up in combating impunity would continue to deepen and evolve, as they had in the years leading up to my work updating the 1997 text. For example, the Updated Principles reflect a then recently heightened awareness of challenges surrounding the inclusion of women and members of other 'groups [that] have been especially vulnerable to human rights violations' in commissions of inquiry.[11] And so I aspired to

[6] UNComHR Res 2004/72, para 20.

[7] See *Independent study on best practices*, n 2, para 5 ('The unique historical experience of each society that has endured ... violations will inevitably shape its citizens' understanding of justice'; 'there is no "one-size-fits-all" response to serious violations of human rights').

[8] This quotation comes from Updated Principle 6, which addresses the establishment of truth commissions. Similar language appears elsewhere, eg Updated Principles 32 and 35.

[9] See, eg, Updated Principle 8.

[10] More typically, however, revisions were made with a view to clarifying relevant Principles. Examples are noted and explained in the *Report of the independent expert*, n 1.

[11] Updated Principle 7(c). See also *Report of the independent expert*, n 1, para 27.

craft a text that provided practical guidance for contemporary challenges, while leaving ample space to accommodate further evolution in our understanding of 'best practices in combating impunity'. Indeed, I believe this volume is all the more valuable because it comes more than a decade after the Principles were updated: it is my understanding that contributing authors will not only elaborate upon the legal foundation of the Principles, but also reflect practice since they were updated in 2005.

Returning to the delicate balance I noted at the outset, while the Updated Principles seek to honour local agency, reflecting in particular the perspectives of victims, they also recognize the elemental importance of clarifying where local discretion ends and legal obligation begins. If these dual commitments exist in some tension, they are hardly irreconcilable; after all, the law the Principles reflect emerged from wide-ranging experience over an extended period. Even as survivors demand remedies responsive to their unique experience of harm, time and again, across disparate regions and cultures, they have derived incalculable benefit from their ability to frame their calls for justice in the language of universal law.[12]

[12] Mr Joinet evoked much the same point in his report proposing the Principles. Those working to secure justice for crimes against the basic law of humanity were, he wrote, 'increasingly aware of the need to back up' their calls for justice 'with reference to standards drawn from experience and recognized by the international community'. *Revised final report prepared by Mr Joinet*, n 2, para 45.

Introduction

Frank Haldemann and Thomas Unger[1]

> The peoples of the earth have ... entered in varying degrees into a universal community, and it has developed to the point where a violation of rights in *one* part of the world is felt *everywhere*. The idea of a cosmopolitan right is therefore not fantastic and overstrained; it is a necessary complement to the unwritten code of political and international right, transforming it into a universal right of humanity. Only under this condition can we flatter ourselves that we are continually advancing towards a perpetual peace.
>
> —Immanuel Kant[2]

We live, it has been said, in an 'age of accountability'.[3] Although an over-simplification, there is some truth in this formulation. In our twenty-first-century world, 'holding perpetrators accountable' and 'ending a culture of impunity' have become central rallying cries for human rights movements across the globe. The battle against impunity has indeed become, as Samuel Moyn puts it, 'one of the unique ethical signatures of our time'.[4] It was not always so, however. Originally concerned with publicly naming and shaming abusive governments, human rights activists did not engage with the issue of impunity until the mid-1980s.[5] The turn to accountability in human rights was therefore not a linear process, but rather a 'dramatic and transformative event' shaped by the special circumstances of the time.[6]

The rise of a global anti-impunity discourse can be traced back to what has been called the 'long decade' of the 1990s, spanning from the formal end of the Cold War (1989/1991) to 2005.[7] This period saw the outbreak of genocidal violence and mass atrocity in many parts of the world, including Rwanda and the former Yugoslavia, but it also witnessed a remarkable number of new international interventions, initiatives, norms, and institutions, each dedicated to fighting the spectre of impunity. At the forefront of these moves was the turn to criminalization as an avenue for human rights enforcement. High-profile trials of former heads of state, including Augusto Pinochet and Slobodan Milošević, testified to a new global trend in world politics towards holding individual

1 We thank Elena Carpanelli for her substantial research contribution to the section dealing with the Principles' drafting history. Warm thanks also to Sandra Krähenmann, Valentina Cadelo, Christof Heyns, and Diane Orentlicher for their insightful comments.

2 I Kant, 'Perpetual Peace: A Philosophical Sketch' in HS Reiss (ed), *Kant, Political Writings* (2nd edn, CUP 1991) 93–130, 107–08 (emphasis in the original).

3 K Sikkink, 'The Age of Accountability: The Global Rise of Individual Criminal Accountability' in F Lessa and LA Payne (eds), *Amnesty in the Age of Human Rights Accountability: Comparative and International Perspectives* (CUP 2012) 19–41.

4 S Moyn, 'Anti-Impunity as Deflection of Argument' in K Engle, Z Miller, and DM Davis (eds), *Anti-Impunity and the Human Rights Agenda* (OUP 2016) 68–94, 68.

5 See P Arthur, 'How "Transitions" Reshaped Human Rights: A Conceptual History of Transitional Justice' (2009) 31 Human Rights Quarterly 321–67, 334.

6 Moyn, n 4, at 69.

7 JH Quataert, *Advocating Dignity: Human Rights Mobilizations in Global Politics* (University of Pennsylvania Press 2009) 16–17.

state officials criminally accountable for human rights violations.[8] But the 'long decade' saw also a global spread of other accountability 'mechanisms', notably truth commissions and reparations programmes, directed at addressing legacies of impunity and pursuing transitional justice.[9]

The United Nations (UN) Set of Principles for the protection and promotion of human rights through action to combat impunity (hereinafter 'the Principles') can be seen as a reflection of this global trend towards accountability.[10] This landmark document is the fruit of several years of study, carried out under the aegis of the UN Commission on Human Rights. Originally drafted by Louis Joinet and updated by Diane Orentlicher, the Principles constitute an authoritative reference point for efforts in the international fight against impunity. Developed in the 1990s and updated in the early 2000s, the Principles emerged in parallel with another key UN document dedicated to victims' rights and state obligations—the Basic Principles on the Right to a Remedy and Reparation for Victims of Gross Violations of International Human Rights Law and Serious Violations of International Humanitarian Law (hereinafter 'Basic Principles on Reparations').[11]

Despite their importance for theory and practice, which has lost some traction in the last years, the thirty-eight Principles to combat impunity have so far not been the subject of a comprehensive academic commentary. The present book seeks to fill this gap. It offers a multi-authored companion to the document, providing a detailed principle-by-principle analysis in the light of the relevant literature and practice. Conceived as a systematic in-depth study of the Principles, the Commentary gathers more than thirty-six authors engaging head-on with a variety of complex theoretical and practical issues currently discussed in the arena of human rights and beyond. Rather than a simple endorsement of the Principles, this book is intended as a multifaceted critical reflection about what the 'fight against impunity' means and involves, as well as about the problems and concerns to which it may give rise. It is hoped that this critical reflection will also contribute to some discussion outside academic circles, and provide some impetus for reform where needed to address the ever-changing landscape in the fight against impunity.

What follows is an introductory discussion, designed to orient readers towards the basic issues and thus set the stage for the more detailed analyses in the subsequent contributions to this Commentary. The central aim, here, will be to place the Principles in their wider historical and political context, and to clarify their conceptual and

[8] For a prominent analysis of this phenomenon, see K Sikkink, *The Justice Cascade: How Human Rights Prosecutions Are Changing World Politics* (Norton 2011).

[9] On the recent spread of reparations politics, see J Torpey, *Making Whole What Has Been Smashed: On Reparations Politics* (Harvard University Press 2006); R Ludi, *Reparations for Nazi Victims in Post-War Europe* (CUP 2012). On the emergence of truth commissions, see PB Hayner, *Unspeakable Truths: Transitional Justice and the Challenge of Truth Commissions* (2nd edn, Routledge 2011). Recent book-length contributions to the ever-expanding literature on transitional justice include C Brants, A Hol, and D Siegel (eds), *Transitional Justice: Images and Memories* (Routledge 2013); S Buckley Zistel and T Koloma Beck (eds), *Transitional Justice Theories* (Routledge 2013); C Lawther, L Moffett, and D Jacobs (eds), *Research Handbook on Transitional Justice* (Edward Elgar Publishing 2017); C Murphy, *The Conceptual Foundations of Transitional Justice* (CUP 2017); N Roht-Arriaza and J Marriezcurrena (eds), *Transitional Justice in the Twenty-First Century: Beyond Truth versus Justice* (CUP 2006); O Simić (ed), *An Introduction to Transitional Justice* (Routledge 2017); R Teitel, *Globalizing Transitional Justice: Contemporary Essays* (OUP 2014).

[10] Updated Set of Principles for the protection and promotion of human rights through action to combat impunity, UN Doc E/CN.4/2005/102/Add.1 (8 February 2005).

[11] Basic Principles and Guidelines on the Right to a Remedy and Reparation for Victims of Gross Violations of International Human Rights Law and Serious Violations of International Humanitarian Law, UNGA Res 60/147, UN Doc A/RES/60/147 (21 March 2006).

normative nature. Moreover, we shall give an overview of the general structure and organization of the Principles, and outline the basic aims and approach of this Commentary. This Introduction will close with some critical reflections on the role, limitations, and opportunities of the Principles in addressing current challenges, especially with respect to 'transitional' societies emerging from prolonged periods of armed conflict or oppression.

Before diving in, however, a *definitional clarification* is in order. Throughout this Introduction, we use the term 'impunity' along the lines suggested by the Principles. While many discussions equate 'impunity' with the absence of criminal justice, the Principles define the term more broadly to mean 'the impossibility, de jure or de facto, of bringing the perpetrators of violations to account' (see definition A). As made explicit in Principle 1, impunity in this sense arises from a failure of the state to meet one of the following four obligations under international human rights law: (i) to investigate serious human rights violations; (ii) to prosecute, try, and duly punish perpetrators of such violations; (iii) to provide victims with effective remedies and reparation for the harm suffered; and (iv) to take the appropriate steps to prevent a repetition of violations. Throughout this Introduction, we employ this broad notion of 'impunity' and, correspondingly, use the term 'anti-impunity' to refer to measures being taken to counter this phenomenon.

A. Drafting the Principles: A Short History

It is tempting to think of law as a 'pure' phenomenon, sealed off from the messy realm of politics, history, and ideology. But as Judith Shklar argued more than fifty years ago, this temptation—she called it 'legalism'—should be resisted or at least questioned.[12] Not only does legalism misguidedly reduce law to a 'closed' system endowed with its own independent logic and integrity, but it also tends to obscure the variety of controversial political purposes behind apparently 'neutral' legal practices and discourses.[13] All this makes legalism an inadequate lens through which to approach law as a complex *social* phenomenon, shaped by historical context and evolving ideas about political legitimacy and authority. With this in mind, the following section approaches the Principles not as something that is just 'there', as a self-contained sphere of practice, but as part of a complex political process within the United Nations.

While the Principles figure prominently in contemporary human rights discourse, their drafting history is often unknown. This has much to do with the fact that there are no *travaux préparatoires* documenting multilateral work of the UN in the arena of human rights. The knowledge of who was behind a particular initiative is therefore often lost or transferred within a very small circle of experts. Some information can be found in sources such as decisions, requests, resolutions by the different multilateral human rights entities, but a systematic review of the drafting history is rarely provided. This leaves room for misinterpretation and distortion of the real meaning, ideas, and dynamics behind this initiative. With the aim to contribute to more clarity, the following pages seek to re-construct the drafting history of the Principles.

[12] JN Shklar, *Legalism: Law, Morals and Political Trials* (Harvard University Press 1964).

[13] For a critical account of the idea of law as a 'closed system', see also R Cotterell, *Law's Community: Legal Theory in Sociological Perspective* (Clarendon Press 1995) 91–110.

As already mentioned, the Principles were developed within the UN Human Rights System throughout the 1990s and early 2000s. The United Nations Commission on Human Rights (hereinafter 'the Commission'), and particularly its Sub-Commission on Prevention of Discrimination and Protection of Minorities (hereinafter 'the Sub-Commission'), played a crucial role in this process. In parallel, human rights experts and civil society exercised considerable influence in shaping the UN anti-impunity agenda. This is particularly true of UN expert Louis Joinet, who was critical in drafting the Principles. States, conversely, played rather a minor role in the elaboration of the Principles since they were actually never negotiated in a multilateral setting. But let us start from the beginning.

In 1991, the question of impunity appeared for the first time on the agenda of the Sub-Commission. It was during its forty-third session that several non-governmental organizations (NGOs) raised the issue, highlighting how impunity prevented any effective protection of human rights and undermined the rule of law in post-dictatorship or post-conflict societies.[14] The initial discussion in the Sub-Commission illustrates well how in its early days the debate on impunity turned around—and was prompted by—the question of amnesties. A few years earlier, in 1985, Mr Joinet, at that time Special Rapporteur on amnesty, had submitted his final report, entitled *Study on amnesty laws and their role in the safeguard and promotion of human rights*, which, according to the author himself, constituted a 'frame of reference that might be of use to the experts of the various specialized international supervisory bodies, in order to enable them to better assess the impact—positive, negative or nil—of an amnesty law cited in justification of authorities'.[15]

In this initial phase, the Sub-Commission requested two of its members, Louis Joinet and El Hadji Guissé, to draft a working paper on the approaches that a study on impunity might take. The paper was submitted to the Sub-Commission in 1992.[16] On this basis, the Sub-Commission requested the co-authors to undertake a study on the impunity of perpetrators of human rights violations.[17] No distinction was made at this point between impunity for violations of civil and political rights on the one hand and economic, social, and cultural rights on the other. Preliminary reports were submitted to the Sub-Commission in 1993 and 1994.[18] In 1994, following a request by the Sub-Commission, the Commission on Human Rights decided to split the study in two. It thus asked the two experts to submit first a report on impunity in the context of civil and political rights and then a study focusing on impunity within the framework of economic, social, and cultural

[14] UN Doc E/CN.4/Sub.2/1991/WP.5 (28 June 1991) para 28.

[15] UN Doc E/CN.4/Sub.2/1985/16/Rev.1 (21 June 1995) para 86.

[16] Sub-Commission decision 1991/110 in UN Doc E/CN.4/Sub.2/1991/65 (24 October 1991) 86; UN Doc E/CN.4/Sub.2/1992/18 (25 August 1992).

[17] Sub-Commission Res 1992/23 (27 August 1992) in UN Doc E/CN.4/Sub.2/1992/58 (14 October 1992) 63 et seq. The Commission on Human Rights endorsed the Sub-Commission's decision with Res 1993/43. See UN Doc E/CN.4/RES/1993/43 (5 March 1993).

[18] See *The administration of justice and the human rights of detainees: The question of human rights of persons subjected to any form of detention or imprisonment. Progress Report on the question of the impunity of perpetrators of human rights violations, prepared by Mr Guissé and Mr Joinet,* UN Doc E/CN.4/Sub.2/1993/6 (19 July 1993) (hereinafter 'Progress Report'). In their preliminary report they suggested subdividing the study into two parts: a first part, concerning the impunity of perpetrators of violations of civil and political rights; and a second part, addressing the impunity of perpetrators of violations of economic, social, and cultural rights.

rights.[19] Interestingly, however, Mr Joinet and Mr Guissé decided to defer the first part of the study (civil and political rights) to a future session and to present to the Sub-Commission, at its forty-sixth session, in 1994, a *Preliminary report on the impunity of perpetrators of violations of economic, social and cultural rights*.[20] The co-Special Rapporteurs' choice to focus on impunity for violations of economic, social, and cultural rights was motivated, in particular, by the complexity of the matter.[21] With this complexity in mind, the Sub-Commission decided to entrust each of the experts with a different part of the study: Mr Joinet was entrusted with the task to complete the study in its first aspect, relating to civil and political rights, while Mr Guissé was requested to address the second aspect, relating to the impunity of perpetrators of violations of economic, social, and cultural rights.[22] From this moment on, the two studies continued separately.

At the Sub-Commission's forty-seventh session, held in 1995, two different reports were presented. Mr Guissé submitted his *Interim report on opposition to the impunity of perpetrators of human rights violations (economic, social and cultural rights)*,[23] whereas Mr Joinet presented a *Progress report on the impunity of perpetrators of violations of civil and political rights*.[24] Pursuing this dual-track approach, both Rapporteurs presented final reports in 1997. Joinet's 1997 report included a Set of Principles for the protection and promotion of human rights through action to combat impunity (hereinafter 'Joinet Principles').[25] The Joinet Principles introduced the well-known *trilogy* of core rights and remedies: the right to know, the right to justice, and the right to reparation and guarantees of non-recurrence.[26] Guissé, for his part, submitted his study on impunity and economic, social, and cultural rights, which included a set of recommendations and suggestions for further action. [27] Based on previous reports, he made the following recommendations: the cancellation of the debt of those countries that had been colonized; the declaration that violations of economic, social, and cultural rights amount to international crimes and, as such, should be subject to international jurisdiction and imprescriptibility; the adoption of an optional Protocol to the International Covenant on Economic, Social and Cultural Rights; and the enactment of measures that protect the vulnerable segments of the population.[28]

Both reports were submitted by the Sub-Commission to the Commission on Human Rights for its consideration and adoption. On the question of impunity for perpetrators

[19] Sub-Commission Res 1993/37 (26 August 1993) in UN Doc E/CN.4/Sub.2/1993/45 (25 October 1993) 80. The Commission on Human Rights endorsed the Sub-Commission's decision with Res UN Doc E/CN.4/RES/1994/44 (4 March 1994).

[20] UN Doc E/CN.4/Sub.2/1994/11 (22 June 1994). In their report, the Special Rapporteurs found that, in light of the mandate received, the following aspects were worth being further analysed: prevention of corruption, role of international financial institutions, economic embargo, and treaty protection of economic, social, and cultural rights.

[21] Ibid, at 2.

[22] Sub-Commission Res 1994/34 (26 August 1994) in UN Doc E/CN.4/Sub.2/1994/56 (28 October 1994) 81.

[23] UN Doc E/CN.4/Sub.2/1995/19 (27 June 1995).

[24] UN Doc E/CN.4/Sub.2/1995/18 (18 June 1995).

[25] See *Question of the impunity of perpetrators of human rights violations (civil and political), Revised final report prepared by Mr Joinet pursuant to Sub-Commission decision 1996/119*, UN Doc E/CN.4/Sub.2/1997/20/Rev.1 (2 October 1997) (hereinafter 'Joinet Report').

[26] See in this volume, 'Preamble', by Theo van Boven.

[27] UN Doc E/CN.4/Sub.2/1997/8 (27 June 1997).

[28] Ibid, at 36 et seq.

of economic, social, and cultural rights, the Sub-Commission even recommended the Commission to establish a mandate for a Special Rapporteur.[29] As to the Joinet Principles, the Sub-Commission recommended to the Commission their transmission to the General Assembly for adoption.[30] At its 1998 session, however, the Commission on Human Rights only took note of the final report submitted by Mr Joinet and the annexed *Set of Principles*.[31] Thus, the Commission never formally endorsed the Principles and they were not transmitted to the General Assembly (in contrast to the Basic Principles on Reparations mentioned later in this section). Similarly, at its 1999 session, the Commission on Human Rights only took note of the final report submitted by Mr Guissé. In addition, despite the Sub-Commission's suggestion, no Special Rapporteur on the impunity of perpetrators of economic, social, and cultural rights was appointed to continue addressing the matter.[32] Despite the end of the Cold War, the split between the 'two blocks' can still be seen in the voting pattern on this question, with western countries all voting against the establishment of a Special Rapporteur on fighting impunity for economic, social, and cultural rights.

From 2000 on, the Commission on Human Rights pushed for updating the Joinet Principles through a Canadian-run initiative. In 2003, it requested the UN Secretary-General to commission a study on best practices to combat impunity. The Secretary-General solicited Professor Diane Orentlicher, a highly regarded human rights scholar, to produce such as study. Having presented her study at the Commission's 2004 session,[33] Orentlicher was appointed to update the Principles to Combat Impunity in light of recent developments and state practice in international law. In 2005, Orentlicher submitted an updated version of the Principles to the Commission on Human Rights.[34] The updated text largely confirms and preserves the Principles as they were proposed in 1997. Revisions particularly reflect not only major institutional developments since 1997, including the establishment of the International Criminal Court (ICC) and the emergence of hybrid courts, but also state practice affirming the central importance of victims' participation in accountability processes. In addition, the Updated Principles advance further the so-called '4th pillar of transitional justice', namely, the guarantees of non-recurrence, by introducing the need to establish effective institutions of civilian oversight over security institutions. In 2005, the Commission on Human Rights took note with appreciation of the Updated Principles, 'as a guideline to assist States in developing effective measures for combating impunity'.[35] Despite this preliminary endorsement, however, the Principles were not formally adopted by the Commission, nor by the General Assembly. As for the Human Rights Council, which succeeded the Commission in 2006, it has—at least so far—not taken any steps towards formal endorsement.

[29] Sub-Commission Res 1997/20 (27 August 1997) in UN Doc E/CN.4/Sub.2/1997/50 (5 November 1997) 52.

[30] Sub-Commission Res 1997/28 (28 August 1997) in UN Doc E/CN.4/Sub.2/1997/50 (5 November 1997) 68.

[31] UN Doc E/CN.4/RES/1998/53 (17 April 1998), adopted without a vote.

[32] UN Doc E/CN.4/RES/1999/58 (28 April 1999). The Commission also decided to continue its consideration of the matter at its fifty-sixth session.

[33] *Independent Study on best practices, including recommendations, to assist states in strengthening their domestic capacity to combat all aspects of impunity, by Professor Diane Orentlicher*, UN Doc E/CN.4/2004/88 (27 February 2004).

[34] Updated Set of Principles, n 10.

[35] United Nations, *Impunity. Resolution adopted by the Commission on Human Rights*, UN Doc E/CN.4/RES/2005/81 (21 April 2005) para 20.

This reluctance to formally endorse the Principles can be explained, at least partly, by the fear of states that such a formalized set of principles would complicate reconciliation processes. According to a widely held view, the Principles are best seen as flexible instruments of guidance with the potential to gradually acquire, through widespread usage, quasi-legal recognition.[36] Some commentators highlight the benefit of such an approach, arguing that a more formalized process may end up watering down well-established standards.[37]

Recent years suggest, however, a decline in usage of the Principles.[38] There are currently no discussions about further updating the Principles, with a view to bringing them into accordance with recent developments or to address potential gaps in the international anti-impunity framework (see 'Concluding Remarks: Debating Anti-impunity' in section F of this chapter); nor are there serious attempts at having the Principles adopted by the UN General Assembly to follow in the footsteps of the Basic Principles on Reparations. However, the Principles have recently gained additional recognition through the creation of a new UN Special Rapporteur mandate dedicated to the promotion of truth, justice, reparation, and guarantees of non-recurrence. Established by the Human Rights Council in 2011, the mandate reflects precisely the four-pillar structure of the Joinet/Orentlicher Principles and thus emphasizes, at least implicitly, its significance at the UN policy level.[39]

Before closing this section, it is worth mentioning the close relationship between the UN Principles to combat impunity and another key human rights document developed in parallel under the auspices of UN Commission on Human Rights—the aforementioned United Nations Basic Principles and Guidelines on the Right to a Remedy and Reparation. Based on the studies of two independent experts, Theo van Boven and Cherif Bassiouni, these Basic Principles and Guidelines were adopted without vote by the UN General Assembly in December 2005. As Theo van Boven notes in this Commentary, these two sets of Principles can be seen as 'twin sets of Principles serving the same agenda but following different tracks in their coming into existence'.[40]

Taking up this idea of synergetic coexistence, Joinet stated in the preparatory documents that his final report should take account of the proposals made by van Boven on the issue of reparations to victims of gross human rights violations.[41] In 1989, the Sub-Commission had tasked van Boven with undertaking a study concerning the right to restitution, compensation, and rehabilitation for victims of gross human rights violations. Following considerable preparatory work, in 1993 van Boven submitted his final report, with proposed Basic Principles and Guidelines on the Right to Reparation for Victims of Gross Violations of Human Rights and Humanitarian Law.

Joinet largely based the section on reparation in the 1996 version and then also in the revised 1997 version of the Principles on van Boven's report.[42] He thus ensured that the reparation section in the Principles to Combat Impunity benefited from and was

[36] Orentlicher, in her *Report of the independent expert to update the Set of Principles to combat impunity, Diane Orentlicher*, UN Doc E/CN.4/2005/102 (18 February 2005) (hereinafter 'Orentlicher Report'), pointed out that the principles received strong affirmation in decisions by international criminal tribunals and human rights treaty bodies. They are also frequently quoted in reports of commissions of inquiry; see also the reference in the *Report of the Secretary-General's Panel of Experts on Accountability in Sri Lanka* (31 March 2011) 266.

[37] International Center for Transitional Justice (ICTJ) Brief, *Transitional Justice in the United Nations Human Rights Council*, June 2011, 4.

[38] Ibid. [39] A/HRC/RES/18/7.

[40] See 'Summary of Findings' in van Boven's contribution to this volume.

[41] See Progress Report, n 18, para 131. [42] Joinet Report, n 25, para 41.

consistent with the Sub-Commission's work on reparation. With respect to the issue of guarantees of non-recurrence, however, Joinet moved away from the van Boven Principles. While van Boven treated guarantees of non-repetition solely as a form of reparation, Joinet introduced the so-called '4th pillar' of transitional justice—a separate and independent category of anti-impunity measures aimed at guaranteeing the non-recurrence of human rights violations. Drawing in particular inspiration from experiences in Latin American transitions, Joinet included here measures aimed at disbanding paramilitary groups, abolishing emergency courts, and purging abusive officials. Orentlicher, for her part, followed this approach in her updated version of the Principles, which draws a clear distinction between the right to reparation (section IV.A.) and guarantees of non-recurrence of violations (section IV.B.).

B. Cosmopolitan Ethics and Fighting Impunity

As noted, the Principles can be profitably linked to the global 'anti-impunity' discourse that gained momentum during the 'long decade' of the 1990s. That discourse, in turn, can hardly be fully appreciated without consideration of another key phenomenon of our times: the rise of cosmopolitanism. The idea that we are all 'citizens of the world', members of the *cosmos*, has a long intellectual history stretching back to Kant, and further to the Roman Stoics.[43] It is only since the 1990s, however, that cosmopolitanism has become established as a broad movement, both intellectual and political, exerting considerable influence over international politics and law.[44] The Principles, informed as they are by the idea of *universal* human rights standards, can be seen as an outgrowth of this new cosmopolitan movement.

The central *moral* claim of cosmopolitanism is that 'there are moral obligations owed to all human beings based solely on our humanity alone, without reference to race, gender, nationality, ethnicity, culture, religion, political affiliation, state citizenship, or other communal particularities'.[45] Moral cosmopolitanism, so understood, embodies the idea that the *individual human beings* should be our primary moral concern, no matter who they are or where they live. From this perspective, then, it makes good sense to extend our moral concern beyond our borders, and not to be indifferent to the needs and suffering of people just because they happen to be 'outsiders'. Perhaps no one captured this cosmopolitan spirit better than the great Enlightenment philosopher Immanuel Kant. In the passage quoted at the start of this Introduction, Kant envisions a 'universal community', where 'a violation of rights in *one* part of the world is felt *everywhere*'.[46] For Kant, establishing some kind of world community—he imagines a federation of peaceful republican states—where individuals have rights as 'citizens of the earth' is a precondition for achieving a peaceful global order (or 'perpetual peace', as he calls it).[47]

[43] See M Nussbaum, 'Kant and Cosmopolitanism' in J Bohman and M Lutz-Bachmann (eds), *Perpetual Peace: Essays on Kant's Cosmopolitan Ideal* (MIT Press 1997) 25–51.

[44] For insightful discussions of the phenomenon, see U Beck, *Cosmopolitan Vision* (Polity Press 2006); R Fine, *Cosmopolitanism* (Routledge 2007); R Pierik and W Werner (eds), *Cosmopolitanism in Context: Perspectives from International Law and Political Theory* (CUP 2010). On the idea of a cosmopolitan 'humanity law', see R Teitel, *Humanity's Law* (OUP 2011).

[45] G Wallace and D Held (eds), 'Editors' Introduction', *The Cosmopolitanism Reader* (Polity Press 2010) 1.

[46] Kant, n 2 (emphasis in the original). [47] Ibid.

Moral cosmopolitanism, so conceived, has increasingly found its way into international legal norms and institutions. The establishment, in 2002, of a permanent international criminal court, The Hague-based ICC, is perhaps most illustrative in this respect. At its core, the ICC rests on the belief that 'unimaginable atrocities', such as crimes against humanity, so 'deeply shock the conscience of humanity' as to be 'of concern to the international community as a whole'.[48] Cosmopolitan ideals, however, also permeate many other areas of international law and politics, including, most relevantly here, human rights. At the heart of contemporary human rights discourses is, if anything, a claim to universality: *all* human beings, so the assumption goes, have basic rights simply by virtue of being human, wherever they live and whatever their nationality, ethnicity, creed, gender, age, or social status.

It is this cosmopolitan idea of all human beings *as* rights-bearers that underlies and shapes the Principles' anti-impunity discourse. True enough, the Principles integrate different moral theories of relevance to the issue of fighting impunity that serve to some extend as a justification for the cosmopolitan idea.[49] For instance, *teleological* (or goal-based) moral theories find some expression in the Principles—as made clear in their Preamble, where a link is made (at least implicitly) between fighting impunity and creating 'just and lasting reconciliation'. But beyond such goal-based considerations, the Principles' fight against impunity has a strong *deontological* (duty-based) dimension to it. As made clear in Principle 1, the Principles' 'anti-impunity' discourse is essentially framed in terms of 'obligations of states to take effective action against impunity'. This 'deontological' perspective, however, is intrinsically bound up with the idea of rights, and specifically human rights. Typically, the state obligations laid down in the Principles correlate with specific rights on the part of the victims of human rights violations: the obligation to investigate violations and preserve memory correlates with the right to truth and the right to know (Principles 2 and 4), the obligation to prosecute and duly punish the perpetrators with the right to justice (Section III), and the obligation to repair the harm suffered with the victims' right to reparation (Principle 31).

Central, here, is the idea of human rights as 'strong' entitlements.[50] The reasoning behind this idea goes something like this: if human rights *matter* as basic entitlements held by all of us by virtue of our being human, they must be *concrete* rights—namely, high-priority claims effectively enforced by state institutions (courts, legislatures, government administration, police forces, and so on), making sure that certain basic human interests are equally protected and that, where violation occurs, reparation or punishment is reliably enforced. But far from an isolated phenomenon, this understanding of rights is best seen as a wider reflection of the international human rights discourse as it evolved throughout the 'long' 1990s. As already mentioned, in the arena of global and regional human rights institutions, there has been a shift in emphasis from naming and shaming human rights violations towards effectively addressing the consequences of such violations. With this

[48] Preamble to the Rome Statute, paras 2 and 4. See also A Duff, 'Authority and Responsibility in International Criminal Law' in S Besson and J Tasioulas (eds), *The Philosophy of International Law* (OUP 2010) 587–604, 601.

[49] Our focus here is on what Ronald Dworkin has referred to as 'goal-based', 'duty-based', and 'rights-based' approaches to ethics. See R Dworkin, *Taking Rights Seriously* (Harvard University Press 1977) 169–70. For an insightful discussion of anti-impunity from the viewpoint of normative ethics, see also M Pensky, 'Two Cheers for the Impunity Norm' (2016) 42 Philosophy and Social Criticism 1–13.

[50] See T Campbell, *Rights: A Critical Introduction* (Routledge 2006) 40.

in view, some commentators have spoken of a new 'age of enforcement',[51] where human rights are not merely declared but concretely realised and enforced. Whether or not this is an accurate characterization of present times, anti-impunity concerns have increasingly become integrated into mainstream human rights theory and practice. Not the least evidence of this is the jurisprudence of the Inter-American Court of Human Rights (IACtHR, about which see more in section C of this commentary).[52]

At the same time, the Principles' cosmopolitan project as sketched out here conflicts with, or at least challenges, the so-called 'classical model of sovereignty'.[53] For much of its life, international law was essentially a system of mere inter-state coexistence predicated on the notion of *sovereign* states, free to run their internal affairs (including the fate of their own nationals) without outside interference. Under such a system, the wrongs done to foreign individuals were irrelevant unless they were taken up by their state of nationality, the assumption being that by acting on their behalf, the state was 'in reality asserting its own rights—its right to ensure, in the person of its subjects, respect for the rule of international law'.[54] In a world of 'cosmopolitanized nations',[55] this model appears increasingly outdated, and is being fundamentally challenged by more individual-centred approaches to sovereignty pushing for a radical redefinition of the concept.[56] The Principles can thus be seen as part of a larger debate on the redefinition of state sovereignty in a global age.

C. Anti-Impunity and International Law

As so far suggested, the Principles' anti-impunity discourse appears closely bound up with a 'strong' notion of rights; a notion that, in complex modern societies, presupposes the existence of a system of *law* through which individual rights can be authoritatively recognized and effectively translated into social reality. The paradigm case of such a system is, of course, the legal order of states.[57] The ambition of the Principles, however, goes further: it is to articulate legal standards of universal concern and, hence, applicable across the borders of nations. This cosmopolitan project, as we have described it in section B, is intrinsically linked to international law.

As commonly understood, international law is essentially built around formal sources as identified in Article 38, paragraph 1 of the Statute of the International Court of Justice

[51] H Rombouts, P Sardaro, and S Vandeginste, 'The Right to Reparation for Victims of Gross and Systematic Violations of Human Rights' in K de Feyter et al (eds), *Out of the Ashes: Reparation for Victims of Gross and Systematic Human Rights Violations* (Intersentia 2005) 345–503, 355 (italics omitted).

[52] *Velásquez-Rodríguez v Honduras* (Merits) IACtHR Series C no 4 (29 July 1988).

[53] See EJ Criddle and E Fox-Decent, *Fiduciaries of Humanity: How International Law Constitutes Authority* (OUP 2016) 5–8.

[54] Permanent Court of International Justice (PCIJ), *Mavrommatis Palestine Concessions*, PCIJ Series A no 2 (1924), at 2.

[55] We take the expression from U Beck and D Levy, 'Cosmopolitanized Nations: Re-imaging in the World Risk Society' (2013) 30(2) Theory, Culture & Society 3–31.

[56] See International Criminal Tribunal for the Former Yugoslavia (ICTY) Appeals Chamber, *Prosecutor v Dusko Tadić* (Decision on the Defence Motion for Interlocutory Appeal on Jurisdiction) IT-94-1-AR72 (2 October 1995) para 97 (holding that a 'state-sovereignty-oriented approach' is being gradually replaced by a 'human-being-oriented approach'); *Report of the Secretary-General on the work of the Organization (A/54/1)*, UN GAOR, 54th Sess, 4th Plenary Meeting, UN Doc A/54/PV.4 (20 September 1999) 1–2.

[57] See also UN Commission on Human Rights, *Commission on Human Rights Resolution 2004/72: Impunity* (21 April 2004) para 20 (requesting UN Secretary-General to appoint an expert 'to update the Set of Principles to reflect recent developments in international law and practice, including international jurisprudence and State practice').

(ICJ). As is well known, Article 38 sets out three principal sources (treaties, custom, and general principles) on the basis of which the ICJ can make its decisions. The Principles, however, do not fit neatly into any of these categories. As noted earlier, no action has been taken to formally adopt the Principles at the level of the UN, and it seems unlikely that they will be translated into a convention or treaty any time soon. As to international custom, it is doubtful that there is a consistent state practice allowing for the conclusion that the Principles, as a whole, can be considered as customary international law binding upon all states irrespective of their treaty commitments or lack thereof. The category of 'general principles', lastly, is controversial and rarely explicitly used in international legal argument.[58] It might be tempting to suggest that the Principles are shared by virtually all, or the majority of, municipal legal systems, and may, therefore, be invoked under this heading; but the legal reality is likely to be much more complex, and by obstinately holding on to a perceived 'general principle' we may end up doing little more than plucking principles out of thin air.

On a traditional analysis of international law, a rule is part of *lex lata* (the law in force) if, and only if, it emanates from one of these recognized formal sources. If it does not, it constitutes at best *lex ferenda*, an ideal projection of what the law ought to be.[59] This distinction becomes less important, however, if we think of international law as a *process* of authoritative decision making, rather than as a rigid system of neutral rules. Prominent international law scholar and former ICJ President Rosalyn Higgins, for instance, has famously advocated such a process-based view of international law. On the 'policy-science approach' she takes, trying to separate 'law as it is' from 'law as it ought to be' is in large measure 'a false dichotomy, a cleavage that we can ourselves banish from existence'.[60] In Higgins' view, international law is not a matter of simply finding 'the correct legal rule' and then applying it in an impartial manner; it involves, rather, a dynamic process of making choices in concrete circumstances, choices that cannot be detached from wider social and political considerations.

This idea of international law as a process, rather than a rigid system of rules, is often discussed under the heading of 'soft law'. Rejecting any simple law/non-law divide, advocates of so-called 'soft law' contend that non-binding international instruments (going by names such as resolutions, declarations, codes of conduct, etc) can play a significant role in the process of *making* international law.[61] While not law per se, these instruments (they suggest) can nonetheless have real effect *within* the international legal system—namely by stimulating the development of legally binding norms and filling interpretive gaps in existing rules.[62]

While the concept is notoriously slippery, soft law may be defined as involving 'instruments that are adopted in an intergovernmental setting and that set forth rules of

[58] For an insightful discussion of the concept, see E Carpanelli, 'General Principles of International Law: Struggling with a Slippery Concept' in L Pineschi (ed), *General Principles of Law—The Role of the Judiciary* (Springer 2015) 125–44.

[59] See, eg, H Thurlway, *The Sources of International Law* (OUP 2014) 165.

[60] R Higgins, *Problems & Process: International Law and How We Use It* (OUP 1994) 10.

[61] For such an argument, see A Boyle and C Chinkin, *The Making of International Law* (OUP 2007) 211–29.

[62] With respect to UN General Assembly Resolutions, see ICJ, *Case Concerning Military and Paramilitary Activities in and against Nicaragua (Nicaragua v United States of America)* (Judgment) [1986] ICJ Rep 14, para 188.

behaviour or other normative standards, but that are not legally binding'.[63] Manifestly enough, the Principles largely fit into this characterization. These are, indeed, normative standards, which were elaborated within the setting of the UN but which, as noted earlier, have still not been formally endorsed by any UN body. From this perspective, the Principles enjoy rather weak legitimacy in the current international system. Yet this should not lead us to underestimate their influence on international law-making *processes*. Widely invoked by human rights scholars and practitioners alike, the Principles have served—and continue to serve—as an important frame of reference for policies and institutional arrangements both within and beyond the UN. And in this sense, they can be considered to be an integral part of contemporary international legal discourse as 'a subtle and evolving interplay of law-making instruments, both binding and non-binding'.[64]

But leaving aside the rather inconclusive discussion about soft law and its legal nature,[65] it may be fruitful at this juncture to ask the related but different question of whether, and to what extent, the Principles are reflective of *existing* international ('hard') law. Regardless of their legal status, are the Principles declarative of existing international norms, or do they rather articulate new obligations—beyond what international law requires? There is no single and clear-cut answer to this question, of course. It rather calls for a careful, separate analysis of each of the 38 Principles in the light of current international law norms and practices; and it is precisely one of the central aims of the present volume to provide such a legal analysis. While leaving such a detailed (principle-by-principle) normative analysis for later, it is important to note here from the outset the somewhat ambivalent nature of the Principles: on the one hand, these Principles are meant to codify *established* legal obligations under international law; on the other hand, they also refer to 'recent developments' and 'emerging principles' of international law.[66] This difference is reflected in the language in which the Principles are written: Principles (or elements thereof) falling within the former category tend to be couched in mandatory terms (such as 'shall', 'must', and 'right to'), while those falling within the latter typically 'avoid categorical language in respect of questions whose resolution is appropriately left to national deliberations'.[67]

However, while each Principle raises interpretative questions of its own and must be appreciated separately, it is possible to identify something like a common theme that runs through the entire set of Principles. This overall theme is perhaps best summed up in Principle 1, which defines impunity as a failure of states to meet the following four state obligations arising from human rights violations:

— to investigate human rights violations and to take appropriate measures to prosecute and punish the perpetrators of such violations;
— to identify the victims and perpetrators of human rights violations;
— to provide victims with effective remedies and to ensure that they receive reparation for the harm suffered; and
— to take the necessary measures to prevent the future recurrence of violations.

[63] J Cerone, 'A Taxonomy of Soft Law: Stipulating a Definition' in S Lagoutte, T Gammeltoft-Hansen, and J Cerone (eds), *Tracing the Roles of Soft Law in Human Rights* (OUP 2016) 15–26, 17.

[64] Boyle and Chinkin, n 61, at vii.

[65] For a seminal critique, see P Weil, 'Vers une normativité relative en droit international? (1981) 86 Revue Générale de Droit International Public 5–47. See also J Klabbers, 'The Redundancy of Soft Law' (1996) 65 Nordic Journal of International Law 167–82; J d'Aspremont, 'Softness in International Law: A Self-Serving Quest for Legal Materials' (2008) 19 European Journal of International Law 1075–91.

[66] Orentlicher Report, n 36, 2 and 5.

[67] Ibid, 2.

The basic assumption at work here is easy to state: if human rights matter, they must not only be respected (by not unduly interfering with them) but they must also be actively secured and implemented. This concern with respecting *and* ensuring human rights guarantees is not peculiar to the Principles: it gained momentum in what we have referred to as the 'long decade' of the 1990s—a phase marked not only by a shift in international human rights discourse away from merely abstract proclamation to concrete realization and implementation, but also by increased attention to the *consequences* of human rights violations. The list of obligations sketched above can been seen as integral to this seemingly new, or at least significant different, understanding of international human rights guarantees as something not only to be proclaimed but to be effectively 'fulfilled' and—if violated—to be adequately *responded* to.[68]

This concern with responding to human rights violations is reflected in recent international human rights practice. General human rights treaties make little explicit reference to the four obligations listed in Principle 2; and yet, in recent years, regional courts and treaty bodies have increasingly tended to read these obligations 'into' the relevant treaty provisions. The UN Committee on Human Rights, for instance, has consistently held that state parties have a duty not only to bring human rights violators to justice, but also to investigate, to compensate victims, and to ensure that such violations do not occur in the future.[69] The ECtHR, for its part, has had occasion to develop substantial jurisprudence on these various dimensions of combating impunity—especially in relation to applications from the new democracies in Central and Eastern Europe, which joined the Convention system after the collapse of the Iron Curtain in 1989/1990.[70] But of all international human rights institutions, it is the IACtHR which has been central in developing an anti-impunity jurisprudence firmly structured around these four types of state obligations. In its landmark case *Velásquez Rodríguez*, the Court famously stated:

> The State has a legal duty to take reasonable steps to prevent human rights violations and to use the means at its disposal to carry out a serious investigation of violations committed within its jurisdiction, to identify those responsible, to impose the appropriate punishment and to ensure the victim adequate compensation.[71]

This passage contains, it has been noted, 'the first truly comprehensive statement of a state's human rights obligations'.[72] It sets the stage for a holistic approach to anti-impunity,

[68] See also European Court of Human Rights (ECtHR), *McCann and others v the United Kingdom* App no 18984/91 (ECHR, 27 September 1995) para 146 (holding that the provisions of the European Convention on Human Rights (ECHR) must be so interpreted and applied as to 'make its safeguards practical and effective').

[69] See Human Rights Committee, General Comment no 31, Nature of the General Legal Obligation Imposed on State Parties to the Covenant, UN Doc CCPR/C/21/Rev.1/Add.13 (26 May 2004). For a detailed analysis of the relevant pronouncements of the Committee, see A Seibert-Fohr, *Prosecuting Serious Human Rights Violations* (OUP 2009) ch 2.

[70] For overviews of the relevant case law, see E Brehms, 'Transitional Justice in the Case Law of the European Court of Human Rights' (2011) 5 International Journal of Transitional Justice 282–303; JA Sweeney, *The European Court of Human Rights in the Post-Cold War Era* (Routledge 2013). On the duty to prosecute under the ECHR in particular, see ECtHR, *Marguš v Croatia* App no 4455/10 (Judgment) (27 May 2014).

[71] IACtHR, *Velásquez-Rodríguez v Honduras* (Merits), n 52, para 174. For an analysis of the Court's anti-impunity jurisprudence, see Seibert-Fohr, n 69, ch 3. See also K Engle, 'Anti-Impunity and the Turn to Criminal Law in Human Rights' (2015) 100 Cornell Law Review 1069–127.

[72] M Freeman, *Truth Commissions and Procedural Fairness* (CUP 2006) 8.

according to which the four state obligations are distinct yet complementary components of 'a fair policy of accountability'.[73] Yet this approach raises questions about what tensions may arise between these various pillars, and how they may be addressed, especially in contexts of transition from armed conflict to negotiated peace.[74] Despite such concerns, the influence of this framework on the international anti-impunity struggle in general, and the Principles in particular, can hardly be overstated.[75] If anything, the Principles are conceptually wedded to such a holistic approach to impunity, which centrally includes, but extends well beyond, the realm of criminal justice.

D. General Structure and Organization of the Principles

The Principles, we have noted, are structured around the four types of state obligations listed in Principle 1—roughly, the duties to prosecute, to disclose the truth, to repair, and to prevent future recurrence of human rights violations. These obligations correspond with the following rights spelled out in the Principles: the right to justice; the right to the truth (or the right to know); the right to effective remedy and reparation; and the right to guarantees of non-recurrence. While the right to the truth and the right to justice are placed under separate headings within the Principles (Sections II and III, respectively), the right to reparation and the right to guarantees of non-recurrence are grouped together under the same general heading (Section IV) but divided out into separate subsections (subsections A and B, respectively)—the underlying assumption apparently being that reparation and non-repetition, while separate issues, constitute complementary aspects of restoring relations broken by serious wrongdoing.[76] Moreover, the set of Principles refers to a variety of measures or institutions through which those four rights may be enforced and realized in practice. Chief among these are four main 'mechanisms':

1. Trials—whether domestic, international, or foreign.
2. Truth-seeking instruments—whether truth commissions, other fact-finding bodies, or archives.
3. Reparations—whether in the form of restitution, financial compensation, or apologies.
4. Institutional reform—including justice and security sector reforms and the removal of former abusers from public positions through vetting procedures.

These institutional measures form a central framework around which the Principles are structured. There is a connection here with the now commonplace notion of 'transitional

[73] JE Méndez, 'Accountability for Past Abuse' (1997) 19.2 Human Rights Quarterly 255–82, 262. See also P de Greiff, 'Theorizing Transitional Justice' in MS Williams, R Nagy, and J Elster (eds), *Transitional Justice, Nomos LI* (New York University Press 2012) 31–77 (making the case for a holistic approach to transitional justice).

[74] On this issue see, in particular, *El Mozote and Nearby Places v El Salvador* (Merits, Reparations and Costs) IACtHR Series C no 252 (25 October 2012), Concurrent Vote, Diego García-Sayán, para 38 (acknowledging that in such contexts a state may not be in a position to comply 'fully and simultaneously' with its various human rights obligations, and that it may be legitimate to weigh these obligations 'in such a way that the satisfaction of some does not affect the exercise of others disproportionately').

[75] The framework has been adopted, for instance, by the African Commission on Human and Peoples' Rights (AComHPR). See, eg, Case no 245/02, *Zimbabwe Human Rights Forum NGO v Zimbabwe* (AComHPR, 15 May 2006) para 144.

[76] See also J Crawford, *The International Law Commission's Articles on State Responsibility: Introduction, Text and Commentary* (CUP 2002) 199.

justice'. Concerned with how societies address an atrocity-ridden past, transitional justice is conventionally understood to revolve around precisely the aforementioned 'mechanisms' or 'pillars', as they are often called. This link between transitional justice and the Principles is anything but coincidental, however. Largely informed by late-twentieth-century transitions to democracy in Latin America and Eastern Europe, the Principles are in an important sense bound up with such contexts of gross human rights violations and transitions from authoritarianism or armed conflict to a more just, more peaceful and decent political order. It is unsurprising, therefore, that the Principles' definitional part proposes clarifications and explanations of what both the phrases 'serious crimes under international law' and 'restoration of or transition to democracy and/or peace' mean.

Following the structure outlined above, the Principles are grouped into three main parts. These are complemented by the Preamble, a definitional part and Principle 1 as the fundamental norm around which the document is organized:

1. The *first* main part ('The Right to Know') articulates relevant general principles (Principles 2–5) and provides detailed information on the establishment, workings, and functions of commissions of inquiry as well as archives as essential instruments for giving effect to the right to know (Principles 6–18).
2. The *second* main part, 'The Right to Justice', is divided into three subsections. While subsection A deals with the general principles applicable to the administration of justice (Principle 19), subsection B deals with the distribution of jurisdiction between national, foreign, international, and internationalized courts (Principles 20–21). Subsection C addresses the issue of whether and under which conditions restrictions on the rule of law may be justified by anti-impunity objectives (Principles 22–30).
3. The *third* main part of the Principles ('The Right to Reparation/Guarantees of Non-Recurrence') comprises a comparatively lesser number of Principles. Section A, dedicated to the right to reparation, clarifies the conditions in which such a right arises and provides details on its scope and the relevant procedures (Principles 31–34). Section B deals with guarantees of non-recurrence, with a specific focus on the reform of state institutions and laws, the disbandment of parastatal armed forces, and the demobilization and social reintegration of children (Principles 35–38).

At this stage, we could include more or less detailed summaries of each Principle and the central findings of this Commentary. We suspect, however, that such a 'condensed' version of the project would not only be of limited interest to the reader but, more importantly, would also run the risk of unhelpfully simplifying—if not distorting—complex issues and arguments. Let us note, however, that each commentary is preceded by a short abstract, providing the reader with summary information about the key findings.

E. Aims and Scope of This Commentary

The present book is designed as a full-scale, Principle-by-Principle commentary to the Principles. Intended as a collective study authored by authors from a variety of backgrounds, the Commentary aims at providing a comprehensive though succinct treatment of the topics covered by the set of Principles. It includes the text of each of the 38 Principles and their detailed commentaries, plus a bibliography of books and cases useful for further study.

The Commentary seeks to provide a thorough and yet accessible guide for those interested in the fight against impunity—scholars, students, and practitioners alike. One of the major challenges of the project, so conceived, consists in combining expertise and complexity of thought with clarity, brevity, and ease of use. Thus, in the interest of succinctness, we asked the authors to comply rigorously with a rather strict word limit.

Clearly, each Principle raises challenges and questions of its own. Some Principles may lend themselves to extended discussion related to broader transitional justice debates, for example, while others may require a focus on legal arguments and procedures. In order to ensure consistency throughout the commentary, however, we asked the authors to utilize the following general structure as a point of reference:

A. **Summary of Findings:** Each commentary provides an abstract of approximately 200 words, which effectively summarizes the main findings.
B. **Contextual and Historical Introduction:** here one finds a historical introduction and the contemporary context in which these Principles are applied. Moreover, this section defines the terminology used and briefly clarifies the nature of the Principle being considered, states its importance in the field, and describes controversial issues or questions.
C. **Theoretical Framework:** Here the normative (legal/ethical) foundation of each Principle is discussed. The authors are asked to consider the influence of international law (including human rights law, international criminal law, and international refugee law) on the interpretation of the relevant Principle. Moreover, this section addresses the relation between particular principles and notions of transitional justice, understood as a comprehensive approach to serious rights violations (including mechanisms of truth-seeking, prosecutions, reparation and guarantees of non-recurrence).
D. **Practice:** In this section, the applications of the various impunity principles in practice is extensively analyzed. Incidents of state practice, case-law (national, regional and international), and views and practice of international organizations and other relevant bodies are covered as exhaustively as possible. Of particular interest, here, are comparative analyses of how particular principles operate in different transitional contexts and policy environments.
E. **Critical Assessment:** In a last section, each Principle is critically discussed, and new perspectives are presented. Authors offer their own views and highlight any debates concerning the future development of the norms in question.

Complying with this general structure was sometimes, and understandably so, a source of difficulty given the complexity and normative diversity of each Principle. It is our hope, however, that this work of distilling the Principles to their essentials contributes to making this Commentary an accessible, user-friendly tool for practitioners and scholars alike.

F. Concluding Remarks: Debating Anti-impunity

In the twenty-first century, the UN Principles to combat impunity have become an integral part of the human rights landscape. Even before being taken 'note of' by the UN Commission on Human Rights in 2005, the Principles shaped—but were also shaped by—human rights politics and activism around the world; especially so in societies, such as Argentina, undergoing 'third-wave' transitions from dictatorship to democracy.[77] As Diane Orentlicher suggested in her independent expert Report, the Principles in the original version drafted by Louis Joinet played 'a singularly influential role' in paving the way for 'remarkable advances in national and international efforts to combat impunity'.[78] Ever since, the Principles have become a reference point for global debates on accountability for human rights violations.[79] Recent years suggest, however, a decline in their usage.[80] More research is needed on this issue, but in practice, anti-impunity objectives often take a backseat to competing policy considerations. The practice of amnesty granting is particularly revealing in this regard. As recent empirical work has suggested,[81] amnesties have not dramatically decreased in number since the late 1980s, and continue to be used in countries facing political crisis—a development rather difficult to reconcile with an anti-amnesty stance as reflected in the Principles, especially in their updated version. In this respect, as in others, political decision making 'on the ground'—especially in situations of mass atrocity and political transitions—may be more 'messy' and prone to political 'trade-offs' than any 'tidy', strictly duty-based normative framework would allow. That might also explain why the Principles have never been formally adopted by the multilateral human rights fora.[82]

Moreover, the anti-impunity framework set out by the Principles has been subject to considerable theoretical debate and contestation. While an important reference point for theory and practice, the anti-impunity framework set up by the Principles is also potentially fraught with disagreement and controversy. Each Principle, in its own way, raises complex theoretical and practical problems, and diversity of views is to be expected when it comes to the question of how best to address them. But beyond a merely punctual criticism of the Principles, a more fundamental criticism may be levelled against the normative project as such, or at least essential parts of it. In what follows, we identify various strands of criticism that may be directed at the anti-impunity project as envisaged by the Principles. In doing so, our purpose is not exhaustiveness but, more modestly, to open a few avenues for thinking critically about the meaning and possible shortcomings of the Principles as a global human rights agenda.

Before pursuing the discussion further, it is worth mentioning that so far—to our knowledge—the Principles have not been subjected to any systematic critique. However, while often not explicitly engaging with the Principles themselves, scholars have increasingly called into question a number of 'core' assumptions on which the contemporary anti-impunity discourse—as reflected in the Principles—supposedly rests. The recent discussion in the burgeoning field of transitional justice is illustrative in this respect. The demand for a stronger inclusion of 'justice from below' perspectives in transitional justice can, for instance, be read more broadly as a critique of (what is perceived to be)

[77] On the origins of the campaign against impunity, see Joinet Report, n 25, at paras 1–6. See also SP Huntington, *The Third Wave: Democratization in the Late Twentieth Century* (Oklahoma University Press 1991).

[78] Orentlicher Report, n 36, at 2.

[79] For references to relevant policy-making instruments and reports by governmental organizations and NGOs, see Roht-Arriaza's commentary to Principle 1 in this volume, para 15.

[80] See ICTJ Brief, n 37, at 4.

[81] See L Mallinder, 'Amnesties' Challenges to the Global Accountability Norm? Interpreting Regional and International Trends in Amnesty Enactment' in Lessa and Payne (eds), n 3, 69; TD Olsen, LA Payne, and AG Reiter, *Transitional Justice in Balance: Comparing Processes, Weighing Efficacy* (United States Institute of Peace 2010) 103–04.

[82] See ICTJ Brief, n 37.

a 'legalistic', 'top-down' perspective on fighting impunity, which supposedly offers 'off-the-shelf' models rather than bespoke solutions to transitions and focuses merely on the consequences and not on the root causes of violations.[83] Moreover, we should mention a recent collection that critically engages with what is referred to as the new 'laser focus on anti-impunity' in human rights.[84] This focus, it is argued, 'has created blindspots in practice and scholarship that result in a constricted response to human rights violations, a narrowed conception of justice, and an impoverished approach to peace'.[85] This collection, however, tends to define 'anti-impunity' narrowly as 'criminalization'. As explained at the beginning of this Introduction, we adopt here a broader understanding of 'anti-impunity' as reflected in Principle 1. On such an understanding, combating impunity revolves around four distinct yet complementary sets of state obligations—to investigate, prosecute and punish, repair, and prevent human rights violations. The critical reflection that follows applies, however, not solely to criminal justice, but also to the broader anti-impunity framework as developed by the Principles.

In what follows, we focus on five sorts of critiques that may be applied to the Principles' anti-impunity framework. We shall refer to them, respectively, as the 'Rigidity Critique', 'Disconnectedness Critique', 'Legalism Critique', 'ESCR Neglect Critique', and 'Beneficiaries Critique'.

1. *Rigidity Critique*: One critique that may be levelled at the Principles is that they provide an excessively rigid framework for dealing with human rights violations, and especially so with respect to societies 'in transition' from dictatorship or armed conflict to a more just and stable order. The Principles, after all, seem to leave little, if any, space for the sort of bargaining and trade-offs that may be required in such contexts to end or constrain violence and enable peaceful adjustment. This issue is often discussed in relation to amnesty. A number of scholars have taken the view that amnesty, even for serious human rights violations, does not 'automatically' amount to a breach of international law.[86] Moreover, it has been argued that taking amnesty simply 'off the table' may be counterproductive, because 'sometimes, peace will only be attainable if justice is sacrificed'.[87] The current discussions in Colombia that move away from amnesties for serious crimes towards a system of reducing the punishment for such crimes might show an alternative model that better squares the demands for justice and peace. It is, however, premature at this stage to make any definite statement in this respect.
2. *Disconnectedness Critique*: Framed in abstractly universal terms, the Principles invite the criticism that they deliver a form of 'justice from above'—remote from and inaccessible to the local communities most effected by violence and conflict.[88] Far from being insensitive to this issue, UN expert Diane Orentlicher stressed in her Report

[83] See K McEvoy and L McGregor (eds), *Transitional Justice from Below: Grassroot Activism and the Struggle for Change* (Hart Publishing 2008). See also D Sharp, 'Addressing Dilemmas of the Local and Global in Transitional Justice' (2014) 29 Emory International Law Review 71–117.

[84] K Engle, Z Miller, and DM Davis, 'Introduction' in K Engle, Z Miller, and DM Davis (eds), *Anti-Impunity and the Human Rights Agenda* (CUP 2016) 1–12, 2.

[85] Ibid.

[86] See M Freeman and M Pensky, 'The Amnesty Controversy in International Law' in F Lessa and LA Payne (eds), n 2, 42–65; L Mallinder, *Amnesty, Human Rights and Political Transitions: Bridging the Peace Justice Divide* (Hart Publishing 2008) 9; W Schabas, *Unimaginable Atrocities: Justice, Politics, and Rights at the War Crimes Tribunals* (OUP 2012) 173–98.

[87] Schabas, n 86, 198.

[88] See McEvoy and McGregor (eds), 83.

'the importance of public consultation in shaping anti-impunity measures', and took pains to strengthen this dimension in the updated version of the Principles.[89] Critics, however, may object that the issue of local ownership remains nonetheless largely sidelined by the effort to articulate a unified, universally applicable scheme for combating impunity that is based on a best practice 'tool box' of pre-determined mechanisms and strategies.

3. *Legalism Critique*: Legalism, as famously defined by Judith Shklar, refers to 'the ethical attitude that holds moral conduct to be a matter of rule following, and moral relationships to consist of duties and rights determined by rules'.[90] One central feature of legalism, so understood, is 'the attendant belief that law is not only separate from political life but that it is a mode of action superior to mere politics'.[91] To some extent, the Principles can be read along these lines—as an institutionalized effort to legally tame political power and prevent arbitrary compromising at the expense of victims of human rights abuse. Legalism has always had its critics, however. It has been criticized, among other things, for exaggerating the power of law to solve complex problems; propagating an unduly abstract idea about people; over-concentrating on the 'state' at the expense of other actors and sites; obscuring the quintessentially political nature of legal decision making; failing to engage with patters of socio-economic injustice and maldistribution; excessively relying on an 'absolutist' vocabulary that rules out compromise.[92]
4. *ESCR Neglect Critique*: The Principles clearly place their focus on civil and political rights (CPR), at the expense of economic, social, and cultural rights (ESCR). This focus can be explained by the Principles' drafting history. As explained earlier, the UN's work on impunity resulted in the elaboration of two separate reports: one focused on ESCR and the other on CPR. Advocates of ESCR, however, will take issue with this division between two groups of human rights. In their view, the common claim that CPR and ESCR are fundamentally different is exaggerated and does not stand up to scrutiny.[93] Economic, social, and cultural rights, so the argument goes, are as essential for the freedom and well-being of the individual as long-established CPR, and should therefore be given equal weight. On this account, then, the Principles' focus on CPR risks misconstruing the anti-impunity project as a human rights agenda by separating, rather than linking, what should be complementary elements of the global struggle against impunity.
5. *Beneficiaries Critique*: A fifth, somewhat related critique that may be addressed to the Principles is that they focus so exclusively on the 'visible' side of human rights abuse as to lose sight of its 'invisible' side. Part of this latter side is the role of beneficiaries—those who eventually benefit materially or socially from large-scale injustice. As Mahmood Mamdani has argued with respect to South Africa's Truth and Reconciliation Commission, a narrow focus on violations of CPR allows those who

[89] Orentlicher Report, n 36, at 6. See also Principles 6, 32, and 35.

[90] Shklar, n 12, at 1.

[91] Ibid, at 8.

[92] For this line of criticism, see D Kennedy, *The Dark Sides of Virtue: Reassessing International Humanitarianism* (Princeton University Press 2004). See also K McEvoy, 'Letting Go of Legalism: Developing a "Thicker" Version of Transitional Justice' in McEvoy and McGregor (eds), n 83, 15–45.

[93] See L Arbour, 'Economic and Social Justice for Societies in Transition' (2007) 40 International Law and Politics 1–27. See also V Mantouvalou, 'In Support of Legalisation' in C Gearty and V Mantouvalou (eds), *Debating Social Rights* (Hart Publishing 2011) 85–171.

benefitted from a grossly unjust system to go away thinking that they had little, if anything, to do with these injustices.[94]

The critiques just outlined vary in emphasis and kind. Some of them are perhaps best described—borrowing from international relations theorist Robert W Cox—as 'problem-solving'.[95] We may, indeed, think of some of these strands of criticism as aimed at solving problems *within* the Principles' anti-impunity framework, while generally accepting the parameters of this framework. Take the 'ESCR Neglect Critique'. As argued in this Commentary,[96] it makes sense for the contemporary interpreter to read the Principles as dealing with violations of *both* CPR and ESCR, despite their initial division into two separate tracks. Take, too, a variant of the 'Legalism Critique'—the claim that the Principles' 'state-centric' perspective does not sufficiently take into account the role of non-state actors. As suggested in this Commentary,[97] there is good ground for arguing that the Principles are best interpreted as applying not only when states commit human rights violations, either directly or indirectly, but also when they fail to protect individuals within their jurisdiction from human rights abuse by *non-state actors*. These are some examples of how critique can serve as a guide to addressing particular problems or shortcomings of the Principles, without, however, calling into question the very framework into which they are organized.

Other critiques—following Cox we may refer to them as 'critical theories'—challenge more fundamentally the prevailing anti-impunity framework. The 'Beneficiaries Critique', for instance, may be understood along these lines. Rather than taking the current anti-impunity framework for granted, the perspective here is 'critical'—directed towards a fundamental reappraisal of the very concepts and categories around which the current anti-impunity discourse is organized.[98] By focusing on the question of 'structural beneficiaries', this critique asks us to radically re-think the question of responsibility for past injustices by moving beyond the victim-perpetrator dichotomy. Something similar may be said about the 'Legalism' and 'Disconnectedness' critiques, both of which aim at moving debates beyond what is perceived as a narrowly 'legalistic', 'from above' perspective on impunity. A more radical critique of the Principles may also fundamentally question their 'state-centric' outlook and call for a shift in perspective towards the recognition of obligations for non-state actors, such as multinational corporations, to provide remedies for their own human rights abuses.[99]

Such wide-ranging critiques need not be rejectionist, however. Even staunch critics may be reluctant to abandon altogether the demand for legal accountability as formulated in the Principles. Instead, they may prefer a reformist strategy, one that builds upon and offers correctives to the existing anti-impunity framework.[100]

[94] See M Mamdami, 'Beyond Nuremberg: The Historical Significance of the Post-Apartheid Transition in South Africa' (2015) 43(1) Politics & Society (2015) 61–88. See also R Meister, 'Human Rights and the Politics of Victimhood' (2002) 16(2) Ethics & International Affairs 91–108.

[95] RW Cox, 'Social Forces, States and World Orders: Beyond International Relations Theory' (1981) 10(2) Millennium 126–52, 128–30.

[96] See Krähenmann, 'Definitions', para 8.

[97] Ibid. See also *González et al ('Cotton Field') v Mexico* (Preliminary objection, merits, reparations and costs) IACtHR Series C no 205 (16 November 2009) para 245.

[98] See Cox, n 95, at 129–30.

[99] See Roht-Arriaza's commentary to Principle 1 in this volume, para 14. See also UN Principles on Business and Human Rights, Annexed to resolution of the Human Rights Council, A/HRC/17/31 (21 March 2011) ('Ruggie Principles').

[100] For such an approach, see McEvoy, n 92, at 29.

A separate issue, however, is whether this or that critique has a point. This is not the place to pursue this discussion in any detail. For the present purpose, we shall focus on one possible counter-argument—the claim that some of the criticisms implicitly or explicitly directed at the Principles fundamentally misunderstand, misconstrue, or misrepresent that which they criticize. Do, we may ask, the various critiques outlined above accurately reflect the Principles as a normative project? To address this question, it is useful to turn to the following statement by Louis Joinet, which features in the afterword to his revised final Report:

> To those who might be tempted to regard the set of principles proposed here as an obstacle to national reconciliation, I would answer this: these principles are not legal standards in the strict sense, but guiding principles intended not to thwart reconciliation but to avoid distortions in certain reconciliation policies so that, once beyond the first stage, which is more concerned with 'conciliation' than reconciliation, the foundations of a 'just and lasting reconciliation' may be laid.
>
> Before a new leaf can be turned, the old leaf must be read! But the campaign against impunity is not just a legal and political issue: its ethical dimension is all too often forgotten.[101]

The statement can be read as a defence of the Principles against some of the critiques sketched above—particularly the so-called 'Rigidity Critique'. There is an understanding here that the Principles are best viewed not as strict legal rules, but rather as 'guiding principles'—flexible and open-ended enough to allow for accommodation and 'conciliation' in times of political transition.[102] Diane Orentlicher takes a somewhat similar stance in her Prologue to the present Commentary. There she explains that in updating the Principles, her aspiration was to provide 'practical guidance for contemporary challenges, while leaving ample space to accommodate further evolution in our understanding of "best practices in combating impunity" '.[103] Moreover, Orentlicher takes pains to stress 'the quintessentially local project of communal reckoning' and the importance of honouring 'the unique experience and agency of each society'.[104] All this may suggest that the critique of the Principles is, to some extent at least, based on a misunderstanding of their very nature and purpose.

There is another side to the matter, however. As noted throughout this Introduction, the Principles refer essentially to a normative cosmopolitan project that defines anti-impunity in terms of global norms, obligations, and rights. At the heart of this project, clearly, is the belief that anti-impunity is too serious a matter to be left to the discretionary disposal of policymakers. The underlying assumption, indeed, is that fighting impunity is not only an option; it is a necessary precondition for creating what Joinet refers to as 'just and lasting reconciliation'. And if this is so, governments are not only permitted to take anti-impunity measures in response to serious human rights abuse; they bear an obligation to do so. Orentlicher aptly puts the point in her Prologue to this Commentary:

[101] Joinet Report, n 25, paras 49–50.

[102] Such a reading may also be supported by the now commonplace distinction between rules and principles. Rules are considered to operate in an 'all-or-nothing affair'—either they apply or they do not, and if they do, they automatically prescribe the legal consequences that follow from a particular set of facts. Principles, by contrast, give reasons for deciding a case in some way, but those reasons are not conclusive and may be outweighed by other principles. For a classic statement, see Dworkin, n 49, 22–31.

[103] Orentlicher, 'Prologue' in this volume.

[104] Ibid.

> [W]hile the Updated Principles seek to honour local agency, reflecting in particular the perspectives of victims, they also recognize the elemental importance of clarifying where local discretion ends and legal obligation begins. If these dual commitments exist in some tension, they are hardly irreconcilable; after all, the law the Principles reflect emerged from wide-ranging experience over an extended period. Even as survivors demand remedies responsive to their unique experience of harm, time and again, across disparate regions and cultures, they have derived incalculable benefit from their ability to frame their calls for justice in the language of universal law.[105]

As Orentlicher suggests, the Principles can be seen as an attempt to reconcile 'local agency' with 'global norms'.[106] Mapping the space 'where local discretion ends and legal obligation begins' is, it seems, a concern very much at heart of the Principles as a cosmopolitan anti-impunity project. It requires, as Orentlicher insists, striking a delicate balance between 'the local' and 'the universal'. How to strike that balance is one of the central challenges facing the human rights movement.[107]

It is a matter of debate, of course, whether or not the Principles strike the 'right' balance. One thing seems sure, however. If the Principles are to be a 'living instrument' rather than a dogmatic tool,[108] critical reflections about why anti-impunity matters and how it matters cannot be ignored. That, at any rate, is the spirit that underlies this Commentary. As noted at the outset, this Commentary is intended to offer a forum for thinking creatively about what 'fighting impunity' may mean, and what it may involve, in the so-called 'age of accountability'. An important part of the project, so conceived, consists of clarifying the precise nature of the legal and conceptual issues at stake and setting out relevant practice. But beyond that, this Commentary offers a space of diversity, where authors holding a variety of views meet and, sometimes, disagree.

It is our hope that the present volume will provide a valuable resource—informing, stimulating, and challenging those involved, or simply interested, in social debates about why and how the global fight against impunity matters.

[105] Ibid.

[106] See DF Orentlicher, 'Settling Accounts Revisited: Reconciling Global Norms with Local Agency' (2007) 1(1) International Journal of Transitional Justice 10–22.

[107] For contributions to this debate, see P Alston, 'Populist Challenge to Human Rights' (2017) 9 Journal of Human Rights Practice 1–15, 8; F Lenzerini, *The Culturalization of Human Rights Law* (OUP 2014); B de Sousa Santos, 'Toward a Multicultural Conception of Human Rights' in B Hernández-Truyol (ed), *Moral Imperialism: A Critical Anthology* (New York University Press 2002) 39–60.

[108] One may refer here to the so-called 'living instrument' doctrine of the ECtHR. For a classic statement, see *Tyrer v the United Kingdom* App no 5856/72 (ECtHR, 25 April 1978) para 31 (holding that the Convention is a 'living instrument' that 'must be interpreted in the light of present-day conditions').

Preamble

Theo van Boven

Recalling the Preamble to the Universal Declaration of Human Rights, which recognizes that disregard and contempt for human rights have resulted in barbarous acts which have outraged the conscience of mankind,

Aware that there is an ever-present risk that such acts may again occur,

Reaffirming the commitment made by Member States under Article 56 of the Charter of the United Nations to take joint and separate action, giving full importance to developing effective international cooperation for the achievement of the purposes set forth in Article 55 of the Charter concerning universal respect for, and observance of, human rights and fundamental freedoms for all,

Considering that the duty of every State under international law to respect and to secure respect for human rights requires that effective measures should be taken to combat impunity,

Aware that there can be no just and lasting reconciliation unless the need for justice is effectively satisfied,

Equally aware that forgiveness, which may be an important element of reconciliation, implies, insofar as it is a private act, that the victim or the victim's beneficiaries know the perpetrator of the violations and that the latter has acknowledged his or her deeds,

Recalling the recommendation set forth in paragraph 91 of Part II of the Vienna Declaration and Programme of Action, wherein the World Conference on Human Rights (June 1993) expressed its concern about the impunity of perpetrators of human rights violations and encouraged the efforts of the Commission on Human Rights to examine all aspects of the issue,

Convinced, therefore, that national and international measures must be taken for that purpose with a view to securing jointly, in the interests of the victims of violations, observance of the right to know and, by implication, the right to the truth, the right to justice and the right to reparation, without which there can be no effective remedy against the pernicious effects of impunity,

Pursuant to the Vienna Declaration and Programme of Action, the following principles are intended as guidelines to assist States in developing effective measures for combating impunity.

A. Summary of Findings

The Preamble to the United Nations (UN) Updated Set of Principles for the protection and promotion of human rights through action to combat impunity was conceived and designed on the premise that this document is to provide guidance to states and other entities in developing effective measures for combating impunity. A leading normative component of the Preamble, further elaborated in the Principles themselves, is the trilogy of the core rights to know, to justice, and to reparation, including guarantees of non-recurrence. Comparison of the Preamble to the UN Updated Set of Principles with the Preamble to the UN Reparation Principles, which together may be considered as twin sets of principles serving the same agenda but following separate tracks in their coming into existence, reveals a lack of coherence and begs the question of increased coordination and cooperation in human rights standard-setting objectives and activities. In concluding remarks, issues are touched upon concerning (i) restorative justice and transformative justice in conflict situations; (ii) retributive justice mechanisms and other accountability tools; and (iii) broad participatory involvement of victims, human rights defenders, and other sectors of civil society.

B. Contextual and Historical Introduction

I. Functions and characteristics of a Preamble

Most if not all normative UN human rights instruments are preluded by a preamble. 1
Preambles should not be considered as being of secondary importance, to be skipped over in order to move directly to the substantive part of the document.[1] Such an approach may well underestimate the functions and characteristics of a preamble, in so far as it serves the purpose of: (i) indicating and explaining the motives leading to the drafting of the document, (ii) providing a broad theoretical framework for the interpretation of the document, (iii) setting out the rationale and the organization of the document.

II. The Report of Special Rapporteur Louis Joinet

Against this background, Louis Joinet, acting as a member of the UN Sub-Commission 2
on Prevention of Discrimination and Protection of Minorities, undertook the task of preparing a set of principles for the protection and promotion of human rights through action to combat impunity. This task was performed through a process of consultations and revisions, and led in 1997 to the presentation of Joinet's final report[2] for submission to the UN Commission on Human Rights. This report, covering an introduction and an overall presentation of a set of principles as well as proposals and recommendations, contained in an Annex II the full text of a Set of Principles for the Protection and Promotion of Human Rights Through Action to Combat Impunity, including the text of a Preamble.[3]

III. The Updated Set of Principles and the evolving notion of 'transitional justice'

A comparison between the text of Joinet's Preamble (1997) and the Preamble to the 3
UN Updated Set of Principles (2005) bears out that the updating process in the years 2003–2005 did not affect, except for a few minor drafting changes, the original text of the Preamble included in Mr Joinet's report.

For purposes of an historical and contextual interpretation of the text of the Preamble, 4
Joinet's motivations and observations may be taken into account in the framework of what were regarded the origins of the campaign against impunity. This should be done, however, against the background of the evolving notion of 'transitional justice' set out by

[1] J Martenson, 'The Preamble of the Universal Declaration of Human Rights and the UN Human Rights Programme' in A Eide et al (eds), *The Universal Declaration of Human Rights: A Commentary* (Scandinavian University Press 1992) at 17–29, at 18–19.

[2] UN Doc E/CN.4/Sub.2/1997/20/Rev.1 (2 October 1997).

[3] Ibid.

the UN Secretary-General in his report to the UN Security Council on the rule of law and transitional justice in conflict and post-conflict societies.[4]

IV. The campaign against impunity

5 The campaign against impunity had strong roots in the 1970s and 1980s in actions of non-governmental organizations (NGOs) in Latin American countries then under dictatorial regimes. Among these NGOs figure prominently the Mothers and Grandmothers of the Plaza de Mayo and the Federation of Associations of Relatives of Disappeared Detainees (FEDEFAM), which received wide public attention and mobilized international action and support, with the Sub-Commission on Prevention of Discrimination and Protection of Minorities as a legitimate UN actor and the International Commission of Jurists and Amnesty International exercising strong moral leadership. The campaign against impunity found further explicit recognition and support at the Vienna World Conference on Human Rights (1993), which in its Programme of Action dedicated two paragraphs to this issue.[5] Indeed, the Preamble to the Updated Set of Principles recalls in its seventh paragraph the recommendation of the Vienna World Conference, which encouraged efforts by the Commission on Human Rights to examine all aspects of the issue, and further observes in its final paragraph that pursuant to the Vienna Declaration and Programme of Action, the Principles are intended as guidelines to assist states in developing effective measures for combating impunity.

V. The orientation and scope of the Principles, including the Preamble, in the broader settings of restoring peace and democracy

6 When, with the passing of time, in 2005, the independent expert Diane Orentlicher presented the UN Updated Set of Principles, she stated that recent developments had strongly affirmed and reinforced a central premise of the Principles: the need for a *comprehensive approach* towards combating impunity.[6] She also noted that experiences had affirmed the importance of promoting *the broad participation of victims and other citizens* in designing policies for combating impunity.[7] Further, she underlined the premise that, while states must meet their obligations under international law, including those reflected in the Principles, there is no 'one-size-fits-all' response to serious violations of human rights.

7 The UN Updated Set of Principles continued to function and retain their significance as they emerged from practices and experiences in post-authoritarian settings, such as those in Latin American countries, but moved more comprehensively to post-conflict contexts and even to settings where conflict is still an ongoing critical phenomenon.[8] The Preamble, initially set out in the context of the UN Sub-Commission's campaign against

[4] UN Doc S/2004/616 (23 August 2004) para 8.

[5] Vienna Declaration and Programme of Action, UN Doc A/CONF.157/23 (12 July 1993) paras 60 and 91.

[6] *Report of the independent expert to update the Set of Principles to Combat Impunity* UN Doc E/CN.4/2005/102 (18 February 2005) (hereinafter '*Report of the independent expert*') para 6.

[7] Ibid, para 7.

[8] See in particular the *Report of the Special Rapporteur on the promotion of truth, justice, reparation and guarantees of non-recurrence, Pablo de Greiff, to the twenty-first session of the Human Rights Council,* UN Doc A/HRC/21/46 (9 August 2012) paras 19–21.

impunity, falls closely into line with the expression 'restoration of or transition to democracy and/or peace' used in the Principles and for that purpose defined in the 'Definitions' section of the Principles.[9]

C. Normative and Theoretical Framework

I. The basic pledge in the UN Charter

The Preamble to the UN Updated Set of Principles refers quite appropriately to the Preamble to the Universal Declaration of Human Rights, and reaffirms the basic pledge, under Article 56 of the UN Charter, of member states to take joint and separate actions for the achievement of universal respect for, and observance of, human rights and fundamental freedoms for all without distinction as to race, sex, language, or religion. This basic pledge is linked to the purposes of the UN spelled out in Article 1 of the UN Charter, relating to the promotion and encouragement of respect for human rights and fundamental freedoms. Accordingly, as the Preamble to the Updated Set of Principles submits, every Member State is through this pledge firmly committed to take effective measures to combat impunity. 8

A remarkable meta-legal notion incorporated and adduced in the Preamble, moving beyond combating impunity, is the notion of *reconciliation* as a means of facing collectively the abuses of the past, and also demanding of victims, survivors, and their families *forgiveness* for wrongs and sufferings encountered by them. Victims and survivors cannot be expected to forgive without full knowledge and acknowledgement of the misdeeds of the perpetrators.[10] Forgiveness and reconciliation appear as meta-legal components in the preambular considerations and substantiate the right to truth or the right to know, being one of the cornerstones of the Impunity Principles. 9

II. The trilogy of core rights

The Preamble reaches the core of its function as a prelude to the UN Updated Set of Principles when expressing the conviction, in the penultimate paragraph, that in order to combat impunity effectively, national and international measures must be taken to achieve the *trilogy* of *the right to know, the right to justice*, and *the right to reparation*.[11] This trilogy of core rights and remedies, widely considered as complementary, reflects the need for a comprehensive approach towards combating impunity. 10

The same trilogy of core rights and remedies also became the foundation of the mandate for the UN Special Rapporteur on the promotion of truth, justice, reparation, and guarantees of non-recurrence established by Resolution 18/7 of the Human Rights Council on 29 September 2011. This Resolution, recalling among other normative 11

[9] Definition of 'restoration of or transition to democracy and/or peace' in Set of Principles for the protection and promotion of human rights through action to combat impunity, UN Doc E/CN.4/2005/102/Add.1 (8 February 2005), under Definition C. This expression refers to situations, within the framework of a national movement towards democracy and peace negotiations in whatever form, by which the actors or parties concerned agree to take measures against impunity and the recurrence of human rights violations.

[10] S Cohen, *States of Denial; Knowing about Atrocities and Suffering* (Polity Press 2001) 238–39.

[11] The trilogy of victims' legal rights was advanced by Special Rapporteur Joinet as a broad strategic framework for action against impunity, and was retained in the Updated Set of Principles. See UN Doc E/CN.4/Sub.2/1997/20/Rev.1 (2 October 1997).

instruments the Set of Impunity Principles and its updated version, may well be regarded as an important tool in support of the Impunity Principles, which continue to serve 'as a guideline to assist States in developing effective measures for combating impunity', as stated in the last preambular paragraph of the Impunity Principles and by the former UN Commission on Human Rights in its endorsement of the Principles.[12] The trilogy of core rights and remedies has turned into a nominal quadruple transitional justice approach in the mandate of the UN Special Rapporteur, in so far as '*guarantees of non-recurrence*' are explicitly added as a distinct category. As a plausible conceptual explanation for the separate mention of guarantees of non-recurrence next to the three core elements of truth, justice, and reparation, it may well be argued that the core elements refer to interrelated modalities, while guarantees of non-recurrence as a preventive device are a function often of a structural nature.[13] The non-recurrence imperative is also implicit in the Preamble to the UN Updated Set of Impunity Principles, where in the second paragraph the warning is made of an ever-present risk that barbarous acts, which have outraged the conscience of mankind, as referred to in the Preamble to the Universal Declaration of Human Rights, may again occur.

III. The interest of victims

12 In the overall perception and structure of the Preamble, *victims* of human rights violations are projected as persons having an interest that the right to know, the right to justice, and the right to reparation be observed. And as the penultimate paragraph of the Preamble underlines, there can be no effective remedy against the pernicious effects of impunity without securing observance of these rights. This vision of primarily linking the interest of victims with combating impunity is properly reflected in the introductory section of the *Report of the independent expert*, where she observed that recent experience has affirmed the central importance of promoting *the broad participation of victims and other citizens* in designing policies for combating impunity as an effective response to victims' actual needs and as a means to reconstitute the full civic membership of those who were denied the protection of the law in the past.[14] This vision, propounded on the basis of the interest of victims in campaigns and policies of combating impunity in a participatory manner which directly and indirectly transpires through the Preamble to the UN Updated Set of Principles, may be compared with the text of the Preamble to the UN Reparation Principles, which, in its language and its thrust, offers more explicitly a victim-oriented perspective, with reaffirmation of the international legal principles of accountability, justice, and the rule of law.[15]

[12] Commission on Human Rights, Resolution (Res) 2005/81 (21 April 2005).

[13] See *Report of the Special Rapporteur on the promotion of truth, justice, reparation and guarantees of non-recurrence, Pablo de Greiff, to the thirtieth session of the Human Rights Council*, UN Doc A/HRC/30/42 (7 September 2015) para 23.

[14] See *Report of the independent expert*, n 6, para 7.

[15] Basic Principles and Guidelines on the Right to a Remedy and Reparation for Victims of Gross Violations of International Human Rights Law and Serious Violations of International Humanitarian Law, adopted by UN General Assembly Res 60/147 (16 December 2005).

D. The Status of the Preamble and the Principles

I. Guidelines to assist states and other entities

The last preambular paragraph of the UN Updated Set of Principles characterizes the Principles as guidelines to assist states in devising effective measures for combating impunity. This function of the Principles, serving as guidelines to assist states, was already developed by Special Rapporteur Joinet in an afterword to his report presented in 1997 to the UN Sub-Commission,[16] where he stated that the Principles are not legal standards in the strict sense but rather provide guidance in a process laying the foundations of a just and lasting reconciliation. In similar vein, the independent expert Diane Orentlicher, in the introduction of her Report to update the Set of UN Impunity Principles, underlined that the Principles are not legally binding in themselves but should nonetheless reflect and comport with pertinent legal standards.[17] In a similar fashion, the UN Commission on Human Rights de facto endorsed the Updated Set of Principles as guidelines to assist states in developing effective measures for combating impunity,[18] and encouraged states, intergovernmental organizations, and NGOs to consider the recommendations and best practices identified in the independent study on impunity[19] and in the Updated Principles.[20] While the Principles in their initial version and in their updated setting may not by and in themselves be regarded as legally binding standards, they do portray the normative baselines for effectively guiding and assisting states and non-state actors, as well as intergovernmental organizations and NGOs, in situations of transitional justice. Consequently, designs and mechanisms elaborated for that purpose are not to be downgraded to the level of a soft form of justice.[21] 13

II. Comparison with the Preamble to the UN Reparation Principles: a critical note

While the Preamble to the UN Updated Set of Principles can be considered as outlining legally and morally the normative basis of the Principles, it lacks the coherence and structure that may be expected from any preamble to a normative human rights instrument. In this respect a comparison is due with the Preamble to the UN Basic Principles and Guidelines on the Right to a Remedy and Reparation for Victims of Gross Violations of International Human Rights Law and Serious Violations of International Humanitarian Law ('the Reparation Principles'), which in their scope and purpose can be considered as a twin instrument to the UN Updated Set of Principles. The Preamble to the UN Reparation Principles follows a logical structure of explaining their object and purpose by listing the underlying relevant normative instruments, by describing the scope of the document in terms of violations and victims, and by qualifying the nature of mechanisms, procedures, and other methods of implementation from a victim-oriented perspective. In contrast to the Preamble to the Updated Set of Principles, its counterpart in the UN Reparation Principles was the subject of negotiations, and was referred to by a number 14

[16] See n 2, para 49. [17] See *Report of the independent expert*, n 6, para 11. [18] See n 12.

[19] *Independent study on best practices, including recommendations, to assist states in strengthening their domestic capacity to combat all aspects of impunity, by Professor Diana Orentlicher*, UN Doc E/CN.4/2004/88 (27 February 2004).

[20] See n 12, para 21. [21] See Report of the Special Rapporteur, n 8, para 19.

of state representatives when clarifying their position on the meaning and the scope of the document.[22]

III. Lack of coherence, consistency, and overall coordination in standard-setting processes

15 In retrospect, and with due respect for the efforts initially invested in the preambular reach of the UN Updated Set of Principles, a few critical notions commend themselves as to the political economy and the organization of a normative instrument that is intended to serve as a set of guidelines to assist states and other entities in developing effective measures for combating impunity. One might wonder whether in the standard-setting process leading to the endorsement of the instrument by the UN Commission on Human Rights in its Resolution 2005/81, the Preamble to the UN Updated Set of Principles would have gained more coherence and consistency if the text had been reviewed in the light of the substantive reflections and the updating considerations of the Impunity Principles themselves, as a mode to link the Preamble more explicitly with the overall vision of the document.[23]

16 Another, more intriguing query that does not touch upon the Preamble itself but which relates to UN human rights standard setting in general and the economy in the design of normative documents, is the co-existence of interrelated instruments concerning respectively the right to remedy and reparation and action to combat impunity. Both instruments received approval by the UN bodies in the same year (2005). In many ways both instruments cover the same ground and were intended to serve interrelated objectives by setting out the following obligations: the obligation to prevent violations; the obligation to investigate, prosecute, and punish perpetrators; the obligation to provide effective access to justice to all individuals alleging a violation; and the obligation to afford full reparation to victims, including guarantees of non-recurrence.[24] The two instruments, referred to in section D.II above as 'twin' instruments, were developed under distinct mandates designed by the UN Commission on Human Rights together with its Sub-Commission. But in the process of standard-setting they followed separate tracks, and no efforts were made to bring these tracks together for the sake of consistency and economy. In fact, the Impunity Principles were finally endorsed in 2005 by the UN Commission on Human Rights, and the Reparation Principles were adopted later in the same year without a vote by the UN General Assembly. While both instruments are aimed at providing normative and substantive guidance to transitional justice processes, the adoption of the Reparation Principles by the widely representative organ of the World Organization enhances the authority of the latter document.

[22] Basic Principles and Guidelines on the Right to a Remedy and Reparation for Victims of Gross Violations of International Human Rights Law and Serious Violations of International Humanitarian Law, 2005, Introductory Note by Theo van Boven, from the website of the United Nations Audiovisual Library of International Law, <www.un.org/law/avl/> accessed 25 November 2017.

[23] Martenson, n 1, recalled (at 19) that in the drafting process of the Universal Declaration of Human Rights, the Preamble was dealt with at the end of the various sessions and thereby had instilled into it the essence of the drafters' substantive reflections and views.

[24] REDRESS, *Implementing Victims' Rights, A Handbook on the Basic Principles and Guidelines on the Right to a Remedy and Reparation*, London, The Redress Trust, March 2006, at 19–42.

E. Some Concluding Remarks

A preamble as an introductory narrative is meant to provide orientation and inspiration for the thrust of the document to which it is a prelude. As suggested in section D of the present commentary, it would have served the quality and the rationale of the Preamble to the Impunity Principles if its text had been subject to review in the updating process. Nevertheless, as attested to under the normative and theoretical framework of the present commentary, the Preamble to the Impunity Principles still offers a number of valuable and striking features, in particular by outlining the trilogy of the core rights to truth, justice, and reparation as the multifaceted and interconnected strategic model to combat impunity further elaborated in the Impunity Principles themselves. From this perspective, a few remarks may be made. 17

First, while the Impunity Principles, including the Preamble, were initially shaped as a transitional justice guide to come to terms with a legacy of large-scale *past* human rights abuses, there is a growing awareness that patterns of restorative justice, in order to overcome the past, are to be complemented by means of transformative justice so as to render economic, social, and political justice to victims belonging to the most vulnerable sectors of society. 18

Second, when the campaign against the culture of impunity was launched in order to serve justice and achieve reconciliation, it was in particular retributive justice and mechanisms of retribution that were envisaged as the most appropriate tools to meet the challenges posed by perpetrators and their accomplices. Over the years it was realized that these challenges may also be encountered by other mechanisms stressing or implying the notions of accountability and acknowledgement. Truth commissions, fact-finding and inquiry exercises, and vetting fall into this category. 19

Third, while states as major subjects of international law and members of the UN carry primary responsibility for combating impunity, there is a growing and commendable practice in many conflict and post-conflict situations of broad participatory involvement of victims, human rights defenders, and other sectors of civil society in promoting and designing policies to combat impunity and insist on accountability. 20

Definitions

Sandra Krähenmann

A. Impunity

'Impunity' means the impossibility, de jure or de facto, of bringing the perpetrators of violations to account—whether in criminal, civil, administrative or disciplinary proceedings—since they are not subject to any inquiry that might lead to their being accused, arrested, tried and, if found guilty, sentenced to appropriate penalties, and to making reparations to their victims.

B. Serious crimes under international law

As used in these principles, the phrase 'serious crimes under international law' encompasses grave breaches of the Geneva Conventions of 12 August 1949 and of Additional Protocol I thereto of 1977 and other violations of international humanitarian law that are crimes under international law, genocide, crimes against humanity, and other violations of internationally protected human rights that are crimes under international law and/or which international law requires States to penalize, such as torture, enforced disappearance, extrajudicial execution, and slavery.

C. Restoration of or transition to democracy and/or peace

This expression, as used in these principles, refers to situations leading, within the framework of a national movement towards democracy or peace negotiations aimed at ending an armed conflict, to an agreement, in whatever form, by which the actors or parties concerned agree to take measures against impunity and the recurrence of human rights violations.

D. Truth commissions

As used in these principles, the phrase 'truth commissions' refers to official, temporary, non-judicial fact-finding bodies that investigate a pattern of abuses of human rights or humanitarian law, usually committed over a number of years.

E. Archives

As used in these principles, the word 'archives' refers to collections of documents pertaining to violations of human rights and humanitarian law from sources including (a) national governmental agencies, particularly those that played significant roles in relation to human rights violations; (b) local agencies, such as police stations, that were involved in human rights violations; (c) State agencies, including the office of the prosecutor and the judiciary, that are involved in the protection of human rights; and (d) materials collected by truth commissions and other investigative bodies.

A. Summary of Findings

The Principles define at the outset a series of key terms that are repeatedly used, namely, 'impunity', 'serious crimes under international law', 'restoration of or transition to democracy and/or peace', 'truth commissions', and 'archives'. The definitions delimit the scope of the Updated Principles. Compared to the Joinet Principles, the Updated Principles adopt a broader notion of 'serious crimes under international law', which also allows the Principles to take into account any future developments. Similarly, as the definition at the outset reveals, the Updated Principles acknowledge the broader role to be played by truth commissions, complementary and distinct from criminal proceedings. At the same time, the definitions illustrate that the Principles are addressed to states and do not provide guidance for investigative mechanisms and archives by international organizations and non-governmental organizations (NGOs).

B. Introduction

1 Key expressions used repeatedly in the Principles are defined at the outset. The meaning of 'serious crimes under international law', 'restoration of or transition to democracy and/or peace', 'truth commissions', and 'archives' is explained '[a]s used in these principles'. These definitions do not purport to provide a generic definition but only a definition for the purposes of the Principles. They provide an interpretation of these expressions in the Principles and thus delimit their scope. In contrast, the key concept of impunity is defined generically, not limited to '[a]s used in these principles'.[1]

2 While the definition of 'impunity' and the definition of 'restoration of or transition to democracy and/or peace' remained unchanged compared to the 1997 Joinet Principles,[2] the Principles revised the definition of 'serious crimes under international law' to reflect developments in international law,[3] and added the definitions for 'truth commissions' and 'archives'.

C. Definitions

I. Impunity

3 The concept of impunity provides the guiding framework for the Principles and distinguishes them from related instruments with a different focus, namely, the 2005 Basic Principles and Guidelines on the Right to a Remedy and Reparations for Victims of Gross Violations of International Human Rights Law and Serious Violations of International Human Rights Law.[4] Nonetheless, the first two reports did not attempt to provide a definition of 'impunity'.[5] Non-governmental organizations advocated for defining the concept.[6] Notoriously difficult to

[1] UN Doc E/CN.4/2005/102/Add.1 (8 February 2005) 'Definitions'.

[2] UN Commission on Human Rights (UNCHR) (Sub-Commission), Set of Principles for the protection and promotion of human rights through action to combat impunity, UN Doc E/CN.4/Sub.2/1997/20/Rev.1 (2 October 1997) Annex II.

[3] UNCHR, *Report of the independent expert to update the Set of Principles to combat impunity*, UN Doc E/CN.4/2005/102 (18 February 2005) para 13 (hereinafter '*Report of the independent expert*').

[4] UNGA Resolution (Res) 60/147, UN Doc A/RES/60/147 (15 December 2005).

[5] UNCHR (Sub-Commission), *The administration of justice and the human rights of detainees. Question of human rights of person subjected to any form of detention or imprisonment* UN Doc E/CN.4/Sub.2/1992/18 (12 August 1992); and UNCHR (Sub-Commission), *The administration of justice and the human rights of detainees. Question of human rights of person subjected to any form of detention or imprisonment. Progress Report on the question of impunity of perpetrators of human rights violations, prepared by Mr Guissé and Mr Joinet, pursuant to Sub-Commission Resolution 1992/23*, UN Doc E/CN.4/Sub.2/1993/6 (19 July 1993).

[6] UNCHR (Sub-Commission), *The administration of justice and the human rights of detainees. Progress Report on the question of the impunity of perpetrators of violations of human rights (civil and political rights), prepared by Mr Joinet, pursuant to Sub-Commission Resolution 1994/34*, UN Doc E/CN.4/Sub.2/1995/18 (28 June 1995) para 4.

define,[7] the proposed definition of 'impunity' underwent several changes during the drafting process. As with many other definitions of the concept,[8] the initial definitions focused on the lack of punishment of perpetrators.[9] Yet, recognizing the close nexus between reparations and accountability,[10] the final 1997 Joinet Principles included the absence of reparations by the perpetrator to victims.[11] Purely descriptive, the definition does not address the consequences of impunity, the reason why impunity needs to be fought, or various manifestations or paths to impunity, such as partial or total impunity or de facto or legal impunity.

4 Conveying the idea that impunity is the opposite of accountability,[12] the definition[13] turns around the individual accountability of the perpetrator, including by providing reparations to victims. In order to ensure such individual accountability, states have to take the measures described in the Principles. In particular, while the definition of 'impunity' in the Principles is the same as in the 1997 Joinet Principles, it must be read together with the new Principle 1.[14] Laying out the general measures states have to take to combat impunity, Principle 1 is significantly broader than what the definition of impunity may convey, in the sense that it goes beyond measures to ensure the accountability of the perpetrator and reparations to victims, and includes the right to truth and the right to an effective remedy.[15] The combination of the definition of 'impunity' with Principle 1 illustrates that impunity invariably involves human rights violations by states in terms of their failure to respond to previous wrongdoing. In addition to Principle 1, Principles 22 (Nature of restrictive measures) and 38 (Reform of laws and institutions contributing to impunity) also explicitly refer to the concept of impunity.

5 Among the human rights bodies that have defined 'impunity', the Inter-American Court of Human Rights (IACtHR) uses a narrower concept. Focusing on individual criminal responsibility, the IACtHR defines 'impunity' as the 'overall lack of investigation, arrest, prosecution and conviction of those responsible for violations of the rights

[7] For an overview of various definitions, see MM Penrose, 'Impunity—Inertia, Inaction, and Invalidity: A Literature Review' (1999) 17 Boston University International Law Journal 269–310, 273–77; and JE Viñuales, 'Impunity: Elements for an Empirical Concept' (2007) 25 Law and Inequality 115–45, 116–18.

[8] For an analysis of the central role played by individual criminal responsibility in the anti-impunity movement, see K Engle, 'Anti-Impunity and the Turn to Criminal Law in Human Rights' (2015) 100 Cornell Law Review 1069–127, 1073–78.

[9] UNCHR (Sub-Commission), *The administration of justice and the human rights of detainees. Progress Report on the question of the impunity of perpetrators of violations of human rights (civil and political rights), prepared by Mr Joinet, pursuant to Sub-Commission Resolution 1995/35*, UN Doc E/CN.4/Sub.2/1996/18 (29 June 1996) 9.

[10] A link that was highlighted in a previous report, see the *1995 Progress Report*, n 6, para 5 and the parallel van Boven study, see UNCHR (Sub-Commission), *Study concerning the right to restitution, compensation and rehabilitation for victims of gross violations of human rights and fundamental freedom. Final Report submitted by Mr Theo Van Boven*, UN Doc E/CN.4/Sub.2/1993/8 (2 July 1993) paras 126–30. See also Viñuales, n 7, who describes these changes in terms of the relationship between punishment and impunity.

[11] See the definition of impunity in the final and the final revised Joinet Principles: UNCHR (Sub-Commission), Set of Principles for the protection and promotion of human rights through action to combat impunity, UN Doc E/CN.4/Sub.2/1997/20 (26 June 1997) Annex II; and revised Set of Principles for the protection and promotion of human rights through action to combat impunity, n 2. In addition, compared to the June 1997 version, the revised Set of Principles changed 'if found guilty, convicted' to 'if found guilty, sentenced to appropriate penalties'.

[12] Penrose, n 7. [13] See n 1. [14] *Report of the independent expert*, n 3, para 16.

[15] See the commentary to Principle 1 in this volume by Naomi Roht-Arriaza.

protected by the American Convention'.[16] Indeed, criminal law mechanisms, including as part of reparations for victims, play a central role in the IACtHR's case law,[17] but the Court has also stressed the complementarity between individual criminal responsibility and state responsibility, with the latter including the right to an effective remedy and the right to truth.[18]

The definition of 'impunity' in the Principles, in particular when read in isolation and not conjunction with Principle 1, may be described as narrow on account of its focus on perpetrators and the absence of punishment.[19] Yet at the same time, the scope of the definition is rather broad and covers all human rights violations, regardless of their gravity, the type of human rights involved, and the suspected perpetrators. 6

The definition of 'impunity' simply refers to human rights 'violations'. In other words, the definition encompasses any human rights violation, regardless of its gravity. In contrast, other related instruments are limited to gross or serious human rights violations, namely, the 2005 Basic Principles and Guidelines on the Right to a Remedy and Reparations for Gross Human Rights Violations and Serious Violations of International Humanitarian Law[20] and the 2011 Council of Europe Guidelines of the Committee of Ministers of the Council of Europe on eradicating impunity for serious human rights violations.[21] Indeed, the limitation in the first studies on impunity to serious or and massive or systematic human rights violations[22] was eventually abandoned.[23] The Preamble to the Principles repeatedly refers to human rights violations in general, without any qualification as to their seriousness or gravity, amongst other matters recalling that the 1993 Vienna Declaration and Programme of Action 'expressed its concern about the impunity of perpetrators of human rights violations'. Moreover, the Principles provide for a series of measures for a particular kind of human rights violations, namely those that amount to 'serious crimes under international law', in Part III.[24] Framed as 'The Right to Justice', Part III in essence focuses on the duty to investigate, prosecute, and duly punish 'serious crimes under international law'. Along the same lines, Principle 8 provides that commissions of inquiry may have jurisdiction to consider all forms of violations of human rights and humanitarian law, but prioritizes violations that amount to serious crimes under international law. The inclusion of all human rights violations further illustrates that the concept of impunity is not limited to criminal justice. In contrast, the 2011 Council of Europe Impunity 7

[16] *Case of Gutiérrez Soler v Colombia* (Judgment) IACtHR Series C no 132 (12 September 2005) para 95 see also *Case of the 'White Van' (Paniagua-Morales et al) v Guatemala* (Judgment) IACtHR Series C no 37 (8 March 1998) para 137.

[17] Engle, n 8, 1080 ff.

[18] *Case of Goibúru et al v Paraguay* (Judgment) IACtHR Series C no 153 (22 September 2006) para 131.

[19] K Hooper, 'The Ending of Impunity and the Fight for Justice for Victims of Human Rights Violations: A Chasm too Great to be Crossed?' (2006) 9 Flinders Journal of Law Reform 181–204, 182.

[20] See n 4.

[21] Council of Europe, Guidelines of the Committee of Ministers of the Council of Europe on Eradicating Impunity for Serious Human Rights Violations (March 2011).

[22] See UNCHR (Sub-Commission) *Question of human rights of person subjected to any form of detention or imprisonment*, n 5, para 13; and UNCHR (Sub-Commission), *The administration of justice and the human rights of detainees*, n 6, para 5. This limitation was modelled after the parallel van Boven study, n 10, para 8.

[23] See the definition proposed in 1996 in UNCHR (Sub-Commission), *The administration of justice and the human rights of detainees*, n 9, at 9.

[24] 'Serious' violations of human rights law are often equated with international crimes, yet this is not necessarily the case. For a clarification of the definition of serious violations under international law, see IM Siatitsa, '"A Serious Violation of International Human Rights Law"—An Attempt to Clarify a Crucial Provision of the Arms Trade Treaty' (2015) 5 European Journal of Human Rights 606–30, 611–23.

Guidelines are geared towards criminal justice, as they only apply to serious violations of human rights, defined rather restrictively as 'those acts in respect of which states have an obligation under the Convention and in the light of the Court's case law, to enact criminal law provisions'.[25]

8 In terms of the type of the rights covered, the reference to violations must be read nowadays as including economic, social, and cultural rights. During the drafting process of the 1997 Joinet Principles, the study was split up into two separate tracks, distinguishing between civil and political rights on the one hand and economic, social, and cultural rights on the other hand. [26] The distinction was maintained in 1997 with the submission of two separate reports: the Joinet Report, with the annexed Joinet Principles focusing on civil and political rights; and the report of Mr El Hadji Guissé on economic, social, and cultural rights.[27] The latter proposed a definition of 'impunity' that was expressly applicable to both civil and political rights and economic, social, and cultural rights.[28] Yet apart from their drafting history, the definition of 'impunity' or the Principles themselves do not mandate a limitation to civil and political rights, despite the difficulties in identifying those responsible for the violation of economic, social, and cultural rights.[29] Without modifying the definition of 'impunity', Professor Orentlicher underscored in her 2004 Progress Report that the Principles apply to economic, social, and cultural rights, and pointed out that 'Recent case law has also helped clarify the nature of States' obligation to combat impunity for serious violations of economic, social and cultural rights.'[30] The confirmation that the Principles apply to economic, social, and cultural rights reflects the general convergence between civil and political rights and economic, social, and cultural rights, including in terms of acknowledging the justiciability of economic, social, and cultural rights, not only for the purposes of establishing state responsibility, but also under international criminal law.[31]

9 Lastly, one might wonder whether the concept of impunity is limited to human rights violations committed by state agents. Indeed, the definition refers to 'perpetrators of violations'. In human rights law, the term 'violations' tends to be associated with violations by state actors. In contrast, for non-state actors, the notion of 'abuses' is often preferred, due to the ongoing discussion of whether—and, if so, in what circumstances and to what extent—non-state actors are bound by human rights law.

[25] Council of Europe, Impunity Guidelines, n 21, at 2.

[26] For an overview of the drafting history of the 1997 Joinet Principles, with a focus on the decision to have two separate studies by two separate rapporteurs, see UNCHR (Sub-Commission), *The realization of economic, social and cultural rights. Final Report on the question of the impunity of perpetrators of human rights violations (economic, social and cultural rights), prepared by Mr El Hadji Guissé, Special Rapporteur, pursuant o Sub-Commission Resolution 1996/24*, UN Doc E/CN.4/Sub.2/1997/8 (27 June 1997) paras 2–5.

[27] See the two separate 1997 reports, UNCHR (Sub-Commission), *The realization of economic, social and cultural rights*, ibid; and *The administration of justice and the human rights of detainees*, n 11.

[28] *The realization of economic, social and cultural rights*, n 26, para 20.

[29] Viñuales, n 7, 117–18. He notes that the definitions proposed by Joinet and Guissé leave 'substantial room for different and possibly conflicting interpretations'.

[30] UNCHR, *Independent study on best practices, including recommendations, to assist states in strengthening their domestic capacity to combat all aspects of impunity, by Professor Diane Orentlicher*, UN Doc E/CN.4/2004/88 (27 February 2004) para 35.

[31] Generally on economic, social, and cultural rights as international crimes, see E Schmid, *Taking Economic, Social and Cultural Rights Seriously in International Criminal Law* (CUP 2015); L van den Herik, 'Economic, Social, and Cultural Rights. International Criminal Law's Blind Spot?' in E Riedel, G Giacca, and C Golay (eds), *Economic, Social, and Cultural Rights in International Law. Contemporary Issues and Challenges* (OUP 2014) 343–66.

Yet the mere use of the term 'violations' does not have any legal consequences in itself.[32] Arguably, the concept of impunity arose in the context of violations committed by state agents or those acting with their connivance, and impunity may be seen as the sign of complicity by the state.[33] Moreover, reflecting these origins, the earlier studies by Joinet were limited to impunity in the context of violations perpetrated by the state, either directly or indirectly.[34] Lastly, the term 'impunity' may be more frequently used in relation to violations committed by states.[35] Yet such a limitation is not inherent in the concept of impunity. Instead, the human rights violations associated with impunity arise due to the failure of the state's positive obligations to ensure human rights, including in relation to non-state actors. The IACtHR has stressed, from the outset, that 'when the State allows private persons or groups to act freely and with impunity to the detriment of the rights recognized by the Convention',[36] the state fails in its duty to ensure human rights.[37] Similarly, the European Court of Human Rights (ECtHR) framed the failure to investigate and punish private actors in terms of impunity.[38] The 2011 Council of Europe Guidelines endorsed this approach when pointing out that the Guidelines 'cover states' obligation to take positive action in respect of non-state actors'.[39]

II. Serious crimes under international law

As already mentioned, some of the Principles provide for a series of measures for violations **10**
that amount to 'serious crimes under international law' in Part III, in particular in respect of the obligation to investigate, prosecute, and duly punish. The definition of 'serious crimes under international law' is thus crucial in order to properly delimit the scope of these obligations.

First, the revised definition of serious crimes under international law brings the def- **11**
inition into line with developments under international law in respect of war crimes.[40] While the 1997 Joinet Principles distinguished between war crimes and grave breaches of international humanitarian law, the revised definition clarifies that grave breaches of the Geneva Conventions and Additional Protocol I are particular types of war crimes.[41] The revision reflects that serious violations of international humanitarian law that attract individual criminal responsibility under international law are war crimes during

[32] A Clapham, 'Protection of Civilians under International Human Rights Law' in H Wilmot, R Marniya, S Sheeran, and W Weller (eds), *Protection of Civilians* (OUP 2016) 141–59, 145.

[33] See Viñuales, n 7, 126.

[34] See the 1993 Report, UNCHR (Sub-Commission), *The administration of justice and the human rights of detainees*, n 5, para 9; and the 1995 Report, UNHCR (Sub-Commission), *The administration of justice and the human rights of detainees*, n 6, para 6.

[35] Viñuales, n 7, in respect of the practice of Amnesty International, at 131.

[36] *Case of Vélasquez Rodríguez v Honduras* (Judgment) IACtHR Series C no 4 (29 July 1988) para 176.

[37] Ibid, para 182. While in the *Vélasquez Rodríguez* case the Court held that the enforced disappearances were carried out by 'agents acting under the cover of public authority' (para 182), in later cases the Court framed in terms of impunity the failure to investigate killings committed by unknown perpetrators that could not be attributed to the state; see *Case of González et al ('Cotton Field') v Mexico* (Judgment) IACtHR Series C no 205 (16 November 2009) paras 242 and 288.

[38] *Opuz v Turkey* (Judgment) (ECtHR, 9 June 2009) para 169.

[39] Council of Europe, Impunity Guidelines, n 21, 7.

[40] UNCHR, *Independent study on best practices*, n 30, para 27.

[41] UNCHR, *Report of the independent expert*, n 3, para 13.

both international and non-international armed conflict,[42] contrary to the traditional assumption that war crimes encompassed only the violations of rules governing international armed conflict.[43] The formulation 'other violations under international humanitarian law that are crimes under international law' allows the Principle to include war crimes that have not been included in the list of war crimes under the Rome Statute,[44] as well as to accommodate future legal developments.

12 Second, compared to the 1997 Joinet Principles, the revised definition significantly expands the scope of serious crimes under international law, most notably by extending them beyond those included in the statutes of international criminal courts, that is, war crimes, genocide, and crimes against humanity. While it remains subject to debate which other acts amount to international crimes,[45] the Principles adopt a broad approach and include 'other violations of internationally protected human rights that are crimes under international law and/or which international law requires States to penalize, such as torture, enforced disappearance, extrajudicial execution, and slavery', in light of the practice of human rights bodies, international criminal courts, national courts, and state practice.[46] Including human rights violations that must be criminalized by states reflects the broader trend in human rights law to resort to requiring criminalization of some human rights violations as a means to ensure human rights.[47] As for war crimes, the open-ended formulation allows the Principles to include the evolving practice of human rights bodies to require such criminalization, such as, for example, servitude in addition to slavery.[48]

III. Restoration of or transition to democracy and/or peace

13 For the Joinet Principles, the definition of 'restoration of or transition to democracy and/or peace' was included at the very last stage,[49] and has remained the same in the Updated Principles. During the drafting period, Joinet had used the concept of 'reference period', which was 'delimited by fixed dates referring to events which marked the appearance and later cessation of a consistent pattern of gross violations of human rights'.[50] Characterized

[42] *The Prosecutor v Duško Tadić* (Appeals Chamber, Decision on the Defence Motion for Interlocutory Appeal on Jurisdiction) (ICTY, 2 October 1995) para 95.

[43] P Gaeta, 'War Crimes and Other "Core" Crimes' in A Clapham and P Gaeta (eds), *The Oxford Handbook of International Law in Armed Conflict* (OUP 2014) 737, 746.

[44] See Art 8 of the Rome Statute of the International Criminal Court (1998). For a discussion of serious violations of international humanitarian law that were not included in the Rome Statute, see K Dörmann, 'War Crimes under the Rome Statute of the International Criminal Court, with a Special Focus on the Negotiations on the Elements of Crimes' (2003) 7 Max Planck Yearbook of the United Nations 341, 345 ff.

[45] For example, a common approach to international crimes includes, in addition to the core crimes in the statute of the International Criminal Court, torture and international terrorism, see A Cassese, P Gaeta, L Baig, M Fan, C Gosnell, and A Whiting, *Cassese's International Criminal Law* (3rd edn, OUP 2013) 18–20. Another question beyond the scope of this chapter would be whether the notion of serious crime under international law is necessarily synonymous with international crimes.

[46] UNCHR, *Report of the independent expert*, n 3, para 13.

[47] For an analysis and critical assessment of how human rights law seeks to affect domestic criminal law, see K Kamber, *Prosecution Human Rights Offences. Rethinking the Sword Function of Human Rights Law* (Brill 2016); and FF Basch, 'The Doctrine of the Inter-American Court of Human Rights Regarding States' Duty to Punish Human Rights Violations and its Dangers' (2007) 23(1) American University International Law Review 195–229. For an in-depth analysis of how the IACtHR developed this approach and influenced other human rights bodies, see Engle, n 8.

[48] ECtHR, *Siliadin v France* (Judgment) (ECtHR, 26 July 2005).

[49] The definition was only added in the very last version, the revised final Joinet Principles, see n 2, 17.

[50] UNCHR (Sub-Commission), *The administration of justice and the human rights of detainees*, n 9, 10.

by patterns of gross human rights violations, the concept of reference period conveyed an idea similar to transitional justice, which is commonly described as 'society's attempts to come to terms with a legacy of human rights violations'.[51] In contrast, the definition of 'restoration of or transition to democracy and/or peace' focuses more on the element of change. Generally, the Joinet reports[52] were more geared towards the transitional context, and in their final version included several references to restoration or transition that were removed during the updating process.[53] The Updated Principles include only two references to restoration or transition to democracy and/or peace, namely, in Principle 18 (Specific measures related to the restoration of or transition to democracy and/or peace) for archives and Principle 38 (Reform of laws and institutions contributing to impunity).

Since only two Principles specifically refer to transitional contexts, all the other Principles have a broader, general application, not limited to such contexts. This approach fits with the broad scope of application of the Principles, which is not limited to serious, massive, or systematic human rights violations that often occur during authoritarian regimes or armed conflicts. 14

Conversely, and more importantly, this also means that the Principles apply to periods of restoration or transition in the same way as outside such periods. With the limited exception of Principle 24, which acknowledges that amnesties may be 'intended to establish conditions conducive to a peace agreement or to foster national reconciliation', the Principles do not include special provisions to accommodate the tensions between peace and justice during periods of restoration or transition. Indeed, the definition of 'restoration or transition to democracy and/or peace' foresees that during such periods, 'the actors or parties concerned agree to take measures against impunity and the recurrence of human rights violations'. At least implicitly, the Principles thus seem to take the approach that peace and justice are mutually complementary. Rather than taking into account the particularities of transitional periods, in particular the right to justice and its criminal law components laid out in Part III, the Principles focus on whether or not human rights violations amount to 'serious crimes under international law'. 15

IV. Truth commissions

The Updated Principles added a definition for 'truth commissions', a term that was not used in the Joinet Principles. Instead, the Joinet Principles used the term 'extrajudicial commissions', but without providing a definition.[54] In the Joinet Principles, the 16

[51] UNSC, *The rule of law and transitional justice in conflict and post-conflict societies*, UN Doc S/2004/616 (23 August 2004) para 8.

[52] UNCHR (Sub-Commission), *The administration of justice and the human rights of detainees*, n 9, with references to the 'reference period' in Principles 13–18, Principle 25, Principle 34, Principle 47, and an interpretative provision that the 'definition of the "reference period" may not be interpreted as exonerating or having exonerated States from applying and observing these Principles during the said period'. See also the discussion on amnesties in UNCHR (Sub-Commission), *The administration of justice and the human rights of detainees* (1995), n 6, paras 19–20.

[53] Cf, eg, Joinet Principle 30 on restrictions on the effects of legislation on repentance related to the restoration of or transition to democracy and/or peace, n 2, at 25, with Updated Principle 28 on restrictions on the effects of legislation on disclosure or repentance, which no longer includes the reference to restoration or transition. Similarly, Updated Principle 7 on guarantees of independence, impartiality, and competence, omits the reference to the process of restoration or transition found in Joinet Principle 6 on guarantees of independence and impartiality for extrajudicial commission of inquiry, n 2, at 18.

[54] UNCHR (Sub-Commission), Set of Principles for the protection and promotion of human rights through action to combat impunity, n 2.

extrajudicial commissions were primarily conceived of as a mechanism without intrinsic value to enable criminal prosecutions, even at a later stage. First, their role was to establish 'the facts so that the truth may be ascertained', and to prevent 'the disappearance of evidence'.[55] Second, such commissions should not be diverted from their purpose and be used as a pretext for not having prosecutions.[56] In contrast, the Updated Principles expanded the role of truth commissions in recognition of their distinct and complementary role in the fight against impunity alongside criminal prosecutions.[57] The Updated Principles also highlight that such truth commissions can play an important role outside transitional contexts.[58]

17 The Updated Principles define 'truth commissions' by their main features, that is, being 'official, non-judicial fact-finding bodies', and their activity, namely, to 'investigate a pattern of abuses of human rights or humanitarian law, usually committed over a number of years'. The definition does not specify that these truth commissions are to be national bodies, which raises the question whether it covers international commissions of inquiry or fact-finding bodies set up by the United Nations (UN) Secretary-General or the Human Rights Council. At first glance, the definition could cover these international mechanisms, which can also play a role in ensuring accountability.[59] Moreover, Principle 7 refers to 'commissions that are international in character'. However, when discussing the definition of 'truth commissions', Professor Orentlicher points out in a footnote that the

> definition would not generally cover commissions of experts appointed from time to time by the Secretary-General to examine a situation involving mass atrocities and to report its conclusions and recommendations. ... The definition included in the revised principles, would, however cover some commissions of inquiry, such as the Commission on the Truth for El Salvador, that have occasionally been appointed by the Secretary-General in implementing the terms of a peace accord.[60]

In addition, both the reports and the Updated Principles stress that such truth commissions should be based on national consultations,[61] which is not generally the case for bodies set up by the UN. In addition, another common element in the definition of 'truth commissions', although not retained in the Updated Principles, is that they are 'officially authorized or empowered by the state'.[62] Yet international mechanisms are frequently set up against the will of the state concerned, and operate without the latter's cooperation.[63] In conclusion, while some truth commissions may be of an international character, in the sense that they include international experts or experts appointed by the UN Secretary-General, international bodies whose mandate and composition are exclusively set up by the UN are excluded from the definition adopted for the purposes of the Principles.

[55] Ibid, Principle 5.
[56] Ibid, para 20.
[57] UNCHR, *Independent study on best practices*, n 30, para 10.
[58] Ibid, para 22.
[59] MC Bassiouni, 'Searching for Peace and Achieving Justice: The Need for Accountability' (1996) 59-4 Law and Contemporary Problems 9–27, 20.
[60] UNCHR, *Report of the independent expert*, n 3, 23, fn 26.
[61] Ibid, paras 19 and 22 and Principle 6.
[62] PB Hayner, *Unspeakable Truths. Transitional Justice and the Challenge of Truth Commissions* (2nd edn, Routledge 2011) 12.
[63] Hence, Hayner excludes the International Commission of Inquiry in Burundi that was established by the UN Security Council, because it 'was not a national endeavour sponsored by the state under review, even if a request for its establishment formally came from the government': ibid, 13.

V. Archives

The Joinet Principles included a series of guidelines for archives but did not include a def- 18
inition.[64] The Updated Principles added such a definition. Archives are defined broadly as 'collections of documents pertaining to violations of human rights and humanitarian law' from a variety of official state sources, and 'materials collected by truth commissions and other investigative bodies'. Hence, for the purposes of the Updated Principles, the term 'archives' includes current documents and is not limited to permanently stored records.[65] Such a broad understanding is consonant with the instrumental role played by archives in the right to know.[66] In addition, in light of the expanded role for truth commissions in the Updated Principles, the definition expressly includes materials collected by them.[67]

Yet in addition to documents collected by official sources and truth commissions, other 19
bodies also collect and maintain archives relevant for violations of human rights and international humanitarian law, for example NGOs, international organizations, including the UN, universities, and also private sector institutions.[68] Reflecting that the Updated Principles are addressed to states, the report accompanying the Updated Principles underlines that 'States must respect and protect the right of non-State organizations and individuals to collect, preserve and make available relevant documents concerning such violations',[69] but their collection of documents is excluded from the definition of archives for the purposes of the Updated Principles. International organisations, NGOs, and other private institutions manage and control their own archives, including in terms of granting access to them.[70] As a consequence, the Principles on preservation, access, and cooperation between archival departments and the courts and non-judicial commissions of inquiry[71] are not applicable to the archives of such organizations. Many NGOs grant access to varying degrees and for different purposes to their archives, and cooperate with truth commissions and courts, but the International Committee of the Red Cross (ICRC) works on the basis of confidentiality,[72] which can lead to tensions with the fight against impunity and victims' rights.[73] Its privilege of non-disclosure is recognized under both national and international law,[74] although it may waive immunity in exceptional circumstances.[75] Similarly, the UN has its

[64] See Set of Principles for the protection and promotion of human rights through action to combat impunity, n 2.

[65] For example, the United Nations Office of the High Commissioner of Human Rights (OHCHR), *Rule-of-Law Tools for Post-Conflict States: Archives* (OHCHR 2015), at 5, distinguishes between records and archives, with archives meaning 'the records of long-term or permanent value as well as the institution that manages them and the building that houses them'.

[66] See Updated Principle 5.

[67] See UNCHR, *Report of the independent expert*, n 3, para 15.

[68] Ibid, para 15; see also *Rule-of-Law Tools*, n 65, at 6.

[69] UNCHR, *Report of the independent expert*, n 3, para 15.

[70] *Rule-of-Law Tools*, n 65, at 6. For example, the United Nations has an Archives and Records Management Section, see <archives.un.org/> accessed 20 May 2017.

[71] See Principles 14–18.

[72] ICRC, 'The International Committee of the Red Cross's (ICRC's) Confidential Approach. Policy Document' (2012) 94-887 International Review of the Red Cross 1135–44.

[73] Indeed, the ICRC has acknowledged that the 'crucial struggle against impunity' and 'victims' demand that justice be done' challenge 'the relevance and effectiveness of the ICRC's traditional confidential approach': ibid, 1136.

[74] See ICRC, 'Memorandum. The ICRC's Privilege of Non-Disclosure of Confidential Information' 97-897/898 (2016) 433, 436 ff with further references, including the recognition of ICRC's privilege of non-disclosure in the jurisprudence of the International Criminal Tribunal for the former Yugoslavia and the International Criminal Tribunal for Rwanda, as well as the Rules of Procedure and Evidence of the International Criminal Court.

[75] Ibid, 443; and ICRC, n 72, 1142.

own security and archiving policy for confidential documents, which does not expressly address the question of cooperation with national judicial and non-judicial investigative bodies.[76] The question would have particular relevance for the documents collected by UN fact-finding or inquiry missions for violations of human rights and humanitarian law, but there is no generally applicable and publicised approach as in the case of the ICRC.[77]

D. Conclusions

20 The definitions provided at the outset delimit the scope of the Principles by explaining how certain terms are to be understood. A closer reading and comparison with the Joinet Principles reveal that the scope of the Principles was extended, such as, for example, in relation to the role played by truth commissions or the notion of serious crimes under international law. At the same time, the definitions foreshadow a series of questions that remain unaddressed in the Principles. First, although the guiding framework for the Principles is the impunity framework, their definition of 'impunity' remains limited and geared towards individual accountability. Second, addressed to states, the Principles do not engage with the role played by international organizations, with the exception of the International Criminal Court, in the fight against impunity in respect of their investigative mechanisms and archives. Third, a similar approach is pursued for NGOs. Fourth, being generally applicable, the Principles offer little guidance in respect of the complexities that characterize the fight against impunity, which arise in transitional contexts.

Bibliography

Bassiouni, MC, 'Searching for Peace and Achieving Justice: The Need for Accountability' (1996) 59-4 Law and Contemporary Problems 9–27.

Eide, A, 'Preventing Impunity for the Violator and Ensuring Remedies for the Victim' (2000) 69 Nordic Journal of International Law 1–10.

Hooper, K, 'The Ending of Impunity and the Fight for Justice for Victims of Human Rights Violations: A Chasm too Great to be Crossed?' (2006) 9 Flinders Journal of Law Reform 181–204.

Méndez, JE, 'Accountability for Past Abuses' (1997) 19 Human Rights Quarterly 255–82.

Morris, MH, 'International Guidelines against Impunity: Facilitating Accountability' (1996) 59 Law and Contemporary Problems 29–39.

Penrose, MM, 'Impunity—Inertia, Inaction, and Invalidity: A Literature Review' (1999) 17 Boston University International Law Journal 269–310.

Viñuales, JE, 'Impunity: Elements for an Empirical Concept' (2007) 25 Law and Inequality 115–45.

[76] UN Secretariat, 'Secretary-General's Bulletin. Information Sensitivity, Classification and Handling', UN Doc ST/SGB/2007/6 (12 February 2007).

[77] For example the Office of the High Commissioner's investigation on Sri Lanka stressed that all witness statements and other confidential material was classified as 'strictly confidential', see UNHRC, *Report of the OHCHR Investigation on Sri Lanka (OISL)*, UN Doc A/HRC/30/CRP.2 (16 September 2015) para 24. The Independent International Commission of Inquiry for Syria illustrates a different approach. It has compiled a list of alleged perpetrators that it shares with the High Commissioner of Human Rights and has shared information with states who were willing to exercise jurisdiction over their nationals who return home after fighting in Syria, see UNHRC, *Report of the Independent International Commission of Inquiry on the Syrian Arab Republic*, UN Doc A/HRC/28/69 (5 February 2015), paras 106–07.

PART I

COMBATING IMPUNITY: GENERAL OBLIGATIONS

Principle 1. General Obligations of States to Take Effective Action to Combat Impunity

Naomi Roht-Arriaza

Impunity arises from a failure by States to meet their obligations to investigate violations; to take appropriate measures in respect of the perpetrators, particularly in the area of justice, by ensuring that those suspected of criminal responsibility are prosecuted, tried and duly punished; to provide victims with effective remedies and to ensure that they receive reparation for the injuries suffered; to ensure the inalienable right to know the truth about violations; and to take other necessary steps to prevent a recurrence of violations.

A. Summary of Findings

Principle 1 is the introduction and cornerstone to the Principles as a whole. It establishes state responsibility for the interrelated obligations outlined in the Principles, and makes clear that these obligations are all mandatory, interrelated, non-hierarchical, and in addition to responsibility for the underlying violations. The Principle arises from then-existing jurisprudence of the regional human rights courts and the United Nations (UN) human rights bodies, and from academic and non-governmental commentary. It has been taken up and developed in national law, donor priorities, and related international soft law since 2005. It has been applied, albeit not explicitly, by the International Court of Justice (ICJ). The Principle contains some ambiguities and weaknesses, which will be detailed in this chapter, but these are due in part to the fast-changing nature of the attitudes of states towards fighting impunity. The Principles were originally drafted at a time of enthusiasm for transitional justice (and its relative, international criminal justice); it is doubtful that their reception would be as enthusiastic were they drafted today.

B. Contextual and Historical Introduction

There was no general principle of state obligation in the 1997 Joinet Principles. The original Principles had a definitions section, followed immediately by the first section, on the right to truth. What became Principle 1 was originally Article 18(1), which was situated in the section on 'right to justice'. It read as follows: 1

DUTIES OF STATES WITH REGARD TO THE ADMINISTRATION OF JUSTICE: Impunity arises from a failure by States to meet their obligations to investigate violations, to take appropriate measures in respect of the perpetrators, particularly in the area of justice, by ensuring that they are prosecuted, tried and duly punished, to provide victims with effective remedies and reparation for the injuries suffered, and to take steps to prevent any recurrence of such violations.

Professor Orentlicher moved Article 18(1) up because it does not refer simply to the right to justice but to all the Principles, and because, while many of the Principles are framed in terms of rights belonging to victims/survivors or to society as a whole, it was 2 important to establish that these rights have corresponding state obligations. The revision also explicitly includes the right to truth, although it does not make clear who exactly the rights holder is. The Principle now refers to state obligations vis-à-vis perpetrators, victims, and, implicitly, the society as a whole. The title also states what the goal is: states should take effective action to combat impunity.

C. Theoretical Framework

3 It is not clear where the origins of 'combating impunity' as a framework came from. The initial Special Rapporteur, Mr Joinet, pointed to the conformation of victims' networks and to conferences in Europe and Latin America in the early 1990s. His initial study was on the evolution of amnesty laws. The 1993 Vienna Declaration on Human Rights, in paragraph 60, reads: 'States should abrogate legislation leading to impunity for those responsible for grave violations of human rights such as torture and prosecute such violations, thereby providing a firm basis for the rule of law.' Paragraph 91 endorses the then Commission on Human Rights' efforts to study the issue.

4 The Principles were intended to restate existing law, not make new law. Principle 1 was by 2004 well established in international human rights law and the law on state responsibility. In 1988, the Inter-American Court on Human Rights (IACtHR), in the landmark *Velásquez Rodríguez* case, held that states had an obligation, as a corollary to their obligation to ensure rights, to investigate, and if warranted prosecute and punish, violations, and to provide remedies to victims.[1] Since that time, the regional human rights courts and commissions, and the expert treaty bodies of the UN, have all reaffirmed the Principle as stated. For example, the European Court of Human Rights (ECtHR), while not going so far as to recognize victims' rights to force prosecutions, does recognize the duties of states to investigate and prosecute serious rights violations.[2] The International Law Commission (ILC) Draft Articles on State Responsibility, while excluding the responsibility of individuals from their ambit, recognizes the responsibility of states to provide reparation and satisfaction for breaches of international obligations.[3] These obligations

[1] *Velásquez Rodríguez v Honduras* (Judgment) IACtHR Series C no 04 (29 July 1988) para 174. This line of jurisprudence has been reiterated and consolidated in subsequent cases, including cases against Peru (*Barrios Altos*), Chile (*Almonacid Arrellano*), Brazil (*Gomes Lund*), Uruguay (*Gelman*) and El Salvador (*El Mozote*). *Case of Barrios Altos v Peru* (Judgment) IACtHR Series C no 87 (30 November 2001); *Case of Luis Alfredo Almonacid Arellano et al v Chile* (Judgment) IACtHR Series C no 154 (26 September 2006); *Case of Gomes Lund et al ('Guerrilha do Araguaia') v Brazil* (Judgment) IACtHR Series C no 219 (24 November 2010); *Case of Juan Gelman et al v Uruguay* (Judgment) IACtHR Series C no 221 (24 February 2011); *Massacres of El Mozote and neighboring locations v El Salvador* (Judgment) IACtHR Series C no 252 (25 October 2012). Orentlicher cites the UN Human Rights Committee's General Comment no 31 to the same effect: *Report of the independent expert to update the Set of Principles to combat impunity*, UN Doc E/CN.4/2005/102 (18 February 2005) at fn 21.

[2] *Case of X and Y v the Netherlands* App no 8978/80 (ECtHR, 26 March 1985); *Case of Benzer and others v Turkey* App no 23502/06 (ECtHR, 24 March 2014) (final) (violation of procedural aspect of Art 2 because no proper investigation was carried out in order to punish). See also African Commission on Human and Peoples' Rights, *Zimbabwe Human Rights NGO Forum v Zimbabwe*, Communication no 245/2002 (2006); UN Human Rights Committee, Observations on Algeria, CCPR/C/109/D/1874/2009, 7 January 2014, para 7.10; CCPR/C/108/D/1796/2008 (11 December 2013) para 8.10; *Quinteros v Uruguay*, Communication no 107/1981; see also General Comment no 31, CCPR/C/21/Rev.1/Add.13 (26 May 2004).

[3] ILC, Draft articles on Responsibility of States for Internationally Wrongful Acts, with commentaries (fifty-third session, 2001). See, eg, Art 58(3) (where crimes against international law are committed by state officials, it will often be the case that the state itself is responsible for the acts in question or for failure to prevent or punish them); Art 41 (states must cooperate to bring to an end breaches of peremptory obligations, including the prohibition on genocide, torture, and war crimes); Art 37 (satisfaction); and Art 31 (reparation).

are rooted both in states' own failure to respect rights and in their failure to protect their inhabitants from violations by others, including private actors. Thus the duties to investigate and provide redress and reparation apply even in cases where a state's own forces were not the only (or even principal) violators. They apply independently of state attribution for the underlying violation.

Parallel proceedings in the UN, especially the van Boven/Bassiouni Basic Principles and Guidelines on the Right to a Remedy and Reparation, and the Principles on Victims of Crime and Abuse of Power, reinforced and enriched the ideas in Principle 1.[4] For example, the Principle refers both to remedies and, as a separate category, to reparations for harm, thus reinforcing the idea that there is both a procedural (access, right to remedy) and a substantive (reparation) aspect to redress for victims. It also refers to 'effective' remedies, thus importing into the Principle the international law on remedies surrounding the requirement of exhaustion of domestic remedies.[5] 5

The great merit of this introductory Principle, as of the revised Principles as a whole, is that it gives equal weight to the different aspects of necessary action in the aftermath of large-scale or systematic violations of human rights or international humanitarian law (IHL). As the Commentary puts it: 6

> Satisfying one of their obligations, such as the duty to ensure prosecution of those responsible for serious crimes under international law, does not relieve States of their independent obligations, including those bearing on reparations, the right to know and, more generally, non-recurrence of violations.

The Principles thus embody what Juan Méndez, in a seminal 1997 article, described as four emerging international law principles, consisting of obligations and correlative rights: 7

> These principles hold that a state is obliged to carry out a number of tasks in response to crimes against humanity. These tasks are:
> 1. to investigate, prosecute, and punish the perpetrators;
> 2. to disclose to the victims, their families, and society all that can be reliably established about those events;
> 3. to offer the victims adequate reparations; and
> 4. to separate known perpetrators from law enforcement bodies and other positions of authority.[6]

This formulation helped shift the discussion from debates over the single best way to deal with the past—international or domestic courts, truth commissions, amnesties or whatever—to a recognition that the issue was one of multiple overlapping yet independent tasks, not of a single response. This is reflected in the UN Secretary-General's 2004 Report on the rule of law and transitional justice.[7] There, the UN's official position reflects the evolution seen in the Principles. The Secretary-General writes: 'Where 8

[4] Basic Principles and Guidelines on the Right to a Remedy and Reparation for Victims of Gross Violations of International Human Rights Law and Serious Violations of International Humanitarian Law, UNGA Res 60/147 of 16 December 2005; Declaration of Basic Principles of Justice for Victims of Crime and Abuse of Power, UNGA Res A/RES/40/34 of 29 November 1985.

[5] See, eg, IACtHR, *Velásquez Rodríguez*, n 1.

[6] J Méndez, 'Accountability for Past Abuses' (1997) 19(2) Human Rights Quarterly 255–82, 261.

[7] UN Office of the Secretary-General, *The rule of law and transitional justice in conflict and post-conflict societies*, UN Doc S/2004/616 (24 August 2004).

transitional justice is required, strategies must be holistic, incorporating integrated attention to individual prosecutions, reparations, truth-seeking, institutional reform, vetting and dismissals, or an appropriately conceived combination thereof.'[8] It is important to note that the Principles do not create hierarchies: each aspect is equally important, although not everything has to be done at once.

9 Principle 1, by linking the fight against impunity to a range of actions, suggests that the obligations to investigate, prosecute, find the truth, provide redress, and avoid recurrence are independent obligations of the state, which means they are not subsumed in the underlying crimes or rights violations. This becomes important, for example, when states have become parties to treaty regimes after the crimes or rights violations have taken place. Despite the fact that the underlying events cannot be the subject of international adjudication due to *ratione temporis* limitations, the continuing failure to comply with the obligations outlined in Principle 1 can still give rise to responsibility since they continue into the present.[9]

D. Practice

10 Since the Updated Principles were issued in 2005, the trends noted in the Commentary have continued, although not in a uniform manner. With respect specifically to the state obligations outlined in Principle 1, an important development was the ICJ decision in *Belgium v Senegal*. There, Belgium claimed that Senegal was failing to comply with its obligations under the 1984 UN Convention Against Torture, to extradite or prosecute former Chadian leader Hisséne Habré, who was living in Senegal. The ICJ found that the obligation to investigate and prosecute was absolute and had to be carried out without undue delay. Furthermore, the Court stated:

> The choice between extradition or submission for prosecution, pursuant to the Convention, does not mean that the two alternatives are to be given the same weight because, while extradition is an option offered to the State by the Convention, prosecution, on the other hand, is an international obligation laid down by the Convention, the violation of which is a wrongful act engaging the responsibility of the State ...[10]
>
> The Court notes that, while Article 7, paragraph 1, of the Convention does not contain any indication as to the time frame for performance of the obligation for which it provides, it is necessarily implicit in the text that it must be implemented within a reasonable time, in a manner compatible with the object and purpose of the Convention, which is why proceedings should be undertaken without delay.[11]

[8] Ibid, para 26.

[9] See, eg, *Moiwana Community v Suriname* (Merits) IACtHR Series C no 124 (15 June 2005) para 43. See also Human Rights Committee, Communication no 491/1992, CCPR/C/45/D/491/1991, para 4.2. A particular application of this idea applies to continuing or permanent crimes like enforced disappearance; there the violation continues until the person or the body is located, up to the present day. See, eg, Supreme Court of Chile, *Case of Miguel Angel Sandoval*, Rol no 517-04, Penal Chamber (17 November 2004).

[10] ICJ, *Questions relating to the Obligation to Prosecute or Extradite (Belgium v Senegal)*, Summary of the Judgment of 20 July 2012, 12.

[11] Ibid, 14.

The UN has further developed its policies in line with the Principles. For example, a 2010 Guidance Note from the UN Secretary-General extensively cites the Principles, and states that the UN shall strengthen its transitional justice activities by, inter alia, 'encouraging the parties to include commitments to protect and promote human rights, combat impunity, and pursue transitional justice in peace agreements'.[12] Between 2006 and 2009 the UN developed a series of specific 'Tools' on aspects of Principle 1, for use by UN personnel and others.[13] The UN Security Council, in resolutions and in presidential statements, has repeatedly referred to the fight against impunity.[14] The UN Human Rights Council in 2011 established the mandate of Special Rapporteur on the promotion of truth, justice, reparation, and guarantees of non-recurrence. The Special Rapporteur is tasked to deal with situations in which there have been gross violations of human rights and serious violations of international humanitarian law. The resolution emphasizes the need for a comprehensive approach to the four elements of the mandate.[15] **11**

Other international actors are beginning to use the framework of the Principles. The European Union (EU) pledged to develop an anti-impunity policy in line with the Principles by 2014.[16] On 16 November 2015, the Council of the EU adopted conclusions affirming the EU's support for transitional justice, and approving the EU's Policy Framework on support to transitional justice. That framework uses the categories set out in the Principles, while linking them to broader processes of peacebuilding and development.[17] The African Union has also been developing a regional transitional justice policy, based on the four interconnected elements mentioned above.[18] **12**

All three regional human rights systems have continuously found that the state has violated the obligation to ensure rights in cases where the obligations to investigate, prosecute, and redress have not been complied with. In a recent decision on the subject, the IACtHR reiterated its long-standing jurisprudence that impediments to serious investigation and prosecution in cases of gross violations like forced disappearances and killings **13**

[12] *Guidance Note of the Secretary-General: United Nations Approach to Transitional Justice* (March 2010) para C(2).

[13] UN Office of the High Commissioner for Human Rights (OHCHR), *The right to the truth* (2008); OHCHR, *Maximizing the legacy of Hybrid Courts* (2008); OHCHR, *Reparations programmes* (2006); OHCHR, *Truth Commissions* (2006); OHCHR, *Mapping the Justice Sector* (2006); OHCHR, *Monitoring Legal Systems* (2006); OHCHR, *Prosecution Initiatives* (2006); OHCHR, *Vetting: An Operational Framework* (2006).

[14] See, eg, UN Security Council Res S/RES/2150 (14 April 2014); Statement of the President of the UN Security Council, S/PRST/2014/5 (21 February 2014).

[15] Res 18/7 of the Human Rights Council (29 September 2011). The mandate is to 'ensure accountability, serve justice, provide remedies to victims, promote healing and reconciliation, establish independent oversight of the security system and restore confidence in the institutions of the State and promote the rule of law in accordance with international human rights law'. Pablo de Greiff is the first Special Rapporteur. His three-year mandate was renewed in 2014 for a further three years.

[16] See Outcome 27(c) of the EU Strategic Framework and Action Plan on Human Rights and Democracy (2012), which calls on the EU to 'Develop policy on transitional justice, so as to help societies to deal with the abuses of the past and fight impunity (truth and reconciliation commissions, reparations, criminal justice, link with ICC), recognising that such policy must allow for tailored approaches to specific circumstances.' Available at <www.consilium.europa.eu/uedocs/cms_data/docs/pressdata/EN/foraff/131181.pdf> accessed 12 January 2018.

[17] European Council, *Council's Conclusions on EU's Support to Transitional Justice*, 16 November 2015 <eeas.europa.eu/archives/docs/top_stories/pdf/the_eus_policy_framework_on_support_to_transitional_justice.pdf> accessed 12 January 2018. The Principles are cited at fn 20. Moreover, the conceptual structure follows that of the Principles.

[18] See African Union Transitional Justice Framework (2014) <www.legal-tools.org/doc/bcdc97/pdf> accessed 12 January 2018; see also, eg, Centre for the Study of Violence and Reconciliation, *Technical Experts' Consultation to Review the African Transitional Justice Policy Framework (Atjf) Agenda* (Nairobi, August 2013).

are not permitted, adding a specific reference to the right to truth.[19] The ECtHR and the African Commission on Human and Peoples Rights (AComHPR) have agreed.[20] A number of countries in Latin America have advanced along all four of the obligations specified in the Principles. Decisions by national courts in Uruguay, Peru, and elsewhere have cited the Principles either for their definition of impunity, or to underscore the international obligation to combat it.[21] In particular, the Principles underlay the Peruvian Supreme Court's conviction of Alberto Fujimori for forced disappearances and killings.[22]

14 The Principles have been recognized as important sources of 'soft law' and as a useful analytical tool by both governments and non-governmental organizations (NGOs). For example, the Swiss Foreign Affairs Ministry designed its Dealing with the Past initiative explicitly around the Principles.[23] The Dutch NGO Impunity Watch developed an instrument for analysing and evaluating degrees of impunity. It states:

> [T]he research instrument is focused on identifying the root causes of impunity: obstacles to processes that have been designed to provide victims with information, criminal justice and reparations as well as obstacles to other measures aimed at avoiding the recurrence of past crimes. This focus follows the recently updated UN Principles.[24]

E. Critical Assessment

15 As already mentioned, the great strength of the Principles in general, and of Principle 1 among them, is their insistence on the multiple overlapping rights of victims, and thus obligations of states, in order to combat impunity. This has been very useful to combat the earlier emphasis on either amnesty or prosecution alone as the two possible poles around which responses to grave international crimes and serious human rights violations can oscillate. The very success of the Principles in broadening the scope of possible state action has also become their weakness, however. Despite continuous protestations and admonitions to the contrary, the rights and obligations detailed in the Principles became seen as a required international 'toolkit' in situations of end of conflict. Truth commissions and trials are viewed as something imposed in peace agreements in order to get foreign funds and a UN imprimatur, rather than as arising from deep, and autochthonous, social

[19] See cases cited in n 1; on the right to truth specifically, see *La Rochela Massacre v Colombia* (Judgment) IACtHR Series C no 163 (11 May 2007) para 195.

[20] See, eg, *Yeter v Turkey* App no 33750/03 (Judgment) (ECtHR, 13 January 2009) para 70; AComHPR, *Zimbabwe Human Rights NGO Forum v Zimbabwe*, Communication no 245/02 (Decision) (21 May 2006) paras 211 and 215.

[21] From Uruguay, see Criminal Judge 19th court, *Case 'Condor Plan' in Uruguay* (José Nino Gavazzo Pereira et al), Sentencia 036, file 98-247/2006, 26 March 2009; from Peru, Constitutional Chamber, *Habeas corpus submitted by María Emilia Villegas Namuche*, File 2488-2002-HC/TC, Extraordinary Writ, 18 March 2004, at 6, 7.

[22] Special Penal Chamber, Superior Court of Justice of Lima, Cases *Barrios Altos, La Cantuta*, and *SIE Basements (Alberto Fujimori Fujimori)*, File A.V. 19-2001, 7 April 2009, at 622–25.

[23] 'The concept of Dealing with the Past stems from the "Principles against impunity", developed by Louis Joinet, which were approved in 1997 by the United Nations Commission on Human Rights in recognition of the rights of victims and the obligations of States in the fight against impunity when massive violations of human rights and international humanitarian law have taken place'. See Swiss Federal Department of Foreign Affairs, 'Dealing with the Past', available at <www.eda.admin.ch/eda/en/home/topics/peasec/peac/confre/depast.html> accessed 12 January 2018.

[24] See Impunity Watch website <www.impunitywatch.org> accessed 17 November 2017.

processes. The perception (and often reality) of external imposition, in turn, makes such processes less likely to meet the goals espoused for them.

Principle 1 imposes very broad responsibilities on states. It does not tie those 16
responsibilities to a showing that the violations are attributable to the state. Thus, even where non-state actors are the principal violators (of IHL, for example), the state retains obligations to ensure (although not necessarily provide) access to remedies and reparations, and access to the truth of the occurrences. This may place a substantial burden on weak states or those emerging from state breakdown. It is worth considering how these obligations intersect with the obligations of private actors (corporations, for instance) to provide remedies for their own violations.[25]

There are a number of weaknesses that are worth pointing out. The Principles are 17
not strong on the interrelationships among the different rights proclaimed, although the Special Rapporteur is now working on this subject. How, for instance, can one balance the demands of extensive reparations against the broad changes required by guarantees of non-repetition, when both entail competing demands on scarce resources? This is perhaps inevitable, as these trade-offs will differ from place to place, yet it would have been helpful to reference some well-known synergies and tensions, for example the need to consider demobilization and reintegration of combatants alongside reparations to non-combatant victims.

There are some ambiguities in the text. For example, Principle 1 expresses a clear pref- 18
erence for criminal prosecution and punishment, yet the definition of 'impunity' refers to the de jure or de facto lack of investigation and sanction—whether in criminal, civil, administrative, or disciplinary proceedings. The definition seems to imply that it is the lack of preliminary investigation of some kind that precludes later criminal prosecution, but administrative or disciplinary proceedings do not necessarily lead to criminal charges, nor are such proceedings a necessary precursor of prosecution.

It is one of the hallmarks of the field that it evolves rather quickly. The Principles as 19
a whole need to grapple with new issues that have come to the forefront since the last revision. Since 2005, for example, there has been much greater emphasis on the role, acceptability, and limitations of informal, 'traditional', or customary justice mechanisms, especially those that eschew imprisonment for other forms of punishment or atonement. These mechanisms, variants of which have appeared in East Timor, Rwanda,[26] Uganda, and elsewhere, combine various aspects of truth-telling, punitive justice, and reparations, and can have connections to local reconciliation and to spiritual or religious practices. They do not fit neatly into the categories delineated in the Principles, although they may fulfil several of the same goals.

Along the same lines, the last ten years or so have seen a debate about how broad 20
the contours of transitional or post-conflict justice should be, in particular around guarantees of non-repetition. In particular, debates abound on the extent to which socio-economic justice and 'transformative' justice for women, indigenous people, or

[25] See, eg, UN Principles on Business and Human Rights, Annexed to resolution of the Human Rights Council, A/HRC/17/31 (21 March 2011).

[26] East Timor's Community Reconciliation Processes, for example, involved group hearings convened by the Commission for Reception, Truth, and Reconciliation alongside traditional local and religious authorities, where those seeking reintegration into their communities and an end to the threat of criminal prosecution could tell their stories and make reparation to their victims. The Gacaca courts in Rwanda were not an informal mechanism but a state-run institution, with some characteristics borrowed from informal dispute resolution.

the poor should be incorporated into, or simply aligned with, anti-impunity measures.[27] The Principles take a modest approach, insisting only on broad public consultation on whatever measures are decided, and on vetting of state institutions, an end to emergency restrictions on liberties, and demobilization of paramilitary groups and child soldiers. This may be appropriate given the wide range of circumstances potentially covered, doubts about whether transitional justice mechanisms can fruitfully engage with wider social reform processes, and the need to remain at a high level of generality. However, current debates around the intersection of these mechanisms with broader security and development concerns indicate that, should the Principles be revised again, they would be more likely to address these issues in addition to others, like curricular reform, corruption, land restitution, and anti-discrimination measures, that have achieved greater play in the last decade.

21 Lastly, the Principles do not grapple with the complexities of trial and punishment that arise once initial barriers to prosecution have fallen away. Some of these are common to all prosecutions, and thus the subject of both hard and soft law on due process and fair trial. However, the question of what constitutes being 'duly punished' in cases of serious crimes under international law has become more urgent as prosecutions, for example in Latin America, have become more common. Can those convicted of serious international crimes be given conditional suspended sentences, or probation, or be imprisoned in luxurious conditions of confinement? If the right to truth and reparations is satisfied through other means, do these sentencing decisions violate international rules requiring proportional punishment for serious crimes, or do they provide permissible flexibility that nonetheless satisfies at least a modicum of victims' aspirations? Is this a purely national decision given the great disparity in national sentencing practices, or are there guideposts? The Colombian experience, both with paramilitaries and more recently with the FARC insurgents, may provide interesting lessons here.

22 Overall, these are not so much criticisms of the Principles per se as indications that the field, in which they are an important marker and touchstone, continues to evolve.

Bibliography

Arbour, L, *Economic and Social Justice for Societies in Transition* (26 October 2006) <chrgj.org/wp-content/uploads/2012/07/WPS_NYU_CHRGJ_Arbour_-Final.pdf> accessed 18 November 2017.

Fletcher, L and Weinstein, H, 'Violence and Social Repair: Rethinking the Contribution of Justice to Reconciliation' (2002) 24 Human Rights Quarterly 573–639.

McEvoy, K and McGregor, L (eds), *Transitional Justice from Below: Grassroots Activism and the Struggle for Change* (Hart Publishing 2009).

Méndez, J, 'Accountability for Past Abuses' (1997) 19.2 Human Rights Quarterly 255–82, 261.

Roht-Arriaza, N, *Impunity in International Law and Practice* (OUP 2005).

Roht-Arriaza, N and Mariezcurrena, J, *Transitional Justice in the Twenty-First Century: Beyond Truth versus Justice* (CUP 2006).

[27] See E Schmid, War crimes related to violations of ESC rights' (2011) 71(3) Heidelberg Journal of International Law 523–42; Z Miller, 'Effects of Invisibility: In Search of the '"Economic" in Transitional Justice' (2008) 2(3) International Journal of Transitional Justice 266–91.

Shaw, R, Waldorf, L, and Hazan, P (eds), *Localizing Transitional Justice: Interventions and Priorities after Mass Violence* (Stanford University Press 2010).

Transitional Justice Institute, *The Belfast Guidelines on Amnesty and Accountability* (2013) <www.transitionaljustice.ulster.ac.uk/documents/TheBelfastGuidelinesonAmnestyandAccountability.pdf> accessed 12 January 2018.

UN Office of the Secretary-General, The rule of law and transitional justice in conflict and post-conflict societies, UN Doc S/2004/616 (24 August 2004).

PART II

THE RIGHT TO KNOW

—

A.

GENERAL PRINCIPLES

Principle 2. The Inalienable Right to the Truth

Dermot Groome

Every people has the inalienable right to know the truth about past events concerning the perpetration of heinous crimes and about the circumstances and reasons that led, through massive or systematic violations, to the perpetration of those crimes. Full and effective exercise of the right to the truth provides a vital safeguard against the recurrence of violations.

A. Summary of Findings

The right to the truth continues to evolve as a human right with both an individual and collective dimension. It arises from the right to know, and obliges governments to establish mechanisms to facilitate the revelation of the truth about serious violations of human rights.[1] The right has been explicitly incorporated into several international instruments and, in 2010, the International Convention for the Protection of All Persons from Enforced Disappearance (ICPPED) became the first treaty to expressly guarantee the right to the truth.

In practice, the right is realized through laws enabling requests for state-held information; archives; truth commissions; national and international courts; and human rights commissions. At this juncture, while the precise contours of the right to truth are still being delineated, it has achieved customary status to the extent that individuals have the right to know the truth about grave violations of human rights affecting them.

As the right to truth continues to evolve, care must be taken to avoid over-broad definitions that ultimately undermine its effectiveness. Its nascent foundations are not sufficiently established and its contours not sufficiently clear to support these aspirationally expansive interpretations. More time is needed for the right, in both its individual and collective dimensions, to develop more precise contours that are more universally accepted.

B. Contextual and Historical Introduction

The right to the truth evolved from the right to know articulated in Article 32 of 1
Additional Protocol I to the Geneva Conventions. The right to know obliges Contracting Parties to fulfil their obligations toward the missing and dead, 'prompted mainly by the right of families to know the fate of their relatives'.[2] Although Article 32's right to know contemplated the specific context of armed conflict, it did not take long before its applicability outside of international humanitarian law came to be considered.[3]

[1] See the commentary to Principle 4 in this volume.

[2] Art 32, Additional Protocol I, Geneva Conventions (1977).

[3] Y Sandoz, 'Commentary to Article 32' in *Commentary on the Additional Protocols of 8 June 1977 to the Geneva Conventions of 12 August 1949* (International Committee of the Red Cross 1987) para 1212.

2 In the 1970s, the UN General Assembly adopted a series of resolutions critical of the repressive regime in Chile engaged in the enforced disappearance of dissidents.[4] Enforced disappearances by other South American[5] regimes during this period also raised public and international awareness about the impact that these disappearances had on the families of victims.[6]

3 In 1992, the General Assembly's Declaration on the Protection of All Persons from Enforced Disappearance called on states to ensure that persons alleging that a relative had been abducted had the right to have that disappearance investigated.[7] In 1997, Louis Joinet, in his Principles to Combat Impunity, defined the right to truth more broadly as one held not only by victims' families but also by society in general. The first of the Joinet Principles, 'The Inalienable Right to the Truth', defined the right broadly to include both an individual and a collective dimension.[8]

4 When Diane Orentlicher updated Joinet's Principles in 2005, she inserted a new first Principle, articulating the general obligations of states to combat impunity; this new Principle includes an explicit reference to the right to the truth.[9] Orentlicher pointed out that while the right to the truth had been 'strongly affirmed' in international law and state practice, 'the contours of this right ha[d] been delineated somewhat differently by various treaty bodies'.[10]

5 Despite variations in definitional 'contour', there is an increasing expectation by the international community that the right to the truth will be a remedial measure used to address allegations of serious human rights abuses. In the same month the revised Principles were published, the then High Commissioner of Human Rights, Louise Arbour, noted with criticism that the negotiations between the Government of Columbia and paramilitary groups 'took place in the absence of a parallel appropriate legal framework that would have guaranteed the right to truth'.[11] Later that year, the High Commissioner prepared

[4] Cf Protection of Human Rights in Chile, UN Doc A/29/3219 (6 November 1974) (no mention of families of the disappeared) with Protection of Human Rights in Chile, UN Doc A/30/3448 (9 December 1975) and Human Rights in Chile, UN Doc A/34/179 (17 December 1979) ('Urges the Chilean authorities to investigate and clarify the fate of persons reported to have disappeared for political reasons, to inform relatives of the outcome . . .').

[5] Brazil, Columbia, Guatemala, Paraguay, Peru, and Venezuela.

[6] On 29 February 1980, the Sub-Commission on Prevention of Discrimination and Protection of Minorities (renamed the Sub-Commission on the Promotion and Protection of Human Rights in 1999) established the Working Group on Disappearances with a universal mandate, a mandate renewed by the Human Rights Council in 2014. See, The Commission on Human Rights Resolution (Res) 20 (XXXVI) Question of Missing and Disappeared Persons (29 February 1980) and Enforced or Involuntary Disappearances, A/HRC/RES/27/1 (1 October 2014).

[7] Declaration on the Protection of All Persons from Enforced Disappearance, UN Doc A/RES/47/133 (18 December 1992).

[8] See L Joinet, Special Rapporteur, *Revised Final Report on Question of the Impunity of Perpetrators of Human Rights Violations (Civil and Political)*, UN Doc E/CN.4/Sub.2/1997/20/Rev.1 (2 October 1997).

[9] See D Orentlicher, *Promotion and Protection of Human Rights, Impunity: Report of the independent expert to update the Set of Principles to Combat Impunity*, UN Doc E/CN.4/2005/102 (18 February 2005) (hereinafter '*Report of the independent expert*'). She also made some minor textual changes to Joinet's Principle 1, the right to the truth, now Principle 2.

[10] *Report of the independent expert*, n 9, para 17.

[11] *Report of the High Commissioner for Human Rights on the Situation of Human Rights in Columbia*, UN Doc E/CN.4/2005/10 (28 February 2005) para 5. See also Commission on Human Rights, Summary Record of the 48th Meeting, UN Doc E/CN.4/2005/SR.48 (21 April 2005) para 21. On 24 November 2016, the Government of Columbia and the FARC leadership signed a final agreement (Acuerdo final para la terminación del conflicto y la construcción de una paz estable y duradera) that included a reference to the fundamental right to the truth. Full text available from Oficina Del Alto Comisionado Para la Paz (Office of

a comprehensive report on the right.[12] Shortly after the report's publication, the General Assembly passed a resolution on the right to remedies for victims of gross violations of human rights, promulgating principles which included the right to the truth.[13] The Organization of American States (OAS) also adopted a resolution that 'recognize[d] the importance of respecting and ensuring the right to the truth'.[14]

In September 2009, the Human Rights Council adopted a resolution on the right to truth, 'recogniz[ing] the importance of respecting and ensuring the right to the truth so as to contribute to ending impunity and to promote and protect human rights'.[15] In 2011, the UN Secretary-General (UNSG) declared 24 March 'Right to Truth Day', to annually commemorate 'the indispensable role of the truth in upholding human rights'.[16] Later that year, the Human Rights Council appointed a new Special Rapporteur on the Promotion of Truth, Justice, Reparation and Guarantees of Non-recurrence.[17] In December 2013, the General Assembly adopted Resolution 68/165 on the Right to the Truth, which encouraged states to ensure that national archival policies facilitated the right and invited the special procedures and other mechanisms of the HRC 'to take into account ... the right to the truth'.[18] 6

C. Theoretical Framework

The evolution of the right to the truth from a humanitarian principle to customary norm is intertwined not only with the right to know, but also with rights related to the access to justice and information, the equal protection of law, and the right to family life. It emanates from essential elements of these rights and operates as a 'meta' right, creating a broadly defined obligation for states to provide effective mechanisms for establishing the truth of serious human rights violations.[19] It has also been conceptualized as part of a state's duty to make reparation for violations of its international obligations.[20] 7

Any emerging principle of customary international law inherently presents definitional difficulties. Absent a deliberate codification process, its definition evolves within a process of emergence and refinement that is evidenced in the practice of states and reliable 8

the High Commissioner for Peace), http://www.altocomisionadoparalapaz.gov.co/procesos-y-conversaciones/Documentos%20compartidos/24-11-2016NuevoAcuerdoFinal.pdf accessed 12 December 2017, [2].

[12] *Study on the right to the truth*, UN Doc E/CN.4/2006/91 (8 February 2006).

[13] See, Basic Principles and Guidelines on the Right to a Remedy and Reparation for Victims of Gross Violations of International Human Rights Law and Serious Violations of International Humanitarian Law, A/RES/60/147 (21 March 2006) para 18 and para 22(b) and (c).

[14] OAS, Right to the Truth, AG/RES. 2175 (XXXVI-O/06) (6 June 2006).

[15] HRC, Right to the Truth, UN Doc A/HRC/12/L.27 (25 September 2009).

[16] UNSG, Statement on Inauguration of 'Right to Truth Day', UN Doc SG/SM/13465, 22 March 2011.

[17] HRC, Special Rapporteur on the Promotion of Truth, Justice, Reparation and Guarantees of Non-recurrence, UN Doc A/HRC/RES/18/7 (13 October 2011).

[18] GA, *Right to the Truth*, UN Doc A/RES/68/165 (18 December 2013).

[19] Pablo de Greiff, the Special Rapporteur on the Promotion of Truth, Justice Reparation and Guarantees of Non-recurrence, recently articulated the right's essential core: '[T]he right to truth should be understood to require States to establish institutions, mechanisms and procedures that are enabled to lead to the revelation of the truth, which is seen as a process to seek information and facts about what has actually taken place'. See P de Greiff, *Report of the Special Rapporteur on the promotion of truth, justice, reparation and guarantees of non-recurrence*, UN Doc A/HRC/24/42 (28 August 2013) (hereinafter 'de Greiff Report') para 20. at 26.

[20] Inter-American Commission on Human Rights, 'The Right to Truth in the Americas' OEA/Ser.L/V/II.152 (2014).

indicia of their acceptance of it as a legal obligation (*opinio juris*).[21] Articulating the precise contours of an emerging customary legal principle can be a prolonged process in which specific lineaments are identified over time, each contributing to a clearer understanding of the right.

9 Early jurisprudence from the International Criminal Tribunal for the former Yugoslavia (ICTY) and the International Criminal Tribunal for Rwanda (ICTR) offers a useful example of this process. When the UN Security Council adopted the ICTY and ICTR statutes in 1993 and 1994 respectively, many of the crimes within the jurisdiction of the ad hoc tribunals had already been committed. The principle of legality required judicial determinations that these crimes already existed in customary law.[22] These courts became 'customary midwives' for many of the criminal prohibitions found in international law today.[23]

10 The definition of 'rape' is one such example. Today, the definition articulated by the *Kunarac* Chamber is broadly accepted as the complete and precise definition of 'rape' found in customary international law. In short, 'rape' is defined as any sexual penetration of the vagina, anus or mouth of the victim without the victim's consent.[24] The precise contours of this definition, however, developed over a series of cases as the facts of individual cases occasioned increasingly precise analysis.[25]

11 In 1989, Theodor Meron recognized that state practice and *opinio juris*, the sources of international law contemplated by Article 38 of the ICJ Statute were not 'comprehensive and immutable', and that '[i]t may well be that these sources will be expanded by, for example, attributing a more direct law-creating role to normative resolutions of the General Assembly'.[26] Meron also considered that another method of 'building customary law' was through the 'general principles of law recognized by civilized nations' referred to in Article 38(1)(c) of the ICJ Statute, a method of particular importance for rights associated with 'the administration of justice and due process'.[27] As Richard Lillich has asserted, the evaluation of the customary status of a human right 'looks not only to traditional but also to new sources of state practice and new expressions of *opinio juris* to determine and

[21] Art 38(1)(b) of the Statute of the International Court of Justice (ICJ) cites as a source of international law, 'international custom, as evidence of a general practice accepted as law'. T Meron, *Human Rights and Humanitarian Norms as Customary Law* (Clarendon Press 1989) 93.

[22] The ICTY statute came into effect on 25 May 1993 with the adoption of UN Security Council (UNSC) Res 827, giving it temporal jurisdiction commencing on 1 January 1991 (UN Doc S/RES/827, 25 May 1993). The ICTR statute came into effect on 8 November 1994 with the adoption of UNSC Res 955 (UN Doc S/RES/955, 8 November 1994), giving it temporal jurisdiction from 1 January 1994.

[23] See G Mettraux, *International Crimes and the ad Hoc Tribunals* (OUP 2005) 14 and generally at 13–18.

[24] See, ICTY, *Prosecutor v Kunarac* (Judgment) IT-96-23-T (2 February 2001) para 460.

[25] The first, post-Second World War case to consider the crime of rape under international law was *Akayesu* in 1998. The Chamber defined the customary international prohibition as 'a physical invasion of a sexual nature, committed on a person under circumstances which are coercive': ICTY, *Prosecutor v Akayesu* (Judgment) ICTR-96-4-T (2 September 1998) paras 597–98. Three months later the *Furundžjia* Chamber brought greater precision to the definition by making clear that the customary definition of 'rape' included forcible oral penetration: ICTY, *Prosecutor v Furundžjia* (Judgment) IT-95-17/1-T (10 December 1998) para 185. During those three months there had been no significant developments with respect to *opinio juris* or state practice in relation to the crime of rape. The definition of 'rape' would be further refined by the *Kunarac* Chamber in 2001, when that Chamber found that under international customary law, the requirement of coercion described by *Akayesu* and *Furundžjia* was more precisely expressed as 'without the consent of the victim': *Kunarac*, n 24. This clarification of the customary definition of 'rape' appropriately reflected the conduct of paramilitaries in Foča, BiH, who held vulnerable women for extended periods and perpetrated non-consensual intercourse on them, often in the absence of explicit indicia of coercion.

[26] Meron, n 21, 88. [27] Ibid.

develop the content and contours of the emerging customary international law of human rights'.[28] This is, in part, a response to the fact that 'state practice and judicial opinions have been slow to recognize or give legal effect to assertions of such norms'.[29]

While the definition of the right to truth is undoubtedly still developing, consideration of relevant, *opinio juris* state practice, other normative indicators such as General Assembly resolutions, and general principles of law makes clear that the core of the right to the truth is a matter of customary international law. Despite variances in the way the right has been expressed and applied, there is a common 'core' of the right that has achieved customary status.[30] 12

The right to the truth emerges from the right to know first articulated in Article 32 of Additional Protocol I to the Geneva Conventions.[31] The customary status of the right to know is settled, and its definition is articulated as follows: 13

> Each party to the conflict must take all feasible measures to account for persons reported missing as a result of armed conflict and must provide their family members with any information it has on their fate.[32]

By virtue of its derivative nature, the right to the truth incorporates this customary core as part of its definition.

In 2010, the ICPPED came into effect. The text of the Convention was adopted by the General Assembly in 2006 and became available for signatures on 6 February 2007. Article 24(2) states: 14

> Each victim has the right to know the truth regarding the circumstances of the enforced disappearance, the progress and results of the investigation and the fate of the disappeared person. Each State Party shall take appropriate measures in this regard.

As of October 2016, ninety-six states have signed the Convention and fifty-three have ratified or acceded to it.[33] This inaugural reference in a widely ratified convention marks an important step in its germination into a customary norm.

[28] R Lillich, 'The Growing Importance of Customary International Human Rights Law' (1995/96) 25(1) Georgia Journal of International and Comparative Law 1–30, 18. at 18.

[29] D Shelton, 'Normative Hierarchy in International Law' (2006) 100(291) *American Journal of International Law* 291–323, 292. Professor Shelton was specifically referring to *jus cogens* norms in this passage. Shelton 'recognizes that states and international institutions increasingly adopt norms or statements of obligations, in nonlegally biding texts': ibid.

[30] See J Méndez, 'The Right to Truth' in C Joyner (ed), *Reining in Impunity for International Crimes and Serious Violations of Fundamental Human Rights: Proceedings of the Siracusa Conference 17–21 September 1998* (Érès 1998) 255–78, 256.

[31] See chapter on 'Principle 4. The Victims' Right to Know'.

[32] International Committee of the Red Cross (ICRC), *Customary International Humanitarian Law*, vol I (ICRC 2005) Rule 117 at 421.

[33] Albania*, Algeria, Angola, Argentina*, Armenia*, Austria*, Azerbaijan, Belgium*, Belize**, Benin, Bolivia (Plurinational State of)*, Bosnia and Herzegovina*, Brazil*, Bulgaria, Burkina Faso*, Burundi, Cabo Verde, Cambodia**, Cameroon, Cape Verde, Central African Republic**, Chad, Chile*, Colombia*, Comoros, Congo, Costa Rica*, Croatia, Cuba*, Cyprus, Czech Republic*, Denmark, Ecuador*, Finland, France*, Gabon*, Germany*, Ghana, Greece*, Grenada, Guatemala, Guinea- Bissau, Haiti, Honduras*, Iceland, India, Indonesia, Iraq**, Ireland, Italy*, Japan*, Kazakhstan**, Kenya, Lao People's Democratic Republic, Lebanon, Lesotho*, Liechtenstein, Lithuania*, Luxembourg, Madagascar, Malawi**, Maldives, Mali*, Malta*, Mauritania*, Mexico*, Monaco, Mongolia*, Montenegro*, Morocco*, Mozambique, Netherlands*, Niger*, Nigeria**, Norway, Palau, Panama*, Paraguay*, Peru**, Poland, Portugal*, Republic of Moldova, Romania, Saint Vincent and the Grenadines, Samoa*, Senegal*, Serbia*, Seychelles**, Sierra Leone, Slovakia*, Slovenia, Spain*, Sri Lanka*, St. Vincent and the Grenadines, Swaziland, Sweden, Switzerland*, Thailand, The former Yugoslav Republic of Macedonia, Togo*, Tunisia*, Uganda, Ukraine**, United Republic of Tanzania, Uruguay*, Vanuatu, Venezuela (Bolivarian Republic of), and Zambia* ('*' denotes ratification; '**' denotes accession). Source: United Nations Treaty Collection. See <https://treaties.un.org/pages/ViewDetails.aspx?src=IND&mtdsg_no=IV-16&chapter=4&clang=_en> accessed 13 January 2018.

15 Prior to the ICPPED, the right to the truth was the subject of numerous regular references in international and regional instruments with varying degrees of normative significance.[34] Several countries, in replying to a note verbale of the OHCHR, took the view that the right was normative in nature.[35] The right to the truth has also been found to be implicit in several rights protected in the International Covenant on Civil and Political Rights (ICCPR), the European Convention on Human Rights (ECHR), the American Convention on Human Rights (ACHR), and the African Charter on Human and Peoples' Rights (ACHPR).[36] As described in section D of this commentary, families of victims have been successful in asserting the right and obtaining tangible relief before commissions and courts with jurisdiction over these conventions, although that relief has been underpinned with rights found explicitly in the conventions. In several cases before the Inter-American Court of Human Rights (IACtHR), state respondents have acknowledged the right to truth and their violation of it. Although the Court declined to accept these acknowledgements as being determinative of whether the right was a conceptually autonomous right, the acknowledgements do indicate that these countries understand the right to the truth as having normative status.[37]

16 The proliferation of truth commissions demonstrates the near-universal value placed on uncovering and documenting the truth about serious violations of human rights. Not irrelevant to any normative analysis are the many national laws that ensure citizens of their right to access information held by their governments.[38] While these laws serve to promote transparency in government, they evidence the same core value and have been employed to uncover human rights abuses.[39]

[34] For examples of references to the right in international instruments see, eg, Art 13(1), Declaration on the Protection of All Persons from Enforced Disappearance, UN Doc A/RES/437/133 (18 December 1992); UNGA Res 44/159, UN Doc A/RES/44/159 (15 December 1989); UNSG, Statement, UN Doc SG/SM/9400 (1 July 2004); UNSC Report, UN Doc S/200/616 (23 August 2004); UNGA Res, Principles and Guidelines on the Right to a Remedy and Reparation for Victims of Gross Violations of International Human Rights Law and Serious Violations of International Humanitarian Law, UN Doc A/RES/60/147 (16 December 2005). See also European Parliament, Recommendation 1056 (1987) on National Refugees and Missing Persons in Cyprus; Res 1414 (2004) on Persons Unaccounted for as a Result of Armed Conflicts or Internal Violence in the Balkans (23 November 2004); Res 1463 (2005) on Enforced Disappearances (3 October 2005). See also OAS Permanent Council, Res OES/Ser.G CP/CAJP-2278/05/rev.4 (23 May 2005).

[35] See *Promotion and Protection of Human Rights: Study on the Right to the Truth*, UN Doc E/CN.4/2006/91 (8 February 2006) at para 21. These states included Argentina, Belarus, Colombia, Cuba Georgia, Mauritius, Peru, Slovenia, Togo, Uruguay, and Venezuela.

[36] See nn 53–65 and the text associated with them.

[37] See, eg, *Blanco-Romero v Venezuela* (Judgment) IACtHR Series C no 138 (28 November 2005) para 62: 'The Court does not consider the right to know the truth to be a separate right enshrined in Articles 8, 13, 25 and 1(1) of the Convention, as alleged by the representatives, and, accordingly, it cannot find acceptable the State's acknowledgement of responsibility on this point. The right to know the truth is included in the right of the victim ... to have the relevant State authorities find out the truth of the facts that constitute the violations and establish the relevant liability through appropriate investigation and prosecution.' See also *Castillo-Páez v Peru* (Judgment) IACtHR Series C no 34 (3 November 1997) paras 85–86.

[38] See, eg, European Union: Art 42 of the Charter of Fundamental Rights of the European Union; US: Freedom of Information Act, § USC para 552; Australia: Freedom of Information Act of 1982; United Kingdom (UK): Freedom of Information Act 2000. It is important to note that the rights of access conferred by these Acts are often limited with respect to documents held by security services.

[39] See, eg, Dominic Kennedy, 'Gays Should Be Hanged, Says Iranian Minister' *The Times* (13 November 2007). In this article, the author employed the UK Freedom of Information Act to access documents, held by the Foreign Commonwealth Office, of a high-level meeting in which a senior Iranian official was asked about recent hangings of two boys alleged to have engaged in homosexual conduct. The official put forward the position that homosexuals should be tortured and executed, something officially denied by Iran.

17 As described in section D of this commentary, the IACtHR has considered the question of whether the right belongs to individuals with a close relationship to the victim, or whether it is also a collective right. While the Court has recognized the importance of the collective dimension, it has stopped short of explicitly recognizing it in a way that would enable those without a sufficiently close relationship to the victim to assert it.[40] The Court has characterized this dimension as an obligation of states rather than a collective right. It is a 'fair expectation' of a democratic society that is served by the relief ordered in cases brought by individuals.[41]

18 Despite variances in the way the right has been expressed and applied, there is a common 'core' of the right that has achieved customary status.[42] The right to truth as a principle of customary international law is best described as: the right of victims and society to know the truth about serious violations of international criminal and human rights law; and the right of victims and those close to victims to require states to affirmatively investigate such violations, as well as to establish judicial and extra-judicial mechanisms capable of ensuring that the complete truth about these violations is revealed.

19 As the right develops and is asserted in different contexts, we can expect to see its core normative definition more broadly articulated and its perimeter more clearly demarcated. It is important to recognize that there will never be perfect parity between the collective and individual interests at stake. For example, in the context of war crimes, victims' families are most often focused on the direct perpetrators of the crime, while the collective's interest may be on those senior officials most responsible for state-sanctioned violations.[43]

D. Practice

20 The right to the truth has been realized through an array of mechanisms, including: archives, truth and fact-finding commissions, regional human rights conventions, domestic and international courts.[44]

21 There have been several ad hoc international fact-finding missions whose mandates have contributed to the realization of both the individual and collective dimensions of the right.[45] State-sanctioned truth commissions have also played an important role in giving practical effect to the right. Overall, the more than forty truth commissions to date have had mixed success, with some dismissed as ineffective and others credited with having made important contributions in the transition from authoritarian rule to democracy.[46]

[40] *Bámaca-Velásquez v Guatemala* (Order of the Court) IACtHR Series C no 70 (25 November 2000) Separate Concurring Opinon of Judge Ramírez, paras 19–22.

[41] *Contreras et al v El Salvador* (Judgment) IACtHR Series C no 232 (31 August 2011) para 170.

[42] See Méndez, n 30, 255–56. See Y Naqvi, 'The Right to the Truth in International Law: Fact or Fiction' (June 2006) 88(862) International Review of the Red Cross 245–73, 267.

[43] See Naqvi, n 42, 251.

[44] In domestic cases the right is realized through application of national laws to uncover and redress grave violations of human rights. For a detailed overview of national cases that followed some of the IACtHR 'right to truth' judgments, see Inter-American Commission on Human Rights, n 20, paras 69–84.

[45] See, eg, Report of the International Independent Fact-Finding Mission on the Conflict in Georgia (September 2009), available at <echr.coe.int/Documents/HUDOC_38263_08_Annexes_ENG.pdf> accessed 12 December 2017; Human Rights in Palestine and Other Occupied Arab Territories, UN Doc A/HRC/12/48 (25 September 2009) ('Goldstone Report') and OHCHR, *Report of the OHCHR Investigation on Sri Lanka (OISL)*, UN Doc A/HRC/30/CRP.2 (16 September 2015).

[46] Truth commissions have been established to investigate events in: Algeria, Argentina, Australia, Bolivia, Burundi, Canada, Chad, Chile, Democratic Republic of Congo, Ecuador, El Salvador, Ethiopia, Germany,

Truth commissions have become a regular response to dealing with serious human rights violations in transitional and post-conflict settings, and while they facilitate a common understanding of events, they alone cannot secure justice for victims.[47]

22 The mandate entrusted to truth commissions of the past 30 years has expanded significantly. While early commissions focused on the enforced disappearance of specific individuals,[48] newer commissions have been given ever more expansive mandates, which include violations of economic and cultural rights.[49] Fulfilling these broad expectations has proved to be challenging.[50]

23 The Special Rapporteur on the Promotion of Truth, Justice, Reparation and Guarantees of Non-recurrence devoted his 2013 report to the challenges faced by truth commissions. While the Special Rapporteur was careful not to diminish the positive aspects of this expansion, he pointed out that overly ambitious mandates may compromise a commission's ability to complete realistically achievable goals. He cautioned against the significant and 'open-ended' expansion of mandates.[51]

24 In addition to state-sanctioned truth commissions, there have been several notable examples of non-state commissions, such as the The Recovery of Historical Memory Project sponsored by the Archdiocese of Guatemala and the commission in Greensboro, North Carolina, established to investigate the deaths of demonstrators against the Klu Klux Klan.[52]

I. Human rights instruments

25 Although the right to truth is not explicitly mentioned in the ICCPR or any of the regional human rights conventions, it has been found to be implicitly embodied in some of the rights guaranteed in these instruments. Under these conventions, the right to the truth operates as a 'meta' right that encompasses those constituent rights that empower next of kin to learn the truth about a family member's fate. The IACtHR has found the right implicit in the ACHR.[53] Similarly, the ECtHR and the Human Rights Chamber

Ghana, Grenada, Guatemala, Haiti, Honduras, Indonesia, Ivory Coast, Kenya, Korea, Liberia, Morocco, Nepal, Nigeria, Panama, Paraguay, Peru, Serbia and Montenegro, Sierra Leone, Solomon Islands, South Africa, South Korea, Sri Lanka, Thailand, Timor Leste, Togo, Uganda, and Uruguay. For an assessment of the work of some of these truth commissions see P Hayner, 'Fifteen Truth Commissions—1974 to 1994: A Comparative Study' (1994) 16 Human Rights Quarterly 597.

[47] See de Greiff Report, n 19, para 26.

[48] See, eg, The National Commission on the Enforced Disappearance of Persons (CONADEP).

[49] See, eg, Commission for Reception, Truth and Reconciliation in East Timor's mandate included violations of a very broad array of international human rights. The enabling document (UNTAET/REG/2001/10) gave the Commission competence to investigate violations of 'international human rights standards' as defined in s 2 of UNAET/REG/1999/1. That section includes a comprehensive list of human rights instruments, including the ICCPR and the International Covenant on Economic, Social and Cultural Rights. Section IV of The Truth and Reconciliation Commission Mandate of Liberia gives the Commission jurisdiction over, inter alia, 'economic crimes, such as the exploitation of natural or public resources to perpetuate armed conflict'.

[50] The Truth and Reconciliation Commission in South Africa was tasked with determining a complete picture of the possible nature, causes, and extent of gross human rights violations. The Commission recognized from the outset that it was impossible to carry out all of its tasks simultaneously, and resorted to a process of prioritizing aspects of its mandate. See South African Truth and Reconciliation Commission, *Final Report*, vol I, ch 4, subs 5, para [34].

[51] See de Greiff Report, n 19, paras 40, 51, and 95.

[52] See Archdiocese of Guatemala, 'Recuperación de la Memoria Histórica (1998) <www.odhag.org.gt/html/Default.htm> accessed 14 January 2018; and Greensboro Truth & Reconciliation Commission, Final Report, 25 May 2006 <www.greensborotrc.org/> accessed 14 January 2018.

[53] See, eg, the following series of cases before the IACtHR: *Blake v Guatemala* IACtHR Series C no 36 (24 January 1998) para 97; *Villagran-Morales et al* IACtHR Series C no 63 (19 November 1999) para 253.6;

of Bosnia and Herzegovina (HRCBiH) have found that the right is embodied in four categories of protections of the ECHR: prohibition of inhuman treatment; access to justice; equal protection of the laws; and right to family life.[54]

Courts have found that a state's failure to disclose the fate of a person in the custody of the state constitutes inhuman treatment with respect to family members. The families of such a person have a right to the truth with respect to the fate of a loved one, and a state's infringement of this right is a violation of the prohibition against inhuman treatment.[55] 26

The ICCPR and regional conventions all protect a person's right of access to justice. Commissions and courts have consistently held that denying a family's right to the truth by failing to adequately investigate and prosecute crimes committed against a loved one 27

Bámaca-Velásquez v Guatemala (Order of the Court) IACtHR Series C no 70 (25 November 2000) paras 159–66, 195, 230; *Barrios Altos v Peru* IACtHR Series C no 75 (14 March 2001) para 51.2(c); *Mapiripán Massacre v Columbia* IACtHR Series C no 134 (15 September 2005) paras 140–46, 195–241, 335.1, 335.5; *Pueblo Bello Massacre v Columbia*, IACtHR Series C no 140 (31 January 2006) paras 163, 169–212, 296.3, 296.4; *Baldeón-Garcia v Peru* IACtHR Series C no 147 (6 April 2006) paras 127–30, 139–69, 218.4, 218.5; *Ximenes-Lopes v Brazil* IACtHR Series C no 149 (4 July 2006) paras 155–63, 262.3, 262.4; *Montero-Aranguren et al v Venezuela (Detention Center of Catia)* (Judgment) IACtHR Series C no 150 (5 July 2006) paras 53, 160.2 (Venezuela acknowledged its violation of Arts 5 and 1(1)); *Goiburú et al v Paraguay (Condor)* IACtHR Series C no 153 (22 September 2006) paras 95–104, 111–33, 192; *La Cantuta v Peru* (Judgment) IACtHR Series C no 162 (29 November 2006) paras 81–98, 122–29, 135–61, 254.5, 254.6; *Anzualdo Castro v Peru* (Preliminary objection, merits, reparations and costs) IACtHR Series C no 202 (22 September 2009) paras 113–14; *Las Dos Erres Massacre v Guatemala* (Preliminary objections, merits, reparations and costs) IACtHR Series C no 211 (24 November 2009) para 213 ('[T]he impunity that persists in the instant case is experienced by the alleged victims as a new traumatic impact, which has been generated by feelings of anger, frustration and even fear of retaliation due to their search for justice.'); *Chitay Nech et al v Guatemala*, IACtHR Series C no 212 (25 May 2010) para 209; and *Manuel Cepeda Vargas v Colombia*, IACtHR Series C no 213 (26 May 2010) para 195.

[54] The ECtHR took a similar approach to the IACtHR in *Cyprus v Turkey*, 2001- IV ECtHR 1 (2001). The HRCBiH has followed the course established by the regional human rights courts and developed criteria for identifying holders of the right. See *Unković v Bosnia and Herzegovina*, Case no CH/99/2150 (Decision on review) (10 May 2002) para 114 and *Srebrenica Cases*, Case no CH/01/8365 (Decision on admissibility and merits) (7 March 2003) paras 181, 191, 202.

[55] The Human Rights Committee has consistently found that the prohibition of cruel treatment found in Art 7 of the ICCPR extends to the suffering caused to families whose relatives have been disappeared or killed while in government custody. See *María del Carmen Almeida de Quinteros et al v Uruguay*, Communication no 107/1981, UN Doc CCPR/C/OP/2 (1990) at 138; *Burkino Faso Miriam Sankara et al* Communication no 1159/2003, UN Doc CCPR/C/86/D/1159/2003 (11 April 2006) 4 November 2006); *Bousroual v Algeria*, CCPR/C/86/D/1085/2002 (15 March 2006); *Titiahonjo v Cameroon*, CCPR/C/91/D/1186/2003 (26 October 2007); and *Zohra Madoui v Algeria*, CCPR/C/94/D/1495/2006 (1 December 2008).

The IACtHR has found similarly with respect to Art 5 of the ACHR in over 14 cases, See, eg, *Blake v Guatemala*, IACtHR Series C no 36 (24 January 1998) paras 114–16; and *Chitay Nech et al v Guatemala*, IACtHR Series C no 212 (25 May 2010) para 209. For a comprehensive list and discussion of the IACtHR's jurisprudence on right to truth, see D Groome, 'Right to Truth in the Fight Against Impunity' (2011) 29 Berkeley Journal of International Law 175.

The ECtHR has found such inhuman treatment to be a violation of Art 3 of the ECHR. See *Cyprus v Turkey* App no 25781/94 (Judgment) [2001] ECHR 1. In May 2014, the Court awarded the surviving family members of missing persons €30,000,000 for Turkey's violation of their right to truth. *Cyprus v Turkey* App no 25781/94 (Judgment) (Just Satisfaction) [2014] ECHR 1 [58].

The HRCBiH has found similarly in its application of Art 3 of the ECHR. See *Srebrenica Cases*, Case nos CH/01/8365 (Decision on Admissibility and Merits) (7 March 2003) paras 181, 191, 202; and *Unković v Bosnia and Herzegovina*, Case no CH/99/2150 (Decision on Review) (10 May 2002) paras 101–19.

Art 5 of the ACHPR has been found to offers similar protection for families of disappeared persons. See *Amnesty International and Others v. Sudan*, Communications nos 48/90 et al (AComHPR, 15 November 1999) para 54. See also *Article 19 v Eritrea*, Communication no 275/2003 (ACHPR, 30 May 2007).

Principle 14 of the Declaration of Human Rights of the Association of Southeast Asian Nations (ASEAN) similarly protects against cruel treatment.

is a violation of the right to access justice.[56] The IACtHR has noted that the obligation to meaningfully investigate gross violations is not discharged by a truth commission, however thorough its work may be,[57]or by military tribunals.[58] Amnesty laws have also been found to improperly infringe on the right to access justice by denying a family's right to truth.[59]

28 Similarly, in cases where a family's efforts to learn the fate of a relative through national legal proceedings are inappropriately thwarted by the government, the Human Rights Committee has found a violation of the guarantee under the ICCPR that all persons are equal under the law.[60]

29 The right to the truth has also been found to encompass rights that protect privacy and family life. Although the ECtHR has found it unnecessary to consider the relationship between the right to the truth and the protection of private and family life under Article 8 of the ECHR,[61] the HRCBiH has held that Article 8 does give families the right to seek information about missing family members.[62] The African Commission on Human and Peoples Rights found similarly that the protection of the family guaranteed by Article 18 of the ACHPR included the family's right to know what had happened to a relative.[63]

30 As described in this section, although regional human rights commissions have asserted the right to the truth as collective right, regional courts have yet to recognize this dimension as right that is enforceable by others who do not have a sufficiently close relationship to the victim.[64] The IACtHR in *Los Dos Erres* noted the importance of this collective

[56] The Human Rights Committee has found such to be a violation of Art 2(3) of the ICCPR. See *Bousroual v Algeria*, UN Doc CCPR/C/86/D/1085/2002 (15 March 2006) [11]; *Zohra Madoui v Algeria*, UN Doc CCPR/C/94/D/1495/2006 (1 December 2008) [8]. The IACtHR has found in over 10 cases that the right to truth was protected under the right of access to justice. See, eg, *Ximenes-Lopes v Brazil*, IACtHR Series C no 149 (4 July 2006) para 262.4. For a complete list and comprehensive discussion of the IACtHR's jurisprudence, see Groome, n 55. The ECtHR came to a similar conclusion with respect to Art 13 of the ECHR—the parallel provision to Arts 8 and 25 of the ACHR. In Cyprus, the court concluded that Turkey's failure to provide Greek-Cypriots with a remedy to contest interference with their rights under Art 8 of the ECHR and Art 1 of Protocol 1 constituted a violation of Art 13: *Cyprus v Turkey* ECHR 2001- IV 1, para 192. See also *Amnesty International and Others v Sudan*, Communication nos 48/90 et al (AComHPR, 15 November 1999) para 51. Principles 3 (equal protection of law) and 5 (right to effective remedy) of the ASEAN Declaration of Human Rights would provide a similar basis for application of a right to the truth.

[57] See *Las Dos Erres Massacre v Guatemala* (Preliminary Objections, Merits, Reparations and Costs) IACtHR Series C no 211 (24 November 2009) para 232.

[58] *Vélez Restrepo and Family v Columbia* (Preliminary Objections, Merits, Reparations and Costs) IACtHR Series C no 248 (3 September 2012) paras 233–52.

[59] *La Cantuta v Perú* (Judgment) IACtHR Series C no 162 (29 November 2006) para 189.

[60] *Burkino Faso, Miriam Sankara et al*, Communication no 1159/2003 , UN Doc CCPR/C/86/D/1159/2003 (11 April 2006) (4 November 2006); see also *Madoui v Algeria* UN Doc CCPR/C/94/D/1495/2006 (1 December 2008) paras 3.4–3.6.

[61] *Cyprus v Turkey*, ECHR 2001- IV 1, para 161.

[62] *Unković v Bosnia and Herzegovina*, Case no CH/99/2150 (Decision on Review) (10 May 2002) para 126. See also *Srebrenica Cases*, Case nos CH/01/8365 et al (Decision on Admissibility and Merits, Bosnia and Herzegovina: Human Rights Chamber for Bosnia and Herzegovina) (7 March 2003) para 181.

[63] *Article 19 v Eritrea*, Communication no 275/2003 (ACHPR, 30 May 2007). See also *Constitutional Rights Project and Another v Nigeria*, Communication nos 143/95 and 150/96 (AComHPR, 5 November 1999). Note, Art 19 of the African Charter on the Rights and Welfare of the Child obliges state parties to gives a child's family members 'essential information concerning the whereabouts of the absent member or members of the family'.

[64] See, eg, *Bámaca-Veláquez v Guatemala* (Order of the Court) IACtHR Series C no 70 (25 November 2000) paras 199–200.

dimension, but suggested that it was already served by the remedies ordered on behalf of the individual claimants.[65]

II. Ad hoc tribunals

Early in its work, the ICTY appreciated its important role in establishing the truth based upon credible and reliable evidence.[66] Although the inquiry undertaken in an international criminal trial is bounded by the crimes charged in the indictment, the trial will adjudicate the material facts of a case to a high standard of proof. 31

During the course of trials at the ICTY and the ICTR, the sworn testimonies of victims, co-perpetrators, international interlocutors, and defendants have been recorded. In some cases, defendants have pleaded guilty, expressing remorse for the crimes they committed. The tribunals have gathered and preserved large volumes of documentary evidence. Exhumation work has also helped identify and return the mortal remains of thousands of victims.[67] 32

III. International Criminal Court

The International Criminal Court (ICC), in implementing its model of restorative justice, has formally granted victims the right to participate fully in proceedings. This right of participation is a fundamental shift from the ICTY and ICTR approach, in which the prosecutor represents the victims' interests. Although the precise form victim participation should take is still evolving, it is an important mechanism for realization of the right to truth.[68] 33

IV. Archives

One final important mechanism for the realization of the right to the truth is the creation and maintenance of accessible archives. National archives, as well as those of truth commissions and international courts, preserve materials that ensure that evidence is available for future study. Principles 14 to 18 deal specifically with the issue of archives. 34

[65] These remedies included: conducting an investigation; publishing the IACtHR's judgment (factual sections); showing a documentary about the massacre; conducting a public ceremony; building a monument commemorating the event; and creating a web page. *Las Dos Erres Massacre v Guatemala* (Preliminary Objections, Merits, Reparations and Costs) IACtHR Series C no 211 (24 November 2009) paras 149, 310.

[66] See LD Johnson, 'Ten Years Later: Reflections on the Drafting' (2004) 2 Journal of International Criminal Justice 368–79, 378. See also *Prosecutor v Karadžić and Mladić* (Review of the Indictments Pursuant to Rule 61 of the Rules of Procedure and Evidence), ICTY, IT-95-5-R6 and IT-95-18-R61 (11 July 1996) para 3.

[67] The International Commission on Missing Persons (ICMP) has been involved in the excavation of over 3,000 mass graves and been at the forefront of using the latest forensic techniques to identify mortal remains. See <www.icmp.int/> accessed 12 December 2017. In December 2014, the foreign ministers of several European countries signed an agreement recognizing the important role that ICMP plays and conferring upon it a legal basis for global operations.

[68] *Prosecutor v Lubanga* (Judgment on the Appeals of the Prosecutor and the Defence against Trial Chamber I's Decision on Victims' Participation of 18 January 2008) ICC-01/04-01/06OA9OA10 (11 July 2008) paras 30, 38, 64, and 97–99.

E. Critical Assessment

35 The development of the right to truth over the past several decades has been marked by different efforts to formulate a legal definition capable of advancing the universally recognized value of accessing the truth about grave violations of human rights. While these efforts have contributed to the normative status of the right, they have been organic and have resulted in a lack of precision. Further complicating the matter is the often interchangeable use of the terms 'right to know', 'right to the truth', and 'right to know the truth', causing confusion with the related but different right—the right to know.[69]

36 Further development of the right to the truth would benefit from more rigorous attention being paid to its definitional contours, and the use of precise terminology that distinguishes it from the right to know and freedom of information laws. A consistent articulation and assertion of the right in a way that is precise and not overbroad will contribute to the great strength and potential it possesses to combat impunity.

Bibliography

Bissett, A, *Truth Commissions and Criminal Courts* (CUP 2012).

Crettol, M, 'The Missing and Transitional Justice: The Right to Know and the Fight against Impunity' (2006) 88(862) International Review of the Red Cross 355–62.

de Greiff, P, *Report of the Special Rapporteur on the Promotion of Truth Justice, Reparation and Guarantees of Non-recurrence*, UN Doc A/HRC/24/42 (28 August 2013).

Freeman, M, *Truth Commissions and Procedural Fairness* (CUP 2006).

Groome, D, 'Right to Truth in the Fight Against Impunity' (2011) 29 Berkeley Journal of International Law 175–99.

Hayner, P, *Unspeakable Truths: Transitional Justice and the Challenge of Truth Commissions* (Routledge 2011).

Inter-American Commission on Human Rights, 'The Right to Truth in the Americas', OEA/Ser.L/V/II.152 (2014).

Méndez, J, 'The Right to Truth' in C Joyner (ed), *Reining in Impunity for International Crimes and Serious Violations of Fundamental Rights* (Association Internationale De Droit Pénal, 1998) [255]–[278].

Naftali, P, 'Crafting a "Right to Truth" in International Law: Converging Mobilizations, Diverging Agendas', *Champ Pénal* vol XIII (2016) 1–20 <journals.openedition.org/champpenal/9245> accessed 12 December 2017.

Naqvi, Y, 'The Right to the Truth in International Law: Fact or Fiction' (2006) 88(862) International Review of the Red Cross 245–73.

[69] See, eg, OHCHR, Right to the Truth, Human Rights Resolution 2005/66, fifty-ninth meeting, 20 April 2005. 'Acknowledging also that the right to the truth may be characterized differently in some legal systems as the right to know or the right to be informed or freedom of information'.

Principle 3. The Duty to Preserve Memory

Julia Viebach

A people's knowledge of the history of its oppression is part of its heritage and, as such, must be ensured by appropriate measures in fulfilment of the State's duty to preserve archives and other evidence concerning violations of human rights and humanitarian law and to facilitate knowledge of those violations. Such measures shall be aimed at preserving the collective memory from extinction and, in particular, at guarding against the development of revisionist and negationist arguments.

A. Summary of Findings

Memorialization has become a key component of transitional justice processes. There has been an observable urge to commemorate human rights violations and international crimes: this has been driven by a 'duty' to remember past injustices and a global demand for remembrance captured in the phrase 'never again'. The Updated Set of Principles has recognized this global memorialization trend and has included the 'Duty to Preserve Memory' under the rubric of 'the right to know'. Principle 3 attests to a people's right to know 'the history of its oppression' as part of its heritage, and calls upon the state's duty to preserve archives and other evidence. These 'measures shall be aimed at preserving the collective memory from extinction'.

In the context of this 'global rush to commemorate', the Updated Set of Principles, particularly 'the duty to preserve memory', signals a move to greater recognition of the role of *collective* memory in transitional processes. However, this chapter argues that the duty to preserve memory has only implicitly been addressed either under symbolic reparations in truth-seeking processes, or under satisfaction in jurisprudence. It is submitted that this approach over-simplifies the collective and societal level and neglects the dangers and complexity of memorialization in transitional contexts.

B. Contextual and Historical Introduction

The year 2015 marked the seventieth anniversary of the liberation of Auschwitz and end of the Second World War. On 26 January 2015, the German Chancellor Angela Merkel remarked that 'Auschwitz concerns us all, today and tomorrow and not only on anniversaries'. Indeed, the Holocaust commemoration has been the driving force behind the impetus to address and *remember* serious international crimes. Since at least the 1980s, the world has witnessed a 'memory imperative',[1] a 'rush to commemorate',[2] 1

[1] D Levy, 'Changing Temporalities and the Internalization of Memory Cultures' in Y Gutman, A Brown, and A Sodaro (eds), *Memory and the Future: Transnational Politics, Ethics and Society* (Palgrave Macmillian 2010) 15–31.

[2] P Williams, *Memorial Museums: The Global Rush to Commemorate Atrocities* (Berg 2007).

or a 'global memory boom'[3] that 'marshals a set of political and normative expectations for the handling of past injustices'.[4] Thus, more and more states, non-governmental organizations, and civil society actors advocate the necessity of commemorating past human rights violations and serious international crimes in order to honour the dead and the disappeared, and to acknowledge the suffering of victims.

2 Despite this global movement to commemorate past injustices, memorialization has been generally overlooked in both international law and the global transitional justice scripts. The legal and transitional processes have simply couched memorialization under the rubric of either the 'right to know the truth' or a (symbolic) reparation framework.

3 The duty to preserve memory has shifted from being a state's obligation owed to the individual victim to society more generally, stressing the aim of preventing both the future reoccurrence of violations and the denial of the past ('guarding against the development of revisionist and negationist arguments'). The collective right of a people to know their history and the heritage of their oppression originates from the first articulation of the Principles in 1997.[5] This collective dimension may explain why, at present, Principle 3 has rarely been addressed explicitly in international legal procedures or transitional justice.

C. Theoretical Framework

4 Principle 3 is interconnected to the 'right to know the truth', which is one of the so-called four pillars of transitional justice, formerly introduced by Louis Joinet.[6] In particular, Principle 3 is related to the principles regarding the preservation of and access to archives bearing witness to violations and to the right to reparation (Joinet Principles 33–42) (Updated Principles 14–18). Significantly, Joinet writes,

> on a collective basis, symbolic measures intended to provide moral reparation, such as formal public recognition by the State of its responsibility, or official declarations aimed at restoring victims' dignity, commemorative ceremonies, naming of public thoroughfares or the erection of monuments, help to discharge the duty of remembrance.[7]

I. UN norm setting: reparations

5 The duty to preserve memory has been conceived of as a form of reparation in UN soft law: Resolution A/RES/60/147[8] identifies *satisfaction* as one of four reparation measures (the others being compensation, rehabilitation, and a guarantee of non-repetition). These include memorial practices 'where applicable', such as 'verification of the facts and full and public disclosure of the truth to the extent that such disclosure does not cause further

[3] P Nora, 'Between Memory and History: Les Lieux de Mémoire' (1989) 26 Representations: Special Issue 'Memory and Counter-Memory' 7–24.

[4] Levy, n 1, 18.

[5] UN Principles to combat impunity, UN Doc E/CN.4/Sub.2/1997/20/Rev.1 (2 October 1997).

[6] Ibid. [7] Ibid, para 42.

[8] Basic Principles and Guidelines on the Right to a Remedy and Reparation for Victims of Gross Violations of International Human Rights Law and Serious Violations of International Humanitarian Law, adopted by the General Assembly in Resolution (Res) A/RES/60/147 (hereinafter 'Basic Principles') on 16 December 2005. The reports by Special Rapporteur of the Sub-Commission, Theo van Boven (van Boven Principles), UN Doc E/CN.4/1997/104 (16 January 1997) and the Special Rapporteur of the Commission on Human Rights, Cherif Bassiouni (Bassiouni Principles), UN Doc E/EC.4/2000/62 (18 January 2000) formed the foundation for the Basic Principles.

harm'; 'the search for the whereabouts of the disappeared and for the bodies of those killed, and assistance in the recovery of the bodies'; 'public apology, including acknowledgement of the facts and acceptance of responsibility'; 'commemorations and tributes to the victims and inclusion of an accurate account of the violations that occurred in the international human rights law and international humanitarian law training and in educational material at all levels'.[9]

II. Transitional justice and the 'duty to preserve memory'

6 In the wider transitional justice discourse, the 'duty to preserve memory' is commonly referred to as *memorialization*. Transitional justice subsumes memorialization under *symbolic reparations* that are directed to the past for a better future; they are meant to right the wrongs of yesterday for a better tomorrow. The status quo ante, however, cannot be restored by monetary compensation: the deeds of the past cannot be undone, and there is no way of accurately measuring the monetary value of humiliation and degradation or of lives taken and dignity lost.[10] Therefore, memorialization, as a form of *symbolic* reparation, is crucial. It is precisely the symbolic and public act of recognition that so importantly confirms victims' experiences as real, and offers them a re-membering into society and a sense of a re-affirmed self.[11]

7 Similar to satisfaction encapsulated in the Basic Principles, practices in this regard include the establishment of memorials, commemoration, and development of history textbooks. For commemoration and the construction of memorials, there is special reference to a *moral* (rather than legal) *obligation* to remember the dead and to give names and faces to the victims so as to ensure that they are not forgotten forever. In this respect, forgiving and forgetting without remembering would implicitly approve the morality of the crimes committed, and even encourage the notion that what is forgotten and has gone unpunished can be repeated without fear.[12] As the entrance of the Dachau concentration camp—today a memorial—a sign reads, 'those who forget the past are doomed to repeat it'. This strand of memorialization corresponds to the legal right to *guarantees of non-repetition* as stated in the Basic Principles.[13]

8 Further, it is widely believed in the transitional justice discourse that memorialization, especially memorials, fosters reconciliation and healing, and prevents re-occurrence through public acknowledgement of victims' suffering and fostering critical thinking and human rights education.[14] Truth and reconciliation commissions in particular have linked

[9] UN General Assembly Res A/RES/60/147, para 8.

[10] M Minow, *Between Vengeance and Forgiveness: Facing History after Genocide and Mass Violence* (Beacon Press 1998) 102–07; F Haldemann, 'Another King of Justice: Transitional Justice as Recognition' in (2008) 41/3 Cornell International Law Journal 675–737, 728–31.

[11] J Viebach, 'Aletheia and the Making of the World: Inner and Outer Dimensions of Memorials in Rwanda' in S Buckley-Zistel and S Schäfer (eds), *Memorials in Times of Transition* (Intersentia 2014) 69–93; CA Nordstrom, *A Different Kind of War Story* (Pennsylvania University Press 1997); R Ibreck, 'The Time of Mourning: The Politics of Commemorating the Tutsi Genocide in Rwanda' in P Lee and P Thomas (eds), *Public Memory, Public Media, and the Politics of Justice* (Palgrave Macmillian 2012) 98–102; JW Booth, *Communities of Memory: On Witness, Identity and Justice* (Cornell University Press 2006).

[12] Derechos 1998, *Without Impunity*, vol 1, no 1 <www.derechos.org/wi/1/1.html> accessed 20 February 2015; JW Booth, 'The Unforgotten: Memories of Justice' (2001) 95/4 American Political Science Review 777–91.

[13] Although the Basic Principles refer to institutional reforms under this heading.

[14] L Bickford and A Sodaro, 'Remembering Yesterday to Protect Tomorrow: How the Current Paradigm of Memorialization Relies on Assumptions about the Relationship between Past and Future' in Gutman et al (eds), n 1, 68–86.

'truth-telling' processes and memory as part of symbolic reparations to reconciliation, healing, and forgiveness. The Sierra Leone Truth and Reconciliation Commission ('Sierra Leone TRC'), for example, stated that 'truth telling and reparations are core components for reconciliation'.[15] Similarly, the high-profile South African Truth and Reconciliation Commission ('South African TRC') equated dealing with the past as knowing the truth of what happened.[16] The preamble to the South African TRC stresses that, 'however painful the experience, the wounds of the past must not be allowed to fester. They must be opened. They must be cleansed ... This is not to be obsessed with the past. It is to take care that the past is properly dealt with for the sake of the future.'[17]

D. Practice

I. Case law

9 Whilst there is no explicit mention of the 'duty to preserve memory' in national or international court judgments to date, there are several judgments issued by the Inter-American Court for Human Rights (IACtHR) that address memorial practices. The IACtHR has ordered the construction of public memorials for past crimes, the location of human remains and their return to their families, and called for measures to prevent reoccurrence in several of its judgments.[18] As Campisi writes, 'the Court mostly relies on the right of the family or the next of kin to preserve their beloved's memory, whose legal justification is primarily linked to the right to know the truth'.[19] Campisi argues that the IACtHR has issued 'ad hoc prescriptions' aimed at restoring the victims' memory as due satisfaction in cases relating to one victim or a limited number of victims. For instance, under non-peculiar reparations, the Court in *Myrna Mack-Chang v Guatemala* held that there was grave human suffering to both the victim and the 'next of kin to the victim'. It ordered:

> The State must also name a well-known street or square in Guatemala City in honour of Myrna Mack Chang, and place a prominent plaque in her memory at the place where she died or nearby, with a reference to the activities she carried out. This will contribute to awakening public awareness to avoid recidivism of facts such as those that occurred in the instant case and to maintain remembrance of the victim.[20]

The Court also ordered the establishment of an annual scholarship in the victim's name at a 'prestigious national university'.[21]

[15] Sierra Leone Truth and Reconciliation Commission, Final Report, *Witness to Truth*, vol 2, ch 4, para 40.

[16] Truth and Reconciliation Commission of South Africa Report, vol 1, ch 1, para 28.

[17] Ibid, para 27.

[18] For location and identification of human remains, see, eg, *Mapiripan Massacre v Columbia* (Merits, reparations and costs) (Judgment) IACtHR Series C no 134 (15 September 2005) para 305; for public acknowledgement, see ibid, *Myrna Mack-Chang v Guatemala* (Merits, reparations and costs) (Judgment) IACtHR Series C no 101 (25 November 2003), and *Plan de Sanchez Massacre v Guatemala* (Merits, reparations and costs) (Judgment) IACtHR Series C no 116 (19 November 2004); for an analysis, see M Campisi, 'From a Duty to Remember to an Obligation to Memory? Memory as Reparation in the Jurisprudence of the Inter-American Court of Human Rights' (2014) 8/1 International Journal of Conflict and Violence 61–74.

[19] Campisi, n 18, 67.

[20] *Myrna Mack-Chang v Guatemala* (Merits, reparations and costs) (Judgment) IACtHR Series C no 101 (25 November 2003), para 286.

[21] Ibid, para 285.

In contrast, when a whole community has suffered from human rights violations, as in the Plan Sanchez Massacre during the Guatemalan conflict, the Court's decisions have been directed at broader memory projects, such as memorials and public acts of recognition.[22] Furthermore, in *Mapiripan Massacre v Columbia*, the Court held that 10

> the State must build an appropriate and dignified monument in remembrance of the facts in the Mapiripán Massacre, as a measure to prevent such grave events happening in the future. Said monument must be placed in an appropriate public space in Mapiripán, within a year of notification of the instant Judgment.[23]

However, such judgments by the Court have arisen from decisions concerning reparations.[24] Thus, rather than asserting the collective dimension of a people's 'knowledge of the history of its oppression', they refer to the individual, namely the victim's, right and the next of kin's right to know the truth, and therefore to the right to satisfaction as part of reparation programmes based on the harm suffered. Nevertheless, 'the trend to memorialization has influenced judicial processes', and 'courts may also see their role as memorial facilitators',[25] thereby strengthening norm setting for a 'duty to preserve memory' through legal judgments. 11

II. Truth commissions

The 'duty to preserve memory' is further ensconced in the practices of truth and reconciliation commissions, particularly their final reports and recommendations. Similar to the IACtHR decisions, the 'duty to preserve memory' is integrated in a reparation framework, with truth commissions generally falling under the rubric of satisfaction.[26] Particularly relevant here is the Sierra Leone TRC, which established its own definition of *symbolic reparations*, thereby acknowledging the link between truth-telling measures, symbolic acts, and reparations: 'They are a clear expression of recognition for the harm suffered. Symbolic reparations can preserve the memory of what happened during the conflict and most importantly, serve as a reminder that society must not allow this to happen again.'[27] 12

Moreover, the Sierra Leone TRC states that memorial measures 'may go a long way to restoring the dignity of victims and facilitating healing and reconciliation'.[28] Based on this definition, the TRC recommended the construction of a National War Memorial and several memorials throughout the country, the organization of commemoration days, the symbolic reburial of victims, and the declaration of a National Reconciliation Day.[29] The TRC's recommendation emphasized that the proposed memorial activities should be undertaken in close consultation with victim groups and, importantly, that memorials 13

[22] Campisi, n 18, 68; *Plan de Sanchez Massacre v Guatemala* (Merits, reparations and costs) (Judgment) IACtHR Series C no 116 (19 November 2004) paras 100, 104.

[23] *Mapiripan Massacre v Columbia* (Merits, reparations and costs) (Judgment) IACtHR Series C no 134 (15 September 2005) para 315.

[24] In the *Mapiripan Massacre v Columbia* case, for example, the Court stated that it 'will order measures of satisfaction to redress non-material damages, those that are non-pecuniary, as well as measures that are public in their scope or repercussions': ibid, para 294.

[25] *Report of the Special Rapporteur in the field of cultural rights*, UN Doc A/HRC/25/49 (23 January 2014), paras 36, 38.

[26] E Naidu and J Torpey, 'Reparations for Human Rights Abuses' in T Cushman (ed), *Handbook of Human Rights* (Routledge 2012) 476–89, 477.

[27] Sierra Leone TRC Final Report, n 15, para 22.

[28] Ibid, para 26.

[29] Ibid, paras 198–202.

can take different forms, such as 'monuments, the renaming of buildings or locations, the transformation of victim's sites into useful buildings for the community, etc'.[30]

14 The prominent South African TRC took a similarly broad approach to reparations, which shall 'facilitate the communal process of remembering and commemorating the pain and the victories of the past. Such measures aim to restore the dignity of victims and survivors.'[31] In its proposal for a reparation and rehabilitation policy, the Sub-Committee on Reparation and Rehabilitation explains how 'The Committee looked at individuals, communities and the nation as a whole when making recommendations to achieve reparation and rehabilitation'.[32] Symbolic reparations were one of the Sub-Committee's measures to facilitate healing and reconciliation in line with the South African idea of ***ubuntu***. It identifies the services and benefits on the individual level as exhumations, reburials, headstones, and tombstones. At the community level, the report lists the renaming of streets and facilities, memorials, and monuments so as to make sure that abuses people have suffered do not happen again. It also mentions culturally appropriate ceremonies, which can include cleansing ceremonies. Under the rubric of national benefits, the proposal includes national days of remembrance and reconciliation, thereby stressing that public remembrance will help bring about reconciliation, 'so that we are able to move forward from the past to the future'.[33]

15 Further truth commissions that included memorialization in their recommendations on symbolic reparation programmes include, amongst others, the Commission on the Truth in El Salvador, the Commission for Historical Clarification in Guatemala, and Tunisia's Truth and Dignity Commission (which is still ongoing).[34]

E. Critical Assessment

16 The normative framework, on which the practices just outlined are built, reveals that Principle 3 itself has not been explicitly recognized by the courts or national policy-makers. Rather, the ideas underpinning the Principle have been implicitly acknowledged through the concepts of reparation, under either the rubric of symbolic reparations during truth-telling processes or the notion of satisfaction in jurisprudence. By failing to engage with the Principle directly, the *collective dimension* of *memory*, referred to in the Principle, remains untouched and under-explored.

17 Yet it is this very collective dimension where concerns about the 'duty to preserve memory' arise. For instance, the IACtHR's decision to order the construction of memorials or public commemoration may exclude other groups of victims and 'create a ranking of legitimacy among victims'.[35] This holds true as well for the practices of truth and reconciliation commissions that legally determine who is to be classed as a victim. Furthermore, in the case of reparations, legally binding decisions, which would usually affect just the parties involved in the case, can affect communities or even entire societies. This is particularly so when the courts make orders for commemoration days

[30] Ibid, para 199.

[31] Truth and Reconciliation Commission of South Africa, *Final Report*, vol 5, s 2, ch 1, 95, para 13.

[32] Truth and Reconciliation Commission of South Africa, Committee on Reparation and Rehabilitation, Summary on Reparation and Rehabilitation Policy, Including Proposal to be Considered by the President <www.justice.gov.za/trc/reparations/summary.htm> accessed 24 November 2017

[33] Ibid, s 3.

[34] PB Hayner, *Unspeakable Truths* (Routledge 2001) 179–80, 311–13.

[35] Campisi, n 18, 69.

to be established or memorials to be built. The individual's demand for remembering and honouring the dead may actually hinder broader social efforts to come to terms with the past.

The IACtHR's decisions, the practices of truth commissions, and the general 'rush to commemorate' mirror the underlying assumption that memorialization contributes to reconciliation and healing.[36] This assumption, however, lacks empirical evidence. In fact, because it is a societal and political endeavour, memorialization can cause more harm than good in societies that are often divided by ethnic group identities or victim-perpetrator hierarchies.[37] Memorialization can easily transform into a battlefield about who, what, how, and to what end the past is remembered. Furthermore, memorials are steady reminders of the past and *materialize* particular group narratives of past injustices—they therefore reach far beyond mere symbolic reparations or satisfaction—they shape group *identities* and 'entire cultural and symbolic landscapes'.[38] **18**

In Burundi, for instance, where a law regarding the establishment of a truth and reconciliation commission was passed in 2013, before the most recent outbreak of political violence, memories of the violent past (1972 and 1993) have fabricated 'Hutu' and 'Tutsi' memories. They are each characterized by their own claims to group victimization that in turn fuel ethnic division and hinder social reconstruction.[39] As an Impunity Watch report importantly outlines, truth-seeking through exhumations, writing history textbooks, and building memorials has often set one side against the other.[40] Therefore, reconciliation and a shared understanding of the violent history of the country are still wanting. Although 'preserving the collective memory from extinction' is legally and morally desirable, in complex post-conflict situations this 'duty' may be more complex and difficult than the Principle suggests. **19**

Whilst Principle 3 is an important first step towards the recognition of collective memory as part of international law, it does not mirror the societal and political realities 'on the ground'. What is needed is a clear definition of collective memory, recognition of its complexity and challenges, and, more importantly, an acknowledgement that memory must be an integral part, in and of itself, of the fight against impunity. At present, there is no UN mechanism in place to identify and advocate for best practices to 'preserve memory'. Therefore, explicit and detailed guidelines ought to be developed based on an independent study on memorialization in post-conflict societies. In that regard, the recent report submitted by Special Rapporteur Farida Shaheed, to the Human Rights Council, offers some fruitful insights and critical reflections.[41] Clearly, though, international law still has to acknowledge the political and societal realities in which it is embedded, and which it seeks to shape and change. **20**

[36] See, eg, the Durban Declaration of the World Conference against Racism, Racial Discrimination, Xenophobia and Related Intolerance.

[37] L Bickford, 'Memoryworks/Memory Works' in C Ramirez-Barat (ed), *Transitional Justice, Culture and Society: Beyond Outreach* (Social Science Research Council 2014) 491–529.

[38] Report of Special Rapporteur, n 25, para 2.

[39] Impunity Watch, 'Lieux de Mémoire, commemorative initiatives and memorials to Burundi's conflict: Invisible and permanent Memories', *Research Brief Perspective Series* (2012) 1–2.

[40] Ibid, 4. [41] Report of Special Rapporteur, n 25.

Bibliography

Antze, P and Lambek, M, *Tense Past: Cultural Essays in Trauma and Memory* (Routledge 1996).

Ashplant, TG, Dawson, G, and Roper M (eds), *The Politics of War Memory and Commemoration* (Routledge 2000).

Barsalou, J and Baxtor, V, *The Urge to Remember: The Role of Memorials in Social Reconstruction and Transitional Justice* (United States Institute of Peace Report, Stabilization and Reconstruction Series No 5, 2007).

Buckley-Zistel, S and Schäfer, S (eds), *Memorials in Times of Transition* (Intersentia 2014).

Coombes, AE, *History after Apartheid: Visual Culture and Public Memory in a Democratic South Africa* (Duke University Press 2003).

Gutman, Y, Brown, A, and Sodaro, A (eds), *Memory and the Future: Transnational Politics, Ethics and Society* (Palgrave Macmillan 2010).

Hamber, B, Ševčenko, L, and Naidu, E, 'Utopian Dreams or Practical Possibilities? The Challenges of Evaluating the Impact of Memorialization in Societies in Transition' (2010) 4/3 International Journal of Transitional Justice 397–420.

Lessa, F, *Memory and Transitional Justice in Argentina and Uruguay: Against Impunity* (Palgrave Macmillian 2013).

Müller, JW (ed), *Memory and Power in Post-War Europe* (CUP 2002).

Osiel, MJ, *Mass Atrocity, Collective Memory and the Law* (Transaction Publishers 1999).

Ramirez-Barat, C (ed), *Transitional Justice, Culture and Society: Beyond Outreach* (Social Science Research Council 2014).

Principle 4. The Victims' Right to Know

Dermot Groome

Irrespective of any legal proceedings, victims and their families have the imprescriptible right to know the truth about the circumstances in which violations took place and, in the event of death or disappearance, the victims' fate.

A. Summary of Findings

The right to know, first articulated in Article 32 of Additional Protocol I to the Geneva Conventions, recognized the basic human need for families to know the fate of missing loved ones. Its applicability beyond the context of international conflicts was appreciated shortly afterwards. The right to know is most often exercised in conjunction with the closely related right to the truth (Principle 2), which not only guarantees families knowledge of the ultimate fate of relatives but also requires a full and fair exposition of what happened, including the existence of human rights violations. The right to know is now a principle of customary international humanitarian law and is best understood as a right extending humanitarian protection to families of the missing. It is evolving to allow others with a legitimate interest to assert it, and in contexts beyond armed conflict.

B. Contextual and Historical Introduction

The inclusion of the right to know in Article 32 of Additional Protocol I[1] was the culmination of earlier efforts to recognize and ameliorate conflict's direct impact on the families of soldiers and detainees.[2] During the discussions surrounding the additional 1

[1] Art 32 of Additional Protocol I to the Geneva Conventions of 1949 states: 'In the implementation of this Section, the activities of the High Contracting Parties, of the Parties to the conflict and of the international humanitarian organizations mentioned in the Conventions and in this Protocol shall be prompted mainly by the right of families to know the fate of their relatives.' See ICRC, Protocol Additional to the Geneva Conventions of 12 August 1949, and relating to the Protection of Victims of International Armed Conflicts (Protocol I) (8 June 1977) 1125 UNTS 3. Additional Protocol II to the Geneva Conventions of 1949 (applicable to internal armed conflicts) includes two obligations related to the right to know: Art 5(2)(b) requires that interned or detained persons 'shall be allowed to send and receive letters'; and Art 8 imposes an affirmative duty to search for the dead. See ICRC, Protocol Additional to the Geneva Conventions of 12 August 1949, and relating to the Protection of Victims of International Armed Conflicts (8 June 1977) 1125 UNTS 609.

[2] See Convention for the Amelioration of the Condition of the Wounded and Sick in Armies in the Field (6 July 1906) Art 4; Convention (IV) respecting the Laws and Customs of War on Land and its annex: Regulations concerning the Laws and Customs of War on Land (18 October 1907) Annex, Arts 14 and 16; Convention Relative to the Treatment of Prisoners of War (27 July 1929) Arts 8, 36, 38, and 41; 1949 Geneva Convention for the Amelioration of the Condition of the Wounded and Sick in Armed Forces in the Field (GC I) 75 UNTS 31, Arts 15 and 16; 1949 Geneva Convention for the Amelioration of the Condition of Wounded, Sick and Shipwrecked Members of Armed Forces at Sea (GC II) 75 UNTS 85, Art 16; 1949 Geneva Convention Relative to the Treatment of Prisoners of War (GC III) 75 UNTS 135, Arts 70, 71, and 122; 1949 Geneva Convention Relative to the Protection of Civilian Persons in Time of War (GC IV) 75 UNTS 287, Arts 25, 26, 106, 107, 129, 130, and 138.

protocols, the Holy See proposed that this fundamental human need to know the fate of family members be explicitly recognized as a right.[3] The text of Article 32 requires parties to meet their obligations with respect to the missing and dead, 'prompted mainly by the right of families to know the fate of their relatives'.[4] The inclusion of this phrase was the subject of much debate, and was ultimately 'adopted after careful reflection, and made in full consciousness'.[5] Articles 33 and 34 of Additional Protocol I set forth in detail the specific obligations of parties giving effect to the right.[6]

2 Although Article 32 contemplated an international conflict, it did not take long before its importance in other contexts was appreciated. Yves Sandoz, in his commentary to Article 32, opined that '[t]he recognition of such a right ... should have further repercussions, particularly with regard to the families of missing persons in non-international armed conflicts and in the framework of human rights, even during internal disturbances or tensions'.[7]

3 In 1985, Louis Joinet first referred to the 'right to know' in this expanded usage.[8] In 1997, when Joinet set out his forty-two Principles to Combat Impunity, he included Principle 1 (The Inalienable Right to the Truth) and Principle 3 (The Victims' Right to Know). Together they broadened the Article 32 right in two ways. First, it was not simply a right to know a loved one's fate but a right to know the full circumstances of the disappearance, and whether there had been a violation of human rights. Second, that it was not simply a right held by individual families but a collective right.[9] When Diane Orentlicher updated the Joinet Principles in 2005, she made no changes to Joinet's articulation of the right to know.[10]

4 A family's right to know the fate of a loved one not only allows it to mourn a loss; the official recognition of that person's fate also allows relatives to resolve associated legal issues, such as the inheritance of property or the ability to remarry.[11] Principle 5

[3] The Vatican delegate, Charles Klein, in proposing the amendment, said 'its purpose was to ... call the attention ... to the suffering caused to families as a result of armed conflicts ... It was not merely a question of feelings but one of respect for a fundamental right which had never been officially recognized'. See Record of Diplomatic Conference on the Reaffirmation and Development of International Humanitarian Law Applicable in Armed Conflicts (Geneva 1974–1977) vol XI (13 March 1975) 363.

[4] Art 32, Protocol I.

[5] Y Sandoz, 'Commentary to Article 32' in *Commentary on the Additional Protocols: of 8 June 1977 to the Geneva Conventions of 12 August 1949* (Martinus Nijhoff 1987) para 1211.

[6] Art 33(1) provides: 'As soon as circumstances permit, and at the latest from the end of active hostilities, each Party to the conflict shall search for the persons who have been reported missing by the adverse Party.' The article specifies the information to be gathered and incorporates by reference Art 138 of GC IV, which in turn states that the information shall be of such 'a character as to make it possible to identify the protected person exactly and to advise his next of kin quickly'. Art 33 concludes by encouraging the parties to work cooperatively in the identification and recovery of the dead from battlefield areas. Art 34 provides that the remains of persons who have died as a result of occupation or hostilities shall be treated in accordance with Art 130 of GC IV (buried in marked, properly maintained individual graves, if possible). In the case of cremations conducted for religious or hygienic reasons, the ashes shall be maintained for transfer to the next of kin.

[7] See Sandoz, n 5, para 1212.

[8] See L Joinet, Special Rapporteur, *Preliminary Report on Study on Amnesty Laws and Their Role in the Safeguard and Promotion of Human Rights*, UN Doc E/CN.4/Sub.2/1985/16 (21 June 1985) para 81.

[9] L Joinet, Special Rapporteur, *Revised Final Report on Question of the Impunity of Perpetrators of Human Rights Violations (Civil and Political)*, UN Doc E/CN.4/Sub.2/1997/20/Rev.1 (2 October 1997).

[10] D Orentlicher, *Report of the Independent Expert to Update the Set of Principles to Combat Impunity*, UN Doc E/CN.4/2005/102/Add.1 (8 February 2005) (hereinafter 'Orentlicher Report'). Orentlicher inserted a new first principle, resulting in the right to know's being renumbered as Principle 4.

[11] See, ICRC, *Missing Persons on the territory of the former Yugoslavia*, April 2008 <www.icrc.org/eng/assets/files/other/missing-newsletter-0408.pdf> accessed 13 January 2018.

of the Joinet/Orentlicher principles asserts the importance of a state's establishing independent and effective judicial institutions, as well as non-judicial processes such as truth commissions, to 'give effect to the right to know'.[12]

C. Theoretical Framework

At present, there is little conceptual or normative difference between the right to know and the right to the truth, and the two phrases are often used interchangeably or as functional equivalents.[13] 5

Although it may not be possible to completely disentangle the concepts of the 'right to the truth' and the 'right to know', the margins between them are best understood in two ways. First, the primary impetus behind the right to know is a humanitarian one—an effort to alleviate suffering for the families of the missing.[14] The primary impetuses behind the right to the truth are justice and avoiding the recurrence of serious violations of human rights.[15] While the right to the truth is often invoked in cases of people who have been forcibly disappeared, it has broad applicability to any situation in which the truth about gross human rights violations is concealed. Second, while there is a general societal interest in families knowing the fate of loved ones, the collective dimension of the right to the truth's exposition of systematic human rights abuses is a core feature of the right.[16] 6

Over time, interpretations regarding the scope of the right to know have changed. The right now not only relates to those missing in conflict or last seen in the custody of the government, but also includes those who are missing as a result of internal displacement,[17] or children who become separated from their families.[18] 7

The determination of those who can assert the right has differed depending upon the court hearing the claim. For example, the European Court of Human Rights (ECtHR) has required the existence of 'special factors' beyond mere familial relationship, while the Human Rights Chamber for Bosnia and Herzegovina (HRCBiH) adopted a more flexible approach, considering a range of factors.[19] In 2010, Article 18(1) of the International 8

[12] See Principle 5, 'Guarantees to give effect to the right to know'.

[13] Orentlicher herself has used the phrases interchangeably: 'As used by Louis Joinet and others, "the right to the truth" or "the right to know" has both an individual and social dimension.' Remarks of D Orentlicher, Human Rights Brief, vol 16, issue 4 (2009) 9–11, 10.

[14] Additional Protocol I to the Geneva Conventions of 1949, Art 32.

[15] Principle 1 of the Joinet/Orentlicher Principles, 'General Obligations of States to Take Effective Action to Combat Impunity', states in relevant part: 'Impunity arises from a failure by States to meet their obligations ... to ensure the inalienable right to know the truth about violations; and to take other necessary steps to prevent a recurrence of violations.'

[16] Orentlicher Report, n 10, para 17.

[17] See Guiding Principles on Internal Displacement, UN Doc E/CN.4/1998/53/Add.2 (11 February 1998). Principle 16 reaffirmed the 'right to know the fate and whereabouts of missing relatives'.

[18] Art 19(3) of the African Charter of the Rights and Welfare of the Child requires states to provide children separated from their families with information regarding their whereabouts.

[19] Cf *Cyprus v Turkey* (Judgment) App no 25781/94 (ECtHR,10 May 2001) para 156 and *Unković v Bosnia and Herzegovina* (Decision on Review) (ECtHR, 10 May 2002) para 114. The ECtHR found that whether a family member of a disappeared person was the subject of an Art 3 violation (prohibition on torture and other inhuman treatment) depended upon the presence of special factors that elevated the suffering beyond 'the emotional distress which may be regarded as inevitably caused to relatives'. Such factors might include the closeness of the familial bond (eg, parent–child bond), whether the family member witnessed the incident, and the efforts of that family member to obtain information about the missing person. The HRCBiH took a more flexible approach, enumerating eight factors that could inform a determination that a particular applicant family member's Art 3 rights had been violated: (i) 'dimension and character of emotional distress ... distinct from

Convention for the Protection of All Persons from Enforced Disappearance guaranteed the right to know for 'any person with a legitimate interest' in information relating to a person deprived of his or her liberty.[20]

D. Practice

9 In practice, the right to know is exercised in several ways: (i) through the mechanisms of international organizations such as the International Committee of the Red Cross (ICRC) and the International Commission on Missing Persons (ICMP); (ii) through the different human rights mechanisms; (iii) through ad hoc truth commissions and other transitional justice mechanisms; and (iv) through the work of international criminal courts.

I. The ICRC and the ICMP

10 The ICRC is the principal agency under international law charged with collecting information about persons missing in internal and international armed conflicts.[21] The right to know the fate of persons missing during international and non-international armed conflicts is a matter of customary international humanitarian law.[22] It is articulated in Rule 117 of Customary International Humanitarian Law as follows:

> Each party to the conflict must take all feasible measures to account for persons reported missing as a result of armed conflict and must provide their family members with any information it has on their fate.[23]

11 The Geneva Conventions oblige belligerents to establish information bureaus to gather information regarding prisoners of war and civilian detainees. This obligation has been incorporated into national military manuals.[24] Belligerents are also required to help families separated during the conflict find each other.[25] In some cases, bilateral and multilateral agreements set out the specific modalities of these international obligations.[26]

12 The ICRC is joined in this important work by the ICMP, established in 1996 to help account for the approximately 40,000 persons missing in the Yugoslav conflict.[27] The

that which would inevitable for all relatives'; (ii) 'proximity of family tie'; (iii) the 'particular circumstances of the relationship between the missing person and the family member'; (iv) the 'extent to which the family member witnessed the events'; (v) the context of the disappearance, eg, during war, as part of an extensive loss of life; (vi) the 'amount of anguish and stressed caused to the family member'; (vii) the role of the family member in efforts to obtain information; and (viii) the tenacity of the family member in 'making complaints, seeking information … and substantiating' the complaint.

[20] Art 18(1) includes a non-exclusive list that includes relatives, representatives, and counsel of the persons deprived of their liberty.

[21] Additional Protocol I, Art 33(3) states that '[i]nformation concerning persons reported missing pursuant … shall be transmitted either directly or through the Protecting Power or the Agency of the International Committee of the Red Cross or national Red Cross (Red Crescent, Red Lion and Sun) Societies'.

[22] See, eg Sandoz, n 5, para 1211; Office for the Coordination of Humantarian Affairs (OCHA) *Guiding Principles on Internal Displacement* (2004) Principle 16(1); Commission on Human Rights, *The Right to the Truth*, Res 2005/66 (20 April 2005); and UNGA Res 3220 (XXIX) (6 November 1974).

[23] ICRC, *Customary International Humanitarian Law*, vol I (ICRC 2005) Rule 117, at 421.

[24] See, eg, United Kingdom, *The Manual of The Law of Armed Conflict* (2004) s 7.38. See also, military manuals for Canada, para 7; Israel, para 11; The Netherlands, para 14; and the USA, para 7.7.4.

[25] Art 26, GC IV.

[26] See, eg, General Framework for Peace in Bosnia and Herzegovina, UN Doc A/50/790 (30 November 1995) (Dayton Peace Accords) Art V of Annex VII.

[27] See ICMP website <www.icmp.int/about-us/history/> accessed 12 December 2017.

ICMP's use of the most advanced scientific identification techniques has earned it a reputation for reliability.[28] The ICMP's mandate now goes beyond the former Yugoslavia to include different parts of the world, and persons missing in natural disasters as well as during conflict.[29] In 2014, the ICMP established itself as an independent international organization. The ICRC and ICMP also support the efforts of national governments to locate and identify the remains of missing persons.[30]

II. Human rights mechanisms

The right to know has been exercised through the UN and regional human rights systems, often concurrently with the right to the truth.[31] The exercise of the right to know has been underpinned by the existing prohibition against inhuman treatment, the right to access to justice, and the right to family life. 13

The Human Rights Committee (HRC) has consistently found that the prohibition of cruel treatment set out in Article 7 of the International Covenant on Civil and Political Rights (ICCPR) extends to the families of persons last seen in government custody[32] or held incommunicado.[33] The ECtHR has taken a similar approach in *Cyprus v Turkey*, concerning Turkey's failure to account for persons missing during its operations in northern Cyprus in 1974. The Court found that Turkey's persistent failure to account for the missing constituted a 'continuing violation of Article 3 [prohibition against inhuman treatment] of the European Convention on Human Rights (ECHR) with respect to the relatives of the missing Greek-Cypriots',[34] Article 5 of the African Charter on Human and People's Rights (ACHPR) provides similar grounds for right to know claims.[35] 14

The second basis on which the right has been exercised rests upon the state's obligation to provide effective access to justice. In cases where families of the missing have sought judicial recourse, the Inter-American Court of Human Rights (IACtHR) has consistently found that the failure to investigate a disappearance constitutes a violation of Articles 1(1), 8(1), and 25(1) ACHR ensuring equal access to justice. The Court found that 'the State's duty to investigate violations of the rights to life and humane treatment is a prerequisite for guaranteeing said rights'.[36] The ECtHR came to a similar conclusion with respect to Article 13 of the ECHR (parallel provision to Articles 8 and 25 of the ACHR).[37] 15

[28] International courts have relied on its forensic work, see, eg, ICTY, *Prosecutor v Popović* (Appeals Judgment) IT-05-88 (30 January 2015) paras 287–91.

[29] The ICMP offered assistance to the countries affected by the tsumani in the Indian Ocean in 2004. See ICMP website <www.icmp.int/where-we-work/asia/> accessed 12 December 2017.

[30] See ICMP website <www.icmp.int/> accessed 12 December 2017. See, eg, Missing Persons Institute of Bosnia and Herzegovina; South African Missing Persons Task Team of the Office of the National Prosecuting Authority; and, in Columbia, the National Institute of Legal Medicine and Forensic Sciences.

[31] For a detailed discussion of these efforts, see this author's commentary to Principle 2 in this volume.

[32] See, eg, HRC, *María del Carmen Almeida de Quinteros et al v Uruguay*, Communication no 107/1981, CCPR/C/OP/2 (21 July 1983) 138. See also HRC, *Bousroual v Algeria*, CCPR/C/86/D/1085/2002 (15 March 2006) para 9.8; and *Zohra Madoui v Algeria*, CCPR/C/94/D/1495/2006 (28 October 2008) para 7.5.

[33] HRC, *Titiahonjo v Cameroon*, CCPR/C/91/D/1186/2003 (26 October 2007). See also *Madoui v Algeria*, n 32, paras 7.4–7.5.

[34] *Cyprus v Turkey* (Judgment) App no 25781/94 (ECtHR,10 May 2001) para 158.

[35] See *Amnesty International and Others v Sudan*, Communication nos 48/90 et al (AComHPR, 15 November 1999) para 54. See also *Article 19 v Eritrea*, Communication no 275/2003 (30 May 2007).

[36] *Ximenes-Lopes v Brazil* (Judgment) IACtHR Series C no 149 (4 July 2006) para 177. See also ibid, paras 260 and 262.4. See also *Villagran-Morales et al* IACtHR Series C no 63 (19 November 1999) para 253.6.

[37] *Cyprus v Turkey* App no 25781/94 (Judgment) (ECtHR, 10 May 2001) para 192. Arts 7 and 26 of the African Charter provide a similar legal basis.

16 The third basis relates to rights protecting family life. The African Commission on Human and Peoples Rights has found that the protection of the family guaranteed by Article 18 of the ACHPR included the family's right to know what has happened to a relative.[38] Article 19 of the African Charter on the Rights and Welfare of the Child obliges state parties to gives a child's family members 'essential information concerning the whereabouts of the absent member or members of the family', and requires family or guardians to be notified 'as soon as possible'.[39]

III. Truth commissions and other transitional justice mechanisms

17 Truth commissions are ad hoc institutions typically established outside of existing judicial institutions. Their formation is a response to serious violations of international humanitarian and human rights law. They are one part of an array of transitional justice mechanisms designed to facilitate a country's move forwards from a time of national crisis. In some cases, the international community has relied on international commissions of inquiry for a similar purpose.[40] Truth commissions have been established in at least 45 countries,[41] and despite significant challenges have played an important part in the transition toward more just societies.[42] The contributions of truth commissions include: empowering victims to provide public testimony of gross violations of human rights; creating a venue for official acknowledgement of atrocities; 'helping set reform priorities'; and building a body of information and evidence that other transitional justice mechanisms can use.[43]

18 Archives charged with preserving and cataloguing the work of truth commissions and other evidence are important 'instruments for realizing the right to truth'.[44] The information collected, as well as the findings of truth commissions, can be a catalyst for other transitional justice initiatives, such as legislating reparations for victims, amending the laws that enabled violations, and establishing watchdog institutions.[45] They can also provide information that can be used in formal investigations and prosecutions.[46] As one author has observed, 'It is their [truth commissions'] contributions to the delivery of these rights [right to the truth, right to justice] that legitimize their place within the transitional justice framework.'[47]

[38] *Article 19 v Eritrea*, Communication no 275/2003 (30 May 2007) para 2013. In this case 18 journalists were detained incommunicado for an extended period of time. See also *Constitutional Rights Project and Another v Nigeria*, Communication nos 143/95 and 150/96 (AComHPR, 15 November 1999).

[39] African Charter on the Rights and Welfare of the Child, Art 19(3) and (4).

[40] See, eg, Office of the High Commissioner for Human Rights (OHCHR), *Report of the OHCHR Investigation on Sri Lanka (OISL)*, UN Doc A/HRC/30/CRP.2 (16 September 2015).

[41] For a complete list of these countries and links to their reports, see United States Institute of Peace <www.usip.org/publications/truth-commission-digital-collection>.

[42] P Hayner, *Unspeakable Truths: Transitional Justice and the Challenge of Truth Commissions* (Routledge 2011).

[43] P de Greiff, *Report of the Special Rapporteur on the promotion of truth, justice, reparation and guarantees of non-recurrence*, UN Doc A/HRC/24/42 (28 August 2013) para 24.

[44] Ibid, para 80. The OHCHR has been instrumental in establishing uniform standards for cataloguing and maintaining archiver material. See OHCHR, *Report of the Office of the High Commissioner for Human Rights on the seminar on experiences of archives as a means to guarantee the right to truth*, UN Doc A/HRC/17/21 (14 April 2011).

[45] O Bakiner, 'Truth Commission Impact: An Assessment of How Commissions Influence Politics and Society' (2014) 8 International Journal of Transitional Justice 6–30, 6, 20.

[46] Ibid, 27.

[47] A Bisset, *Truth Commissions and Criminal Courts* (CUP 2012) 13.

IV. International criminal justice mechanisms

International courts have also played an important part in realizing the right to know. The investigative and forensic work of prosecutors at the ad hoc tribunals and other courts has made an important contribution towards helping families learn the ultimate fate of loved ones.[48] The International Criminal Court (ICC), with its greater rights of victim participation, is likely to become an important avenue for families to exercise their right to know. Article 68(3) of the Rome Statute gives victims the right to express their views and concerns whenever their personal interests are affected. Although this right has been broadly interpreted by ICC judges,[49] victim participation also raises practical concerns about efficiency and fairness to an accused.[50] 19

E. Critical Assessment

The right of families to know the fate of missing relatives, whether they are missing as the result of conflict or serious human rights violations, is an important right that meets a significant humanitarian need for the families of the missing. It is often exercised in conjunction with the broader right to the truth, and the distinction between the two has in many ways eroded. 20

One way in which the right may develop further is in application to non-state actors, such as international organizations and corporations. In 2014, the Committee on the Rights of the Child concluded that Articles 7 and 8 of the Convention on the Rights of the Child[51] gave children fathered by Catholic priests the 'right to know' the identity of their biological fathers, despite confidentiality agreements signed by their mothers.[52] 21

International corporations whose activities result in the unexplained disappearance of people may also be deemed to have an obligation to give effect to the right to know. For example, the families of the passengers of Malaysian Airlines flight MH370 still suffer the effects of not knowing what happened to their loved ones. Although the airline and several governments continue their efforts, it may be possible for the families to assert their right to know should the search ever be abandoned. 22

Bibliography

Bissett, A, *Truth Commissions and Criminal Courts* (CUP 2012).

Crettol, M, 'The Missing and Transitional Justice: the Right to Know and the Fight against Impunity', International Review of the Red Cross, vol 88 no 862 (2006) 355–62.

de Greiff, P, *Report of the Special Rapporteur on the Promotion of Truth Justice, Reparation and Guarantees of Non-recurrence*, UN Doc A/HRC/24/42 (28 August 2013).

Freeman, M, *Truth Commissions and Procedural Fairness* (CUP 2006).

Groome, D, 'Right to Truth in the Fight Against Impunity' (2011) 29 Berkeley Journal of International Law 175–99.

48 See, ICTY, *Prosecutor v Popović* (Judgment) IT-05-88-T (10 June 2010) paras 608 et seq.

49 C Van den Wyngaert, 'Victims Before the International Criminal Courts: Some Views and Concerns of an ICC Trial Judge' (2011) 44 Case Western Reserve Journal of International Law 475–96, 83.

50 Ibid, 487–88.

51 Convention on the Rights of the Child (20 November 1989) 1577 UNTS 3.

52 Committee on the Rights of the Child, *Concluding observations on the second periodic report of the Holy See*, UN Doc CRC/C/VAT/CO/2 (25 February 2014) para 34.

Hayner, P, *Unspeakable Truths: Transitional Justice and the Challenge of Truth Commissions* (Routledge 2011).

Inter-American Commission on Human Rights, 'The Right to Truth in the Americas', OEA/Ser.L/V/II.152 (2014).

ICRC, *Customary International Humanitarian Law*, vol I (ICRC 2005) Rule 117.

Méndez, J, 'The Right to Truth' in C Joyner (ed), *Reining in Impunity for International Crimes and Serious Violations of Fundamental Rights* (Association Internationale De Droit Pénal 1998) 255–78.

Naftali, P, 'Crafting a "Right to Truth" in International Law: Converging Mobilizations, Diverging Agendas' *Champ Pénal* vol XIII (2016) 1–20 <journals.openedition.org/champpenal/9245> accessed 12 December 2017.

Naqvi, Y, 'The Right to the Truth in International Law: Fact or Fiction', International Review of the Red Cross, vol 88, no 862 (2006) 245–73.

Sandoz, Y, 'Commentary to Article 32' in *Commentary on the Additional Protocols: of 8 June 1977 to the Geneva Conventions of 12 August 1949* (Martinus Nijhoff 1987) para 1211.

Principle 5. Guarantees to Give Effect to the Right to Know

Thomas Unger

States must take appropriate action, including measures necessary to ensure the independent and effective operation of the judiciary, to give effect to the right to know. Appropriate measures to ensure this right may include non-judicial processes that complement the role of the judiciary. Societies that have experienced heinous crimes perpetrated on a massive or systematic basis may benefit in particular from the creation of a truth commission or other commission of inquiry to establish the facts surrounding those violations so that the truth may be ascertained and to prevent the disappearance of evidence. Regardless of whether a State establishes such a body, it must ensure the preservation of, and access to, archives concerning violations of human rights and humanitarian law.

A. Summary of Findings

Since the Joinet Principles, there has been a clear expansion, in both theory and practice, of guarantees to give effect to the right to know. This is reflected in Principle 5. Guarantees include judicial and non-judicial mechanisms. The focus of Principle 5 is on courts, truth commissions, and archives. Criminal justice is given a privileged position. The list in Principle 5 follows, therefore, a clear human rights understanding on what guarantees should look like in the fight against impunity.

This approach, which aims for guarantees as a form of absolute justice, is at odds with a conception of transitional justice as a 'vehicle for crafting complex compromises'. It also fails to reconcile with guarantees for the right to know that are found in other fields, such as in the area of humanitarian law. The primacy given to criminal justice in Principle 5 also neglects theoretical and practical concerns regarding the adequacy of criminal justice to give effect to the right to know. Recent practice further shows some decrease in the effectiveness of truth commissions. The issue of archives is in practice often only an afterthought and needs to be reinvigorated.

A revised version of Principle 5 should move from a static institutional framework, which prescribes a holistic transitional justice tool-box approach, to a more dynamic functional approach, which looks creatively at what kind of existing and new interventions could take on the function of guarantees to give effect to the right to know. Such an approach would enable the making of linkages to other fields, such as peace-building and development, and thus respond more adequately to contextual challenges, especially in situations of fragility. It would also allow more space for informal processes that are trusted and used more frequently by local communities in the aftermath of atrocities. A functional approach would further allow that guarantees grow more organically along the way and take into account long-term, even inter-generational, needs that serious human rights violations trigger in a society.

B. Contextual and Historical Introduction

1 Principle 5 lists guarantees that states must take to give effect to the right to know. The Principle does not present an exhaustive list of mechanisms that could fulfil such a guarantee, but highlights the judiciary and truth commissions (or other commissions of inquiry), as well as archives, as possible institutions. From a literal reading of the Principle there seems to be, however, a certain hierarchy of mechanisms suggested, by assigning only a complementary nature to non-judicial processes and giving a primary role to the judiciary in guaranteeing the right to know. Among the non-judicial processes, the preservation of and access to archives is considered equally mandatory.

2 There is a progressive difference between the set of Principles drafted by Joinet and that updated by Orentlicher. Principle 4 of the Joinet Principles (current Principle 5) linked the right to know more clearly to the issue of enforced disappearances.[1] This can be explained from an historical perspective. Early experiences indicate that truth commissions in the 1980s and 1990s, especially in Latin America, had very narrow mandates, giving these commissions predominantly a fact-finding and victims-tracing function for cases concerned with disappeared persons.[2] Principle 4 in the Joinet Principles also does not assign a role to the courts in guaranteeing the right to know. The Principle speaks only about 'extrajudicial commissions of inquiry'. The Principle in the Joinet version is also a prelude to the more specific part in the Principles addressing standards for the establishment and operation of extrajudicial commissions of inquiry, such as guarantees for their independence and impartiality, guarantees for persons implicated, and guarantees for witnesses and victims.

3 Building on this, Principle 5 of the Updated Principles is up-graded to a stand-alone principle. It reflects the focus on criminal justice as a guarantee for the right to know that existed in the early 2000s, especially with the entry into force of the Rome Statute in 2002. Principle 5 also reflects the growing experience on truth commissions since the Joinet Principles. It assigns to truth commissions, alongside the victims-tracing function, a strong fact-finding function for all kinds of serious human rights violations, not only enforced disappearances. Furthermore, it emphasizes the role of truth-seeking mechanisms to prevent the disappearance of evidence, therefore reinforcing the tendency in the early 2000s to look at the right to know from a criminal justice perspective.

4 Interesting is that Orentlicher still makes a distinction between the right to the truth, which is the focus of Principle 2, and the right to know, on which Principle 5 suggests specific guarantees. Only for the latter are guarantees prescribed in the Set of Principles.[3]

5 To sum up, in the Orentlicher Updated Principles, guarantees to give effect to the right to know for serious human rights violations are mainly associated with fact-finding by an independent and impartial judiciary or a truth commission, or the preservation of and access to archives. Primacy is given to judicial processes, while non-judicial processes, such as truth commissions, are seen as complementary measures.[4] It is worth mentioning

[1] Louis Joinet, Special Rapporteur, *Revised Final Report on the question of the impunity of perpetrators of human rights violations (civil and political)*, UN Doc E/CN.4/Sub.2/1997/20/Rev.1 (2 October 1997).

[2] See the National Commission on the Enforced Disappearance of Persons (CONADEP) in Argentina, Decree/Decreto 187/83 (15 December 1983).

[3] See UN Doc E/CN.4/2005/102/Add.1 (8 February 2005), Principle 5, p 7. See also the commentary to Principle 2 in this volume, by Dermot Groome.

[4] This approach is followed by the Office of the High Commissioner for Human Rights (OHCHR) *Rule-of-Law Tools for Post-Conflict Situations: Truth Commissions* (OHCHR 2006) 27.

that this approach is somehow at odds with the 2004 Report of the UN Secretary-General on the rule of law and transitional justice, which calls for a comprehensive and integrated approach to transitional justice, including the right to know.[5] The 2004 Report does not stipulate any hierarchy among and within the four pillars respectively. This approach is also followed by the 2011 Human Rights Council Resolution establishing the mandate of the UN Special Rapporteur on the promotion of Truth, Justice, Reparation and Guarantees of non-recurrence.[6] This leads to some in-consistency among different international policy documents.

Recent years have seen few standard-setting developments related to the question of guarantees for the right to know. The bi-annual Human Rights Council Resolution on the right to truth sponsored by Argentina has focused on areas such as forensics[7] and on archives,[8] but without specific standard-setting elements. On archives, the UN Special Rapporteur in 2015 published a set of general recommendations on archives and truth commissions, addressing a current gap in standards setting in this area.[9] 6

C. Theoretical Framework

Looking first at the different legal sources of the right to know and its interpretation, we find only very little guidance as to what appropriate guarantees should look like in order to give effect to this right. In the case of specific treaty obligations, the International Convention for the Protection of All Persons from Enforced Disappearance (ICPPED)[10] reaffirms in Article 24 the right of each victim to know the truth about the enforced disappearance, but leaves it to each state party to take 'appropriate measures in this regard'. In some specific cases, however, the Convention mandates criminal justice as the appropriate mechanism.[11] 7

The soft law standards that have been developed by the Human Rights Council and the General Assembly in the area of the right to know have generally placed the right in the context of contributions to end impunity. This provides for a clear purpose that the right to know should fulfil, namely to lead to accountability, understood in the majority of case as criminal accountability.[12] This approach at the international level has 8

[5] See Report of the Secretary-General, The rule of law and transitional justice in conflict and post-conflict societies,UN Doc S /2004/616 (23 August 2004).

[6] UNHRC Resolution (Res) 18/7 (13 October 2011), preambular para 10.

[7] UNHRC Res 10/26 (27 March 2009).

[8] UNHRC Res 21/7 (10 October 2012); UNGA Res 68/165 (2 December 2013).

[9] *Report of the Special Rapporteur on the promotion of truth, justice, reparation and guarantees of non-recurrence*, UN Doc A/HRC/30/42 (7 September 2015), Annex, 'Set of general recommendations for truth commissions and archives', 27.

[10] International Convention for the Protection of All Persons from Enforced. Disappearance (open for signature 6 February 2007, entered into force 23 December 2010) 88 UNTS 25 (ICPPED).

[11] See Art 6 ICPPED.

[12] UNHRC Res 12/12 (12 October 2009), para 1 and Res 9/11, para 1; UNGA Res 68/165 (2 December 2013) , operative para 1; UN Doc E/CN.4/2006/91 (8 February 2006) and UN Doc A/HRC/5/7 (7 June 2007), both documents with further references; CAT/C/COL/CO/4 (2010) para 27; UN Doc A/HRC/16/48 (26 January 2011), para 39; UN Doc A/HRC/22/52 (1 March 2013), paras 23–26, 32–34; UN Doc A/HRC/7/3/Add.3 (15 January 2008), para 82; UN Doc A/HRC/14/23 (20 April 2010), para 34; see also jurisprudence of Inter-American Court for Human Rights (IACtHR) in *Digest of Latin American Jurisprudence on International Crimes* (Due Process of Law Foundation 2010) 251; JE Méndez, 'In Defense of Transitional Justice' in AJ McAdams (ed), *Transitional Justice and the Rule of Law in New Democracies* (Notre Dame Press 1997) 1–27.

informed the way guarantees have been designed in practice, namely, focusing mainly on institutions that provide some form of investigative and redress function, such as courts and truth commissions, with a strong bias towards addressing serious civil and political rights violations.[13]

9 Some critics of this approach, which gives primacy to criminal accountability, have highlighted the impossibility of 'perfect justice' in times of transitions and called for a more pragmatic, compromise-driven approach that takes into account context-specific dilemmas.[14] Guarantees under such an approach are much broader than the current transitional justice tool-box, and include in some cases amnesties, traditional justice models, and community-based reconciliation processes. This conception of transitional justice as a 'vehicle for crafting complex compromises' is somehow at odds with the above-mentioned fight against impunity approach under international law, which calls for 'absolute justice'.[15] A discussion of guarantees has to take into account these existing differences.

10 Regarding the role of criminal justice as a guarantee for the fulfilment of the right to know, critics have contested from very early on the truth-seeking potential of criminal trials in the face of mass atrocities, in particular due to the inherent limitations of trials, which by their very nature seek individual criminal responsibility by establishing the guilt of individual perpetrators beyond reasonable doubt.[16] Current debates on criminal justice acknowledge these limitations, and move more in the direction of seeing trials as a process of accounting within a society that has been tormented by serious abuse and less as vehicles for punishment.[17] Current discussions in Colombia around the peace agreement, however, still show tensions between a more absolutist understanding of human rights prosecution and a more pragmatic approach based on compromises that need to be made regarding perfect justice in post-conflict situations.[18]

11 Lastly, there are different theoretical understandings between human rights approaches towards guarantees seeking to give effect to the right to know and approaches taken in this respect in the humanitarian field. In case of an international armed conflict, Additional

[13] DM Sharp, 'Emancipating Transitional Justice from the Bonds of the Paradigmatic Transition' (2014) 9(1) *International Journal of Transitional Justice* 150–69; L Arbour, 'Economic and Social Justice for Societies in Transitions' (2007) 40:1 International Law and Politics 1–28. For the context of archives, see the commentary to Principle 14 in this volume.

[14] Sharp, n 1; F Ní Aoláin (2017), *Transitional Justice and the European Convention on Human Rights* (Geneva Academy Briefing No 10).

[15] The impunity approach has recently been allied with an emerging emphasis in transitional justice on transformative and holistic transitional justice, which seeks, at least in some cases, to address inequality and marginalization: see P Gready and S Robbins, 'From Transitional to Transformative Justice: A New Agenda for Practice' (2014) 8(3) International Journal of Transitional Justice 339–61. However, others have argued for a more pragmatic approach to transitional justice and the concern of 'overloading' the capacity of transitional justice: see, eg, P McAuliffe, 'The Prospects for Transitional Justice in Catalyzing Socioeconomic Justice in Postconflict States: A Critical Assessment in Light of Somalia's Transition' (2014) 14:2 Northeast African Studies 77–110; K Andrieu, 'Dealing with a "New" Grievance: Should Anticorruption be Part of the Transitional Justice Agenda' (2012) 11:4 Journal of Human Rights 537–57; L Waldorf, 'Anticipating the Past: Transitional Justice and Socio-Economic Wrongs' (2012) 21:2 Social and Legal Studies 171–86.

[16] M Minow, *Between Vengeance and Forgiveness: Facing History After Genocide and Mass Violence* (Beacon Press 1998) 25.

[17] RA Duff, *Process, not Punishment: The Importance of Criminal Trials for Transitional and Transnational Justice*, Draft on file with the author; see also MA Drumbl, *Atrocity, Punishment, and International Law* (CUP 2007); P Seils, *Squaring Colombia's Circle, The Objectives of Punishment and the Pursuit of Peace*, International Center for Transitional Justice (ICTJ) Briefing, June 2015.

[18] Seils, n 17.

Protocol I to the Geneva Convention lists, in Section III on 'Missing and Dead Persons', several guarantees that need to be taken into account in order to fulfil 'the right of families to know the fate of their relatives'.[19] These mainly include measures in respect of victim tracing, but also measures in the event of death, exhumation of human remains, as well as preservation and access to grave sites. Measures listed therein, however, regard the issue of the right to know entirely as a humanitarian concern, while justice and the fight against impunity are not viewed as part of this perspective. Yet the linkages between the scope and nature of guarantees under a human rights approach and those under humanitarian law need to be explored further without the one colonizing the other.

D. Practice

The following paragraphs will look at some practical trends regarding the guarantees listed in Principle 5. The list of issues does not claim to be comprehensive, but it is intended to give a flavour of some of the current practical challenges regarding guarantees that give effect to the right to know. 12

Principle 5 mentions truth commissions as one of the appropriate mechanisms that provide a guarantee for the right to know. The last decades have seen a steady increase in officially state-sanctioned truth commissions.[20] Truth seeking has also been extensively used at the international level through international commissions of inquiry and fact-finding missions. In spite of the increase in use of truth commissions, their effectiveness on the ground has been questioned. The UN Special Rapporteur, in his 2013 Report, highlights a series of alarming practical challenges truth commissions are currently facing, including the selection of commissioners, a trend of overly broad mandates, and the lack of follow up to commissions' recommendations.[21] 13

Recent years have also seen challenges to implementing transitional justice mechanisms, including guarantees for the right to know, in conflict and post-conflict situations. The usage in these situations constitutes a shift to their original usage in post-authoritarian contexts. The origin of the transition (eg authoritarianism or conflict) generates differences in the needs that transitional justice mechanisms, including measures that are intended to give effect to the right to know, are meant to address. For example, part of the aim of transitions in post-authoritarian situations in Latin American countries of the Southern Cone was understood in terms of the recovery of both institutions and traditions that had been brutally disrupted by dictatorship.[22] Truth seeking contributed to this endeavour by addressing the wide-scale denial of responsibility of previous regimes.[23] Denial does 14

[19] Protocol Additional to the Geneva Conventions of 12 August 1949, and related to the protection of victims of international armed conflicts (hereinafter 'Protocol I') (8 June 1977) 1125 UNTS 3.

[20] Examples of state-sponsored truth-seeking processes include, among others: the National Commission on Disappeared persons (CONADEP) in Argentina; the Truth and Reconciliation Commission in South Africa; the Commission for Reception, Truth and Reconciliation (CAVR) in East Timor; the Truth and Reconciliation Commission in Peru; the Equity and Reconciliation Commission in Morocco; the Truth and Reconciliation Commission in Sierra Leone. For more on state-sponsored truth commission, see: M Freeman, *Truth Commissions and Procedural Fairness* (CUP 2006); NJ Kritz (ed), *Transitional Justice: how emerging democracies reckon with former regime*, vols I–III (United States Institute of Peace Press 1995); PB Hayner, *Unspeakable Truths: Confronting State Terror and Atrocity* (2nd edn, Routledge 2011).

[21] *Report of the Special Rapporteur on the promotion of truth, justice, reparation and guarantees of non-recurrence*, UN Doc A/HRC/24/42 (28 August 2013).

[22] Ibid, para 27. [23] Ibid, para 28.

not play the same role in post-conflict settings. What is often needed in such situations, from the perspective of the right to know, are measures and processes that explain the causes and consequences of the conflict, especially giving visibility to marginalization and inequality.[24]

15 There is still a trend in practice that measures in the area of the right to know are designed on the basis of pre-established formulae that take a holistic approach to dealing with the past, including the full implementation of the four pillars of transitional justice. These approaches are, however, not fitting the context in which they are supposed to be applied.[25] One current example is the Central African Republic, where the peace agreement foresees the implementation of the whole four-pillar structure of transitional justice, in a country that has a central government without power, weak or non-existing institutions, most of its territory controlled by different non-state actors, and no real civil society.[26] But even countries like Colombia, which are more sophisticated in terms of institutionalization, struggle to meet a holistic transitional justice approach.[27] Even in cases where national consultations are organized on transitional justice lines, such as in Tunisia, the outcome or the agenda is often pre-determined by the demands of the international community regarding what such consultations should say on justice, including the right to know.[28]

16 A final area where there have been increasing challenges is the participation of victims. The importance of putting victims at the centre of transitional justice, including in truth-seeking processes, is now widely accepted.[29] Without the participation of victims, consensus has emerged that measures and processes of transitional justice will lack internal and external legitimacy. Victims have, however, played only a peripheral role in transitional justice, and encounter great difficulties in influencing the design, implementation, and outcomes of its processes, including those institutions listed in Principle 5. In practice, processes are also often overly focused on institutions, informal processes are frequently overlooked, victims are marginalized, and effective protection systems are not available. The finding of a recent empirical study by Impunity Watch is that despite a clear policy focus in recent years on victim participation in transitional justice mechanisms, its actual impact and effectiveness remain uncertain and illusive.[30]

E. Critical Assessment

17 From Principle 4 of the Joinet Principles to current Principle 5, there has been a clear expansion of guarantees to give effect to the right to know. Guarantees include judicial and non-judicial mechanisms. The focus is on courts, truth commissions, and archives. Criminal justice is given a privileged position. Reparations are not given a specific

[24] Arbour, n 13, 8.

[25] V Nesiah, Research Report (2016), *Transitional Justice Practice: Looking Back, Moving Forward, Scoping Study* (Impunity Watch) 49.

[26] For background on transitional justice and the Central African Republic, see the website of Centre for Humanitarian Dialogue <www.hdcentre.org/activities/central-african-republic/> accessed 22 November 2017.

[27] Seils, n 16.

[28] Impunity Watch, *Victim participation in Tunisia's transitional justice process* (2015) <www.impunitywatch.org/docs/6.Victim_participation_report_ENG_SR_131015_FINAL.pdf> accessed 22 November 2017.

[29] *Report of the Special Rapporteur on the promotion of truth, justice, reparation and guarantees of non-recurrence*, UN Doc A/HRC/34/62 (27 December 2016).

[30] The study is on file with author. The publication of the study is scheduled for early 2018.

function as a guarantee for the right to know. The list in Principle 5 reflects a traditional human rights understanding on what guarantees should look like.

18 As has been shown elsewhere in this volume, the expansion of guarantees for the right to know has been effected without a full understanding of the contours of the right.[31] There are also some concerns, both in theory and in practice, that have been raised here on the appropriateness of the 'classical' transitional justice tool-box reflected in Principle 5, to adequately address the challenges faced in the aftermath of mass atrocities. The challenges increase when these mechanisms are applied to situations of conflict or in contexts where there is a high degree of fragility and instability. The current framework also has a bias towards reckoning only with civil and political rights violations. The question whether the mechanisms proposed in Principle 5 would be functionally adequate to address economic social and cultural rights violations is thus left open.

19 Ways to move forward could include a change of perspective. A revised version of Principle 5 could move from the heavy and rather static institutional framework, which prescribes a holistic transitional justice tool-box approach, to a more dynamic functional approach that looks creatively at what kind of existing and new interventions could take on the function of guarantees to give effect to the right to know. Such an approach would enable linkages to other fields, such as peacebuilding and development, and thus respond more adequately to contextual challenges, especially in situations of fragility.[32] It would also allow more space for informal processes that are trusted and used more frequently by local communities in the aftermath of atrocities. A functional approach would also allow guarantees to grow more organically along the way, and take into account long-term, even inter-generational, needs that serious human rights violations trigger in a society.

20 The goal of a revised version of Principle 5 should be to look rather for 'good enough' approaches that fit the context, especially in situations of fragility or failed states, and not for 'best practice' models, which even western governments would not be able to meet. A more moderate approach will also help to manage expectations, provide space for local solutions, and show some concrete progress on the ground. Leading organizations in the field of transitional justice, such as the ICTJ, are currently re-thinking their strategic approach towards transitional justice, moving away from integrated or holistic approaches towards a broader set, or a 'basket of ideas', in the area of acknowledgement, accountability, and reform, that will vary widely in implementation, depending on the local context.[33] Discussions on appropriate guarantees to give effect to the right to know should be seen in this light.

Bibliography

Andrieu, K, 'Dealing with a "New" Grievance: Should Anticorruption Be Part of the Transitional Justice Agenda' (2012) 11:4 Journal of Human Rights 537–57.

[31] See the commentary to Principle 2 in this volume, by Dermot Groome.

[32] See, eg, the approach taken in the EU policy on transitional justice, linking transitional justice, development, and peacebuilding: Council of the European Union, *EU's support to transitional justice—Council conclusions* (16 November 2015) <data.consilium.europa.eu/doc/document/ST-13576-2015-INIT/en/pdf> accessed 22 November 2017.

[33] International Center for Transitional Justice (ICTJ), *Pursuing Justice in Changing Times*, Strategic Plan 2015–2018.

Arbour, L, 'Economic and Social Justice for Societies in Transitions' (2007) 40:1 International Law and Politics 1–28.

Council of the European Union, *EU's support to transitional justice—Council conclusions* (16 November 2015) <data.consilium.europa.eu/doc/document/ST-13576-2015-INIT/en/pdf>.

Drumbl, MA, *Atrocity, Punishment, and International Law* (CUP 2007).

Freeman, M, *Truth Commissions and Procedural Fairness* (CUP 2006).

Gready, P and Robbins, S, 'From Transitional to Transformative Justice: A New Agenda for Practice' (2014) 8(3) International Journal of Transitional Justice 339–61.

Hayner, PB, *Unspeakable Truths: Confronting State Terror and Atrocity* (2nd edn, Routledge 2011).

Impunity Watch, *Victim Participation in Tunisia's transitional justice process* (2015) at <www.impunitywatch.org/docs/6.Victim_participation_report_ENG_SR_131015_FINAL.pdf>.

McAuliffe, P, 'The Prospects for Transitional Justice in Catalyzing Socioeconomic Justice in Postconflict States: A Critical Assessment in Light of Somalia's Transition' (2014) 14:2 Northeast African Studies 77–110.

Méndez, JE, 'In Defense of Transitional Justice' in AJ McAdams (ed), *Transitional Justice and the Rule of Law in New Democracies* (1997) 1–27.

National Commission on the Enforced Disappearance of Persons (CONADEP) in Argentina, Decree/Decreto 187/83 (15 December 1983).

Nesiah, V, Research Report (2016), *Transitional Justice Practice: Looking Back, Moving Forward, Scoping Study* (Impunity Watch).

Ní Aoláin, F (2017), *Transitional Justice and the European Convention on Human Rights* (Geneva Academy Briefing No 10).

Report of the Special Rapporteur on the promotion of truth, justice, reparation and guarantees of non-recurrence, UN Doc A/HRC/24/42 (28 August 2013).

Report of the Special Rapporteur on the promotion of truth, justice, reparation and guarantees of non-recurrence, UN Doc A/HRC/30/42 (7 September 2015), Annex, 'Set of general recommendations for truth commissions and archives'.

Report of the Special Rapporteur on the promotion of truth, justice, reparation and guarantees of non-recurrence, UN Doc A/HRC/34/62 (27 December 2016).

Seils, P, *Squaring Colombia's Circle, The Objectives of Punishment and the Pursuit of Peace*, ICTJ Briefing, June 2015.

Sharp, DM, 'Emancipating Transitional Justice from the Bonds of the Paradigmatic Transition' (2014) 9(1) International Journal of Transitional Justice 150–69.

Waldorf, L, 'Anticipating the Past: Transitional Justice and Socio-Economic Wrongs' (2012) 21:2 Social and Legal Studies 171–86.

B.

COMMISSIONS OF INQUIRY

Principle 6. The Establishment and Role of Truth Commissions

Ilya Nuzov and Mark Freeman[1]

To the greatest extent possible, decisions to establish a truth commission, define its terms of reference and determine its composition should be based upon broad public consultations in which the views of victims and survivors especially are sought. Special efforts should be made to ensure that men and women participate in these deliberations on a basis of equality.

In recognition of the dignity of victims and their families, investigations undertaken by truth commissions should be conducted with the object in particular of securing recognition of such parts of the truth as were formerly denied.

Introduction

There are three main recommendations contained in Principle 6. Before discussing them in detail, it is important to make two general observations.

First, Principle 6 is limited in scope to one kind of commission of inquiry: the truth commission. It does not purport to apply to commissions of inquiry more broadly.

Second, the Principle focuses on two separate aspects of truth commissions, which are treated separately in this chapter: their establishment (paragraph 1) and their role (paragraph 2). In this regard, its scope overlaps with other principles, including Principle 8, which deals with the terms of reference of commissions of inquiry and thus a priori with a truth commission's establishment and role.

I. Paragraph 1 of Principle 6

A. Summary of findings

Public debate on the establishment of a truth commission tends to arise through a variety of channels, including the media, the non-governmental organization (NGO) sector, and victim groups. It is common for national and international conferences to be organized in order to consider the question. Politicians may incorporate the idea into their electoral campaigns. 1

The practice of broad consultations with the public in defining the mandate and appointing commissioners is a relatively recent phenomenon. State practice shows that truth commissions can begin their work with a greater initial legitimacy when they emerge through a process of consultation with civil society, including victim groups, and after careful consideration of what kind of commission and commissioners would be most appropriate for the particular context.[2] The principal downside of consultation is the length of time it can require. 2

[1] The authors would like to thank Clara Martinez Ginès for her research support.

[2] Office of the United Nations High Commissioner for Human Rights (OHCHR), *Rule-of-Law Tools for Post-Conflict States. Truth Commissions*, UN Doc HR/PUB/06/1 (2006) (hereinafter 'Rule of Law Report') 7;

B. Historical and contextual background

3 The first paragraph of Principle 6 deals with the establishment of truth commissions. It is aspirational: it recommends criteria that can be applied '[t]o the greatest extent possible'. The paragraph encompasses three different aspects of the issue: the preliminary 'decision to establish a truth commission' (ie the social and political process, or debate, about whether and why a country may benefit from the establishment of a truth commission), the subsequent creation of its 'terms of reference' (ie its formal legal mandate), and the related determination of its 'composition' (ie, the selection of the commissioners and any other equivalent posts within the commission). Regarding all three, Principle 6 advocates the importance of 'broad consultations', emphasizing the need to seek the views of 'victims and survivors especially'. The paragraph also recommends that consultations and deliberations take place on a basis of equality among men and women.

4 This first paragraph of Principle 6 did not appear in the original Joinet Principles. This may be because broad consultations with the public were not common at the time Louis Joinet was writing about truth commissions. However, the expectation of broad participation by victims and other citizens in designing policies for combating impunity (including for truth commissions) has increased with time.[3] As such, the 2005 Commentary on the Updated Principles recommends that 'the decision whether to establish a truth commission should be the product of national deliberations when local conditions allow such deliberations to take place freely and safely'.[4]

5 The aspirational nature of Principle 6 reflects numerous practical challenges of carrying out broad consultations, which are often difficult in transitional contexts in which victims or survivors of repression still fear for their safety (eg, El Salvador), or in which an open consultation process could jeopardize a fragile accord or behind-the-scenes negotiations.

6 Some of the earliest truth commission mandates were established by presidential decrees, without public or victim consultations. As a practical matter, a presidential decree can be put in place more quickly than ordinary legislation, and can mitigate the negative influence of a legislature dominated by political parties that are hostile to the truths a commission eventually could expose. At the same time, the legislative process can potentially generate broader political support for a commission and, as such, result in greater political legitimacy.[5]

7 In general, today more emphasis is placed on the benefits of building a broad base of support for a commission among several important constituencies, including human rights groups, victim organizations, and other independent actors—even if the process involves inconvenient delays.

Report of the Special Rapporteur on the promotion of truth, justice, reparation and guarantees of non-recurrence, Pablo de Greiff, UN Doc A/HRC/24/42 (28 August 2013) (hereinafter 'Report of the Special Rapporteur') paras 58–59.

[3] *Report of the independent expert to update the Set of Principles to combat impunity, Diane Orentlicher, Updated set of principles for the protection and promotion of human rights through action to combat impunity,* UN Doc E/CN.4/2005/102 (8 February 2005) (hereinafter 'Commentary to the Updated Principles') para 7.

[4] Ibid, para 22.

[5] Rule of Law Report, n 2, at para 12. See also M Freeman, *Truth Commissions and Procedural Fairness* (CUP 2006) 27–28.

C. Theoretical framework

Although there is no legal requirement to create truth commissions, states have a variety of obligations to investigate international crimes and human rights abuses when they are committed,[6] and to disclose the truth surrounding these violations.[7] A truth commission can constitute one means of making good on these obligations.[8] 8

The Commentary to the Updated Principles and other soft law sources assert that broad participation in deliberations for the establishment of truth commissions can serve several purposes in the fight against impunity.[9] First, public participation (including by former combatants) can inspire greater public support for the resulting policy and increase trust in government institutions. Second, participation of victims can help ensure that policies for combating impunity effectively respond to actual needs and help restore a sense of citizenship to those denied the protection of the law in the past. Third, broad consultations can serve as a guarantee that policies for combating impunity are themselves rooted in processes that ensure some form of public accountability.[10] 9

The principle that policies for combating impunity should be informed by public consultations is grounded in the notion that there is no 'one-size-fits-all' response to serious violations of human rights. The UN Secretary-General has noted that the fight against impunity must above all 'be based on national assessments, national participation 10

[6] Some treaties provide for the duty to investigate explicitly. See, eg, UN General Assembly, International Convention for the Protection of All Persons from Enforced Disappearance (ICED), UNGA A/RES/61/177, 20 December 2006, Art 6; Geneva Convention for the Amelioration of the Condition of the Wounded and Sick in Armed Forces in the Field (12 August 1949) 75 UNTS 31, Art 49; Geneva Convention for the Amelioration of the Condition of Wounded, Sick and Shipwrecked Members of Armed Forces at Sea (12 August 1949) 75 UNTS 85, Art 50; Geneva Convention Relative to the Treatment of Prisoners of War (12 August 1949) 75 UNTS 135, Art 129; Geneva Convention Relative to the Protection of Civilian Persons in Time of War, 12 August 1949 (75 UNTS 287) Art 14; Convention Against Torture and Other Cruel, Inhuman or Degrading Treatment or Punishment, UNGA Res 39/46 (10 December 1984) 1465 UNTS 85, Art 12. By contrast, human rights treaty bodies usually derive this obligation from the substantive provisions of their respective treaties. See, eg, Human Rights Committee, *General Comment 6: The Right to Life (Art 6)* (30 April 1982) para 4; ECtHR, *Cyprus v Turkey* (Judgment) (ECtHR, 10 May 2001), paras 131–32 (Art 2, right to life); *Velásquez-Rodríguez v Honduras* (Judgment) (Merits) IACtHR Series C no 1 (29 July 1988) para 181 (Art 1, obligation to respect rights provided for in the convention).

[7] The right to truth has been expressly mentioned in connection with other established rights in a number of international treaties and soft law instruments. See, eg, Additional Protocol I to the Geneva Conventions of 12 August 1949 (AP I); ICED, Art 24(2); The United Nations Basic Principles and Guidelines on the Right to a Remedy and Reparation for Victims of Gross Violations of International Human Rights Law and Serious Violations of International Humanitarian Law, UN Doc A/RES/60/147 (21 March 2006) Arts 11(c), 24; United Nations Human Rights Commission, Res 9/11, Right to the truth, UN Doc A/HRC/RES/9/11 (24 September 2008); OHCHR, *Study on the right to truth*, UN Doc E/CN.4/2006/91 (8 February 2006). This right has also been reaffirmed by international courts. See, eg, *Al Nashiri v Poland*, App no 28761/11 (Judgment) (ECtHR, 24 July 2014) para 495; *Myrna Mack Chang v Guatemala* (Judgment) (Merits, reparations and costs) IACtHR Series C no 101 (25 November 2013) para 274; *Bámaca Velásquez v Guatemala* (Judgment) (Merits) IACtHR Series C no 70 (25 November 2000) para 77. For the emergence of right to truth as an independent right in and of itself, see, eg, Y Naqvi, 'The right to the truth in international law: fact or fiction?' International Review of the Red Cross, vol 88, no 862, June 2006, 245–273, 256–57.

[8] See, eg, OHCHR, Res 2005/66, Right to the truth, UN Doc E/CN.4/RES/2005/66.

[9] The *UN Manual on the Effective Prevention and Investigation of Extra-Legal, Arbitrary and Summary Executions* (hereinafter '*UN Manual*'), although applicable more broadly to commissions of inquiry, provides that the public should be notified about the establishment of the commission through a broad publicity campaign: Art 11.

[10] Commentary to the Updated Principles, n 3, para 7.

and national needs and aspirations'.[11] There is accompanying literature on the notion of 'localizing' transitional justice processes.[12]

11 In the view of the OHCHR, consultative processes should pursue two basic aims: increasing the understanding of a truth commission and strengthening its terms of reference.[13] As a means to avoid an elite-driven process, the OHCHR recommends incorporating views from all parts of a country (even the most remote or inaccessible ones) and from 'all major sectors, especially those communities most affected by the violence'.[14]

12 Public involvement in the development of a truth commission's terms of reference can also be a useful way to enable the introduction of new elements drawn from past truth commission experiences in other countries.

13 One of the defining characteristics of truth commissions is their relative independence from the state. But independence is partly a question of fact and partly a question of perception. The sponsoring authority must enjoy the minimal credibility necessary to avoid a commission's being rejected before its birth for lack of independence. Public support for the establishment of a truth commission as expressed through the presence of a vigorous and engaged civil society—and in particular representative victims' groups, human rights groups, religious leaders, and intellectuals—can help imbue a commission with greater legitimacy.[15]

14 Truth commissions will tend to garner the greatest support if their members, and not merely their mandates, are determined through a consultative process. Among other options, the process 'may include inviting nominations from the public and forming a representative selection panel (appointed by a variety of sectors and societal groupings) to vet the nominations and interview the finalists, recommending the final commissioners to the appointing authority'.[16]

15 A meritorious appointment process can enhance the ability of future triers of fact to have confidence in the commission's findings, inasmuch as the reliability of any commission's findings will depend in part on having had a membership considered to be independent and impartial.

16 Concerning gender equality in participation, numerous UN resolutions and reports confirm the heightened focus on incorporating women's experiences and views in transitional contexts.[17]

D. Practice

17 Many of the earliest truth commissions arose through presidential decrees, with the president setting out the commission's mandate without much public debate.[18] In Argentina

[11] Ibid, para 9.

[12] On recent debates regarding the need to 'localize' transitional justice, see, eg, K McEvoy and L McGregor (eds), *Transitional Justice from Below: Grassroots Activism and the Struggle for Change* (Hart Publishing 2008).

[13] Rule of Law Report, n 2, 7. [14] Ibid.

[15] M Freeman and P Hayner, 'Truth–Telling' in *Reconciliation after Violent Conflict: A Handbook* (Institute for Democracy and Electoral Asistance, 2003) 129.

[16] Rule of Law Report, n 2, 14.

[17] See, eg, UN Security Council Res 1325 (31 October 2000) and 1820 (19 June 2008); Report of the Secretary-General, *The rule of law and transitional justice in conflict and post-conflict societies*, UN Doc S/2004/616 (23 August 2004), para 3; Report of the OHCHR, *Analytical Study Focusing on Gender-Based and Sexual Violence in Relation to Transitional Justice*, UN Doc A/HRC/27/21 (30 June 2014) (hereinafter 'Analytical Study on Gender-Based Violence') para 21.

[18] P Hayner, *Unspeakable Truths. Transitional Justice and the Challenge of Truth Commissions* (2nd edn, Routledge 2011) 210.

and Chile, the new civilian presidents decided that passing national legislation in Congress would either take too much time, or require too many compromises. Both commissions have been considered highly successful nonetheless. The commissions in Haiti, Sri Lanka, Chad, Nepal, and Uganda were also put in place through presidential action, with little public debate on their terms of reference.[19]

Today, it is more common for truth commissions to arise through legislation (eg Kenya, Brazil). One of the most famous commissions, the South African Truth and Reconciliation Commission, was established by the elected parliament after considerable input from civil society, two international conferences to explore the transitional justice policies instituted in other countries, and hundreds of hours of public and private hearings.[20] **18**

In Nepal, the initial executive order for a truth commission was successfully challenged in the Supreme Court, which ordered the Government to amend the prospective commission with the help of organizations representing victims' interests and human rights experts.[21] The subsequent Parliamentary Act created two separate commissions, which represented an improvement from the previous version.[22] **19**

As officially-sponsored bodies, the state in which a truth commission operates necessarily plays a formal role in the appointment of commissioners. In the 1980s and 1990s, the members of most truth commissions were appointed through procedures that relied on the good judgement of the appointing authority, with little consultation of civil society. This was the case, for example, in Bolivia, Argentina, Chad, Chile, Haiti, Morocco, Sri Lanka, and Uganda. Since then, the selection of commissioners has increasingly operated through more creative and consultative processes.[23] This was the case in Sierra Leone, Peru, Timor-Leste, Ivory Coast, Liberia, Togo, and Kenya. In Canada, the Truth and Reconciliation Commission's mandate explicitly called for consultations with the organizations representing indigenous victims' interests.[24] **20**

South Africa set an important precedent by the broad public debate that accompanied both the drafting of the truth commission's terms of reference and the public nomination and selection process for its commissioners.[25] Inspired by this precedent, in Sierra Leone candidates were vetted by the former armed opposition, the president, the religious community, and human rights groups.[26] In Ecuador, a number of commissioners were selected directly by NGOs. In Togo, the president asked for nominations from a number of civil society organizations and chose from among them, resulting in a more independent body.[27] Likewise, a national consultative process, led by a steering committee of representatives of human rights, women's and other civil society groups, helped to refine the terms of reference and the composition of the Commission for Reception, Truth, and Reconciliation in East Timor.[28] By contrast, commissioners of the DRC's Truth and **21**

[19] Ibid, 210–11; Track Impunity Always (TRIAL) Report, *Written Information for the Consideration of Nepal's Second Periodic Report by the HRC*, CCPR/C/NPL/2 (February 2014) para 14.

[20] Hayner, n 18, 27. [21] TRIAL Report, n 19, para 15.

[22] OHCHR Technical Note, 'The Nepal Act on the Commission on Investigation of Disappeared Persons, Truth and Reconciliation' (2014) 2071.

[23] Freeman and Hayner, n 15, 129.

[24] Mandate for The Truth and Reconciliation Commission of Canada, Section 5, <www.trc.ca/websites/trcinstitution/index.php?p=7>.

[25] Freeman and Hayner, n 15, 129. [26] Hayner, n 18, 212. [27] Ibid, 212–13.

[28] Ibid, 39–40.

Reconciliation Commission were appointed with little consultation, and were widely perceived as dependent on political allegiances to the parties involved in the country's peace process.[29]

22 Women's voices have not tended to have a profound influence on the mandate or composition of truth commissions, whether in terms of prioritizing women's experiences at the investigation stage, or in terms of the ratio of female commissioners.[30] Few commissions have had a reasonable balance of male and female commissioners (South Africa being an early exception to the rule). Only one of the seventeen commissioners in Morocco was female, and only one of fifteen in the case of South Korea. The Liberian case may point the way forward: the commission's mandate required a certain number of women as members.[31] Since then, positive examples such as Ivory Coast (five out of ten commissioners are women) and Tunisia (the commission is chaired by a woman) have arisen. The Peruvian Truth and Reconciliation Commission established a special gender unit, while commissions in South Africa, Haiti, Kenya, Liberia, Morocco, Sierra Leone, the Solomon Islands, and East Timor conducted specific investigations of gender-based and sexual violence.[32]

E. Critical assessment

23 Truth commissions are inherently flexible and can be crafted to respond to the specific needs and circumstances of the country. While much can be learned from prior experiences in other parts of the world, it is important that any new truth commissions primarily emerge from a process of strategic planning and reflection grounded in local realities.

24 Though commendable, the recent emphasis on broad consultations has risked making consultation an end in and of itself, resulting in the delay or non-implementation of truth commissions. In places such as Nepal and Burundi, for example, there has been nearly a full decade of consultation mechanisms and processes regarding the establishment of truth commissions, resulting in a massive delay in implementation.

25 Any future revision of the first paragraph of Principle 6 should reflect the point that consultations should be broad-based *but expeditious*. The priority objective should be to establish a truth commission that is credible, but this does not necessarily require a prolonged consultation process, as readers of the current principle could wrongly infer. Tempo matters.

[29] E Gonzalez and H Varney (eds), *Truth Seeking: Elements of Creating an Effective Truth Commission* (Amnesty Commission of the Ministry of Justice of Brazil; International Center for Transitional Justice 2013) 15.

[30] This is particularly true with respect to the earlier truth commissions, such as those in Guatemala and Chile. F Ni Aoláin, D Haynes and N Cahn, *On the Frontlines: Gender War, and the Post-Conflict Process* (OUP 2011) 186.

[31] See An Act to Establish the Truth and Reconciliation Commission of Liberia (2005), s 7.

[32] Report of the Special Rapporteur, n 2, para 36; C Bell and C O'Rourke, 'Does Feminism Need a Theory of Transitional Justice? An Introductory Essay' (2007) 1.1 International Journal of Transitional Justice 23–44, 28; Analytical Study on Gender-Based Violence, n 17, paras 17–23; *Independent study on best practices, including recommendations, to assist States in strengthening their domestic capacity to combat all aspects of impunity*, UN Doc E/CN.4/2004/88 (27 February 2004) para 19(f).

II. Paragraph 2 of Principle 6

A. Summary of findings

Truth commissions generally have been consistent in their focus on helping to recognize the dignity of victims and their families, establishing and acknowledging the truth, and revealing disputed or hidden parts of a recent period of abuse. This has been particularly so with respect to uncovering outgoing regimes' practices of enforced disappearances and extrajudicial killings. It has been comparatively less so for violations that occurred in chaotic civil war contexts. 26

As an official investigative body with a focus on victims, a truth commission can help increase recognition of the dignity of victims through statement-taking and public hearings, especially if the latter are widely broadcast. Regarding its investigative priorities, there is a valid case to be made for truth commissions to seek political and social acknowledgement of truths that were formerly denied. At the same time, since the truth of certain events cannot emerge until after a commission's investigations are completed (in the absence of early and detailed confessions), a better focus is on the investigation of the most contested events and practices in order to clarify facts. Acknowledgement or recognition of those facts comes afterwards, and depends on many other variables outside a commission's control. 27

B. Historical and contextual background

The second paragraph of Principle 6, which is virtually unchanged from Louis Joinet's original formulation, focuses on the role more than on the establishment of truth commissions. The word 'role' (which appears in the title of Principle 6) is a reference to the functional end-goal that a commission is expected to serve: 'securing recognition of such parts of the truth as were formerly denied'. However, the paragraph is narrower in scope than might first appear. It does not deal with the wider range of potential objectives that a truth commission mandate might specify—from reconciliation to justice to institutional reform—nor with the equally wide range of activities that it might undertake—from victim reparation assessments to the organization of public debates and conferences. Instead, it deals only with a commission's 'investigations', and advocates that these should be conducted with the primary objective of acknowledgement of formerly-denied truths out of respect for 'the dignity of victims and their families'.[33] 28

Because truth commissions are commissions of inquiry, their primary function, a priori, is to investigate. They may be defined as: 29

> *Ad hoc*, autonomous, and victim-centered commission of inquiry set up in and authorized by a state for the primary purposes of (1) investigating and reporting on the principal causes and consequences of broad and relatively recent patterns of severe violence or repression that occurred in the state during determinate periods of abusive rule or conflict, and (2) making recommendations for their redress and future prevention.[34]

At their best, truth commissions are able to provide a measure of impartial, historical clarification capable of significantly overcoming false or revisionist accounts of the past.[35]

[33] For more on the role of 'recognition' in truth-telling, see, eg, F Haldemann, 'Another King of Justice: Transitional Justice as Recognition' (2008) 41.3 Cornell International Law Journal 675–737.

[34] Freeman, n 5, 18.

[35] Ibid, 39.

30 Truth commissions can be instrumental in investigating the whereabouts of missing persons who have disappeared during periods of armed conflict or state repression. Many of the earliest commissions arose after the fall of regimes that concealed or denied the widespread practice of enforced disappearances.[36]

31 In practical terms, an enormous amount of a truth commission's time and resources is dedicated to statement taking. Many truth commissions also conduct public hearings, public outreach, academic-style research, police-like investigation, data processing, quantitative analysis, and selected exhumations.

32 Statement taking is important in at least two ways: it advances a commission's truth-seeking objectives, and it provides an opportunity for victims and others to describe their traumatic experiences within a caring and safe environment. In the absence of statement taking, it is very difficult for a truth commission to fulfil its mission. When done well, statement taking can afford a moment of private recognition of what previously may have been denied.

33 Public hearings constitute a unique public platform for victims to recount their experiences, and thus can serve as an indirect form of acknowledgement and moral restoration for past suffering. When they are broadcast on national television and radio, they can have unrivalled impact on public awareness about past abuses. In the best cases, they can generate a society-wide debate and foster greater public sympathy for victims. These in turn can contribute to processes of recognition and reconciliation, helping secure public support for other transitional justice reforms.

C. Theoretical framework

34 As noted in the commentary to Principle 4 in this volume, public authorities have an obligation to investigate, establish, and acknowledge the truth about serious abuses of human rights and violations of international humanitarian law.[37] Principle 6 suggests that truth commissions with robust investigative capacity can help states fulfil these obligations.

35 A truth commission is a body whose essential mission is 'the vindication of human rights'.[38] As such, it must respect the fundamental dignity of all those it encounters or investigates. It is not enough merely to respect 'the dignity of victims and their families'.

D. Practice

36 Truth commissions can have a wide range of objectives. Typically they emphasize the investigation or clarification of serious past violations and the prevention of future violations. Few commissions have had an explicit objective of revealing formerly denied parts of a country's history of violations (although several early truth commissions were mandated to look only into disappearances, such as those in Argentina, Uruguay, and Sri Lanka).[39]

37 Some commission mandates (eg, Ecuador) have called for the declassification of archives.[40] This is another means of contributing to the fulfilment of the recommendation to investigate that part of the truth which has previously been denied.

[36] Hayner, n 18, 21.
[37] See 'Principle 4. The Victims' Right to Know' by Dermot Groome.
[38] Freeman, n 5, 146.
[39] Hayner, n 18, 75.
[40] Peru Truth Commission to Impede Impunity, Ministerial Accord no 305, 3 May 2007, Art 2(b) <www.usip.org/sites/default/files/ROL/Mandato%20de%20Ecuador.pdf>.

The call for truth often leads to the discovery of burial sites. The Peruvian truth commission documented 4,600 clandestine burial sites throughout the country—a number that surprised even the commissioners.[41] This kind of discovery can also help in overcoming formerly denied truths. 38

In South Africa, the Truth and Reconciliation Commission took testimony from over 21,000 victims and witnesses, 2,000 of whom appeared in public hearings.[42] Media coverage of the Commission was extensive, thus contributing to public awareness, if not always recognition, of formerly-denied truths. In addition to its research and investigations, the Morocco Equity and Reconciliation Commission held a number of victim hearings, which were broadcast nationally (as well as regionally on Al-Jazeera television). The Peruvian truth commission was the first in Latin America to organize victim-centred public hearings. 39

Some truth commissions' work has compelled national heads of state to issue broad public apologies (eg, Peru) or individualized apologies to victims (eg, Chile). Depending on the perceived sincerity of such apologies, these may constitute a form of moral reparation for victims and a recognition of their inherent human dignity.[43] 40

E. Critical assessment

Truth commissions are official bodies that focus on victims—on their experiences, views, needs, and preferences. Yet even the most successful ones have been criticized for 'holding the mission of reconciliation above that of finding the truth'.[44] Although a reasonable balance between these must be found, a truth commission would do well to keep front and centre its larger objective of providing a measure of impartial, historical clarification to counter false or revisionist accounts of the past. 41

Since what is fact and what is myth cannot be predetermined, a preferable formulation of the second paragraph of Principle 6 would place the priority on investigation of the most contested events and practices. This would avoid the inference that, ex ante, a truth commission has at hand the facts that would enable it to know which denials are legitimate and which are not. 42

Bibliography

Freeman, M, *Truth Commissions and Procedural Fairness* (CUP 2006).

Freeman, M and Hayner, P, 'Truth–Telling' in *Reconciliation after Violent Conflict: A Handbook* (Institute for Democracy and Electoral Assistance 2003).

Gonzalez, E and Varney, Howard (eds), *Truth Seeking: Elements of Creating an Effective Truth Commission* (Amnesty Commission of the Ministry of Justice of Brazil; International Center for Transitional Justice 2013).

Haldemann, F, 'Another King of Justice: Transitional Justice as Recognition' (2008) 41.3 Cornell International Law Journal 675–737.

Hayner, P, *Unspeakable Truths. Transitional Justice and the Challenge of Truth Commissions* (2nd edn, Routledge 2011) 211.

[41] Hayner, n 18, 37. [42] <www.usip.org/publications/truth-commission-south-africa>.

[43] On the meaning of apologies in transitional contexts, see, eg, N Tavuchis, *Mea Culpa: A Sociology of Apology and Reconciliation* (Stanford University Press 1991); N Smith, *I Was Wrong: The Meanings of Apologies* (CUP 2008).

[44] Hayner, n 18, 28.

McEvoy, K and McGregor, L (eds), *Transitional Justice from Below: Grassroots Activism and the Struggle for Change* (Hart Publishing 2008).

Naqvi, Y, 'The right to the truth in international law: fact or fiction?', International Review of the Red Cross, vol 88, no 862, June 2006.

Nesiah, V et al, International Center for Transitional Justice Report, *Truth Commissions and Gender: Principles, Policies and Procedures* (July 2006).

Ni Aoláin, F, Haynes, D, and Cahn, N, *On the Frontlines: Gender War, and the Post-Conflict Process* (OUP 2011).

Report of the independent expert to update the Set of Principles to combat impunity, Diane Orentlicher, Updated set of principles for the protection and promotion of human rights through action to combat impunity, UN Doc E/CN.4/2005/102 (8 February 2005).

Report of the Special Rapporteur on the promotion of truth, justice, reparation and guarantees of non-recurrence, Pablo de Greiff, UN Doc A/HRC/24/42 (28 August 2013).

Smith, N, *I Was Wrong: The Meanings of Apologies* (CUP 2008).

Tavuchis, N, *Mea Culpa: A Sociology of Apology and Reconciliation* (Stanford University Press 1991).

Principle 7. Guarantees of Independence, Impartiality, and Competence

Ilya Nuzov and Mark Freeman[1]

Commissions of inquiry, including truth commissions, must be established through procedures that ensure their independence, impartiality and competence. To this end, the terms of reference of commissions of inquiry, including commissions that are international in character, should respect the following guidelines:

(a) They shall be constituted in accordance with criteria making clear to the public the competence and impartiality of their members, including expertise within their membership in the field of human rights and, if relevant, of humanitarian law. They shall also be constituted in accordance with conditions ensuring their independence, in particular by the irremovability of their members during their terms of office except on grounds of incapacity or behaviour rendering them unfit to discharge their duties and pursuant to procedures ensuring fair, impartial and independent determinations;

(b) Their members shall enjoy whatever privileges and immunities are necessary for their protection, including in the period following their mission, especially in respect of any defamation proceedings or other civil or criminal action brought against them on the basis of facts or opinions contained in the commissions' reports;

(c) In determining membership, concerted efforts should be made to ensure adequate representation of women as well as of other appropriate groups whose members have been especially vulnerable to human rights violations.

A. Summary of Findings

There are four main recommendations in Principle 7. Before discussing them, it is worth making some more general observations.

First, the Principle applies to commissions of inquiry in general, and not merely to national truth commissions. Second, it is focused on three separate but interrelated aspects of commissions of inquiry: their 'independence, impartiality and competence'. Third, it is concerned with the need for guarantees of these aspects in two different realms: the process leading to a commission's establishment, and the commission's ultimate terms of reference. As such, the Principle's scope overlaps with Principle 6, which deals with the establishment of truth commissions, and Principle 8, which deals with the mandates of commissions of inquiry.

Paragraphs (a) and (b) of Principle 7 come almost word for word from Louis Joinet's original formulation of the Impunity Principles; only paragraph (c) is distinctive.

[1] The authors would like to thank Clara Martinez Ginès for her research support.

B. Contextual and Historical Introduction

1 The values addressed by Principle 7—independence, impartiality, and competence—are commonly included in the domestic legislation and mandates applicable to most commissions of inquiry. However, these values must be measured against a commission's actual conduct. With respect to truth commissions, just over half could be characterized as truly independent and impartial.

2 Concerning the composition of commissions of inquiry, at least one commissioner is likely to have expertise and experience in human rights and/or humanitarian law. Most, however, will come from a wider range of educational and professional backgrounds, including law, academia, psychology, and medicine. Competence does not require in-depth expertise in human rights.

3 Ensuring the irremovability of commissioners helps to protect them from undue influence, and enables them to perform their functions impartially and independently. Most commissions have rules that require commissioners to disclose actual or apparent conflicts based on financial or personal interests (and to recuse themselves from decisions when appropriate). Many also require commissioners and staff to swear to carry out the commission's mandate in good faith and perform assigned duties impartially and independently. Reduction of conflicts of interest can also be achieved by requiring commissioners to serve strictly in their personal capacities. This does not necessarily entail resigning from an existing post.

4 While some states have made concerted efforts to ensure the representation of vulnerable groups, and especially of women as members of commissions of inquiry, the practice is not pervasive. Yet commissions will tend to enjoy greater public support when the members represent a broad spectrum of constituencies, ethnic or religious groups, and genders.

5 The chapeau of Principle 7 preserves the main aim of what was formerly Principle 6 of the original Joinet Principles, namely, to guarantee the legitimacy and public support of commissions of inquiry by ensuring their independence, impartiality, and operational competence.[2]

I. Paragraph (a) of Principle 7

6 Paragraph (a) of Principle 7 deals with a blend of concepts. It provides that commissions of inquiry should be created using criteria that give the public confidence in the 'competence and impartiality' of the commissioners ('members').

7 For any 'human rights investigation', the members of the body in question logically require a certain level of expertise on the topic. If not individually then certainly collectively, the members of a human rights-related commission of inquiry should be minimally competent and professionally qualified in the tasks that will be required of them—in this instance, to investigate the commission of human rights violations, humanitarian ones, or both.

8 When it comes to commissions of inquiry, the principle of competence also implies a level of self-sufficiency. Commissions with robust investigative powers—such as the

[2] *Report of the independent expert to update the Set of Principles to combat impunity, Diane Orentlicher, Updated set of principles for the protection and promotion of human rights through action to combat impunity,* UN Doc E/CN.4/2005/102 (8 February 2005) (hereinafter 'Commentary to the Updated Principles') para 24.

power to compel the disclosure of evidence or to ensure the protection of witnesses and victims—can be described as more competent than those that lack the same powers, inasmuch as they do not depend excessively on the state to carry out essential functions.

On the theme of impartiality, the first sub-paragraph of Principle 7 provides no guidance. In general, impartiality refers to the absence of a bias that may arise, for example, on account of a commissioner's pecuniary interest or prior personal involvement in cases under investigation.[3] As such, independence and impartiality are not synonymous; an independent commission of inquiry is not necessarily an unbiased one. However, the factors that tend to increase the appearance and reality of independence will help to increase the appearance and reality of impartiality.[4] **9**

Lastly, on the theme of independence, paragraph (a) of Principle 7 advocates the need for conditions that ensure the 'irremovability' of commissioners during their terms of office, 'except on grounds of incapacity or behaviour rendering them unfit to discharge their duties and pursuant to procedures ensuring fair, impartial and independent determinations'. According to the Commentary to the Updated Principles, this should be understood as referring solely to legitimate grounds for removal, such as corrupt behaviour.[5] **10**

Providing for the irremovability of commissioners helps to ensure the individual and institutional autonomy a commission of inquiry requires. A commission whose composition or mandate can be frivolously changed, dissolved, or curtailed is one lacking in independence. **11**

Commissions of inquiry provide for the irremovability of commissioners in different ways. Regarding truth commissions, in South Korea commissioners could not be 'retired, suspended, demoted, or removed ... except in instances involving confirmation of punishment or disciplinary action'.[6] In Mauritius, a commissioner could be removed only for infirmity of body or mind, incompetence, or misbehaviour. Similar provisions existed in South Africa and Ghana, although the latter provided for removal only in cases of incompetence or other unspecified reasons. **12**

However, a commission's grade of independence can be inadequate in other ways. For example, a commission that is subject to the direct control of any single political faction or governmental organ cannot be considered truly independent (eg the committees of inquiry created in Algeria and Lebanon to establish the fate of disappeared persons were considered mere 'interfaces' between the public and the government).[7] **13**

The choice of commissioners is another relevant criterion in assessing the degree of a commission's independence. First, the original Joinet Report rightly noted that '[a] wide **14**

[3] M Freeman, *Truth Commissions and Procedural Fairness* (CUP 2006) 138. With respect to impartiality of judges, the European Court of Human Rights (ECtHR) elaborated that in addition to the absence of personal conviction or prejudice, impartiality also requires objectively adequate guarantees to exclude any legitimate doubt in this respect: *Findlay v United Kingdom* (Judgment) (ECtHR, 25 February 1997) para 73. Thus, the presence of a military judge in a non-military tribunal created the appearance of the judge's impartiality: *Incal v Turkey* (Judgment) (ECtHR, 9 June 1998) paras 72–73.

[4] This is underscored by the coupling of these terms in most human rights treaties. See, eg, Art 10 of the Universal Declaration of Human Rights, which refers to an 'independent and impartial tribunal'. See also Art 40(2)(b)(iii) of the Convention on the Rights of the Child, Arts 18 and 26 of the American Declaration of the Rights and Duties of Man, Art 8(1) and (5) of the American Convention on Human Rights, Art 6(1) of the European Convention on Human Rights, and Arts 7(1) and 26 of the African Charter of Human and Peoples' Rights.

[5] Commentary to the Updated Principles, n 2, para 25.

[6] Art 16.

[7] Freeman, n 3, 133, fn 192.

range of opinions among commission members also makes for independence'.[8] Second, commissions tend to be more independent when commissioners are selected through a procedure that operates partly at arm's length from the sponsoring government. By contrast, a unilateral appointment process is more likely to reduce the appearance of independence—although it may be otherwise where, for example, a president is seen to be the highest moral authority in a state.[9]

15 Financial security is another relevant criterion in measuring independence. In this respect, Principle 7 overlaps with Principle 11.

II. Paragraph (b) of Principle 7

16 Paragraph (b) of Principle 7 does not use the terms 'independence', 'impartiality', or 'competence', but effectively relates to the first two of these. It calls for commissioners to enjoy the privileges and immunities necessary for their protection, 'including in the period following their mission'. It also makes a special plea to shield commissioners from potentially retributive criminal or civil actions based on the commission's reports.

17 States create commissions of inquiry with the ostensible understanding that a commissioner should face appropriate legal penalties for any serious misbehaviour. At the same time, being a commissioner should not expose one to unreasonable legal risk. Commissioners, as well as staff, should have express immunity from adverse legal proceedings for all actions, decisions, and omissions made in good faith in the course of the inquiry.[10] This can help ensure that they (i) report their findings to the government and the public without fear or favour, and (ii) are held accountable for serious misconduct but not for merely taking unpopular actions.

III. Paragraph (c) of Principle 7

18 Paragraph (c) of Principle 7 does not deal, explicitly or implicitly, with the norms of 'independence', 'impartiality', or 'competence'. It simply calls for 'concerted efforts' in the selection of a commission's members, to ensure 'adequate representation of women as well as of other appropriate groups whose members have been especially vulnerable to human rights violations'. This is a normative plea with no obvious relation to the objectives of an independent, impartial, and competent commission of inquiry.

C. Theoretical Framework

19 Although there are no multilateral human rights treaties that explicitly address national commissions of inquiry, there are relevant international standards that, broadly speaking,

[8] L Joinet, *Question of the impunity of perpetrators of human rights violations (civil and political)*, Report prepared as special procedures following sub-Commission decision 1996/119, UN Doc E/CN.4/Sub.2/1997/20/Rev.1 (26 June 1997) para 21.

[9] This was the case in South Africa, where President Mandela added two members to the country's Truth and Reconciliation Commission who did not pass through the full selection process.

[10] This is provided for expressly under the Promotion of National Unity and Reconciliation Act, 1995 (South Africa), s 41(2). See also Law 04/018 (DRC), Art 47; Commissions of Inquiry Law, s 24 in 'Israel: Commission of Inquiry Law and Amendments' (1983) 22(3) ILM 658–66, 662, which provides that commissioners 'have every immunity granted by law to a Judge'.

are applicable.[11] The 1899 and 1907 Hague Conventions for the Pacific Settlement of International Disputes ('Hague Conventions') provide what seems the first international codification of standards applicable to commissions of inquiry. Article 9 of both treaties urges parties who have not been able to come to an agreement by diplomacy to 'institute an International Commission of Inquiry, to facilitate a solution of these disputes by elucidating the facts by means of an impartial and conscientious investigation'. Additional Protocol I to the Geneva Conventions of 1949 likewise envisions the institution of an International Fact-Finding Commission, consisting of 'members of high moral standing and acknowledged impartiality'.[12]

The procedural standards in the Hague Conventions serve as the main benchmarks in the area of non-judicial fact finding. Their influence is apparent in the design of the International Labour Organization Commission of Inquiry mechanism, as well as the UN Declaration on Fact-Finding in the Field of Maintenance of International Peace and Security.[13] The latter provides that fact finding must be 'comprehensive, objective, impartial and timely'. As a guarantee of their independence, members of fact-finding missions are to be accorded 'all immunities and facilities needed for discharging their mandate'.[14] **20**

The Hague Conventions are now supplemented by the Permanent Court of Arbitration's Optional Rules for Fact-Finding Commissions of Inquiry. To ensure the appointment of 'independent and impartial' commissioners,[15] Article 5 requires each to 'submit a declaration confirming his or her independence from the parties'. **21**

Numerous soft law sources offer guidance on questions of independence, impartiality, and competence. The UN Principles on the Effective Prevention and Investigation of Extra-Legal, Arbitrary and Summary Executions (1989) recognize that standing investigative bodies of the state may sometimes lack the capacity or impartiality to conduct a fair investigation.[16] In such instances, they require governments to appoint an 'independent commission of inquiry or similar procedure', comprising members 'chosen for their recognized impartiality, competence and independence as individuals'.[17] To ensure impartiality, Principle 10 entitles such bodies to 'all the necessary budgetary and technical resources for effective investigation'. **22**

The Belgrade Minimum Rules of Procedure for International Human Rights Fact-Finding Missions (the 'Belgrade Rules') provide a similar bundle of minimal procedures to protect the integrity of human rights fact finding. With respect to the selection of fact-finders, they recommend that 'the fact finding mission should be composed of persons who are respected for their integrity, impartiality, competence and objectivity and who are serving in their personal capacities'.[18] **23**

[11] Notably, truth commissions may be charged with the tasks of fact finding as well as identifying the perpetrators of violations of human rights or international humanitarian law (see Principle 8), raising methodological and legal issues pertaining to the relationship between the standards of proof used by human rights, international humanitarian law, and international criminal law bodies which Principle 7 does not address. For more on this relationship, see, eg, BG Rahcharan, *International Law and Fact Finding in the Field of Human Rights* (Brill Nijhoff 2014); S Vezzani, 'Fact-Finding by International Human Rights Institutions and Criminal Prosecution' in F Pocar, M Pedrazzi, and M Frulli (eds), *War Crimes and the Conduct of Hostilities: Challenges to Adjudication and Investigation* (Edward Elgar Publishing 2013) 349–68.

[12] Art 90 of Additional Protocol I. The impartiality requirement also appears in the Convention Against Torture, Art 12, which obliges each state party to conduct 'a prompt and impartial investigation' of an act of torture under its jurisdiction.

[13] GA Res A/RES/46/59 (9 December 1991). [14] Ibid, Annex, paras 3, 23.

[15] Art 4, para 4. [16] UN Doc E/1989/89 (24 May 1989). [17] Ibid, Principle 11.

[18] Section II, Rule 4.

24 With respect to irremovability, the concept first appears in Joinet's original Principles. Updated Principle 7 simply expands the rule by drawing from Principles 18 to 20 of the UN Basic Principles on the Independence of the Judiciary (1985).[19] The Belgrade Rules also provide that 'Any person appointed a member of the fact finding mission should not be removed from membership except for reasons of incapacity or gross misbehaviour.'[20]

25 With respect to the recommendation to ensure adequate representation of women and vulnerable groups, in her commentary on Principle 7, Orentlicher asserts that '[t]he aims of the Principles can be effectively achieved only when concerted efforts are made to ensure that men and women participate on an equal basis in the development and implementation of policies for combating impunity'.[21]

26 Numerous UN resolutions and reports affirm the heightened focus on incorporating women's experiences and views in transitional contexts.[22] Orentlicher asserts that fair representation of women on truth commissions—'who often number disproportionately among victims and are sometimes the target of violations'—is likely to enhance victims' confidence in the proceedings.[23]

D. Practice

27 The adherence to values espoused in Principle 7 is difficult to measure in practice. Some commissions of inquiry may enjoy considerable structural independence, yet lack the ideological independence to conduct a truly independent investigation. By contrast, others lacking in structural independence may find ways to overcome such constraints and conduct a truly independent investigation. For instance, in Germany, two-thirds of the members of the Commission of Inquiry on 'Working through the History and Consequences of the SEC Dictatorship' were parliamentarians, represented in proportion to their political parties' presence within the parliament. The presence of these members does not, however, appear to have negated the Commission's independence in the eyes of the public.[24]

28 Most truth commission mandates explicitly emphasize the need for independence in the work of the commission (eg Ghana, Togo, Honduras), its membership (eg Mauritius, Liberia, Kenya, Tunisia), or both (eg, South Korea).[25] The section on the 'Independence of the Commission' in the Kenyan legislation states that the commission 'shall not

[19] UN Doc A/CONF.121/22/Rev.1 (13 December 1985). [20] Rule no 6.

[21] Commentary to the Updated Principles, n 2, para 8; Report of the OHCHR, *Analytical Study Focusing on Gender-Based and Sexual Violence in Relation to Transitional Justice*, UN Doc A/HRC/27/21 (30 June 2014) (hereinafter 'Analytical Study on Gender-Based Violence') para 24.

[22] See, eg, UNSC Res 1325 (31 October 2000) and 1820 (19 June 2008); *Report of the Special Rapporteur on the promotion of truth, justice, reparation and guarantees of non-recurrence, Pablo de Greiff*, UN Doc A/HRC/24/42 (28 August 2013), para 36; Report of the Secretary-General, *The rule of law and transitional justice in conflict and post-conflict societies*, UN Doc S/2004/616 (23 August 2004) para 3; Analytical Study on Gender-Based Violence, n 21, para 24.

[23] Commentary to the Updated Principles, n 2, para 27. [24] Freeman, n 3, 133.

[25] See, eg, Mauritius: Truth and Justice Commission Act 2008, s 3(4); Ghana: National Reconciliation Commission Act of 2002, s 8(1)(a); Solomon Islands: Truth and Reconciliation Commission Act 2008, Art 12; Liberia: An Act to Establish the Truth and Reconciliation Commission of Liberia, 2005, s 39(a); South Korea: Framework Act on Clearing Up Past Incidents for Truth and Reconciliation by Law No 7542, 31 May 2005, Arts 3, 8 ; Kenya: Truth, Justice and Reconciliation Commission Bill 2008, cl 21(2); Tunisia: Loi organique n° 2013-53 du 24 Décembre 2013 relative à l'attribution et l'organisation de la justice transitionnelle, Art 21, <www.legislation-securite.tn/fr/node/32961>.

be subject to the direction or control of any person or authority'. A similar provision appeared in Mauritius, Togo, and South Korea.[26]

Impartiality standards for commissions of inquiry tend to be addressed to individual commissioners, rather than the commission in its entirety. For example, section 9(1) of the UK Inquiries Act 2005 prohibits the appointment of a commissioner if that person has: 29

(a) a direct interest in the matters to which the inquiry relates, or
(b) a close association with an interested party,

unless, despite the person's interest or association, his appointment could not reasonably be regarded as affecting the impartiality of the inquiry panel.

If there is an appearance of bias on the part of individual commissioners, this could partly be mitigated by ensuring equal representation, within the commission, of persons holding the opposite bias. This was the approach taken in Chile, where the truth commission comprised eight commissioners; half were known as public sympathizers of the military government, and half as opponents. However, the more common approach is to appoint foreign nationals (eg, El Salvador, Guatemala, and Sierra Leone) or commissioners representative of a broad cross-section of religious, racial, cultural, and socio-economic communities (eg, South Africa, East Timor),[27] in order to augment perceptions of impartiality. 30

By contrast, commissions are less likely to be considered unbiased if their members represent only a narrow range of a country's main identity groups (eg the former Federal Republic of Yugoslavia, where all of the original commissioners were ethnic Serbs; or Uganda, where most of the original commissioners came from ethnic groups that were persecuted under the previous regimes).[28] 31

In order to reinforce impartiality, commission mandates sometimes contain provisions requiring a commissioner with a financial or personal interest in the matter to disclose the interest and recuse herself from the proceedings.[29] Other mandates require commissioners to take an oath to perform their duties impartially (eg the truth commissions in East Timor, Kenya, and Mauritius).[30] 32

Another approach to reduce bias is to appoint a retired judge as the head of the commission. This practice is especially prevalent in Commonwealth jurisdictions. 33

With respect to commissioner immunity, Commonwealth commissions of inquiry tend to provide full immunity, whereas truth commission practice is more varied. For instance, while the Mauritian truth commission's mandate precluded liability, prosecution, action, or suit in respect of 'any matter or thing done by a commissioner', the legislation in Kenya (clause 24(1)) and the Solomon Islands (Article 13) provided immunity only 34

[26] See Mauritius Act, n 25, s 3; section 3.1 of La Commission Vérité, Justice et Réconciliation du Togo, Décret Présidentiel n° 2009-046/PR du 25 février 2009; South Korea Act, n 25, Art 12.

[27] East Timor: UN Transitional Administration in East Timor (UNTAET) Regulation 2001/10, UN Doc UNTAET/REG/2001/01 (31 January 2001), s 4.1; see also Kenya Truth, Justice and Reconciliation Commission Bill 2008, cl 10.

[28] E Wiebelhaus-Brahm, *Truth Commissions and Transitional Societies: The Impact on Human Rights and Democracy* (Routledge 2010) 106.

[29] Ghana: National Reconciliation Commission Act, 2002, Act 611, Art 6(5); Liberia: An Act to Establish the Truth and Reconciliation Commission of Liberia, 2005, s 23; Law 04/018 (2004) Concerning the Organization, Powers and Functions of the Truth and Reconciliation Commission (DRC), Art 45; South Korea Act, n 25, Art 11.

[30] Kenya Bill, n 25, cl 14; Mauritius Act, n 25, s 3(5).

for acts performed in 'good faith'.[31] This preserved the possibility of judicial review, which can be important, since its absence would leave an accused person without legal recourse in respect of any bad-faith actions by a commission.

35 A final dimension of impartiality relates to a commission's mandate, which must avoid explicit bias. For example, a commission should not have a title that, itself, pre-judges responsibility, such as the truth commission in Chad, which was called the *Commission d'Enquête sur les Crimes et Détournements Commis par l'Ex Président Habré, ses co-Auteurs et/ou Complices*. Likewise, a truth commission mandate that skips over key periods of past abuse in a way that implies partisan or ethnic bias will tend to undermine the appearance of impartiality. For example, the truth commission in Panama excited controversy by providing a temporal jurisdiction that implicitly excluded examination of violations that may have been committed by the incumbent president's spouse (who was a prior president) or US forces following their invasion of Panama in December 1989.[32]

36 Regarding the issue of commissioner competence, there are different theories about what is required for an investigation of human rights violations. Section 8(1)(a) of the UK Inquiries Act 2005, which deals with commissions of inquiry on issues both related and unrelated to human rights, requires an assessment of the 'necessary expertise' of prospective commissioners during the appointment process. With truth commissions, some mandates expressly call for experience or knowledge of human rights (eg, clause 10 of the Kenyan mandate requires at least three of the commissioners to have at least fifteen years' experience in human rights; Article 20 of the Tunisian legislation calls for two representatives of organizations defending human rights). Others simply ensure a strong representation of human rights experts in the moment of commissioner selection.

37 It is uncommon for commissions to include provisions regarding gender equity. Exceptionally, the Kenya Commission obliges the selection panel in charge of appointments to 'have regard to principles of gender equity and regional balance'.[33]

E. Critical Assessment

38 In transitional contexts in which truth recovery and justice claims arise, the objective of victim-centredness may come into tension with the principle of impartiality. Elevated attention to victim interests and perspectives risks making a commission less attentive to important issues of procedural fairness for implicated persons, such as the need to afford a right of reply before attributing individual responsibility in a final report. A truth commission must remain steadfast in its adherence to the value of impartiality, while still allocating special attention to victims in line with Principle 7.

39 The norm of independence is well established by many different judicial, quasi-judicial, and non-judicial bodies and commissions of inquiry. The Updated Principles simply mirror longstanding practice. It would be difficult to suggest a new standard on such issues.

40 By contrast, the issue of competence could have benefited from better articulation in Principle 7. The text could have distinguished between the collective competence that

[31] See also Mauritius Act, n 25, s 14(1).

[32] In December 2014, Panamanian President Juan Carlos Varela announced the creation of a truth commission to investigate the US invasion.

[33] Kenya Bill, n 25, cl 10.

needs to exist in a commission of inquiry, on the one hand, and any individual member's competence on the other. As such, a reformulated Principle 7 could expressly emphasize the need to ensure a 'diversity of competences among the members', in conformity with the commission's specific mandate.

Bibliography

Freeman, M, *Truth Commissions and Procedural Fairness* (CUP 2006).

Joinet, L, *Question of the impunity of perpetrators of human rights violations (civil and political)*, Report prepared as special procedures following sub-Commission decision 1996/119, UN Doc E/CN.4/Sub.2/1997/20/Rev.1. (26 June 1997).

Rahcharan, BG, *International Law and Fact Finding in the Field of Human Rights* (Brill Nijhoff 2014).

Vezzani, S, 'Fact-Finding by International Human Rights Institutions and Criminal Prosecution' in F Pocar, M Pedrazzi, and M Frulli (eds), *War Crimes and the Conduct of Hostilities: Challenges to Adjudication and Investigation* (Edward Elgar Publishing 2013) 349–68.

Wiebelhaus-Brahm, E, *Truth Commissions and Transitional Societies: The Impact on Human Rights and Democracy* (Routledge 2010) 106.

Principle 8. Definition of a Commission's Terms of Reference

Alison Bisset

To avoid conflicts of jurisdiction, the commission's terms of reference must be clearly defined and must be consistent with the principle that commissions of inquiry are not intended to act as substitutes for the civil, administrative or criminal courts. In particular, criminal courts alone have jurisdiction to establish individual criminal responsibility, with a view as appropriate to passing judgement and imposing a sentence.

In addition to the guidelines set forth in principles 12 and 13, the terms of reference of a commission of inquiry should incorporate or reflect the following stipulations:

(a) The commission's terms of reference may reaffirm its right: to seek the assistance of law enforcement authorities, if required, including for the purpose, subject to the terms of principle 10 (a), of calling for testimonies; to inspect any places concerned in its investigations; and/or to call for the delivery of relevant documents;

(b) If the commission has reason to believe that the life, health or safety of a person concerned by its inquiry is threatened or that there is a risk of losing an element of proof, it may seek court action under an emergency procedure or take other appropriate measures to end such threat or risk;

(c) Investigations undertaken by a commission of inquiry may relate to all persons alleged to have been responsible for violations of human rights and/or humanitarian law, whether they ordered them or actually committed them, acting as perpetrators or accomplices, and whether they are public officials or members of quasi-governmental or private armed groups with any kind of link to the State, or of non-governmental armed movements. Commissions of inquiry may also consider the role of other actors in facilitating violations of human rights and humanitarian law;

(d) Commissions of inquiry may have jurisdiction to consider all forms of violations of human rights and humanitarian law. Their investigations should focus as a matter of priority on violations constituting serious crimes under international law, including in particular violations of the fundamental rights of women and of other vulnerable groups;

(e) Commissions of inquiry shall endeavour to safeguard evidence for later use in the administration of justice;

(f) The terms of reference of commissions of inquiry should highlight the importance of preserving the commission's archives. At the outset of their work, commissions should clarify the conditions that will govern access to their documents, including conditions aimed at preventing disclosure of confidential information while facilitating public access to their archives.

A. Summary of Findings

Clear terms of reference are essential in enabling effective truth seeking and in avoiding jurisdictional and operational conflict between courts and commissions.[1] In practice, overlapping mandates and requirements to access the same resources to fulfil their objectives have the potential to bring courts and commissions into conflict. Past practice, although limited, demonstrates the difficulties of coordinating their operations and aligning their powers. Although Principle 8 provides for the creation of strong commissions, which complement court proceedings, it offers no guidance on *how* to

[1] This commentary focuses on truth commissions and criminal courts as the most commonly used transitional justice mechanisms. For a definition of truth commissions, see PB Hayner, *Unspeakable Truths: Transitional Justice and the Challenge of Truth Commissions* (2nd edn, Routledge 2011) 11–13. For explanation of the

coordinate their proceedings. Indeed, its stipulations that commissions should possess quasi-judicial powers and the abilities to investigate all violations increase the likelihood of overlap in investigations and, therefore, the potential for operational tension.

B. Contextual and Historical Introduction

The importance of creating commissions with clear terms of reference that ensure delineation between their role and that of courts was recognized within the Joinet Principles. 1 The earliest commissions had been used as an alternative to criminal justice, often due to fragile political settlements and national amnesty laws within transitional states. They had narrow mandates and weak, if any, truth-seeking powers. Some of the Latin American commissions had been considered a success in relation to their investigation of enforced disappearances.[2] However, the lack of powers led some to accuse truth commissions of fostering a culture of impunity.[3] It was not until South Africa employed its truth and reconciliation model in the mid-1990s that wider support for commissions began to grow. As the South African model was adopted and adapted elsewhere, commission mandates broadened to enable the investigation of all violations, rather than focusing on a particular set of crimes, such as killings or torture. Likewise, commissions began to be created with quasi-judicial powers to enhance truth seeking.

The new millennium brought important developments in the way that commissions 2 were used in transitional states. The programmes implemented in East Timor and Sierra Leone saw them established alongside prosecutorial institutions as a complement to criminal justice.[4] More recent practice has continued in a similar vein, with national truth commissions being created in states where International Criminal Court (ICC) investigations are underway.[5] However, dual use presents new challenges, in that two different bodies may now concurrently investigate the most serious human rights violations, creating the potential for conflicts of jurisdiction.

C. Theoretical Framework

A commission's terms of reference will affect the nature and depth of its investigations, 3 regulate its relations with other bodies, and ultimately influence the impact and perception of its work. The terms of reference are set by the authority that creates the commission.[6] They set the commission's length of operation, geographic scope and subject matter, outline any investigative powers with which it is to be endowed and may additionally regulate its relationship with judicial institutions.

It is generally considered that commissions should be given broad terms of reference that 4 enable them to concentrate on the abuses that society at large, and victims in particular,

distinction between truth commissions and other forms of national human rights commissions of inquiry, see M Freeman, *Truth Commissions and Procedural Fairness* (CUP 2006) 53–58.

[2] *Report of the Special Rapporteur on the promotion of truth, justice, reparation and guarantees of non-recurrence, Pablo de Greiff*, UN Doc A/HRC/24/42 (28 August 2013) 11–12 (hereinafter '*Report of the Special Rapporteur*').

[3] JD Tepperman, 'Truth and Consequences' (2002) 81 Foreign Affairs 128–45, 131.

[4] On the need for multiple transitional justice mechanisms, see *Report of the UN Secretary-General on the Rule of Law and Transitional Justice in Conflict and Post Conflict Societies*, UN Doc S/2004/616 (23 August 2004) para 8 (hereinafter '*Report of the UN Secretary-General*').

[5] With varying degrees of success, this practice can be seen in DRC, Kenya, Côte d'Ivoire, Libya and Mali.

[6] Freeman, n 1, 27–28.

consider the most serious.[7] This may encompass a wide variety of violations,[8] but has typically resulted in a focus on rights protecting physical and mental integrity.[9] The ability to investigate across the spectrum of violations committed assists the commission in its task of establishing the broadest possible account of the past and contributing to the fulfilment of the right to truth.[10]

5 It is also important for commissions to be able to investigate and document the roles played by all parties involved in past violations, whether they are state or non-state actors. The ability of commissions to provide an overarching view of responsibility for past violations is considered one of their key strengths and, longer term, may contribute to reform of implicated institutions and guarantees of non-repetition.[11] Endowing commissions with truth-seeking powers is believed to be a key means of ensuring effective and independent investigations.[12] The extent of a commission's powers may influence the strength and reach of its investigations, enabling it to obtain information from sectors of society that might not otherwise offer testimony, such as former perpetrators and vulnerable victims. Powers to access information may also help a commission to overcome reluctance among state institutions to share sensitive material.

6 There is a general belief that commissions should complement judicial proceedings[13] and that, unless protected from disclosure for reasons of confidentiality, commission information should be available for use by courts.[14] However, where commission proceedings are ongoing, commissioners may prefer not to share information as it may inhibit perpetrator participation in the truth-seeking process.[15] There are also serious questions around whether compelled self-incriminating information obtained under commission powers should be available to judicial bodies.[16] Protecting certain categories of information from disclosure also has implications for archiving. Terms of reference should provide commissions with the powers to regulate access to their documents. The ability to access archives is considered an essential element of the exercise of the right to truth.[17] It must, however, be balanced with the rights of individuals to privacy and reputation.[18]

[7] Office of the United Nations High Commissioner for Human Rights (OHCHR), *Rule-of-Law Tools for Post-Conflict States: Truth Commissions* (United Nations 2006) 9.

[8] In some cases economic and social violations have been included. See An Act to Establish the Truth and Reconciliation Commission of Liberia, 2005, s 4(a); Kenya, Truth, Justice and Reconciliation Act 2008, s 6(n) and (o).

[9] PB Hayner, *Unspeakable Truths: Facing the Challenge of Truth Commissions* (Routledge 2001) 316–19.

[10] OHCHR, *Study on the Right to Truth, Report of the Office of the United Nations High Commissioner for Human Rights*, UN Doc E/CN.4/2006/91 (8 February 2006) paras 33–40.

[11] *Report of the Special Rapporteur on the promotion of truth, justice, reparation and guarantees of non-recurrence*, UN Doc A/67/368 (13 September 2012).

[12] E González and H Varney (eds), *Truth Seeking: Elements of Creating an Effective Truth Commission* (Amnesty Commission of the Ministry of Justice of Brazil; International Center for Transitional Justice 2013) 12; OHCHR, n 7, 10–11.

[13] *Report of the UN Secretary-General*, n 4.

[14] González and Varney, n 12, 24; OHCHR, n 7, 27.

[15] *Witness to Truth: Report of the Sierra Leone Truth and Reconciliation Commission*, (Graphic Packaging Ltd, 2004) vol 3B, ch 6, para 59 (hereinafter '*Witness to Truth*'); PRIDE, 'Ex-Combatant Views of the Truth and Reconciliation Commission and the Special Court for Sierra Leone', A Study in Partnership with the International Center for Transitional Justice, Freetown (12 September 2002) 19.

[16] A Bisset, 'Rethinking the Powers of Truth Commissions in Light of the ICC Statute' (2009) 7 Journal of International Criminal Justice 963–82.

[17] OHCHR, n 10, para 52.

[18] Universal Declaration of Human Rights, UNGA Res 217 A(III), Art 12; International Covenant on Civil and Political Rights (adopted 16 December 1966, entered into force 23 March 1976) 999 UNTS 171, Art 17;

D. Practice

The requirements of Principle 8 are reflected in modern practice. Most recent commissions have been given broad mandates to investigate all types of violations.[19] Some have raised concerns that such broad mandates are difficult for commissions to fulfil within their limited lifespans.[20] However, this development seems to be intended to remedy problems with many early commissions, which were permitted only to investigate disappearances, excluding a large number of other abuses from investigation and distorting the final account of the types and numbers of violations committed.[21] Since the South African Truth and Reconciliation Commission (TRC) was created with a wealth of truth-seeking powers, commissions have routinely been endowed with powers of subpoena, search and seizure and witness protection, often bolstered by court-administered penalties where orders are not complied with.[22] 7

Reporting demonstrates deliberation on the roles of state actors,[23] rebel groups[24] and terrorist organizations[25] in past violations, as well as analysis of the involvement of international corporations.[26] Final reports also show that commissions have given detailed consideration to how their information ought to be archived and the measures needed to protect information received confidentially.[27] In a number of states, commissions and judicial institutions have built cooperative relationships, with the commission forwarding information relating to human rights crimes.[28] There is also evidence of successful use of the findings of the commissions of Chad,[29] Chile,[30] Guatemala[31] and Sierra Leone,[32] in a variety of judicial proceedings. 8

Yet past practice also demonstrates that there are considerable difficulties inherent in designing a transitional model that effectively combines prosecutions and truth seeking 9

Convention on the Rights of the Child (adopted 20 November 1989, entered into force 2 September 1990) 1577 UNTS 3, Art 16; Convention for the Protection of Human Rights and Fundamental Freedoms (ECHR, as amended) (adopted 4 November 1950, entered into force 3 September 1953) 213 UNTS 221, Art 8; American Convention on Human Rights (adopted 22 November 1969, entered into force 11 July 1978) 1144 UNTS 123, Arts 11 and 14.

[19] Hayner, n 1, App 2, Chart 3. [20] *Report of the Special Rapporteur*, n 2, para 40.

[21] P Schey, D Shelton, and N Roht-Arriaza, 'Addressing Human Rights Abuses: Truth Commissions and the Value of Amnesty' (1997) 19 Whittier Law Review 325–44, 332.

[22] Freeman, n 1, App 1, Table A.1. Note, however, that international commissions of inquiry are not routinely equipped with such powers. See, eg, *Report of the International Commission of Inquiry on Darfur to the United Nations Secretary-General* (2005) paras 10 and 528.

[23] *Guatemala, Memory of Silence: Report of the Commission for Historical Clarification* (1999).

[24] *Final Report of the Truth and Reconciliation Commission for Liberia* (2009) vol 2.

[25] Peru, *Informe Final de la Comisión de la Verdad y Reconciliación* (2003).

[26] *Witness to Truth*, n 15, vol 3B, ch 2.

[27] *Final Report*, n 24, 334; *Witness to Truth*, n 15, vol 3B, ch 6.

[28] On the Argentinean, Haitian, and Pervian arrangements, see: Trial of the Members of the Former Military Junta, reprinted in NJ Kritz, *Transitional Justice: How Emerging Democracies Reckon with Former Regimes*, III: *Laws, Rulings and Reports* (United States Institute of Peace Press 1995) 483–84; République d'Haiti, *Rapport de la Commission Nationale de Vérité et de Justice* (2001) ch 2; Institutional Cooperation Agreement Between the Prosecutor's Office and the Truth and Reconciliation Commission, Lima (15 August 2002).

[29] Human Rights Watch, 'The Case Against Hissène Habré, An African Pinochet', May 2006.

[30] Ampliación y funadamentación del Auto ordenando la prisión provisional incondicional de AUGUSTO PINOCHET y su detención, Madrid (18 October 1998).

[31] Rights Action/NISGUA (Network in Solidarity with Guatemala), 'Arrest Warrants Against Former Military Officials' (12 November 2006).

[32] Special Court for Sierra Leone (SCSL), *Prosecutor v Charles Ghakay Taylor* (Trial Chamber) (Decision on prosecution motion for admission of extracts of the report of the Truth and Reconciliation Commission of Sierra Leone) SCSL-03-1-T (19 February 2009).

without compromising one or the other. In order to carry out their investigations, courts and commissions are frequently dependent on the same resources, raising difficult questions around access to witnesses, evidence contamination and competing requests for information.[33] These problems are exacerbated by the creation of commissions with truth-seeking powers. A situation arises where two bodies possess the ability to exercise judicial powers, often simultaneously, in relation to the same crimes and individuals, making conflicts of jurisdiction a real possibility.

10 Sequencing of operations and division of labour have been suggested as means of avoiding conflict. However, to delay criminal trials until after a commission has completed its work, or vice versa, will inevitably deny one body the momentum that is present at the point of transition.[34] Dividing work between the two is also undesirable. Assigning the most serious cases exclusively to criminal courts will hinder a truth commission from developing a coherent picture of the conflict as a whole. It therefore seems preferable, where possible, to run the two processes simultaneously, even though this comes at the cost of potential operational difficulties.

11 The difficulties of coordination and avoiding jurisdictional conflict can be seen in the experiences of past commissions. In South Africa, the focus on creating a strong commission with a wide mandate and robust powers[35] meant that truth seeking was pursued at the expense of criminal justice and judicial bodies were inadequately resourced.[36] Where the commission was conducting investigations, prosecuting bodies had to stay their proceedings and incriminating information obtained by the commission was not admissible in subsequent court proceedings. [37]

12 In East Timor, imposing an obligation on the commission to make information available to prosecutorial institutions meant that it could not exercise powers to compel the provision of self-incriminating information[38] or guarantee the confidentiality of testimony, hampering its truth-seeking abilities.[39] In Sierra Leone, the commission's attempts to exercise its powers to interview detainees in the custody of the Special Court led to protracted legal proceedings.[40] Ultimately, the commission was denied access to the detainees on the ground that appearance before the commission might jeopardize the right to a fair trial. These judgments provide a precedent for the limitation of truth commission operations where they are perceived to threaten prosecutorial proceedings,

[33] On the International Criminal Tribunal for the former Yugoslavia's (ICTY's) opposition to a truth commission for Bosnia, see ICTY, Press release, 'The ICTY and the Truth and Reconciliation Commission in Bosnia and Herzegovina' (17 May 2001).

[34] A Bisset, L Moxham, and J van Zyl Smit, *The Rule of Law and Transitional Justice in Nepal: Options for Co-ordinating a Truth Commission, Criminal Justice Mechanisms and Personnel Reforms* (Bingham Centre Working Paper 2014/02), Bingham Centre for the Rule of Law, BIICL, London, April 2014, 18–19.

[35] Promotion of National Unity and Reconciliation Act 1995, ss 29–32.

[36] J Klaaren and H Varney, 'A Second Bite at the Amnesty Cherry? Constitutional and Policy Issues Around Legislation for a Second Amnesty' (2000) 117 South African Law Journal 572–93, 575; J Sarkin, *Carrots and Sticks: The TRC and the South African Amnesty Process* (Intersentia 2004) 127–34.

[37] Promotion of National Unity and Reconciliation Act 1995, s 31(3).

[38] UNTAET Regulation 2001/10, ss 17.1 and 17.2.

[39] *Chega!*, Report of the Commission for Reception, Truth and Reconciliation for East Timor (January 2006) pt 2, paras 23–24.

[40] SCSL, *Prosecutor v Samuel Hinga Norman* (Pre-Trial Chamber) (Decision on the Request by the Truth and Reconciliation Commission of Sierra Leone to Conduct a Public Hearing with Samuel Hinga Norman) SCSL-03-08-PT-101 (29 October 2003); SCSL, *Prosecutor v Samuel Hinga Norman* (Appeals Chamber Decision on Appeal by the Truth and Reconciliation Commission for Sierra Leone and Chief Samuel Hinga Norman JP) SCSL-03-08-PT-122-I and II (28 November 2003).

regardless of the consequences for truth seeking. However, the tension surrounding the competing interests of courts and commissions around certain categories of witnesses and the information they possess remains unresolved.

E. Critical Assessment

The stipulations of Principle 8 appear innocuous. However, the experiences of South Africa, East Timor and Sierra Leone demonstrate the practical difficulties associated with endowing commissions with wide mandates and truth-seeking powers, where there are also efforts to pursue criminal justice. Care must be taken in designing terms of reference that commissions are neither permitted to dominate the transitional programme, as in South Africa, nor compromised in their truth-seeking capabilities through obligations to cooperate with prosecutorial institutions, as in East Timor. 13

The overlapping nature of investigations points to the need for some regulation in their relationship. This is particularly important where commissions possess truth-seeking powers. There must be clear parameters for their use, which ensure compatibility with contemporaneous court proceedings. To maintain the legitimacy and fairness of judicial proceedings, truth-seeking powers should not extend to those indicted by prosecutorial bodies. Equally, information gathered through the exercise of truth-seeking powers should be safeguarded, both during commission operations and afterwards through protection of archived material. To obtain information under those powers and then make it available to a judicial body may undermine commission credibility. Ultimately, the aim must be to maintain the integrity of both bodies. 14

Provision should be made for an independent third party to resolve any conflict that does arise. The situation that occurred in Sierra Leone, where the SCSL determined the outcome of the dispute, is unsatisfactory. It is impossible for one transitional justice mechanism to objectively evaluate an issue in which its powers are challenged and proceedings threatened. Recourse to a neutral and impartial body should be available for the resolution of any emerging dispute.[41] 15

To date, the challenges in coordinating courts and commissions have arisen at the national level. In future, commission proceedings may take place alongside those of the ICC, raising new dilemmas and debates. 16

Bibliography

Boister, N, 'Failing to Get to the Heart of the Matter in Sierra Leone? The Truth Commission is Denied Unrestricted Access to Chief Hinga Norman' (2004) 2 Journal of International Criminal Justice 1100–17.

Burgess, P, 'Justice and Reconciliation in East Timor: The Relationship Between the Commission for Reception, Truth and Reconciliation and the Courts' (2004) 15 Criminal Law Forum 135–58.

Hayner, PB, *Unspeakable Truths: Transitional Justice and the Challenge of Truth Commissions* (2nd edn, Routledge 2011) chs 8 and 9.

[41] A Bisset, *Truth Commissions and Criminal Courts* (CUP 2012) 190.

Nesbitt, M, 'Lessons from the Sam Hinga Norman Decision of the Special Court for Sierra Leone: How Trials and Truth Commissions Can Co-Exist' (2007) 8 German Law Journal 977–81.

Pedain, A, 'Was Amnesty a Lottery? An Empirical Study of the Decisions of the Truth and Reconciliation Commission's Committee on Amnesty' (2004) 121 South African Law Journal 785–828.

Roht-Arriaza, N and Mariezcurrena, J (eds), *Transitional Justice in the Twenty-First Century: Beyond Truth Versus Justice* (CUP 2006).

Sarkin, J, *Carrots and Sticks: The TRC and the South African Amnesty Process* (Intersentia 2004).

Schabas, WA, 'The Relationship Between Truth Commissions and International Courts: The Case of Sierra Leone' (2003) 25 Human Rights Quarterly 1035–66.

Tejan-Cole, A, 'Complementary and Conflicting Relationship between the Special Court for Sierra Leone and the Truth and Reconciliation Commission' (2003) 6 Yale Human Rights and Development Law Journal 139–59.

Principle 9. Guarantees for Persons Implicated

Alison Bisset

Before a commission identifies perpetrators in its report, the individuals concerned shall be entitled to the following guarantees:

(a) The commission must try to corroborate information implicating individuals before they are named publicly;
(b) The individuals implicated shall be afforded an opportunity to provide a statement setting forth their version of the facts either at a hearing convened by the commission while conducting its investigation or through submission of a document equivalent to a right of reply for inclusion in the commission's file.

A. Summary of Findings

Identification of those responsible for past violations constitutes an important element of a commission's historical account and contributes to the fulfilment of the right to truth. However, the consequences of being named in a final report can be significant, impacting on an individual's reputation, family life and privacy. Before commissions publish findings in relation to specific persons, best practice dictates that information implicating individuals be corroborated and that they be afforded a right to reply to the allegations against them. Such requirements impose administrative burdens on commissions, which often have limited resources and short temporal mandates. Past practice evidences difficulty in adhering to these standards, sometimes resulting in the exclusion from the report of some or all of the names of those identified during investigations and thereby limiting the scope of the published truth. Nevertheless, where commissions cannot meet these minimum standards, they should not name individuals, in order to protect the rights of those implicated and the integrity of the commission itself.

B. Contextual and Historical Introduction

The need to provide those implicated with guarantees of procedural fairness has long been 1
recognized. It was included within the Joinet Principles[1] and remains largely unchanged within the text of the Updated Principles. The issue of whether to name those deemed responsible in the final report is one of the most controversial in truth commission operation. It highlights a fundamental tension between the rights of the individual to privacy and reputation[2] and the public's right to know.[3] There remains no settled practice on naming. Some commissions, such as those in Chad, El Salvador and Liberia, listed the

[1] *Question of the impunity of perpetrators of violations of human rights (civil and political rights): final report prepared by Mr L Joinet, pursuant to Subcommission resolution 1995/35*, UN Doc E/CN.4/Sub.2/1996/18 (29 June 1996) (hereinafter 'Joinet Principles') Principle 8.

[2] M Freeman, *Truth Commissions and Procedural Fairness* (CUP 2006) 95–96.

[3] See the commentary to Principle 2 in this volume.

names of those concluded to have committed the worst violations in their final reports. Others, such as those in Haiti and Peru, took a more cautious approach, forwarding confidential lists of those implicated to prosecuting authorities. The Argentinean commission attempted to reach a compromise, making no findings of its own on individual culpability but quoting victim testimony, which included the names of those accused. Others still have withheld names altogether, finding themselves prevented from making findings on specific individuals under their enacting legislation.[4]

2 Even where there are no legislative barriers, a number of factors influence the decision to name names. Political pressure, security risks, the quality of the sources and the resource implications of carrying out investigations in sufficient depth to reach findings on individuals all impact. To enable flexibility, the best practice is considered to be for a commission's terms of reference to allow but not require the identification of perpetrators.[5] However, where the decision to name individuals is taken, it is widely agreed that commissions should adhere to standards that ensure procedural fairness and respect for the due process rights of those alleged to have committed violations.[6]

C. Theoretical Framework

3 Freeman identifies three main justifications for naming.[7] First, exposing the truth concerning who was responsible for past violations is a key element of the truth-telling process. Second, assigning individual responsibility can act as a measure of accountability, which is particularly important where there is little chance of criminal trials. Third, naming individuals may contribute to victims' sense of justice through the provision of official acknowledgement of past suffering.[8] The importance of identifying those responsible for past violations has been confirmed by human rights courts and monitoring bodies in their consideration of the rights of victims to an effective remedy[9] and the obligations of states to guarantee human rights,[10] as well as in relation to the wider right to truth.[11] However, the public interest in knowing the truth about the past must be balanced with the rights of those implicated. International human rights law protects the rights to privacy, family life and respect for reputation under a host of instruments.[12] Being implicated in the perpetration of past human rights violations in a commission's report may have far-reaching

[4] For discussion of these approaches, see PB Hayner, *Unspeakable Truths: Transitional Justice and the Challenge of Truth Commissions* (Routledge 2011) 121–42.

[5] OHCHR, *Rule-of-Law Tools for Post-Conflict States: Truth Commissions* (United Nations 2006) 22. See, *contra*, Amnesty International, *Truth, Justice and Reparation: Establishing an Effective Truth Commission*, AI Index: POL 30/009/2007 (June 2007) at 42.

[6] See section C of this commentary.

[7] Freeman, n 2, 271.

[8] On truth commissions and acknowledgement, see JR Quinn, *The Politics of Acknowledgement: Truth Commissions in Uganda and Haiti* (University of British Columbia Press 2010).

[9] *Aksoy v Turkey* App no 21987/93 (Judgment) (ECtHR, 18 December 1996) para 98; Human Rights Committee, *Rodríguez v Uruguay*, Communication no 322/1988, CCPR/C/51/D/322/1988 (1994) para 14.

[10] *Velásquez-Rodríguez* (Judgment) IACtHR Series C no 4 (29 July 1988) para 174.

[11] Human Rights Committee, *Concluding Comments on Guatemala*, UN Doc CCPR/C/79/Add.63, para 25; IACtHR, *Monseñor Oscar Arnulfo Romero and Galdamez v El Salvador*, Case 11.481, Report N° 37/00, OEA/Ser.L/V/II.106 Doc 3 rev at 671 (1999) para 148. Note the concerns raised by the OHCHR on extending the right to truth to include the identification of individuals: OHCHR, *Study on the Right to Truth, Report of the Office of the United Nations High Commissioner for Human Rights*, UN Doc E/CN.4/2006/91 (8 February 2006) para 39.

[12] Universal Declaration of Human Rights, UNGA Res 217 A(III), Art 12; International Covenant on Civil and Political Rights (adopted 16 December 1966, entered into force 23 March 1976) 999 UNTS 171,

consequences for an individual's reputation and family life.[13] Naming might also impact on an individual's employment through dismissal from public service or a temporary bar on future reemployment due to the link between commissions' findings and other transitional initiatives, such as vetting.[14]

It is therefore understood that commissions should conduct their proceedings in accordance with standards that ensure fairness. Although they are not courts, with no ability to make findings on civil or criminal guilt, their operation raises a range of due process related issues. It has also been argued that in order for commissions to contribute to the rule of law, they themselves must operate in accordance with rule of law standards.[15] There is agreement that it is not necessary for commissions to adhere to the strict standards of criminal trials, with which due process is normally associated, because the consequences of being named by a commission are much less severe than those of being found guilty in a court.[16] However, it has been argued convincingly that where similar rights are implicated, due process standards "provide a useful benchmark of fairness" for commissions.[17] It is considered that commissions should notify those to be named of the allegations against them, afford them a right to reply, either in writing or in person, and make clear in the final report that the findings do not constitute judgments of legal or criminal guilt.[18] In addition, commissions must try to corroborate the implicating information before publicly naming individuals.[19] Corroboration, while not a requirement of international criminal law,[20] is considered important in commission proceedings because they do not operate to the strict procedural and evidentiary standards of criminal trials.[21] 4

D. Practice

As with all aspects of truth commission operation, differing transitional circumstances and priorities mean that no two commissions have adopted exactly the same procedures in relation to assigning individual responsibility. Modern practice reveals a general adherence to a balance of probabilities standard in making findings,[22] leading some commissions to name individuals where it is more probable than not that the allegations 5

Art 17; Convention on the Rights of the Child (adopted 20 November 1989, entered into force 2 September 1990) 1577 UNTS 3, Art 16; Convention for the Protection of Human Rights and Fundamental Freedoms (European Convention on Human Rights, as amended) (adopted 4 November 1950, entered into force 3 September 1953) Art 8; American Convention on Human Rights (adopted 22 November 1969, entered into force 18 July 1978) 1144 UNTS 123, Arts 11 and 14.

[13] Hayner, n 4, 122.

[14] P de Greiff and A Mayer-Rieckh, *Justice as Prevention: Vetting Public Employees in Transitional Societies* (Social Science Research Council 2007) chs 12 and 13.

[15] *Report of the Special Rapporteur on the promotion of truth, justice, reparation and guarantees of non-recurrence*, UN Doc A/67/368 (13 September 2012) paras 72–73.

[16] OHCHR, n 5, 21; Human Rights Watch, 'Recommendations to the Truth and Reconciliation Commission' (January 1998) 4.

[17] Freeman, n 2, 110.

[18] E González and H Varney (eds), *Truth Seeking: Elements of Creating an Effective Truth Commission* (Amnesty Commission of the Ministry of Justice of Brazil; International Center for Transitional Justice 2013) 26; OHCHR, n 5, 21–22; Amnesty International, n 5, 38.

[19] Note the difference with the Joinet Principles, which required two sources for corroboration: Joinet Principles, n 1, Principle 8.

[20] M Klamberg, *Evidence in International Criminal Trials* (Brill 2013) 179–82.

[21] Freeman, n 2, 281.

[22] Also referred to as the 'preponderance of evidence'.

against them are true.[23] The South African Truth and Reconciliation Commission (TRC) is one example. Its approach was to decide which 'version was the more probable, reasonable or likely, after taking all the available evidence into account'.[24] It required only one reliable source[25] to corroborate victims' accounts and determine individual responsibility.[26] Other commissions have sought to work to a higher standard. In El Salvador, the commission required two credible and independent sources on which to base findings against individuals, and created three categories of evidence: 'overwhelming', 'substantial', and 'sufficient'. Only where the evidence was 'substantial' or 'overwhelming' were individuals named in the final report.[27]

6 Recent commissions have used data management systems to record information relating to violations. These databases enable the identification of common links between statements and simultaneous examination of several accounts of the same event, making them useful tools for corroboration.[28] However, even with such systems at their disposal, commissions often find corroboration a difficult task. As the TRC for Sierra Leone explained, time constraints coupled with incomplete witness details and unknown whereabouts can make corroborating many statements impossible.[29]

7 Providing implicated persons with notification and a right to reply has also proved problematic. Commissions have not generally been obligated under their enacting legislation to provide these procedural safeguards. The closest example can be found in South Africa's establishing Act, which required the TRC to provide those implicated with an opportunity to submit representations to the Commission within a specified time or to give evidence at a hearing.[30] The requirements of this clause led to legal proceedings[31] and a ruling that those expected to be named during public hearings should be given sufficient notice so as to allow them to be present to hear the evidence, have the opportunity to rebut it, and see the demeanour of the witness. It was also held that immediate cross-examination was permissible and that alleged perpetrators ought to be afforded a prior view of the findings the Commission intended to publish.[32]

8 Following the decision, the South African TRC gave twenty-one days' written notice to those likely to be implicated in hearings and allowed cross-examination of witnesses. However, many of those implicated could not be traced and the TRC had to delete from its report the names of a large number of alleged perpetrators and descriptions

[23] *Chega!*, Report of the Commission for Reception, Truth and Reconciliation for East Timor (January 2006) pt 2, paras 34–35; *Final Report of the Truth and Reconciliation Commission for Liberia* (2009) vol 1, s 2, pt C (hereinafter 'Liberia TRC Report').

[24] *Truth and Reconciliation Commission of South Africa Report* (Truth and Reconciliation Commission, distributed by Juta and Co, 2002) vol 1, ch 4, s 155, 91 (hereinafter 'TRC Report').

[25] On the types of evidence that commissions should ideally rely, see Freeman, n 2, 276–80.

[26] Hayner, n 4, 142.

[27] *From Madness to Hope: The Twelve Year War in El Salvador: Report of the Commission on the Truth for El Salvador*, UN Doc S/25500 (1 April 1993), Annex. The Sierra Leone TRC also required 'overwhelming' evidence before making findings on individuals. See *Witness to Truth: Report of the Sierra Leone Truth and Reconciliation Commission* (Graphic Packaging Ltd, 2004) vol 2, ch 2, para 5 (hereinafter '*Witness to Truth*').

[28] *Witness to Truth*, n 27, vol 1, ch 5, 151; *Chega!*, n 23, pts 7 and 8; Liberia TRC Report, n 23, vol II, 85–89.

[29] *Witness to Truth*, n 27, vol 1, ch 5, 151.

[30] Promotion of National Unity and Reconciliation Act 1995, s 30(1).

[31] *Nieuwoudt v Chairman, South African Truth and Reconciliation Commission* (1996) 2 All SA 660 (SE); *Du Preez and Van Rensburg v Chairman, South African Truth and Reconciliation Commission*, Case no 4443/96 (Cape of Good Hope Provisional Division, 30 April 1996), 1996 (3) SA 997 (C).

[32] *Du Preez and Van Rensburg v Chairman, South African Truth and Reconciliation Commission*, 1997 (3) SA 204 (SCA).

of the incidents in which they were allegedly involved.[33] The Commission was critical of the ruling, its imposition of administrative burdens and the requirements for cross-examination, which it concluded had a traumatizing effect on victims who testified.[34] This perhaps explains the direction in current standards that although implicated persons should have a right to reply to allegations, this does not necessarily entail any right to confront their accusers.[35]

Commissions established subsequently have also encountered difficulties in providing a right to reply. The Timorese Commission for Reception, Truth, and Reconciliation (CAVR) documented practical issues associated with investigating violations committed by citizens of another country, a lack of functioning postal and telephone systems, absence of official records and problems of common naming.[36] It decided to forward the list of those alleged to have been involved in serious violations to the Prosecutor-General, and replaced the names with a code in the final report.[37] The Kenyan Truth, Justice and Reconciliation Commission (TJRC) also found it impossible to notify all of those implicated in the 54,000 allegations it received. It concentrated on those alleged to have committed the most serious violations and the frequency with which they appeared in testimony. Only those who were given the opportunity to respond were named in the final report.[38] 9

Lastly, the majority of commissions have stated that their findings do not amount to civil or criminal culpability. Some have explained that they have made factual findings in relation to responsibility and accountability.[39] Others have referred to different categories of responsibility, such as political, historical and moral.[40] Freeman cautions against assigning individual responsibility for legally defined violations, such as torture or genocide.[41] However, not all commissions have adhered to this standard, thereby blurring the line between factual and legal findings.[42] 10

E. Critical Assessment

Making express findings on the responsibility of specific individuals is not the only means of including names within the final report. Hayner suggests that, similar to the approach taken in Argentina, commissions might take on a reporting role, summarizing information received and including names mentioned in testimony where they hold credibility.[43] While this might ease the administrative burdens associated with corroboration and providing a right to reply, the danger of falsely accusing individuals persists. Alternatively, a commission might assign institutional responsibility in a way that infers the responsibility 11

[33] TRC Report, n 24, vol 5, ch 6, 260.

[34] Ibid, vol 1, 185. On this point, see A du Bois-Pedain, *Transitional Amnesty in South Africa* (CUP 2007) 185.

[35] On the impact of overly juridical proceedings on witnesses in Ghana, see N Valji, *Ghana's National Reconciliation Commission: A Comparative Assessment* (International Center for Transitional Justice 2006) pt V.

[36] *Chega!*, n 23, pt 2, para 34.

[37] Ibid, paras 37–39. The list was also sent to the President, with a recommendation that those named be prohibited from holding public office.

[38] *Report of the Truth, Justice and Reconciliation Commission* (TJRC 2013) vol 1, ch 2 para 61. See also *Witness to Truth*, n 27, vol 1, ch 5, 154–55; Liberia TRC Report, n 23, vol II, 190.

[39] *Witness to Truth*, n 27, vol 2, ch 2, para. 7.

[40] *Chega!*, n 23, pt 2, para 40.

[41] Freeman, n 2, 295–96.

[42] TRC Report, n 24, vol 5, 244; Liberia TRC Report, n 23, vol ii, ch 11.

[43] Hayner, n 4, 143.

of particular individuals. For example, the Chilean commission documented the involvement of specific groups, such as military units, in past violations,[44] leading readers to infer that members of those groups might have been responsible for those violations. The commissions for Peru and Sierra Leone did something similar, documenting specific crimes and the individuals and units in charge of the areas in which the crimes were committed at the relevant time.[45] Again, however, this is not a risk free approach as some individuals may be tarnished simply through membership of the named institutions.

12 Ultimately, the decision of whether and how to name individuals must be left to individual commissions. It is an important one that can bring serious repercussions for those implicated and for the credibility of the commission. It necessitates a delicate balancing of the various rights and interests involved against the requirements of the commission's mandate, as well as consideration of the practical factors that might facilitate or impede the naming process. Where the decision to name individuals is made, commissions must, in order to ensure fairness to those implicated and to maintain their own integrity, adhere to minimum standards of corroboration and due process. Naming individuals brings onerous procedural and administrative requirements for commissions, which are very often time and resource constrained. Yet commissions may make an important contribution to the needs for accountability and justice within transitional states by publishing findings on the role of individuals.

Bibliography

Boraine, A, *A Country Unmasked: Inside South Africa's Truth and Reconciliation Commission* (OUP 2001) ch 6.

Buergenthal, T, 'The United Nations Truth Commission for El Salvador' (1994) 27 Vanderbilt Journal of Transnational Law 497–544.

Freeman, M, *Truth Commissions and Procedural Fairness* (CUP 2006) ch 7.

Hayner, PB, *Unspeakable Truths: Transitional Justice and the Challenge of Truth Commissions* (Routledge 2011) ch 10.

Keller, AN, 'To Name or Not to Name? The Commission for Historical Clarification in Guatemala, Its Mandate and the Decision not to Identify Individual Perpetrators' (2001) 13 Florida Journal of International Law 289–319.

Seils, P, 'The Limits of Truth Commissions in the Search for Justice: An Analysis of the Truth Commissions of El Salvador and Guatemala and their Effect in Achieving Post-Conflict Justice' in MC Bassiouni (ed), *Post-Conflict Justice* (Transnational Publishers 2002) 775–95.

[44] *Report of the Chilean National Commission on Truth and Reconciliation* (University of Notre Dame Press 1983) App II.

[45] Peru, *Informe Final de la Comisión de la Verdad y Reconciliación* (2003) Annex; *Witness to Truth*, n 23, vol I, para 34.

Principle 10. Guarantees for Victims and Witnesses Testifying on Their Behalf

Alison Bisset

Effective measures shall be taken to ensure the security, physical and psychological well-being, and, where requested, the privacy of victims and witnesses who provide information to the commission.

(a) Victims and witnesses testifying on their behalf may be called upon to testify before the commission only on a strictly voluntary basis;
(b) Social workers and/or mental health-care practitioners should be authorized to assist victims, preferably in their own language, both during and after their testimony, especially in cases of sexual assault;
(c) All expenses incurred by those giving testimony shall be borne by the State;
(d) Information that might identify a witness who provided testimony pursuant to a promise of confidentially must be protected from disclosure. Victims providing testimony and other witnesses should in any event be informed of rules that will govern disclosure of information provided by them to the commission. Requests to provide information to the commission anonymously should be given serious consideration, especially in cases of sexual assault, and the commission should establish procedures to guarantee anonymity in appropriate cases, while allowing corroboration of the information provided, as necessary.

A. Summary of Findings

The majority of commissions have taken considerable care to create systems that enable victims and witnesses to testify in safe and supportive environments, often employing specific staff to provide psychological assistance or forging links with relevant external agencies. Although few have had the resources to develop formal protection schemes, they have used their powers to grant confidentiality and prevent disclosure to allow victims and witnesses to testify securely. However, commissions must exercise caution in granting confidentiality, and ensure that they do not offer a level of protection that they cannot guarantee. In particular, commissions must be aware of the possibility of requests to access confidential information, both during and beyond their lifespans, by national and international judicial bodies, as well as from a variety of individuals under freedom of information regimes. Where absolute confidentiality cannot be offered, this should be made clear so that victims and witnesses can make informed decisions on whether to share their accounts.

B. Contextual and Historical Introduction

The participation of victims and witnesses in truth-seeking processes is essential and a 1
fundamental means of uncovering the truth about the past. Many commission mandates have included gathering victim testimony as a key objective, and some have specifically

instructed the commission to provide victims with a forum in which to give their accounts of the abuses suffered and to restore their dignity.[1] The testimony of victims and witnesses is also very often a commission's primary resource. In the aftermath of serious violations, many have found that official, state-held records and documents relating to investigations have been destroyed or tampered with, thereby excluding an important source of information.[2] Without testimony, commissions are unlikely to be able to fulfill their broader mandates of establishing a historical record of past violations.

2 For victims and witnesses, the opportunity to share their experiences can be beneficial[3] and provide official acknowledgement of their suffering.[4] Of course, sharing accounts of past violations is also likely to be traumatic for those testifying[5] and some may prefer not to do so. Others may be fearful of repercussions or social stigma and require guarantees of confidentiality, or even anonymity, before sharing their stories. In light of the complex personal and external factors that influence the decision to testify, both the Joinet[6] and Updated Principles[7] recognize that victims and witnesses should never be subject to a commission's powers of compulsion and should only participate in truth telling on a voluntary basis.[8] However, the Updated Principles afford broader and more detailed protection to victims and witnesses than was given under the Joinet Principles. In particular, the Updated Principles recognize the need to safeguard psychological well-being as well as physical security,[9] and expand the circumstances in which testimony might be given anonymously, making it a routine consideration rather than an exception.[10]

C. Theoretical Framework

3 The need to protect witnesses testifying in relation to past human rights violations can be seen in a range of international instruments. Although related to international criminal

[1] Chile, Supreme Decree no 355, Creation of the Commission on Truth and Reconciliation, Santiago (25 April 1990), Art 4(a); Sierra Leone, Truth and Reconciliation Commission Act 2000, s 6(2); Kenya, Truth, Justice and Reconciliation Commission Act 2008, s 5(g)–(h); Act Establishing the Truth and Reconciliation Commission of Liberia 2005, s 4(b).

[2] See *Truth and Reconciliation Commission of South Africa Report* (Truth and Reconciliation Commission, distributed by Juta and Co 2002) (hereinafter 'TRC Report') vol 1, ch 8; *Report of the International Commission of Inquiry on East Timor to the Secretary-General*, UN Doc A/54/726, S/2000/59 (31 January 2000) para 134; *Bringing them Home: Report of the National Inquiry into the Separation of Aboriginal and Torres Strait Islander Children from Their Families* (Commonwealth of Australia 1997) pt 1.

[3] B Hamber, 'The Burdens of Truth: An Evaluation of the Psychological Support Services and Initiatives Undertaken by the South African Truth and Reconciliation Commission' (1998) 55 American Imago 9–28.

[4] M Minow, *From Vengeance to Forgiveness: Facing History after Genocide and Mass Violence* (Beacon Press, 1998), 58.

[5] AR Chapman, 'Truth Commissions as Instruments of Forgiveness and Reconciliation' in RG Helmick and RL Peterson (eds), *Forgiveness and Reconciliation: Religion, Public Policy and Conflict Transformation* (Templeton Foundation Press, 2002) 257–79; R Picker, *Victims Perspectives about the Human Rights Violations Hearings* (Centre for the Study of Violence and Reconciliation 2005).

[6] *Question of the impunity of perpetrators of violations of human rights (civil and political rights): final report prepared by Mr. L. Joinet, pursuant to Subcommission resolution 1995/35*, UN Doc E/CN.4/Sub.2/1996/18 (29 June 1996) (hereinafter 'Joinet Principles') Principle 9(a).

[7] *Report of the independent expert to update the Set of principles to combat impunity, Diane Orentlicher, Updated Set of principles for the protection and promotion of human right through action to combat impunity*, UN Doc E/CN.4/2005/102/Add.1 (8 February 2005) (hereinafter 'Updated Principles') Principle 10(a).

[8] Joinet Principles, n 6, Principle 9(a); Updated Principles, n 7, Principle 10(a).

[9] Updated Principles, n 7, Principle 10.

[10] Ibid, Principle 10(d).

proceedings, the statutes of the ad hoc tribunals[11] and the International Criminal Court (ICC) make provision for witness protection and the courts have departments dedicated to the support and protection of witnesses involved in proceedings. The UN Principles on the Right to a Remedy and Reparation recognize the right to a remedy as encompassing a right of access to justice, which in turn places a responsibility upon states to take measures to protect the privacy of victims and their representatives and to ensure their safety from intimidation and retaliation before, during and after judicial, administrative, or other proceedings.[12] International institutions and organizations also consider the protection of victims and witnesses an essential element of effective truth seeking.[13]

Although not the subject of binding legal instruments, the notion that victims of past violations should receive any necessary medical, psychological or social assistance is also internationally recognized.[14] The Basic Principles on the Right to a Remedy and Reparation consider rehabilitation in the form of medical and psychological care as a means of reparation.[15] This has also been confirmed by the Inter-American Court of Human Rights (IACtHR), which stated that the medical, psychological and psychiatric care that may be required by victims of human rights violations must be provided without cost and immediately.[16] 4

D. Practice

Many commissions operate in volatile settings, in which there may be real or perceived threats to the safety of those who testify and their families. As a result, a number of commissions have had powers of witness protection.[17] Some have created specific witness 5

[11] Statute of the International Criminal Tribunal for the Prosecution of Persons Responsible for Serious Violations of International Humanitarian Law Committed on the Territory of the former Yugoslavia since 1991, established pursuant to Security Council Resolution 827, UN Doc S/RES/827 (25 May 1993), (1993) 32 ILM 1159 (as amended), Art 22; Statute of the International Criminal Tribunal for the Prosecution of Persons Responsible for Genocide and Other Serious Violations of International Humanitarian Law Committed in the Territory of Rwanda and Rwandan Citizens Responsible for Genocide and Other Such Violations Committed in the Territory of Neighbouring States, between 1 January 1994 and 31 December 1994, established pursuant to Security Council Resolution 955, UN Doc S/RES/955 (8 November 1994), (1994) 35 ILM 1598 (as amended), Art 21; Rome Statute of the International Criminal Court (1998) 2187 UNTS 3, Art 68. The Rome Statute provides for the creation of a Victims and Witnesses Unit within the Registry. Under Art 43(6), the Unit will consult with the Office of the Prosecutor to provide protective measures, security arrangements, and counselling for victims, witnesses and 'others who are at risk on account of testimony given by such witnesses'.

[12] Basic Principles and Guidelines on the Right to a Remedy and Reparation for Victims of Violations of International Human Rights and Humanitarian Law annexed to General Assembly (GA) Res A/C.3/60/L.24 (16 December 2005), Principle 12(b).

[13] Office of the United Nations High Commissioner for Human Rights (OHCHR), *Rule-of-Law Tools for Post-Conflict States: Truth Commissions* (United Nations 2006) 23–24; E González and H Varney (eds), *Truth Seeking: Elements of Creating an Effective Truth Commission* (Amnesty Commission of the Ministry of Justice of Brazil; International Center for Transitional Justice 2013) 26.

[14] UN Declaration of Basic Principles of Justice for Victims of Crime and Abuse of Power, GA Res 40/34 (29 November 1985) Principle 14; Basic Principles and Guidelines on the Right to a Remedy and Reparation, n 12, Principle 24.

[15] Basic Principles and Guidelines on the Right to a Remedy and Reparation, n 12, Principle 21.

[16] IACtHR, *Annual Report of the Inter-American Court of Human Rights* (2010), OAS, San José, Costa Rica, 11.

[17] South Africa, Promotion of National Unity and Reconciliation Act, 1995, s 35; Act to establish the Truth and Reconciliation Commission of Liberia 2005, s 26(n); UNTAET Regulation No 2001/10 on the Establishment of a Commission for Reception, Truth and Reconciliation in East Timor, UN Doc UNTAET/REG/2001/10 (13 July 2001) s 36.1.

protection programmes. The South African Truth and Reconciliation Commission's (TRC's) was the most sophisticated, with safe houses, bodyguards and increased policing, where necessary.[18] Peru's commission reached an agreement with the Prosecutor's Office for the provision of witness protection on request[19] and Timor-Leste ensured a police presence at public hearings.[20] However, even where commissions possess the power of witness protection, few have the resources to develop strong programmes.[21]

6 A number of commissions have therefore sought to protect testifying victims and witnesses through guarantees of confidentiality. The Guatemalan truth commission's proceedings were kept confidential so as to guarantee the safety of witnesses.[22] Sierra Leone's TRC could receive information on a confidential basis, [23] and Kenya's Truth, Justice and Reconciliation Commission (TJRC) had powers to conduct private hearings[24] and withhold the identities of those involved.[25] The Sierra Leone Truth and Reconciliation Commission (SLTRC) recounted the importance of confidentiality in its investigations, explaining that it enabled those afraid of persecution by perpetrators to share their accounts.[26] Confidentiality was important for women who had experienced sexual violence, as the stigma that accompanies such violations can make it difficult to discuss experiences publicly.[27] This issue is also documented by the Kenyan TJRC, which noted that men who came forward to testify about sexual violations would do so only in private hearings.[28] Children also routinely testify in confidential sessions.[29]

7 In granting confidentiality, commissions must be clear about the extent of any guarantee they can offer. For example, the Commission for Reception, Truth, and Reconciliation (CAVR) in Timor-Leste had confidentiality powers but could also be compelled to disclose information to the Office of the General Prosecutor. The Special Court for Sierra Leone (SCSL) understood its powers as enabling it to issue binding orders to the any institution, including the SLTRC.[30] Although it did not attempt to access confidential commission information in practice, such an eventuality was possible. Where commission proceedings overlap those of the ICC, it is possible that the Court may seek to access confidential commission testimony through its powers to request information from its states parties.[31] Where there are no trials at the national level, third states might pursue

[18] PB Hayner, *Unspeakable Truths: Transitional Justice and the Challenge of Truth Commissions* (Routledge 2011) 232.

[19] Institutional Cooperation Agreement between the Prosecutor's Office and the Truth and Reconciliation Commission, Lima (15 August 2002) s II.

[20] M Freeman, *Truth Commissions and Procedural Fairness* (CUP 2006) 260.

[21] See *Final Report of the Truth and Reconciliation Commission for Liberia* (2009) (hereinafter 'Liberia TRC Report') vol II, 62.

[22] Agreement on the establishment of the Commission to clarify past human rights violations and acts of violence that have caused the Guatemalan Population to suffer, Oslo (17 June 1994), (1997) 36 ILM 283.

[23] Truth and Reconciliation Commission Act 2000, s 7(3).

[24] Truth, Justice and Reconciliation Act 2008, s 25(2). [25] Ibid, s 25(4).

[26] *Witness to Truth: Report of the Sierra Leone Truth and Reconciliation Commission* (Graphic Packaging Ltd 2004) (hereinafter *Witness to Truth*) vol 1, ch 5, para 22.

[27] Ibid, vol 1, ch 3, para 27.

[28] *Report of the Truth, Justice and Reconciliation Commission* (TJRC 2013) vol IIA, ch 6, para 19.

[29] Ibid, para. 9. This was also the case in Liberia; see Liberia TRC Report, n 21, 71–72.

[30] *Prosecutor v Samuel Hinga Norman* (Appeals Chamber) (Decision on Appeal by the Truth and Reconciliation Commission) SCSL-03-08-PT-122-I and II, para 4. This position was never accepted by the SLTRC. See *Witness to Truth*, n 26, ch 6, para 66. See also WA Schabas, 'A Synergistic Relationship: The Sierra Leone Truth and Reconciliation Commission and the Special Court for Sierra Leone' (2004) 15 *Criminal Law Forum* 3–54, 36–39.

[31] A Bisset, *Truth Commissions and Criminal Courts* (CUP 2012) ch 4.

prosecution and request information under mutual legal assistance treaties.[32] At the national level, freedom of information regimes may enable access to commission records.[33] Commissions should explain that while the likelihood of such disclosure is relatively low, it is possible. The careful approach of the Timorese CAVR is of note in this regard. It informed every deponent of the possible uses of statements, allowing individuals to decide whether their statement could be included in the final report, whether it would be accessible through the commission's archives and whether to give information confidentially or anonymously.[34] Indeed, particularly where the violations are of a sexual nature, commissions should consider the possibility of anonymity in order to enable all those who wish to testify to do so, while exercising caution in basing findings on anonymous testimony.

Guarantees of confidentiality also bring questions about how information is to be protected in the long term. Where it is given confidentially, the details of the statement giver will not be included in the commission's final report,[35] though the statement and identity of its giver are likely to remain in the commission's archives.[36] A number of commissions have therefore been instructed in their enacting legislation to protect confidential legislation upon dissolution.[37] The Liberian TRC Act attached a twenty-year prescription to documents classified as 'confidential' by the commission and these were categorized accordingly in the final report.[38] The SLTRC noted in its report the possibility that the SCSL or another criminal justice mechanism might in future seek access to the information archived under guarantees of confidentiality. While it considered that its own enacting legislation prohibited such access, it nevertheless recommended that Parliament never permit reform of those provisions so as to enable criminal justice mechanisms to obtain confidential information. Disclosure, it considered, would be a violation of privacy and in the cases of vulnerable witnesses, could expose them to the risk of reprisal or persecution. [39] 8

The need to provide emotional and psychological support to those testifying is something almost all commissions have been aware of. In South Africa, staff were employed to provide support to those giving testimony at public hearings[40] and the TRC established a system to refer traumatized victims to external agencies for additional support.[41] The Ghanaian commission provided counselling[42] and the Moroccan commission opened 9

[32] Ibid, ch 5. Requests for information might be made, eg, under: the European Convention on Mutual Assistance in Criminal Matters, 1959 ETS 30; Scheme Relating to Mutual Assistance in Criminal Matters within the Commonwealth 1986 (Commonwealth Secretariat, London, LMN (86)) 13; Inter-American Convention on Mutual Assistance in Criminal Matters, OAS TS 75; EU Convention on Mutual Assistance on Criminal Matters [2000] OJ C197/01.

[33] See, eg, the United States of America Freedom of Information Act (FOIA) 1967; the South African Promotion of Access to Information Act, Act no 2 of 2000; England, Wales, and Northern Ireland, Freedom of Information Act 2000.

[34] *Chega!*, Report of the Commission for Reception, Truth and Reconciliation for East Timor (January 2006) pt 1, para 150.

[35] *Witness to Truth*, n 26, vol 1, ch 5, para 24.

[36] See, eg, Liberia TRC Report, n 21, vol 2, 334–35.

[37] Decreto Supremo No 065-2001-PCM, Creación de la Comisión de la Verdad en el Perú, Lima, Peru (2 June 2001) Art 7; Sierra Leone: Truth and Reconciliation Commission Act 2000, s 19(2)(a)(ii); Kenya: Truth, Justice and Reconciliation Act 2008, s 52(2).

[38] Liberia TRC Report, n 21, 334–35.

[39] *Witness to Truth*, n 26, vol 3B, ch 6, para 68.

[40] TRC Report, n 2, vol 1, ch 6, 146.

[41] Ibid, vol 1, ch 10.

[42] *Ghana National Reconciliation Commission Final Report* (2004), vol 1, ch 2, section 2.3.3.5.2 and vol 2, ch 2, section 2.5.3.1.

a medical unit to assist victims suffering physical or psychological illness as a result of the violations they had suffered.[43] The CAVR for Timor-Leste established a Victim Support Division and referred those with urgent needs to external sources of support.[44] The Liberian TRC created a Psycho-Social Unit to provide support for those testifying in public hearings[45] and sought to secure support for statement givers who were part of the Diaspora Project in the UK and US.[46] Despite their importance, psychological counselling and associated support services are not always readily available in transitional states. The South African TRC noted the lack of available services outside urban areas[47] and the Liberian TRC found difficulties in securing support for those testifying as part of the Diaspora Project from Ghana.[48]

E. Critical Assessment

10 The limited temporal mandates of commissions make it impossible for them to deal with the longer-term consequences for victims and witnesses who have testified and the protection of confidentially received information. The impact of participation in truth-seeking proceedings is an under-researched area.[49] Yet whatever the impact, commissions with short-term mandates and limited resources will likely be ill-placed to respond. While they must be aware of the need to support victims at the time of giving testimony, it is equally, and perhaps more important that, as suggested by the Moroccan commission, transitional states take responsibility for ensuring long-term access to appropriate services post testifying.[50] It has also been suggested that greater attention needs to be paid to more culturally relevant forms of support, such as from traditional healers, religious leaders and community elders, particularly as resort to formal psychological counselling arguably stems from western notions of how best to respond to trauma.[51] However, there has been little research on the impact of culture on trauma recovery, making firm conclusions on the appropriateness of psychological treatment difficult. Future commissions should be open to direction from new studies that may give guidance on how best to provide support in different contexts.

11 Confidentiality raises even more complex issues. It has become both an essential means of protecting victims and witnesses and a truth-seeking tool, but the information obtained through this power may, as discussed in section D, be subject to requests for disclosure under a host of legal regimes. It is foreseeable that as the pursuit of criminal justice for the worst violations gains momentum, particularly under the ICC regime, there may be requests for access to confidential information where it is perceived as relevant to prosecutorial proceedings. It may prove very difficult for state authorities to resist such requests, especially where they are made in accordance with international treaty obligations. However, disclosure would raise serious questions about the privacy of the

[43] Kingdom of Morocco, Justice and Reconciliation Commission, *National Commission for Truth, Justice and Reconciliation, Summary of the Final Report* (2006) 37.

[44] *Chega!*, n 34, pt 10. [45] Liberia TRC Report, n 21, vol 2, 37. [46] Ibid, 84.

[47] TRC Report, n 2, vol 1, ch 10, 289. [48] Liberia TRC Report, n 21, 84.

[49] Most studies that have been conducted have focused on South Africa, making it difficult to draw general conclusions.

[50] Kingdom of Morocco, Justice and Reconciliation Commission, *National Commission for Truth, Justice and Reconciliation, Summary of the Final Report* (2006) 45.

[51] Hayner, n 18, 156–57.

victim or witness who provided the statement, not to mention the credibility of the commission itself. As yet, there have not been attempts by prosecuting bodies to access information received under guarantees of confidentiality but it seems naive to assume that this will never be the case. Some consider that all information should be available on a confidential basis to judicial bodies.[52] It can also be argued to the contrary that in the interests of robust truth seeking and to uphold the privacy and dignity of victims testimony received confidentially should not be subject to disclosure.

Selected Bibliography

Allan, A and Allan, M, 'The South African Truth and Reconciliation Commission as a Therapeutic Tool' (2000) 18 Behavioral Sciences and the Law 459–77.

Bisset, A, 'Confidential Truth Commission Information before the ICC: Extending Rule 73(4) Protections' (2012) 18 New England Journal of International and Comparative Law 207–25.

Bisset, A, 'Truth Commissions: A Barrier to the Provision of Judicial Assistance? (2010) 10 International Criminal Law Review 647–78.

Byrne, C, 'Benefit or burden: Victims' Reflection on TRC Participation'(2004) 10 Peace and Conflict: Journal of Peace Psychology 237–56.

De La Rey, C and Owens, I, 'Perceptions of Psychosocial Healing and the Truth and Reconciliation Commission in South Africa' (1998) 4 Peace and Conflict: Journal of Peace Psychology 257–70.

Hamber, B, 'Forgiveness and Reconciliation: Paradise Lost or Pragmatism?' (2007) 13 Peace and Conflict: Journal of Peace Psychology 115–25.

Millar, G, 'Between Western Theory and Local Practice: Cultural Impediments to Truth-Telling in Sierra Leone' (2011) 29 Conflict Resolution Quarterly 177–99.

Stein, DJ et al, 'The Impact of the Truth and Reconciliation Commission on Psychological Distress and Forgiveness in South Africa' (2007) 43 Social Psychiatry and Psychiatric Epidemiology 462–68.

[52] Amnesty International, *Truth, Justice and Reparation: Establishing an Effective Truth Commission*, AI Index: POL 30/009/2007 (June 2007) V.D.

Principle 11. Adequate Resources for Commissions

Howard Varney

The commission shall be provided with:

(a) Transparent funding to ensure that its independence is never in doubt;

(b) Sufficient material and human resources to ensure that its credibility is never in doubt.

A. Summary of Findings

There is considerable international law supporting Principle 11. This ranges from instruments that require an effective remedy be provided to victims of human rights violations, to instruments which specifically impose a duty on member states to provide adequate resources to investigative mechanisms.[1] Best practice suggests that there is a clear link between political will and the extent of resources provided to an investigation. There is also a connection between an investigative body's capacity to deliver, and its budget and resources. It is proposed that commissions be permitted to be heard in the determination of their resources; and that they be sufficiently resourced to enable them to perform their functions competently. Comparative experience demonstrates that, in most cases, commissions that are not adequately resourced will be unable to complete their mandates. Investigative commissions are, by their nature, very costly exercises, as the entire investigative machinery has to be set up from scratch. This commentary cautions against proceeding with commissions of inquiry where adequate support is not guaranteed. Such commissions are unlikely to deliver the truth or meet their objectives, and are likely to be discredited in the eyes of the public.

B. Contextual and Historical Introduction

1 Principle 11, 'Adequate Resources for Commissions', is one of the most fundamental Principles to Combat Impunity ('the Impunity Principles'). The history of this topic is replete with examples of inadequately resourced investigative commissions. In most cases national authorities have been unable to meet the budgetary demands of commissions. This has forced some commissions to seriously curtail their activities, while others have sought funding from donors in the international community.

2 Without the necessary resources, no commission can function optimally. In order to give meaningful effect to principles such as the right to the truth, a commission must have sufficient support to carry out its mandated tasks. Without the necessary financial, human, and physical resources, a commission cannot be expected to meet its mandate.

[1] In this commentary the reference to investigative mechanisms or commissions refers to both truth commissions and commissions of inquiry that investigate human rights abuses. Mandates of truth commissions are generally more extensive than those of other investigative commissions, often covering greater temporal periods and subject matters.

'Adequate resources' suggests that a commission should have sufficient support to enable the commissioners and staff to comply with their legal mandate without compromising the commission's independence and autonomy.[2] Autonomy for a commission means that it has control over its own finances and may make its own decisions in respect of the allocation of its resources.[3] The question of autonomy is inextricably linked to the independence of a commission.[4] Without adequate support, a commission of inquiry cannot be said to be genuinely independent, since it is likely to be susceptible to inappropriate functional relationships with other bodies. Moreover, its ability to set its own policy and strategic priorities will be severely eroded. 3

C. Theoretical Framework

There are several international law instruments governing the investigation of human rights violations that oblige state parties to adequately resource the responsible investigative agency. 4

I. Competent authorities

The right to an effective remedy following a violation of human rights is upheld by Article 8 of the UN Declaration of Human Rights;[5] and by Article 2(3) of the International Covenant on Civil and Political Rights,[6] which requires that a determination of rights be carried out by competent authorities.[7] Such competent authorities include commissions of inquiry.[8] Implicit in the term 'competent authorities' is the notion that such authorities must be adequately resourced to carry out their legal mandates. 'Competence' includes not only the legal authority to make a determination of rights, but also the actual capacity to carry out the necessary investigations. 5

II. Explicit duty

Other international instruments have explicitly imposed a duty on states to adequately fund investigative mechanisms. The International Convention for the Protection of All Persons from Enforced Disappearance[9] and the Declaration on the Protection of all Persons from Enforced Disappearance both mention that the investigative authorities shall have 'the necessary powers and resources to conduct the investigation effectively'.[10] 6

[2] E González and H Varney, *Truth Seeking Elements of Creating an Effective Truth Commission* (International Center for Transitional Justice 2013) 16.

[3] Ibid. [4] See commentary to Principle 7 in this volume.

[5] UN General Assembly (GA), Universal Declaration of Human Rights, UN Doc A/RES/217(III)[A] (10 December 1948) Art 8.

[6] UNGA, International Covenant on Civil and Political Rights (ICCPR), UN Doc A/RES/2200A (XXI) (16 December 1966).

[7] Ibid, Art 2(3)(b).

[8] See also the UN Basic Principles and Guidelines on the Right to a Remedy and Reparation for Victims of Gross Violations of International Human Rights Law and Serious Violations of International Humanitarian Law, UN Doc A/RES/60/147 (16 December 2005), Item 22(d), which stipulates that victims of gross violations of international human rights law and serious violations of international humanitarian law are entitled to an 'official declaration'. Such official declaration could also be made by a commission of inquiry.

[9] UNGA, International Convention for the Protection of All Persons from Enforced Disappearance, UN Doc A/RES/61/177 (12 January 2007) Art 12.

[10] UNGA, Declaration on the Protection of all Persons from Enforced Disappearance, UN Doc A/RES/47/133 (12 February 1993) Art 13(2).

The UN Principles on the Prevention and Investigation of Summary Executions and those on the Investigation of Torture stipulate that investigators must have 'all the necessary budgetary and technical resources for effective investigation'.[11] All these instruments establish a clear link between an investigative body's capacity to deliver and its budget and resources. Lastly, the United Nations Manual on the Effective Prevention and Investigation of Extra-Legal, Arbitrary and Summary Executions stipulates:

> [I]nvestigators should have the support of adequate technical and administrative personnel, as well as access to objective, impartial legal advice to ensure that the investigation will produce admissible evidence for later criminal proceedings. … [I]nvestigators should receive the full scope of the Government's resources and powers. Finally, investigators should have the power to seek help from the international community of experts in law, medicine and forensic sciences.[12]

7 The UN Convention against Corruption imposes an obligation on each state party to ensure that bodies tasked with the investigation of corruption are provided with the 'necessary material resources and specialized staff, as well as the training that such staff may require to carry out their functions'.[13]

III. Funding principles

8 Although commissions carry out different functions from courts, commissions, like courts, must act independently and impartially. In the conduct of their activities they must also apply a measure of procedural fairness. Accordingly, certain principles relating to financing and budgeting, which have their origins in international soft law pertaining to courts, also apply in large part to commissions.

9 These principles include that financial support must be sufficient to enable a commission to perform its functions competently[14] and to function without an excessive workload.[15] Secondly, a commission should have an opportunity to be heard and to participate in the determination of its budget and resourcing.[16] Lastly, the control of monies allocated to a commission must be exercised by the responsible commission staff.[17]

IV. Political will

10 A report published by the Organisation for Economic Co-operation and Development (OECD) [18] noted that while operationalizing specialized anti-corruption institutions is expensive in the longer term, it would be 'even more costly to set up a specialised body

[11] United Nations Economic and Social Council, *Principles on the Effective Prevention and Investigation of Extra-Legal, Arbitrary and Summary Executions*, UN Doc E/RES/1989/65 (14 July 1989) Annex 10; and UNGA, *Principles on the Effective Investigation and Documentation of Torture and Other Cruel, Inhuman or Degrading Treatment or Punishment*, UN Doc 1/RES/55/89 (22 February 2001) Art 3(a).

[12] United Nations Manual on the Effective Prevention and Investigation of Extra-Legal, Arbitrary and Summary Executions, UN Doc E/ST/CSDHA/.12 (1991) III.A.

[13] UNGA, United Nations Convention against Corruption, UN Doc A/58/422 (31 October 2003) Art 6(2), (2004) 43 ILM 37.

[14] Latimer House Guidelines for the Commonwealth on Parliamentary Supremacy and Judicial Independence (1998).

[15] Syracuse Draft Principles on the Independence of the Judiciary, 1981 (International Association of Penal Law and ICJ) 25.

[16] European Charter on the Statute for Judges, Council of Europe, DAJ/DOC (98) 23, para 1.6.

[17] Latimer House Guidelines, n 14, II 2.

[18] OECD, *Specialised Anti-Corruption Institutions: Review of Models* (2008) 17.

and then fail to provide it with adequate resources, hence hindering its performance. This consequently results in the failure to obtain and maintain public confidence.'[19]

The OECD emphasized in the same report that 'It is genuine political commitment, coupled with adequate resources, powers and staff, which are as crucial as formal independence, if not more so, to the success of an anti-corruption institution.'[20] 11

Alston, the former Special Rapporteur on Extrajudicial, Summary, or Arbitrary Executions, noted that the 'adequacy of resources' provided at the inception of a commission can be a 'useful indicator of the good faith of the government and perhaps also of its potential effectiveness'.[21] 12

González and Varney recommend that the initial funding allocation to a commission be on a provisional basis to support the start-up phase, and that subsequent funding be subject to estimates that reflect the operational plans of the commissioners.[22] The law establishing the South African Truth and Reconciliation Commission required it to consult with the audit commission before submitting annual estimates of revenue and expenditure to the relevant authority for approval.[23] 13

D. Practice

Support for commissions has ranged from the extravagant to the negligible.[24] The Bloody Sunday Inquiry (also known as the 'Savile Inquiry') into the deaths of 14 people sat for 12 years and reportedly cost more than £190 million.[25] The Commission of Inquiry into the Crimes and Misappropriations Committed by Ex-President Habré, his Accomplices and/or Accessories in Chad cost less than $500,000 and investigated some 3,780 killings and many other violations.[26] Truth Commission budgets have ranged from $1 million for the National Commission for Truth and Reconciliation in Chile, to nearly $18 million per year for the South African Truth and Reconciliation Commission.[27] 14

I. Costly exercise

Investigative commissions are, by their nature, costly exercises. In most cases the entire investigative machinery has to be set up from scratch, and often for a limited period of time.[28] A number of factors will impact on the total cost of a commission. These include the extent of the legal mandate of a commission, including its temporal jurisdiction, its geographic scope, and the scale of the incidents and violations to be investigated. Other 15

[19] Ibid, 27. [20] Ibid, 24.

[21] P Alston, *Report of the Special Rapporteur on Extrajudicial, Summary or Arbitrary Executions* (Human Rights Council 2008) para 30.

[22] González and Varney, n 2.

[23] Promotion of National Unity and Reconciliation Act no 34 of 1995, s 46(5).

[24] See Chart 4, 'A Comparison of Resources and Responsibilities' for budgets of various truth commissions in P Hayner, *Unspeakable Truths: Transitional Justice and the Challenge of Truth Commissions* (2nd edn, Routledge 2011) 268. See also P De Grieff, *Report of the Special Rapporteur on the Promotion of Truth, Justice, Reparation and Guarantees of Non-recurrence, Pablo de Greiff*, UN Doc A/HRC/24/42 (26 August 2013) [73] at 1–20.

[25] G Warner, 'Why did the Savile Inquiry cost almost twenty times the 9/11 Commission?' *Telegraph* (18 June 2010).

[26] NJ Kritz (ed), *Transitional Justice: How Emerging Democracies Reckon with Former Regimes*, vol 3, *Laws, Rulings, and Reports* (United States Institute of Peace Press 1995) 54 and 80.

[27] Hayner, n 24, 268–73. [28] González and Varney, n 2.

factors include the commission's duration of operations and the anticipated size of the commission.

16 Finances have to be found to cover the salaries of commissioners and skilled and experienced staff, including lawyers, forensic investigators, and other professionals. The salary budget for the Sierra Leone Truth and Reconciliation Commission consumed some 75 per cent of the entire budget.[29] Importing foreign skills can add considerable cost. Two of the five commissioners in the Solomon Islands Truth and Reconciliation Commission were foreign nationals, and those two commanded a significant proportion of the total staffing budget and 73 per cent of the money allocated for commissioner salaries. [30]

17 Resources are needed to support a number of time-consuming and laborious activities. These include investigations and research, the design and building of a database, statement-taking, data entry and analysis, public and closed hearings, outreach and communications, preparation, publication, and distribution of a report. Additional costs include administrative and logistical support, security and witness protection, transcription and translation services, information technology, office space, travel, and accommodation. Some commissions are required to provide legal representation to witnesses,[31] while others are required to provide legal assistance to interested parties so that they may participate meaningfully in the proceedings.[32]

II. Impact of inadequate resources

18 Hayner observed that truth commissions frequently run short of funds.[33] This even includes well-supported truth commissions, such as those of South Africa and Guatemala.[34]

19 The failure to adequately resource a commission can undermine its operations and ultimately prevent it from achieving its objectives. In Sri Lanka, the International Independent Group of Eminent Persons (IIGEP) concluded that the inquiries of the Commission of Inquiry to Investigate and Inquire into Alleged Serious Violations of Human Rights, which was appointed by the President in 2006, were not conducted in accordance with basic international norms and standards.[35] Amongst the reasons for this conclusion was the fact that the Commission had insufficient funding, no independent budget, and was entirely reliant on the Presidential Secretary for its finances.[36] The Commissioners worked part-time and investigators were seconded from government departments.[37] The IIGEP also noted that there was no effective victim and witness protection programme. Although such a unit existed in name, it had little funding, lacked trained staff, and was unable to offer protection, or even legal representation, to victims

[29] Final Report of the Truth and Reconciliation Commission for Sierra Leone, vol 1, ch 4, para 77.

[30] ICTJ, *Preliminary Contribution on the Comparative Analysis of the Costs of Administering Truth Commissions* (ICTJ 2009).

[31] Promotion of National Unity and Reconciliation Act no 34 of 1995 (SA), s 34(1).

[32] See *Magidiwana and Another v President of the Republic of South Africa and Others* (37904/2013) [2013] ZAGPPHC 292, [2014] 1 All SA 76 (GNP) (14 October 2013); and *Reference Guide for Judges Appointed to Commissions of Inquiry* (Canadian Judicial Council 2011) 9.

[33] Hayner, n 24, 216. [34] Ibid, 217.

[35] Concluding Public Statement, International Independent Group of Eminent Persons (15 April 2008) 1(e).

[36] Ibid.

[37] H Varney, 'Reflections on Commissions of Inquiry: How Does the Presidential Commission of Inquiry Compare with International Best Practice?', vol 18, issues 239 & 240 Law Society Trust Review (September 2007).

and witnesses.[38] As a result, no vital witnesses came forward. The Commission closed before it could finalize its investigations.[39]

The Truth and Reconciliation Commission for Sierra Leone prepared a budget of just under $10 million, but ultimately it had to make do with a 'bare bones budget' of approximately $4 million.[40] Internal mismanagement caused by the employment of unqualified staff in the start-up phase, as well as financial irregularities, dented the Commission's credibility and compounded its funding crisis.[41] As a result of the failure to raise sufficient funds, the Commission had to scale back its operations significantly. It had to reduce its planned staff complement by more than 25 per cent, and cut back on vehicles, equipment, information technology, and even fuel for the generator.[42] Operational units were reduced in size and merged, resulting in some organizational disjuncture.[43] 20

Inadequate funding, as well as the slow release of monies, severely impacted on the ability of the Commission to carry out its activities optimally.[44] Nonetheless, the Sierra Leone experience stands as proof that much can be achieved even with marginal support. Thierry Cruvellier noted that the report of the Commission constituted a 'small miracle', and that 'no one could have predicted such a logically structured, abundantly detailed, and well written report two years ago when the Commission almost dissolved itself'.[45] Several of the report's recommendations have been implemented.[46] 21

III. Sources of funding

Funds for a commission's budget can come from a variety of sources, including foreign and private sources. Alston notes that international assistance will be appropriate where a government demonstrates a desire to establish an effective commission but lacks the necessary expertise, funding, and resources.[47] Funding from the international community should be permitted so long as no unreasonable or questionable conditions are attached to it. Whereas the early truth commissions in countries such as Argentina and Chile were fully funded by their national governments, others, such as El Salvador and East Timor, have been fully funded by the international community, while Guatemala, South Africa, and Liberia relied on a mix of national and international funding.[48] The Peruvian Truth and Reconciliation Commission funded 50 per cent of its budget by using funds recovered from secret bank accounts of corrupt former officials.[49] 22

While national funding provides for local ownership, it is not a realistic possibility in many cases. Poor countries, struggling to emerge from conflict and rebuild institutions, will require support from the international community if they are to carry out competent 23

38 IIGEP Concluding Statement, n 35, 1(b).

39 B Matthews, 'The limits of international engagement in human rights situations: the Case of Sri Lanka' (2009) 82.4 Pacific Affairs 593–96.

40 Report of the Sierra Leone Truth and Reconciliation Commission, vol 1, ch 4, paras 71, 75, and 90, App 2, para 13.

41 Ibid, vol 1, 'Introduction', para 7; and vol 1, ch 4, para 66.

42 Ibid, vol 1, ch 4, paras 77 and 85.

43 Ibid, vol 1, ch 4, para 80.

44 Ibid, vol 1, ch 4, para 90.

45 T Cruvellier, 'Truth Report Spares No Parties' *International Justice Tribune* (18 October 2004).

46 See the Recommendations Matrix <www.sierraleonetrc.org/index.php/resources/recommendations-matrix> accessed 18 November 2017.

47 Alston, n 21, para 54.

48 Hayner, n 24, 217; and CAVR of Timor-Leste Donors List <www.cavr-timorleste.org/en/donors.htm> accessed 18 November 2017.

49 Gonzàlez and Varney, n 2, 32.

investigations. Where foreign funding tops up a national budget, specific projects can be sponsored, which can add considerable value to the truth-seeking exercise.

IV. Transparency

24 Transparency and good governance demand that commissions should comply with financial regulations governing the use of public funds; and that the sources of all funding should be disclosed.[50] The truth commissions of South Africa and Peru provide good examples of funding transparency. The South African report provides details of its budget-planning processes, itemized expenditure, sources and types of income, as well as its full balance sheets.[51] The Peruvian Commission is one of the few commissions that disclosed the salaries of each individual staff member on its website.[52]

E. Critical Assessment

25 While Principle 11 has not received much attention by way of research and academic study, it can nonetheless be described as a foundational principle. Unless this principle is complied with, the operations of a commission are likely to be stillborn or severely undermined. None of the other Principles to Combat Impunity, as they apply to commissions, can be properly sustained if adequate resources are not forthcoming.

26 While there will be exceptions where commissions excel notwithstanding limited support, it is not advisable to proceed with a commission of inquiry where the necessary resources are not available or guaranteed. Commissions that lack the basic support are unlikely to deliver any meaningful answers, and are likely to be discredited in the eyes of the public. The failure to provide adequate support to a commission must call into question the real intentions of the enabling authority.

27 National commissions that require support from the international community need to demonstrate that they are serious about truth seeking; and that they have the necessary competence to responsibly manage the commission and its resources.

28 Principle 11 takes on even greater significance given the recent trend in legal mandates of truth commissions that have extended the ambit of inquiry well beyond the violation of civil and political rights. Truth commissions in Kenya, Tunisia, and elsewhere have been required to investigate the root causes of conflict, including the violation of economic, social, and cultural rights.[53] These requirements have serious implications for the extent of resources required to support such commissions, which need considerably more expertise and time to carry out their mandates. This suggests that those designing legal frameworks should consider the question of the availability of finances and support before finalizing the investigative mandate of commissions.

[50] Ibid. [51] South African Truth and Reconciliation Commission Final Report, vol 1, 301.

[52] Comisión de la Verdad y Reconciliación (Perú), 'Financial Information' <www.cverdad.org.pe/ingles/lacomision/ifinanciera/pdfs/planillaenero03.pdf> accessed 18 November 2017.

[53] See Truth, Justice and Reconciliation Commission Act no 6 of 2008, <http://kenyalaw.org/kl/fileadmin/pdfdownloads/Acts/TruthJusticeandReconciliationCommissionAct_.pdf> accessed 18 November 2017; and Organic Law on Establishing and Organizing Transitional Justice (No 53, 2013) <http://www.ohchr.org/Documents/Countries/TN/TransitionalJusticeTunisia.pdf> accessed 18 November 2017.

Bibliography

Alston, P, *Report of the Special Rapporteur on Extrajudicial, Summary or Arbitrary Executions* (Human Rights Council 2008).

Gonzàlez, E and Varney, H, *Truth Seeking Elements of Creating an Effective Truth Commission* (ICTJ 2013).

Hayner, P, *Unspeakable Truths: Transitional Justice and the Challenge of Truth Commissions* (2nd edn, Routledge 2011).

Organisation for Economic Co-operation and Development, *Specialised Anti-Corruption Institutions: Review of Models* (2008).

United Nations Manual on the Effective Prevention and Investigation of Extra-Legal, Arbitrary and Summary Executions, UN Doc E/ST/CSDHA/.12 (1991).

Principle 12. Advisory Functions of the Commissions

Isabel Robinson and Howard Varney

The commission's terms of reference should include provisions calling for it to include in its final report recommendations concerning legislative and other action to combat impunity. The terms of reference should ensure that the commission incorporates women's experiences in its work, including its recommendations. When establishing a commission of inquiry, the Government should undertake to give due consideration to the commission's recommendations.

A. Summary of Findings

The advisory function of truth commissions is a core aspect of the forward-looking dimension of truth-telling and truth-seeking processes. It is one of the most concrete ways in which truth commissions can achieve their goals of facilitating the rebuilding of society and preventing further violence.[1] In particular, the advisory function provides an important way of ensuring that truth commissions pay attention to the experiences and roles of women in transitioning societies. Additionally, the advisory function of truth commissions is one key area where commissions intersect with other measures aimed at combating impunity, including reparations, criminal prosecutions, and institutional reform.

Although there are numerous challenges in ensuring that the recommendations of truth commissions are implemented, recommendations can make an important contribution to the process of transformation and regeneration of society. In most cases, recommendations are more likely to be implemented if they are both realistic and specific, and if implementation is effectively monitored by an independent body.

B. Contextual and Historical Introduction

1 The recommendations of a truth commission are the advice that the commission wishes to provide to the head of state, executive, legislature, and other bodies.[2] They are usually contained within the final report of a truth commission, and can include institutional, administrative, legislative, constitutional, and other measures, for example: reform of previously abusive institutions, such as the police, army, and judiciary; development of

[1] P Hayner, *Unspeakable Truths: Transitional Justice and the Challenge of Truth Commissions* (Routledge 2011) 23 and 182.

[2] In rare cases, truth commissions have also issued recommendations to other states or the 'international community'. See The Timor-Leste Commission for Reception, Truth and Reconciliation for East Timor (CAVR), *Chega! The Final Report of the Timor-Leste Commission for Reception, Truth and Reconciliation (CAVR)* (2013), 2575–77 <http://chegareport.net/Chega%20All%20Volumes.pdf> accessed 21 November 2017; and *Witness to Truth: Report of the Sierra Leone Truth and Reconciliation Commission*, vol 2 (Graphic Packaging Ltd 2004) ch 3, 205–24 (hereinafter '*Witness to Truth*') <www.sierraleonetrc.org/index.php/view-the-final-report/download-table-of-contents/volume-two> accessed 21 November 2017.

an administrative reparations programme; criminal prosecutions; ratification of international human rights treaties; legislative reform in natural resource industries; dissemination of the commission's report; and preservation of the commission's archives.

Historically, the advisory function of truth commissions has been a defining characteristic of almost all commissions to date. As such, this function was also included in the original version of the Principles ('the Joinet Principles') from 1997.[3] However, in contrast to the Updated Principles, the original Principle 11 pinpointed the material scope of the advisory function, underlining three objectives for the recommendations of a truth commission: (i) to encourage perpetrators to admit their guilt; (ii) to invite the Government to accede to international treaties; and (iii) to propose legislative or other measures—directed at the army, police, judicial system, and democratic institutions—to prevent recurrence of violations. Similarly to the Updated Principle 12, the original Principle 11 also underlined the importance of adopting a gender-sensitive approach that responds to the specific experiences of women.[4] 2

Although most truth commissions have exercised an advisory function, the number and complexity of recommendations have varied considerably: while many of the earlier commissions focused on recommendations regarding criminal prosecution, more recent commissions have developed elaborate recommendations regarding the establishment of reparations programmes as well as legal and institutional reform. For example, the Sierra Leone Truth and Reconciliation Commission (SLTRC) compiled 108 pages of recommendations encompassing 118 topics under 17 subject headings.[5] Some truth commissions have also included specific recommendations on how the findings of the commission should be disseminated, including that the findings of the commission be incorporated into the national school and university curricula.[6] 3

One of the most controversial aspects of the advisory functions of truth commissions has been the legal status and enforceability of recommendations. Despite the enabling laws of several commissions, which have provided for the mandatory implementation of recommendations,[7] recommendations are by definition not binding. In line with the principle of separation of powers, as set out under the constitutions of many states, the recommendations of a truth commission cannot be binding on the executive arm of government. This has been affirmed in Liberia, where the Supreme Court struck down the sections in the truth commission law that provided for mandatory implementation of the commission's recommendations.[8] 4

[3] *Question of the impunity of perpetrators of human rights violations (civil and political): Revised final report prepared by Mr Joinet pursuant to Sub-Commission decision 1996/119*, UN Doc E/CN.4/Sub.2/1997/20/Rev.1 (2 October 1997) Annex II, Principle 11.

[4] Principle 11 specifically underlined the need, where applicable, to recommend reparations for violations of the fundamental rights of women and prevention of their recurrence.

[5] See *Witness to Truth*, n 2, 180–83.

[6] *Guatemala: Memory of Silence*, Report of the Commission for Historical Clarification, para 36 <https://www.aaas.org/sites/default/files/migrate/uploads/mos_en.pdf> accessed 20 January 2018; *Witness to Truth*, n 2, 203.

[7] Examples include the laws establishing the truth commissions in El Salvador, Sierra Leone, Liberia, and Kenya.

[8] *Williams v Minister of Justice, Attorney General, Independent National Human Rights Commission and Government of Liberia*, Supreme Court of the Republic of Liberia, 21 January 2011, <www.mediafire.com/?u1n6zkqoxl1zn3o> accessed 21 November 2017. See also 'Liberian Supreme Court Squashes Truth and Reconciliation Commission Ban on Politicians' *African Press Agency* (24 January 2011) <http://archive.is/9NKp> accessed 21 November 2017.

5 Despite this, Principle 12 of the Updated Principles states explicitly that governments should undertake to give due consideration to the recommendations of truth commissions. The United Nations High Commissioner for Human Rights supports this approach, and has encouraged states to implement and monitor implementation of recommendations.[9] In practice, there are several ways in which truth commissions can encourage governments to give due consideration to their recommendations. For example, by recommending that the government formally respond to its final report within a specified or reasonable time period; and that it publish its response in a publicly available document, such as the government gazette or a government white paper.

6 Truth commissions could also recommend that the parliament or national assembly of a country convene a special sitting within a specified or reasonable time period, to debate the government's response to the final report and to consider any further action that the assembly may wish to take.[10]

C. Theoretical Framework

7 The advisory function of truth commissions aims to identify reforms and transitional measures that can be undertaken at a legal, political, institutional, and administrative level, which will help to prevent further conflict and violence. As such, it is central to the state's legal obligation to take effective measures to prevent future human rights violations and ensure the corresponding right of victims to guarantees of non-recurrence.[11] Additionally, recommendations may help to facilitate national reconciliation, by helping to restore civic trust in public institutions.[12]

8 Within the current international framework, truth commissions are regularly located within liberal peacebuilding processes, which seek to cultivate liberal democratic political systems.[13] Thus, the recommendations of truth commissions usually relate to liberal democratic goals, including, for example, good governance, respect for human rights, and strengthening the rule of law. Accordingly, the advisory function of a truth commission may often intersect with parallel development and peacebuilding processes. In this regard, the Special Rapporteur on the promotion of truth, justice, reparations, and guarantees of non-recurrence has advised that truth commissions 'will need to engage earlier with

[9] UN Commission on Human Rights, Human Rights Resolution (Res) 2005/66, Right to the Truth, UN Doc E/CN.4/RES/2005/66 (20 April 2005).

[10] In Sierra Leone, the TRC Follow-Up Project persuaded the Clerk of Parliament to set aside one day in the parliamentary calendar on which no other business but the TRC report and recommendations would be considered. An unprecedented Special Session of the Sierra Leone Parliament on the TRC Report and Recommendations was held on 14 November 2005. See TRC Follow-Up Project: Sierra Leone (West Africa), *Witness Final Report—January 2006*, 41 <www.sierraleonetrc.org/images/docs/sl_trc_follow_up_final-report-jan06.pdf> accessed 21 November 2017.

[11] See the commentary to Principle 35 in this volume.

[12] National reconciliation is understood here as the process of reaffirming shared norms and values at a community level, and rebuilding civic trust in state institutions and state officials. See P de Greiff, 'The Role of Apologies in National Reconciliation Processes: on Making Trustworthy Institutions Trusted' in M Gibney, R Hassman-Howard, J-M Coicaud, and N Stiener (eds), *The Age of Apology: Facing up to the Past* (University of Pennsylvania Press 2008) 120–36.

[13] K Andrieu, 'Political Liberalism after Mass Violence: John Rawls and a "Theory" of Transitional Justice' in S Buckley-Zistel, T Koloma Bec, C Braun, and F Mieth, *Transitional Justice Theories* (Routledge 2014) 85–104, 88. See also CL Sriram, 'Justice as Peace? Liberal Peacebuilding and Strategies of Transitional Justice' (2007) 21(4) Global Society 579–91; P de Greiff, 'Theorizing Transitional Justice' in M Williams, R Nagy and J Elster (eds), *Transitional Justice* (New York University Press 2011) 31–77.

different government agencies and development agents regarding the articulation of their recommendations in actionable ways'.[14]

In line with a comprehensive approach to transitional justice,[15] the advisory functions of a truth commission are one key area where truth-telling and truth-seeking processes intersect with other transitional justice mechanisms, including reparations, vetting, criminal prosecutions, and institutional reform. Recommendations regarding prosecution, pardons, and vetting may be particularly controversial, especially if individuals are identified publicly. As discussed in the commentary to Principle 9 in this volume, recommendations of this type will require specific measures to ensure procedural fairness for individuals who are named in a commission's report.[16] 9

As emphasized in Principle 12, truth commissions should pay attention to women's experiences when developing recommendations.[17] The focus on women is reflected in other Principles,[18] as well as in key international documents,[19] and is a response to the 'gender-blind' approach of previous truth commissions.[20] 10

D. Practice

The recommendations of truth commissions have varied considerably, ranging from vague recommendations, such as improving economic justice, raising awareness, and increasing capacity and resources, to detailed recommendations on rules of evidence in criminal prosecutions and judicial tenure. For example, the Commission in El Salvador issued detailed recommendations regarding reform of the judiciary, in order to ensure independence in the appointment process and adequate training for judges.[21] 11

12. In line with Principle 12, some truth commissions have developed recommendations that specifically respond to the experiences of women.[22] For example, in Timor-Leste, the

[14] See *Report of the Special Rapporteur on the Promotion of Truth, Justice, Reparation and Guarantees of Non-recurrence, Pablo de Greiff*, UN Doc A/HRC/24/42 (26 August 2013) para 73.

[15] See *Report of the Special Rapporteur on the Promotion of Truth, Justice, Reparation and Guarantees of Non-recurrence, Pablo de Greiff*, UN Doc A/HRC/21/46 (9 August 2012) paras 22–27; Office of the United Nations High Commissioner for Human Rights (OHCHR), *Rule-of-Law Tools for Post-Conflict States: Truth Commissions* (OHCHR 2006) 5.

[16] Regarding the naming of individuals and procedural fairness, see generally M Freeman, *Truth Commissions and Procedural Fairness* (CUP 2006).

[17] S Buckley-Zistel, *Truth Commissions, Human Rights and Gender. Normative Changes in Transitional Moments* (2 May 2014) <www.ssrn.com/abstract=2432164> or <www.dx.doi.org/10.2139/ssrn.2432164> accessed 19 January 2018; M Albertson Fineman and E Zinsstag (eds), *Feminist Perspectives on Transitional Justice: From International and Criminal to Alternative Forms of Justice* (Intersentia 2013) (especially ch 9); J West, 'Rethinking Representations of Sexual and Gender-Based Violence: A Case Study of the Liberian Truth and Reconciliation Commission' (2013) 14(4) Journal of International Women's Studies 109–23.

[18] See Principles 6, 7, 8(d), 32, 35.

[19] UN Secretary-General, *Guidance Note of the Secretary-General: United Nations Approach to Transitional Justice* (UN 2010) 5; UN Secretary-General, *The rule of law and transitional justice in conflict and post-conflict societies*, UN Doc S/2011/634 (12 October 2011) para 22.

[20] Many earlier commissions focused on human rights violations typically committed against men, and failed to reflect the experiences of women. See, eg, E Schmid, 'Liberia's Truth Commission Report: Economic, Social, and Cultural Rights in Transitional Justice' (2009) XXIV The Fletcher Journal of Human Security 5–28, 16–17.

[21] *From Madness to Hope: the 12-year war in El Salvador: Report of the Commission on the Truth for El Salvador* (15 March 1993) 171 <www.usip.org/sites/default/files/file/ElSalvador-Report.pdf> accessed 20 January 2018.

[22] *Witness to Truth*, n 2, 168–76; Equity and Reconciliation Commission, *Rapport Final: Eléments de Consolidation des Reformes et de la Réconciliation*, vol 4, 40–41, <http://www.cndh.org.ma/fr/rapport-final-de-lier/livre-4-elements-de-consolidation-des-reformes-et-de-la-reconciliation> accessed 20 January 2018 (recommendations on reforming the Family Code).

CAVR recommended legislative reform on domestic violence, and measures to recognize and support the role of women in the prevention and resolution of conflicts and in peacebuilding.[23] Additionally, the CAVR recommended that at least 50 per cent of reparations should go to women.[24] In this way, the CAVR sought to recognize and address the gender inequities that existed during the statement-taking process.

13 Another key element underpinning the practice of truth commissions is the importance of local participation and ownership.[25] To date, several truth commissions have adopted a participatory approach to the exercise of their advisory function, for example by soliciting proposals for recommendations through written submissions, and by convening special hearings to obtain expert advice on thematic areas. In Guatemala, the Commission convened a conference with over 400 participants, including legislators and key civil society leaders, to draft the Commission's recommendations.[26] A participatory approach is reinforced in Principle 35, and is a vital part of ensuring a bottom-up approach to transitional justice.[27]

14 It is important to consider how truth commissions have attempted to ensure effective monitoring of the implementation of their recommendations. Such processes are not addressed by Principle 12 but have proved necessary for sound accountability and to help to provide an incentive for implementing the recommendations.[28]

15 In Sierra Leone, the TRC law foresaw the establishment of a follow-up body, but this role was in fact taken on by the Human Rights Commission (HRC), which was established pursuant to the TRC's recommendation.[29] In coordination with the UN Integrated Office in Sierra Leone (UNIOSIL), the HRC developed a 'recommendations matrix', which analysed the status of implementation of the TRC recommendations.[30] The draft matrix was validated by a National Consultative Conference in 2007 and reviewed again in 2010.[31] This matrix has been identified as a good model for monitoring mechanisms.[32] In addition, civil society groups played a key role in lobbying the Government on certain recommendations.[33] As a result, a number of key recommendations dealing with the rights of women and children and the combating of corruption, including disclosure of assets and independent corruption prosecutions, have been implemented.[34]

[23] *Chega!* n 2, 12–13. [24] Ibid, 39.

[25] See, eg, UN Secretary-General, *The Rule of Law and Transitional Justice in Post-Conflict Societies*, UN Doc S/2004/616 (23 August 2004).

[26] Hayner, n 1, 192.

[27] Bottom-up theories of transitional justice have developed as a critical response to top-down approaches modelled on a dominant international script. See, eg, P Lundy and M McGovern, 'Whose Justice? Rethinking Transitional Justice from the Bottom Up' (2008) 35(2) Journal of Law and Society 265–92.

[28] *Report of the Special Rapporteur*, n 14, para 78.

[29] Prior to this, the non-governmental organization Witness also launched a Follow-Up Project in May 2005. See *Witness Final Report—January 2006*, n 10.

[30] Human Rights Commission of Sierra Leone and United Nations Integrated Peace-building Office in Sierra Leone (UNIPSIL), 'Matrix on the Status of Implementation of the Truth and Reconciliation Commission Recommendations', 2010, <www.sierraleonetrc.org/index.php/resources/recommendations-matrix> accessed 20 January 2018.

[31] Ibid. [32] *Report of the Special Rapporteur*, n 14, para 78.

[33] An example of civil society lobbying was the compilation by local musicians of an album highlighting the TRC recommendations. The album was launched in the national stadium in 2007. See The Patriotic Vanguard, 'CD on TRC Recommendations to be launched Saturday', 10 May 2007 <http://www.thepatrioticvanguard.com/cd-on-trc-recommendations-to-be-launched-saturday> accessed 22 November 2017.

[34] Recommendations Matrix, n 30, 6–10.

In contrast to Sierra Leone, the national human rights commission in Morocco (the CCDH) was charged with implementing the recommendations of the Equity and Reconciliation Commission, which submitted its final report in December 2005.[35] Many advocates were critical of this delegation, given that the CCDH had limited powers to implement legislative or administrative changes.[36] Despite this, Morocco was extremely efficient in implementing the Commission's recommendations on reparations, including individual compensation[37] and provision of healthcare.[38] In addition, the CCDH developed a Community Reparation Programme, which coordinated a range of projects in eleven provinces, including, for example, income-generating projects and projects aimed at building local capacity.[39] The CCDH issued two reports on implementation, describing the activities undertaken to implement the recommendations and the status of implementation.[40] 16

E. Critical Assessment

Although most truth commissions develop recommendations, the key challenge is that implementation remains weak or non-existent in the majority of cases.[41] The failure to implement recommendations often gives rise to a view that commissions are established in order to address criticism of government inaction, without the government actually doing anything. This in turn promotes public disillusionment and fatigue with commissions. 17

The failure to implement recommendations can often be ascribed to a lack of political will. For example, many of the recommendations of the South African TRC have not been implemented, including those relating to reparations and investigation/prosecution of cases.[42] In a court application launched during 2015 to compel the South African prosecuting authority to make a decision in an enforced disappearance case, a former chief prosecutor conceded that the cases recommended by the TRC for criminal investigation were not taken forward because of political interference.[43] The South African state has also claimed that it is unnecessary to proceed with comprehensive reparations recommended by the TRC when the state already has ongoing programmes that provide essential services, such as social welfare.[44] 18

[35] The national human rights commission, the Advisory Council on Human Rights (CCDH), was nominated by the King of Morocco as the body responsible for implementation of the Commission's recommendations.

[36] Hayner, n 1, 44.

[37] *Follow-Up Report on the Implementation of Equity and Reconciliation Commission Recommendations: Main Report* (CCDH, December 2009) 55 <www.cndh.org.ma/sites/default/files/documents/follow_UP_IER.pdf> accessed 22 November 2017.

[38] Ibid, 59. [39] Ibid, 62–76. [40] Ibid.

[41] See the example of Kenya: 'A Study of Commissions of Inquiries in Kenya', AfriCOG Reports 2007 <www.africog.org/reports/Commissionsofinquirypaper.pdf> accessed 19 January 2018. See also Hayner, n 1, 193.

[42] H Varney, 'Transitional Justice, Criminal Justice and Exceptionalism in South Africa' in M Reed and A Lyons (2010) *Contested Transitions: Dilemmas of Transitional Justice in Colombia and Comparative Experience* (International Center of Transitional Justice and Ministry of Foreign Relations of Norway 2010) 281–99.

[43] *Nkadimeng v National Director of Public Prosecutions and Others*, Case no 35554/2015, High Court of South Africa, Gauteng Division. See the affidavit of Vusi Pikoli <www.southernafricalitigationcentre.org/cases/ongoing-cases/south-africa-challenging-npa-inaction-for-trc-related-prosecutions/> accessed 20 January 2018.

[44] Declaration by Justice Minister Penuell Maduna on Apartheid Litigation in the United States, dated 11 July 2003, before The Honourable Mr Justice John E Sprizzo, United States District Judge, New York, attached as appendix 2a in *Esther Kiobel, et al v Royal Dutch Petroleum Co, et al, Brief of the Governments of the Kingdom of the Netherlands and the United Kingdom of Great Britain and Northern Ireland as Amicus Curaie in support of Neither Party*, No 10-1491, Supreme Court of the United States of America <www.sdshhlaw.com/pdfs/Governments%20of%20the%20Kingdom%20of%20the%20Netherlands%20and%20the%20Kingdom%20of%20Great%20Britain%20and%20Northern%20Ireland.pdf> accessed 22 November 2017.

19 The expansion in the mandates of contemporary truth commissions also means that commissions are regularly expected to develop complex recommendations on comprehensive structural reform.[45] It is questionable as to whether most commissioners are adequately prepared to do this. Most commissions do not possess the expertise to devise the actual roll-out plan of government programmes.

20 Recommendations that resonate with communities are likely to be the subject of mobilization and lobbying. Such recommendations stand a reasonable prospect of being implemented. In particular, recommendations that are specific,[46] feasible, linked to findings, addressed to specific office holders, and which have measurable short-, medium-, or long-term goals, will facilitate implementation and monitoring. Recommendations should identify the problem or issue that they seek to address, and indicate how they will do so. In some cases, it may also be appropriate to prioritize which recommendations should be implemented first. For example, the SLTRC organized its recommendations into three categories for implementation: 'imperative'; 'work towards'; and 'seriously consider'.[47]

21 In addition, recommendations should be practical and realistic, taking into account the available resources and capacity. This does not mean that commissions should only make recommendations that the government will be willing to implement. However, it is important to emphasize that recommendations should not aim to address all of the shortcomings in society.

22 Effective monitoring can encourage governments to implement recommendations. Although there are a number of institutional possibilities, it appears that official monitoring is best carried out by an existing statutory body, such as a national human rights commission, which is likely to have the resources and authority to monitor human rights and related developments.[48] Importantly, monitoring should not be carried out by the same body charged with implementing the recommendations. The actual facilitation and coordination of recommendations involving government programmes ought to take place at the heart of government, rather than by a standalone body located outside of government.

23 Ultimately, it is up to a vigilant civil society to monitor and scrutinize the government's performance in implementing the recommendations of a truth commission. Such monitoring ought to be sector-driven by civil society groups that can focus on the recommendations that impact on their programmes and constituencies. Focused lobbying can target relevant government departments and ministries, as well as legislative committees and individual members of the legislature. Innovative ways of monitoring include the publishing of periodic scorecards, which assess performance in respect of the implementation of selected recommendations. Civil society organizations can also serve the function of '*monitoring the monitors*', evaluating whether the government body assigned to monitoring implementation is actually doing so in an impartial and critical manner.

[45] According to the UN Special Rapporteur on the promotion of truth, justice, reparation and guarantees of non-recurrence, it is no surprise that 'commissions are finding it increasingly difficult to satisfy growing expectations'. See *Report of the Special Rapporteur*, n 14, para 94.

[46] Hayner, n 1, 193. [47] *Witness to Truth*, n 2, 119–21.

[48] In Sierra Leone where a follow-up body was mandated by law, no such entity was established. The SLTRC, recognizing the unlikelihood of such a body being established, recommended that the national human rights commission be tasked with follow-up and monitoring. See *Witness to Truth*, n 2, 204.

Bibliography

de Greiff, P, 'The Role of Apologies in National Reconciliation Processes: on Making Trustworthy Institutions Trusted' in M Gibney, R Hassman-Howard, J-M Coicaud, and N Stiener (eds), *The Age of Apology: Facing up to the Past* (University of Pennsylvania Press 2008) 120–36.

Equity and Réconciliation Commission, *Rapport Final: Eléments de Consolidation des Reformes et de la Réconciliation*, vol 4, 40–41, <http://www.cndh.org.ma/fr/rapport_final-de-lier/livre-4-eléments-de-consolidation-des-reformes-et-de-la-reconciliation>.

Freeman, M, *Truth Commissions and Procedural Fairness* (CUP 2006).

From Madness to Hope: the 12-year war in El Salvador: Report of the Commission on the Truth for El Salvador (15 March 1993) <www.usip.org/sites/default/files/file/ElSalvador_Report.pdf>.

Guatemala: Memory of Silence, Report of the Comission for Historical Clarification, <https://www.aaas.org/sites/default/files/migrate/uploads/mos_en.pdf>.

Hayner, P, *Unspeakable Truths: Transitional Justice and the Challenge of Truth Commissions* (Routledge 2011).

Human Rights Commission of Sierra Leone and United Nations Integrated Peace-buidling Office in Sierra Leone (UNIPSIL), 'Matrix on the Status of Implementation of the Truth and Reconciliation Commission Recommendations', 2010 <www.sierraleonetrc.org/index.php/resources/recommendations-matris>.

Lundy, P and McGovern, M, 'Whose Justice? Rethinking Transitional Justice from the Bottom Up' (2008) 35(2) Journal of Law and Society 265–92.

OHCHR, *Rule-of-Law Tools for Post-Conflict States: Truth Commissions* (OHCHR 2006).

Report of the Special Rapporteur on the Promotion of Truth, Justice, Reparation and Guarantees of Non-recurrence, Pablo de Greiff, UN Doc A/HRC/24/42 (26 August 2013).

Report of the Special Rapporteur on the Promotion of Truth, Justice, Reparation and Guarantees of Non-recurrence, Pablo de Greiff, UN Doc A/HRC/21/46 (9 August 2012).

Schmid, E, 'Liberia's Truth Commission Report: Economic, Social, and Cultural Rights in Transitional Justice' (2009) XXIV The Fletcher Journal of Human Security 5–28.

Sriram, CL, 'Justice as Peace? Liberal peacebuilding and Strategies of Transitional Justice' (2007) 21(4) Global Society 579–91.

The Timor-Leste Commission for Reception, Truth and Reconciliation for East Timor (CAVR), *Chega! The Final Report of the Timor-Leste Commission for Reception, Truth and Reconciliation (CAVR)* (2013) <http://chegareport.net/Chega%20All%20Volumes.pdf>.

TRC Follow-Up Project: Sierra Leone (West Africa), *Witness Final Report—January 2006*, 41 <www.sierraleonetrc.org/images.docs/sl_trc_follow_up_final_report_jan06.pdf>.

Witness to Truth: Report of the Sierra Leone Truth and Reconciliation Commission, available at <www.sierraleonetrc.org/index.php/view-the-final-report/download-table-of-contents/volume-two>.

Principle 13. Publicizing the Commission's Reports

Catherine Harwood and Carsten Stahn

For security reasons or to avoid pressure on witnesses and commission members, the commission's terms of reference may stipulate that relevant portions of its inquiry shall be kept confidential. The commission's final report, on the other hand, shall be made public in full and shall be disseminated as widely as possible.

A. Summary of Findings

The principle of publicity is a crucial component of the United Nations (UN) Updated Impunity Principles.[1] Full publication and wide dissemination of a report realizes the right to the truth. An authoritative account of violations might also promote accountability and reconciliation. A final report should be widely accessible, taking into account cultural and technological contexts. However, this principle is not unlimited. Commissions may receive information confidentially, and may exclude some information from reports for security reasons and to avoid interference with witnesses and commissioners. The term 'security reasons' could be further defined to guide interpretation and prevent undue censorship. In practice, political considerations have barred the publication of some reports, which impedes the *raison d'être* of commissions.

B. Contextual and Historical Introduction

1 Principle 13 is articulated in terms similar to Principle 12 of the earlier Joinet Principles, which was explained in the Introduction to those Principles as follows:[2]

> While there may be reasons to keep the commissions' proceedings confidential, in part to avoid pressure on witnesses and ensure their safety, the commissions' reports should be published and publicized as widely as possible.

2 Principle 13 specifies a closed list of reasons for confidentiality, rather than the open-ended exception implied in the Introduction to the Joinet Principles. A report that examined the application and further implementation of the Joinet Principles referred to the principle of publicity in a general way and did not examine the scope of exceptions.[3] The general principle of publicity is reaffirmed in other fact-finding and

[1] Updated Set of Principles for the Protection and Promotion of Human Rights through Action to Combat Impunity, UN Doc E/CN.4/2005/102/Add.1 (8 February 2005) (hereinafter 'Updated Impunity Principles').

[2] *Revised final report prepared by Mr Joinet pursuant to Sub-Commission decision 1996/119*, UN Doc E/CN.4/Sub.2/1997/20/Rev.1 (2 October 1997) para 24.

[3] *Independent Study on Best Practices, Including Recommendations, to Assist States in Strengthening Their Domestic Capacity to Combat All Aspects of Impunity, by Diane Orentlichter*, UN Doc E/CN.4/2004/88 (27 February 2004) paras 19(b) and (i).

transitional justice guidance documents.[4] Principle 13 applies to both truth commissions and commissions of inquiry with a narrower investigative focus on specific situations or incidents.[5] National commissions are established by states, while international and regional[6] commissions are established by intergovernmental organizations.

C. Theoretical Framework

I. Overview of normative dimensions

Principle 13 gives practical effect to international norms associated with transitional justice processes,[7] particularly the right to the truth (Principle 2); the duty to preserve memory (Principle 3); and the right of victims to know the circumstances of violations (Principle 4). Dissemination of reports may also have wider transitional justice effects. Truth-seeking mechanisms may assist societies to come to terms with the past, promote reconciliation, and prevent recurrence of violations.[8] A credible and authoritative account of violations may promote accountability, particularly as findings of serious violations may trigger a state's legal duty to investigate and prosecute atrocities amounting to international crimes. 3

II. Confidential portions of an inquiry

Principle 13 accepts that aspects of an inquiry may be confidential for security reasons or to avoid pressure on witnesses and commissioners. Protecting the safety of victims and preventing intimidation are of paramount concern for commissions. The tenet 'do no harm' applies,[9] and UN General Assembly declarations affirm rights of victims and human rights defenders to protection from retaliation.[10] However, many commissions do not have the mandate or resources for witness protection programmes.[11] Victims' and witnesses' safety could be jeopardized if their identities were revealed. In addition, commissioners and staff can face security risks when investigating situations 4

[4] Office of the United Nations High Commissioner for Human Rights (OHCHR), *Commissions of Inquiry and Fact-Finding Missions on International Human Rights and Humanitarian Law: Guidance and Practice*, UN Doc HR/PUB/14/7 (February 2015) 92; *Siracusa Guidelines for International, Regional and National Fact-Finding Bodies* (Intersentia 2013) Guideline 13.9 (hereinafter '*Siracusa Guidelines*'); MC Bassiouni and D Rothenberg (eds), *The Chicago Principles on Post-Conflict Justice* (International Human Rights Law Institute 2008) 24 (hereinafter '*Chicago Principles*').

[5] Updated Impunity Principles, 'Definitions, D. Truth commissions' and Principle 7; and 'Introduction' in this volume.

[6] This commentary does not discuss fact-finding missions of regional human rights commissions.

[7] *Guidance Note of the Secretary-General: United Nations Approach to Transitional Justice* (March 2010) 3.

[8] Updated Impunity Principles, Principles 2 and 3.

[9] OHCHR, n 4, 75. For example, *Report of the Detailed Findings of the Commission of Inquiry on Human Rights in the Democratic People's Republic of Korea*, UN Doc A/HRC/25/CRP.1 (7 February 2014) para 29 (hereinafter '*North Korea Report*').

[10] *Basic Principles and Guidelines on the Right to a Remedy and Reparation for Victims of Gross Violations of International Human Rights Law and Serious Violations of International Humanitarian Law*, General Assembly (GA) Res 60/147, UN Doc A/RES/60/147 (16 December 2005), para 10; UNGA Res 53/144 (9 December 1998); UNGA Res 40/34 (29 November 1985).

[11] C Petrigh, 'Protection of Victims, Witnesses and Staff in Monitoring, Reporting and Fact-Finding Mechanisms', Program on Humanitarian Policy and Conflict Research Working Paper, 7 February 2014 <ssrn.com/abstract=2392493> accessed 15 November 2017.

of violence or instability,[12] but may also be threatened following publication of the report.[13]

5 While 'pressure' refers to interference and intimidation, the term 'security reasons' is less clear. In addition to safety, it might also include national security. Indeed, Principle 16 accepts that access to archives may be denied on this ground, subject to strict conditions and judicial review.[14] If access to archives may be refused for national security reasons, the same rationale might also apply to aspects of the inquiry itself. However, the International Center for Transitional Justice (ICTJ)'s view is that '[s]ecrecy laws, like national security considerations, should not apply to any matter that is the subject of a truth commission inquiry'.[15] Lack of guidance on the parameters of this exception might attract diverse unilateral interpretations, and even misuse.

III. Full publication and wide dissemination

6 Recent fact-finding guidelines require publication of final reports.[16] A 1991 declaration on UN fact-finding activities in matters of international peace and security is ambivalent in this respect,[17] but a recent guidance document provides that UN commissions' reports should 'generally be public' in order to 'contribute to the historical recording of events, strengthen the calls for accountability and promote implementation of the recommendations'.[18] Although the UN Updated Impunity Principles require 'full' publication, the required contents are not specified. Other guidelines recommend that reports set out the mandate, working methods, a detailed record of events and findings of violations, as well as recommendations where mandated to do so.[19]

7 Publication should be context-sensitive. Where possible, a report should be translated into local languages.[20] Dissemination must occur through 'media that are technically and culturally accessible'.[21] Truth commissions' reports can be disseminated through media such as radio and television,[22] and findings can be integrated into the education curriculum.[23]

8 A commission's mandate generally ends when it delivers its report. Responsibility to release the report usually rests with the mandating authority, which for truth commissions is usually the executive or legislative branch of government.[24] It is unclear whether states have the same duty vis-à-vis international and regional commissions created without their consent. In these cases, responsibility likely lies with mandating authorities.

[12] P Hayner, *Unspeakable Truths* (2nd edn, Routledge 2010) 230.

[13] Human Rights Watch, 'Peru: President of Truth Commission Receives Death Threats', 6 October 2005 <www.hrw.org/news/2005/10/05/peru-president-truth-commission-receives-death-threats> accessed 15 November 2017.

[14] See the contribution on Principle 16 in this volume.

[15] ICTJ, *Truth-Seeking: Elements of Creating an Effective Truth Commission* (ICTJ 2013) 26.

[16] *Siracusa Guidelines*, n 4, Guideline 13.9.

[17] *Declaration on Fact-finding by the United Nations in the Field of the Maintenance of International Peace and Security*, GA Res 46/59 (9 December 1991) Art 26.

[18] OHCHR, n 4, 92.

[19] *Siracusa Guidelines*, n 4, Guideline 13; *Chicago Principles*, n 4, at 41. See also ICTJ, n 15, at 65.

[20] OHCHR, n 4, at 92. The ICTJ suggests that civil society may undertake translation: ICTJ, n 15, 53.

[21] Orentlicher, n 3, para 19(i). [22] *Chicago Principles*, n 4, 41. [23] Ibid, 42.

[24] M Freeman, *Truth Commissions and Procedural Fairness* (CUP 2006) 27.

D. Practice

I. Confidential portions of an inquiry

9 International commissions have reported that witnesses feared reprisals by concerned states[25] and that authorities pressured witnesses.[26] While these issues are particularly pertinent for commissions established without the consent of the states concerned, they are not limited to them. The Sierra Leone Truth and Reconciliation Commission (SLTRC) observed that some witnesses sought anonymity to avoid retaliation by perpetrators, while others were afraid of rejection by their communities.[27] A Sri Lankan truth commission was itself criticized for failing to protect witnesses and contributing to witness intimidation.[28]

10 Commissions have frequently adopted confidentiality measures to protect witnesses and victims, such as holding private interviews,[29] substituting anonymizing identifiers for names,[30] and excising particulars such as locations and dates from reported testimonies.[31] Some terms of reference also provide that commissions cannot be compelled to disclose confidential information.[32] Some inquiries were conducted strictly confidentially,[33] while others had a combination of public and private hearings.[34] An international commission on Eritrea classified witness interviews as 'strictly confidential', so that the informed consent of witnesses was necessary before their information could be shared with third parties.[35]

11 The UN Updated Impunity Principles permit the identification of suspected perpetrators, provided that the commission seeks to corroborate information implicating the individual and he or she is afforded a right of reply.[36] A few commissions have named suspected individuals in their reports.[37] However, many commissions have instead prepared confidential lists of suspects to safeguard due process and protect victims and witnesses.[38]

[25] *North Korea Report*, n 9, para 34; *Report of the Detailed Findings of the Commission of Inquiry on Human Rights in Eritrea*, UN Doc A/HRC/29/CRP.1 (5 June 2015) para 27 (hereinafter '*Eritrea Report*').

[26] *Report of the International Commission of Inquiry on Darfur to the United Nations Secretary-General*, UN Doc S/2005/60 (1 February 2005) para 35 (hereinafter '*Darfur Report*').

[27] *Witness to Truth: Report of the Sierra Leone Truth and Reconciliation Commission* (Graphic Packaging Ltd 2004) vol 1, ch 5, para 22.

[28] *Report of the Secretary-General's Panel of Experts on Accountability in Sri Lanka* (31 March 2011) para 335 <www.un.org/News/dh/infocus/Sri_Lanka/POE_Report_Full.pdf> accessed 15 November 2017.

[29] For example, *North Korea Report*, n 9, para 35; *Eritrea Report*, n 25, para 36.

[30] *Report of the UN Fact-Finding Mission on the Gaza Conflict*, UN Doc A/HRC/12/48 (25 September 2009) para 159(b) (hereinafter '*Gaza Report*').

[31] *Eritrea Report*, n 25, para 37.

[32] Truth and Reconciliation Commission Act 2000 (Sierra Leone); UNTAET Regulation 2001/10 (Timor-Leste); Truth and Reconciliation Commission Act 2008 (Solomon Islands); Truth and Reconciliation Commission of Liberia Mandate, s 26(m) (Liberia TRC).

[33] *Darfur Report*, n 26, para 13; *Eritrea Report*, n 25, para 29.

[34] *North Korea Report*, n 9; *Gaza Report*, n 30, para 164.

[35] *North Korea Report*, n 9, para 30.

[36] Updated Impunity Principles, Principle 9.

[37] For example, *From Madness to Hope: the 12-year war in El Salvador: Report of the Commission on the Truth for El Salvador*, UN Doc S/25500 (1 April 1993); *Final Report of the Truth, Justice, and Reconciliation Commission of Kenya*, vol IV (Truth Justice and Reconciliation Commission 2013); *Report of the International Commission of Inquiry mandated to establish the facts and circumstances of the events of 28 September 2009 in Guinea*, UN Doc S/2009/693 (18 December 2009).

[38] For example, *Darfur Report*, n 26, para 526. See OHCHR, n 4, 14; and Freeman, n 24, 273–76.

12 In relation to wider security exceptions, some national inquiries relating to the 'war on terror' have been subject to stringent secrecy regulations protecting national security.[39] In other circumstances, entire reports were suppressed for public safety reasons.[40] Regional human rights courts have cautioned that notions of 'state secrecy' and national security must not be used to obstruct the truth.[41] While truth commissions might decide that information should remain confidential for national security reasons,[42] due to the confidentiality of such decisions, it is difficult to identify the extent to which this has occurred in practice.[43]

II. Full publication

13 Brahm writes that political will to publish reports tends to falter when commissions scrutinize sitting governments.[44] As the examples set out in this subsection illustrate, when states are reluctant to publish reports, civil society plays a crucial role in bringing them to light. Non-governmental organizations (NGOs) have pressured mandating authorities to publish reports, and where suppression continues, have sometimes facilitated 'unofficial' public release. For instance, the reports of truth commissions in Nigeria and the Solomon Islands remain officially unpublished and were released by NGOs.[45]

14 Although most truth commissions' reports are published in a timely manner, some were delayed, and others remain unpublished. For example, a truth commission in Timor-Leste delivered its report in October 2005,[46] but it was only published in 2006 after serious riots.[47] In the South African context, both the African National Congress and former president FW de Klerk sought injunctions to prevent publication of sections of the TRC's report.[48] In 1993, the Zimbabwean Government refused to publish a report of a commission for fear of triggering further violence,[49] and NGOs published an alternative report in 1997.[50] The 2005 report of an Algerian commission on enforced disappearances[51] remains unpublished, although the Government has issued some reparations.

[39] For example, Protocol Between the Iraq Inquiry and Her Majesty's Government regarding Documents and Other Written and Electronic Information (UK), s 7; Commission of Inquiry into the Actions of Canadian Officials in Relation to Maher Arar Rules of Procedure and Practice (Canada), rules 43–56.

[40] See para 14 of this commentary.

[41] For example, *El-Masri v Former Yugoslav Republic of Macedonia* App no 39630/09 (Judgment) (ECtHR, 13 December 2012) para 191 and *Myrna Mack Chang v Guatemala* (Judgment) IACtHR Series C no 101 (25 November 2003) para 181.

[42] Freeman, n 24, 182.

[43] For a discussion of truth commissions' disclosure obligations in the International Criminal Court (ICC) context, see A Bisset, *Truth Commissions and Criminal Courts* (CUP 2012) 112–15 and 120–25.

[44] E Brahm, 'Truth Commissions', *Beyond Intractability* (June 2004).

[45] *Human Rights Violations Investigation Commission Report* (1 January 2005) <www.dawodu.com/oputa1.htm> accessed 15 November 2017; and *Confronting the Truth for a better Solomon Islands* (February 2012) <pacificpolicy.org/files/2013/04/Solomon-Islands-TRC-Final-Report-Vol1.pdf> accessed 15 November 2017.

[46] *Chega!, Report of the Timor-Leste Commission for Reception, Truth and Reconciliation* (CAVR) (January 2006).

[47] ICTJ, n 15, 66.

[48] A du Bois-Pedain, 'Communicating criminal and political responsibility in the TRC process' in F du Bois and A du Bois-Pedain (eds), *Justice and Reconciliation in Post-Apartheid South Africa* (CUP 2008) 62–89, 73.

[49] Zimbabwe Commission of Inquiry into the Matabeleland Disturbances; Hayner, n 12, 242.

[50] Legal Resources Foundation and the Catholic Commission for Justice and Peace, *Breaking the Silence, Building True Peace* (1997) <archive.org/details/BreakingTheSilenceBuildingTruePeace> accessed 21 November 2017.

[51] Ad Hoc Inquiry Commission in Charge of the Question of Disappearances.

International commissions of inquiry have had a better track record, perhaps because they 15
do not depend on the states concerned for publication. Almost all UN commissions' reports have been publicly released; an exception is a commission on Côte d'Ivoire established by the Security Council in 2004.[52] Human Rights Watch states that the report was not released due to concerns that its findings would 'derail peace negotiations'.[53] It remains unpublished, although an unofficial version is available online.[54] By contrast, access to UN commission archives is extremely limited.[55]

Regional commissions have not enjoyed the same success. Of four prominent regional 16
commissions established to date, three have published final reports.[56] The African Union agreed to release an inquiry report on South Sudan more than a year after its completion,[57] having previously decided to defer publication due to concerns that it would obstruct peace efforts.[58] An Arab League commission on Darfur did not issue a report and its statements of violations were retracted.[59] This limited practice does not permit generalizations, but in these cases it seems that diplomatic concerns took priority over truth seeking.

III. Wide dissemination

Methods of dissemination have been varied, with some innovative approaches. Most 17
reports, especially those of recent inquiries, are published online. Some truth commissions only issued a written report,[60] while others utilized media such as video,[61] radio,[62] and theatrical performances.[63] Some commissions made a version of the report for children[64] and also disseminated information beyond the final report. The South African TRC broadcast some live hearings on television. Several commissions have made selected witness testimonies and transcripts available online.[65]

States have not always complied with dissemination requirements. For instance, only 18
1,575 copies of the report of a Haitian commission of inquiry were ever made, apparently due to political sensitivities surrounding the report.[66] Some reports were published

[52] *Statement by the President of the Security Council*, UN Doc S/PRST/2004/17 (25 May 2004).

[53] Human Rights Watch, 'Côte d'Ivoire: Act Swiftly on UN Inquiry' (15 June 2011) <www.hrw.org/news/2011/06/15/cote-divoire-act-swiftly-un-inquiry> accessed 15 November 2017.

[54] *Rapport sur la situation des droits de l'homme en République de Côte d'Ivoire depuis le 19 septembre 2002 jusqu'au 15 octobre 2004 conformément aux dispositions de l'annexe VI de l'Accord de Linas-Marcoussis et à la Déclaration du président du Conseil de Sécurité du 25 mai 2004 (PRST/2004/17)* <fr.wikisource.org/wiki/Rapport_de_la_Commission_d%E2%80%99enqu%C3%AAte_internationale_sur_les_all%C3%A9gations_de_violations_des_droits_de_l%E2%80%99homme_en_C%C3%B4te_d%E2%80%99Ivoire> accessed 15 November 2017.

[55] For example, *Secretary-General's Bulletin: Commission for Historical Clarification*, UN Doc ST/SGB/1999/6 (8 June 1999); *Eritrea Report*, n 25, para 30.

[56] Independent International Fact-Finding Mission on the Conflict in Georgia (European Union); Independent Fact Finding Committee on Gaza (League of Arab States); and Commission of Inquiry on South Sudan (African Union).

[57] Communiqué of the Peace and Security Council, Doc no PSC/AHG/COMM.1(DXXVII) (26 September 2015) para 25.

[58] Communiqué of the Peace and Security Council, Doc no PSC/AHG/COMM.1(CDLXXXIV) (29 January 2015) para 9.

[59] N Hasbani, 'About The Arab Stance Vis-à-vis Darfur' *Al-Hayat* (21 March 2007).

[60] For example, Liberia TRC.

[61] For example, CAVR and SLTRC.

[62] For example, CAVR and South Africa TRC.

[63] For example, South Africa TRC.

[64] For example, SLTRC and CAVR.

[65] For example, SLTRC, Liberia TRC, North Korea Commission, and Gaza Commission.

[66] A Chapman and P Ball, 'The Truth of Truth Commissions: Comparative Lessons from Haiti, South Africa, and Guatemala' (2001) 23(1) Human Rights Quarterly 1–43, 35.

by private companies, which yielded mixed results. The report of an Argentinian truth commission became a best-seller,[67] while the South African TRC's report was inaccessible for much of the population due to its expense.[68] Some states created follow-up mechanisms to publish commissions' reports and maintain archives, which fostered wide dissemination.[69]

19 Some reports have been translated into local languages. United Nations commissions' reports are routinely translated into other UN languages, but some have also been translated into other relevant languages.[70] A national commission in Kyrgyzstan urged the Government to translate its summary into Kyrgyz and Uzbek,[71] but this was not done. According to Amnesty International, the failure to translate the report 'contributed to biased and selective interpretations of the report and fuelled further distrust and alarm'.[72]

E. Critical Assessment

20 Full publication promotes transparency and accountability.[73] However, the principle of publicity should also accommodate legitimate grounds of confidentiality. Some truth commissions have extensive subpoena powers and may hold highly sensitive information that attracts confidentiality.[74] That said, the term 'security reasons' is prone to over-broad interpretation, and commissions should treat requests for confidentiality for reasons of national security with caution, to guard against excessive censorship. Certain proceedings and information may need to stay confidential to protect the safety of vulnerable individuals and guard against intimidation. Moreover, identification of individual suspects engages issues of procedural fairness,[75] which are not much emphasized in the UN Updated Impunity Principles but are acknowledged in practice.[76] In any case, these exceptions do not permit the suppression of entire reports.

21 Appropriate modes of publication and dissemination maximize access for affected communities. Online publication of reports should now be standard practice. Wide dissemination of truth commissions' reports may be best achieved through an independent and well-resourced follow-up mechanism.

22 In practice, truth commissions and international commissions of inquiry have generally complied with Principle 13, while national and regional commissions have faced greater difficulties. Truth commissions may experience less obstruction when they are established after regime change, and perhaps also as a result of the high political cost of suppressing their reports. The UN has an (almost) unblemished record of publishing reports, but emerging practice of regional organizations is less encouraging. Reports of

[67] Hayner, n 12, 46.

[68] H van der Merwe and A Chapman, 'Did the TRC Deliver?' in H van der Merwe and A Chapman (eds), *Truth and Reconciliation in South Africa: Did the TRC Deliver?* (University of Pennsylvania Press 2008) 241–79, 253.

[69] Post-CAVR Technical Secretariat (Timor-Leste) and Transfer Committee (Peru).

[70] For example, *North Korea Report*, n 9, was translated into Korean and Japanese.

[71] *Report of the Independent International Commission of Inquiry into the Events in Southern Kyrgyzstan in June 2010* (2011) 89.

[72] Amnesty International, 'Kyrgyzstan: Dereliction of Duty' (8 June 2012) 6 <www.amnesty.org/en/documents/EUR58/001/2012/en> accessed 15 November 2017.

[73] Freeman, n 24, 145.

[74] For example, Truth and Reconciliation Commission Act 2000 (Sierra Leone), Art 8(1)(a).

[75] Freeman, n 24, 268.

[76] See para 11 of this commentary; and Freeman, n 24, 268 et seq.

national commissions have been particularly vulnerable to suppression. This practice is contrary to Principle 13 and the general spirit of the UN Updated Impunity Principles. To avoid such outcomes, the power to publish reports could reside with commissions themselves or other independent bodies. Where this power remains with reluctant mandating authorities, civil society plays a crucial role in urging publication and acting as an alternative conduit for public release as a means of last resort.

Bibliography

Chapman, A and Ball, P, 'The Truth of Truth Commissions: Comparative Lessons from Haiti, South Africa, and Guatemala' (2001) 23(1) Human Rights Quarterly 1–43.

Farson, S and Pythian, M, (eds), *Commissions of Inquiry and National Security: Comparative Approaches* (Praeger 2011).

Freeman, M, *Truth Commissions and Procedural Fairness* (CUP 2006).

Grace, R, 'Communication and Report Drafting in Monitoring, Reporting, and Fact-finding Missions', HPCR Working Paper, Program on Humanitarian Policy and Conflict Research at Harvard University (July 2014).

Hayner, P, *Unspeakable Truths* (2nd edn, Routledge 2010).

International Center for Transitional Justice, *Truth-Seeking: Elements of Creating an Effective Truth Commission* (2013).

Lawry-White, M, 'The Reparative Effect of Truth Seeking in Transitional Justice' (2015) 64(1) International and Comparative Law Quarterly 141–77.

Macklin, A, 'From Cooperation, to Complicity, to Compensation: The War on Terror, Extraordinary Rendition, and the Cost of Torture' (2008) 10(1) European Journal of Migration and Law 11–30.

Office of the United Nations High Commissioner for Human Rights, *Commissions of Inquiry and Fact-finding Missions on International Human Rights Law and International Humanitarian Law: Guidance and Practice*, UN Doc HR/PUB/14/7 (February 2015).

Program on Humanitarian Policy and Conflict Research, *HPCR Advanced Practitioner's Handbook on Commissions of Inquiry* (March 2015).

C.

PRESERVATION OF AND ACCESS TO ARCHIVES BEARING WITNESS TO VIOLATIONS

Principle 14. Measures for the Preservation of Archives

Valentina Cadelo and Trudy Huskamp Peterson

The right to know implies that archives must be preserved. Technical measures and penalties should be applied to prevent any removal, destruction, concealment or falsification of archives, especially for the purpose of ensuring the impunity of perpetrators of violations of human rights and/or humanitarian law.

A. Summary of Findings

Preservation of archives is an integral part of the right to know the truth.[1] Technical measures and penalties must prevent any removal, destruction, concealment, or falsification of archives to ensure that there will be no impunity for perpetrators of violations of human rights and/or humanitarian law.

Preservation of governmental and non-governmental archives requires both the prevention of destruction and the taking of active steps to prolong the life of the materials. Records need to be appraised, with the records of long-term importance selected and protected as archives.

Preserving archives is particularly important during periods of governmental transition and regime change. Authorities need to order the preservation of vulnerable government records and provide for their transfer to the custody to a trusted archival institution, preferably the national archives.

B. Contextual and Historical Introduction

'Archives' is a word that must be understood in context. In some countries and languages, 1
the term 'archives' is synonymous with 'records'. Technically speaking, however, the two terms are distinct. The term 'records' is meant to indicate any documentary materials, regardless of physical form or characteristics, made or received and maintained by an institution in pursuance of its legal obligations or in the transaction of its business. 'Archives' refers to records of long-term or permanent value, as well as to the institution that manages them and the building that houses them.[2] The word 'archives', as used in the Principles, partly reflects this distinction, and indicates any body of documents concerning violations of human rights and humanitarian law that are found in the custody of governments (national, provincial, and local), as well as of truth commissions and other investigative bodies and non-governmental institutions.[3]

[1] See commentaries to Principles 2–5 in this volume.

[2] See Office of the United Nations High Commissioner for Human Rights (OHCHR), *Rule-of-Law Tools for Post-Conflict States: Archives* (United Nations 2015) 5.

[3] For more information on the notion of archives as enshrined in the Principles, see the commentary on 'Definitions' in this volume.

2 While archives have been preserved for more than 4,000 years,[4] modern archival philosophy and practices developed in nineteenth-century Europe. It was, however, with the massive production of records during the Second World War and the changing technologies used to create documentary material that more attention was eventually given to the need to decide what to save and what to destroy, a function that archivists call 'appraisal'.[5] The second half of the twentieth century, therefore, saw archivists writing thousands of commentaries on the subject, with most experts agreeing that only records with enduring value need to be retained as archives.[6]

3 Although the preservation of archives dates back centuries, for an equally long time archives have been destroyed in many ways. In 1996, the International Council on Archives (ICA), the worldwide organization of archivists and an official partner of UNESCO on behalf of the world's archival profession, documented the worldwide loss of archives due to 'war, civil unrest, fire, flooding or other catastrophies, by simple neglect and lack of interest . . ., by financial constraints, by the lack of training or of cost-effective conservation methods'.[7]

4 In response to these challenges, over the last twenty years a number of important initiatives have been put in place to help ensure the preservation of archives, especially in the aftermath of armed conflict and/or in case of change of regime.[8] Along these lines, an important set of legal standards has been emerging in order to reinforce states' obligations to ensure preservation and access to archives, most of which have been reflected in the text of Principle 14.

5 First, it is today widely acknowledged that states have a primary obligation to ensure that archives are preserved. Importantly, the term 'preserved' has both a negative and a positive connotation. On the one hand, it means 'not destroyed'; on the other, it means the active interventions needed to prolong the life of archival material. Both senses are present in Principle 14.

6 Second, because records as evidence of alleged human rights violations are found in a wide variety of institutions, from military to commercial to religious, states must have an archival policy that ensures that all archives pertaining to human rights held by all types

[4] E Posner, *Archives in the Ancient World* (Harvard University Press 1972) especially ch 1.

[5] Both governmental and non-governmental institution archivists issue 'general schedules' that give instructions on the period of retention of records that are common throughout an organization, such as travel orders, procurement documents, and personnel files. More highly specialized records (eg, land titles or annual housing surveys) have a separate instruction. General and specific schedules apply both to records that exist and records of the same type that will be created in the future (until the schedule is revised or superceded). If records have not yet been scheduled, or if they are the records of an unusual activity unlikely to be repeated, the records are simply appraised when the activity is completed.

[6] If the creating office no longer needs the records and all administrative and financial needs have been met, records can be destroyed unless they have enduring value as evidence of what the institution did, or because they contain information not easily available elsewhere about persons, places, things, and phenomena.

[7] L Auer, 'Archival Losses and Their Impact on the Work of Archivists and Historians' in *Archivum XLII: Memory of the World at Risk: Archives Destroyed, Archives Reconstituted* (KG Sauer 1996) 1–10.

[8] In 1993, for instance, the ICA, in cooperation with UNESCO, established a working group with the mandate to investigate practice relating to the management of the archives of the state security services of former repressive regimes. An updated version of the first report, published in 1995, was released in 2009. See A González Quintana, *An Updated and Fuller Version of the Report Prepared by UNESCO and International Council of Archives (1995), Concerning the Management of the Archives of the State Security Services of Former Repressive Regimes* (ICA 2009). See also the Universal Declaration on Archives, adopted by UNESCO on 10 November 2011, where the preservation of archives is recognized as a 'vital necessity for supporting . . . accountability and transparency, for protecting citizens' rights, for establishing individual and collective memory, for understanding the past, and for documenting the present to guide future actions'.

of institutions are preserved and protected. Accordingly, Principle 14 refers to 'archives' in general, without—as does Principle 17—specifically referencing state archives.[9]

Third, as preservation activities may include a wide range of measures, the expression 'technical measures' for preserving archives, included in Principle 14, should be understood as comprising a great variety of tools, such as measures for preserving paper (including maps, drawings, and posters), electronic records (such as e-mail and word-processing records and databases), still photographs, film, video and audio tapes, and the use of microform and scanning technologies.[10] 7

Fourth, while states have the duty to enforce penalties to prevent any removal, destruction, concealment, or falsification of archives, Principle 14 reinforces this obligation if such conduct results in impunity for those responsible for violations of human rights and/or humanitarian law. 8

C. Theoretical Framework

Principle 14 is a fundamental corollary to the right to the truth. Preserving archives containing information on violations of human rights and humanitarian law is instrumental in enabling victims to realize their right to know the truth about the violations from which they suffered. 9

Despite the important role archives play in giving effect to this right, relatively little interpretation of Principle 14 is yet found in international law. While, during the last decade, multiple international courts and human rights mechanisms have helped to define the contours of the right to the truth, the Inter-American Court of Human Rights (IACtHR) acted as a pioneer in affirming the strict link existing between the preservation of archives and the right to the truth. 10

In 2006, the IACtHR, in the case of *Goiburú et al v Paraguay*, noted 'positively' that the 'preservation, classification and systematization' of the 'Terror Files' of the Alfredo Stroessner regime constituted 'an important effort for establishing and acknowledging the historic truth of the events that occurred in the Southern Cone during several decades'.[11] Following that case, further jurisprudence has slowly been developing, on the premise that states have a duty to preserve archives and documents to prevent impunity, especially in cases of violations of human rights and/or international humanitarian law.[12] Interestingly, although most of the existing cases do not expressly address such a duty 11

[9] In addition to the state responsibility to preserve non-state archives, see *Report of the Independent Expert to update the Set of Principles to combat impunity, Diane Orentlicher*, UN Doc E/CN.4/2005/102 (18 February 2005) para 15, where it is stated also that states must respect and protect the right of non-state organizations and individuals to collect, preserve, and make available relevant documents concerning such violations.

[10] See OHCHR, n 2, at 18. Over the past few years, many new technologies and tools have been developed to provide new solutions for preserving archives and documents. However, these tools may also bring risks, unless sufficient professionalism is exercised in handling data. For an overview of the opportunities and risks of new technologies in documenting human rights violations and violations of international humanitarian law, see Swisspeace, *Conference report: Securing Archives at Risk* (November 2015) para 1.7.

[11] *Goiburú et al v Paraguay* (Judgment) IACtHR Series C no 153 (22 September 2006) paras 61(121) and 170, regarding records of the Ministry of Interior seized by court order in 1992.

[12] Concerning the national jurisprudence, see, eg, Constitutional Court of Hungary, *Magyar Közlöny* (Decision) (13 July 2006) 2006/84, ruling that 'the government is under a general obligation to maintain records because failure to do so would seriously and directly restrict the right of access to information'.

per se, a reasonably clear position was taken by the European Court of Human Rights (ECtHR) in the 2011 case of *Kamburov v Bulgaria*, where the Court declared that

> the destruction of documents created by the security services of the former communist regime would not only prevent the regime's victims from consulting the ones which concern them, but would also infringe the general interest of the post-communist society in Bulgaria to carry out a much needed historical reassessment of the events that occurred during that era.[13]

12 The growing attention paid by international organizations and human rights mechanisms to the creation, organization, and management of archives as a means to guarantee the right to the truth has also resulted in a number of guidelines and resolutions, which have further consolidated the meaning of Principle 14 under international law.[14]

13 In resolutions concerning the right to the truth, for instance, the Organization of American States (OAS) has agreed that while states have some flexibility within their domestic law and practice, they

> should preserve records and other evidence concerning serious violations of human rights and of international humanitarian law so as to facilitate knowledge thereof, investigate allegations, and provide victims with access to an effective remedy in accordance with international law, in order to prevent these violations from occurring again in the future, among other reasons ...[15]

14 In a similar vein, UN agencies/mechanisms are now frequently addressing the duty of states to protect archives.[16] Particularly illustrative is, for instance, the 2015 OHCHR *Rule-of-Law Tool for Post-Conflict States: Archives*, which provides a comprehensive set of considerations for the management and preservation of archives of transitional

[13] *Kamburov v Bulgaria* App no 14336/05 (Decision) (ECtHR, 6 January 2011) para 56. See also *Rad v Romania* App no 9742/04 (Decision) (ECtHR, 9 June 2009) para 43. It is also worth noting that while the ECtHR has not yet pronounced explicitly on the issue of preservation of archives as such, it did so implicitly in a number of other cases. First, when dealing with the right to access information, the Court has repeatedly stated that any storage of information by states parties shall be regulated by law and, as such, shall not result in violation of the European Convention on Human Rights. See, eg, *Kamburov v Bulgaria*, para 56 (as this would have constituted an obstacle to the right to remedy of the victim). It could thus be argued that, in the Court's view, the actions of any national archival system shall not facilitate impunity, especially in cases of violations of human rights falling under the state's jurisdiction. Second, it is further worth noting that in cases of enforced disappearances, the Court constantly has affirmed that the absence of any records in cases of detention and the subsequent lack of official trace of the detainees' whereabouts or fate must be considered a most serious failing, since it enables those responsible for an act of deprivation of liberty to conceal their involvement in a crime, to cover their tracks, and to escape accountability for the fate of a detainee. See, amongst others, *Kurt v Turkey* (Judgment) (ECtHR, 25 May 1998) para 125.

[14] In 2009, the OHCHR released a report reiterating the crucial role of preserving archives in implementing the right to the truth, and the need for states to preserve government records at all levels and set up mechanisms to protect and manage documents effectively. See *Right to the Truth, Report of the Office of the High Commissioner for Human Rights*, UN Doc A/HRC/12/19 (21 August 2009) para 2. Notably, the Report set forth a series of considerations for preserving archives that are the most important to transitional justice processes, and at the same time it emphasized the need for states to establish a comprehensive national archival system. See ibid, paras 12–15, 26–31.

[15] See OAS, *Right to the truth*, AG/RES 2822 (4 June 2014). See also the previous resolutions adopted by the OAS General Assembly, such as *Right to the truth*, AG/RES 2800 (5 June 2013), *Right to the truth*, AG/RES 2595 (8 June 2010), and *Right to the truth*, AG/RES 2406 (3 June 2008).

[16] Among most recent resolutions, see: UN General Assembly, *Right to the truth*, A/RES/68/165 (21 January 2014) para 10; Human Rights Council, *Right to the truth*, A/HRC/RES/21/7 (10 October 2012), para 10. Among reports, see *Report of the Office of the United Nations High Commissioner for Human Rights on the seminar on experiences of archives as a means to guarantee the right to the truth*, UN Doc A/HRC/17/21 (14 April 2011) paras 8–19. The need to preserve archives has also been raised in the context of protection of cultural heritage: see *Report of the Special Rapporteur in the field of cultural rights*, UN Doc A/71/317 (9 August 2016).

justice institutions, as well as some interesting reflections on the role of the international community.[17]

Equally useful are the recent recommendations on archives by the UN Special Rapporteur on the promotion of truth, justice, reparation and guarantees of non-recurrence, which reiterate the call for states to provide a comprehensive archival practice and which emphasize the crucial role that truth-seeking mechanisms might have in that context.[18] 15

Ultimately, it is worth noting that the importance of preserving archives as fundamental tools for exercising the right to the truth has increasingly been acknowledged in a number of soft law documents issued by international non-state actors. Among others, particularly insightful are the ICA *Basic Principles on the Role of Archivists and Records Managers in Support of Human Rights*, which provide a powerfully advanced framework of action for governments, institutions, and archivists in terms of protection of records on human rights violations, with specific attention paid to the duty to preserve archives of transitional justice institutions.[19] 16

D. Practice

State practice on public records and archives has varied widely, with different legislative measures and policies being put in place in the last few years. Destruction of archives, for instance, has been prohibited by freedom of information and memory laws in an increasingly large number of states.[20] Particularly illustrative in this regard is, for instance, the Model Inter-American Law on Access to Public Information, which makes it 'a criminal offence to willfully destroy or alter records after they have been the subject of a request of information',[21] and an administrative offence to destroy records without authorization.[22] 17

[17] OHCHR, n 2, 37–41.

[18] See *Report of the Special Rapporteur on the promotion of truth, justice, reparation and guarantees of non-recurrence, Pablo de Greiff*, UN Doc A/HRC/30/42 (7 September 2015) (hereinafter '*Report of the Special Rapporteur*') Annex, 27–30.

[19] The ICA Basic Principles were endorsed by the ICA Programme Commission in Seoul, in September 2016, as a working document for discussion, publicizing, and use by archivists. Notably, under Principle 5, it is stated that states shall not only protect state archives, but indeed also have many options for supporting preservation and access to non-governmental archives, such as making forceful public statements on preservation and access, enacting legislation requiring such archives to be preserved, obtaining court rulings that require specific archives to be preserved, providing monetary support for non-governmental archives, conducting surveys and creating databases to identify for the public where relevant archives are located, taking donations of private sector archives, or providing a 'safe haven' trusted repository for endangered archives. Further, under Principle 6, institutions, archivists, and records managers should also ensure that the archives of temporary bodies established to assist in transitional justice are protected and preserved, both while the entity exists and after it closes; lastly, public notice should be given prior to the disposal of any archives from these bodies.

[20] For a comprehensive overview on memory laws, see U Belavusau and A Gliszczyńska-Grabias (eds), *Law and Memory: Addressing Historical Injustice by Legislation and Trials* (CUP forthcoming). With respect to freedom of information laws, see, among others, R Perlingeiro, *Information Access Laws in the World* (Editora da Universidade Federal Fluminense 2014).

[21] OAS, *Model Inter-American Law on Access to Public Information*, AG/RES 2607 (8 June 2010), Appendix, Art 66. The Model Law was elaborated by the Group of Experts on Access to Information (coordinated by the Department of International Law of the Secretariat for Legal Affairs), pursuant to OAS, *Access to Public Information: Strengthening Democracy*, AG/RES/2514 (4 June 2009).

[22] AG/RES 2607, n 21, Appendix, Art 67(f). Under Art 67(e), it is also an administrative offence to 'fail to create a record either in breach of applicable regulations and policies or with the intent to impede access to information'.

18 Most Central and Eastern European countries in the process of transition have passed laws regulating the management of archives of their former repressive governments, which clearly provide for what is to happen to these institutional records and require their preservation when documentation of serious violations of human rights is included therein.[23] Similar approaches are characteristic of numerous Latin American countries, where authorities have adopted laws and/or initiated measures aimed at preserving national archives and records in order to address victims' claims to know the truth about repression and, at the same time, ensure accountability for serious violations of human rights and humanitarian law.[24]

19 Interestingly, while current state practice is mostly linked to the protection of archives and records by public institutions—such as archives of the State Security Services, the archives of special tribunals, those of prisons or concentration camps, military archives, archives of law enforcement agencies, and those of the judiciary—most recently, attention has also being paid to the protection of archives of truth commissions and other inquiry mechanisms.[25]

20 While the importance of the above-mentioned practices should not be underestimated, a number of challenges remain. To start with, internationally, practices arguably are fragmented, with different measures being put in place depending on the specific context. Moreover, there is a general lack of consistency in the disposition of archives, especially in relation to transitional justice mechanisms, such as truth commissions.[26]

21 Further challenges result from the fact that records of a government are generally assumed to be its property, and consequently are inalienable and imprescriptible, and may be destroyed or retained at its discretion. Courts routinely order preservation of records relevant to ongoing litigation, but often these orders cover a small set of specific material. Principle 14, however, demands retention of blocks of archives, the responsibility for which properly lies in legislative powers, such as enacted by the Germans for the Stasi archives in 1989.[27] With a view to overcoming similar challenges, in Colombia, as

[23] Among others, note the Spanish Historical Memory Law, which provides explicitly for the preservation of archives and records containing information relating to the Civil War and Franco's dictatorship era. See *Ley de Memoria Histórica* or *La Ley por la que se reconocen y amplían derechos y se establecen medidas en favor de quienes padecieron persecución o violencia durante la Guerra Civil y la Dictadura*, which was adopted by the Congress of Deputies on 31 October 2007. See also González Quintana, n 8, 26, 82–85.

[24] See González Quintana, n 8, 82–85. For an overview on the practice of Brazil, Paraguay, and Guatemala in particular, see G Citroni, 'El Derecho a la verdad y el acceso a los archivos: logros y retos' in H van Engen, G Janssens, G Kwanten and KM Pompe (eds), *Archives without borders—Proceedings of the International Congress in The Hague, August 30–31, 2010* (Vlaamse Vereniging voor Bibliotheek-, Archief- en Documentatiewezen, Sectie Archieven 2012) 237–55.

[25] Thanks to the crucial role played by such mechanisms in assisting countries to confront their past in situations of transition, over the last few years a number of initiatives have been implemented in order to ensure the preservation of and access to their records. See, amongst others, the cases of Chile, El Salvador, South Africa, and Peru, where the records collected by the respective truth commissions have all been put under protection. For an overview of the role of truth commissions archives and the need to ensure their preservation, see B Jones and I Oliveira, 'Truth Commission Archives as "New Democratic Spaces"' (2016) 8 Journal of Human Rights Practice 6–24.

[26] See *Report of the Special Rapporteur*, n 18, para 97.

[27] See Act regarding the records of the State Security Service of the former German Democratic Republic (STASI Records Act) of December 1991 <www.bstu.bund.de/SharedDocs/Downloads/EN/StUG_englisch_2012.pdf?__blob=publicationFile> accessed 22 June 2017; for disposition of the records of temporary international criminal courts, see T Huskamp Peterson, *Temporary Courts, Permanent Records* (2008) <www.wilsoncenter.org/sites/default/files/TCPR_Peterson_HAPPOP02.pdf> accessed 22 June 2017.

part of its responsibilities following the peace agreement with the FARC rebel group, the National Center of Historical Memory and the General Archives of the Nation issued the Documentary Management Protocol of the files referring to grave and overt violations of Human Rights and violations of International Humanitarian Law, on the occasion of the armed conflict. The Protocol established the criteria and measures that all state entities are required to follow in order to identify, protect, and guarantee access to information on human rights records, historical memory, and armed conflict, including temporary suspension of the destruction of records.[28]

Lastly, the records of government-sponsored truth, vetting, and compensation commissions should be appraised. Due to the acutely sensitive nature of these records, general government-wide appraisal schedules should be applied very carefully, and the normal period for retention of disposable records might be lengthened so that the records are available to answer any questions that might arise in the future. 22

E. Critical Assessment

What steps can reformers take to preserve records of former repressive governments from intentional destruction? In the period of chaos after a change of regime, it may be difficult to find an authority that has the power to compel protection, but activists should seek to have the head of government, the legislative body, or a court issue both a temporary protective order and an order to transfer custody of vulnerable records to a responsible new body: the national archives, a special temporary body, or a non-archival government body. For example, when the Guatemala police archives were located in July 2005, the Human Rights Ombudsman (Procuraduria de los Derechos Humanos (PDH)) obtained a civil court order to safeguard the documents and authorize access; the PDH then created a unit called the Archivo Historico de la Policia Nacional (AHPN). In 2009, Inter-Institutional Cooperation Agreement 24-2009 transferred the police archives from the Ministry of the Interior to the Ministry of Culture and Sport, and the AHPN now sits organizationally within the Archivo General de Centroamérica, Guatemala's national archives.[29] Whichever custodial option is selected, the authorities, responsibilities, and duration of custody of the archives must be clearly and publicly stated. 23

And what of the preservation of non-government archives of importance to human rights? The Updated Principles against Impunity require states to take 'effective action' to protect records that provide evidence of gross violations of human rights; they do not confine this responsibility to the records of *state* bodies. States must have an archival policy that ensures that archives pertaining to human rights held by all types of organizations are protected, and this, in turn, means that states must think of the archives not as solely historical government records, but also as a national archival system protecting the 24

[28] See Protocolo de gestión documental de los archivos referidos a las graves y manifiestas violaciones a los Derechos Humanos, e Infracciones al Derecho Internacional Humanitario, ocurridas con ocasión del conflicto armado interno (February 2017) <www.centrodememoriahistorica.gov.co/en/noticias/noticias-cmh/ya-esta-disponible-el-protocolo-de-gestion-documental-de-archivos-de-derechos-humanos> accessed 22 June 2017.

[29] K Weld, *Paper Cadavers: The Archives of Dictatorship in Guatemala* (Duke University Press 2014); *From Silence to Memory: Revelations of the Archivo Historico de la Policia Nacional* (University of Oregon Libraries 2013) xxxiv–xxxv <scholarsbank.uoregon.edu/xmlui/bitstream/handle/1794/12928/ahpn_final_20130620.pdf?sequence=3> accessed 22 June 2017.

documentary heritage of the country. Some non-governmental institutions will be comfortable maintaining their own archives, with the associated costs; others will be comfortable donating their records to national archives; while still others will be wary of doing so. It may be useful for the country to establish a new archival institution within the national system for the explicit purpose of holding non-governmental materials (including personal papers) in accordance with the wishes of the donors.

25 A key preservation problem is to find a secure place to store a *copy* of sensitive records important to the struggle against impunity, particularly if the political situation in the country is volatile. In 2013, the Swiss Federal Council approved a revision to its Law on the Protection of Cultural Property, granting Swiss Federal agencies with the legal authority to provide a 'safe haven' for the temporary storage of cultural property, including archives, seriously threatened in other countries, including in situations of disaster and emergency. By enacting this much-needed law, Switzerland became the first country in the world to offer this official protection.[30]

26 Preserving archives from immediate destruction when regime change happens must be a cooperative venture involving the creators of the records, concerned citizens, and archivists. Once the immediate threat to the records has receded, legislators need to ensure adequate funding for archival preservation; architects and engineers must ensure that the physical structure housing the archives has structural integrity, proper temperature and humidity, and good security controls; archivists must intervene to ensure the stability of the materials; computer specialists must ensure that digital records continue to be intelligible and reliable; and, most important, citizens must monitor and demand support for the archival institution. Preservation is never finished; as long as the materials exist, preservation is a process to be managed, not a one-time problem to be solved.

Bibliography

Archivum XLII: Memory of the World at Risk: Archives Destroyed, Archives Reconstituted (KG Sauer 1996).

Cox, D, 'Burn After Viewing: The CIA's Destruction of the Abu Zubaydah Tapes & The Law of Federal Records' (2011) 5 Journal of National Security Law & Policy 131–77.

Forde, H, Preserving Archives (Facet Publishing 2007).

International Council on Archives, Committee on Disaster Prevention, 'Guidelines on Disaster Prevention and Control in Archives' (2011) <www.ica.org/en/ica-study-n%C2%B011-guidelines-disaster-prevention-and-control-archives>.

International Council on Archives, Committee on Legal Matters, 'Draft Principles for Archives and Records Legislation' (2004) <www.ica.org/en/draft-principles-archives-and-record-legislation-2004>.

[30] For more information on the Swiss legislation on cultural property, see <www.babs.admin.ch/en/aufgabenbabs/kgs.html> accessed 22 June 2017. Notably, on 11 October 2017, Swiss authorities signed an headquarters agreement with the International Alliance for the Protection of Heritage in Conflict Areas (ALIPH), which was created on 8 March 2017. The ALIPH aims to support the implementation of programmes to prevent the destruction of cultural property, and of emergency measures to protect cultural property threatened with destruction, damage, or looting as a result of armed conflict, as well as to contribute to rehabilitation efforts, see <www.admin.ch/gov/en/start/documentation/media-releases.msg-id-68386.html> accessed 27 November 2017.

Jost, H-P, 'Concevoir un bâtiment d'archives: Une method', International Council on Archives (2003) <www.ica.org/en/designing-archive-building-method>.

Peterson, T Huskamp, *Final Acts: A Guide to Preserving the Records of Truth Commissions* (Johns Hopkins University Press 2005) <https://www.wilsoncenter.org/sites/default/files/Petersonfinpdf.pdf>.

Peterson, T Huskamp, *Securing Police Archives: A Guide for Practitioners* (Swisspeace 2013) <www.swisspeace.ch/fileadmin/user_upload/Media/Publications/Essentials/Essential_2_2013_Peterson_Securing_Police_Archives_A_Guide_for_Practitioners_2013.pdf>.

Principle 15. Measures for Facilitating Access to Archives

Valentina Cadelo and Trudy Huskamp Peterson

Access to archives shall be facilitated in order to enable victims and their relatives to claim their rights.

Access shall be facilitated, as necessary, for persons implicated, who request it for their defence.

Access to archives should also be facilitated in the interest of historical research, subject to reasonable restrictions aimed at safeguarding the privacy and security of victims and other individuals. Formal requirements governing access may not be used for purposes of censorship.

A. Summary of Findings

Access to archives is central to the exercise of human rights, yet it remains a much contested area. Principle 15 reinforces this premise, by requiring states to adopt measures that facilitate access to archives for victims, persons implicated in human rights violations, and individuals doing historical research.

While the theoretical and best practice framework for access to archives exists, the implementation of Principle 15 is far from satisfactory. Important challenges persist due to the reluctance of states to provide access to information, often linked to national security concerns. Access for defence purposes and for academic research continues to be impeded, and bedevils the work of transitional justice institutions.

Archival description can help identify records that will be useful, and special masters may help courts resolve archives-heavy cases. States shall also enact reasonable restrictions to protect privacy and security; however, these may not impede the exercise of fundamental human rights or be used for the purposes of censorship.

B. Contextual and Historical Introduction

1 Access is the availability of records/archives for consultation as a result both of legal authorization and the existence of finding aids. While archives are neutral, the use of them is not. Authorizing access to archives, particularly those of governments, is a political act. Sweden's Freedom of the Press Act of 1766 was the world's first law governing access to information,[1] but the idea that the public has a right to know what is in government records has its roots in Article 37 of the French Revolution's Decree of 7 Messidor II: 'Every citizen is entitled to ask in every depository … for the production of the documents it contains.'[2] However, not until the last third of the twentieth century were laws on access

[1] See J Mustonen (ed), *The World's First Freedom of Information Act. Anders Chydenius' Legacy Today* (Anders Chydenius 2006).

[2] E Posner, 'Some Aspects of Archival Development since the French Revolution' in K Munden (ed), *Archives and the Public Interest: Selected Essays of Ernst Posner* (Public Affairs Press 1967) 23–35.

to government records enacted in many national governments, and in some sub-national governments too.

Today, access to archives is considered crucial to the exercise of individual rights such as the right to information, the right to fair trial, and the right to know the truth about the circumstances in which human rights violations took place and, in the event of death or disappearance, the victims' fate.[3] Accordingly, archives shall be made accessible to victims and relatives, any person allegedly implicated in human rights violations who might request access to them for his/her defence, and more generally, in the interest of historical research, in order to ensure an undistorted written record of the past. Bearing in mind privacy and security concerns for the individuals involved, reasonable restrictions may apply, on the condition, however, that applicable requirements may not result in censorship. 2

Principle 15 reflects this understanding, and it refers to 'archives' without—as does Principle 17—specifically referencing *state* archives; the Principle, then, must apply to *all* archives that hold records relating to human rights matters. While the term 'archives' usually brings paper to mind, audio and video recordings, satellite images, photographs taken by cellphones, and databases of all kinds are also archival holdings that can provide crucial information for the human rights researcher. Decisions on the rules for access usually are made at the upper levels of the institution that created the records, whether a government, a business, a faith-based body, or non-governmental organization, and archivists execute the decisions. 3

C. Theoretical Framework

In the 1980s, the collapse of Latin American dictatorships and the end of the Cold War created new demands for access to government archives. The subsequent decades witnessed the development of a number of international standards that provide a foundation for governmental and non-governmental access policies. 4

The International Council on Archives (ICA) in particular developed a series of positions on access to archives, starting with a code of ethics (1996), a set of principles for a national archives law (1996, updated 2004), a UNESCO-funded study on archives of security services (1997), a set of principles on access to (principally) government archives (1998), and a Universal Declaration on Archives (2010, endorsed by UNESCO in 2011), all of which had statements on access to archives. In 2012, the ICA adopted the *Principles of Access to Archives*, covering all archives, governmental and non-governmental, supplemented in 2014 by the *Technical Guidance on Managing Archives with Restrictions* and in 2016 by the *Basic Principles on the Role of Archivists and Records Managers in Support of Human Rights*.[4] 5

In the context of Principle 15, the most relevant sources of interpretation are arguably Principles 2 and 6 of the ICA *Principles of Access to Archives*. Principle 2 reads, in part, '[u]sers have the right to know whether or not a specific series, file, item or portion of an item exists, even though it is withheld from use, or if it has been destroyed', a position consistent with the Inter-American Court of Human Rights (IACtHR)'s holding 6

[3] Office of the United Nations High Commissioner for Human Rights (OHCHR), *Rule-of-Law Tools for Post-Conflict States: Archives* (United Nations 2015) 1.

[4] The documents cited are available on the ICA website <www.ica.org/en> accessed 22 June 2017.

in *Gomes Lund et al v Brazil* that the state must take 'all measures' to show whether or not the records exist.[5] Principle 6 of the ICA *Principles of Access to Archives* specifically references the Updated Set of Principles against Impunity: 'Institutions holding archives ensure that victims of serious crimes under international law have access to archives that provide evidence needed to assert their human rights and to document violations of them, even if those archives are closed to the general public.'[6]

7 That access to archives is instrumental to the exercise of core individual rights, and therefore shall be facilitated to the extent possible, has been widely recognized in jurisprudence as well. In a series of cases, the IACtHR held that 'every person, including the next of kin of the victims of grave violations of human rights, has the right to the truth';[7] and in *Myrna Mack Chang v Guatemala*, the Court held that in cases of human rights violations, 'resorting to official secret with respect to submission of the information required by the judiciary may be considered an attempt to privilege the "clandestinity of the Executive branch" and to perpetuate impunity'.[8] In a similar vein, the European Court of Human Rights (ECtHR) elaborated a particularly rich jurisprudence on the right to access state-held information and archives dealing with past regimes,[9] and analogous developments can be traced in the practice of international human rights bodies, such as the UN Human Rights Committee (HRC).[10]

8 The OHCHR has foregrounded the centrality of access to archives, convening a seminar in 2011 on the experiences of archives as a means to guarantee the right to the truth,[11] and producing a *Rule-of-Law Tool for Post-Conflict States* specifically on archives in 2015, which set forth important standards in terms of archives law, particularly on legal

[5] *Gomes Lund at al v Brazil* (Judgment) IACtHR Series C no 219 (24 November 2010) para 211, where it was held that 'The State cannot seek protection in arguing the lack of existence of the requested documents; rather, to the contrary, it must establish the reason for denying the provision of said information, demonstrating that it has adopted all the measures under its power to prove that, in effect, the information sought did not exist.'

[6] Notably, the ICA *Basic Principles on the Role of Archivists and Records Managers in Support of Human Rights* reiterate in their respective Principle 6 that 'governments shall ensure that access is provided to their archives concerning violations of human rights and humanitarian law', and specifically makes reference to the universal recognition of the right of individuals to access information held by a public authority.

[7] See commentaries to Principles 4 and 5 in this volume.

[8] *Myrna Mack Chang v Guatemala* (Judgment) IACtHR Series C no 101 (25 November 2003) para 181.

[9] Notably, the ECtHR jurisprudence concerned not only documents relating to past regimes and still held by states, but more generally any personal information at a state's disposal. In this context, violations have been found with regard to many articles of the European Convention on Human Rights (ECHR), mostly Article 8(1) (right to respect for private and family life), but also Article 10 (freedom of expression), Article 3 (prohibition of torture or other inhuman or degrading treatment or punishment) and Article 13 (right to an effective remedy). For an overview of the main findings, see section D of this commentary.

[10] The HRC has not yet dealt specifically with the right to access to archives and other state-held information in the context of a transition. Nevertheless, it has developed a clear position with regard to the general right to access information, which has been recognized as part of the right freedom of expression under Art 19 of the International Covenant on Civil and Political Rights (ICCPR) and of the right to privacy and family life under Art 17 ICCPR. Furthermore, the denial of access to state-held information has also in some cases been considered a violation of Art 7 ICCPR on the prohibition of torture or other cruel, inhuman or degrading treatment with respect to the families of the victims. It also bears noting that the HRC expressed its position on the gathering and storage of information by states, as well as on the access to state-held information, in two of its General Comments: see General Comment no 16 on Article 17 (the right to respect privacy, family, home and correspondence and protection of honour and reputation), 1988, para 10; General Comment no 34 on Article 19 (freedom of opinion and expression), UN Doc CCPR/C/CG/34, 2011, paras 18–19.

[11] See *Report of the Office of the High Commissioner for Human Rights on the seminar on the experiences of archives as a means to guarantee the right to the truth*, UN Doc A/HRC/17/21 (14 April 2011).

authorizations to access records, while at the same time ensuring that access is balanced with guarantees for privacy and security for the individuals named in the records.[12]

Alongside legal authorization, important standards have also developed with regard to the second element of effective access, which is adequate archives description. Indeed, finding aids produced by archivists allows researchers to key in on the records of most significance to their investigation and point to unlikely sources of information, such as the Turkish Cypher Office records, which provide information on the Armenian genocide, and the Chilean Ministry of Foreign Affairs records, which provide information on processes used by the secret police.[13] The ICA has international standards for the description of archives and provides open source software for description.[14] Conversely, lack of arrangement and description can impair human rights processes. For example, in 2010, the ECtHR instructed Romania to implement a mechanism for compensating victims of Communist-era property confiscation:[15] while foot-dragging and government corruption were the main culprits, a records problem contributed to the lack of progress; an audit in early 2012 found that 'the files of the real owners of properties dispossessed by the Communists lie abandoned in the archives of the Property Restitution Agency', which allowed people with 'forged ownership documents or inheritance papers' to obtain properties or 'illegal payments worth hundreds of millions of euros'.[16] 9

D. Practice

While the theoretical and best practice framework for access to archives exists, the implementation of Principle 15 is far from satisfactory. International and national courts have taken a variety of positions on access. **10**

The ECtHR was one of the pioneers in this field, delivering an extensive number of judgments relating to access to archives in the last few years. It repeatedly held that access to state-held information must be granted to all interested persons through a procedure that is effective and accessible.[17] Furthermore, denial of access to state-held information concerning previous regimes would be considered a violation of the ECHR if this **11**

[12] See OHCHR, n 3, 14, 18–20.

[13] See AK Gregorian, 'Akçam Says Turkish Archives Show Genocide Planning By Central Government' *Mirror-Spectator* (22 October 2012) <www.mirrorspectator.com/2012/10/22/akcam-says-turkish-archives-show-genocide-planning-by-central-government/> accessed 22 June 2017; Mauricio Weibel Barahona, 'Pinochet lideraba red de espionaje que cruzó caminos con el Vaticano, el FBI y la prensa internacional' *El Mostrador* (2 August 2012) <www.elmostrador.cl/pais/2012/08/02/pinochet-lideraba-red-de-espionaje-que-cruzo-caminos-con-el-vaticano-el-fbi-y-la-prensa-internacional/> accessed 22 June 2017.

[14] ICA, *General International Standards Archival Description* (1 September 2011). The open source software is developed by Artefactual Systems in collaboration with the ICA Program Commission (PCOM) and a growing network of international partners: see J Bushey, 'International Council on Archives (ICA) "Access to Memory" (AtoM): Opensource software for archival description' (2012) 2 *Archivi & Computer* <www.ICA-AtoM.org/download/ICA-AtoM_JBushey.pdf> accessed 22 June 2017.

[15] Considering the scale of the problem, the Court gave a pilot judgment, in which it requested the adoption of measures capable of affording adequate redress to all the persons affected by the restitution laws. See *Maria Atanasiu and others v Romania* (Judgment) (ECtHR,12 October 2010).

[16] See 'Romania Restitution Law Angers Communists' Victims' *Balkan Insight* (18 April 2012) <www.balkaninsight.com/en/article/romania-plans-controversial-new-properties-restitution-law> accessed 22 June 2017.

[17] See, eg, *Haralambie v Romania* (Judgment) (ECtHR, 27 October 2009) paras 79 and 96; *Antonieta Tudor v Romania* (Judgment) (ECtHR, 24 September 2013) para 39; *Joanna Szulc v Poland* (Judgment) (ECtHR, 13 November 2012) para 87.

prevented the development of historical research;[18] analogously, refusal to give information to the family of victims of human rights violations perpetrated by previous regimes was also deemed to amount, in certain circumstances, to a violation of the Convention.[19] Interestingly, the Court stated that it is almost impossible for the state to deny access to information gathered by previous regimes on the basis of national security reasons, and in any case it is for the state to prove that such national interest still exists. Also, it twice ruled that withholding documents from the court is a violation of the ECHR.[20]

12 In parallel to these rulings, the IACtHR reiterated many times that there is a right to the truth in cases of human rights violations, for both the families of the victims and the public at large.[21] On this basis, the Court therefore derived an obligation for states to disclose state-held information, refusal of which constitutes a violation of the American Convention on Human Rights (ACHR).[22] It bears noting that the IACtHR also found that states have an obligation to cooperate with the judiciary by disclosing the necessary documents, and that they cannot invoke reasons of state security or the unproven alleged destruction of records in order to shield themselves from this obligation.[23]

13 Practice at the national level has proved to be more challenging. For example, a court in Spain, reviewing inquiries into the history of the Spanish Civil War, declared that determining historic truth is not the role of courts.[24] A US Court of Appeals ruled in 2014 that the Central Intelligence Agency could withhold the draft of volume V of the Agency's history of the 1961 failed invasion of Cuba at the Bay of Pigs as 'predecisional and deliberative'; the US Congress subsequently legislated that such a privilege cannot be used for items more than 25 years old.[25] Other cases, coming from the Russian Federation and Hungary, also show the on-going reluctance of authorities to provide access to information because of security reasons.[26] Conversely, Latin American courts seemed to be

[18] *Kenedi v Hungary* (Judgment) (ECtHR, 26 May 2009) paras 43 and 45.

[19] *Janowiec and others v Russia* (Judgment) (ECtHR, 16 April 2012) para 166; and *Janowiec and others v Russia* (Judgment) (ECtHR Grand Chamber, 21 October 2013) paras 186–89. Notably, in the first decision by the Chamber in 2012, the withholding of documents by the Soviet regime, relating, first, to the fate of the applicants' relatives because of security reasons and then because of the foreign nationality of the applicants, combined with the cold attitude of Russian authorities in dealing with such requests, was considered to amount to a violation of Art 3 ECHR on the prohibition of torture and other inhuman and degrading treatment and punishment. The decision was subsequently reversed in the 2013 Grand Chamber decision because of the lack of competence *ratione temporis*. Nevertheless, the case remains of great importance because of the possibility to link the denial of access to state-held information to a violation of the Convention.

[20] See, eg, *Janowiec v Russia* (Judgment) (ECtHR Grand Chamber, 21 October 2013) paras 215–16 (records relating to Katyn massacre in 1940); *Husayn (Abu Zubaydah) v Poland* (Judgment) (ECtHR, 24 July 2014) (Polish records on secret prisons). In both cases the Court found that this amounted to a violation of Art 38 ECHR.

[21] Amongst others, see *Myrna Mack Chang v Guatemala*, n 8.

[22] See, eg, *Bámaca-Velásquez v Guatemala* (Judgment) IACtHR Series C no 70 (25 November 2000) para 160; *Jose Miguel Gudiel Alvarez and others v Guatemala (Diario Militar case)* IACtHR Series C no 253 (20 November 2012) paras 269, 302.

[23] See, eg, *Myrna Mack Chang v Guatemala*, n 8; *Gomes Lund et al v Brazil*, n 5, paras 202 and 211; *Contreras v El Salvador* (Judgment) IACtHR Series C no 232 (31 August 2011) paras 169, 171 and 173.

[24] See 'Baltasar Garzon cleared over his Franco-era crimes inquiry' *Guardian* (2 February 2012) <www.theguardian.com/world/2012/feb/27/baltasar-garzon-cleared-franco-crimes/print> accessed 22 June 2017.

[25] See Freedom of Information Act 5 USC § 552 (b) (5) <www.justice.gov/oip/freedom-information-act-5-usc-552> accessed 22 June 2017.

[26] On Russia see, eg, *International Memorial Society v Russian Minister of Interior*, decision of the Cassation Chamber of the Supreme Court (24 March 2011). On Hungary see *Constitutionality of various acts of primary and secondary legislation to archives and classification regimes*, decision of the Constitutional Court (22 June 1994).

less willing to accept national security as an excuse to deny access to documents about past human rights abuses, and accordingly have ordered the disclosure of information for public interest purposes as well as in the context of criminal proceedings.[27]

Meanwhile, the international community has undertaken important steps in relation to access to archives/records. For instance, in 2012, the Human Rights Council requested the OHCHR to 'collect information on good practices in the establishment, preservation and provision of access to national archives on human rights, and to make the information received publicly available in an online database'.[28] Notably, the same call was reiterated one year later, by the General Assembly.[29] Moreover, a number of Special Rapporteurs have increasingly included archival issues and demands for access to archives in their reports.[30] 14

Despite these important developments, challenges remain when it comes to accessing specific categories of archives. Access to records of the military and the intelligence services is manifestly inadequate in most states. Some are said to be 'lost', but, for example, in 2013, thirty years after Argentina's dictatorship ended, the Minister of Defence announced that the records of the military junta had been 'found' in the basement of the headquarters of the Air Force.[31] Declassification of military and intelligence records is a major constraint on access; a 2014 survey of eighteen national archives in the European Union found that only one country (Greece) has a law that provides for automatic declassification of all classified national security information after a given number of years, while eleven countries reported no automatic declassification.[32] Freedom of information acts, while essential to good government and helpful in some human rights cases, have also proved to be a weak, slow tool when requesting sensitive records, and completely inadequate when government bodies deny the existence of records.[33] 15

[27] See, eg, in Mexico the cases against the Procuraduría General de la República before the Instituto Federal de Acceso a la Información Pública y Protección de Datos, decisions of 2009 and 2010; and in Guatemala, *The Prosecution in the Trial of Rios Montt v Ministry of National Defence*, decision of the Constitutional Court (5 March 2008). Unfortunately the situation seems to have reversed most recently, after the disappearance case concerning 43 Mexican students in the city of Iguala in 2014.

[28] Human Rights Council, *Right to the Truth*, Res A/HRC/RES/21/7 (27 September 2012) para 11.

[29] General Assembly, *Right to the Truth*, Res A/RES/68/165 (28 December 2013) para 11. As at the date of writing, however, only a limited number of state members and institutions have responded to the call. See OHCHR web page on national archives on human rights <www.ohchr.org/EN/Issues/Truth/Pages/TruthIndex.aspx> accessed 22 June 2017.

[30] See, eg, *Report of the Special Rapporteur in the field of cultural rights*, UN Doc A/68/296 (9 August 2013) paras 46–48 (access to archives for historical memory); *Report of the Special Rapporteur on the promotion of truth, justice, reparation and guarantees of non-recurrence*, UN Doc A/HRC/24/42 (28 August 2013) paras 80–88 (truth commissions archives); *Report of the Special Rapporteur on the promotion and protection of the right to freedom of opinion and expression*, UN Doc A/68/362 (4 September 2013) (the right to access information and the right to the truth); *Report of the Special Rapporteur on the implications for human rights of the environmentally sound management and disposal of hazardous substances and wastes*, UN Doc A/HRC/30/40 (8 July 2015) (on the right to information on hazardous substances and waste).

[31] Tess Bennett, '"Secret" Military Dictatorship Documents Discovered in Basement' *The Argentina Independent* (5 November 2013) <www.argentinaindependent.com/currentaffairs/secret-military-dictatorship-documents-discovered-basement/> accessed 22 June 2017.

[32] Surveys by the European Board of National Archivists (2014) <www.archivi.beniculturali.it/index.php/cosa-facciamo/relazioni-internazionali/eag-ebna-meeting-torino-2014/item/1231-surveys-on-military-and-intelligence-archives-and-on-the-regulation-of-the-archival-profession-in-eu-countries> accessed 22 June 2017.

[33] See, eg, S Aftergood, 'An Inquiry into the Dynamics of Government Secrecy' (2013) 48 Harvard Civil Rights-Civil Liberties Law Review 511–30.

16 Persons implicated who request access to archives for their defence also encounter problems. Defence lawyers for a soldier on trial for war crimes filed a criminal complaint against Bosnia's Defence Minister for denying access to the Ministry's archives, even though the lawyers had an 'access permit' from the court. The Ministry claimed that the country's data protection legislation states that 'only members of the Bosnian presidency, presidents and vice presidents of the country's two political entities, judges, prosecutors and general attorneys can gain access to data at all levels of confidentiality without a security check'.[34]

17 Academic researchers routinely complain of the difficulties they have in obtaining access to records for study. A case currently before the ECtHR concerns a Russian historian who, along with the archivist who provided him with the records, was convicted in a Russian court for violating 'personal and family secret' information while studying cases of ethnic Germans who were repressed and committed to special settlements in the Arkhangelsk oblast during and after the Second World War.[35]

18 Furthermore, access to electronic records presents new challenges. The International Standards Organization in November 2016 released a standard on electronic discovery and production of electronically stored data.[36] Future judicial proceedings will surely rely in some measure on electronic records discovered through data-mining and data-retrieval techniques; however, at present sophisticated data mining is costly and requires specialized expertise. The use of special masters to assist courts faced with electronic discovery matters is an emerging trend in the US.[37]

19 But access clearly can make a difference. Two former police officers in Guatemala were sentenced in 2010 to forty years in prison over the disappearance of a union leader twenty-six years earlier; of the 750 documents used in evidence in the case, 667 came from police archives discovered in 2005.[38] Sometimes access to one agency's records can point to records in other archives; for example, in August 2013 the US Federal Bureau of Investigation responded to a request for information on Noam Chomsky, a famous dissident, which showed that a Central Intelligence Agency file on Chomsky once existed, something the Agency had always denied.[39] And access to records of one government may

[34] 'War Crimes Lawyers Target Bosnian Defence Minister', *Balkan Insight* (28 June 2013) <www.balkaninsight.com/en/article/war-crimes-defence-files-complaint-against-bosnian-minister?utm_source=Balkan+Transitional+Justice+Daily+Newsletter&utm_campaign=3aafd09703-RSS_EMAIL_CAMPAIGN&utm_medium=email&utm_term=0_561b9a25c3-3aafd09703-311109073> accessed 22 June 2017.

[35] See *Suprun v Russia* App no 58029/12, still pending.

[36] See <www.iso.org/standard/63081.html> accessed 22 June 2017. See also American National Standards Institute (13 November 2013) <www.ansi.org/news_publications/news_story.aspx?menuid=7&articleid=3789> accessed 22 June 2017.

[37] NB Fischer and RN Lettieri, 'Creating the Criteria and the Process for Selection of E-Discovery Special Masters in Federal Court' *The Federal Lawyer* (February 2011) <www.fedbar.org/Image-Library/webinar-files/Creating-the-Criteria.pdf> accessed 22 June 2017.

[38] Organismo Judicial, Guatemala, C-01069-1997-00001 Oficial Tercero, Tribunal Octavo de Sentencia Penal, Narcoactividad y Delitos Contra el Ambiente, Guatemala, Judgment of 28 October 2010, <www2.gwu.edu/~nsarchiv/NSAEBB/NSAEBB337/Document1.pdf> accessed 22 June 2017; and M McDonald, 'Long-hidden archives help Guatemala war crimes trials' *Reuters* (8 February 2012) <www.reuters.com/article/2012/02/08/us-guatemala-archives-idUSTRE8172D220120208> accessed 22 June 2017.

[39] J Hudson, 'After Multiple Denials, CIA Admits to Snooping on Noam Chomsky' *Foreign Policy* (13 August 2013) <thecable.foreignpolicy.com/posts/2013/08/13/after_multiple_denials_cia_admits_to_snooping_on_noam_chomsky> accessed 22 June 2017.

shed light on human rights violations in another; for example, the trial of former Peruvian President Fujimori used declassified US archives as part of the prosecutor's evidence.[40]

E. Critical Assessment

At minimum, governments must require state bodies holding archives to describe the 20
holdings so that users can know what exists, even if it is not publicly available. This description could be carried out by the staff of those archives, the national archives, or, if ordered by a court, by archivists acting as special masters of the court.

States need to ensure that the rules for access to exculpatory or other information can 21
be provided to persons directly if the request is not in the context of actual or potential litigation. And they need to ensure that the security classifications are not used as an arbitrary bar to access for defence purposes.

With the continued difficulties in gaining access to archives, it is no surprise that a 22
number of important records are leaked. For example, someone in Guatemala leaked the '*Diario Militar*', a set of photographs with identifications of persons seized by a military death squad (most were killed), as well as the military plans of 'Operation Sofía', a counterinsurgency campaign that resulted in massacres of unarmed Mayan civilians, and which displaced hundreds of thousands more as they fled the Army's attacks on their communities during the early 1980s: both sources were used in prosecutions.[41] The substantial leak of US military and State Department records by former Army soldier Chelsea (Bradley) Manning included items that were helpful to the truth commission in Honduras. And the massive leak of records from the US National Security Agency (NSA) by former contract employee Edward Snowden led the American Civil Liberties Union to file a lawsuit challenging the constitutionality of the NSA's mass call-tracking programme.[42] Until Principle 15 is observed in national and international bodies, leaks will continue to be an unofficial access strategy.

Bibliography

González Quintana, A, *The Management of the Archives of the State Security Services of Former Repressive Regimes* (International Council on Archives 2009) <www.ica.org/en/the-management-of-the-archives-of-the-state-security-services-of-former-repressive-regimes>

International Council on Archives, *Basic Principles on the Role of Archivists and Records Managers in Support of Human Rights* (2016) <www.ica.org/en/basic-principles-role-archivists-and-records-managers-support-human-rights>.

International Council on Archives, *Code of Ethics* (1996) <www.ica.org/en/ica-code-ethics>.

[40] 'Archive expert testifies in Fujimori Trial', National Security Archive Electronic Briefing Book no 256 (9 September 2009) <www2.gwu.edu/~nsarchiv/NSAEBB/NSAEBB256/> accessed 22 June 2017.

[41] See 'The Guatemalan Death Squad Diary and the Right to Truth', National Security Archive Electronic Briefing Book no 378 (3 May 2012) <www2.gwu.edu/~nsarchiv/NSAEBB/NSAEBB378/> accessed 22 June 2017; 'Operation Sofia: Documenting Genocide in Guatemala', National Security Archive Electronic Briefing Book no 297 (2 December 2009) <www2.gwu.edu/~nsarchiv/NSAEBB/NSAEBB297/> accessed 22 June 2017.

[42] American Civil Liberties Union, Brief for Plaintiffs-Appellants (3 July 2014) <www.aclu.org/sites/default/files/assets/corrected_brief_of_plaintiffs-appellants_-_final_stamped_03_07_2014.pdf> accessed 22 June 2017.

International Council on Archives, *Universal Declaration on Archives* (2010) <www.ica.org/en/universal-declaration-archives>.

International Council on Archives, *International Standard for Archival Description (General)* <www.ica.org/en/isadg-general-international-standard-archival-description-second-edition>.

International Council on Archives, *Principles of Access to Archives* (2012) <www.ica.org/en/access>.

International Council on Archives, *Technical Guidance on Managing Archives with Restrictions* (2014) <www.ica.org/en/technical-guidance-managing-archives-restrictions-0>.

OHCHR, *Report of the Office of the United Nations High Commissioner for Human Rights on the seminar of experiences of archives as a means to guarantee the right to truth*, UN Doc A/HRC/17/21 (14 April 2011) <www2.ohchr.org/english/bodies/hrcouncil/docs/17session/A-HRC-17-21.pdf>.

OHCHR, *Rule-of-Law Tools for Post-Conflict States: Archives* (United Nations 2015) <www.ohchr.org/Documents/Publications/HR_PUB_14_4_Archives_en.pdf>.

Peterson, T Huskamp, *Application of ISAD(G) for Human Rights Archives* (International Council on Archives 2012) <www.ica.org/en/application-isadg-human-rights-archives>.

Principle 16. Cooperation Between Archive Departments and the Courts and Non-Judicial Commissions of Inquiry

John D Ciorciari

Courts and non-judicial commissions of inquiry, as well as investigators reporting to them, must have access to relevant archives. This principle must be implemented in a manner that respects applicable privacy concerns, including in particular assurances of confidentiality provided to victims and other witnesses as a precondition of their testimony. Access may not be denied on grounds of national security unless, in exceptional circumstances, the restriction has been prescribed by law; the Government has demonstrated that the restriction is necessary in ademocratic society to protect a legitimate national security interest; and the denial is subject to independent judicial review.

A. Summary of Findings

Official archives can provide crucial evidentiary foundations for truth and accountability efforts, shedding light on individual abuses and the policies and bureaucratic practices in which those acts were embedded. Nevertheless, states routinely withhold relevant documents from courts and commissions of inquiry, usually invoking national security concerns. Domestic freedom of information (FOI) laws and international human rights law have only begun limiting states' ability to withhold files concerning gross human rights violations. Norms governing the balance between access and privacy protection also remain underdeveloped in human rights law and practice.

B. Contextual and Historical Introduction

Archival materials have been central to pursuing justice for gross human rights abuses, 1
from Nuremberg to more recent trials in Argentina, Cambodia, and Guatemala. They have furnished crucial information for official and unofficial truth commissions, such as the 1992 German commission to investigate crimes of the East German Communist Party and the civil society report *Brasil: Nunca Mais*, detailing abuses of Brazil's military regime.[1] However, the state secrets privilege and related legal principles have given states wide-ranging discretion to refuse access to courts, commissions, and their investigators. The International Covenant on Civil and Political Rights (ICCPR), major regional human rights instruments, and most of the ninety-five extant national FOI laws encourage information sharing, but also permit broad disclosure exemptions on national security and other grounds.[2] Moreover, secrecy laws have become more common since the mid-1990s,

[1] L Bickford, 'Unofficial Truth Projects' (2007) 29 Human Rights Quarterly 994–1035, 1006.

[2] International Covenant on Civil and Political Rights 1966 (ICCPR) 99 UNTS 771, Art 19(3); European Convention for the Protection of Human Rights and Fundamental Freedoms 1950 (ECHR), ETS no 5, 213 UNTS 221, Art 10(2); American Convention on Human Rights 1969, OAS Treaty Series no 36, 1144 UNTS 123, Art 13(2) (all enabling exceptions to disclosure on grounds of national security and public order). See

largely offsetting the wave of FOI legislation that preceded them.[3] In many countries, an executive agency needs only assert a national security risk to refuse access. Key questions include the level of anticipated harm governments must demonstrate, whether such harm must be balanced against public interests in disclosure, and whether courts should review executive agency decisions.

2 Disclosure also raises privacy concerns. Fear of disclosing personal details and subjecting innocent parties to harm led the International Tracing Service to seal myriad Nazi files for sixty years, and prompted the Paraguayan 'Archive of Terror' to publish only a small sample of its many files online. The challenge is to prevent privacy breaches without also hiding information needed to clarify human rights abuses. International law offers few guidelines for courts, commissions, and investigators on how to protect privacy while promoting a full and fair vetting of the evidence.

3 Principle 16 addresses these issues, updating a similar provision in Louis Joinet's 1997 Principles. Diane Orentlicher refined Joinet's assertion that 'national security may not be invoked to prevent access',[4] adding that restrictions may be permissible, in 'exceptional circumstances', when 'prescribed by law', 'necessary in a democratic society to protect a legitimate national security interest', and 'subject to independent judicial review'.[5] Orentlicher also added a sentence on the need to respect privacy, particularly relating to confidential testimony.

C. Theoretical Framework

3 Access to archives helps uphold several related human rights norms. These include the duty to prosecute serious crimes, the right of victims, their loved ones, and the public to know the truth about gross human rights abuses, and fair trial rights, since archival materials may be exculpatory and contribute to a full vetting of the evidence. In a 2011 report, the Office of the United Nations High Commissioner for Human Rights (OHCHR) noted that states use multiple means to address gross human rights violations, including prosecutions, truth-seeking initiatives, and other measures, and '[e]very one of these mechanisms relies on archives'.[6] A 2012 UN Human Rights Council resolution likewise noted 'the importance of archives to the ability of victims to realize their right to the truth, to judicial accountability and non-judicial truth-seeking processes, and for reparations'.[7]

4 Principle 16 also draws attention to two key challenges of managing archival access—respecting legitimate national security needs and protecting privacy. With respect to national security, the Principle's requirement for independent judicial review renders it

also JD Ciorciari and J Franzblau, 'Hidden Files: Archival Sharing, Accountability, and the Right to the Truth' (2014) 46 Columbia Human Rights Law Review 1–84, 15–23.

[3] A Roberts, *Blacked Out: Government Secrecy in the Information Age* (CUP 2006) 129–30.

[4] Set of Principles for the protection and promotion of human rights through action to combat impunity, UN Doc E/CN.4/Sub.2/1997/20/Rev.1 (2 October 1997) Annex II, Principle 15.

[5] Principle 16. See also Johannesburg Principles on National Security, Freedom of Expression and Access to Information (1996).

[6] OHCHR, *Report of the Office of the United Nations High Commissioner for Human Rights on the seminar on experiences of archives as a means to guarantee the right to the truth*, UN Doc A/HRC/17/21 (14 April 2011) paras 6, 20–40, 49.

[7] UN Human Rights Council Res 21/7, *Right to the Truth*, UN Doc A/HRC/RES/21/7 (10 October 2012) para 10.

more demanding than the ICCPR and other major human rights instruments, which merely require that restrictions be prescribed by law and necessary to protect national security or public order.[8] Principle 16's forward-leaning position rightly reflects an understanding that national security and public order exemptions are easily abused by states keen to avoid embarrassment or self-incrimination.

International human rights law has only begun to limit state discretion to withhold documents on national security grounds. In 2010, the Inter-American Court of Human Rights (IACtHR) held in *Gomes Lund v Brazil* that governments cannot invoke national security to refuse information requested by courts or other authorities in human rights cases.[9] It also found that non-disclosure must be subject to review by an entity other than the originating agency.[10] The European Court of Human Rights (ECtHR) has issued supporting decisions, most notably in *Janowiec and Others v Russia*,[11] in which the Court held that Russia had violated the law by refusing to produce documents pertaining to the Katyn massacre. The International Convention on Enforced Disappearances, which took effect in 2010, requires states parties to provide authorities with access to documents relevant to investigations of disappearances.[12] In 2009, the Council of Europe adopted the unprecedented Convention on Access to Official Documents, which would require disclosure when an 'overriding public interest'[13] exists and subject non-disclosure to review by a court or other independent body.[14] 5

When states do disclose archives, Principle 16 emphasizes the need for privacy measures to prevent unwarranted release of sensitive personal information (or disinformation) and honour pledges to victims or witnesses who agree to testify under a condition of confidentiality.[15] Major human rights instruments likewise allow limited non-disclosure to protect individual rights and reputations.[16] In a 2013 report, UN special rapporteur Pablo de Greiff encouraged states to maximize access 'in compliance with the rights to privacy and personal security', and to share best practices using '[t]echnological advances in archiving that allow for selected blocking of parts of documents'.[17] Yet de Greiff rightly stressed that balancing access with privacy norms 'is not easy to achieve'[18]—among other things, it raises important questions about the defendant's right to confront his accusers. 6

In 2015, de Grieff issued a set of recommendations for truth commissions and archives, stressing the importance of archival preservation, accessibility, and privacy protections. He concluded by reiterating that archives relevant to gross violations of human rights 'may not be denied to the public on grounds of national security unless the restriction is in full compliance with international human rights law'[19]—the latest formulation of the evolving international standard. 7

[8] See n 2.

[9] *Gomes Lund et al v Brazil* (Judgment) IACtHR Series C no 219 (24 November 2010) para 202.

[10] Ibid.

[11] *Janowiec and Others v Russia* (Judgment) (ECtHR, 21 October 2013) paras 213–16.

[12] International Convention for the Protection of All Persons from Enforced Disappearance 2007, UN Doc A/61/488, Art 12.

[13] Council of Europe Convention on Access to Official Documents 2009, CETS no 205, Art 3(2). The Convention has obtained eight of the ten required ratifications to enter into force.

[14] Ibid, Art 8.

[15] See also Principle 10(d) (highlighting the importance of respecting pledges of confidentiality to witnesses).

[16] See n 2.

[17] *Report of the Special Rapporteur on the promotion of truth, justice, reparation, and guarantees of non-recurrence, Pablo de Greiff*, UN Doc A/HRC/24/42 (28 August 2013) para 106.

[18] Ibid, para 84.

[19] *Set of general recommendations for truth commissions and archives*, UN Doc A/HRC/30/42 (7 September 2015) Annex, para 25.

D. Practice

I. Access to archival materials

7 Archival access remains a major challenge in practice. Over-classification is pervasive,[20] as states routinely withhold files to avoid criticism or self-incrimination. Courts generally defer to executive agencies, asserting security imperatives, and court-ordered release of classified information is rare, even in democracies.[21] Change has begun, however. Freedom of information laws adopted in Mexico and Peru (2002), Guatemala (2008), Uruguay (2009), and Brazil (2011) all prohibit the withholding of documents describing grave human rights violations.[22] Peru's information law also grants courts, Congress, the Comptroller, and the Human Rights Ombudsman access to other files exempted from disclosure, subject to the rules for handling classified information.[23] Human rights ombudsmen for Slovenia and Bosnia and Herzegovina likewise have the explicit authority to access classified materials.[24] In Mexico, a domestic court recently ruled that the Government must release files about a 2010 massacre of Mexican migrants by the Zetas drug cartel.[25]

8 Some international courts, including the International Criminal Tribunals for the former Yugoslavia and Rwanda (ICTY and ICTR respectively), have used their authority to order states to produce documents.[26] The ICTY and International Criminal Court (ICC) rules of procedure and evidence enable states to object on national security grounds and discuss mitigating measures.[27] Ultimately, if a state refuses to comply, international tribunals have only a weak enforcement mechanism—referring non-compliance to the Security Council or Assembly of States Parties (in the case of the ICC).[28] The ECtHR has similar powers and limitations.[29] It has challenged Russian secrecy claims in cases on disappearances in Chechnya, but has no easy means of enforcing compliance.[30] The IACtHR and hybrid criminal courts, such as those in Cambodia and Sierra Leone,

[20] See, eg, J Sims, 'Too Many Secrets?' *The American Interest* (2 February 2012); D Curtin, 'Overseeing Secrets in the EU: A Democratic Perspective' [2014] Journal of Common Market Studies 684–700.

[21] See, eg, M Fuchs, 'Judging Secrets: The Role Courts Should Play in Preventing Unnecessary Secrecy' (2006) 58 Administrative Law Review 132–76, 163–68.

[22] K Doyle, *Mexico's New Freedom of Information Law* (10 June 2002) <nsarchive2.gwu.edu/NSAEBB/NSAEBB68/> accessed 22 November 2017; Law on Access to Public Information, Decree no 57/2008 (Guatemala), 2008, Art 24; Law on Access to Public Information, Law no 18381 (Uruguay), 2009, Art 12; Law on Access to Public Information, Law no 12.527 (Brazil), 2011, Art 21.

[23] Ley de Transparencia y Accesso a la Información Pública (Peru), Ley no 27806 (as amended, 2003) Art 15C.

[24] Law on the Human Rights Ombudsman of Bosnia and Herzegovina, Dayton Accords, annex VI (1995), Art 28; Classified Information Act (Slovenia), Law no 50/06 (2006), Art 3.

[25] Distrito Federal, Ciudad de México, Juicio de amparo 1371/2013, Sentencia de 11 abril 2014, 54–58.

[26] See, eg, ICTY, *Prosecutor v Blaškić* (Order to the Republic of Croatia for the Production of Documents) IT-95-14 (21 July 1998); ICTR, *Prosecutor v Bizimungu, Decision on Prosper Mugiraneza's Motion Regarding Cooperation with the Republic of Burundi* ICTR-99-50-T (30 October 2008). On the courts' authority, see Ciorciari and Franzblau, n 2, 33–36.

[27] ICTY Rules of Procedure and Evidence (rev 50), r 54 *bis* (A), (E), (F); ICC Rules of Procedure and Evidence, rr 72(4)–(5), 93(4).

[28] ICTY, *Prosecutor v Tihomar Blaskic* (Judgment on the Request of the Republic of Croatia for Review of the Decision of Trial Chamber II of 18 July 1997) IT-95-14 (28 October 1997) paras 25–31; Rome Statute of the International Criminal Court, 1998, Arts 72(7)(a)(i)–(ii), 87(7).

[29] Art 38 ECHR; ECtHR, Rules of Court, rr 44A–44C (as amended, entered into force 1 January 2016).

[30] See, eg, *Musikhanova and Others v Russia* (Judgment) (ECtHR, 4 December 2008) para 107; *Sasita Israilova and Others v Russia* (Judgment) (ECtHR, 28 October 2010) para 145.

lack even the power to issue binding orders.[31] Across the board, international courts rely heavily on voluntary state disclosure for archival information.

Most truth commissions have had insufficient access to secret state files as well. The South African Truth and Reconciliation Commission (TRC) was empowered to 'inspect' and 'retain' any 'article or thing' relevant to its investigations,[32] but chose to allow the military to sift archival records before disclosing them, reflecting the political difficulty of obtaining archival access.[33] Guatemala's Historical Clarification Commission and Peru's TRC both lacked the power to order documents, and were denied access to security and intelligence documents.[34] Likewise, Canada's TRC has been frustrated by government reluctance to transfer millions of federal records.[35] Still, some progress is evident. In 2011, Brazil created a truth commission with explicit authority to access all government documents to investigate Cold War-era crimes.[36] By late 2012, the commission had obtained collections of once-secret documents detailing the chain of command of the internal security services and disappearances by the military.[37] 9

In 2013, the Open Society Justice Initiative and twenty-one other leading civil society organizations and academic institutes unveiled the Global Principles on National Security and the Right to Information, developed through a series of consultative meetings with hundreds of experts from more than seventy states and intended as guides for the reform of state practices. These guidelines—agreed in Tshwane, South Africa—assert that courts and investigators should have access to all information, including classified information, needed to perform their duties, and that national security can justify non-disclosure only when prescribed by law, necessary in a democracy to protect a legitimate security interest, and subject to independent review.[38] The Tshwane Principles thus reflect strong civil society support for the major components of Principle 16. The formidable challenge is to translate that support into laws and rules that are enforced and implemented effectively. 10

II. Privacy protections

Privacy continues to raise challenges for domestic and international proceedings. The case surrounding Stasi wiretap recordings of former German Chancellor Helmut Kohl highlighted the difficulty of balancing individuals' right to privacy and the 'right to the truth' of victims and the public. The eventual result was release of files redacted to conceal 11

[31] IACtHR, Rules of Procedure, r 25 (as amended 8–22 March 2013); Special Court for Sierra Leone, Rules of Evidence and Procedure, r 8 (as amended 31 May 2012); Extraordinary Chambers in the Courts of Cambodia, Internal Rules (rev 9), r 5.

[32] Promotion of National Unity and Reconciliation Act no 34 of 1995 (South Africa) (hereinafter 'South Africa TRC Act'), s 29.

[33] D McKinley, *The State of Access to Information in South Africa* (Center for the Study of Violence and Reconciliation 2004) 17.

[34] On Guatemala, see C Tomuschat, 'Clarification Commission in Guatemala' (2001) 23 Human Rights Quarterly 233–58, 249–51.

[35] M Kennedy, 'Truth commission lacks access to documents' *Ottawa Citizen* (26 October 2013).

[36] Lei da Comissão da Verdade (Brazil), Ley no 12528/2011 (19 November 2011) Art 4(II).

[37] P Duffy, 'National Truth Commission Presents Its First-Year Findings' *Transitional Justice in Brazil* (25 November 2013) <transitionaljusticeinbrazil.com/2013/11/25/national-truth-commission-presents-its-first-year-findings/> accessed 22 November 2017.

[38] The Global Principles on National Security and the Right to Information, Tshwane, South Africa (12 June 2013) (hereinafter 'Tshwane Principles'), Principles 3, 6, 10.

details about private persons—a compromise solution that sought to minimize privacy intrusions while still contributing significantly to the historical record.[39]

12 Truth commission mandates generally include commitments to protect privacy, particularly for those who testify under pledges of confidentiality, but lack specific guidance on when and how to redact official records and archives used in the proceedings.[40] International criminal tribunals have also taken numerous measures to ensure victim and witness privacy and confidentiality—including the use of courtroom screens, *in camera* proceedings, and sometimes redaction of court documents[41]—but have only begun to define the contours of what types of information may be redacted and on what specific grounds.[42]

13 Archival projects also continue to wrestle with questions pertaining to access and privacy. As the Impunity Principles recommend,[43] the Stasi files and similar archives in Hungary, Slovakia, and elsewhere have developed access schemes differentiating among investigators, family members, and researchers in efforts to uphold privacy norms.[44] Using redaction and differential access to separate legitimate human rights and historical inquiries from inappropriate ones is resource-intensive, and inevitably requires difficult value judgements. The Internet adds new potential for archives to contribute to memory and justice, and poses new challenges for managing access.[45]

E. Critical Assessment

14 Principle 16 highlights an important weak link in the human rights regime, and rightly stresses the need for privacy protection and independent judicial review of access restrictions. Yet after a decade of developments in human rights law, the Principle merits strengthening. Like the Tshwane Principles and several Latin American states, updated Impunity Principles should insist on disclosure of any file relevant to gross human rights violations, noting the ample means courts and commissions possess to take legitimate security concerns into account. Instead of requiring governments merely to show that a document has security value—which agencies do easily by invoking 'mosaic' theories and citing superior knowledge of threats—the law should mandate disclosure of files to any credible court or commission able to demonstrate their relevance to an inquiry into gross human rights violations. In addition to promoting archival access, this scheme is more amenable to judicial review.

15 Little organized guidance exists at the international level on how courts and commissions should address the other major challenge Principle 16 identifies—balancing archival access with privacy concerns. The Impunity Principles do not themselves define

[39] M Sabrow, 'The Quarrel over the Stasi Files' in AM Eckert (ed), *Institutions of Public Memory* (German Historical Institute 2007) 46–52.

[40] See, eg, Truth and Reconciliation Commission of Liberia Mandate, National Transitional Legislative Assembly (12 May 2005) Art 25; South Africa TRC Act, n 32, Art 11.

[41] See C McLaughlin, 'Victim and Witness Measures of the International Criminal Court: A Comparative Analysis' (2007) 6 Law and Practice of International Courts and Tribunals 189–220.

[42] See B Kuschnik, 'International Criminal Due Process in the Making: New Tendencies in the Law of Non-Disclosure before the ICC' (2009) 9 International Criminal Law Review 173–82.

[43] See Principles 15, 17(b).

[44] See JD Ciorciari, 'Archiving Memory after Mass Atrocities', Rapoport Center Working Paper Series no 4/2012 (2012) 25–29.

[45] Ibid, 29.

'privacy' and could usefully be updated to include a clearer functional definition. The Tshwane Principles, which countenance limited non-disclosure when needed to protect victims and witnesses, also include little specific guidance on the standards to apply.[46] The same is true of UN Special Rapporteur de Greiff's 2015 recommendations for truth commissions and archives. However, national and international courts and archives have established a variety of systems for managing privacy concerns. This remains an area ripe for further international dialogue and consolidation of best practices.

Bibliography

Ciorciari, JD and Franzblau, J, 'Hidden Files: Archival Sharing, Accountability, and the Right to the Truth' (2014) 46 Columbia Human Rights Law Review 1–84.

Fuchs, M, 'Judging Secrets: The Role Courts Should Play in Preventing Unnecessary Secrecy' (2006) 58 Administrative Law Review 132–76.

González Quintana, A, *Archival Policies in the Protection of Human Rights* (ICA 2009).

International Council on Archives (ICA), *Principles of Access to Archives* (ICA 2012).

Peterson, T Huskamp, *Securing Police Archives: A Guide for Practitioners* (Swisspeace 2013).

Roberts, A, *Blacked Out: Government Secrecy in the Information Age* (CUP 2006).

[46] Tshwane Principles, n 38, Preamble, Principle 10(6)(b).

Principle 17. Specific Measures Relating to Archives Containing Names

Valentina Cadelo and Trudy Huskamp Peterson

(a) For the purposes of this principle, archives containing names shall be understood to be those archives containing information that makes it possible, directly or indirectly, to identify the individuals to whom they relate;

(b) All persons shall be entitled to know whether their name appears in State archives and, if it does, by virtue of their right of access, to challenge the validity of the information concerning them by exercising a right of reply. The challenged document should include a cross-reference to the document challenging its validity and both must be made available together whenever the former is requested. Access to the files of commissions of inquiry must be balanced against the legitimate expectations of confidentiality of victims and other witnesses testifying on their behalf in accordance with principles 8 (f) and 10 (d).

A. Summary of Findings

'State archives' encompasses an enormous variety of records. Names in state archives appear in many locations, not all of which are captured by indexing. Archives must be searched using a strategy that is different from that of searching the active records of a government institution; search strategies differ for paper, audiovisual, and electronic records. Data-mining techniques for electronic records can recover some but not all names, although at a relatively high cost.

Against this background, all persons are entitled to know whether their names appear in state archives and, if so, by virtue of their right to access, shall be given the opportunity to challenge the validity of the information concerning them.

Access rules shall permit the eventual release of all records, including records challenging the validity of the information in the file. Commissions of inquiry, in particular, need to set specific access rules for their records, protecting not only the victims and witnesses but also commission staff members and alleged but unproven perpetrators.

B. Contextual and Historical Introduction

1 Naming names: the quintessence of the collaborator. Storing names: the essence of security services. While the Argentine writer Jacobo Timerman called himself 'a prisoner without a name in a cell without a number', his Czech counterpart, Milan Kundera, thought, 'Police files are our only claim to immortality.' Principle 17 links them all: the names named, the names stored, and the publicly unnamed prisoners.

2 A name is any unique personal identifier, from a proper name to an identity card number to a description that fits only one person. The important limitation in Principle 17(b) is that the name must be in 'State archives'. This includes records from the national government level (including its branches throughout the country and its diplomatic missions and military outposts around the world) to that of the smallest village

or rural township. It includes records of contractors carrying out government functions, such as security guard forces and defence contractors. It includes records in the custody of the creating government institution, as well as records held by an official state archives.

Names and identifiers are found in applications, declarations, inquiries and complaints, interviews, claims, reports, contracts, lists, registers, invoices, certificates, payments, examinations, questionnaires, hearings, agreements, wills, leases, licences, and permits, etc. These records are created by agencies in an enormous variety of contexts: civil status and affiliation (births, deaths, marriages, divorces, adoptions); health (medical facilities, social security, drug treatment); wealth and income (taxation, banking, wages, and salaries); crime and punishment (police, courts, prisons, prosecutors, amnesties, and pardons); employment records; censuses and surveys; immigration and border control, and more.[1] The records may be paper, electronic, cartographic, and audiovisual. The name may or may not be indexed. The file may be on the person or on another person, an organization, a subject, an event or a transaction, or it may simply be a chronological file. The name may be linked to a physical item: fingerprints, iris recognition images, and DNA samples. 3

Principle 17 supposes that finding where a person's name appears in state archives is a manageable burden for governments. In many cases, however, this is not true (see section D). If, after a search, a record on the person is located, it may include inaccurate or false information; documents containing surveillance information in files from security services are particularly likely to raise this issue. In these cases, the person often demands the correction or expunging of the item, an action that is not contemplated by Principle 17. 4

It is important to be clear about what is at stake when demands are made to expunge records. First, expunging falsifies everyone's history. If the item relates to the political behaviour of a former totalitarian regime, destroying these files will allow the whitewashing of the past, with no evidence to the contrary, making future debates about what the regime did a matter of argument without proof. Only by retaining the US FBI file on Martin Luther King, Jr, for example, is it possible to know the extensive harassment he suffered while leading the US civil rights movement in the 1950s and 1960s. At the same time, the proposal to destroy could cover information that is entirely accurate, as well as information that is false, in which case truthful records would also be eliminated. A person could ask to have his personnel file deleted, thereby eliminating the evidence that he, as a soldier, was present at the site of a massacre. Second, scientific work that depends on identifying persons and links between groups would be severely hampered or rendered impossible. Medical research into disease often requires linking known cases to identify patterns; sociological research on settlements and ethnic conflict relies on information about people in context. Historical research needs identification of individuals, whether actors or observers. Research in many fields is accomplished by linking databases of names to create patterns that provide insights unattainable without those connections. Destroying or anonymizing archives makes these studies impossible—and all of us poorer. 5

But if the item or the file is not to be destroyed, what is the alternative? Principle 17 is clear: the person can submit a statement of clarification, and this statement will 6

[1] Drawn from lists in T Cook, *The Archival Appraisal of Records Containing Personal Information: A Ramp Study with Guidelines* (UNESCO April 1991) PGI-91/WS/3, 15–16.

be made available whenever the original file is provided to a researcher. The archival custodian should accept the submission, create a new file in which the submission is placed, and place a cross-reference in the original file indicating that a parallel file exists. This cross-reference will be incorporated in both the paper and electronic files, and the archivists will ensure that the parallel file is always given to researchers who request the original file. This ensures that the file the researcher sees is precisely that created by the agency—no whitewashing of the past—but it still provides the opportunity to contest the information.

7 The procedures adopted shall include adequate measures for the protection of confidentiality of any other person whose identity can be determined from the records in the file requested. Principle 17 incorporates this aspect by making reference to the files of commissions of inquiry in particular, where ensuring the confidentiality of victims and other witnesses testifying on their behalf in accordance with Principles 8(f) and 10(d) is of utmost importance.

C. Theoretical Framework

8 Principle 17 requires states to provide specific safeguards to individuals who exercise their right of access to archives, in particular to know whether their personal information is included therein. While its origins may arguably be found in the so-called 'habeas data', a judicial remedy used only by some Latin American countries,[2] the Principle reflects contemporary standards relating to access to archives,[3] freedom of information, data protection, and any other situation regarding rights to privacy.[4]

9 The theory that there is a right to know of the existence of personal information kept in archives of oppressive regimes was asserted emphatically at the end of the 1980s and beginning of the 1990s as a consequence of the fall of authoritarian regimes and the corresponding opening of archives of past regimes to the public. 'I want my file' was the slogan of those groups of citizens who occupied the offices of the Stasi on 15 January 1990, carrying placards demanding 'Security for our documents' and 'Freedom for my file'.[5] In response to these challenges, many states emerging from repressive regimes adopted legislation to regulate access to information held in their archives, with particular consideration given to circumstances where police or repressive information services kept information on individuals and where political, ideological, ethical, or racial repression had affected the personal, family, or professional life of the persons concerned.[6]

[2] A Guadamuz, 'Habeas Data: The Latin-American Response to Data Protection' 2000 (2) *The Journal of Information, Law and Technology*.

[3] See commentary to Principle 15 in this volume.

[4] It is now widely recognized that both the right to information and the right to privacy are fundamental human rights, which are protected by the main human rights treaties and arguably have developed as norms of customary international law. While both rights may overlap, data protection standards aim to protect the personal privacy that people have against the possible collection and misuse of their personal data by data processors in an unauthorized manner. For an overview of the existing legal framework on the freedom of information, see <www.Right2INFO.org>, a website launched by the Open Society Justice Initiative in 2008. On the right to privacy, see A Rengel, *The General Right to Privacy as a Norm of International Law* (Nijoff 2013).

[5] E Ketelaar, 'Access; the democratic imperative' (2006) 34(2) Archives and Manuscripts 62–81.

[6] See, eg, the Stasi Records Act of 29 December 1991, which forms the legal basis for the work of the Federal Commissioner for the Records of the State Security Service of the former German Democratic Republic. Under Art 13, those affected and third parties have the right to information, inspection, and to request documents. See also A González Quintana, *An Updated and Fuller Version of the Report Prepared by UNESCO*

In calling for a right of access to personal data kept in state archives, as well as the possibility to challenge the validity of such data, Principle 17 requires the state to adopt specific procedures and safeguards to protect personal information from unauthorized access, in order to ensure respect for the rights, fundamental freedoms, and dignity of persons to whom the information relates, in accordance with international human rights law. International standards relating to the right to information and the right to privacy thus must be given due consideration in interpreting this Principle. 10

While access to records shall be granted to any individual under the procedure already described, the last sentence of Principle 17(b) provides for specific guarantees in the event that the records concerned are those collected by a commission of inquiry, in accordance with Principles 8(f) and 10(d). Principle 8(f) instructs commissions of inquiry to clarify 'the conditions that will govern access to their documents, including conditions aimed at preventing disclosure of confidential information while facilitating public access to their archives';[7] however, if the commission has not clarified those conditions, appropriate government authorities must do so, establishing conditions reflecting both international norms on privacy and local cultural values. And although Principle 17(b) speaks only of the names of victims and witnesses, other persons, such as staff members of the commission (whose personnel files are within the commission's administrative records) and persons who have been accused but not proved to be perpetrators, also have privacy rights that must be respected, in accordance with international human rights law. 11

The conditions that are established when an inquiry commission is active or when it has just completed its work will necessarily be more stringent than those required several decades later. Principle 10(d) would close records of confidential witnesses for eternity; this is not sensible. It may be necessary to protect these identities until the witnesses are dead; in some nations, the rule would be to protect personal information for twenty years after death; yet in others, the risk of possible retribution by families or social units might require an even longer delay.[8] However, at some time in the future, such records can be made known. 12

Bearing in mind these challenges, recent years have seen the increasing development of soft law documents regulating the management of names and other personal data stored in archives. The International Council on Archives (ICA) has arguably issued most of the relevant standards, particularly the 2014 ICA *Technical Guidance on Managing Archives with Restrictions*, which gives detailed information on the techniques that can be employed for review and redaction of personal data included in archives, and the 2016 ICA *Basic Principles on the Role of Archivists and Records Managers in Support of Human Rights*, which explicitly prescribe safeguards to be adopted in order to balance the right to know the truth with the need to protect the privacy of identifiable persons.[9] 13

and International Council on Archives (1995), Concerning the Management of the Archives of the State Security Services of Former Repressive Regimes (International Council on Archives 2009) 82–85.

[7] See commentary to Principle 8 in this volume.

[8] See commentary to Principle 10 in this volume.

[9] The documents are both available on the ICA website <www.ica.org/> accessed 22 June 2017.

D. Practice

14 The question of whether a person's name exists in state archives and, if so, what the consequences shall be, has become entangled with debates over privacy, principally in Europe.[10]

15 Particularly worth mentioning in this regard is the jurisprudence of the European Court of Human Rights (ECtHR), which has pronounced on the issue from different viewpoints. To start with, the ECtHR found violations of Article 8(1) of the European Convention on Human Rights (ECHR) in a number of cases in which access to documents was denied to the person who was the subject of the documents. In the 2009 *Haralambie v Romania* case, for instance, the Court declared that the existence of a file containing information about the applicant which might be of a personal or intimate nature, and his interest in having access to that file, fell under the scope of application of Article 8, because the possible inaccuracy of the information might jeopardize his reputation and because the purpose of such files was to 'terrorize the population'. The Court further held that the mechanism to grant access to these documents, even if enshrined in national legislation, was not accessible and effective because of the consistent delays in access to the file.[11]

16 At the same time, in other cases the Court not only indicated what constitutes an effective and accessible procedure for access, but also underlined the necessity to enable any person to refute the content of the information contained in state archives. By way of example, in the 2000 *Rotaru v Romania* case, the Court stated that there must be an effective remedy to challenge the validity of information held and used by states,[12] a position subsequently reiterated in 2012 when, in the *Joanna Szulc v Poland* case, the Court stressed the requirements of such a procedure, which must, in its view, 'enable an interested party to have access to all relevant and appropriate information which would allow that party to effectively counter any allegations ... [and] the procedure shall equally provide for a possibility to correct any erroneous entries in the relevant files'.[13]

17 Ultimately, the ECtHR supported the destruction of records containing names. In its 2011 decision in the case *Association '21 Decembre 1989' and others v Romania*, the Court noted 'the absence of safeguards in the domestic legislation to guarantee that information obtained through secret surveillance was destroyed as soon as it was no longer needed to achieve the required purposes', and the fact that because the files still existed, the applicant was at risk of having his telephone calls intercepted.[14]

[10] For the purpose of this chapter, the practice cited here is limited to Europe only. For more case law and practice, see, eg, <www.Right2INFO.org> accessed 22 June 2017, n 4.

[11] *Haralambie v Romania* (Judgment) (ECtHR, 27 October 2009) paras 79 and 96. The Court came to similar conclusions in other cases. See, eg, *Antonieta Tudor v Romania* (Judgment) (ECtHR, 24 September 2013) para 39.

[12] *Rotaru v Romania* (Judgment) (ECtHR, 4 May 2000) paras 67 and 71.

[13] *Joanna Szulc v Poland* (Judgment) (ECtHR, 13 November 2012) para 87. The question of what is then to be considered an effective remedy in the challenging of the content of state-held information is, however, rather left unclear by the Court. In the 2011 *Kamburov v Bulgaria* decision, for example, the Court took a different position on the matter, and declared that in order to be effective it is not necessary for such a remedy to allow the applicant to obtain a formal rectification or annulment of the incriminated order concerning his punishment (see *Kamburov v Bulgaria* (Decision) (ECtHR, 6 January 2011) para 57).

[14] *Association '21 Decembre 1989' and others v Romania* (Judgment) (ECtHR, 25 May 2011) para 121. The case dealt generally with investigations into deaths that took place during the 1990 revolution. Amongst other issues, the Court dealt with the question of whether the state was authorized to hold personal information gathered by the previous regime. The Court found that the holding of private information about the applicants

Other European institutions also have addressed the issue of the holding of names and 18
personal information by state agents. In 2012, the European Commission proposed to revise its General Data Protection Regulation to allow 'data subjects' to 'obtain from the controller the erasure of personal data relating to them and the abstention from further dissemination of such data', so long as the agency that holds the information no longer needs it for its legitimate business. After vigorous protests from the press, archivists, and scientific researchers, the proposal was modified to permit 'archives to continue operating on the basis of the same principles as today. … In short, the right to be forgotten is not absolute and does not affect historical research or the freedom of the press.'[15]

Then came *Google Spain SL, Google Inc v Agencia Española de Protección de Datos,* 19
Mario Costeja González before the Court of Justice of the European Union. In 2013, the Advocate General issued an opinion stating that the current European Union Data Protection Directive 'does not establish a general "right to be forgotten" '.[16] However, in 2014 the Court ruled that Google was responsible for removing, from name-based search results, any links to personal information that are 'inadequate, irrelevant or no longer relevant, or excessive'.[17] It is unclear what impact that decision will have on the management of state archives in Europe.

Ultimately, in Europe, the destruction of archives containing names has repeat- 20
edly proved to be a very sensitive issue whenever authorities have attempted to promote similar policies. For instance, the Government of Hungary proposed in 2011 to give people the security files held on them during the communist era, which could then be retained or destroyed as each person chose. Archival organizations protested to the Hungarian authorities.[18] The Society of Greek Archivists, noting that Greece destroyed its police security files after the end of the Colonels' dictatorship, and thereby that 'an important part of our history … is forever lost', argued that preservation of these types of records 'supports an accurate account of the past and ensures that collective and, even worst, selective amnesia do not prevail'.[19] The ICA quoted the Updated Principles against Impunity in its letter opposing the Hungarian Government's proposal.[20] The law was not passed.

by secret services for sixteen years after its gathering amounted to a violation of Art 8 ECHR (right to respect for private and family life).

[15] Memo, European Commission, 'Data Protection Day 2014: Full Speed on EU Data Protection Reform' (27 February 2014) <europa.eu/rapid/press-release_MEMO-14-60_en.htm> accessed 22 June 2017.

[16] Case C-131/12 *Google Spain SL, Google Inc v Agencia Española de Protección de Datos, Mario Costeja González* (Reference for a preliminary ruling from the Audiencia Nacional (Spain) lodged on 9 March 2012) [2012] OJ C165/11 <eur-lex.europa.eu/LexUriServ/LexUriServ.do?uri=OJ:C:2012:165:0011:0012:EN:PDF> accessed 22 June 2017.

[17] Case C-131/12 *Google Spain SL, Google Inc v Agencia Española de Protección de Datos, Mario Costeja González* (Judgment) (CJEU, Grand Chamber, 13 May 2014) <curia.europa.eu/juris/document/document.jsf?text=&docid=152065&pageIndex=0&doclang=en&mode=req&dir=&occ=first&part=1&cid=276941> accessed 22 June 2017.

[18] See 'Closing down history: The Hungarian government's unorthodox approach to its secret-police archives' *The Economist* (28 February 2011) www.economist.com/blogs/easternapproaches/2011/02/hungarys_secret-police_archives> accessed 22 June 2017.

[19] Letter, Nestor Bamidis to Ambassador of the Republic of Hungary in Greece, 26 February 2011, copy posted along with other messages of protest at <hungarianarchives.wordpress.com/2011/03/page/2/> accessed 22 June 2017.

[20] Copy in author's possession.

E. Critical Assessment

21 Most records in state archives are not organized or indexed by name. Standard archival practice is to describe records by the creating institution and then by the functional context in which the records were created (for example, Archives of the National Police, Second Corps, San Diego Station, Records of control of vehicles). Archives obtain indexes, paper and electronic, when they accession the records from the creating institution, but archivists are unlikely to index archives further, particularly not at an item level. This means that those requesting the records should know what institution was likely involved, and the broad outlines of its organization and functions, in order to determine in which part of the institution's records to search for files or items containing the particular name. The archival institution should both provide the researcher with the finding aids it has created and explain what finding aids (indexes, databases) have been transferred with the records.

22 Searching audiovisual materials is more complex than searching textual records, unless the material has a caption, yet a photograph of a demonstration may make it possible to identify the colonel in charge of the troops; analysis of a sound recording of a conversation may identify the speakers or the person mentioned. New technology promises to make it possible to use photographs of a person's eyes to see and identify who is in his line of sight (the 'indirect' identification required by Principle 17).

23 Sometimes, however, even with electronic systems, names are not simple to find. Names appear in variant forms; names are in fields that are not easily searchable. As the world learned in 2013 from the Edward Snowden disclosures, the technological capacities of security agencies permit an astonishing mass of data in transmission to be sifted for names and unique personal identifiers.[21] However, the majority of electronic records in state control are stored off-line, some in deep storage. Further, many employees use electronic 'shoeboxes', from e-mail in personal mailboxes to word-processing documents maintained on the desktop, or use personal mobile devices for business purposes; searching these applications requires a complex procedure to locate the relevant institutional information while protecting private data.

24 Principle 17 raises problems in the breadth of its potential implications, the difficulty of locating all archives with names and unique personal identifiers, and the increasing confusion in the public mind between right to know where a name appears, the right to data privacy with regard to names, the security of electronic archives containing names, and the right of the government's archival institution to retain records containing names.

25 Searching all current and stored systems in state archives is a major undertaking. Processing costs are significant. To require governments to conduct a search for a name wherever it appears in *all* state archives is an unsustainable demand and an unreasonable burden. However, if Principle 17 is interpreted to mean that a person has the right to ask a specific government agency to search the records in its custody, using its available indexes and current technology, this would limit the burden, although it would likely miss items. It would surely pick up a person's name that was used as the title of the file, but it might miss the name in a paper-based list of names or as a bystander in a photograph. This is a

[21] See the massive coverage by the *Guardian*, 'The NSA files/us-news' <www.theguardian.com/us-news/the-nsa-files> accessed 22 June 2017.

classic risk management dilemma that must be resolved by governments, while the search parameters need to be clearly explained to those who request information.

Lastly, Principle 17 raises specific challenges with regard to archives of commissions of 26
inquiry. Using the conditions established by the commission concerned or other government authorities, archivists will review the records to identify where protected information is located and then undertake careful processing to make sure that such information is not disclosed. This is, however, a slow, complex process, and the time to complete it should not be underestimated when plans are made for the future release of the truth commission/commissions of inquiry records.

Bibliography

Cook, T, The Archival Appraisal of Records Containing Personal Information: A Ramp Study with Guidelines, UNESCO: April 1991, PGI-91/WS/3.

International Association of Privacy Professionals <www.privacyassociation.org/>.

International Council on Archives, *Basic Principles on the Role of Archivists and Records Managers in Support of Human Rights* (2016) <www.ica.org/en/basic-principles-role-archivists-and-records-managers-support-human-rights>.

International Council on Archives, *Technical Guidance on Managing Archives with Restrictions* (2014) <www.ica.org/en/technical-guidance-managing-archives-restrictions-0>.

Nissenbaum, H, 'Privacy as Contextual Integrity' (2004) 79 Washington Law Review 101–39 <crypto.stanford.edu/portia/papers/RevnissenbaumDTP31.pdf>.

Open Society Justice Initiative <www.Right2INFO.org/>.

UNGA Res 45/95, Guidelines for the regulation of computerized personal data files (14 December 1990) <www.un.org/documents/ga/res/45/a45r095.htm>.

United Nations General Assembly, *The right to privacy in the digital age*, Report of the Office of the United Nations High Commissioner for Human Rights, UN Doc A/HRC/27/37 (30 June 2014) <www.ohchr.org/EN/HRBodies/HRC/RegularSessions/Session27/Documents/A.HRC.27.37_en.pdf>.

Principle 18. Specific Measures Related to the Restoration of or Transition to Democracy and/or Peace

John D Ciorciari

(a) Measures should be taken to place each archive centre under the responsibility of a specifically designated office;

(b) When inventorying and assessing the reliability of stored archives, special attention should be given to archives relating to places of detention and other sites of serious violations of human rights and/or humanitarian law such as torture, in particular when the existence of such places was not officially recognized;

(c) Third countries shall be expected to cooperate with a view to communicating or restituting archives for the purpose of establishing the truth.

A. Summary of Findings

Transitional states emerging from civil conflict or widespread repression offer crucial opportunities to challenge impunity, give effect to the right to the truth, and renew social contracts based on democratic norms and the rule of law. As Principle 18 suggests, seizing those opportunities requires protecting and preserving, inventorying, and analysing archives of the old regime, often in the face of formidable political challenges and capacity constraints. Making that process transparent and effective necessitates both clear lines of domestic responsibility and assistance from third countries. A number of states in Europe, Latin America, and elsewhere have indeed established domestic authorities and worked with third countries to build effective archives of past state-inflicted terror. Nevertheless, international and domestic laws continue to impose only weak duties on transitional states and third countries to take the necessary measures. Stronger norms are imperative if post-conflict of newly democratizing states are to build effective archives of past repression.

B. Contextual and Historical Background

1 Principle 18 emerged largely as part of an effort to respond to archival challenges and opportunities in post-authoritarian states. Those issues came to the fore as the 'third wave' of democratization in Europe, Latin America, and elsewhere brought new leaders with incentives and opportunities to illuminate abuses of the *ancien régime* and signal breaks from the past. In 1995, UNESCO and the International Council on Archives (ICA) issued a path-breaking study on how archives detailing past state repression can contribute to truth, accountability, and political reform.[1] Louis Joinet's 1997 Principles on combating impunity asserted that archives shall be placed under the responsibility of a specific person, recommended that special attention be given to places of detention,

[1] A González Quintana, *Archives of the Security Services of Former Repressive Regimes* (UNESCO 1997).

especially those not officially recognized, and invited third countries to cooperate in restituting relevant files.[2] Diane Orentlicher strengthened those provisions by asserting that archives should be the responsibility of a designated 'office', recommending that that special attention also be given to 'other sites of serious violations of human rights and/or humanitarian law such as torture', and stating that third countries 'shall be expected to cooperate' by communicating or restituting archival materials.[3] Subsequent reports by the UN Office of the High Commissioner for Human Rights (OHCHR) have echoed the call for special attention to archives in transitional periods.[4]

States emerging from repressive rule face acute archival challenges. Outgoing officials 2
sometimes burn or shred incriminating documents to cover their tracks, as occurred in East Germany, the Soviet Union, South Korea, and South Africa.[5] In 2011, Egyptian authorities reportedly destroyed files at the State Security Police headquarters before demonstrators stormed the facility to stop them.[6] Sensitive files can also be hidden or neglected when agencies refuse to release them, or if archival laws and policies do not create clear responsibility for assembling and preserving them. For years, troves of documents detailing atrocities in Pol Pot's Cambodia and Guatemala's civil war decayed in back rooms of government facilities, before human rights investigators discovered and organized them into usable archives.[7]

Post-conflict societies face additional obstacles. Records are sometimes lost in the fog of 3
war or during messy transitions toward peace, as when looting and fires destroyed most of the Iraqi National Library and Archives after the 2003 US-led invasion.[8] War-torn states often inherit particularly weak, dysfunctional government institutions, including archival agencies. Economic deprivation and myriad state-building needs make developing sound archival institutions a formidable task. Moreover, multiple factions normally commit human rights violations during armed conflicts, complicating efforts to obtain robust coverage of abuses from state archives alone.[9]

[2] Set of Principles for the protection and promotion of human rights through action to combat impunity, UN Doc E/CN.4/Sub.2/1997/20/Rev.1 (2 October 1997), Annex II, Principles 13–15.

[3] See Updated Impunity Principle 18.

[4] OHCHR, *Report of the Office of the High Commissioner for Human Rights, Right to the Truth*, UN Doc A/HRC/5/7 (7 June 2007), para 63; OHCHR, *Report of the OHCHR on the seminar on experiences of archives as a means to guarantee the right to the truth*, UN Doc A/HRC/17/21 (14 April 2011), paras 6–9.

[5] See, eg, ES Danielson, *The Ethical Archivist* (Society of American Archivists 2010) 19, 41; V Harris, '"They Should Have Destroyed More": The Destruction of Public Records by the South African State in the Final Years of Apartheid, 1990–1994' in R Cox and D Wallace (eds), *Archives and the Public Good* (Society of American Archivists 2002) 205–06.

[6] K Doyle, 'Egyptians Seize Secret Police Files' *Unredacted* (10 March 2011) <https://unredacted.com/2011/03/10/egyptians-seize-secret-police-files/> accessed 22 November 2017.

[7] K Doyle, 'The Atrocity Files: Deciphering the archives of Guatemala's dirty war' *Harper's Magazine* (December 2007) 52; JD Ciorciari with Y Chhang, 'Documenting the Crimes of Democratic Kampuchea' in J Ramji and B Van Schaack (eds), *Bringing the Khmer Rouge to Justice* (Edwin Mellen Press 2005) 221–306, 226.

[8] J Spurr, 'Indispensable Yet Vulnerable: The Library in Dangerous Times', report for the Middle East Librarians Association (10 August 2005).

[9] On differences between post-authoritarian and post-conflict settings, see *Report of the Special Rapporteur on the promotion of truth, justice, reparation, and guarantees of non-recurrence, Pablo de Greiff*, UN Doc A/HRC/21/46 (9 August 2012), paras 15–18.

C. Theoretical Framework

4 Principle 18 reflects an understanding that archives are keys to advancing accountability, the right to truth, and other elements of a successful transition to peace and/or democracy. A 2003 resolution of the International Conference of the Round Table on Archives noted that for states transitioning to democracy, archives serve as 'evidence supporting victims' rights for reparation; as an essential element of collective memory; as a means of determining responsibilities for rights violations; and as a basis for reconciliation and universal justice'.[10] Archivist Antonio González Quintana, expanding on the 1995 ICA-UNESCO report, similarly characterizes archives as 'a means of understanding the past', 'a form of justice for the victims', and as 'tools of information' to help victims pursue accountability and democratic rights.[11]

I. Responsible archival agencies

5 The 1995 ICA-UNESCO report recommended establishing dedicated commissions to manage archival processes in transitional states, foreshadowing Principle 18.[12] Clear lines of responsibility are essential for transparency, accountability, and public trust. International law could promote this norm by requiring national laws that specify offices responsible for sensitive archival collections, and furnish those offices with the legal authority and resources to enforce compliance among the agencies creating relevant records. Thus far, the OHCHR and UN Human Rights Council have merely encouraged states—particularly new democracies—to pass archives laws as expeditiously as possible and pursue the institutional capacity to safeguard their archival collections.[13]

II. Special attention to detention centres and other sites of serious violations

6 Archives are particularly crucial for advancing accountability and the right to the truth with respect to detention centres and other sites of serious violations, especially those cloaked in official secrecy. In these cases, security agencies are especially apt to destroy files or refuse to transfer them to an archive. In theory, international human rights law could prohibit destruction or the withholding of files relating to detention centres and other sites of serious alleged violations, or subject agency decisions to review by a court or independent administrative authority. However, no such binding provision exists.

II. Third-country cooperation

7 Third countries can advance transitional processes by returning archives taken during wartime, or by opening their own files. International law and archival ethics provide overlapping normative bases for restitution of archives seized during war or occupation. The 1954 Hague Convention and 1970 UNESCO Convention declare archives the

[10] Resolutions of the Delegates' Meeting of the International Council on Archives, Cape Town, 24 October 2003, s 3.

[11] A González Quintana, *Archival Policies in the Protection of Human Rights* (ICA 2009) 27–28.

[12] González Quintana, n 1, s 3.2.3.

[13] Report of the OHCHR, *Right to the Truth,* UN Doc A/HRC/12/19 (21 August 2009) para 6; UN Human Rights Council Res 21/7, *Right to the Truth*, UN Doc A/HRC/RES/21/7 (10 October 2012) para 10.

cultural property of the state that produced them,[14] and UNESCO has deemed archives 'the inalienable and indefeasible property' of the state.[15] According to the archival principle of inalienability, archives may only be alienated by an act of the legislature of the originating state and must otherwise be returned.[16] International law does permit seizure of documents 'demanded by the necessities of war' and enables occupying powers to administer the state,[17] including measures to preserve archives and other cultural property.[18] Nevertheless, UNESCO has outlined the prevailing legal and ethical view that '[m]ilitary and colonial occupation do not confer any special right to retain archives acquired by virtue of that occupation'.[19]

Third countries can also disclose their own files, which can shed important light on 8
human rights violations—especially those involving international participation, such as 'Operation Condor' in Latin America and the programme of extraordinary renditions since 9/11. However, domestic and international law do not impose clear third-party disclosure obligations. The National Security Archive in Washington, DC and other civil society groups have used domestic freedom of information (FOI) laws to assist truth and accountability efforts in transitional states, but the US FOI law and most other extant FOI laws give states broad discretion to withhold files on national security and other grounds. The same is true of mutual legal assistance treaties (MLATs) designed to facilitate international cooperation in criminal proceedings. Regional human rights courts and conventions, UN human rights bodies, and domestic legislation have begun imposing limited duties on states to disclose files relevant to human rights cases within their borders, but they have yet to address third-country files.[20]

D. Practice

I. Responsible archival agencies

A number of states have established clear responsibility for the management of archives 9
relating to past human rights abuses. In Germany, a 1991 law established a federal commissioner to manage the Stasi (secret police) archives and related records of the former East German security services.[21] The commissioner's role has helped safeguard archival

[14] Convention for the Protection of Cultural Property in the Event of Armed Conflict 1954 (1954 Hague Convention), 249 UNTS 240, Art 1; Convention on the Means of Prohibiting and Preventing the Illicit Import, Export and Transfer of Ownership of Cultural Property 1970, 823 UNTS 231, Art 1.

[15] UNESCO, *Report on the Possibility of Transferring Documents from Archives Constituted within the Territory of Other Countries*, Doc CC.76/WS/9 (April 1976), s 5.2.

[16] See Executive Committee of the International Council on Archives, *The View of the Archival Community on Settling Disputed Archival Claims* (April 1995) para 4(a).

[17] Hague Convention Respecting the Laws and Customs of War on Land, Regulations on Respecting the Customs of War on Land 1907, TS no 539, Annex, Arts 23, 43, 53.

[18] 1954 Hague Convention, n 14, Art 5(2). Some experts argue that temporary removal can help ensure survival of sensitive archives, but the OHCHR concludes that '[e]xcept in extreme cases, this course of action is inappropriate in a post-conflict period', partly because it denies the transitional state an opportunity to build archival capacity. See also Report of the OHCHR, n 13, para 14.

[19] UNESCO, n 15, s 3.1.1.

[20] See JD Ciorciari and J Franzblau, 'Hidden Files: Archival Sharing, Accountability, and the Right to the Truth' (2014) 46 Columbia Human Rights Law Review 1–84, 9–38.

[21] Act Regarding the Records of the State Security Service of the Former German Democratic Republic (Stasi Records Act), Arts 35–38, Federal Law Gazette 1991, 2272.

access, order, and public legitimacy.[22] In Paraguay, the Supreme Court established a special centre to manage the 'Archives of Terror' depicting abuses during the Stroessner military regime.[23] Other transitional states have transferred files of past repression to national archives or specialized institutions. Ukrainian presidential decrees passed Communist Party and KGB records to the national archives in 1991,[24] and the 1996 National Archives of South Africa Act provided a legal and institutional foundation for that country's effort to preserve archives of repression under Apartheid.[25] The Franco files at Spain's National Historical Archive, the Argentine National Archive of Memory, and the Historical Archives of the Hungarian State Security are prominent examples of specialized bodies.

10 A number of other states dealing with legacies of severe past repression—such as Cambodia, Latvia, Libya, and Mexico—have passed archives laws in recent years, partly to promote more responsible, accountable management of sensitive official records. Such laws give national archives authority to obtain, retain, and make accessible agency records of historical value.[26] However, as the head of Egypt's National Library and Archives and others have lamented, agencies often fail to retain or transfer important files, and archives have few tools to force them to do so.[27] Experience in Mexico and Russia also shows that recalcitrant agencies and archivists can bury unfavourable information with incomplete inventories and other tactics.[28] More than progressive archives laws are needed; strong civil society engagement and international cooperation aimed at solidifying best practices are also imperative in this area.

II. Special attention to detention centres and other sites of serious violations

11 Where states have paid special attention to records concerning secret detention centres and other sites of gross human rights violations, that focus has reaped dividends. For example, the Tuol Sleng Archives in Cambodia, concerning the notorious Khmer Rouge secret prison in Phnom Penh, have preserved evidence of the voluminous atrocities there and contributed mightily to the eventual criminal conviction of its chief, Duch.[29] The 2006–07 release by the International Tracing Service of Nazi records, including millions

[22] See G Bruce, 'East Germany' in L Stan (ed), *Transitional Justice in Eastern Europe and the Former Soviet Union* (Routledge, 2009) 15–36.

[23] Resolution no 81 of the Supreme Court of Paraguay (26 March 1993).

[24] See, eg, Decree of the Presidium of Verkhovna Rada of Ukraine on Passing of Archives of Communist Party of Ukraine to Subordination of the Main Archival Administration under the Cabinet of Ministers of Ukraine (27 August 1991).

[25] V Harris, 'Archives' in C Villa-Vicencio and D du Toit (eds), *Truth & Reconciliation in South Africa: 10 Years on* (David Philip 2006) 53–58. See also Promotion of Access to Information Act no 2 of 2000, South Africa (2 February 2000), Art 11 (providing for a right of access to information in the files).

[26] See, eg, Archives Law (Latvia), entered into force 1 January 2011, Arts 4, 6–11; Ley Federal de Archivos (Mexico), 21 January 2012, Arts 14–17.

[27] M Saad, 'Head of Egypt National Archives: State institutions illegally dispose of documents' *Ahram Online* (29 October 2013) <english.ahram.org.eg/NewsContentP/18/84935/Books/Head-of-Egypt-National-Archives-State-institutions.aspx> accessed 22 November 2017.

[28] WG Rosenberg, 'Politics in the (Russian) Archives: The "Objectivity Question", Trust, and the limitations of Law' (2001) 64 American Archivist 78–95, 78, 94; 'The Dead of Tlatelolco: Using the archives to exhume the past', National Security Archive Electronic Briefing Book no 201 (1 October 2006).

[29] Extraordinary Chambers in the Courts of Cambodia, *Case 001* (Trial Chamber Judgment) (26 July 2010) paras 149, 647–48.

of pages of concentration camp documents, has enabled researchers to uncover information about little-known secret Nazi camps and torture sites.[30]

III. Third-country cooperation

Third countries have sometimes returned archives taken during war or occupation, such as the Russian return of 'trophy archives' taken from Central Europe during and after the Second World War,[31] and the US return of Haitian documents confiscated during the 1994 US intervention in Haiti.[32] However, states often keep files seized during war or occupation, and international law imposes no clear sanctions. The US still holds documents seized during the 1989 Panama intervention,[33] and US officials asserted in 2011 that international law does not set a time frame for returning Iraqi Ba'athist records taken to the US after the fall of Saddam Hussein.[34] The Iraqi records, some of which now reside at the Hoover Institution in California, have generated legal and ethical debate, as the head of Iraq's National Library and Archives requested their return and won public support from the American and Canadian archival associations.[35] Principle 18 suggests that restitution of archives taken from transitional states should occur promptly, but state practice remains decidedly mixed, making it difficult to conclude that prompt restitution is part of customary international law. 12

Principle 18 also calls on third countries to 'communicate' archives by advertising their existence and content. Important examples of voluntary disclosure exist, including US schemes to declassify documents pertaining to human rights abuses in Chile and Guatemala.[36] However, such disclosure remains the exception rather than the norm and has not been done out of a sense of *opinio juris*. 13

E. Critical Assessment

Principle 18 identifies important aspects of archival practice in transitional periods but stops short of asserting state duties to take the necessary steps. Further progress in this area will require incentivizing preservation and disclosure by both the home state and third countries. International human rights bodies and civil society groups, including archival associations, should advance the principle that third countries bear legal and ethical duties to share archives detailing certain gross human rights violations beyond their borders. At the same time, disclosure advocates should work with states to develop palatable means of implementation. 14

[30] See, eg, PA Shapiro, 'Vapniarka: The Archive of the International Tracing Service and the Holocaust in the East' (2013) 27 Holocaust and Genocide Studies 114–37, 119–25.

[31] See PK Grimsted, 'Why Do Captured Archives Go Home? Restitution Achievements under the Russian Law' (2010) 17 International Journal of Cultural Property 291–333, 292.

[32] CS Wren, 'US Agrees to Return Documents Soldiers Confiscated in Haiti' *New York Times* (7 December 1995).

[33] See D Cox, 'The Lost Archives of Noriega: Emancipating Panamanian Human Rights Documents in US Military Custody' (2014) 32 Boston University International Law Journal 57–89, 59–69.

[34] D Cox, 'National Archives and International Conflicts: The Society of American Archivists and War' (2011) 74 American Archivist 451–81, 467.

[35] J Gravois, 'Disputed Iraqi Archives Find a Home at the Hoover Institution' *Chronicle of Higher Education* (23 January 2008).

[36] Ciorciari and Franzblau, n 20, 40–48.

15 The supporting role of non-state organizations also merits greater attention. Some governments have supplemented their capacity to inventory and preserve records of past repression by partnering with non-state actors. For example, the Documentation Center of Cambodia was created in 1995, and has managed Khmer Rouge records with the consent of Cambodian authorities. In Guatemala, outside experts and the University of Texas have helped the Historical Archive of the National Police preserve and disseminate its files and insulate them from political risk. These partnerships with civil society and academic institutions provide potentially crucial supports for the legitimacy and efficacy of archival efforts in transitional states.

Bibliography

Ciorciari, JD and Franzblau, J, 'Hidden Files: Archival Sharing, Accountability, and the Right to the Truth' (2014) 46 Columbia Human Rights Law Review 1–84.

Cox, R and Wallace, D (eds), *Archives and the Public Good* (Society of American Archivists 2002).

Danielson, ES, *The Ethical Archivist* (Society of American Archivists 2010).

González Quintana, A, *Archival Policies in the Protection of Human Rights* (ICA 2009).

Harris, V *Archives and Justice: A South African Perspective* (Society of American Archivists 2007).

Office of the UN High Commissioner for Human Rights, *Rule-of-Law Tools for Post-Conflict States: Archives* (United Nations 2015).

PART III

THE RIGHT TO JUSTICE

—

A.

GENERAL PRINCIPLES

Principle 19. Duties of States with Regard to the Administration of Justice

Kai Ambos

States shall undertake prompt, thorough, independent and impartial investigations of violations of human rights and international humanitarian law and take appropriate measures in respect of the perpetrators, particularly in the area of criminal justice, by ensuring that those responsible for serious crimes under international law are prosecuted, tried and duly punished.

Although the decision to prosecute lies primarily within the competence of the State, victims, their families and heirs should be able to institute proceedings, on either an individual or a collective basis, particularly as *parties civiles* or as persons conducting private prosecutions in States whose law of criminal procedure recognizes these procedures. States should guarantee broad legal standing in the judicial process to any wronged party and to any person or non-governmental organization having a legitimate interest therein.

A. Summary of Findings

Principle 19 focuses on states' (criminal) justice obligations regarding serious human rights violations. The duty to carry out criminal proceedings in these cases, as expressed, albeit not unambiguously, in paragraph 1 follows from this very duty of states under international law, that is, from treaty obligations, customary international law, or as a general principle of international law. This duty has long been recognized by regional human rights courts and international human rights bodies.

Paragraph 2 reflects the growing tendency in national and international criminal procedure to strengthen the position of victims of international crimes. This tendency is also reflected in domestic criminal procedure, especially of civil law jurisdictions, where victims for decades have the status of *parties civiles* with extensive participatory rights. At the international level, this tendency has been taken up by the International Criminal Court (ICC), which, contrary to the more common law-inspired UN ad hoc tribunals, grants victims broad participation rights. Principle 19 goes beyond that in extending these rights 'to any person or non-governmental organization having a legitimate interest'.

In sum, it can be safely concluded that the fight against impunity through criminal proceedings and the victims' role therein has steadily advanced and found its most comprehensive reflection in the regime of the ICC.

B. Contextual and Historical Introduction

Under Principle 19, states have a duty to ensure that those responsible for serious crimes 1
under international law are prosecuted, tried, and duly punished. According to paragraph 1, the necessary measures are not limited to the area of criminal justice, but the latter seems to be considered the most comprehensive and efficient way ('particularly') to bring

justice to the victims.[1] The individual criminal responsibility of the perpetrators of such violations has long been recognized in international (criminal) law.[2] This is predicated on the assumption that criminal prosecution and punishment for these crimes reduces impunity and is the most promising approach to prevent future crimes. Of course, this assumption finds its limits in transitional justice processes, where (criminal) justice often has to give way to broader peace interests.

2 Today the fight against impunity is the explicit aim of the ICC[3] and a major goal of the United Nations (UN).[4] However, the duty to prosecute lies primarily with the domestic justice system, with regional or international mechanisms being subsidiary or complementary.[5] In this context the establishment of an 'International Criminal Law Section' within the restructured African Court of Justice and Human Rights[6] deserves special attention, especially as regards its relationship with the ICC and the complementarity principle.

3 The Updated Set of Principles expands the list of 'serious crimes under international law'[7] as compared to the original 1997 Joinet Principles.[8] According to the new author of the Principles, Diane Orentlicher, this expansion reflects the national and international jurisprudence and the opinions of treaty bodies, as well as the text of the relevant treaties and resolutions of the General Assembly and other UN bodies.[9] However, it must not be overlooked that, even after the adoption and entry into force of the ICC Statute, no uniform, comprehensive list of crimes entailing a duty to prosecute exists. On the contrary, the existence of such a duty and its precise scope are still controversial. We shall return to this issue in section C of this commentary.

4 Paragraph 2 of Principle 19 concerns victims' participation in accountability proceedings. The Statutes of the International Criminal Tribunal for the former Yugoslavia (ICTY) and the International Criminal Tribunal for Rwanda (ICTR) did not provide for explicit victim participation *stricto sensu*, that is, participation beyond testifying as witnesses (including the respective rules on victims and witness protection).[10] By contrast, the ICC Statute and the ICC Rules of Procedure and Evidence (RPE) grant victims special participatory rights. In the same vein, paragraph 2 of Principle 19 provides that 'victims, their families and heirs should be able to institute proceedings'. In contrast to Principle 20 paragraph 2 of the original 1997 Principles, the new wording of paragraph 2

[1] For (supplementary) alternatives to criminal justice, see K Ambos, 'The Legal Framework of Transitional Justice: A Systematic Study with a Special Focus on the Role of the ICC' in K Ambos, J Large, and M Wierda (eds), *Building a Future on Peace and Justice* (Springer 2009) 19–103, MNN 12–18.

[2] On the history, see K Ambos, *Treatise on International Criminal Law*, vol I: *Foundations and General Part* (OUP 2013) 2 et seq.

[3] Cf Preamble and Art 5, ICC Statute.

[4] Rome Statute of the ICC, A/CONF.183/9 of 17 July 1998, updated doc at <www.icc-cpi.int>. See only General Assembly (GA) Resolution (Res) A/RES/67/1 (30 November 2012) para 22.

[5] See Principle 20; para 10 of the Preamble, Arts 1, 17 ICC Statute.

[6] Cf Art 6 of the Statute of the African Court of Justice and Human and Peoples' Rights, Annex to the Protocol on Amendments to the Protocol on the Statute of the African Court of Justice and Human Rights, adopted at the Malabo summit (26/27 June 2014).

[7] See the commentary in this volume, 'Definitions', section C.II.

[8] *Set of Principles for the protection and promotion of human rights through action to combat impunity, Revised Final Report prepared by Mr Joinet pursuant to Sub-Commission decision 1996/119*, UN Doc E/CN.4/Sub.2/1997/20/Rev.1 (2 October 1997) (hereinafter 'Joinet Principles') Annex II.

[9] *Report of the independent expert to update the Set of Principles to combat impunity, Diane Orentlicher*, UN Doc E/CN.4/2005/102 (18 February 2005) (hereinafter 'Orentlicher Report') para 13.

[10] B McGonigle Leyh, *Procedural justice?—Victim Participation in International Criminal Proceedings* (Intersentia 2011) 137 et seq.

pays regard to the fact that some domestic procedural systems, especially of common law origin, may not provide for such a mechanism. Irrespective of the domestic law, however, paragraph 2 obliges states to grant broad legal standing to 'any' wronged party and to 'any person or non-governmental organization', as long as these can demonstrate 'a legitimate interest'. Legal standing has to be ensured at 'all appropriate stages of the criminal proceedings'.[11] 'Broad legal standing' in this sense can only be interpreted as participatory rights of some sort. Thus, paragraph 2 strives, in essence, to extend the *partie civil* model to all domestic systems.

Moreover, the Updated Principle drops the requirement that the non-governmental organizations (NGOs) representing the victims must produce 'recognized long-standing activities on behalf of the victims concerned'.[12] This appears, at first sight, quite broad, but it is justified with the alleged fact that often, 'during periods of restoration of or transition to democracy and/or peace, the most effective domestic NGOs may not have been able to establish themselves on a long-standing basis'.[13] Instead the 'legitimate interest' appears as the decisive criterion; it will have to be determined with regard to the declared aims of the organization, its official statements, and its work with the victims. 5

C. Theoretical Framework

I. Duty to prosecute

Paragraph 1 of Principle 19 provides for a duty to prosecute ('shall'), although the wording is not completely straightforward for two reasons. First, as already noted, it does not limit accountability measures to criminal prosecution but only lays a special emphasis on these measures ('particularly . . .'). Second, criminal justice is to be understood broadly, allowing for a series of 'alternative' accountability measures going beyond criminal justice measures *stricto sensu*.[14] In any case, the last part of paragraph 1 ('ensuring that . . .') makes clear that the focus lies on criminal prosecution and punishment. 6

As already pointed out, there is no homogeneous, all-inclusive source from which the duty to prosecute international crimes can be inferred. In terms of *treaties* within the meaning of Article 38(1)(a) of the Statute of the International Court of Justice (ICJ), one particularly relevant treaty is the ICC Statute. As is well known, the ICC has complementary jurisdiction over the crime of genocide, crimes against humanity, and war crimes—the so-called international core crimes.[15] Although states parties to the ICC Statute are not explicitly obliged to transfer these crimes into their domestic law, on a factual level such a duty can be inferred from the principle of complementarity under Article 17 of the ICC Statute. Against this background, it can be argued that at least the ICC states parties have accepted a duty to prosecute with regard to the ICC crimes.[16] Further, there are several so-called suppression conventions that oblige states parties to criminalize the respective conduct under their domestic penal laws.[17] With regard to the 'serious crimes' referred 7

[11] Orentlicher Report, n 9, para 37.

[12] Joinet Principles, n 8, Principle 20, para 2.

[13] Orentlicher Report, n 9, para 37.

[14] Cf Ambos, n 1, MNN 7 et seq.

[15] Arts 5–8 ICC Statute. The crime of aggression (Art 8*bis* ICC Statute) is not of interest here, since it does not protect individual human rights but peace, security, and the well-being of the world. Cf K Ambos, *Treatise on International Criminal Law*, vol II: *The Crimes and Sentencing* (OUP 2014) 184 et seq.

[16] Critical of such a duty, SMH Nouwen, *Complementarity in the Line of Fire: The Catalysing Effect of the International Criminal Court in Uganda and Sudan* (CUP 2013) 36–40.

[17] On the terminology and relevant treaty crimes, see Ambos, n 15, 222 et seq.

to by Principle 19, these international conventions are the Geneva Conventions[18] and Additional Protocol I thereto,[19] the Genocide Convention,[20] the Torture Convention,[21] the Slavery Convention,[22] and the Convention for the Protection of All Persons from Enforced Disappearance.[23] While the conventions may differ in the framing of the concrete criminalization obligation and state parties have usually discretion how to comply with such an obligation, they must ensure that the respective conduct is covered in their domestic criminal law and adequately punished. Thus, given the large number of states parties to these conventions, it is fair to say that the great majority of states are bound by an explicit duty to prosecute the said crimes, notwithstanding their constitutional arrangements to make such a duty effective domestically.

8 The international and regional human rights conventions do not contain provisions that explicitly oblige states to institute criminal proceedings against offenders. The respective treaty bodies have concluded, however, that an accordant duty can be inferred from the general provisions, which oblige states parties to protect and ensure human rights. We shall return to this question in section D.

9 A duty to prosecute may also be derived from *customary international law* within the meaning of Article 38(1)(b) of the ICJ Statute. Although it is relatively easy to make out a respective *opinio juris* of states to prosecute serious human rights violations (eg, by invoking resolutions of UN bodies and the corresponding statements of states in these forums), it is much more difficult to claim a coherent state practice in this regard, given the widespread human rights violations that are often neither investigated nor prosecuted, nor even explicitly exempted from punishment (eg, by an amnesty). The existence of a customary law duty depends, therefore, on the importance of state practice in the creation of such a duty. It can safely be concluded if one downplays the actual state practice and stresses the *opinio juris*, or if one interprets states' accession to a treaty as an expression of state practice in the form of a 'Verbalpraxis' (verbal practice).[24] From this perspective one may infer a customary duty from the growing accession to the ICC Statute, since it reflects the acceptance of a 'duty of every State to exercise its criminal jurisdiction over those responsible for international crimes'.[25] In contrast, with regard to other crimes

[18] Art 49, First Geneva Convention of 1949, 75 UNTS 31; Art 50, Second Geneva Convention of 1949, 75 UNTS 85; Art 129, Third Geneva Convention of 1949, 75 UNTS 135; Art 146, Fourth Geneva Convention of 1949, 75 UNTS 287.

[19] Art 85, Protocol Additional to the Geneva Conventions of 12 August 1949, and relating to the Protection of Victims of International Armed Conflicts, 1125 UNTS 3.

[20] Arts IV, V, Convention on the Prevention and Punishment for the Crime of Genocide, 78 UNTS 277.

[21] Art 4, Convention against Torture and Other Cruel, Inhuman or Degrading Treatment or Punishment, 1465 UNTS 85.

[22] Arts 6, 4, Supplementary Convention on the Abolition of Slavery, the Slave Trade, and Institutions and Practices Similar to Slavery, 3 UNTS 266.

[23] Preamble, Arts 3, 7, 9, International Convention for the Protection of All Persons from Enforced Disappearance, GA Res A/Res/61/177 of 20 December 2006.

[24] H Kreicker, 'Grundfragen der nationalen Strafverfolgung völkerrechtlicher Verbrechen' in A Eser, U Sieber, and H Kreicker (eds), *Nationale Strafverfolgung völkerrechtlicher Verbrechen/National Prosecution of International Crimes*, vol VII (Max Planck Institute for Foreign and International Criminal Law 2006) 7–34, 13.

[25] Para 6 of the Preamble to the ICC Statute. See also H Gropengießer and J Meißner, 'Amnesties and the Rome Statute of the International Criminal Court' (2005) 5 International Criminal Law Review 267–300, 272 et seq; JK Kleffner, *Complementarity in the Rome Statute and National Criminal Jurisdictions* (OUP 2008) 8 et seq; D Robinson, 'Serving the Interests of Justice: Amnesties, Truth Commissions and the International Criminal Court' (2003) 14 European Journal of International Law 481–505, 491–93. More cautious C Kress,

not covered by the ICC Statute (namely torture, enforced disappearance, extrajudicial executions, and slavery as isolated acts), a similarly unambiguous state (verbal) practice, and thus a customary duty to prosecute, cannot be identified.[26]

Last but not least, such a duty for the small number of states not bound by treaty obligations may be based on *general principles* of international law within the meaning of Article 38(1)(c) of the ICJ Statute. Such general principles can be deduced from rules that are found in practically every legal system. Their global existence demonstrates the fundamental importance of these rules. Furthermore, soft law, that is, resolutions and statements of international and regional institutions, can be an indication for such general principles. In fact, in particular in the field of human rights, general principles may be drawn from an all-over assessment of international 'soft law', as a kind of '*opinio iuris* without concordant state practice'.[27] As to the acts in question, it can be concluded that they are criminal under almost every domestic system, and apart from that, states regularly confirm the need to punish such acts in public statements or through the approval of resolutions of international and regional bodies. Thus, it follows that there exists a general principle of international law that states are under an obligation to investigate and prosecute acts of torture, enforced disappearance, extrajudicial executions, and slavery.[28] 10

It is sometimes argued that a duty to prosecute serious crimes (or extradite the offender, *aut dedere aut iudicare*)[29] may be inferred from the character of these crimes as *jus cogens*, since this generates a respective duty *erga omnes*.[30] However, the *jus cogens* nature of certain crimes does not, automatically, entail a duty to prosecute these crimes. It only means that the underlying prohibition and the ensuing criminalization cannot be derogated, and that states may prosecute these crimes domestically even if there exists no jurisdictional link. 11

Principle 19 may have to be applied in a more flexible manner in transitional justice processes. Here the admissibility of limitations to criminal prosecution often depends on a difficult balancing exercise, which, by means of a threefold proportionality test, aims to reconcile the conflicting interests of peace and justice.[31] Probably the most important 12

'International Criminal Law' in R Wolfrum (ed), *Max Planck Encyclopedia of Public International Law* (online edition: OUP 2008–) para 18 ('emergence of a customary duty').

[26] Cf K Ambos, 'Völkerrechtliche Bestrafungspflichten bei schweren Menschenrechtsverletzungen' (1999) 37 Archiv des Völkerrechts 318–56, 328 et seq. On the controversial customary international law status of the obligation to extradite or prosecute, see also the recent Final Report of the ILC's Working Group on the Obligation to extradite or prosecute (*aut dedere aut judicare*), A/CN.4/L.844 (5 June 2014) paras 8 et seq (with further references), stating a certain disagreement concerning a respective *opinio juris* with regard to an all-embracing duty. On the widespread amnesty practice, see L Mallinder, *Amnesty, Human Rights and Political Transitions* (Hart Publishing 2008).

[27] Cf originally B Simma, 'International Human Rights and General International Law: A Comparative Analysis' in *Collected Courses of the Academy of European Law*, vol IV: *Book 2* (*1994*) 153–236, 225. For further references and a discussion, see Ambos, n 2, 76.

[28] See previously Ambos, n 26, 332 et seq.

[29] The relationship between these two limbs—prevalence of one of the two or equal weight—depends on the 'context and applicable legal regime in particular situations', and is thus case-specific (ILC Final Report, n 26, paras 4, 13 (distinguishing at paras 6 et seq between four types of conventions pursuant to a 2010 survey by the Secretariat and, at paras 11, 38 et seq, between two types following the Separate Opinion of Judge Yusuf in ICJ, *Belgium v Senegal, Questions relating to the Obligation to Prosecute or Extradite*, Judgment of 20 July 2012, [2012] ICJ Rep 422)); in some conventions, the prosecution obligation may, in line with the so-called 'Hague formula', prevail over the extradition option (see, eg, regarding Art 7(1) CAT, *Belgium v Senegal, ibid*, paras 94–95).

[30] MC Bassiouni, 'International Crimes: *Jus Cogens* and *Obligatio Erga Omnes*' (1996) 59 Law and Contemporary Problems 63–74, 65 et seq.

[31] Cf Ambos, n 2, 420–21, with further references.

normative argument for such a flexible approach can be found in Article 6(5) of Additional Protocol II to the Geneva Conventions, which allows, 'at the end of hostilities', for the 'broadest possible amnesty' for the participants of the respective armed conflict. Of course, this provision has to be interpreted as only covering legal acts in combat and those breaches of international humanitarian law (IHL) that have been committed as a necessary consequence of the armed conflict, that is, excluding IHL violations.[32] Also, the transitional justice flexibility is not unlimited: if the duty to prosecute and punish the international core crimes, as already explained, indeed exists, it remains, in principle, valid during such processes and must be addressed by a complex package of (broad) justice measures, which, ultimately, guarantee the accountability of the most responsible perpetrators.[33]

II. Victim participation

13 The duty to prosecute is inextricably linked with the victims' right to justice. In fact, the victims' participation in the respective (criminal) proceedings—from the early stages of investigation to the sentencing phase—is an important part of their right to justice. The extent of victim participation varies in the different legal systems. Whether and to what extent their participation, including the institution of proceedings as *parties civiles*, is envisaged in domestic law largely depends on the legal tradition and approach of the respective systems.[34] In a nutshell, one can say that civil law jurisdictions normally provide for this possibility—with differences in detail, of course—while common law jurisdictions only grant victims the possibility to be heard after the actual trial, for example in sentencing or parole hearings.[35]

14 While so far no comprehensive UN convention on the rights of victims of human rights violations has been adopted, there are some important soft law instruments,[36] and above all, the ICC regime demonstrates how the participation of victims can be established throughout criminal proceedings. Victims may submit information regarding the alleged commission of international crimes to the Prosecutor of the ICC in order to trigger investigations under Articles 13(c) and 15 of the ICC Statute. Furthermore, they have the opportunity to make representations to the Pre-Trial Chamber that decides on the authorization of an investigation under Article 15(3) and (2) of the ICC Statute, or to submit observations in proceedings on jurisdiction or admissibility under Article 19(3) and (2) of the Statute. According to Article 68(3) of the ICC Statute, victims have the right to present their views and concerns to the judges at any stage of the proceedings.[37] The Chambers have, however, discretion to determine the concrete modalities of this form

[32] Ibid, n 2, 425–26, with further references.

[33] For a detailed analysis with further references see Ambos, n 1, 19 et seq.

[34] McGonigle Leyh, n 10, 65 et seq, 79 et seq; J Doak, *Victims' Rights, Human Rights and Criminal Justice: Reconceiving the Role of Third Parties* (Hart Publishing 2008) 156 et seq; D Donat-Cattin, 'Article 68' in O Triffterer and K Ambos (eds), *Commentary on the Rome Statute of the International Criminal Court* (3rd edn, Beck/Hart Publishing 2016) MN 5.

[35] JP Pérez-León Acevedo, *Victims' Status at International and Hybrid Criminal Court—Victims' Status as Witnesses, Victim Participants/Civil Parties and Reparation Claimants* (Åbo Akadmi University Press 2014) 51 et seq.

[36] See, eg, Declaration of Basic Principles of Justice for Victims of Crime and Abuse of Power, UN Doc A/RES/40/34 (29 November 1985); Basic Principles and Guidelines on the Right to a Remedy and Reparation for Victims of Gross Violations of International Human Rights Law and Serious Violations of International Humanitarian Law, UN Doc A/RES/60/147 (16 December 2005).

[37] For the application process, see Rule 89 RPE ICC.

of participation on a case-by-case-basis, taking into account, inter alia, whether or not the victims are represented by a lawyer or have requested anonymity. So far, all Chambers have insisted on a common legal representative,[38] which means that one lawyer acts in the interests of all, or at least in the interests of a certain group of victims participating in the proceedings. At the trial stage, victims' representatives are, as a rule, granted the right to make opening and closing statements, to attend all public court sessions, to question witnesses, experts, and the accused, and to tender, examine, and challenge evidence.[39] In addition, victims may be allowed to file written submissions on the sentencing principles to be applied by the Chamber in the relevant case.[40] They also have the right, as a concretization of Article 68(3) of the ICC Statute, to be heard in special sentencing or reparation hearings.[41] Last but not least, the ICC is the first international criminal court that has the power to order a convicted person to make reparations to victims, under Article 75 of the ICC Statute.[42] In addition, the ICC's Assembly of States Parties has set up a Trust Fund for Victims, which assists the Court in the implementation of its reparation orders and provides general assistance to victims of international crimes.[43]

Similarly, some of the hybrid or new tribunals established in the last fifteen years (Extraordinary Chambers in the Courts of Cambodia, Special Tribunal for Lebanon, Special Panels of the Dili District Court [East Timor], Kosovo Specialist Chambers) provided victims with strong participatory rights.[44] Depending on the respective tribunal, victims may file complaints, participate as civil parties, or serve as witnesses. In contrast, the Special Court for Sierra Leone adopted a common law-featured system based on the procedural provisions of the ICTR, and therefore confined the victims' role to that of mere witnesses. However, victims at least had the possibility to be heard by the Truth and Reconciliation Commission that operated parallel to the Court.[45] Thus, in sum, it can be said that the position of victims has been strengthened in international criminal proceedings, and the implementation of these participatory mechanisms may serve as a blueprint for further domestic developments. **15**

The position of victims has also been strengthened at the regional level. The European Union has issued Directive 2012/29/EU,[46] which imposes binding obligations on all **16**

[38] See Rule 90(2) ICC RPE.

[39] See, in particular, *Prosecutor v Lubanga* (Judgment on the Appeals of the Prosecutor and the Defence against Trial Chamber I's Decision on Victims' Participation of 18 January 2008) ICC-01/04-01/06-1432 (11 July 2008) para 109; *Prosecutor v Lubanga* (Decision on Victims' Participation) ICC-01/04-01/06-1119 (18 January 2008) paras 105 et seq. For a detailed treatment and references to the divergent case law, see S Bock, *Das Opfer vor dem Internationalen Strafgerichtshof* (Duncker & Humblot 2010) 440 et seq; McGonigle Leyh, n 10, 225 et seq; Pérez-León Acevedo, n 35, 302 et seq; K Ambos, *Treatise on International Criminal Law*, vol III (OUP 2016) 187 et seq.

[40] *Prosecutor v Lubanga* (Scheduling Order Concerning Timetable for Sentencing and Reparations) ICC-01/04-01/06-2844 (14 March 2012) para 3.

[41] Cf Rule 143 RPE; McGonigle Leyh, n 10, 301–02.

[42] Donat-Cattin, n 34, MNN 1 et seq; in more detail on the ICC's reparation scheme, E Dwertmann, *The Reparation System of the International Criminal Court* (Martinus Nijhoff Publishers 2010); Bock, n 39, 555 et seq.

[43] Arts 75(2), 79 ICC Statute.

[44] For a detailed comparative analysis, see Pérez-León Acevedo, n 35, 287 et seq; cf also McGonigle Leyh, n 10, 148 et seq; JC Ochoa, *The Rights of Victims in Criminal Justice Proceedings for Serious Human Rights Violations* (Martinus Nijhoff 2013) 212 et seq.

[45] Cf Art 16 of the Lomé Agreement ('to provide a forum for ... the victims ... to tell their story').

[46] Directive 2012/29/EU of the European Parliament and of the Council of 25 October 2012 Establishing Minimum Standards on the Rights, Support and Protection of Victims of Crime, and Replacing Council Framework Decision 2001/220/JHA, [2012] OJ L315/57.

member states regarding minimum standards on information, support, protection, and participation of victims. Especially noteworthy is Article 11, according to which victims have the right to a review of a decision not to prosecute. Hereby, victims are given active participatory rights and are able to control decisions of the competent state organs. Further, under Article 10 victims have the right to be heard and, in principle, under Article 16, are entitled to obtain a decision on compensation in the course of the proceedings.

D. Practice

17 Although human rights conventions do usually not expressly oblige states parties to investigate and punish violations of the respective human rights, human rights courts and treaty bodies have for quite some time read into the 'respect and ensure' and 'right to remedy' provisions of the conventions a positive duty to prosecute serious human rights violations.[47]

18 The first seminal judgment was handed down by the Inter-American Court of Human Rights (IACtHR) in *Velásquez-Rodriguez*.[48] The Court held that Article 1(1) ACHR contains the obligation to 'prevent, investigate and punish any violation of the rights recognized by the Convention and, moreover, if possible attempt to restore the right violated and provide compensation as warranted for damages resulting from the violation'.[49] This view was confirmed by a series of subsequent judgments of the Court.[50] Most importantly, the Court has ruled on the duty to prosecute with regard to enforced disappearances, extra-judicial executions, and torture.[51] Thus, for example, in *Rodríguez Vera et al v Colombia* (regarding the disappeared from the Palace of Justice in the context of the events of 1985), the Court held that the duty to prosecute wrongful acts that violate rights recognized in the Convention is derived from the obligation to ensure respect for the human rights protected by the Convention, under Articles 1(1) and 2 ACHR.[52] In that sense, illusory measures that only appear to meet the formal requirements of justice should be avoided.[53]

[47] Art 2(1), (3), International Covenant on Civil and Political Rights (ICCPR), 999 UNTS 171; Arts 1(1) and 25, American Convention on Human Rights (ACHR), OAS Treaty Series no 36, 1144 UNTS 123; Arts 1 and 13, European Convention on Human Rights (ECHR), 213 UNTS 222. For a thorough analysis of the case law and the legal rationale behind the decisions, see A Seibert-Fohr, *Prosecuting Serious Human Rights Violations* (OUP 2009).

[48] *VelásquezRodríguez v Honduras* (Judgment) IACtHR Series C no 4 (29 July 1988).

[49] Ibid, para 166; see also paras 162 et seq.

[50] See also, *Barrios Altos v Peru* (Judgment) IACtHR Series C no 75 (14 March 2001) paras 41 et seq; *Massacres of El Mozote and nearby Places v El Salvador* (Judgment) IACtHR Series C no 252 (25 October 2012) paras 143 et seq; *Osorio Rivera y Familiares v Perú* (Judgment) IACtHR Series C no 274 (26 November 2013) para 177; *Veliz Franco y otros v Guatemala* (Judgment) IACtHR Series C no 277 (19 May 2014) paras 183, 250–51; *Tenorio Roca y ostros v Perú* (Judgment), IACtHR Series C no 314 (22 June 2016) paras 142, 168; *Valencia Hinojosa y otros v Ecuador* (Judgment), IACtHR Series C no 327 (29 November 2016) para 131; *Pacheco León y otros v Honduras* (Judgment), IACtHR Series C no 342 (15 Novenber 2017) paras 74 et seq. For a comprehensive analysis of this case law, see K Ambos and E Malarino (eds), *Sistema interamericano de protección de los derechos humanos y derecho penal internacional* (3 vols, Konrad Adenauer Stiftung 2010, 2011, and 2013) <www.cedpal.uni-goettingen.de/index.php/investigacion/grupo-latinoamericano-de-estudios-sobre-derecho-penal-internacional> accessed 17 November 2017.

[51] E Ferrer Mac-Gregor and CM Pelayo Möller, 'Artículo 1. Obligación de respetar los derechos' in C Steiner and P Uribe (eds), *Convención Americana sobre Derechos Humanos. Comentario* (Temis and Konrad Adenauer Stiftung 2014) 42–68.

[52] *Rodríguez Vera et al (the disappeared from the Palace of Justice) v Colombia* (Judgment) IACtHR Series C no 287 (14 November 2014) para 459.

[53] Ibid; *Heliodoro Portugal v Panama* (Judgment) IACtHR Series C no 186 (12 August 2008) para 203; *Manuel Cepeda Vargas v Colombia* (Judgment) IACtHR Series C no 213 (26 May 2010) fn 225.

19 For the IACtHR, the states parties' compliance with the obligation to investigate is crucial. Thus, in *Heliodoro Portugal*, the Court held that the obligation to investigate must be assumed by the state as its own legal duty, not as a step taken by private interests that depend upon the initiative of the victim or his family.[54] In *Radilla Pacheco* the Court also clarified that this obligation persists as long as there is uncertainty about the fate of the disappeared persons.[55] In *Manuel Cepeda*, the Court held that the principle of proportionality requires states to 'ensure that the sentences imposed and their execution do not constitute factors that contribute to impunity, taking into account aspects such as the characteristics of the crime, and the participation and guilt of the accused'.[56] This means that the Court inquires whether a certain sentence is appropriate (proportional) in light of the gravity of the crime and the culpability of the defendant, thereby invoking a concept of positive (proactive) proportionality in the sense of guaranteeing a minimum sentence. In addition, in the Court's view, the obligation to conduct investigations 'is an obligation of means rather than of results',[57] which the state has to fulfil *ex officio*. In other words, the investigation may not necessarily lead to a conviction; it may also well produce an acquittal. Further, the Court has stressed that the obligation is not only of a preventive nature with a view to future human rights violations, but also retrospectively owed to the victims and their relatives.[58]

20 Similarly, the European Court of Human Rights (ECtHR) moved from its originally more conservative approach of interpreting the ECHR as only granting negative rights of defence against the state to a more progressive positive approach, according to which member states have a positive obligation to institute an effective official investigation that is capable of leading to the identification and punishment of those responsible.[59] The Court has clarified that in cases of serious human rights violations this duty not only reflects the state obligation to respect and ensure the rights of the Convention, but also

[54] *Heliodoro Portugal v Panama*, n 53, para 144; see also *Radilla Pacheco v Mexico* (Judgment) IACtHR Series C no 209 (23 November 2009) para 233; *Anzualdo Castro v Peru* (Judgment) IACtHR Series C no 202 (22 September 2009) para 123; *Gelman v Uruguay* (Judgment) IACtHR Series C no 221 (24 February 2011) para 184.

[55] *Radilla Pacheco v Mexico*, n 54, para 233; see also *Contreras et al v El Salvador* (Judgment) IACtHR Series C no 232 (31 August 2011) para 129. In connection with the duty to investigate crimes against humanity, see also *La Cantuta v Peru* (Judgment) IACtHR Series C no 162 (29 November 2006) para 157; *Almonacid Arellano et al v Chile* (Judgment) IACtHR Series C no 154 (26 September 2006) paras 99 and 111; *Las Dos Erres Massacre v Guatemala* (Judgment) IACtHR Series C no 211 (26 November 2009) paras 233–234; *Massacres of el Mozote and nearby places v El Salvador* (Judgment) IACtHR Series C no 25 (25 October 2012) paras 243 et seq, 299; *Comunidad Campesina de Santa Bárbara v Perú* (Judgment) IACtHR Series C no 299 (1 September 2015) paras 217 et seq, 221.

[56] IACtHR, *Manuel Cepeda Vargas v Colombia* n 53, para 150 and fn 210.

[57] IACtHR, *Gelman v Uruguay* (Judgment), n 54, para 184; see also *Valle Jaramillo et al v Colombia* (Judgment) IACtHR Series C no 192 (27 November 2008) para 100; *García Prieto et al v El Salvador* (Judgment) IACtHR Series C no 168 (20 November 2007) para 99; *Heliodoro Portugal v Panama*, n 53, para 144; *Rosendo Cantú et al v Mexico* (Judgment) IACtHR Series C no 216 (31 August 2010) para 175; *Gelman v Uruguay* (Judgment) IACtHR Series C no 221 (24 February 2011) para 184; *Veliz Franco et al v Guatemala* (Judgment) IACtHR Series C no 277 (19 May 2014) para 183; *Landaeta Mejías Brothers et al v Venezuela* (Judgment) IACtHR Series C no 281 (27 Aug 2014) para 216.

[58] IACtHR, *Bámaca-Velásquez v Guatemala* (Judgment) IACtHR Series C no 70 (25 November 2000) para 129; *Moiwana Community v Suriname* (Judgment) IACtHR Series C no 124 (15 June 2005) para 204; *Miguel Castro-Castro Prison v Peru* (Judgment) IACtHR Series C no 160 (25 November 2006) para 441; *Veliz Franco et al v Guatemala* (Judgment) IACtHR Series C no 277 (19 May 2014 paras 183–184; *Rochac Hernández et al v El Salvador* (Judgment) IACtHR Series C no 285 (14 October 2014) para 140.

[59] See *McCann and Others v the United Kingdom* (Judgment) (ECtHR, 27 September 1995) para 161; *Kaya v Turkey* (Judgment) (ECtHR, 19 February 1998) para 86; *El-Masri v the former Yugoslav Republic of Macedonia* (Judgment) (ECtHR, 13 December 2012) para 182; *Marguš v Croatia* (Judgment) (ECtHR,

constitutes an effective remedy and thereby a right of the victim.[60] More recently, the Strasbourg Court held that 'in order to be "effective" … an investigation must firstly be adequate. That is to say it must be capable of leading to the establishment of the facts and, where appropriate, the identification and punishment of those responsible.'[61] The Court furthermore held that 'the authorities must take whatever reasonable steps they can to secure the evidence concerning the incident'.[62] The positive obligation to proceed in the case of serious human rights violations and the demand for effective investigations has been a constant recognition in the case law of the Court.[63]

21 The Human Rights Committee (HRC) has equally assumed an affirmative duty of states to investigate alleged human rights violations and to punish the violators.[64] The failure to investigate alleged breaches might in itself constitute a breach of the Pact. The Committee further observed that mere administrative proceedings are not sufficient in cases of serious violations of human rights but that criminal proceedings are necessary.[65] Although the HRC does not consider that victims have a right to criminal prosecution, it implicitly acknowledges thorough investigations as an effective remedy.[66] More recently the HRC held, confirming its position on the right to an effective remedy, that a human rights violation must be investigated promptly, thoroughly, and impartially by the competent authorities, and appropriate action must be taken against those responsible.[67] For

27 May 2014) paras 125, 127; *Husayn (Abu Zubaydah) v Polen* (Judgment) (ECtHR, 24 June 2014) paras 540–43 and *passim; Bouyid v Belgium* (Judgment) (ECtHR, 28 September 2015) paras 114–23; see also *Jeronovics v Latvia* (Judgment) (ECtHR, 5 July 2016) paras 118–22; *Armani da Silva v the United Kingdom* (Judgment) (ECtHR, 30 March 2016) paras 229–39; *Ceesay v Austria* (Judgment) (ECtHR, 16 November 2017) paras 88–91. On *El-Masri* and *Husayn*, see K Ambos, 'The European Court of Human Rights and extraordinary renditions' (2015) 5 European Criminal Law Review 107–21.

[60] *Kaya v Turkey*, n 59, para 107; *Husayn (Abu Zubaydah) v Polen*, n 59, paras 540–43.

[61] *Ceesay v Austria* (Judgment) (ECtHR, 16 November 2017) para 88; *Cangöz and others v Turkey* (Judgment) (ECtHR, 26 April 2016) para 114; see also *Armani da Silva v the United Kingdom* (Judgment) (ECtHR, 30 March 2016) para 229; *Mustafa Tunç and Fecire Tunç v Turkey* (Judgment) (ECtHR, 14 April 2015) para 172; *Giuliani and Gaggio v Italy* (Judgment) (ECtHR, 24 March 2011) para 301.

[62] *Ceesay v Austria* (Judgment) (ECtHR, 16 November 2017) para 90; *Mustafa Tunç and Fecire Tunç v Turkey* (Judgment) (ECtHR, 14 April 2015) para 174; *Giuliani and Gaggio v Italy* (Judgment) (ECtHR, 24 March 2011) para 301.

[63] For the most recent case law, see *Ceesay v Austria* (Judgment) (ECtHR, 16 November 2017) paras 88–90; *M Özel and others v Turkey* (Judgment) (ECtHR, 17 November 2015) paras 187–90; *Abakarova v Russia* (Judgment) (ECtHR, 15 October 2015) para 70 (s V); *Zoltai v Hungary and Ireland* (Decision) (ECtHR, 29 September 2015) paras 27–29; *Mustafa Tunç and Fecire Tunç v Turkey* (Judgment, 14 April 2015) paras 171–82; *Association for the Defence of Human Rights in Romania–Helsinki Committee on behalf of Ionel Garcea v Romania* (Judgment) (ECtHR, 24 March 2015) para 67; *Asiye Genç v Turkey* (Judgment) (ECtHR, 27 January 2015) paras 68–72.

[64] For example, HRC, General Comment no 20 (1992), paras 13–15; General Comment no 31 (2004), paras 15, 18; *Purna Maya v Nepal*, Communication no 2245/2013, UN Doc CCPR/C/119/D/2245/2013, paras 12.2–12.4; *Dalisa Dovadzija and Sakiba Dovdzija v Bosnia and Herzegovina*, Communication no 2143/2012, UN Doc CCPR/C/114/D/2143/2012, para 11.5; *Nijaru v Cameroon*, Communication no 1353/2005, UN Doc CCPR/C/89/D/1353/2005, para 8; *Saker v Algeria*, Communication no 992/2001, UN Doc CCPR/C/86/D/992/2001, para 11. On the evolution of the HRC's jurisprudence, see Seibert-Fohr, n 47, 11 et seq.

[65] See, eg, HRC, *Bautista de Arellana v Colombia*, Communication no 563/1993, UN Doc CCPR/C/55/D/563/1993, paras 8.2, 10; *Coronel et al v Colombia*, Communication no 778/1997, UN Doc CCPR/C/76/D/778/1997, paras 6.2, 10.

[66] Cf Seibert-Fohr, n 47, 22 et seq.

[67] See, eg, HRC, *Mamatkarim Ernazarov v Kyrgyzstan*, Communication no 2054/2011, UN Doc CCPR/C/113/D/2054/2011, para 9.6; *Dmitry Tyan v Kazakhstan*, Communication no 2125/2011, UN Doc CCPR/C/119/D/2125/2011, para 11; *MacCallum v South Africa*, Communication no 1818/2008, UN Doc CCPR/C/100/D/1818/2008, para 6.7; *Sathasivam/Saraswathi v Sri Lanka*, Communication no 1436/2005, UN Doc CCPR/C/93/D/1436/2005, paras 6.3 and 6.4; HRC, *Kamela Allioua and Fatima Zohra Kerouane v Algeria*,

the HRC, an effective remedy for direct victims and family member must include a criminal investigation that brings to justice those responsible.[68]

E. Critical Assessment

Paragraph 1 of Principle 19 is predicated on a duty to prosecute, but such a duty is neither uncontested nor clearly defined. As we have seen, such a duty can only be inferred from a combination of different sources, and only with regard to the core crimes; with regard to mere transnational crimes it may, at best, be derived from general principles of international law. The inference of such a duty from the 'ensure' and 'effective remedy' provisions of human rights treaties is not free from doubt since rights may also be 'ensured' through other mechanisms, and such mechanisms may constitute 'remedies' within the meaning of these provisions. Thus, to establish a comprehensive and uniform duty to prosecute an international convention, clearly defining such a duty would be necessary. It would, of course, only apply to the states parties, and it would, as in the case of the ICC Statute, take considerable time until such a convention could claim broader allegiance and validity. Apart from that, as already mentioned, the wording of paragraph 1 is not completely clear. Last but not least, transitional justice situations call for a more flexible approach, offering a more sophisticated justice package, going beyond mere criminal justice. 22

While the tendency to strengthen victims' participation in international criminal proceedings can generally be seen as a positive development, it must not be overlooked that criminal trials are primarily concerned with establishing the guilt of the accused, and the respective criminal process is characterized by a complex system of checks and balances organizing the relationship between the primary participants (prosecution, defence, judge), leaving little room to accommodate the interests of victims as a fourth participant. Apart from this rather conceptual consideration, each additional participant tends to prolong the proceedings, and indeed an important practitioner has voiced the criticism that victims' participation effectively slows down international criminal proceedings.[69] In any case, victims' rights always have to be balanced against the fair trial rights of the accused. 23

Communication no 2132/2012, UN Doc CCPR/C/112/D/2132/2012, para 9; HRC, *M.T. v Uzbekistan*, Communication no 2234/2013, UN Doc CCPR/C/114/D/2234/2013, paras 7.4–7.5; HRC, *Mejdoub Chani v Algeria*, Communication no 2297/2013, UN Doc CCPR/C/116/D/2297/2013, para 9.

[68] See, eg, HRC, *Rafik Belamrania v Algeria*, Communication no 2157/2012, UN Doc CCPR/C/118/D/2157/2012, para 8; *Urtmatbek Akunov v Kyrgyzstan*, Communication no 2127/2011, UN Doc CCPR/C/118/D/2127/2011, para 10; *Ernesto Benitez Gamarra v Paraguay*, Communication no 1829/2008, UN Doc CCPR/C/104/D/1829/2008, paras 7.5 and 9; *Zyuskin v Russian Federation*, Communication no 1605/2007, UN Doc CCPR/C/102/D/1605/2007, para 13.

[69] Cf C van den Wyngaert, 'Victims Before International Criminal Courts—Some Views and Concerns of an ICC Trial Judge' (2011) 44 Case Western Reserve Journal of International Law 475–96, 493–94; but contra *Prosecutor v Bemba Gombo*, ICC-01/05-01/08-2140 (23 February 2012), Partly Dissenting Opinion of Judge Sylvia Steiner on the Decision on the Supplemented Applications by the Legal Representatives of Victims to Present Evidence and the Views and Concerns of Victims, para 8 ('at no point can their participation be seen as having had a negative impact on the expeditiousness of the trial').

Bibliography

Ambos, K, 'Völkerrechtliche Bestrafungspflichten bei schweren Menschenrechtsverletzungen' (1999) 37 Archiv des Völkerrechts 318–56.

Ambos, K, 'The Legal Framework of Transitional Justice: A Systematic Study with a Special Focus on the Role of the ICC' in K Ambos, J Large, and M Wierda (eds), *Building a Future on Peace and Justice* (Springer 2009) 19–103.

Ambos, K, 'The European Court of Human Rights and extraordinary renditions' (2015) 5 European Criminal Law Review 107–21.

Ambos, K, *Treatise on International Criminal Law*, vol III (OUP 2016).

Ambos, K and Böhm, ML, 'Tribunal Europeo de Derechos Humanos y Corte Interamericana de Derechos Humanos. ¿Tribunal tímido vs Tribunal audaz?' in E Ferrer Mac-Gregor and A Herrera García (eds), *Diálogo Jurisprudencial en Derechos Humanos entre Tribunales Constitucionales y Cortes Internacionales* (Tirant lo Blanch 2013) 1057–88.

Beigbeder, Y, *International Justice against Impunity: Progress and New Challenges* (Martinus Nijhoff 2005).

Bock, S, *Das Opfer vor dem Internationalen Strafgerichtshof* (Duncker & Humblot 2010).

Doak, J, *Victims' Rights, Human Rights and Criminal Justice: Reconceiving the Role of Third Parties* (Hart Publishing 2008).

Ferrer Mac-Gregor, E and Pelayo Möller, CM, 'Artículo 1. Obligación de respetar los derechos' in C Steiner and P Uribe (eds), *Convención Americana sobre Derechos Humanos. Comentario* (Temis and Konrad Adenauer Stiftung 2014).

Grover, SC, *The European Court of Human Rights as a Pathway to Impunity for International Crimes* (Springer 2010).

International Law Commission, Final Report of the ILC's Working Group on the Obligation to extradite or prosecute (*aut dedere aut judicare*), A/CN.4/L.844 (5 June 2014).

McGonigle Leyh, B, *Procedural Justice?—Victim Participation in International Criminal Proceedings* (Intersentia 2011).

Mallinder, L, *Amnesty, Human Rights and Political Transitions* (Hart Publishing 2008).

Ochoa, JC, *The Rights of Victims in Criminal Justice Proceedings for Serious Human Rights Violations* (Martinus Nijhoff 2013).

Orentlicher, DF, '"Settling Accounts" Revisited: Reconciling Global Norms with Local Agency' (2007) 1 International Journal of Transitional Justice 10–22.

Pérez-León Acevedo, JP, *Victims' Status at International and Hybrid Criminal Court—Victims' Status as Witnesses, Victim Participants/Civil Parties and Reparation Claimants* (Åbo Akadmi University Press 2014).

Seibert-Fohr, A, *Prosecuting Serious Human Rights Violations* (OUP 2009).

Triffterer, O and Ambos, K (eds), *Rome Statute of the International Criminal Court: a Commentary* (3rd edn, Beck/Hart Publishing 2016).

van den Wyngaert, C, 'Victims Before International Criminal Courts—Some Views and Concerns of an ICC Trial Judge' (2011) 44 Case Western Reserve Journal of International Law 475–96.

B.

DISTRIBUTION OF JURISDICTION BETWEEN NATIONAL, FOREIGN, INTERNATIONAL, AND INTERNATIONALIZED COURTS

Principle 20. Jurisdiction of International and Internationalized Criminal Tribunals

William A Schabas

It remains the rule that States have primary responsibility to exercise jurisdiction over serious crimes under international law. In accordance with the terms of their statutes, international and internationalized criminal tribunals may exercise concurrent jurisdiction when national courts cannot offer satisfactory guarantees of independence and impartiality or are materially unable or unwilling to conduct effective investigations or prosecutions.

States must ensure that they fully satisfy their legal obligations in respect of international and internationalized criminal tribunals, including where necessary through the enactment of domestic legislation that enables States to fulfil obligations that arise through their adherence to the Rome Statute of the International Criminal Court or under other binding instruments, and through implementation of applicable obligations to apprehend and surrender suspects and to cooperate in respect of evidence.

A. Summary of Findings

There is a presumption that national courts are primarily responsible for the prosecution of serious international crimes. International or internationalized criminal courts should step in only when the national institutions fail in this respect. In some cases, the international criminal courts have primacy, while in others they may only exercise jurisdiction when the shortcomings of the national system have been established, an approach described as 'complementarity'. Formulation of the relationship suggests tension and conflict, but in practice it is often marked by cooperation and even synergy, a feature insufficiently developed in the Updated Set of Principles. Obligations of cooperation are also fundamental, because the international institutions cannot function if they are unable to obtain evidence and secure the custody of suspects. The obligations result from a tangled web of international treaties of general application, international human rights instruments, customary norms, and detailed provisions of the statutes of the relevant international bodies.

B. Contextual and Historical Introduction

International and 'internationalized' criminal courts are a recent phenomenon by contrast with national courts that have existed since ancient times. Isolated examples of criminal trials with an international dimension have been found in medieval times, but the real beginnings of international and internationalized courts, in the sense we understand them today, date to little more than a century ago. From the early nineteenth century there are many examples of international arbitration tribunals with authority to rule on disputes between states. They are the forerunners of the permanent institutions of the 1 twentieth century, the Permanent Court of International Justice and the International Court of Justice (ICJ). The role of these bodies in addressing impunity should not be overlooked. In some cases they have managed to confront issues that have largely escaped national and international criminal courts. For example, in its famous Advisory Opinion on the Wall in the Occupied Palestinian Territory, the ICJ might be said to have acted in some sense like an international truth commission.

2 The international and internationalized criminal tribunals with jurisdiction over individuals for war crimes and other atrocities can be traced to efforts at the end of the First World War under the Treaties of Versailles and Sèvres, although the institutions were never actually set up. After the Second World War, two international military tribunals, one located in Nuremberg and the other in Tokyo, held trials of major war criminals. A permanent international criminal court was contemplated in the 1948 Genocide Convention but its establishment was delayed for half a century. In the early 1990s, as international law focused greater attention on problems of impunity and accountability for serious violations of international humanitarian law and human rights, the United Nations Security Council set up international criminal tribunals with respect to the conflicts in the former Yugoslavia and Rwanda, and, several years later, prompted the creation of a similar institution for Sierra Leone. The United Nations (UN) also created judicial mechanisms as part of its larger administration of the territories of East Timor and Kosovo, and negotiated an agreement with Cambodia regarding 'extraordinary' chambers of its national courts in which foreign judges and prosecutors participated. Negotiation of the Rome Statute of the International Criminal Court (ICC)[1] concluded in 1998. It entered into force in 2002, and the Court soon began its judicial activities.

3 The Set of Principles uses the terms 'international and internationalized criminal tribunals' but does not define them. Shortly before the Updated Set of Principles was adopted, the Secretary-General issued his Report on *The rule of law and transitional justice in conflict and post-conflict societies*, where reference is made to 'a wide range of special criminal tribunals', including 'ad hoc international criminal tribunals', 'mixed tribunals', and national courts where there is international participation.[2] Elsewhere in the same document he referred to 'international and hybrid criminal tribunals'.[3] It is beyond the scope of this commentary to parse all of the distinctions that arise from this terminology. There is no great difficulty with the concept of 'international criminal tribunals', because these must be set up by mechanisms of international law, namely treaties (the case of the ICC and the Special Court of Sierra Leone) and by decision of the United Nations Security Council (the case of the ad hoc tribunals for the former Yugoslavia and Rwanda). There is probably no entirely satisfactory formula for identifying 'internationalized criminal tribunals'. Diane Orentlicher described

> a new breed of court comprising both national and international elements, a trend exemplified by the establishment of the Special Court for Sierra Leone, the Special Panels for Serious Crimes in Timor-Leste, and courts in Kosovo established under the authority of the United Nations Interim Administration Mission in Kosovo; and the likely establishment of other internationalized courts, including the Extraordinary Chambers in the Courts of Cambodia.[4]

[1] Rome Statute of the International Criminal Court, (2002) 2187 UNTS 90 (hereinafter 'Rome Statute').

[2] Report of the Secretary-General, *The rule of law and transitional justice in conflict and post-conflict societies*, UN Doc S/2004/616 (3 August 2004), para 38.

[3] Ibid, para 40.

[4] *Report of the independent expert to update the Set of Principles to combat impunity, Diane Orentlicher*, UN Doc E/CN.4/2005/102, para 39.

Participation of foreign judges is probably too broad a criterion given that this is a rather common feature of many national jurisdictions, notably those of the Commonwealth. Nor is the fact that they exercise jurisdiction over serious international crimes, because Principle 20 specifically deals with the obligation of national courts to exercise jurisdiction over such offences. Principle 20 juxtaposes national courts with international and internationalized courts, suggesting some sort of coexistence. But probably what was envisaged was the operation of international or internationalized criminal courts even in the total absence of national courts capable of exercising concurrent jurisdiction, as was the case in East Timor and Kosovo for some time.

C. Theoretical Framework

Principle 20 is one of three provisions in Part III of the Updated Set of Principles, which 4
is entitled 'The Right to Justice'. Within that Part there are two subheadings. Principle 20 falls under the second of them, 'Distribution of jurisdiction between national, foreign, international and internationalized courts'. Principle 20 is concerned with 'international and internationalized courts'. It governs the relationship between such institutions and 'national courts'. The role of 'foreign' courts exercising universal jurisdiction appears to be reserved for Principle 21. 'Serious crimes under international law' are defined at the beginning of the Updated Set of Principles.[5]

The word 'impunity', also defined at the beginning of the Updated Set of Principles, 5
implies punishment or some similar sanction. It inexorably directs us towards judicial activity of criminal courts, or the lack of it. It may therefore seem surprising that in the Updated Set of Principles so little attention is devoted to the work of courts and tribunals. Bringing perpetrators to account also involves 'civil, administrative or disciplinary proceedings', but references to persons being 'accused, arrested, tried and, if found guilty, sentenced to appropriate penalties' leaves little doubt that criminal justice is at the core of the issue of impunity.[6]

The first sentence of Principle 20 is addressed to the national justice system. It affirms 6
that it 'remains the rule' that states have primary responsibility in this regard. The language echoes recital 6 of the Preamble to the Rome Statute, 'recalling that it is the duty of every State to exercise its criminal jurisdiction over those responsible for international crimes'.[7] This duty stems from two sources. In various forms, treaties dealing with international crimes impose an obligation upon states parties to investigate and prosecute offences, as well as to cooperate with other states that are prepared to exercise criminal jurisdiction. Examples include Article 5 of the Genocide Convention and the grave breach provisions of the 1949 Geneva Conventions (Articles 49–50, 50–51, 129–130, and 146–147) and Additional Protocol I (Articles 11 and 85). More recent treaties, like the UN Torture Convention[8] and the UN Convention on Enforced Disappearance, also contain provisions to this effect.[9] It can be argued that the obligation also exists under

[5] <Set of Principles for the protection and promotion of human rights through action to combat impunity, UN Doc E/CN.4/2005/102/Add.1 (8 February 2005), 'Definitions', B.

[6] Ibid, 'Definitions', A.

[7] Rome Statute, Preamble, para 6.

[8] Convention against Torture and Other Cruel, Inhuman or Degrading Treatment or Punishment (1987) 1465 UNTS 85, Art 5(5).

[9] International Convention for the Protection of All Persons from Enforced Disappearance (2010) 2716 UNTS 3, Art 9(2).

customary international law.[10] Moreover, the requirement that states investigate and prosecute serious international crimes is a corollary of their duty to address all serious crimes against the person imposed by international human rights law, in particular as a consequence of the protection of the right to life and the prohibition of ill-treatment. This has been regularly confirmed in case law of the European Court of Human Rights, the Inter-American Court of Human Rights, and the United Nations Human Rights Committee.[11]

7 The second sentence of Principle 20 is addressed to the international and internationalized criminal tribunals. It states that they may exercise 'concurrent jurisdiction' in two circumstances: when national courts cannot offer satisfactory guarantees of independence and impartiality, or when such courts are materially unable or unwilling to conduct effective investigations or prosecutions. This must be understood as being permissive rather than as an exhaustive enumeration of conditions under which international and internationalized courts may exercise concurrent jurisdiction.

8 Some international criminal tribunals operate on the basis of primacy, meaning that when they decide to proceed, the national court must defer to them. The ad hoc tribunals for the former Yugoslavia and Rwanda function on this basis. The rule of primacy is set out in each tribunal's Statute, which is an annex to a Security Council decision. Accordingly, the national court must decline jurisdiction where the international court opts to proceed.[12] The other approach is designated 'complementarity'. Set out in detail in Article 17 of the Rome Statute, it requires the ICC to declare a case inadmissible and defer to the national jurisdiction unless the latter is unwilling or unable to investigate and prosecute the case. Amongst other criteria, Article 17 says that unwillingness may be established if proceedings 'were not or are not being conducted independently or impartially, and they were or are being conducted in a manner which, in the circumstances, is inconsistent with an intent to bring the person concerned to justice'.

9 Whether primacy or complementarity is adopted, there must also be a rule to prevent a second prosecution for the same offence. Known as the *ne bis in idem* principle, it is set out in several human rights instruments, including the International Covenant on Civil and Political Rights[13] and Protocol no 7 of the European Convention on Human Rights.[14] Statutes of international criminal tribunals generally prevent the *bis* in both directions, blocking prosecution at the national level where the case has been finally judged by the international tribunals, as well as preventing the international tribunal from proceeding if there is a final judgment at the national level.

10 The last sentence of Principle 20 requires that states 'fully satisfy their legal obligations' with respect to international and internationalized criminal tribunals. This refers generally to cooperation in the investigation of alleged crimes, and the apprehension of

[10] M Scharf, 'Aut dedere aut judicare' in Rüdiger Wolfrum (ed), *The Max Planck Encyclopedia of Public International Law*, vol I (OUP 2012) 749–54, paras 6–9.

[11] *Šilih v Slovenia* App no 71463/01 (ECtHR, Grand Chamber, 9 April 2009) para 153; *McCann and Others v the United Kingdom* (ECtHR, 27 September 1995) paras 157–64, Series A no 324; *Pestaño et al v Philippines*, UN Doc CCPR/C/98/D/1619/2007, para 7.2; *González v Argentina*, UN Doc CCPR/C/101/D/1458/2006, para 9.4; *Velásquez-Rodríguez v Honduras* (Merits) IACtHR Series C no 4 (29 July 1988); *Godínez-Cruz v Honduras* (Merits) IACtHR Series C no 5 (20 January 1989).

[12] *Prosecutor v Tadić* (Decision on the Defence Motion for Interlocutory Appeal on Jurisdiction) IT-94-1-AR72 (2 October 1995) para 56.

[13] International Covenant on Civil and Political Rights, (1976) 999 UNTS 171, Art 14(7).

[14] Protocol no 7 to the Convention for the Protection of Human Rights and Fundamental Freedoms, ETS 117, Art 4.

suspects and their transfer to the international jurisdiction. Very detailed rules in this area are set out in Part 9 of the Rome Statute. Problems may arise in this respect when a suspect may have a claim to immunity, a matter governed by special rules of international law. In 2002, the ICJ said that rules governing head-of-state immunity do not apply before 'certain international criminal tribunals', citing the ICC and the ad hoc tribunals for the former Yugoslavia and Rwanda as specific examples.[15]

D. Practice

Failure of the national jurisdiction to observe the obligation to bring perpetrators to justice is at the root of international concerns with the problem of impunity. This has led to the establishment of international and internationalized courts. The legal obligation to prosecute is rarely debated before national courts. They are reluctant to intervene in the discretion of prosecutors. In many jurisdictions prosecution is conditional upon some sort of political approval or authorization. Probably many cases that fulfil the terms of serious international crimes are in fact dealt with at the national level as ordinary crimes. Arguably, this amounts to compliance with the international obligation, although the International Criminal Tribunal for Rwanda (ICTR) was not satisfied when Norway proposed to try for murder a suspect who had already been indicted for genocide by the international tribunal.[16] There is barely a trace, in national jurisdictions, of the obligation set out in the treaties. For example, although the Geneva Conventions have been nearly universally ratified, there have been essentially no prosecutions at the national level for grave breaches. 11

Principle 20 has been violated in some cases by the United Nations Security Council itself. In a perverse application of Article 16 of the Rome Statute, two resolutions of the Council blocked the ICC from exercising jurisdiction over nationals of non-party states.[17] On the two occasions when the Council has referred situations to the Court, pursuant to Article 13(b) of the Statute, it has carved out exceptions and required that certain suspects be brought to justice only before the courts of their nationality. Such a requirement is incompatible with obligations under the relevant treaties, including the Geneva Conventions and the Genocide Convention. 12

Respect for the obligation to transfer suspects to the international institutions has generally depended upon political factors. In the former Yugoslavia, for example, there was considerable evidence to indicate that some states, or elements within their government and military establishments, were assisting persons in the evasion of justice. When suspects were brought to the International Criminal Tribunal for the former Yugoslavia (ICTY) in The Hague, there was obstruction in the production of relevant evidence.[18] The fact that the ICTR focused its prosecutions on members of the former regime meant that cooperation at the national level was generally more forthcoming. 13

[15] Arrest Warrant of 11 April 2000 (Democratic Republic of the Congo v Belgium) (Judgment) [2002] ICJ Rep 3, para 61.

[16] *Prosecutor v Bagaragaza* (Decision on Rule 11*bis* Appeal) ICTR-05-86-AR11*bis* (30 August 2006).

[17] UN Doc S/RES/1593 (31 March 2005), para 6; UN Doc S/RES/1970 (26 February 2011), para 6.

[18] *Prosecutor v Blaškić* (Judgment on the Request of the Republic of Croatia for Review of the Decision of Trial Chamber II of 18 July 1997) IT-95-14-AR108*bis* (29 October 1997).

14 Similar patterns present themselves in the work of the ICC. The Democratic Republic of the Congo willingly transferred suspects who led anti-government militias. In Kenya, on the other hand, where senior officials, including the country's President, were charged, the Prosecutor ultimately admitted defeat, contending that official connivance prevented the production of evidence and the protection of witnesses.

15 In contrast with the primacy of the ICTY and ICTR, the complementarity of the ICC has manifested itself in serious contestation at the international level. Where governments did not object, it was sometimes the accused who argued that the case should remain at the national level. But some shrewd accused persons seem to have calculated that they were better off in The Hague. The result in the case of Thomas Lubanga, for example, was that the admissibility of the case was essentially conceded by all concerned parties. In Libya, on the other hand, a Pre-Trial Chamber gave the national authorities the chance to deal with the prosecution of a former official.[19]

16 Immunities have occasionally proved to be an obstacle, although their importance may have been exaggerated. Only a handful of the many hundreds of suspects who have been charged at the international level had an arguable claim to immunity. The notion is offensive, but in practice it has little impact on the operation of the international criminal courts.

E. Critical Assessment

17 During the late 1990s and the first decade of the new century, at any given time there were many trials under way at the international level. This has declined because of the closing of the institutions for the former Yugoslavia, Rwanda, and Sierra Leone, and because of the poor level of productivity of the ICC. This does not necessarily signal a more acute problem of impunity, however. Recent years have also shown a heightened attention to national prosecutions, including the establishment of more robust and focused domestic institutions. In the states of the former Yugoslavia, as the work of the Tribunal progressed, there were renewed initiatives at the national level, including the establishment of specialized tribunals with international involvement. The ICTY developed a practice of transferring less important cases to the national courts. There were somewhat similar developments in Rwanda. Before authorizing transfer to the national courts, the ICTR insisted upon significant judicial reforms at the domestic level.

18 Principle 20 may suggest a relationship of tension and conflict between the national and the international criminal courts. But at the ICC, the adjective 'positive' was affixed to the term 'complementarity', denoting a more benign and constructive relationship between the two levels, directed at both assisting and encouraging states to assume their primary responsibility to bring perpetrators of atrocity crimes to justice. To some extent, then, the national and the international are not rivals but rather partners in the campaign against impunity. This dimension is not sufficiently developed within the Updated Set of Principles.

[19] *Prosecutor v Gaddafi et al* (Judgment on the appeal of Mr Abdullah Al-Senussi against the decision of Pre-Trial Chamber I of 11 October 2013 entitled 'Decision on the admissibility of the case against Abdullah Al-Senussi') ICC-01/11-01/11 OA 4 (24 July 2014).

Bibliography

Ferdinandusse, W, *Direct Application of the International Criminal Law in National Courts* (Asser 2006).
Mallinder, L, *Amnesty, Human Rights and Political Transitions: Bridging the Peace and Justice Divide* (Hart Publishing 2008).
Romano, CPR, Nollkaemper, A, and Kleffner, JK (eds), *Internationalized Criminal Court* (OUP 2004).
Schabas, WA, *Unimaginable Atrocities: Justice, Politics, and Rights and the War Crimes Tribunals* (OUP 2012).
Schabas, WA, *The UN International Criminal Tribunals* (CUP 2006).
Stahn, C (ed), *The Law and Practice of the International Criminal Court* (OUP 2015).

Principle 21. Measures for Strengthening the Effectiveness of International Legal Principles Concerning Universal and International Jurisdiction

Paola Gaeta

States should undertake effective measures, including the adoption or amendment of internal legislation, that are necessary to enable their courts to exercise universal jurisdiction over serious crimes under international law in accordance with applicable principles of customary and treaty law.

States must ensure that they fully implement any legal obligations they have assumed to institute criminal proceedings against persons with respect to whom there is credible evidence of individual responsibility for serious crimes under international law if they do not extradite the suspects or transfer them for prosecution before an international or internationalized tribunal.

A. Summary of Findings

Principle 21 deals with both the establishment by states of universal criminal jurisdiction and any legal obligations to prosecute or to extradite (*aut dedere aut judicare*) states may have assumed. The Updated Set of Principles does not provide for a definition of universal criminal jurisdiction, and there are divergent views on the meaning of this formula. A certain number of treaties contain the obligation for states to establish jurisdiction when they refuse extradition and the suspect is present on their territories. This form of extraterritorial jurisdiction may overlap with the notion of universal jurisdiction when the latter is made conditional upon the presence of the suspect on the territory of the state. A certain number of treaties also contain the obligation for states to exercise jurisdiction, namely to prosecute the suspect when he or she is found on their territories and he or she is not extradited. The relationship between *dedere* and *judicare* might vary depending on the formulation of the relevant treaty obligation. Surrendering a suspect to an international criminal court might be in some cases a violation of the treaty obligation, contrary to what Principle 21 suggests. It is controversial whether states can assert 'pure' universal criminal jurisdiction, and whether the *aut dedere aut judicare* treaty-based formula is opposable to non-state parties. Arguably, universal criminal jurisdiction can fully serve the purpose of 'closing the impunity' gap to the extent that international functional immunities are not applicable to persons who have committed crimes while acting *qua* state agents.

B. Contextual and Historical Introduction

1 Principle 21 consolidates Principles 20–22 of the 1997 Set of Principles to combat impunity and contains two main innovations. First, in paragraph 1, it provides that states should enable their courts to exercise universal jurisdiction over serious crimes under

international law in accordance with 'applicable principles of customary and treaty law'. The corresponding Principle in the 1997 Set of Principles was instead formulated in a more cautious way. It referred to the exercise of universal criminal jurisdiction by states, but only on the basis of a treaty provision; absent such a clause, it recognized that states could exercise *extraterritorial jurisdiction* over serious crimes under international law in accordance with their domestic laws.[1] Second, paragraph 2 of Principle 21 recalls that states must fully implement the obligations to prosecute or extradite persons accused of serious international crimes they have assumed (under international law). However, it clarifies that transferring these persons for prosecution before an international or internationalized criminal tribunal constitutes an alternative to extradition. This option was not mentioned in the 1997 Set of Principles.

The broader formulation on universal criminal jurisdiction in paragraph 1 of Principle 21 is part of the process geared towards the fight against impunity that started to unfold in the late 1990s.[2] According to the supporters of this process, the exercise by states of universal criminal jurisdiction is a crucial tool for bringing to justice perpetrators of serious crimes under international law and to close the so-called 'impunity gap'.[3] The reason is clear. These are crimes that exhibit a sort of 'system criminality',[4] in that they are normally perpetrated by state officials with the acquiescence, tolerance, or support of the authorities of the state. Domestic prosecutions in the state where the crimes have been committed or of nationality of the perpetrators are therefore unlikely. The expansion of the reach of national criminal jurisdiction on the basis of the principle of universal criminal jurisdiction would instead allow persons allegedly responsible for these crimes to be brought on to the docket.[5] The more so if one considers that there is no international criminal court or tribunal that has automatic and mandatory jurisdiction over international crimes, independently of where they are committed or by whom.[6] 2

[1] See Principles 20 and 22 of the 1997 Set of Principles. As is clear, the expression 'extraterritorial jurisdiction' is not equivalent to 'universal jurisdiction'. The former is used to refer to jurisdiction exercised in relation to events occurring abroad, which might have as a basis—in addition to universal jurisdiction—one of the following: (i) the so-called active personality principle (ie when the person allegedly responsible for a crime is a national of the state asserting jurisdiction); (ii) the so-called passive personality principle (ie when the victim of a crime is a national of the state asserting jurisdiction); (iii) the so-called protective principle (ie when the crime is committed against the state asserting jurisdiction). It is therefore noteworthy that the 1997 Set of Principles did not expressly refer to the possibility for states to exercise universal jurisdiction absent a treaty provision, but preferred to use a more general formulation.

[2] D Luban, 'After the Honeymoon: Reflections on the Current State of International Criminal Justice' (2013) 11 Journal of International Criminal Justice 505–15.

[3] See, eg, C Hall, 'The Role of Universal Jurisdiction in the International Criminal Court System' in M Bergsmo (ed), *Complementarity and the Exercise of Universal Criminal Jurisdiction for Core International Crimes* (Torkel Opshal Academic EPublisher 2010) 201–32. See also A Cassese, '"Foreword": Symposium on the "Twist and Turns of Universal Jurisdiction"' (2006) 4 Journal of International Criminal Justice 559–60, 559, who asserts that universal criminal jurisdiction, together with the exercise of jurisdiction by international criminal courts and tribunals, 'is the only alternative to the impunity resulting from insistence on jurisdiction by the territorial or national state'.

[4] BVA Röling, 'The Significance of the Laws of War' in A Cassese (ed), *Current Problems of International Law* (Giuffrè 1975) 133–55, 137.

[5] For further elaboration on this point, see P Gaeta, 'The Need Reasonably to Expand National Criminal Jurisdiction over International Crimes' in A Cassese (ed), *Realizing Utopia: The Future of International Law* (OUP 2012) 596–606.

[6] The only permanent criminal court created so far, the International Criminal Court (ICC), can exercise its jurisdiction only when certain preconditions exists, unless the jurisdiction is triggered by the UN Security Council (see Art 12 of the Rome Statute of the International Criminal Court (2002) 2187 UNTS 3 (hereinafter 'Rome Statute')).

3 The arrest in London of General Augusto Pinochet for crimes committed in Chile while he was in power, further to a Spanish warrant issued on the basis of universal criminal jurisdiction,[7] undoubtedly contributed to disseminating and reinforcing this view. Other triggering factors were the investigations initiated in some countries in application of the provisions on universal jurisdiction of the UN Torture Convention,[8] and the civil complaints of human rights abuses brought in the United States (US) on the basis of the universal jurisdiction clause contained in the 'rediscovered' 1789 Alien Tort Statute.[9]

4 In mirroring these developments, however, paragraph 1 of Principle 21 has also taken into account the controversy that sparked in diplomatic and academic circles on the scope of universal criminal jurisdiction. The complaints filed in some countries against current or former foreign top-level state officials triggered this controversy.[10] The Democratic Republic of Congo (DRC) had also brought a case against Belgium before the International Court of Justice (ICJ), to challenge the legality under international law of the issuance by Belgium of an arrest warrant against its acting Minister for Foreign Affairs (the *Arrest Warrant* case). For the DRC, the exercise of universal jurisdiction by Belgium was in violation of international law because excessive, and also constituted a violation of the sovereign immunities protecting ministers of foreign affairs from foreign criminal jurisdiction while they were in office.[11] The Court eventually did not pronounce on the claim on universal jurisdiction,[12] but even a cursory look

[7] On the Pinochet case, also for further reference, see A Gattini, 'Pinochet Cases' in *Max Planck Encyclopedia of Public International Law*, online at Oxford Public International Law <opil.ouplaw.com/view/10.1093/law:epil/9780199231690/law-9780199231690-e859> accessed 22 November 2017.

[8] The Convention against Torture and Other Cruel, Inhuman or Degrading Treatment or Punishment (1987) 1465 UNTS 85 ('UN Torture Convention') entered into force in 1987, and national laws implementing its provisions on the repression of the crime of torture on the basis of universal jurisdiction started to be applied one decade later. For instance, in The Netherlands, in 1996 and 1997, relatives of the victims brought complaints to Dutch authorities against Désiré Bouterse for the torture and summary execution of fifteen people in Surinam. At the end, the case was dismissed on 18 September 2001 by the Supreme Court of The Netherlands, since it found that there was no legal basis for prosecution: the UN Torture Convention had not yet entered into force at the time of the alleged events (8–9 December 1982), neither had the Dutch Implementation Act of the UN Torture Convention. The decision of the Dutch Supreme Court is available on the International Crimes Database of the TMC Asser Institute <www.internationalcrimesdatabase.org/Case/1082> accessed 22 November 2017.

[9] See, eg, *Kadic v Karadžić*, 70 F 3d 232, 244 (2d Cir 1995). For a detailed account of the 'use' of the Alien Tort Statute by human rights advocacy centres, see B Stephens, 'The Curious History of the Alien Tort Statute' (2014) 89 Notre Dame Law Review 1467–1543.

[10] After Pinochet, victims of serious human rights violations started filing judicial complaints against other prominent former or incumbent high-level foreign state officials in countries adopting a broad interpretation of the universality principle (primarily Belgium and Spain). For instance, in Belgium the list includes, to name just a few, the then Israeli Prime Minister Ariel Sharon (for his role in the Sabra and Shatila massacre); the former Chinese President Jiang Zemin (for international crimes allegedly committed against Falungong practitioners); and the former US President George W Bush and the then Secretary of Defense Dick Cheney (for war crimes allegedly committed in the 1991 Gulf War). On the practice by non-governmental organizations (NGOs) of bringing complaints on behalf of the victims of international crimes against current or former foreign state officials, see L Reydams, *The Application of Universal Jurisdiction in the Fight Against Impunity*, Report to the EU Directorate-General for External Policies (2016), especially at 16–20.

[11] *Arrest Warrant of 11 April 2000 (Democratic Republic of the Congo v Belgium)* Application instituting proceedings (17 October 2000), available at the website of the ICJ <www.icj-cij.org/files/case-related/121/7081.pdf> accessed 22 November 2017.

[12] See *Arrest Warrant of 11 April 2000 (Democratic Republic of the Congo v Belgium)* (Judgment) (ICJ, 14 February 2002), available at the website of the ICJ <www.icj-cij.org/files/case-related/121/121-20020214-JUD-01-00-EN.pdf> accessed 22 November 2017.

at the individual opinions of the judges appended to the judgment reveals how divisive the matter was.[13]

The other innovation contained in Principle 21 is the assertion that transferring a suspect to an international or internationalized criminal tribunal is an option for states to comply with their obligations to prosecute or extradite persons suspected of being responsible for serious crimes under international law. In her Report to the Human Rights Commission, Diane Orentlicher underlined that the revised text of the relevant Principle 'reflect[ed] recent developments in international criminal law', including the entry into force of the Rome Statute of the ICC and the establishment of other international or internationalized tribunals. She thus made it clear that, 'in accordance with relevant sources of legal obligation, including resolutions of the Security Council, the Rome Statute, and the statute of internationalized tribunals, under some circumstances States' obligations must be satisfied by searching for, arresting and transferring indicted suspects to one of these tribunals'.[14] This stand can be fully appreciated if one considers that—at the time of the adoption of the Updated Set of Principles—it was evident that international/internationalized criminal courts and tribunals would not be able to discharge their mandate fully and effectively in the absence of judicial cooperation by states. For instance, as regards the International Criminal Tribunal for the former Yugoslavia (ICTY), major perpetrators of serious international crimes, such as Ratko Mladić and Radovan Karadžić, were still at large: they were the world's most wanted men for the Srebrenica massacre and the siege of Sarajevo, and arrest warrants by the ICTY were pending on them for more than a decade.[15] 5

In this context, paragraph 2 of Principle 21 therefore does not hesitate to clarify that the surrender of suspects to an international or internationalized criminal tribunal is a way for states to implement their obligations to prosecute or extradite under international law, such as the ones contained in the 1949 Geneva Conventions for the protection of victims of warfare. As will be clarified, however, this approach raises some problematic issues from a theoretical point of view. 6

[13] In his Separate Opinion, Judge Guillaume contended that under international law a state can exercise universal jurisdiction only over the crime of piracy and in the situation of 'subsidiary' jurisdiction provided for by some treaties when the alleged offender is present in the territory of the forum state. In his Dissenting Opinion, Judge Oda argued instead that universal criminal jurisdiction was 'being increasingly recognized', while Judge Ranjeva, in his Declaration, contended that without treaty-based permission, Belgium could not have exercised criminal jurisdiction the way it did. According to Judge Koroma, universal criminal jurisdiction is available not only for piracy, but also for war crimes, crimes against humanity, the slave trade, and genocide. Almost in the same vein, Judges Higgins, Kooijmans, and Buergenthal, in their Joint Separate Opinion, argued that while international law does not expressly authorize universal criminal jurisdiction when the alleged offender is not present in the territory of the forum state, at the same time there is no evidence that it prohibits it when such jurisdiction is asserted and exercised over persons accused of serious international crimes. The text of the Opinions and Declarations appended to the Judgment is available at the website of the ICJ, n 12.

[14] *Report of the independent expert to update the set of principles to combat impunity*, UN Doc E/CN.4/2005/102 (18 February 2005) paras 39 and 44.

[15] On 25 July 1995, both Mladić and Karadžić were accused by the ICTY of genocide, crimes against humanity, and violations of the laws and customs of war. On 15 November 1995, they were further accused of serious breaches of humanitarian law committed by the Bosnian Serb forces during the siege of and capture of the security zones in Srebrenica in July 1995, of genocide, and of crimes against humanity. Karadžić was arrested in Serbia in July 2008 and transferred to The Hague. Mladić was instead arrested by Serbian authorities and transferred to The Hague in May 2011.

C. Theoretical Framework

I. The definition and scope of 'universal jurisdiction'

7 The Updated Set of Principles does not define what is meant by 'universal jurisdiction' in criminal matters. This is regrettable since this issue is so controversial that one may contend that there is 'no generally accepted definition of universal jurisdiction in conventional or customary international law'.[16] What is instead clear from the wording of paragraph 1 of Principle 21 is that it makes reference to the jurisdiction of a state to undertake, that is to enact, criminal legislation or adopt other measures, based on the universality principle. This evidently allows national courts to adjudicate cases based on national criminal legislation having such a broad scope (the so-called 'jurisdiction to adjudicate'). Paraphrasing a commentator,[17] 'universal jurisdiction' is used in the Updated Set of Principles as shorthand for 'universal prescriptive jurisdiction'.

8 In defining universal jurisdiction, there are two major schools of thought. First, according to one view, universal jurisdiction must be defined in a 'negative' way: it would consist in the possibility for a state to establish criminal jurisdiction over a crime irrespective of its place of commission (the so-called *territoriality principle*), or of the nationalities of the alleged perpetrator or of the victim (respectively, the so-called *active nationality* and *passive personality principles*).[18] A second view adds a further element to this negative definition, namely, the *nature* of the crime: universal jurisdiction would thus be that asserted and exercised *solely* because of the specific nature of certain crimes, in the absence of any other link between the prosecuting state and the crime.[19]

9 Under both definitions, it is nevertheless unclear at what moment the assessment of the place of commission of the offence or the nationality of the perpetrator or the victim should be made, so as to identify the absence of any link between the *forum* state and the crime. Some scholars expressly declare that the relevant time is the moment of the commission of the crime.[20] If one follows this view, therefore, national criminal legislation that applies to individuals who have been naturalized after the commission of the crime abroad[21] is in fact providing for universal criminal jurisdiction, although in a

[16] See the Dissenting Opinion of Judge van den Wyngaert to the Judgment of the ICJ in the *Arrest Warrant* case, n 12, para 44.

[17] See R O'Keefe, 'Universal Jurisdiction. Clarifying the Basic Concept' (2004) 2 Journal of International Criminal Justice 735–60, 745.

[18] See, eg, International Law Association, *Final Report on the Exercise of Universal Jurisdiction in Respect of Gross Human Rights Offences* (London, 25–29 July 2000); the AU-EU Expert, *Report on the Principle of Universal Jurisdiction* (Brussels, 16 April 2009) para 9, which makes reference to the absence of any vital interests of the state exercising jurisdiction; the Resolution of the Institut de droit international on universal criminal jurisdiction with regard to the crime of genocide, crimes against humanity and war crimes, adopted on 26 August 2005 at the Krakow Session by the 17th Commission of the Institute. This negative definition is also propounded by many scholars: see, also, for further reference, O' Keefe, n 17, 745–46.

[19] See, eg, the *Princeton Principles on Universal Jurisdiction* (Program in Law and Public Affairs, Princeton University 2001) <lapa.princeton.edu/hosteddocs/unive_jur.pdf> accessed 22 November 2017, Principle 1 of which defines universal jurisdiction as 'criminal jurisdiction based solely on the nature of the crime, without regard to where the crime was committed, the nationality of the alleged or convicted perpetrator, the nationality of the victim, or any other connection to the state exercising such jurisdiction'.

[20] O' Keefe, n 17, 742–44. For the author, this is in order to avoid the violation of the principle of retroactive application of criminal laws. On this point see, however, n 23.

[21] The assertion and exercise of criminal jurisdiction on account of the nationality of the *forum state* acquired by the alleged offender after the commission of the crime abroad and established at the time of the prosecution, is expressly envisaged in the legislation of some countries to prosecute war crimes committed during the Second World War by Germans who subsequently changed their nationality. See, eg, in the UK, the

'masked form'. From the national point of view, however, these criminal laws are often considered as application of the active nationality principle, taking the beginning of the criminal prosecution as the relevant moment of assessment of the nationality link.[22] This example shows that one cannot take it for granted that, for the purpose of defining universal jurisdiction, the assessment of the absence or existence of any jurisdictional link between a state and a crime should necessarily be made by looking at the moment of the commission of the crime.[23]

10 Paragraph 1 of Principle 21 does not expressly mention any condition that should exist for a state to establish universal jurisdiction. On the face of it, one could thus argue that it upholds a broad notion of universal jurisdiction, one that has been termed 'absolute' or 'pure', to indicate that a state may also possess criminal jurisdiction and initiate criminal proceedings in cases where the suspect is *not* present in the territory of the forum state and in the absence of any other connection with the crime.[24] Paragraph 1, however, clarifies that the measures adopted by states to enable their national courts to exercise universal jurisdiction should be 'in accordance with applicable principles of customary and treaty law'. This caveat implicitly recognizes that the establishment of universal jurisdiction may be not unfettered but is subject to conditions, such as the presence of the suspect in the territory of the state or, eventually, other conditions.

II. The principle *aut dedere aut judicare*

11 The principle of universal jurisdiction, if made conditional on the presence of the suspect in the territory of the state, may overlap and is often confused with the principle *aut dedere aut judicare*, which literary means 'either extradite or punish'. This principle was formulated by Hugo Grotius and Emer de Vattel, who developed the notion that the state which has the custody of persons responsible for crimes violating natural law and of concern to humankind should either punish them or surrender them to the country requesting extradition. The Spanish jurist Diego Covarrubias y Leyva extended this theory further. In *Practicarum Quaestionum* (1775), he argued that under the natural law common to all nations, the court of the *locus deprehensionis* (the place where the alleged

1991 War Crimes Act, s 1 <www.legislation.gov.uk/ukpga/1991/13/pdfs/ukpga_19910013_en.pdf> accessed 24 November 2017. See also the The Australian War Crimes Act of 1945 (Preamble and Section 11) <www.legislation.gov.au/Details/C2010C00110> accessed 24 November 2017.

[22] See, eg, the UK War Crimes Act 1991, s 1 of which allows proceedings to be brought for offences constituting violations of the laws and customs of war committed during the period beginning with 1 September 1939 and ending with 5 June 1945 in a place which at the time was part of Germany or under German occupation, against persons who were on 8 March 1990, or have subsequently become, British citizens or resident in the United Kingdom, the Isle of Man, and any of the Channel Islands. For an in-depth discussion of the temporal dimension of the principle of active nationality and the issues to which it gives rise, see Z Deen-Racsmany, 'The Nationality of the Offender and the Jurisdiction of the International Criminal Court' (2001) 95 American Journal of International Law 606–23, especially at 612–15.

[23] The question of whether the principle banning retroactive application of criminal law will be violated by a state that takes into account the nexus that exists at the moment of the initiation of the prosecution is linked to whether one considers the rules on heads of jurisdiction as belonging to *substantive* or to *procedural* criminal law. See, on this matter, B Swart, 'La place des critères traditionnels de compétence dans la poursuite des crimes internationaux' in A Cassese et al, *Juridictions nationales et crimes internationaux* (PUF 2002) 567–87, 583–86.

[24] See, eg, the *Princeton Principles*, n 19, comment on Principle 1(1). See also A Cassese et al, *Cassese's International Criminal Law* (OUP 2013) 278. In their individual Opinions in the *Arrest Warrant* case (n 12), some judges have preferred to use the expression 'universal jurisdiction *in absentia*' to refer to the criminal jurisdiction exercised without the suspect's being present in the territory of the state (see, eg, the individual Opinions of Judges Guillaume, Ranjeva, Rezek, and van den Wyngaert).

culprit is found) has a duty either to extradite or punish (*vel remittere ... vel punire*) all dangerous criminals, thus coining for the first time the formula currently better known as *aut dedere aut judicare*.[25]

12 The *aut dedere aut judicare* principle can be used as a basis to establish criminal jurisdiction, thus constituting a conditional form of universal jurisdiction. Under this variant, universal jurisdiction has thus features in common with the so-called 'representation principle' (or 'vicarious administration of justice'), whereby the criminal jurisdiction of the state applies to cases where an alleged offender is found on its territory and extradition to a more directly involved state is denied, or there is a presumption or confirmation from the latter that it will not request extradition.[26]

13 There are treaties in criminal matters that expressly require state parties to establish their jurisdiction over the relevant prohibited offence on the basis of the *aut dedere aut judicare* formula. This is, for instance, the case for the 1984 UN Torture Convention, Article 5(2) of which stipulates that each state party shall take 'such measures as may be necessary to establish its jurisdiction over [offences amounting to torture] in cases where the alleged offender is present in any territory under its jurisdiction and it does not extradite him'. This formula is known as the 'Hague formula', since it was taken from the 1970 Hague Convention,[27] and is also included in other treaties dealing with so-called 'terroristic crimes'.[28] A variant of the Hague formula is also provided in Article 9(2) of the 2006 International Convention for the Protection of All Persons from Enforced Disappearance: in the *dedere* prong, this provision adds surrendering the alleged offender to an international criminal tribunal, the jurisdiction of which the relevant state party to the Convention has recognized.

14 The obligation imposed on states *to establish* criminal jurisdiction when the person is found in the territory and he or she is not extradited must be distinguished from the obligation they might have acquired *to exercise* criminal jurisdiction under the same conditions. The latter is an obligation that—as a matter of principle—is independent from the head of criminal jurisdiction. In other words, the obligation to exercise jurisdiction under the *aut dedere aut judicare* principle can also be imposed on the state having a direct link with the crime, such as territoriality or the nationalities of the offender or of the victim.

15 While it is controversial whether a rule of customary international law obliges states to prosecute or extradite persons suspected of international crimes, there are at least sixty-one multilateral conventions in criminal matters that contain this rule.[29] Clearly enough,

[25] For the necessary references, see L Reydams, *Universal Jurisdiction. International and Municipal Legal Perspectives* (OUP 2003) 29.

[26] See *amplius*: M Henzelin, *Le principe de l'universalité en droit pénal international* (Bruylant 2000) 30–32.

[27] See Art 4(2) of the Hague Convention for the Suppression of Unlawful Seizure of Aircraft (1970) 860 UNTS 105 ('1970 Hague Convention').

[28] See, amongst others, Art 5(2) of the Convention for the Suppression of Unlawful Acts against the Safety of Civil Aviation (1975) 974 UNTS 177; Art 5(3) of the International Convention against the Taking of Hostages (1983) 1316 UNTS 205; Art 6(4) of the Rome Convention for the Suppression of Unlawful Acts against the Safety of Maritime Navigation (1992) 1678 UNTS 221; Art 3(2) of the Convention on the Safety of United Nations and Associated Personnel (1999) 2051 UNTS 361; Art 6(4) of the International Convention for the Suppression of Terrorist Bombings (2001) 2149 UNTS 256.

[29] For instance, the International Law Commission (ILC) did not agree on the existence of an international custom as source of the obligation *aut dedere aut judicare*. In addition, in the Sixth Committee, several delegations contended that there is no such an obligation under customary international law. See Final Report of the ILC on its work on *The Obligation to Extradite or to Prosecute (Aut Dedere Aut Judicare)* (2014) II International Law Commission Ybk, Part Two, paras 51–52. As for the multilateral conventions containing

however, none of these conventions requires states to *punish* a person accused of a relevant crime. The *judicare* prong shall be therefore understood as corresponding to the obligation to prosecute (*prosequi*), if not—as we shall see—less than that.[30]

The relevant provisions of these conventions differ in the way they formulate the relationship between extradition and prosecution.[31] In some conventions the obligation to prosecute is triggered only by a prior request for extradition that has been refused. This obligation is, however, usually imposed only on the state that has no direct link with the offence but finds the offender on its territory. The primary obligation for this state is extradition (to a state having a direct link with the offence), and the obligation to prosecute stems from the failure to extradite.[32] By contrast, in other conventions priority is given to prosecution by the state finding the suspect on its territory, independently from a prior request for extradition. In these conventions, extradition is an option offered in order to be relieved from the obligation to prosecute.[33] 16

It is worth mentioning that the conventions adopting this second approach, differently from those belonging to the first category, usually impose the obligation to prosecute on every state party that finds a suspect on its territory, including on states having a direct link with the offence. However, and importantly, they differ from these conventions in another respect. Instead of imposing an obligation to prosecute *stricto sensu*, they merely oblige the state which finds the suspect on its territory to submit the case to its competent authorities for the purpose of prosecution. This formulation clearly permits the prosecuting authorities of the relevant state to exercise prosecutorial discretion, when such a possibility is envisaged under the domestic legal system.[34] 17

The *aut dedere aut judicare* obligations embedded in the system of criminal repression established by the grave breaches provisions of the 1949 Geneva Conventions (GCs) deserve separate analysis because of their unique features.[35] Under such system, state parties are obliged 'to search for' persons who have allegedly committed, or have ordered to be 18

the obligation *aut dedere aut judicare*, see *Survey of multilateral conventions which may be of relevance for the work of the International Law Commission on the topic 'The Obligation to Extradite or Prosecute (Aut Dedere Aut Judicare)'*, prepared by the UN Secretariat, UN Doc A/CN.4/630 (18 June 2010) (hereinafter '*Survey of multilateral conventions*') para 4.

[30] See para 17. [31] *Survey of multilateral conventions*, n 29, paras 126–36.

[32] See, eg, Art 9(2) of the 1929 International Convention for the Suppression of Counterfeiting of Currency 112 LNTS 371, which imposes only on states not having a direct link with the offence the obligation to institute proceedings if a request for extradition has been refused. For the other conventions containing a similar provision, see *Survey of multilateral conventions*, n 29, para 28.

[33] See, eg, Art 7 of the 1970 Hague Convention (n 27), which has been the model for a relevant number subsequent conventions, such as the UN Torture Convention. For a list of the other relevant conventions, see *Survey of multilateral conventions*, n 29, para 108.

As for the 1984 UN Torture Convention, this interpretation has been upheld by the ICJ in *Question Relating to the Obligation to Prosecute or Extradite Case (Belgium v Senegal)* (Judgment) (20 July 2012), [2012] ICJ Rep 422, para 95.

[34] With respect to Art 7(1) of the UN Torture Convention, see the Judgment of the ICJ in the *Question Relating to the Obligation to Prosecute or Extradite Case*, n 33, para 90. It is worth mentioning, however, that under Art 12, whenever an act of torture has allegedly been committed 'in any territory under the jurisdiction' of a state party, the latter is obliged to proceed *ex officio* to a prompt and impartial investigation. In addition, if seized with a complaint by an alleged victim of torture, it must ensure that the competent state authorities examine the case promptly and impartially. As the present author has argued elsewhere, the obligations on the territorial state are therefore stricter than those incumbent upon other states parties: see P Gaeta, 'National Prosecution of International Crimes: International Rules on Grounds of Jurisdiction' in *Studi in diritto internazional in onore di Gaetano Arangio-Ruiz* (Editorial Scientifica 2004) 1923–43, 1938.

[35] See Arts 49, 50, 129, and 146 of the four 1949 GCs (GCs I–IV).

committed, a grave breach; to bring these persons before their own courts; or to 'hand over' such persons to other state party for trial, 'in accordance with the provisions of its own legislation', provided that such other state party 'has made out a prima facie case'.[36] The obligation to bring persons responsible for grave breaches before own courts is clearly an obligation to prosecute, should a state party find in its territories a person responsible for a grave breach and collect sufficient evidence against him or her.[37] Arguably, therefore, the prosecuting authorities of state parties cannot exercise prosecutorial discretion and shall prosecute alleged offenders if they have collected sufficient evidence.[38] The handing over to another state party (*dedere*) limb is instead an option that relieves the state from the obligation to prosecute. At the same time, the two requirements for handing over the suspect to another state weaken the system of repression of grave breaches. In fact, a state party may well decline to try a person for lack of evidence and at the same time refuse to hand over the suspect to another state, either because it considers the crimes a political offence (for which extradition is usually excluded) or because of other obstacles provided for in its national legislation.[39]

19 The conventional wisdom is that the GCs establish a system of 'mandatory universal jurisdiction' over grave breaches. This expression is used to mean two things at the same time, namely, that state parties are obliged to establish their criminal jurisdiction based on the universality principle and to exercise it. The grave breaches provisions do not envisage the assertion and exercise of universal criminal jurisdiction by state parties in clear-cut terms. This interpretation stems from the *incipit* of the provisions, which establishes the obligations upon 'each High Contracting Party' to search for, to bring before own courts, or to hand over, regardless of any link with the place of commission of a grave breach or the nationality of the offender. The preparatory works also support this view. The main problematic issue concerns how broad universal criminal jurisdiction should be under the grave breaches system: are the aforementioned obligations triggered only by the presence of an alleged offender on the territory of the state, or regardless of it?[40]

20 Admittedly, the grave breaches provisions do not expressly make these obligations conditional upon the presence of the suspect on the territory of the state. However, as the present author has noticed elsewhere, conceiving of the mandatory exercise of universal criminal jurisdiction without the suspect's ever entering the territory of the state seems both excessive and contrary to state practice. Arguably, the grave breach provisions do not require the presence of the accused in the territory of the state because they are *also* meant to apply to states with a direct connection to the grave breach (for instance territoriality, or the nationality of the alleged perpetrator or the victim). The presence of the accused on the territory of the forum state is usually not requested in the national

[36] For a commentary, see P Gaeta, 'Grave Breaches of the Geneva Conventions' in A Clapham et al, *The 1949 Geneva Conventions: A Commentary* (OUP 2015) 615–46.

[37] Clearly, this is an obligation to prosecute and not to punish: it will be for the competent national courts to assess the criminal responsibility of the accused, in accordance with the relevant procedural guarantees.

[38] This view is also endorsed in the ICRC, *Commentary on the First Geneva Convention: Convention (I) for the Amelioration of the Condition of the Wounded and Sick in Armed Forces in the Field*, 2nd edn, 2016 (hereinafter '*ICRC Commentary of 2016*') <ihl-databases.icrc.org/ihl/full/GCI-commentary> accessed 24 November 2017 (see Comment on Art 49, para 2862). At the same time, the ICRC notes that prosecutorial discretion and similar requirements or procedures 'are helpful in avoiding actions that are not founded in law, but should not be used by States Parties to bring political considerations into play, or as a way of evading their duties to search for and either prosecute or extradite an alleged offender' (Comment on Art 49, para 2866).

[39] See GIAD Draper, 'The Geneva Conventions of 1949' (1965-I) 114 RCADI 59–165, 159.

[40] See Gaeta, n 36, 639.

criminal legislation of states having a direct link with the crime, and to insert it in the grave breaches provisions would have run counter to the main objective of the system of repression set forth by the GCs and Additional Protocol I. Therefore, the silence of the grave breaches provisions concerning the presence requirement does not necessarily mean that these provisions oblige state parties to adopt and exercise the broadest form of universal jurisdiction. At the same time, it cannot be contended that the 'voluntary' exercise of such a broadest form of universal jurisdiction is necessarily 'illegal' under the GCs.[41]

III. Transferring the suspect to an international or an internationalized criminal court or tribunal

21 The question arises whether the state having the custody of the suspect can be relieved of its treaty obligations to prosecute or extradite by surrendering him or her to a competent international/internationalized criminal court or tribunal. The Updated Set of Principles expressly envisages this option, which, however, is usually not included in the *aut dedere aut judicare* provision of the relevant conventions.[42]

22 A variety of authorities support the stand taken in the Updated Set of Principles. For instance, with respect to the grave breaches provisions of the 1949 GCs, the *Pictet Commentary* asserts that the 'handing over of the accused to an international penal tribunal, the competence of which is recognized by the Contracting Parties', is not excluded by the provisions at stake.[43] The same view has been taken by the *ICRC Commentary of 2016*.[44] Similarly, the ILC has followed the same approach both in its 1994 Draft Statute for an International Criminal Court[45] and, more recently, in the context of its work on the obligation to extradite or prosecute.[46]

23 Arguably, however, there may be situations where the surrender of the alleged offender to a competent international court or tribunal might be in breach of the conventional obligations incumbent upon the surrendering state. For instance, one might think of a person allegedly responsible for a grave breach of the GCs, who is a national of a state that has not accepted the jurisdiction of the ICC. The state of nationality of the offender could indeed claim that, because the option of surrendering a suspect to a competent international criminal court is not foreseen in the GCs, the custodial state will violate its obligations by surrendering the suspect to the ICC.[47]

[41] Ibid, 639–40. According to the *ICRC Commentary of 2016*, n 38, 'the practice since 1949 shows that some States, while having extended the principle of universal jurisdiction to grave breaches, have made prosecution conditional on the presence, temporary or permanent, of the alleged offender in the territory of the State Party' (Comment on Art 49 GC I, para 2866).

[42] An exception is the 2006 Convention for the Protection of All Persons from Enforced Disappearance, Art 11(1) of which expressly envisages the possibility for s state party to surrender the suspect 'to an international criminal tribunal whose jurisdiction it has recognized'. See para 13.

[43] J Pictet (ed), *Geneva Convention for the Amelioration of the Condition of the Wounded and Sick in Armed Forces in the Field: Commentary* (ICRC 1952) 366.

[44] See *ICRC Commentary of 2016*, n 38, Comment on Art 49 GC I, para 2887.

[45] *Report of the International Law Commission on the Work of its 46th Session* (2 May–22 July 1994) (1994) II *International Law Commission* Ybk, Part Two, at 64.

[46] ILC, *Report of the Working Group on the Obligation to extradite or prosecute (aut dedere aut judicare)* A/CN.4/L. 829 (22 July 2013) 15, paras 33–34. However, it has pointed out (ibid, 34) that this would be possible unless 'a different intention appears from the treaty or is otherwise established', as provided for in Art 28 of the 1969 Vienna Convention on the Law of Treaties 1155 *UNTS* 331.

[47] Under Art 90(4) of the Rome Statute, regulating cases of competing requests for extradition and surrender to the ICC, if the state requesting extradition is a state not party to the Rome Statute, 'the requested State, if it is not under an international obligation to extradite the person to the requesting State, shall give

24 The issue can instead be framed differently for cases of surrender to the tribunals directly established by the Security Council, such as the ICTY and the International Criminal Tribunal for Rwanda (ICTR). These are subsidiary bodies of the Security Council, endowed with judicial authority that stems from binding decisions of the Security Council. All members of the UN are obliged to accept the jurisdiction of these Tribunals and to comply with their requests for surrender. Under Article 103 of the UN Charter, the latter prevail over any other international obligations of UN member states, including the obligation to prosecute or surrender as stipulated in the grave breaches provision or other relevant *aut dedere aut judicare* obligations. This means, for instance, that states that have surrendered persons suspected of a grave breach to the ICTY cannot be considered responsible for a violation of the *aut dedere aut judicare* obligations as framed in the GCs.

D. Practice

25 According to a recent study, a majority of states establish universal criminal jurisdiction, often subjecting it to a variety of conditions, such as the presence of the suspect in the territory of the state.[48] There is no uniformity with regard to the crimes that come under the purview of this form of jurisdiction: while there are countries where universal jurisdiction applies to domestic and international crimes alike, other limits it to certain international crimes, or provide that universal jurisdiction applies if envisaged or made mandatory by an international convention to which they are party.[49]

26 The concept of universal criminal jurisdiction is therefore not problematic per se. There are, however, at least two controversial aspects that concern the application and exercise of universal jurisdiction, namely: (i) whether universal criminal jurisdiction can be asserted absent a treaty provision, and for which crimes; and (ii) whether it can be 'pure' universal jurisdiction, that is, established or exercised without any link with the state such as the presence of the suspect on its territory.

27 These and other issues have given rise to intensive academic debate,[50] to studies by NGOs,[51] and to codification efforts by private institutions.[52] The Sixth Committee of

priority to the request for surrender from the Court, if the Court has determined that the case is admissible'. As the present author has already argued elsewhere, things are not different when the Security Council triggers the jurisdiction of the ICC. Even in cases of referrals by the Security Council, the source of the ICC powers and authority will remain the Rome Statute, and states not parties to the Rome Statute will continue not to be subject to the Rome Statute. See Gaeta, n 36, 637.

[48] See V Thalmann, 'Conditions to the Exercise by National Courts of Universal Jurisdiction over International Crimes' (PhD thesis, University of Geneva 2017) (on file with the present author) pt 2, ch 1.

[49] Ibid.

[50] For instance, using the function 'search the title' of the catalogue of the Peace Palace Library, 304 hits appear for the words 'universal jurisdiction', sixteen hits for the words 'universal criminal jurisdiction', sixty-four hits for the words 'compétence universelle', and five hits for the words 'giurisdizione universale' (which is almost 400 hits in English, French, and Italian).

[51] See, eg, Amnesty International, *Ending Impunity: Developing and Implementing a Global Action Plan Using Universal Jurisdiction* (2009) and *A Preliminary Survey of Legislation around the World—2012 Update*; Human Rights Watch, *Universal Jurisdiction in Europe: The State of Art* (2006); Redress and the International Federation for Human Rights (FIDH), *Update on Universal Jurisdiction: Fighting Impunity Worldwide* (2009), to name just a few.

[52] See the *Princeton Principles on Universal Jurisdiction*, n 19, and the Resolution of the Institut de droit international on universal criminal jurisdiction with regard to the crime of genocide, crimes against humanity and war crimes, n 18.

the General Assembly has been examining the issue of 'The scope and application of the principle of universal jurisdiction' since 2009, while other international organizations have issued resolutions on the matter.[53] The African Union and the European Union also established an advisory Technical Ad hoc Expert Group, to provide a description of the legal notion of the principle of universal jurisdiction, outline its respective application, and make recommendations for fostering a better mutual understanding of the purpose and the practice of universal jurisdiction.[54]

With respect to serious crimes under international law, the question whether customary international law allows states to exercise universal criminal jurisdiction clearly arises when there is no treaty basis for universal criminal jurisdiction.[55] The question is also relevant when a treaty basis exists and universal jurisdiction is exercised over a national of a state not party to the relevant treaty. In the UN Sixth Committee, some states claimed that customary international law allows universal jurisdiction for genocide, crimes against humanity, war crimes, torture, and piracy, while others contended that it is limited to piracy, genocide, and torture, or to piracy only.[56] In the case *Certain Criminal Proceedings in France (Republic of the Congo v France)*, the Republic of the Congo contended, inter alia, that the proceedings for crimes against humanity and torture commenced in France on the basis of universal jurisdiction against the President and the Minister of the Interior of the Republic of the Congo and against other individuals, constituted a violation of the principle of sovereign equality among states. According to the Republic of the Congo, universal criminal jurisdiction could be exercised only on the basis of a treaty, which did not exist for crimes against humanity. As for torture, the Republic of the Congo argued that the relevant provision was not applicable vis-à-vis a national of a state not party to the UN Torture Convention (as the Republic of the Congo was at the time).[57] The case was discontinued and the ICJ did not have the opportunity to pronounce itself on this issue. In the *Arrest Warrant* case, however, some judges had asserted that universal jurisdiction can be asserted only on the basis of a treaty,[58] while other judges took the 28

[53] For instance, see African Union, *Decision on the Report of the Commission on the Abuse of the Principle of Universal Jurisdiction*, Doc Assembly/AU/14(XI), 11th session of the Assembly of the African Union, Sharm El-Sheikh (Egypt).

[54] The AU-EU Expert Report, n 18.

[55] The Convention for the Prevention and Repression of the Crime of Genocide 78 *UNTS* 277 obliges the state on whose territory acts of genocide have been committed to bring persons charged with such acts before its own courts (Art VI). The possibility to include prosecution on the basis of the universality principle was considered, but was not retained because of the opposition of many states: see N Robinson, *The Genocide Convention. A Commentary* (Institute of Jewish Affairs 1960) 82–83. As for crimes against humanity, there is at the moment no convention dealing with the prevention and criminal repression of crimes against humanity. Since 2014, the ILC has been working on the topic, and in 2016 it provisionally adopted a series of articles, including draft Art 6, which includes the so-called 'Hague formula' mentioned at para 13: see ILC, *Report on the Work of the Sixty-eighth Session* (2 May–10 June and 4 July–12 August 2016), UN Doc A/71/10, 245. Also for war crimes not amounting to grave breaches, including war crimes committed in non-international armed conflict, there is no convention dealing in general with their prevention or criminal repression.

[56] See *The scope and application of the principle of universal jurisdiction. Report of the Secretary-General prepared on the basis of comments and observations of governments*, UN Doc A/65/181 (29 July 2010) paras 27–28.

[57] See Application by the Republic of the Congo filed on 9 December 2002, available at the website of the ICJ <www.icj-cij.org/en/case/129/institution-proceedings> accessed 24 November 2017. See also the position taken the Republic of the Congo at the oral phase of the proceedings on interim measures, verbatim record, 28 April 2003, CR 2003/20.

[58] See the individual Opinions in the *Arrest Warrant* case, n 12, of Judges Guillaume, Ranjeva, and Judge ad hoc Bula-Bula.

opposite stand and endorsed the exercise of universal criminal jurisdiction under customary international law.[59]

29 If one recognizes that universal criminal jurisdiction is allowed under customary international law, the question arises of whether this can be 'absolute' universal criminal jurisdiction. In the *Arrest Warrant* case, some judges contended that under international law this is a permissible form of criminal jurisdiction.[60] A number of other authorities also support this view.[61]

30 However, the presence of the suspect on the territory of the state is requested in most criminal legislations, either as a basis to establish jurisdiction or as a requirement for its exercise.[62] In Europe, Belgium and Spain, which in the past applied 'absolute' universal criminal jurisdiction, subsequently restricted its scope by amending the relevant national provisions. In Belgium the amendment occurred in 2003, because the broad field of application of the law providing universal jurisdiction 'gave rise to a politicization of the law which was considered improper'.[63] In Spain, the amendments to restrict expressly universal jurisdiction as provided by Article 23(4) of Organic Act no 6/1985[64] were prompted, inter alia, by a decision of the Spanish Constitutional Court, which interpreted this provision as providing *unconditional* universal criminal jurisdiction.[65] In Germany, where the 2002 Code of Crimes against International Law also applies with respect to crimes committed abroad that bear no connection with Germany,[66] the prosecutor systematically dismisses complaints where there is a lack of a strong and objective link with Germany.[67] In light of these developments, the question of whether states can assert 'absolute' universal jurisdiction seems now less topical than it was in the aftermath of the Pinochet case, having lost significance in practice.[68]

[59] See the Joint Separate Opinion of Judges Higgins, Kooijmans, and Buergenthal, and the Dissenting Opinion of Judge ad hoc Van den Wyngaert, ibid.

[60] See the Dissenting Opinion of Judge ad hoc van den Wyngaert (ibid, paras 50 et seq), as well as the Joint Separate Opinion of Judges Higgins, Kooijmans, and Buergenthal, who, however, contended that 'absolute' universal jurisdiction is subject to a number of safeguards (ibid, para 59).

[61] See, inter alia, the AU-EU Expert Report, n 18, para 9; Principle 1 of the 2001 *Princeton Principles on Universal Jurisdiction*, n 19; the 2005 Resolution of the Institut de droit international, n 18, which in para 3 requests the presence of the alleged offender in the territory of the state, 'apart from acts of investigation and requests for extradition'.

[62] See Thalmann, n 48, pt 3, ch 2, para 1.

[63] Observation of Belgium to the Sixth Legal Committee of the UN General Assembly <www.un.org/en/ga/sixth/65/ScopeAppUniJuri_StatesComments/Belgium_E.pdf>, para 14. It is also explained, however, that the 2003 Act amending the relevant legislation 'did not affect universal jurisdiction where it was already envisaged under domestic law for a number of offences or where required under international treaty or customary law' (para 16).

[64] Art 23(4) of Organic Act no 6/1985, originally providing for absolute universal jurisdiction was amended in 2009, to restrict universal jurisdiction to cases to which Spain had 'a relevant connecting link' or where the alleged perpetrator was present in Spain. The second amendment occurred in 2014, limiting universal jurisdiction to persons residing in Spain or to persons who are in Spain, and where Spain has denied an extradition request. See submission by Spain to the Sixth Committee of the UN General Assembly <www.un.org/en/ga/sixth/71/universal_jurisdiction/spain_e.pdf> accessed 24 November 2017.

[65] Decision no 237/2005, *Guatemala Genocide case*, Constitutional Tribunal, 26 September 2005 <ihl-databases.icrc.org/applic/ihl/ihl-nat.nsf/0/6CDD72AEA4C2FC4AC1257102003B836B> accessed 24 November 2017.

[66] Submission of Germany to the Sixth Legal Committee of the UN General Assembly <www.un.org/en/ga/sixth/65/ScopeAppUniJuri_StatesComments/Germany.pdf> accessed 24 November 2017, para 2.

[67] See Reydams, n 10, 19–20.

[68] See F Lafontaine, 'Universal Jurisdiction—The Realistic Utopia' (2012) 10 Journal of International Criminal Justice 1277–1302, 1281.

Overall, prosecutions of cases concerning serious crimes under international law based on universal jurisdiction are rare and have mainly taken place in western countries.[69] In most cases they were brought against so-called 'low-cost defendants', namely former Nazis, or Rwandans, or former Yugoslavs, namely persons accused of crimes the repression of which was already decided by the Security Council through the establishment of ICTY and ICTR, or persons not 'protected' by their state of nationality.[70] Outside Europe, the case in Senegal against Hissène Habré stands out, being the first trial against a former foreign head of state for serious crimes under international law besides having taking place in an African country.[71] 31

Arguably, however, universal jurisdiction will continue to be mainly a European concern in the near future. The 2003 EU Council Decision on the investigation and prosecution of genocide, crimes against humanity and war crimes, obliges EU member states to investigate and prosecute persons who are trying to enter and reside in the EU, if suspected of being criminally responsible of one of the aforementioned crimes.[72] It is likely that the forced migration crisis with which Europe is currently confronted will also make it necessary for the law enforcement authorities of EU member states to deal with universal jurisdiction cases, perhaps less spectacular than the one against Hissène Habré, but no less important in the fight against impunity.[73] 32

E. Critical Assessment

Universal criminal jurisdiction is not an 'innovative' form of jurisdiction, specifically envisaged for the repression of serious crimes under international law. It has old origins, which can be traced back to the Justinian Code[74] and the statutes and practice of the medieval Italian and German cities.[75] At the international level, its applicability to certain 33

[69] See Reydams, n 10, 15.

[70] See M Langer, 'The Diplomacy of Universal Jurisdiction: the Political Branches and the Transnational Prosecution of International Crimes' (2011) 105 AJIL 1–49, 5. See also Reydams, n 10, 14–16.

[71] Hissène Habré was convicted on 30 May 2016 by the Extraordinary African Chambers established in February 2013 in the Senegalese court system by Senegal and the African Union to prosecute 'the person or persons' most responsible for international crimes committed in Chad between 1982 and 1990, the period where Chad was under the rule of Habré. The Chambers sentenced him to life in prison for his role in torture, rape, war crimes, and crimes against humanity. On 27 April 2017, the Appeals Chamber in the Extraordinary African Chambers confirmed his conviction for war crimes, crimes against humanity, and torture, but acquitted him of rape.

[72] Council Decision 2003/335/JHA of 8 May 2003 on the investigation and prosecution of genocide, crimes against humanity and war crimes [2003] OJ L118/12, paras 6–7.

[73] See Reydams, n 10, 20.

[74] See H Donnedieu de Vabres, *Les principes modernes du droit pénal international* (Librairie du Récueil Sirey 1928) 135–36, where he explains that the Justinian Code (Lib III, tit XV) conferred jurisdiction on criminal tribunals solely because of the custody of the alleged culprit (the so-called *forum deprehensionis* principle). Another author has noted, however, that the jurisdiction based on the principle of the *forum deprehensionis* was subsidiary to that based on the place of commission of the crime (so-called 'territorial jurisdiction'). In the event of a request for extradition by the authorities of the place of commission of the crime, the jurisdiction of the latter therefore prevailed. See G Guillaume, 'La compétence universelle. Formes anciennes et nouvelles' in *Mélanges offerts à Georges Levasseur* (Gazette du Palais, 1992) 22–36, 24 ff.

[75] See M Henzelin, n 26, 72–79, who also explains that in the German medieval legislation and practice, the *judex deprehensionis* constituted a head of jurisdiction on its own, on the same footing as that based on the place of the commission of the crime (*locus commissi delicti*).

criminal offences has long been recognized. One might think, for instance, of piracy,[76] but also of other offences defined in multilateral conventions containing an express provision on universal jurisdiction.[77] In addition, there are states that (subject to certain conditions) establish unilaterally universal jurisdiction over domestic offences, such as murder or rape.[78]

34 At first sight, it may therefore come as a surprise that universal jurisdiction, once applied to serious crimes under international law such as genocide, crimes against humanity and war crimes, has generated so much controversy. Should not the crimes of most serious concern to the international community attract the widest form of criminal jurisdiction so as to enhance the possibilities of repression?

35 Arguably, the crux of the matter is represented by the specific features of the crimes under consideration. As already noted,[79] these crimes are often the expression of 'system criminality', in that they are committed by state officials in furtherance of, or with the support or tolerance of, the apparatus of the state as such. The debate over universal jurisdiction has thus mainly originated from domestic cases involving foreign former or sitting senior state officials, which has contextually raised the question of respect for the sovereign international immunities protecting them.

36 The issues of the applicability of the international rules on immunities before domestic courts and of the conditions and scope of universal jurisdiction are thus closely intertwined. Arguably, should international immunities (particularly the so-called functional immunities[80]) continue to apply in the field of national repression of international crimes, the *rationale* of the establishment of universal jurisdiction over such crimes would be seriously undermined. Without a waiver from the state to which the official belongs or belonged, foreign domestic courts could not prosecute any foreign former or sitting state officials accused of a serious crime under international law. The domestic pillar in the existing system of repression of international crimes would be thus principally confined to the prosecution of individuals who have acted in a private capacity (such as members of non-state armed actors) and other 'low-cost' defendants. They would be the main category of persons falling under universal jurisdiction.

Bibliography

Bassiouni, C et al, *Aut Dedere Aut Judicare: The Duty to Extradite or Prosecute in International Law* (Martinus Nijhoff 1995).

Donnedieu de Vabres, H, 'Le système de la répression universelle: Ses origines historiques—ses formes contemporaines' (1922-1923) Revue critique de droit international privé 533–64.

Gaeta, P, 'The Need Reasonably to Expand National Criminal Jurisdiction over International Crimes' in A Cassese (ed), *Realizing Utopia: The Future of International Law* (OUP 2012).

[76] See the *Harvard Research Draft Convention on Jurisdiction with Respect to Crime* in (1935) 29 AJIL 563. Art 102 of the UN Convention on the Law of the Sea also recognizes that piracy is subject to universal jurisdiction.

[77] In pre-Second World War multilateral conventions, see, eg, Art 9 of the 1929 Convention for the Suppression of Counterfeiting Currency, and Art 8 of the 1936 Convention for the Suppression of the Illicit Traffic in Dangerous Drugs. On these provisions, see Reydams, n 25, 44–46.

[78] See Amnesty International, *Universal Jurisdiction. A Preliminary Survey of Legislation around the World* (2011) 16.

[79] At para 2.

[80] See in the commentary to Principle 27 in this volume, paras 22–23.

Henzelin, M, *Le principe de l'universalité en droit pénal international: Droit et obligation pour les Etats de poursuivre et juger selon le principe de l'universalité* (Helbing & Kichtenhahn/Bruylant 2000).

Lafontaine, F, 'Universal Jurisdiction—the Realistic Utopia' (2012) 10 Journal of International Criminal Justice 1277–1302.

Langer, M, 'Universal Jurisdiction is Not Disappearing: The Shift from "Global Enforcer" to "No Safe Haven" Universal Jurisdiction' (2015) 13 Journal of International Criminal Justice 1–12.

O'Sullivan, A, *Universal Jurisdiction in International Law: The Debate and the Battle for Hegemony* (Routledge, 2017).

Reydams, L, *Universal Jurisdiction: International and Municipal Perspectives* (OUP 2003).

Reydams, L, 'The Rise and Fall of Universal Jurisdiction' in WA Schabas et al (eds), *Handbook of International Criminal Law* (Routledge 2011).

Scharf, M, 'Application of Treaty-Based Universal Jurisdiction on Nationals of Non-Party States' (2000-2001) 35 New England Law Review 363–82.

Van Steenbergher, R, 'The Obligation to Extradite or Prosecute Clarifying its Nature' (2011) 9 Journal of International Criminal Justice 1089–1116.

GAETA

C.

RESTRICTIONS ON RULES OF LAW JUSTIFIED BY ACTION TO COMBAT IMPUNITY

Principle 22. Nature of Restrictive Measures

Giulia Pinzauti

States should adopt and enforce safeguards against any abuse of rules such as those pertaining to prescription, amnesty, right to asylum, refusal to extradite, *non bis in idem*, due obedience, official immunities, repentance, the jurisdiction of military courts and the irremovability of judges that fosters or contributes to impunity.

A. Summary of Findings

Principle 22 is an umbrella provision listing certain rules or principles in national legal systems, in themselves legitimate, which might impede the criminal prosecution or other scrutiny of human rights violations by domestic courts. These rules and principles include those regulating prescription (statutory limitations), amnesty, the right to asylum, extradition, *non bis in idem* (double jeopardy), due obedience, official immunities, repentance, the jurisdiction of military courts, and the irremovability of judges. The list is not exhaustive, and other examples can be imagined, especially tailored to the unique characteristics of particular jurisdictions. The common thread is that certain exceptions or qualifications to these rules may be justified by the need to combat impunity. Principle 22 is best understood as an overarching guideline to states on the nature of the safeguards and restrictions that they may need to adopt and enforce in order to counter impunity more effectively. Accordingly, the Updated Principles do not impose any strict obligation. It is up to each state to decide the measures that are most appropriate in its own national context and in light of other relevant considerations, such as the need to maintain a lasting peace or to foster national reconciliation.

B. Contextual and Historical Introduction

Restrictive measures under section C of the Updated Principles aim to remove barriers to the prosecution of international crimes by domestic courts, which under Principle 20 have the primary responsibility to bring to justice the alleged perpetrators of serious crimes under international law. 1

Although the idea was already included in the Joinet Principles[1] that restrictions to, or qualifications of, certain legal rules may be desirable or necessary to support efforts to counter impunity, it has since undergone significant changes. 2

First, the list of legal doctrines, principles, or rules whose abuse or misuse might foster or contribute to impunity has been expanded, both by expressly identifying new principles of relevance, such as *non bis in idem* and official immunities, and by making 3

[1] *Set of Principles for the protection and promotion of human rights through action to combat impunity, Revised Final Report prepared by Mr Joinet pursuant to Sub-Commission decision 1996/119*, UN Doc E/CN.4/Sub.2/1997/20/Rev.1 (2 October 1997) (hereinafter 'the Joinet Principles') Principle 23.

clear that the list is non-exhaustive, as evidenced by the prefatory words 'such as'. In particular, adding the reference to *non bis in idem*, which is further developed in Principle 26(b), brings the Updated Principles into line with the statutes of international and mixed courts and tribunals tasked with the prosecution of serious crimes under international law.[2] These instruments allow for exceptions to the *non bis in idem* rule when a person has been previously tried, for the purpose of shielding that person from criminal responsibility, if the proceedings were not impartial or independent, or if the case was not diligently prosecuted. Similarly, including official immunities was fitting in light of the considerable attention they received as the prosecution of international crimes by foreign courts became more frequent in the late 1990s and early 2000s. The *Yerodia* case before the International Court of Justice, where the Court held that an incumbent Minister of Foreign Affairs charged with the commission of international crimes was entitled to personal immunity, is a paramount example of the relevance of jurisdictional immunities. It is not surprising that this case had a formative influence on the Updated Principles.[3]

4 Second, the reference to *in absentia* procedures, which appeared in Principle 23 of the Joinet Principles, is no longer included in the text of Principle 22 of the Updated Principles. This amendment appears to reflect a more global view, affording greater deference to philosophical differences between legal systems. The Joinet Principles suggested that a state's failure to acknowledge trials *in absentia* could foster or contribute to impunity, particularly when coupled with the state's refusal to cooperate with prosecuting authorities in other countries. By contrast, the Updated Principles now appear to recognize that whereas *in absentia* proceedings are seen as appropriate, with suitable safeguards, in some states, they are virtually alien to other legal traditions.[4] This amendment should, of course, not be taken to imply that states can abuse the lack of proceedings by default in their own legal system to frustrate their obligation to cooperate with investigations undertaken *in absentia* in other states.

5 Lastly, the Updated Principles place greater emphasis on the effectiveness of restrictive measures than did the Joinet Principles. Thus, Principle 22 now clarifies that states should not only introduce appropriate safeguards and restrictive measures, but also enforce them in practice.

[2] Statute of the International Tribunal for the Prosecution of Persons Responsible for Serious Violations of International Humanitarian Law Committed in the Territory of the Former Yugoslavia since 1991, UNSC Res 827 (25 May 1993) Art 10; Statute of the International Criminal Tribunal for Rwanda, UNSC Res 955 (8 November 1994) Art 9; Rome Statute of the International Criminal Court (adopted 17 July 1998, entered into force 1 July 2002) 2187 UNTS 90 (hereinafter 'Rome Statute') Art 20(3); Statute of the Special Court for Sierra Leone, Annex to the Agreement between the United Nations and the Government of Sierra Leone on the Establishment of a Special Court for Sierra Leone (adopted 16 January 2002, entered into force 12 April 2002) 2178 UNTS 138, Art 9.

[3] *Case concerning the Arrest Warrant of 11 April 2000 (Democratic Republic of the Congo v Belgium)* [2002] ICJ Rep 3. The Court did not clarify whether functional immunities bar jurisdiction for the perpetration of international crimes (para 61). See also *Independent Study on best practices, including recommendations, to assist states in strengthening their domestic capacity to combat all aspects of impunity, by Professor Diane Orentlicher*, UN Doc E/CN.4/2004/88 (27 February 2004) (hereinafter 'Independent Study') para 52.

[4] *Report of the independent expert to update the Set of Principles to combat impunity, Diane Orentlicher*, UN Doc E/CN.4/2005/102 (18 February 2005), paras 10, 46.

C. Theoretical Framework

One of the basic tenets of the Updated Principles, expressed in Principle 1, is that states are obliged to combat impunity through the proper administration of criminal and civil justice. The prosecution and punishment of the offender is one of an array of measures designed to provide redress for victims and to re-establish the force of societal norms.[5] Ensuring the right to justice requires states not only to investigate violations and take appropriate measures in respect of the perpetrators, but also to adopt and enforce restrictive measures to ensure that judicial mechanisms do not favour impunity.[6] As van Boven puts it, 'where national or international society allows [the perpetrators of international crimes] to go unpunished and to benefit from policies or practices of impunity, the very fundamentals of justice are seriously jeopardized'.[7] 6

Accordingly, to give effect to the general duty in Principle 1, states should adopt and enforce safeguards against any misuse or abuse of the procedural and other rules by which their legal systems are administered. The rules to which such safeguards or restrictive measures may apply are diverse. They include, for example, those regulating the maximum time for initiating criminal or civil proceedings (statutory limitations, or prescription);[8] judicial cooperation and the allocation of responsibilities in apprehending and prosecuting alleged offenders (asylum, extradition);[9] second prosecutions (*non bis in idem*);[10] the extinction or mitigation of criminal responsibility (amnesty and other measures of clemency, mitigating factors such as superior orders and repentance);[11] jurisdiction and judicial independence (jurisdictional immunities, competence of specialized courts such as military courts, irremovability of judges).[12] 7

Many of these rules or principles are essential facets of the rule of law in modern societies. However, this does not mean that they may not be vulnerable to misuse or abuse, particularly in transitional justice contexts. Principle 22 thus provides a helpful emphasis on the importance of the proper administration of justice, and the prudent application of broad procedural and other principles and rules to ensure that they do not foster or otherwise contribute to impunity. 8

The specific safeguards or restrictive measures appropriate for each of the rules and principles illustrated in Principle 22 are justified by different legal and ethical considerations. In other words, there is no normative unity underpinning these various doctrines. They will thus be analysed separately elsewhere in this volume.[13] Very generally, however, it bears noting that the restrictive measures called for by the Updated Principles are not absolute prohibitions or prescriptions for the legal principles or rules in question. 9

[5] N Roht-Arriaza, 'Punishment, Redress, and Pardon: Theoretical and Psychological Approaches' in N Roht-Arriaza (ed), *Impunity and Human Rights in International Law and Practice* (OUP 1995) 13–23, 23.

[6] J Abrams and M Morris, 'Assessing Efforts to Develop International Principles or Guidelines on Accountability. Report of the Rapporteurs' in CC Joyner (ed), *Reining in Impunity for International Crimes and Serious Violations of Fundamental Human Rights: Proceedings of the Siracusa Conference, 17–21 Semptember 1998* (Érès 1998) 345–57, 347.

[7] T van Boven, 'Accountability for International Crimes: The Victims' Perspective' in Joyner (ed), n 6, 349–57, 349.

[8] See the commentary to Principle 23 in this volume.

[9] See the commentaries to Principles 25–26 in this volume.

[10] See the commentary to Principle 26 in this volume.

[11] See the commentaries to Principles 24, 27–28 in this volume.

[12] See the commentaries to Principles 27, 29–30 in this volume.

[13] See the commentaries to Principles 23–30 in this volume.

Rather, with appropriate constraints, it is for the states concerned to strike an appropriate balance between accountability for international law-breaking and other relevant considerations, such as the need to re-establish peace and foster national reconciliation, or legitimate interests in judicial economy, procedural certainty, expeditious legal proceedings, and so on, as the circumstances demand. Further considerations that states need to factor into their decision-making process may include victims' rights.[14]

D. Practice

10 Recent years have seen an increase in domestic efforts to combat impunity through criminal prosecution, particularly as a result of the entry into force of the Rome Statute.[15] These efforts have been marked by states' action not only to close gaps in national legislation on international crimes, but also to remove barriers to domestic prosecutions, including by reforming laws governing statutory limitations, amnesty, asylum, the administration of justice by military tribunals, and so forth.[16]

11 Practice concerning the application of these safeguards or restrictive measures is not uniform across national legal systems. Rather, states have responded differently to the question of impunity for past crimes in light of their history, culture, legal tradition, and the capacity of the domestic system. Moreover, the approach to implementing restrictive measures relevant to one barrier to prosecution is not necessarily apt for the safeguards relevant to another. This follows from the diverse nature of the rules and principles at issue, and the legal context in which they operate. Therefore, the application of restrictive measures in practice will be analysed in more detail in the following chapters in relation to each legal rule or principle.

E. Critical Assessment

12 The list of safeguards in Principle 22, although long, is not exhaustive and must not be considered as such. Rather, it is best understood as providing illustrative guidelines to states on the nature of the safeguards or restrictive measures that they may need to implement in respect of existing rules in order to ensure that accountability may be pursued fairly and effectively. At the same time, such measures may be necessary but not sufficient to meet the challenges to the administration of justice in particular states, in specific circumstances.

13 Other rules that might generally merit consideration for possible additional restrictive measures include the law regulating the standing afforded to victims. This follows from the emphasis given to reparation for victims as one of the key accountability measures under the Updated Principles, together with the right to know and the right to justice. In this connection, the ability of victims to bring a claim is a prerequisite for their enjoyment of the right to reparation. Likewise, legal doctrines precluding judicial scrutiny, at least in civil claims if not criminal cases, of certain executive acts (known as the 'political question' doctrine, or similar) may also require additional safeguards, given the potential

[14] See the commentaries to Principles 4, 19, 31–34 in this volume.

[15] Independent Study, n 3, para 24.

[16] Ibid, paras 45–49; C Grammer, 'The Rome Statute Regime as a Mainspring of International Criminal Law' (2004) 64 ZaöRV 1059–76, 1072.

for their misuse or abuse to obscure conduct by the military or in the context of foreign affairs.[17]

Lastly, it must be recalled that Principle 22—and section C of the Updated Principles more generally—addresses only legal rules in domestic systems that may obstruct the pursuit of accountability for the perpetrators of international crimes. Yet there are, of course, many extra-legal factors that may contribute to impunity, or at least result in the achievement of only partial accountability, which are not addressed. These include political, resource, and practical constraints, quite apart from the difficulty of marshalling a will to act in the first place.[18] Arguably, these obstacles to effective justice may be even more difficult to surmount than the legal impediments, often requiring concerted action by other states or the international community as a whole. 14

Bibliography

Deen-Racsmány, Z, 'A New Passport to Impunity? Non-Extradition of Naturalized Citizens versus Criminal Justice' (2004) 2 Journal of International Criminal Justice 761–84.

Delmas-Marty, M, 'La responsabilité pénale en échec (prescription, amnistie, immunités)' in A Cassese and M Delmas-Marty (eds), *Juridictions nationales et crimes internationaux* (Presses universitaires de France 2002) 613–52.

Joyner CC (ed), *Reining in Impunity for International Crimes and Serious Violations of Fundamental Human Rights: Proceedings of the Siracusa Conference, 17–21 September 1998* (Érès 1998).

Morris, MH, 'International Guidelines against Impunity: Facilitating Accountability' (1996) 59 Law and Contemporary Problems 30–39.

Orakhelashvili, A, 'Between Impunity and Accountability for Serious International Crimes: Legal and Policy Approaches' (2008) 55 Netherlands International Law Review 207–32.

Roht-Arriaza, N, 'Special Problems of a Duty to Prosecute: Derogation, Amnesties, Statutes of Limitation and Superior Orders' in N Roht-Arriaza (ed), *Impunity and Human Rights in International Law and Practice* (OUP 1995) 57–70.

[17] Determining some issues as non-justiciable on the basis that they concern a 'political question' is typical of the US system, although the precise scope and application of the doctrine is by no means clear: see, eg *Marbury v Madison*, 5 US 137 (1803), 163–70; *Baker v Carr*, 369 US 186 (1962), 211, 217; *Zivotofsky v Clinton*, 123 SCt 1421 (2012), 1426–31, 1431–35 (concurring). Equivalent notions may be found in the French concept of *actes de gouvernement*, which are not subject to judicial scrutiny (by administrative courts), or the so-called *atti di governo* in the Italian legal system. In England and Wales, the power of judicial review—which is the principal means of challenging administrative decision-making and vindicating human rights—is no longer circumscribed by the source of the decision-maker's authority (eg a royal prerogative) but 'simply [by] whether the nature and subject matter of the decision is amenable to the judicial process', decided on a case-by-case basis: *R v Secretary of State for the Home Department, ex p Bentley* [1994] QB 349, 363.

[18] MH Morris, 'International Guidelines against Impunity: Facilitating Accountability' (1996) 59 Law and Contemporary Problems 30–39, 30–31.

Principle 23. Restrictions on Prescription

Giulia Pinzauti

Prescription—of prosecution or penalty—in criminal cases shall not run for such period as no effective remedy is available.

Prescription shall not apply to crimes under international law that are by their nature imprescriptible.

When it does apply, prescription shall not be effective against civil or administrative actions brought by victims seeking reparation for their injuries.

A. Summary of Findings

Statutory limitations, which are intended to protect the rights of the accused, represent a major hurdle to the prosecution of international crimes by domestic courts, and thus to fulfilling the victims' rights to justice and, potentially, effective reparation. State practice does not appear uniform in attempting to balance these competing interests. It may now be widely accepted that specific rules of customary international law prohibit the application of statutory limitations to core international crimes, such as genocide and certain war crimes and crimes against humanity. Yet it is much less clear that corresponding rules have crystallized in customary law in respect of *all* international crimes, let alone other gross violations of human rights. However, rules prohibiting the application of statutory limitations may be contained in specific treaties (for example, in relation to enforced disappearance). They have also been recognized by human rights supervisory bodies through their interpretive practice in construing general human rights treaties. In any event, even when statutory limitations formally apply, courts may choose to assuage their effects by 'stopping the clock' while no effective remedy is available, or by characterizing certain forms of conduct as 'continuing' crimes.

B. Contextual and Historical Introduction

1 Statutory limitations (*prescription*, in French) are legal norms regulating the effects of the passage of time in domestic systems. In criminal law, they provide for a maximum timeframe, or prescription period, within which criminal proceedings can be instituted or sentences enforced. Thus, if an action is not commenced in a timely fashion, a defendant can invoke a statutory limitation as a bar to prosecution or the enforcement of a sentence even if he is actually culpable.[1]

2 That the application of statutory limitations to international crimes is problematic became apparent in the 1960s, when several civil law countries saw prescription periods

[1] On the notion of statutory limitations, see generally RA Kok, *Statutory Limitations in International Criminal Law* (TMC Asser Press 2007).

begin to elapse, risking potential impunity for crimes committed during the Second World War.[2] This concern led to the adoption of the 1968 UN Convention on the Non-Applicability of Statutory Limitations to War Crimes and Crimes against Humanity, and following instruments.[3] Since then, there has been an ongoing debate as to whether such non-applicability was or is mandated by a general rule of customary international law, or is left to the will of states. A related question concerns the crimes, if any, that are subject to such rule. Furthermore, there is no agreement on the temporal scope of the rule, and specifically on whether it applies retroactively or only to future crimes. Such issues have obvious implications for the principle of legality, as well as other procedural questions.

Notwithstanding these conceptual ambiguities, the idea that international crimes 3
should not be time-barred was already recognized in Principle 24 of the Joinet Principles, and has remained substantially unchanged in the text of the Updated Principles. An important difference, however, concerns the definition of the international crimes concerned. The updated definition of 'serious crimes under international law' in the 'Definitions' section of the Principles is much broader, in that it includes torture, enforced disappearance, extrajudicial execution, and slavery, amongst others. Principle 23, however, does not clearly specify which international crimes are not subject to statutory limitations; it only states that certain crimes 'are by their nature imprescriptible'. This reflects the ongoing debate, and accommodates the fact that different instruments may set out different rules for some of the offences included in the updated definition.[4] Principle 23 may thus be considered *de lege ferenda* rather than the biding codification of law.

C. Theoretical Framework

The primary purpose of statutory limitations is protecting defendants from stale claims 4
that might be difficult to counter. In particular, with the passage of time the gathering of evidence becomes more difficult, as it may no longer be available, or may in any event be hard to find and preserve. Significant delays in criminal action may thus impair the accused's right to a fair trial. For the same reasons, the passage of time may also reduce the effectiveness of criminal prosecution. In addition, criminal proceedings tend to lose legitimacy as time passes. Since such delays may be due to the prosecuting officers' failure to gather evidence or to find the culprit in a timely fashion, the preventive and deterrent effect of punishment dwindles as time goes by, as may its moral authority. The need for the social reintegration of the offender may also diminish, especially if the time elapsed has not been marked by further offending. For all these reasons, it is widely seen as fair and appropriate to bar prosecutions if they are not initiated within a reasonable time after the commission of the offence.[5]

[2] C van den Wyngaert and J Dugard, 'Non-applicability of Statute of Limitations' in A Cassese, P Gaeta, and JRWD Jones (eds), *The Rome Statute of the International Criminal Court: A Commentary*, vol 1 (OUP 2002) 873–88, 874.

[3] See section D of this commentary. On the status of ratifications of these instruments, see para 8.

[4] *Report of the independent expert to update the Set of Principles to combat impunity, Diane Orentlicher*, UN Doc E/CN.4/2005/102 (18 February 2005) (hereinafter 'Report'), para 47.

[5] A Cassese, *International Criminal Law* (OUP 2003) 316; M Delmas-Marty, 'La responsabilité pénale en échec (prescription, amnistie, immunités)' in A Cassese and M Delmas-Marty (eds), *Juridictions nationales et crimes internationaux* (Presses universitaires de France 2002) 613–52, 617.

5 Yet these justifications, which may be reasonable for some common crimes, may not hold so good for the most serious international crimes. In such circumstances, even if difficulties in the gathering of evidence persist when proceedings are delayed, this may not be sufficient to justify barring those proceedings altogether given the particular interests at stake. First, there is a much stronger case for punishing the perpetrators of serious international crimes, even if after the lapse of much time, in light of their extraordinary gravity and exceptional nature. Second, unlike common crimes, which tend only to affect a particular community, international crimes generally have a much broader impact, offending the international community as a whole. Accordingly, as Cassese aptly noted, it would be incongruous to subject them to the statutory limitations in force in a particular state, be it the territorial state or the state of nationality of the victim or of the perpetrator.[6] Third, delays in initiating legal proceedings with respect to international crimes are often not due simply to a lack of prosecutorial diligence. A range of independent factors may commonly impede or delay the initiation or fruition of such proceedings, including political circumstances, legal impediments, or victims' or witnesses' psychological difficulties in facing the past. Yet all of these things may change with the passage of time, and the public policy interest in confronting international crimes, as well as the interests of justice, may warrant prosecutorial action.[7] In line with the above, statutes of limitations can be suspended (to prolong the prescription period) for such time as a regime is in power or victims have no effective remedy.[8]

6 Principle 23 concerning statutory limitations must also be interpreted in the light of the extent of any positive duty to prosecute international crimes. For obvious reasons, statutory limitations are irreconcilable with such a duty, where it applies. However, there is no general duty to prosecute all international crimes.[9]

7 Lastly, where statutes of limitation apply, they may potentially affect victims' right to reparation. Addressing this concern, paragraph 3 of Principle 23 provides that prescription of criminal offences shall have no effect on civil or administrative actions initiated by victims. This provision further advances the position set out in the UN Basic Principles and Guidelines on the Right to a Remedy and Reparation (2005), which provide that time limitations applicable to civil claims and other procedures 'not constitut[ing]' international crimes 'should not be unduly restrictive'.[10]

D. Practice

I. Multilateral treaties

8 Four multilateral treaties specifically provide for the non-applicability of statutory limitations to (some) international crimes. The first is the 1968 UN Convention, to which fifty-five states are party at the time of writing. Article 1 of the Convention provides that war crimes, crimes against humanity, genocide, eviction by armed attack or occupation,

[6] Cassese, n 5, 318. [7] Delmas-Marty, n 5, 617–18.

[8] This technique was adopted, eg, by Control Council Law no 10 (1945) for the period from 30 January 1933 to 1 July 1945. Statutes suspending the prescription period for certain international crimes were also adopted in The Netherlands (1947), Germany (1965), and the Czech Republic (1993).

[9] See the commentary to Principle 19 in this volume.

[10] *Basic Principles and Guidelines on the Right to a Remedy and Reparation for Victims of Gross Violations of International Human Rights Law and Serious Violations of International Humanitarian Law*, annexed to UNGA Res 60/147 (16 December 2005) para 7.

and inhuman acts resulting from the policy of apartheid shall not be subject to statutes of limitation, 'irrespective of the date of their commission'.[11] This temporal clause, and the Convention's perceived broad material scope, are said to be the reasons for states' reluctance to ratify it.[12] In 1974, the Council of Europe adopted the European Convention on the Non-Applicability of Statutory Limitations to War Crimes and Crime against Humanity.[13] This Convention has a more limited material and temporal scope than the 1968 UN Convention. First, it only applies to genocide, crimes against humanity, grave breaches and other violations of rules or customs of international law 'of a comparable nature'. Second, its applicability to past crimes is confined to crimes that have not already become prescribed; other than that, the Convention applies to crimes committed *after* its entry into force. Notwithstanding the Convention's more limited scope, it has been ratified by only eight European states to date. Arguably, this is due to the fact that by the time the Convention entered into force (in 2003), most European states already had domestic legislation in place on the non-applicability of statutory limitations to some international crimes and did not feel the need to ratify this instrument.[14] All in all, although support for the two conventions is modest, they have had the further benefit of prompting other states to adopt relevant national legislation.[15]

More recently, the 1994 Inter-American Convention on Forced Disappearance of Persons, providing specifically in Article VII that the prosecution of forced disappearances shall not be subject to statutes of limitation,[16] was somewhat more successful, being ratified by fifteen Latin American states. **9**

The 1998 Rome Statute seems to mark the high point in treaties addressing the non-applicability of statutes of limitation, forbidding their use for all crimes within the jurisdiction of the Court, namely, genocide, crimes against humanity, war crimes, and aggression.[17] One hundred and twenty-four states are presently parties to the Rome Statute. However, it should be noted that the Statute's prohibition applies only to the crimes which it establishes—some of which are more restrictive than their counterparts in customary international law.[18] Statutory limitations applying to crimes within the jurisdiction of the Court would thus raise questions as to the state's ability to prosecute those **10**

[11] Convention on the Non-Applicability of Statutory Limitations to War Crimes and Crimes against Humanity (adopted 26 November 1968, entered into force 11 November 1970) 754 UNTS 73.

[12] Kok, n 1, 96–100; SD Murphy, *Second Report on Crimes Against Humanity by Sean D. Murphy, Special Rapporteur*, International Law Commission, A/CN.4/690 (21 January 2016) para 70; RH Miller, 'The Convention on the Non-Applicability of Statutory Limitations to War Crimes and Crimes against Humanity' (1971) 65 AJIL 476–501, 486–93.

[13] European Convention on the Non-Applicability of Statutory Limitations to War Crimes and Crime against Humanity (adopted 25 January 1974, entered into force 27 June 2003) ETS No 82.

[14] Kok, n 1, 101–02. [15] Ibid, 376.

[16] Inter-American Convention on Forced Disappearance of Persons (adopted 6 September 1994, entered into force 28 March 1996) OAS Treaty Series no 68. The prohibition in Art VII, however, is not absolute.

[17] Rome Statute of the International Criminal Court (adopted 17 July 1998, entered into force 1 July 2002) 2187 UNTS 90 (hereinafter 'Rome Statute') Art 29.

[18] For example, the notion of crimes against humanity in Art 7 of the Rome Statute is narrower than in customary international law, in that the Statute requires that the conduct at issue be carried out 'pursuant to or in furtherance of a State or organizational policy to commit' a widespread or systematic attack directed against any civilian population. This requirement narrows down the scope of the notion of 'widespread or systematic attack' under customary international law. For a comparison between the Rome Statute's definitions of international crimes and customary international law, see A Cassese and P Gaeta, *Cassese's International Criminal Law* (3rd rev edn, OUP 2013) 79–83, 105–08, 129–30.

crimes domestically.[19] Moreover, like the 1974 European Convention, the Rome Statute is expressly prospective in its application.

11 Various other instruments, including the 1948 Genocide Convention, 1949 Geneva Conventions, the 1977 Additional Protocols thereto, and the 1996 International Law Commission Draft Code of Crimes against the Peace and Security of Mankind, make no mention of statutory limitations.

12 Many of the leading human rights treaties, such as the European Convention on Human Rights, the International Covenant on Civil and Political Rights (ICCPR), the American Convention on Human Rights (ACHR), and the Convention against Torture and other Cruel, Inhuman or Degrading Treatment and Punishment, are likewise silent. However, their supervisory bodies have interpreted those instruments as prohibiting the applicability of rules of prescription to gross human rights violations constituting international crimes. For example, the Strasbourg organs have concluded that war crimes and crimes against humanity are imprescriptible since, in their view, this rule was laid down in the Nuremberg Charter (although this conclusion is open to criticism).[20] The Inter-American Court of Human Rights (IACtHR) took a step further. In a seminal judgment, *Barrios Altos*, it held that 'provisions on prescription ... are inadmissible' under the ACHR because they prevent the investigation and punishment of those responsible for serious human rights violations, which are prohibited because they violate non-derogable human rights.[21] The Court's case law characterizing enforced disappearance as a continuing crime is also of crucial relevance, because it provides that the prescription period does not start running until the remains or whereabouts of the victim are discovered.[22]

13 The ECtHR also considered whether the retroactive extension of prescription periods is compatible with the principle of legality. In *Coëme and others v Belgium*, where domestic law treated statutory limitations as procedural rules, the Court held that amendments extending limitation periods did not infringe the principle of legality. This was subject in each case to the original limitation period's not yet having expired. The Court did not, however, pronounce on the legality of statutes retroactively extending limitation periods for offences that are no longer punishable because the limitation period has elapsed.[23]

[19] WA Schabas, 'Article 29: Non-applicability of Statute of Limitations' in O Triffterer and K Ambos (eds), *The Rome Statute of the International Criminal Court: A Commentary* (3rd edn, CH Beck/Hart Publishing/ Nomos 2016) 1107–10, at MN 8.

[20] *X v Germany* (Decision) (Admissibility) (ECommHR, 6 July 1976) 115–16; *Touvier v France* (Decision) (Admissibility) (ECommHR, 13 January 1997) 161; *Papon v France* (Decision) (Admissibility) (ECtHR, 15 November 2001); *Kolk and Kislyiy v Estonia* (Decision) (Admissibility) (ECtHR, 17 January 2006) 9. For a criticism of the ECtHR's analysis see A Cassese, 'Balancing the Prosecution of Crimes against Humanity and Non-Retroactivity of Criminal Law: The *Kolk and Kislyiy v Estonia* Case before the ECHR' (2006) 4 Journal of International Criminal Justice 410–18, 414.

[21] *Chumbipuma Aguirre and others v Peru* (Judgment) (Merits) IACtHR Series C no 75 (14 March 2001) para 41. This statement was reiterated in subsequent decisions. In the context of the ICCPR, see also Human Rights Committee, Concluding Observations on Argentina (3 November 2000) para 9 (holding that 'gross violations of civil and political rights during military rule should be prosecutable as for as long as necessary, with applicability as far back in time as necessary to bring their perpetrators to justice').

[22] See, eg, *Blake v Guatemala* (Judgment) IACtHR Series C no 27 (2 July 1996) paras 30–34.

[23] *Coëme and others v Belgium* (Judgment) (ECtHR, 22 June 2000) para 149. For a discussion of whether statutes of limitations are considered substantive or procedural rules see para 16 of this commentary.

II. Domestic legislation and case law

Domestic legislation on statutory limitations is also far from uniform. While statutes of limitation may be relatively typical in civil law countries, they may be unknown (or inapplicable to serious crimes) in at least some common law countries. Moreover, different jurisdictions have responded in different ways to the specific challenge of fighting impunity for international crimes. In her study, Kok concluded that, by 2006, 146 states had adopted legislation excluding the applicability of statutory limitations to crimes under international law, or serious criminal offences.[24] Yet of these states, many have been selective in choosing which crimes are *not* time-barred, perhaps revealing a trend to give better protection for genocide and crimes against humanity, to the exclusion of war crimes. Domestic law continues to evolve rapidly, however, as more states accede to the Rome Statute and implement its broad protection for statutory crimes into domestic law. 14

Domestic courts in European and Latin American countries have disapplied statutory limitations to international crimes committed during the Second World War, the Communist era, and the period of military *juntas*. In doing so, some courts discerned and relied on the existence of relevant customary rules,[25] while others looked to domestic law.[26] Courts in common law countries have also denied defences based on staleness of the offence or abuse of process in relation to prosecutions initiated many years after the fact, on the ground that the passage of time does not a priori cause evidence to be unavailable or unreliable. Thus, each case has to be decided on its own, in light of all the relevant circumstances.[27] 15

The suspension or disapplication of statutes of limitation may raise questions regarding its compliance with the principle of legality (non-retroactivity of criminal law). This depends on whether statutory limitations are considered substantive rules, to which the legality principle applies, or procedural ones, which instead can be applied immediately to pending proceedings.[28] It also depends on whether the offences in question are already prescribed at the time when the limitation statute is modified. 16

III. The practice of UN organs

The practice of UN organs also supports the non-applicability of statutory limitations to selected international crimes. In 1967, the General Assembly affirmed that 'the application to war crimes and crimes against humanity of the rules of municipal law relating to the period of limitation for ordinary crimes is a matter of serious concern to world public opinion, since it prevents the prosecution and punishment of persons responsible for those crimes'.[29] More recently, Regulation 2000/15, adopted by the UN Transitional 17

[24] Kok, n 1, 75–85, 375.

[25] For example, France, Court of Cassation, *Barbie* (Decision) (26 January 1984) (in relation to crimes against humanity; note that in a subsequent decision the Court did not accept this rule with respect to war crimes); Argentina, Supreme Court, *Scwammberger* (20 March 1990) (confirming an earlier decision by the Federal Court of La Plata).

[26] See, eg, Italy, Supreme Court of Cassation, *Priebke* (Judgment) (16 November 1998) 41.

[27] For a discussion of these cases, see Kok, n 1, 365–66.

[28] This characterization varies from state to state. For a survey of domestic legislation and case law, see Kok, n 1, 297–304; C van den Wyngaert, 'War Crimes, Genocide and Crimes against Humanity—Are States Taking National Prosecutions Seriously?' in MC Bassiouni, *International Criminal Law*, vol III (2nd edn, Transnational Publishers 1999) 227–38, 236.

[29] Question of the punishment of war criminals and of persons who have committed crimes against humanity, A/RES/2338 (XXII) (18 December 1967). See also Question of the punishment of war criminals and of persons who have committed crimes against humanity, A/RES/2712 (XXV) (15 December 1970) and

Administration in East Timor, establishing panels with exclusive jurisdiction over serious criminal offences, has disapplied statutory limitations to genocide, war crimes, crimes against humanity, and torture. By contrast, however, it provides that the other crimes within the panels' jurisdiction (murder and sexual offences) are subject to the applicable law.[30] Likewise, the Cambodian legislation establishing the Extraordinary Chambers in the Courts of Cambodia provides for the non-application of statutory limitations to war crimes and crimes against humanity—even though this is not expressly required, apparently, in the preceding international agreement between the UN and Cambodia.[31]

18 Lastly, the *Furundžija* Trial Chamber at the Internation Criminal Tribunal for the former Yugoslavia (ICTY) has observed that one of the consequences of the *jus cogens* character of the prohibition of torture is that it may not be covered by a statute of limitations.[32]

E. Critical Assessment

19 The varying expressions of state practice, and its frequent grounding in domestic law, militate against discerning a general rule or principle of customary international law prohibiting the application of statutory limitations to *all* international crimes. The better view seems to be that specific customary rules provide for the non-applicability of statutory limitations to certain core crimes, such as genocide, and certain war crimes and crimes against humanity.[33] The adoption of the Rome Statute may ultimately prove very significant in this process, given its wider ratification and the possibility that it contributes to the grounding of an independent customary rule. More widely, practice concerning the non-applicability of statutory limitations to other gross human rights violations not constituting core international crimes is more limited. However, this trend in human rights jurisprudence may also continue, potentially leading to the crystallization of additional customary rules in the future.

20 From a moral standpoint, arguably, no international crime should be subject to statutory limitations. The case law of domestic courts seems to show that the problems posed by the passage of time can be solved, or adequately addressed, on a case-by-case basis.[34] Consequently, statutory limitations are not a priori necessary to protect the rights of the accused. Nor are they necessarily justified on the grounds of public policy, given the unique characteristics of international crimes and the gravity of the harm they cause. For

Question of the punishment of war criminals and of persons who have committed crimes against humanity, A/RES/2840 (XXVI) (18 December 1971).

[30] UNTAET/REG/2000/15 (6 June 2000) s 17.

[31] Law on the Establishment of the Extraordinary Chambers, with inclusion of amendments as promulgated on 27 October 2004 (NS/RKM/1004/006) Arts 4–5.

[32] ICTY, *Prosecutor v Anto Furundžija* (Trial Chamber) IT-95-17/1-T (10 December 1998) para 157. *Furundžija* does not consider the implications of the inapplicability of statutory limitations for the principle of legality discussed at para 16 of this contribution.

[33] In agreement, see, eg, Cassese, n 5, 319; P Gaeta, 'War Crimes Trials before Italian Criminal Courts: New Trends' in H Fischer, K Kress, R Lüder (eds), *International and National Prosecution of Crimes under International Law: Current Developments* (Spitz 2001) 764–68; van den Wyngaert and Dugard, n 2, 879, 887. For Bassiouni, there can be no statutory limitations for violations of *jus cogens*, such as crimes against humanity, genocide, war crimes, and torture; see MC Bassiouni, 'Accountability for Violations of International Humanitarian Law and Other Serious Violations of Human Rights' in MC Bassiouni (ed), *Post-Conflict Justice* (Transnational Publishers 2002) 3–54, 25.

[34] Kok, n 1, 366. See also van den Wyngaert, n 28, 236.

similar reasons, states abrogating statutory limitations for international crimes should refrain from introducing arbitrary distinctions between them by implementing such reforms selectively.

While statutory limitations remain for certain international crimes in many states, an extension of the prescription period or the enactment of a suspension statute constitute desirable intermediate steps before the total abrogation of the statutes of limitations in question. Additionally, even where legislatures act slowly or reluctantly, practice shows that national judges can often assuage the deleterious effects of statutory limitations by the ordinary exercise of their powers, for example by considering the prescription period suspended while no effective remedy is available or while the accused absconds from justice; and by considering certain offences as continuing crimes. Of course, in so doing domestic courts should strike an appropriate balance between the offender's right to legal certainty and the interest of society in prosecuting past crimes. 21

Bibliography

Bassiouni, MC, 'Accountability for Violations of International Humanitarian Law and Other Serious Violations of Human Rights' in MC Bassiouni (ed), *Post-Conflict Justice* (Transnational Publishers 2002) 3–54.

Cassese, A and Delmas-Marty, M, *Juridictions nationales et crimes internationaux* (Presses universitaires de France 2002).

Kok, R, *Statutory Limitations in International Criminal Law* (TMC Asser Press 2007).

Miller, RH, 'The Convention on the Non-Applicability of Statutory Limitations to War Crimes and Crimes against Humanity' (1971) 65 American Journal of International Law 476–501.

Murphy, SD, Second Report of the Special Rapporteur on Crimes Against Humanity, International Law Commission, A/CN.4/690 (21 January 2016).

Page, MG, 'Article 29 of the Rome Statute as a Crystallization of Customary International Law' in S Yee (ed), *International Crime and Punishment: Selected Issues*, vol 2 (University Press of America 2004) 1–53.

Schabas, WA, 'Article 29: Non-applicability of statute of limitations' in O Triffterer and K Ambos (eds), *The Rome Statute of the International Criminal Court: A Commentary* (3rd edn, CH Beck/Hart Publishing/Nomos 2016) 1107–10.

van den Wyngaert, C and Dugard, J, 'Non-applicability of Statute of Limitations' in A Cassese, P Gaeta, and JRWD Jones (eds), *The Rome Statute of the International Criminal Court: A Commentary*, vol 1 (OUP 2002) 873–88.

Principle 24. Restrictions and Other Measures Relating to Amnesty

Ilia Maria Siatitsa and Marieke Wierda

Even when intended to establish conditions conducive to a peace agreement or to foster national reconciliation, amnesty and other measures of clemency shall be kept within the following bounds:

(a) The perpetrators of serious crimes under international law may not benefit from such measures until such time as the State has met the obligations to which principle 19 refers or the perpetrators have been prosecuted before a court with jurisdiction—whether international, internationalized or national—outside the State in question;

(b) Amnesties and other measures of clemency shall be without effect with respect to the victims' right to reparation, to which principles 31 through 34 refer, and shall not prejudice the right to know;

(c) Insofar as it may be interpreted as an admission of guilt, amnesty cannot be imposed on individuals prosecuted or sentenced for acts connected with the peaceful exercise of their right to freedom of opinion and expression. When they have merely exercised this legitimate right, as guaranteed by articles 18 to 20 of the Universal Declaration of Human Rights and 18, 19, 21 and 22 of the International Covenant on Civil and Political Rights, the law shall consider any judicial or other decision concerning them to be null and void; their detention shall be ended unconditionally and without delay;

(d) Any individual convicted of offences other than those to which paragraph (c) of this principle refers who comes within the scope of an amnesty is entitled to refuse it and request a retrial, if he or she has been tried without benefit of the right to a fair hearing guaranteed by articles 10 and 11 of the Universal Declaration of Human Rights and articles 9, 14 and 15 of the International Covenant on Civil and Political Rights, or if he or she was convicted on the basis of a statement established to have been made as a result of inhuman or degrading interrogation, especially under torture.

A. Summary of Findings

Amnesties may take many forms, but they continue to be a controversial measure. Historically, they were considered a valuable tool to end conflicts or to ease transitions to democracy, for instance in Argentina, Chile, and South Africa. Since the Second World War, it has been possible to speak of an emerging legal norm that prohibits amnesties for international crimes, including genocide, war crimes, crimes against humanity, and serious violations of international human rights law. Various developments point to the formation of this norm, prominent among which is the establishment of the International Criminal Court (ICC). Principle 24 of the UN Impunity Principles adopted this approach to amnesties. However, the reality is that state practice on amnesties remains inconsistent. In this sense, the debate on amnesties remains unresolved and is still fundamental.

B. Contextual and Historical Introduction

The term 'amnesty' derives from the Greek word '*amnesia*', meaning 'forgetfulness' or 'oblivion'. An amnesty can be defined as a legal measure that has the effect of 'prospectively barring criminal prosecution, and in some cases, civil actions against certain individuals or categories of individuals in respect of specified criminal conduct committed before the amnesty's adoption', or 'retroactively nullifying legal liability previously established'.[1] Amnesties can take various forms.[2] 1

2 Historically, amnesties were considered a valuable tool to end conflicts. To this end, amnesties were granted in a wide variety of countries and contexts. In some situations, an amnesty was deemed necessary to allow for a peaceful transition to democracy. A well-known example is South Africa, where a Truth and Reconciliation Commission was empowered to grant individuals amnesty in exchange for the truth.[3]

3 The scope of amnesties may vary. The widest are 'blanket' (or 'unconditional') amnesties, encompassing broad categories of beneficiaries and broad categories of crimes, such as the Lomé Amnesty of 1999, which provided for 'free pardon and reprieve for all combatants and collaborators in respect of anything done by them in the pursuit of their objectives'.[4] 'Self-amnesties', which describe laws or decrees passed unilaterally by governments or individuals to shield themselves from prosecution, are often similar to 'blanket' amnesties.[5] There can also be 'pseudo-amnesties'[6] or '*de facto*' amnesties. They both have the same result of tacitly granting amnesties. Examples are the *Punto Final* law and Due Obedience Law of Argentina, passed in 1986–87, which did not grant amnesty but effectively prevented the investigation and prosecution of serious violations of human rights.[7] Lastly, 'limited' or 'conditional' amnesties may require individual applications, and can be made conditional on fulfilling different demands, such as acknowledgement of crimes, non-repetition of crimes or further violence, assisting in a truth-seeking process, return of stolen assets, or participation in reparations for victims.

[1] Office of the United Nations High Commissioner for Human Rights (OHCHR), *Rule-of-Law Tools for Post-Conflict States, Amnesties* (United Nations 2009) (hereinafter '*Rule-of-Law Tools*') 5.

[2] Amnesties can take the form of executive decrees or legislation, but an amnesty should be distinguished from a pardon, which exempts a criminal from serving his or her sentence 'without expunging the underlying conviction' (*Rule-of-Law Tools*, n 1, 5). An amnesty should be also differentiated from the granting of exile, such as Nigeria offered to Charles Taylor in 2003. It should be equally distinguished from diplomatic or head-of-state immunities, which serve as a procedural bar to jurisdiction but do not absolve their beneficiaries from all liability.

[3] Promotion of National Unity and Reconciliation Act 34 of 1995, 19 July 1995.

[4] Another recent example of a blanket amnesty is that brokered by the Gulf Cooperation Council and granted by the Yemeni Parliament on 21 January 2012 to the President of Yemen and his senior aides for crimes committed during his thirty-three-year reign.

[5] L Mallinder, *Amnesty, Human Rights and Political Transitions; Bridging the Peace and Justice Divide* (Hart Publishing 2008) 6.

[6] They refer to 'statutes designed to have the same effect as amnesties … while avoiding the damning name of amnesty': G Meintjes and JE Méndez, 'Reconciling Amnesties with Universal Jurisdiction' (2002) 2 International Law Forum du Droit International 76–97, 85.

[7] The *Punto Final* law set a sixty-day limit on the initiation of new criminal complaints in regard to Argentina's 'dirty war', whereas the Due Obedience Law created an irrefutable presumption that lower-ranking military officers acted under superior orders. They were both annulled by the Argentinian Constitutional Court. P Engstrom and G Pereira, 'From Amnesty to Accountability: The Ebb and Flow in the Search for Justice in Argentina' in F Lessa and LA Payne (eds), *Amnesty in the Age of Human Rights Accountability: Comparative and International Perspectives* (CUP 2012) 97–122.

4 The idea that amnesties contribute to impunity developed gradually after the Second World War and consolidated in the late 1990s.[8] By the time of the Updated Impunity Principles, the amnesties debate was inextricably linked to the obligation of states to prosecute, try, and punish perpetrators of international crimes. Principle 24(a) declares that perpetrators of serious crimes under international law may not benefit from amnesties until the state fulfils its obligations under the duty to prosecute. It does not refer to the distinction between conditional and unconditional amnesties.[9] The independent expert, Diane Orentlicher, concluded that 'recent decisions have reaffirmed the incompatibility of amnesties that lead to impunity with the duty of states to punish serious crimes under international law'.[10] This was a significant development from the 1997 Joinet Principles, where Principle 32 (currently Principle 24) provided that 'Amnesty cannot be accorded to perpetrators of violations before the victims have obtained justice by means of an effective remedy.'[11]

5 Paragraph (b) of Principle 24 links the permissibility of amnesties to the right to reparation and the right to know. Principle 24(c) refers to the fact that an amnesty should not be imposed on individuals prosecuted for acts covered by freedom of expression, and Principle 24(d) specifies that individuals should be able to refuse an amnesty if their right to fair trial has not been respected. Hence, the Principles disregard the use of amnesty as a tool for the safeguarding and promotion of human rights.[12] An example may be an amnesty for 'political crimes' that allows former political dissidents to return from exile.[13]

6 The 2005 Impunity Principles may have adopted a restrictive approach to amnesties, but in the continually evolving debate, voices advocating for a more flexible approach to amnesties are increasing.[14] For instance, the 2013 Belfast Guidelines on Amnesty and Accountability, compiled by a group of experts, underlined the various positive objectives amnesty laws can have and advocated for the use of conditional amnesties as a tool to achieve accountability.[15]

[8] See Lessa and Payne (eds), n 7.

[9] Following Principle 19, which underlines the obligation of states to prosecute those responsible for serious crimes under international law, it appears that under Principle 24, any amnesty for international crimes would be impermissible in all circumstances. On the relevance of conditions for assessing the legality of amnesties, see W Schabas, *Unimaginable Atrocities* (OUP 2012) 188.

[10] *Report of the independent expert to update the Set of Principles to combat impunity, Diane Orentlicher*, UN Doc E/CN.4/2005/102 (18 February 2005) 15, para 50; *Independent study on best practices, including recommendations, to assist states in strengthening their domestic capacity to combat all aspects of impunity, by Professor Diane Orentlicher*, UN Doc E/CN.4/2004/88 (27 February 2004) 11, para 28.

[11] *Question of the impunity of perpetrators of human rights violations (civil and political), Revised final report prepared by Mr Joinet pursuant to Sub-Commission decision 1996/119*, UN Doc E/CN.4/Sub.2/1997/20/Rev.1 (2 October 1997) 8, para 32.

[12] In 1983, the UN Sub-Commission on Prevention of Discrimination and Protection of Minorities asked Louis Joinet to prepare a study on 'the importance that the promulgation of amnesty law could have for the safe-guard and promotion of human rights and fundamental freedoms.' UN Sub-Commission on Prevention of Discrimination and Protection of Minorities, Res 1983/34, 6 September 1983. See Study on amnesty laws and their role in the safeguard and promotion of human rights. Preliminary report by Mr Louis Joinet, Special Rapporteur, UN Doc E/CN.4/Sub.2/1985/16 (21 June 1985), para 1.

[13] Albanian amnesty law (Law no 7660), 14 January 1993.

[14] Amongst others, M Freeman, *Necessary Evils: Amnesties and the Search for Justice* (CUP 2009); W Schabas, 'Amnesty, the Sierra Leone Truth and Reconciliation Commission and the Special Court for Sierra Leone' (2004) 11 UC Davis Journal of International Law and Policy 145–69.

[15] *The Belfast Guidelines on Amnesty and Accountability* (University of Ulster Transitional Justice Institute 2014), Part A: General Principles, Guidelines 4(a) and 5.

C. Theoretical Framework

7 Despite the Impunity Principles' rigid approach, currently no international convention prohibits the adoption of amnesties as such. Article 6(5) of Additional Protocol II to the Geneva Conventions of 1949[16] even encourages states, in the context of internal armed conflict, to 'grant the broadest possible amnesty to persons who have participated in the armed conflict' at the end of hostilities. Even though, in 2005, the International Committee of the Red Cross (ICRC) proposed a reformulation, which would provide for the 'exception of persons suspected of, accused of or sentenced for war crimes',[17] the prohibition of amnesties is rather inferred through other obligations in international law.

I. Amnesty and the obligation to prosecute

8 Principle 24 requires that no amnesty should take precedence over the obligation of states to prosecute, try, and punish the perpetrators of serious crimes under international law. The Impunity Principles therefore directly connect the obligation to prosecute with the prohibition of amnesties. The position that blanket amnesties for war crimes, crimes against humanity, genocide, and serious violations of international human rights should be considered impermissible stems from treaty obligations establishing the obligation to prosecute.[18]

9 Various international treaties explicitly require criminal prosecution of individuals responsible for specific crimes. The 1949 Geneva Conventions require signatories to criminalize grave breaches and prosecute or extradite persons who commit them (*aut dedere aut judicaire*). The 1951 Genocide Convention likewise binds Contracting Parties to enact domestic legislation and to provide for effective penalties.[19] The 1984 Convention against Torture and the 2006 Convention on Enforced Disappearance also establish a duty to prosecute.[20]

10 However, it can seldom be argued that these treaties, while they definitely establish the state's duty to prosecute, provide a sufficient legal basis for assessing the impermissibility of amnesties.[21] First, their scope is limited to specific crimes. For instance, the duty to prosecute under 1949 Geneva Conventions applies only to grave breaches committed in international armed conflict, while the legal status of the duty to prosecute war crimes

[16] Protocol Additional to the Geneva Conventions of 12 August 1949, and relating to the Protection of Victims of Non-International Armed Conflicts (Protocol II) (8 June 1977) 1125 UNTS 609.

[17] J-M Henckaerts and L Doswald-Beck (eds), *Customary International Humanitarian Law* (ICRC 2005) Rule 159.

[18] M Freeman and M Pensky, 'The Amnesty Controversy in International Law', in Lessa and Payne (eds), n 7, 42–65, 42.

[19] Convention on the Prevention and Punishment of the Crime of Genocide (9 December 1948) 78 UNTS 277, Art 5. Also, the Convention on the Non-Applicability of Statutory Limitations to War Crimes and Crimes Against Humanity, ratified by fifty-five states, provides that state parties will ensure that 'statutory or other limitations shall not apply to the prosecution and punishment' of war crimes and crimes against humanity. Convention on the Non-Applicability of Statutory Limitations to War Crimes and Crimes Against Humanity (26 November 196) 754 UNTS 73.

[20] See Convention against Torture and Other Cruel, Inhuman or Degrading Treatment or Punishment (10 December 1984) 1465 UNTS 85 (hereinafter 'Convention against Torture') Art 7(2); and International Convention for the Protection of All Persons from Enforced Disappearance (20 December 2006) 2716 UNTS 3 (hereinafter 'Convention on Enforced Disappearance'), Art 11(2).

[21] Freeman and Pensky, n 18, 46–48.

in internal armed conflict as well as crimes against humanity—both found in customary international law—is less clear.[22]

11 Second, the establishment of a duty to prosecute does not prescribe an obligation to prosecute in all circumstances. Non-prosecution does not automatically imply a violation of the obligation to prosecute. For example, the Convention against Torture and the Convention on Enforced Disappearance grant national authorities a degree of discretion in how to conduct their prosecutions, for instance in allowing for the selection and prioritization of cases by objective and transparent criteria.[23] Principle 24 provides that no perpetrator of a serious crime of international law can benefit from an amnesty until the state fulfils its obligations under the duty to prosecute. However, fulfilling these duties does not always lead to prosecution and conviction. In addition, especially in transitional justice contexts, the authorities have inevitably to prioritize and select certain cases over others due to the large number of cases. They occasionally adopt prosecutorial strategies to this end. In such circumstances, cases that are left pending might in theory be opened at a certain point. However, considering the prosecutors' workload, it may often not be possible to deal with all of them. Such situations resemble *de facto* amnesties.

12 Scholars and human rights organizations refer to an emerging customary international law norm that prohibits amnesties, and argue that the *jus cogens* and *erga omnes* nature of the prohibition of certain crimes renders amnesties for those crimes impermissible.[24] However, the *jus cogens* and *erga omnes* character of a norm does not as such establish an obligation to prosecute.[25]

13 Lastly, state practice is not sufficiently consistent to support the establishment of a customary rule prohibiting amnesties.[26] State practice indicates that amnesties are still widely used.[27] The Special Court for Sierra Leone (SCSL), therefore, while it referred to a 'crystallizing' norm, added that the view that it had crystallized 'may not be entirely correct'.[28] The Trial Chamber of the Extraordinary Chamber of the Courts of Cambodia (ECCC) concluded that state practice is 'arguably insufficiently uniform to establish an absolute prohibition in relation to [amnesties]'.[29]

II. Amnesty and the right to remedy

14 Unconditional amnesties are also considered impermissible under international human rights law because they violate the right to an effective remedy.[30] Paragraph (b) of Principle

[22] The ICRC, in its study of customary law, concluded that amnesties for serious violations of international humanitarian law would be incompatible with the customary rule obliging states to investigate and prosecute persons suspected of having committed war crimes in non-international armed conflicts: see Henckaerts and Doswald-Beck (eds), n 17, Rule 158.

[23] *The Belfast Guidelines*, n 15, Guideline 6(c).

[24] Human Rights Watch, *The Meaning of 'the Interests of Justice' in Article 53 of the Rome Statute*, Policy Paper (June 2005) 9.

[25] An *erga omnes* obligation potentially gives a state the right to investigate a crime, it does not automatically mean that a state has a corresponding duty. Similarly, a *jus cogens* norm cannot create additional obligations. See A Seibert-Fohr, *Prosecuting Serious Human Rights Violations* (OUP 2009) 252–54.

[26] See section D of this commentary; Freeman and Pensky, n 18, 51–57.

[27] Mallinder, n 5, ch 3.

[28] SCSL, *Prosecutor v Kallon and Kamara* (Decision on Challenge to Jurisdiction: Lomé Accord Amnesty) SCSL-2004-15-AR72(E) and SCSL-2004-16-AR72(E) (13 March 2004) para 82.

[29] ECCC, *Prosecutor v Ieng Sary*, Case File No 002/19-09-2007/ECCC/TC (Decision on Ieng Sary's Rule 89 Preliminary Objections (*ne bis in idem* and amnesty and pardon)) (3 November 2011) paras 49 and 53.

[30] Amongst many others, see Art 2(3) of the International Covenant on Civil and Political Rights (16 December 1966) 999 UNTS 171.

24 reaffirms that amnesties shall not affect the victims' right to reparation and the right to know. Regional human rights courts have held on many occasions that amnesties deny victims their right to an effective remedy.

The Inter-American Court on Human Rights (IACtHR) has repeatedly rejected broad, unconditional amnesties in its jurisprudence, amongst others in Argentina, Chile, Guatemala, El Salvador, Peru, Uruguay, and Brazil.[31] In the *Barrios Altos* case, it held that 'all amnesty provisions, provisions on prescription and the establishment of measures designed to eliminate responsibility are inadmissible, because they are intended to prevent the investigation and punishment of those responsible for serious human rights violations'.[32] The European Court of Human Rights (ECtHR), in *Marguš v Croatia*, after examining international practice on the duty to prosecute and the jurisprudence of the IACtHR on amnesties, reached the conclusion that '[a] growing tendency in international law is to see ... amnesties [for acts which amounted to grave breaches of fundamental rights] as unacceptable because they are incompatible with the unanimously recognised obligation of States to prosecute and punish grave breaches of fundamental human rights'.[33] 15

Other human rights bodies have also affirmed this position.[34] The Human Rights Committee considered that the right to guarantee an effective remedy for violations of the International Covenant on Civil and Political Rights includes a duty to investigate allegations of violations and bring perpetrators to justice, including in cases of crimes against humanity.[35] The Committee also stated that states may not 'relieve perpetrators from personal responsibility' by means of an amnesty.[36] 16

If, as noted, the illegality of amnesties under international human rights law is directly connected to the duty to investigate and prosecute as a right to an effective remedy for the victims, this foundation for the prohibition of amnesties has its limits. First, the right to a remedy merely requires the state to conduct an effective investigation that may or may not lead to prosecution. Already, what constitutes an effective investigation remains ambiguous; thus, it adds an additional layer of difficulty. Second, the duty to investigate and prosecute is not the only form the right to a remedy takes. Amnesties 17

[31] See, amongst many others, *Velásquez-Rodriguez v Honduras* (Merits) IACtHR Series C no 4 (29 July 1988) para 165; *Barrios Altos v Peru* (Merits) IACtHR Series C no 75 (14 May 2001) para 41; *Myrna Mack Chang v Guatemala* (Merits, Reparations and Costs) IACtHR Series C no 101 (25 November 2003) para 153; *Almonacid-Arellano et al v Chile* (Merits) IACtHR Series C no 154 (26 September 2006) para 114; *Gomes Lund ('Guerrilha Do Araguaia') v Brazil* (Preliminary Objections, Merits, Reparations, and Costs) IACtHR Series C no 219 (24 November 2010) para 174; *Gelman v Uruguay* (Merits and Reparations) IACtHR Series C no 221 (24 February 2011) para 241.

[32] *Barrios Altos v Peru*, n 30, para 41. See also the more recent decision, *Massacres of El Mozote and Nearby Places v El-Salvador* (Merits, Reparations and Costs) IACtHR Series C no 252 (25 October 2012) para 283.

[33] *Marguš v Croatia* (Judgment, Grand Chamber) (ECtHR, 27 May 2014) para 139. In numerous cases before *Marguš*, the ECtHR has affirmed that the right to an effective remedy entails the right to a thorough and effective investigation. See, amongst others, *Aksoy v Turkey* (Judgment) (ECtHR, 18 December 1996) para 98.

[34] The African Commission on Human and Peoples Rights (AComHPR) has similarly held that a remedy for violations of the African Charter on Human and Peoples' Rights (Nairobi, 27 June 1981, CAB/LEG/67/3 rev.5) entails investigation and criminal prosecution, along with compensation: AComHPR, *Social and Economic Action Center et al v Nigeria*, Communication no 155/96 (AComHPR, 27 May 2002); *Mouvement Burkinabe des Droits de l'Homme et des Peuples v Burkina Faso*, Communication no 204/97 (AComHPR, 7 May 2001). See also AComPHR, *Zimbabwe Human Rights NGO Forum v Zimbabwe*, Communication no 245/02 (Decision) (21 May 2006) paras 211 and 215.

[35] UN Human Rights Committee, General Comment no 31 [80], UN Doc CCPR/C/21/Rev.1/Add.13 (26 May 2004).

[36] Ibid.

from criminal proceedings might not necessarily be incompatible with the right to reparation.[37] Reparation, particularly in the form of compensation, can come through judicial and non-judicial means.[38]

18 To date, to the knowledge of the authors, no human rights court has ruled on the legality of a conditional amnesty. However, the ECtHR, in the above-mentioned *Marguš* case, went on to add:

> Even if it were to be accepted that amnesties are possible where there are some particular circumstances, such as a reconciliation process and/or a form of compensation to the victims, the amnesty granted to the applicant in the instant case would still not be acceptable since there is nothing to indicate that there were any such circumstances.[39]

Thus, it seems to acknowledge the possibility that conditional amnesties might be permissible under the European Convention[40] if other forms of reparation (such as a reconciliation process and/or a form of compensation) were in place. However, the Court's approach should be assessed cautiously; it cannot be interpreted as implying that a state could evade any obligation simply by providing monetary compensation to the victims.

III. Amnesties in international criminal law

i. Amnesties before international criminal tribunals

19 Developments in the field of international criminal law lent further weight to the position that amnesties for international crimes should be considered impermissible. The establishment of the International Criminal Tribunal for the former Yugoslavia (ICTY) in 1993 and the International Criminal Tribunal for Rwanda in 1994, as well as the establishment of hybrid tribunals in East Timor, Kosovo, Sierra Leone, and Cambodia, also contributed to increased recognition that amnesties should no longer be granted. In 1998, a Trial Chamber of the ICTY held that the fact that torture is prohibited by a peremptory norm of international law means that an amnesty for torture should be considered null and void under international law.[41] The hybrid tribunals of Sierra Leone[42] and Cambodia[43] both ruled that the national amnesties in those countries were not applicable. The SCSL noted that states are under a duty to prosecute crimes violating *jus cogens* norms, and that the Sierra Leone amnesty could not include crimes covered by universal jurisdiction.[44]

ii. Impact of the Rome Statute of the International Criminal Court

20 The Preamble to the Rome Statute of the ICC[45] provides that 'the most serious crimes of concern to the international community as a whole must not go unpunished', but the

[37] Freeman and Pensky, n 18, 48–49.

[38] L Mallinder, 'Can Amnesties and International Justice be Reconciled?' (2007) 1 The International Journal of Transitional Justice 208–30.

[39] *Marguš v Croatia*, n 33, para 139.

[40] European Convention for the Protection of Human Rights and Fundamental Freedoms, as amended by Protocols nos 11 and 14, Council of Europe, 4 November 1950, ETS 5.

[41] ICTY, *Prosecutor v Anto Furundzija* (Judgment) IT-95-17/1-T (10 December 1998) para 155.

[42] SCSL, *Prosecutor v Kallon and Kamara*, n 28, para 82. This decision was upheld in other cases before the SCSL.

[43] ECCC, *Prosecutor v Ieng Sary*, n 29.

[44] SCSL, *Prosecutor v Kallon and Kamara*, n 28, paras 71, 82 and 84.

[45] Rome Statute of the International Criminal Court (17 July 1998) 2187 UNTS 3 (hereinafter 'Rome Statute').

remainder of the Rome Statute is silent on the question of how the Court should treat amnesties. South African delegates raised the issue of amnesties during the Rome Statute negotiations, but it found no consensus and, therefore, no expression in the Statute.[46] Nonetheless, the ICC is not bound by domestic amnesties, and should a person, accused by the ICC, be a beneficiary of an amnesty, the Court can consider that amnesty as proof of 'the purpose of shielding the person from criminal responsibility'.[47]

A nonpaper drafted by the US delegation for a preparatory conference in August 1997 tabled the suggestion that the ICC should recognize amnesties to facilitate transitions to democracy, which led to the eventual inclusion of Article 53 in the Statute.[48] Article 53 allows the Prosecutor to discontinue an investigation or prosecution if she or he deems that it is 'in the interests of justice' to do so, subject to the review of the Pre-Trial Chamber. These words were allegedly inserted in the Rome Statute to allow for 'creative ambiguity' in possibly recognizing amnesties.[49] Subsequently, however, a policy paper by the Office of the Prosecutor gave the concept a narrower interpretation. The paper states that 'there is a difference between the concepts of the interests of justice and the interests of peace', and finds that 'the latter falls within the mandate of institutions other than the Office of the Prosecutor', that is, the Security Council. [50] Voices opposing such a narrow interpretation have been raised and argue that justice in Article 53 is not necessarily limited to criminal justice but may be translated to include alternative forms of justice, such as truth commissions.[51] In addition, it has been argued, contrary to the Office of the Prosecutor, that the notion of the 'interests of justice' cannot be completely separated from the concept of the 'interests of peace'.[52] Therefore, it could be interpreted as allowing the Prosecutor to refrain from investigating or prosecuting in order to facilitate a peace-making process.[53] However, the Office of the Prosecutor does not seem for the moment to intend to change its position. 21

IV. The right to refuse amnesty

Principle 24, in paragraphs (c) and (d), refers to scenarios where the imposition of amnesty is unfair, abusive, or otherwise illegitimate. Paragraph (c) provides that 'amnesty cannot be imposed on individuals prosecuted or sentenced for acts connected with the peaceful exercise of their right to freedom of opinion and expression'. Paragraph (d), in turn, has as its focus individuals convicted of crimes other than those addressed by paragraph (c). These individuals, it is stated, have a right to refuse amnesty and to request a 22

[46] There were those who 'had misgivings about laying down an iron rule for all time, mandating prosecutions as the only acceptable response in all situations'. See D Robinson, 'Serving the Interests of Justice: Amnesties, Truth Commissions and the International Criminal Court' (2003) 14 European Journal of International Law 481–505, 483.

[47] Art 17(2)(a), Rome Statute.

[48] M Scharf, 'The Amnesty Exception to the Jurisdiction of the International Criminal Court' (1999) 31 Cornell International Law Journal 507–27, 508.

[49] Ibid, 522.

[50] The policy paper also argued that that the interests of victims 'will generally weigh in favor of prosecution': Office of the Prosecutor, *Policy Paper on the Interests of Justice* (September 2007) 1–2.

[51] K Ambos, 'The Legal Framework of Transitional Justice: A Systematic Study with a Special Focus on the Role of the ICC' in K Ambos, J Large, and M Wierda (eds), *Building a Future on Peace and Justice* (Springer 2009) 19–103, 40–49 and 85.

[52] Schabas, n 9, 191. [53] Ibid, 191.

retrial if they have been convicted without a fair trial, or if convicted on the basis of a statement that may have been made under torture.

23 To conclude, elements to contradict the legality of amnesties, reflected in Principle 24, are found in various branches of international law, and some transnational actors and agencies have taken a strong stance against the use amnesties in cases of serious human rights violations. The UN, for instance, takes the position that it cannot condone amnesties for war crimes, crimes against humanity, genocide, or serious violations of international humanitarian or human rights law.[54] It first took this position in Sierra Leone during the peace agreement negotiated at Lomé, in the aftermath of the Rome Statute negotiations.[55] Today, UN mediators are instructed not to endorse peace agreements containing such amnesties, even though they might not always apply this in practice.[56] The Security Council has often referred to the responsibility of states to end impunity and prosecute international crimes.[57] However, state practice on amnesties does not seem to align with these views.

D. Practice

24 As mentioned, states continue to resort to amnesties to end armed conflicts, or even issue them subsequently. A comprehensive study by Louise Mallinder of over 500 situations has highlighted that amnesties, including for international crimes, remain a reality in today's world.[58] National courts have upheld amnesty laws in recent years in Uganda, Spain, and Brazil.[59] Spain transitioned out of three decades of violent civil war during the Franco era by means of an amnesty law passed in 1977, based on the 'Pact of Forgetting' or *El Pacto del Olvido*. In 2010, Judge Baltasar Garzón was disbarred on charges that he abused his power when he began investigations into mass graves.[60] Amnesty was also granted as part of the peace agreement between Felimo and Renamo in Mozambique, in a law promulgated in 1992.

25 A Spanish court held that the notorious General Pinochet's self-amnesty in Chile of 1978 did not prevent the exercise of universal jurisdiction by Spanish courts.[61] Yet recent years have also seen a number of broad 'self-amnesties'. In February 2007, the National Assembly of Afghanistan passed a law on 'National Reconciliation, General Amnesty and National Stability', which contained a broad self-amnesty. In Libya, in May 2012, the National Transitional Council passed Law 38, which stated in Article 4 that that 'there shall be no penalty for military, security, or civil actions dictated by the February 17 revolution performed by revolutionaries with the goal of promoting or protecting the revolution'. Nevertheless, as the Pinochet example indicates, at least 'self-amnesties' are highly

[54] *Report of the UN Secretary-General. The rule of law and transitional justice in conflict and post-conflict societies*, UN Doc S/2004/616 (23 August 2004) paras 10 and 6(c). See also *Rule-of-Law Tools*, n 1.

[55] *Report of the Secretary-General on the establishment of a Special Court for Sierra Leone*, UN Doc S/2000/915 (4 October 2000) para 23.

[56] United Nations Guidance for Effective Mediation (September 2012). See also *Rule-of-Law-Tools*, n 1, 27.

[57] ComHR Res 2005/81 on Impunity (21 April 2005) para 20.

[58] Mallinder, n 5, 404.

[59] Constitutional Court of Uganda, *Thomas Kwoyelo Alias Latoni v Uganda*, HCT-00-ICD-Case no 20/10, Constitutional Petition no 036/11 (22 September 2011); Supremo Tribunal Federal, ADPF 153- arguicao de descumprimento de preceito fundamental, 2010 (Brazil); Tribunal Supremo, Setencia Absolutoria, Sentencia no 101/2012 (27 February 2012) (Spain).

[60] G Tremlett, 'Baltasar Garzón cleared over his Franco-era crimes inquiry' *Guardian* (27 February 2012).

[61] Spanish Sala de lo Penal de la Audiencia Nacional, *Pinochet* case (5 November 1998).

susceptible to subsequent legal challenge by virtue of their lack of legitimacy, and are also unlikely to be recognized by international tribunals or third states.[62]

'Self-amnesties' ought to be contrasted with democratically endorsed amnesties. 26
These types of amnesties may be better able to withstand legal challenges, as the *AZAPO* case demonstrated in South Africa.[63] Uganda too has an amnesty that was proposed by victim communities. The Supreme Court of Uganda, while denying amnesty to Thomas Kwoyelo, held that the Ugandan Amnesty Act 2000 was not granting 'blanket' amnesties and thus remained valid.[64] A more controversial example of an amnesty arguably approved by referendum is the Algerian Charter for Peace and National Reconciliation of 2006.[65] Approval through democratic process alone may not in itself change the illegal nature of an amnesty, as several conditions need to be fulfilled for any amnesty law to be permitted.[66]

In some countries, amnesties were framed in such a way as to exclude international 27
crimes such as war crimes and crimes against humanity, including in Suriname, Nicaragua, Guatemala, the Federation of Bosnia and Herzegovina, Venezuela, Côte d'Ivoire, the Philippines, the DRC, Tunisia, and Poland.[67] Increasingly, states are also including provisions prohibiting amnesties in their constitutions.[68] But it is not yet possible to discern a general trend to this effect.

E. Critical Assessment

Amnesties continue to be a divisive topic. The overview of the theoretical framework in 28
section C demonstrates the tendency of international law to consider amnesties—or at least blanket-unconditional amnesties—impermissible. The trend towards a prohibition on amnesties for international crimes may have reached its zenith during the 2010 ICC Statute Review Conference in Kampala. In a panel intended to effect 'stocktaking' on peace and justice, Ken Roth, from Human Rights Watch, spoke of a 'paradigm shift', in which amnesties were considered 'no longer an option' and 'mediators had to find ways to

[62] French Cour de Cassasion, *Ely Ould Dah* (23 October 2002) Bull Crim 2002, no 195, 725.

[63] South African Constitutional Court, *Azanian Peoples Organization (AZAPO) and Others v President of the Republic of South Africa and Others* (CCT17/96), 25 July 1996. See also ECtHR, *Marguš v Croatia*, n 33, para 139.

[64] In 2011, Uganda's Constitutional Court, in the *DPP v Thomas Kwoyelo* case, upheld the Ugandan Amnesty Act 2000, ordering the prosecutor to stop the proceedings against Kwoyelo. However, the prosecutor appealed the decision, which was overturned, as mentioned above, by the Supreme Court. *Uganda v Thomas Kwoyelo*, Supreme Court of Uganda, Constitutional Appeal No 1 of 2012 (8 April 2015).

[65] The Algerian Government passed a presidential decree, bypassing the Parliament, allowing for broad amnesty for any governmental security forces. The opposition armed groups were given the opportunity to surrender in exchange for amnesty. The referendum that was held before the decree did not explicitly mention the broad amnesties for security forces. Joint statement by Amnesty International, Human Rights Watch, the International Center for Transitional Justice, and the International Federation for Human Rights, 'Algeria: New Amnesty Law Will Ensure Atrocities Go Unpunished' (28 February 2006).

[66] IACtHR, *Gelman v Uruguay*, n 31, paras 238–39.

[67] Suriname's 1992 Act providing for the granting of amnesty, Decree no 5544; Nicaragua's Amnesty Law, 1993; Guatemala's National Reconciliation Law, 18 December 1996; Federation of Bosnia and Herzegovina's Law of 1999 on Amnesty, 3 December 1999; Venezuela's 2000 Law of General Political Amnesty, 17 April 2000; Côte d'Ivoire's 2003 Amnesty Law, August 2003; Philippines' 2007 Proclamation no 1377, 6 September 2007; Democratic Republic of Congo's 2009 Law of Amnesty, 7 May 2009; Tunisia's Legislative Decree no 2011-11 granting amnesty; Poland's 1998 Act on the Institute of National Remembrance, 18 December 1998.

[68] Art 28(1), Ethiopian Constitution, 8 December 1994; Art 29, Constitution of the Bolivarian Republic of Venezuela, December 1999; Art 80, Constitution of Ecuador, 28 September 2008.

convince parties to come to the negotiating table against a backdrop of actual or possible indictments'.[69] Principle 24 encapsulates this anti-amnesty stance.

29 Yet, as discussed in section D, state practice reveals a much more complex reality, and recent developments indicate that the debate on amnesties, even for international crimes, remains unsettled. This debate is complicated by the fact that in some situations, peace and justice may come into direct conflict. In the words of former Prosecutor Louise Arbour, this 'requires compromise—both sides have to give'.[70] In any event, experience indicates that it is impossible to try all those who may be involved in international crimes, so that selection and prioritization is necessary.[71] Amnesties can therefore be useful for persons who may be unlikely to be tried because they fall outside the selection criteria. For instance, the Secretary-General has noted that 'carefully crafted amnesties can help in the return and reintegration' of displaced persons and former fighters in the aftermath of conflict, and 'should be encouraged' as long as they do not extend to international crimes.[72]

30 Most recently, in *Massacres of El Mozote and Nearby Places v El-Salvador*, the IACtHR drew a distinction between self-amnesties granted at the end of dictatorships and amnesties used to end civil wars.[73] In a Separate Opinion, Judge Diego Garcia Sargan said that when negotiating the end to an armed conflict, '[s]tates must weigh the effect of criminal justice both on the rights of the victim and on the need to end the conflict'.[74] In *Tarbuk v Croatia*, the ECtHR held that even for violations of the right to life, a state may enact any amnesty it deems necessary, provided it balances the legitimate interests of the state against the interests of individual members of the public.[75] This suggests that an amnesty or 'stay on prosecutions' would comply with the ECHR, provided that effective, prompt, independent, and transparent investigations were conducted. The *Marguš* case seems to affirm the understanding that conditional amnesties for any crimes might not violate the right to an effective remedy.[76]

31 The recently proposed *Belfast Guidelines* similarly advocate keeping the door open to conditional amnesties. The authors of the *Guidelines* argue that massive human rights violations give rise to different obligations, including the obligations to investigate, prosecute, provide remedies for victims, prevent the recurrence of the crimes, and ensure the effective protection of human rights.[77] The authors support the view that, rather than prioritizing one, states should seek to balance these various obligations, in particular the obligation to investigate and the obligation to prevent recurrence. In order to be considered as legitimate, at a minimum, amnesties must be made conditional on the rights of victims to truth and reparation, as recognized in Principle 24(b). According to one study, since 1990 the vast majority of amnesties were accompanied by reparations

[69] Moderator's Summary of Stocktaking of international criminal justice, Peace and Justice, RC/11, 23 September 2010, paras 29 and 31.

[70] L Arbour, 'Doctrine Derailed? Internationalism's Uncertain Future: International Crisis', Group's Global Briefing (28 October 2013).

[71] See M Bergsmo (ed), *Criteria for Selecting and Prioritizing Core International Crimes Cases, Forum of International Criminal and Humanitarian Law* (2nd edn, Torkel Opsahl Academic EPublisher 2010).

[72] *Report of the UN Secretary-General*, n 54, para 32.

[73] *Massacres of El Mozote and Nearby Places v El-Salvador*, n 32, paras 287–300.

[74] Ibid, Concurring Opinion of Judge Diego Garcia-Sayan, paras 26–27.

[75] *Tarbuk v Croatia* (Judgment) (ECtHR, 11 December 2012) para 50.

[76] ECtHR, *Marguš v Croatia*, n 33, para 139.

[77] *The Belfast Guidelines*, n 15. William Schabas strongly criticizes blank statements against amnesties as not reflecting practice and for not being pragmatic: Schabas, n 14.

measures.[78] Also, Mark Freeman provided an extensive guide, with specific design choices to ensure that an amnesty is legitimate.[79]

Finally, recent practice indicates that states are developing alternatives to amnesties. In Colombia, a range of initiatives sought to balance peace and justice while avoiding amnesties, including an initiative offering reduced sentences to demobilizing paramilitaries;[80] a constitutional amendment that allows for case selection and prioritization, as well as alternative sentences against members of the FARC as part of the Havana peace process;[81] and a Prosecutorial Directive that regulates the prioritization of cases according to who bears the greatest responsibility for crimes. The IACtHR held that the reduced sentencing scheme introduced by Colombia under the Justice and Peace Law (975) was not in violation of the Convention.[82] Post-conviction leniency may be a desirable alternative to amnesties, as it leaves less room for impunity. 32

Bibliography

Dugard, J, 'Dealing with Crimes of a Past Regime: Is Amnesty Still an Option?' (1999) 12 Leiden Journal of International Law 1003–15.

Freeman, M, *Necessary Evils: Amnesty and the Search for Justice* (CUP 2009).

Lessa, F and Payne, LA, Amnesty in the Age of Human Rights Accountability: Comparative and International Perspectives (CUP 2012).

Mallinder, L, Amnesty, Human Rights and Political Transitions: Bridging the Peace and Justice Divide (Hart Publishing 2008).

Mallinder, L, 'Can Amnesties and International Justice be Reconciled?' (2007) 1 The International Journal of Transitional Justice 208–30.

Orentlicher, D, 'Settling Accounts: The Duty to Prosecute Human Rights Violations of the Prior Regime' (1991) 100 Yale Law Journal 2539–2615.

Robinson, D, 'Serving the Interests of Justice: Amnesties, Truth Commissions and the International Criminal Court' (2003) 14 European Journal of International Law 481–505.

Roht-Arriaza, N and Gibson, L, 'The Developing Jurisprudence on Amnesty' (1998) 20 Human Rights Quarterly 843–84.

Schabas, W, *Unimaginable Atrocities* (OUP 2012).

Scharf, M, 'The Amnesty Exception to the Jurisdiction of the International Criminal Court' (1999) 31 Cornell International Law Journal 507–27.

Stahn, C, 'Complementarity, Amnesties and Alternative Forms of Justice: Some Interpretative Guidelines for the International Criminal Court' (2005) 3 Journal of International Criminal Justice 695–720.

Zalaquett, J, 'Balancing Ethical Imperatives and Political Restraints: The Dilemma of New Democracies Confronting Past Human Rights Violations' (1992) 43 Hastings Law Journal 1425–38.

[78] Mallinder, n 5. [79] Freeman, n 14.

[80] Justice and Peace Law of Colombia (Law 975), 22 July 2005.

[81] Legal Framework for Peace (Legislative Act 1/2012), 14 June 2012. The Legal Framework for Peace also included a reference to suspended sentences, but the Constitutional Court ruled that suspended sentences were not permissible for those most responsible for crimes against humanity, genocide, and war crimes committed in a systematic manner: Constitutional Court Decision C-579/13, para 8.4.9. The whole agreement is on hold after the rejection of the Peace Agreement during the referendum on 2 October 2016.

[82] *Rochela Massacre v Colombia* (Merits, Reparations and Costs) IACtHR Series C no 163 (11 May 2007).

Principle 25. Restrictions on the Right of Asylum

Colin Harvey

Under article 1, paragraph 2, of the Declaration on Territorial Asylum, adopted by the General Assembly on 14 December 1967, and article 1 F of the Convention relating to the Status of Refugees of 28 July 1951, States may not extend such protective status, including diplomatic asylum, to persons with respect to whom there are serious reasons to believe that they have committed a serious crime under international law.

A. Summary of Findings

In the global struggle against impunity, Principle 25 emerges from a concern that the institution of asylum might be used to evade criminal justice and accountability. The imperative that underpins the Principle is to ensure that there are no 'safe havens' where, for example, war criminals and those who have committed crimes against humanity are shielded from justice. It should be read in a holistic way that views denial of status as one piece of the jigsaw of accountability. The systems in place to support international refugee protection have long recognized the aim, and need not impede attempts to combat impunity. As Principle 25 notes, the 1951 Convention relating to the Status of Refugees[1] indicates when status will not be applicable. To be clear: if there are 'serious reasons for considering' that a person has committed a war crime then this person is denied the title 'refugee', and thus the guarantees that flow from the legal regime. This does not mean that the individual loses other human rights entitlements; impunity must always be challenged in a rights-compliant manner. While practical difficulties can emerge (on questions, for example, around prosecutions), neither international refugee law nor international human rights law necessarily hinders lawful, proportionate, and human rights-compliant efforts to tackle impunity effectively. In fact, international refugee law has always explicitly acknowledged this.

B. Contextual and Historical Introduction

1 Principle 25 has not substantively changed, and should be read in the context of the evolution of the Principles as a whole and, in particular, as part of the development of 'restrictions' that can be justified in attempts to combat impunity.[2] There is a clear

[1] Convention relating to the Status of Refugees (hereinafter 'Refugee Convention') (28 July 1951) 189 UNTS 137.

[2] See Principle 22, which refers to 'any abuse of rules', and D Orentlicher, *Report of the independent expert to update the Set of Principles to combat impunity*, UN Doc E/CN.4/2005/102 (18 February 2005) paras 45–57. Other than numbering, the Principle is unchanged, see *Question of the impunity of perpetrators of human rights violations (civil and political), Final report prepared by Mr Joinet pursuant to Sub-Commission decision 1996/119*, UN Doc E/CN.4/Sub.2/1997/20 (26 June 1997) Annex II; and for the revised final report see UN Doc E/CN.4/Sub.2/1997/20/Rev.1 (2 October 1997).

connection to Article 1F of the Refugee Convention, and thus to the exclusion clauses of refugee law. This is significant, as it provides a treaty-based reference for any restrictions, but it also imports the difficulties around the interpretation and application of Article 1F (given the absence of an authoritative international adjudicative body for refugee law). The Principle must be located as one part of a more systematic attempt to address impunity. For example, it makes little sense to insist on exclusion from refugee status without following through on the right to justice (Principles 19–22).

The Principle is connected to a long-standing recognition in international refugee law of circumstances when an individual *must* be excluded from status, and it confirms that the right to seek asylum has historically contained similar limitations.[3] It is in Principle 26 that explicit awareness of *non-refoulement* is displayed, in the context of extradition, and there it is clear that the alternative must be prosecution. Principle 25 is primarily focused essentially on denial of status, with Principle 26 reflecting a plain acceptance of the limits placed on possible return by international human rights law. Tensions can surface, in particular on this question of return. States remain unwilling, at the international level, to accept in treaty form a legally binding right of the individual to be *granted asylum*. The right to grant asylum appears to remain wedded to state sovereignty, but this must now be viewed (and even questioned) in the context of increasingly strong guarantees on *non-refoulement*.[4] International human rights law prohibits return in certain circumstances. Therefore, where this prohibition applies, thought will turn to legitimate alternatives, such as prosecution. 2

International human rights law now embraces robust and inclusive standards for displaced persons, and supplements the refugee regime in significant ways. International refugee law provides a concept of refugee status linked to a 'well-founded fear of being persecuted' test. This must be for a 'Convention reason' and, although subject to purposive interpretation, it remains limited in its reach. Refugee law also includes a qualification to the cornerstone of global refugee protection; the *non-refoulement* principle in Article 33 of the Refugee Convention. International human rights law has developed *non-refoulement* guarantees that are 'absolute'; where the relevant tests are met then return is not permitted, and there is no need to base the claim on a 'Refugee Convention reason'.[5] So, there are circumstances where return may be permissible under international refugee law but strictly prohibited under international human rights law. That is why it is increasingly necessary to consider the impact of both regimes. 3

Exclusion from refugee status signals a bar to the protective reach of international refugee law (and it aligns with emerging trends in international criminal law), but it does not necessarily equate to expulsion, extradition, or return; equally, it does not mean that action to combat impunity is prohibited. It primarily means that the steps that are next taken are not constrained by this regime (as the person is not a 'refugee'). 4

[3] JC Hathaway and CJ Harvey, 'Framing Refugee Protection in the New World Disorder' (2001) 34 Cornell International Law Journal 257–320, 318: 'From its inception, international refugee law has ... accepted the need to reconcile each state's duty to protect involuntary migrants with its responsibility to avoid the infiltration by international criminals and fugitives from justice through refugee law.'

[4] See M-T Gil-Bazo, 'Asylum as a General Principle of International Law' (2015) 27 International Journal of Refugee Law 3–28.

[5] Race, religion, nationality, membership of a particular social group, or political opinion.

C. Theoretical Framework

5 Displacement is one of the main consequences of conflict, and post-conflict societies are often faced with the fact that many will have fled. That means that those suspected of being responsible for serious crimes under international law may be living elsewhere, and thus hidden within populations of displaced persons. Victims and survivors (and thus potential witnesses) may also be among those forced to flee. This situation arises in many transitional settings, and international law has established mechanisms for facilitating accountability in such circumstances, including extradition.[6] Principle 25 reflects an ethical concern that those responsible for committing a serious crime under international law should not be granted asylum (including diplomatic asylum) or refugee status ('protective status'). As with international refugee law, the Principle does not prescribe what should happen next, and that is why it must be read in the light of the other Principles. States have been urged, for example, to ensure that where entry is denied or deportation sought (for exclusion-related reasons), more is done to make sure that people will in fact be prosecuted.[7] This remains one of the principal practical dilemmas.

6 Return may not be permissible for human rights reasons, for example because of the risk of torture. In such instances the obligation to prosecute may arise (or states may wish to exercise a 'discretion' to prosecute by making use of the concept of universal jurisdiction), but as with extradition, there can be practical difficulties, with the result that individuals may be left 'in limbo'.[8] This outcome has, for example, been described as a 'fundamental system error in international law'.[9] That is precisely why Principle 25 must be read in the context of the objectives of the Updated Principles, to ensure that (where possible) there is accountability, whether this occurs in the state itself or elsewhere.

7 International law secures a normative (and institutional) basis for the protection of refugees and asylum-seekers. It embraces the fundamental nature of the principle of *non-refoulement*,[10] and spells out the rights that apply. The global struggle against impunity is conducted on the basis of a desire to preserve the integrity of this 'protective system'. The Universal Declaration of Human Rights (UDHR) 1948 includes the 'right to seek and enjoy in other countries asylum from persecution'.[11] It is qualified, and 'may not be invoked in the case of prosecutions genuinely arising from non-political

[6] As the experience regarding Rwanda demonstrated, extradition can be prevented for human rights reasons: see J Rikhof, *The Criminal Refugee: The Treatment of Asylum Seekers with a Criminal Background in International and Domestic Law* (Republic of Letters Publishing BV 2012) 470.

[7] D Orentlicher, *Independent study on best practices, including recommendations, to assist states in strengthening their domestic capacity to combat all aspects of impunity*, UN Doc E/CN.4/2004/88 (27 February 2004) para 55.

[8] J Reijven and J van Wijk, 'Caught in Limbo: How Alleged Perpetrators of International Crimes who Applied for Asylum in the Netherlands are Affected by a Fundamental System Error in International Law' (2014) 26 International Journal of Refugee Law 248–71, 249.

[9] Ibid, 263.

[10] G Gilbert, 'Exclusion under Article 1F since 2001: Two steps backwards, one step forward' in V Chetail and C Bauloz (eds), *Research Handbook on International Law and Migration* (Edward Elgar Publishing 2014) 519–40, 526, arguing that it is 'an accepted rule of customary international law if not a peremptory norm'. See also T Gammeltoft-Hansen and JC Hathaway, '*Non-Refoulement* in a World of Cooperative Deterrence' (2015) 53 Columbia Journal of Transnational Law 235–84.

[11] Art 14(1), UNGA Res 217 A, 10 December 1948. At the regional level see: American Convention on Human Rights (ACHR) 1969, Art 22(7), OAS, 22 November 1969; African Charter on Human and Peoples' Rights 1981, Art 12(3), 27 June 1981, CAB/LEG/67/3 rev 5, (1982) 21 ILM 58; Charter of Fundamental Rights of the European Union 2000, Art 18, [2012] OJ C326/391.

crimes or from acts contrary to the purposes and principles of the United Nations'.[12] This is further confirmed, as noted, in the UN Declaration on Territorial Asylum 1967, which states that the right 'may not be invoked' where there are 'serious reasons for considering' that a person 'has committed a crime against peace, a war crime or a crime against humanity, as defined in international instruments drawn up to make provision in respect of such crimes'.[13] As indicated, the 1951 Convention relating to the Status of Refugees and the 1967 Protocol relating to the Status of Refugees[14] provide a status-based system of international protection for refugees. Those outside their country of nationality or habitual residence, who have a well-founded fear of being persecuted for a 'Convention reason', are unable or unwilling to avail of state protection, and do not fall within any of the exclusion clauses, are refugees for the purposes of the 1951 Refugee Convention.[15] There is clear provision for the concept of exclusion from refugee status[16] and, for example, several states 'have established specialized war crimes units within their immigration departments' to ensure that the implications of these commitments are taken seriously.[17] Article 1F of the Convention lists the grounds for exclusion:

> The provisions of this Convention shall not apply to any person with respect to whom there are *serious reasons for considering* that:
> (a) he [she] has committed a crime against peace, a war crime, or a crime against humanity, as defined in international instruments drawn up to make provision in respect of such crimes;
> (b) he [she] has committed a serious non-political crime outside the country of refuge prior to his [her] admission to that country as a refugee;
> (c) he [she] has been guilty of acts contrary to the purposes and principles of the United Nations. (emphasis added)

Recognition as a refugee does not end the conversation (and it is a status that may be 8
cancelled or revoked). Article 2 of the 1951 Refugee Convention provides that refugees have duties to the country they are in, with particular reference to conformity with 'laws and regulations as well as to measures taken for the maintenance of public order'. Article 33 contains both the *non-refoulement* obligation[18] and a limitation (applicable to those *who are refugees*, and with the primary intention of protecting the security of the asylum state).[19] States are prohibited from expelling or returning a refugee '*in any manner whatsoever* to the frontiers of territories where his [her] life or freedom would be threatened on

[12] Art 14(2) UDHR. See S Kapferer, 'Article 14(2) of the Universal Declaration of Human Rights and Exclusion from International Refugee Protection' (2008) 27 Refugee Survey Quarterly 53–75.

[13] UN General Assembly, Declaration on Territorial Asylum, 14 December 1967, AS/RES/2312 (XXII), Art 1(2).

[14] (31 January 1967) 606 UNTS 267.

[15] Art 1(A)(2). There is an ongoing debate in refugee law on the question of whether exclusion should be considered before inclusion, see, eg, D Kosar, 'Inclusion before Exclusion or Vice Versa: What the Qualification Directive and the Court of Justice Do (Not) Say' (2013) 25 International Journal of Refugee Law 87–119. Whatever view is taken, practically speaking, there is little sense bothering with the exclusion clauses if refugee status is not at least being considered.

[16] This was not new, see the Constitution of the International Refugee Organization 1946, Annex 1, pt II.

[17] Rikhof, n 6, 370. These include: Canada, The Netherlands, Australia, US, UK, and New Zealand.

[18] Art 33(1). See also Declaration of States Parties to the 1951 Convention and or its 1967 Protocol relating to the Status of Refugees, UN Doc HCR/MMSP/2001/09 (16 January 2002) para 4.

[19] Art 33(2): 'The benefit of the present provision may not, however, be claimed by a refugee whom there are reasonable grounds for regarding as a danger to the security of the country in which he is, or who, having been convicted by a final judgment of a particularly serious crime, constitutes a danger to the community of that country.'

account of his [her] race, religion, nationality, membership of a particular social group or political opinion'.[20] No reservations are permitted to Article 33.[21] Article 32 deals with the expulsion of a refugee, and limits this to grounds of national security or public order, with due process protections included.

9 The 1969 Convention on the Specific Aspects of Refugee Problems in Africa incorporates exclusion clauses that endorse the approach in the 1951 Refugee Convention, with a further exclusion of those who have been 'guilty of acts contrary to the purposes and principles of the Organization of African Unity'.[22] There is an express prohibition on 'subversive activities against any Member State'[23] that is underlined in the 1981 African Charter on Human and Peoples' Rights.[24] The European Union Qualification Directive 2011 (recast) acknowledges exclusion in the context of international protection (refugee status and subsidiary protection) in language that goes beyond the text of the 1951 Refugee Convention.[25] For example, 'particularly cruel actions, even if committed with an allegedly political objective, may be classified as serious non-political crimes',[26] and there is reference to the Preamble to the UN Charter and Articles 1 and 2,[27] as well as incitement.[28] An exclusion provision is also adopted for a 'person eligible for subsidiary protection' that covers, amongst other things (when there are 'serious reasons for considering'), those who have committed 'a crime against peace, a war crime, or a crime against humanity'.[29] The Directive goes even further, to include those who are a danger to security or the community, and it captures a broader range of potential fugitives from justice.[30] This confirms that states still regard exclusion provisions as essential to the integrity of the protection system.

10 Refugee law therefore provides that in defined circumstances status should not be applied. That approach is reinforced when, for example, the EU trends already noted are considered; the EU applies exclusion to refugee recognition and claims for subsidiary protection. In order to protect the integrity of the international protection system, it is accepted that those who have committed war crimes or crimes against humanity, for example, do not deserve the status 'refugee'—even where they would otherwise meet the definition. In this way, international refugee law advances the global struggle against impunity. But that is where the contribution of refugee law effectively ends, and a more complex legal and practical picture can emerge.

11 The next stage must then be viewed in the context of the development of the principle of *non-refoulement*, and the general advances made in international human rights law.[31]

[20] Art 33(1) (emphasis added). [21] Art 42.

[22] (10 September 1969) 1001 UNTS 45, Art I(5)(c). [23] Art II(1).

[24] OAU Doc CAB/LEG/67/3 rev 5, 1520 UNTS 217, (1982) 21 ILM 58, Art 12(3) and Art 23(2)(a): '[A]ny individual enjoying the right of asylum under Article 12 ... shall not engage in subversive activities against his country of origin or any other State party to the present Charter.'

[25] EU Directive 2011/95/EU of 13 December 2011 on standards for the qualification of third-country nationals or stateless persons as beneficiaries of international protection, for a uniform status for refugees or for persons eligible for subsidiary protection, and for the content of the protection granted (recast) [2011] OJ L337/9, Art 12.

[26] Ibid, Art 12(2)(b); this also 'applies to persons who incite or otherwise participate in the commission of crimes or acts mentioned therein' (ibid, Art 12(3)).

[27] Ibid, Art 12(2)(c), [28] Ibid, Art 12(3). [29] Ibid, Art 17.

[30] Ibid, Arts 17(1)(d) and (3).

[31] See generally n 10; JC Hathaway, 'Leveraging Asylum' (2010) 45 Texas International Law Journal 503–36; E Lauterpacht and D Bethlehem, 'The Scope and Content of the Principle of *Non-Refoulement*' in E Feller, V Türk, and F Nicholson (eds), *Refugee Protection in International Law: UNHCR's Global Consultations on International Protection* (CUP 2003) 87–163.

For example, an explicit treaty-based commitment can be found in the UN Convention against Torture and Other Cruel, Inhuman or Degrading Treatment or Punishment 1984:

> No State Party shall expel, return ('refouler') or extradite a person to another State where there are substantial grounds for believing that he [she] would be in danger of being subjected to torture.[32]

Regional refugee and human rights instruments include this protection either directly or indirectly (thus even when it is not expressly mentioned in the text);[33] UN treaty-monitoring bodies (following the example of the European Court of Human Rights (ECtHR)) have been prepared to read in or acknowledge the obligation.[34] In addition to this, the ECtHR, for example, is prepared to interpret Article 6 of the Convention (fair trial rights) to prevent extradition to face a trial where there is a real risk of a flagrant denial of justice.[35]

Refugee law, and the struggle against impunity, must be read and interpreted with 12
these trends in mind; it is equally apparent that international human rights law—with its increasing insistence on the absolute nature of *non-refoulement*—has overtaken the specialist regime in certain spheres.

D. Practice

The exclusion clauses of refugee law have been subjected to extensive examination and 13
consideration.[36] This has intensified as part of an enhanced focus on confronting 'terrorist

[32] (10 December 1984) 1465 UNTS 85, Art 3. A substantial jurisprudence has emerged from the UN Committee against Torture on Art 3 and *non-refoulement*: see UN Committee against Torture, *General Comment 1: Implementation of Article 3 of the Convention in the Context of Article 22*, UN Doc A/53/44, Annex IX; UN Committee against Torture: *PSB and TK v Canada*, Communication no 505/2012 (2015), CAT/C/55/D/505/2012; *FB v The Netherlands* Communication no 613/2014 (2015), CAT/C/56/D/613/2014; *NTW v Switzerland*, Communication no 414/2007 (2012), CAT/C/48/D/414/2010; *Jahani v Switzerland*, Communication no 357/08 (2011), CAT/C/46/D/357/2008. See also the International Convention for the Protection of all Persons from Enforced Disappearance 2006 (20 December 2006) 2716 UNTS 3, Art 16 of which provides: '1. No State Party shall expel, return ('refouler'), surrender or extradite a person to another State where there are substantial grounds for believing that he or she would be in danger of being subjected to enforced disappearance.'

[33] See, eg, Convention on the Specific Aspects of Refugee Problems in Africa 1969, Art II(3); ACHR 1969, Art 22(8); European Union Charter of Fundamental Rights 2000, Art 19(2); Inter-American Convention to Prevent and Punish Torture 1985 (9 December 1985), OAS Treaty Series no 67, Art 13(4); Arab Charter on Human Rights 2004 (22 May 2004), (2005) 12 IHRR 893, Art 28. In the Council of Europe, the ECtHR interprets the Convention to include the principle of non-return: see *Tarakhel v Switzerland* (2015) 60 EHRR 28; *Hirsi Jamaa and others v Italy* (2012) 55 EHRR 21; *MSS v Belgium and Greece* (2011) 53 EHRR 2.

[34] See, eg, the UN Human Rights Committee: *HEAK v Denmark*, Communication no 2343/2014, CCPR/C/114/D/2343/2014; *MI v Sweden*, Communication no 2149/2012, CCPR/C/108/D/2149/2012; *X v Denmark*, Communication no 2007/2010 (2014), CCPR/C/110/D/2007/2012; *Hamida v Canada*, Communication no 1544/2007 (2010), CCPR/C/98/D/1544/2007; *Ahani v Canada*, Communication no 1051/2002 (2004), CCPR/C/80/D/1051/2002; UN Committee on the Elimination of Discrimination against Women, General Recommendation no 32: *On the gender-related dimensions of refugee status, asylum, nationality and statelessness of women*, (2014) CEDAW/C/GC/32; UN Committee on the Rights of the Child, *General Comment 6: Treatment of Unaccompanied and Separated Children Outside their Country of Origin* (2005), CRC/GC/2005/6.

[35] European Convention on Human Rights (ECHR) (4 November 1950) ETS no 5. *Othman (Abu Qatada) v UK* (2012) 55 EHRR 1; *Othman v Secretary of State for the Home Department* [2013] EWCA Civ 277; Treaty on Mutual Assistance on Criminal Matters between UK and Jordan, Cm 8612 (2013). See also *Soering v UK* (1989) 11 EHRR 439.

[36] See, eg, JC Hathaway and M Foster, *The Law of Refugee Status* (CUP 2014) ch 7.

acts' and the increasing international desire to tackle impunity. The UN Security Council has, for example, called on states to ensure that there is no 'safe haven' for those involved in terrorism.[37] One result of this pressure is more intense interest in exclusion.

14 The United Nations High Commissioner for Refugees (UNHCR) offers guidance on how these exclusion clauses should be interpreted, and an extensive body of case law exists at the national level applying the clauses in practice. In explaining their purpose, the UNHCR states:

> The rationale for the exclusion clauses, which should be borne in mind when considering their application, is that certain acts are so grave as to render their perpetrators undeserving of international protection as refugees. Their primary purpose is to deprive those guilty of heinous acts, and serious common crimes, of international refugee protection and to ensure that such persons do not abuse the institution of asylum in order to avoid being held legally accountable for their acts.[38]

It is plain to see why they are referenced in Principle 25. They are triggered when there are 'serious reasons for considering' that an individual has committed any of the listed acts. As noted, it is also possible for an existing grant of refugee status to be cancelled or revoked. Rikhof, for example, suggests that an indictment by an 'international institution' will usually be regarded as conclusive on the exclusion question, but that problems can then arise if the person is subsequently acquitted. Although evidence must be provided for exclusion to apply, it plainly (given the formulation in the Convention) does not mean 'guilt', in the usual criminal law sense. The logic and integrity of refugee law dictates, however, that there genuinely are *serious reasons for considering*.

15 There is an awareness that Article 1F exclusion could be deployed more extensively than is merited. While recognizing the need to protect the integrity of the refugee regime, the risk of abuse is noted.[39] There is evidence of judicial awareness of this need for caution and care. In *Ezokola*, the Canadian Supreme Court addressed the meaning of Article 1F(a).[40] The applicant had been excluded from refugee status as a result of his work as an adviser in the Government of the Democratic Republic of Congo—a regime that was responsible for crimes against humanity. The question here was whether staying in his role amounted to personal and knowing participation. In attempting to move away from 'guilt by association', the Supreme Court stressed the importance of the individual's actual involvement, and whether he or she voluntarily made a knowing and significant contribution.

16 The UK Supreme Court has also insisted on a careful approach. In *Al-Sirri; DD*, the Court insisted that Article 1F(c) should be approached with caution, and there was a high threshold before exclusion could be applied.[41] Here the questions raised related to the use of the exclusion provisions in counter-terrorism (Al-Sirri had a history of involvement

[37] UNSC Res 1624, UN Doc S/RES/1624 (14 September 2005) 'and also *recalling* that the protections afforded by the Refugees Convention and its Protocol shall not extend to any person with respect to whom there are serious reasons for considering that he has been guilty of acts contrary to the purposes and principles of the United Nations'.

[38] UNHCR, Guidelines on International Protection no 5: *Application of the Exclusion Clauses: Article 1F of the 1951 Convention relating to the Status of Refugees*, HCP/GIP/03/05 (4 September 2003) para 2.

[39] Hathaway and Foster, n 36.

[40] *Ezokola v Canada (Citizenship and Immigration)* 2013 SCC 40; [2013] 2 SCR 678. See also, *Pushpanathan v Canada (Citizenship and Immigration)* [1998] 1 SCR 982 (involving Art 1F(c)).

[41] *Al-Sirri v Secretary of State for the Home Department; DD (Afghanistan) v Secretary of State for the Home Department* [2012] UKSC 54.

with a terrorist organization that was proscribed in the UK) and in situations where UN-mandated forces are attacked (in this instance the International Security Assistance Force in Afghanistan). The Supreme Court stressed the importance of individual responsibility, the need for clear and credible evidence, and whether the actions had an international impact. It is worth observing that in these cases it was accepted that both applicants could not be returned for human rights reasons; the sole question related to exclusion from refugee status. This insistence on the need to avoid generalized presumptions and promote case-by-case assessment is also evident in *JS*.[42] This case involved exclusion under Article 1F(a) and membership of the 'Tamil Tigers'. It was accepted by all concerned that mere membership was not enough, but the question was what else was required. This case made clear that the analysis needs to include: an assessment of the nature of the organization; whether it was proscribed; when the person was recruited; how long he or she had remained and whether leaving was possible; his or her position and rank; and his or her knowledge, personal involvement, and role. There is also the question of whether the acts could be classed as war crimes or crimes against humanity; in this case the Court highlighted when this would and would not be appropriate.

The Court of Justice of the EU in *B and D* addressed the questions raised by exclusion of **17**
those who are involved in, or who support, organizations that are on the EU list of groups engaged in terrorist acts (in this instance, PKK and DHKP).[43] Again, the Court noted the need for individual assessment of the specific facts, and that mere membership would not be enough. There must be evidence of the true role of the individual, and although it did not rule out the use of presumptions for those who held senior positions, they must remain presumptions and should not be definitive.

For exclusion to apply there must be an evidential basis for it ('serious reasons for **18**
considering'), and this must be tied in a clear and convincing way to individual responsibility for the precise actions envisaged in Article 1F. Generalized presumptions are unhelpful, and suspicion, speculation, or anecdotal evidence will not be enough.

The human rights regimes have been confronted with these questions, largely on the **19**
question of removal, expulsion, or extradition (and not the direct issue of the denial of status). In these cases, and irrespective of what the individual may have done or been accused of, the ECtHR, for example, requires that the relevant tests are applied—even where this can cause intense irritation for states seeking removal. If there are substantial grounds for believing that there is a real risk of torture or inhuman or degrading treatment, for example, then return is not an option. This is also true where there is a real risk of a flagrant breach of Article 6 ECHR (fair trial) rights on return. In *Chahal*, the majority refused to envisage—in an Article 3 ECHR assessment—a balancing exercise that would see a fair balance test applied to the risk of ill-treatment judged against the severity of the national security risk.[44] The Court has continued to stress the 'absolute' nature of the prohibition and to resist the invitation to build in such a balancing test.[45]

[42] *R (JS (Sri Lanka)) v Secretary of State for the Home Department* [2010] UKSC 15.

[43] Joined Cases C-57/09 and C-101/09 *Bundesrepublik Deutschland v B and D* [2010] ECR I-10979 (exclusion clauses of the 2004 version of the Directive). See also Case C-373/13 *HT v Land Baden-Württemberg* [2016] 1 CMLR 6.

[44] *Chahal v UK* (1997) 23 EHRR 413.

[45] *Saadi v Italy* (2009) 49 EHRR 30, para 138: 'It must therefore reaffirm the principle stated in the Chahal judgment that it is not possible to weigh the risk of ill-treatment against the reasons put forward for the expulsion in order to determine whether the responsibility of a state is engaged under art 3, even where such treatment is inflicted by another state. In that connection, the conduct of the person concerned, however

It has indicated that this takes the Convention beyond the protections of refugee law.[46] It is equally plain, however, that the Court is open to accepting Convention-compliant mechanisms for securing removal (such as sufficiently robust diplomatic assurances).

20 The UN Human Rights Committee has usefully also noted the problems that can arise where the focus on exclusion clouds domestic assessments of the nature and reality of the risk on return. In *Hamida*, the Committee concluded that there was a real risk of a violation of Article 7 of the International Covenant on Civil and Political Rights,[47] and stressed that the domestic authorities in this case had been too concerned with exclusion.[48]

21 In *Othman (Abu Qatada)*, the ECtHR held that return to Jordan would breach Article 6 (there would be no breach of Article 3);[49] there were substantial grounds to believe that a real risk existed of a trial where 'torture evidence' would be used.[50] In the extradition context, involving return to Rwanda for trials relating to genocide, the Court has held, for example (in the correct circumstances), that these returns need not be in a violation of Convention rights.[51]

E. Critical Assessment

22 Principle 25 reflects a desire to ensure that the institution of asylum is not used to avoid facing the responsibility to challenge and combat impunity. The contribution that international refugee law makes is to deny refugee status in such contexts. The international system designed for refugees protects those who face persecution if returned to another state. Refugee law offers an international framework of support to those with a well-founded fear of being persecuted for a 1951 Refugee Convention reason, but it also excludes those who fall within Article 1F. If a person comes within this provision, he or she is excluded and therefore outside the scope of the Convention's protective reach—even where a well-founded fear of being persecuted in the state of origin still exists. While this is refugee law's role in combating impunity, the regime does not

undesirable or dangerous, cannot be taken into account, *with the consequence that the protection afforded by art 3 is broader than that provided for in arts 32 and 33 of the 1951 United Nations Convention relating to the Status of Refugees*.' (footnotes omitted and emphasis added)

[46] Ibid. [47] (16 December 1966) 999 UNTS 171.

[48] *Hamida v Canada*, UNHRC Communication no 1544/2007 (2010), CCPR/C/98/D/1544/2007, para 8.5: 'In the present communication the Committee observes that the material before it shows that, when the author's claims were considered by the State party's authorities, much weight was given to the fact that the Convention relating to the Status or [*sic*] Refugees did not apply to him and *it appears that inadequate consideration was given to the specific rights of the author under the Covenant and such other instruments as the Convention Against Torture*.' (emphasis added)

[49] *Othman (Abu Qatada) v UK* (2012) 55 EHRR 1. See *Aswat v UK* App no 62176/14 (inadmissible) (ECtHR, 29 January 2015), where concerns expressed in an earlier judgment about extradition to the US had been addressed (for the earlier case, see *Aswat v UK* (2014) 58 EHRR 1). See also *Ahmad and Others v UK* (2013) 56 EHRR 1.

[50] See *Othman (Abu Qatada)*, n 49, para 267: 'For the foregoing reasons, the Court considers that the admission of torture evidence is manifestly contrary, not just to the provisions of Article 6, but to the most basic international standards of a fair trial. It would make the whole trial not only immoral and illegal, but also entirely unreliable in its outcome. It would, therefore, be a flagrant denial of justice if such evidence were admitted in a criminal trial.'

[51] *Ahorugeze v Sweden* (2012) 55 EHRR 2, the Court held that extradition would not violate Arts 3 or 6 ECHR, and the case contains useful information on the history of various extradition and transfer requests involving Rwanda.

indicate what should happen next, precisely because it is a *disapplication provision.* However, a strong signal has been transmitted: the state believes that there are 'serious reasons for considering' that the person has, for example, committed war crimes or crimes against humanity, or been guilty of acts contrary to the purposes and principles of the UN. Prosecution is one logical next step, but that is often not what happens, and this requires much further reflection if the objectives of the Updated Principles are to be realized.

Human rights law now provides guarantees that are not tied to particular 'Convention 23 reasons' for ill-treatment, which (in certain contexts) will apply even where exclusion from refugee status arises. The international refugee protection system remains fragile, and is consistently threatened by attempts to undermine existing guarantees. It is vital that the struggle against impunity does not end in the erosion of this system. That is why the integrity of the 'exclusion tests' should not be undermined; the law should not be abused by inappropriate use.

Practical challenges do arise (in cases where, for example, return to the state of 24 origin is not possible and where there may be an unwillingness to prosecute), but these should not impede the global effort to confront impunity and ensure accountability. Mechanisms (including those built into international refugee law) do exist to support both the continuing integrity of international protection and the goals of international criminal justice. In considering the next steps in the discussion, more thought might be given to the post-exclusion phase (when a person has been excluded from refugee status and what precisely happens next) and what can be done to combat impunity in ways that fully respect human rights norms, including *non-refoulement.* International refugee law, properly interpreted, continues to make a contribution, and Principle 25 reflects this fact.

Bibliography

Chetail, V, 'Are Refugee Rights Human Rights? An Unorthodox Questioning of the Relations between Refugee Law and Human Rights Law' in R Rubio-Marín (ed), *Human Rights and Immigration* (OUP 2014) 19–72.

Gilbert, G, 'Exclusion under Article 1F since 2001: Two steps backwards, one step forward' in V Chetail and C Bauloz (eds), *Research Handbook on International Law and Migration* (Edward Elgar Publishing 2014) 519–40.

Gilbert, G, 'Running scared since 9/11: refugees, UNHCR and the purposive approach to treaty interpretation' in JC Simeon (ed), *Critical Issues in International Refugee Law* (CUP 2012) ch 3.

Gilbert, G, 'Current Issues in the Application of the Exclusion Clauses' in E Fuller, V Türk, and F Nicholson (eds), *Refugee Protection in International Law: UNHCR's Global Consultation on International Protection* (CUP 2003) 425–78.

Goodwin-Gill, GS and McAdam, J, *The Refugee in International Law* (3rd edn, OUP 2007) 162–97.

Hathaway, JC and Foster, M, *The Law of Refugee Status* (CUP 2014) ch 7.

Hathaway, JC and Harvey, CJ, 'Framing Refugee Protection in the New World Disorder' (2001) 34 Cornell International Law Journal 257–320.

Juss, S Singh, 'Complicity, Exclusion, and the "Unworthy" in Refugee Law' (2012) 31 Refugee Survey Quarterly 1–39.

HARVEY

Rikhof, J, 'Exclusion Law and International Law: *Sui Generis* or Overlap' (2013) 20 International Journal on Minority and Group Rights 199–232.

Rikhof, J, *The Criminal Refugee: The Treatment of Asylum Seekers with a Criminal Background in International and Domestic Law* (Republic of Letters Publishing BV 2012).

Singer, S, *Terrorism and Exclusion from Refugee Status in the UK* (Brill Nijhoff 2015).

Zimmerman, A (ed), *The 1951 Convention relating to the Status of Refugees and its 1967 Protocol: A Commentary* (OUP 2011) on Article 1F and Article 33, paragraph 2.

Principle 26. Restrictions on Extradition/*Non Bis in Idem*

Robert Roth

(a) Persons who have committed serious crimes under international law may not, in order to avoid extradition, avail themselves of the favourable provision generally relating to political offences or of the principle of non-extradition of nationals. Extradition should always be denied, however, especially by abolitionist countries, if the individual concerned risks the death penalty in the requesting country. Extradition should also be denied where there are substantial grounds for believing that the suspect would be in danger of being subjected to gross violations of human rights such as torture; enforced disappearance; or extra-legal, arbitrary or summary execution. If extradition is denied on these grounds, the requested State shall submit the case to its competent authorities for the purpose of prosecution;

(b) The fact that an individual has previously been tried in connection with a serious crime under international law shall not prevent his or her prosecution with respect to the same conduct if the purpose of the previous proceedings was to shield the person concerned from criminal responsibility, or if those proceedings otherwise were not conducted independently or impartially in accordance with the norms of due process recognized by international law and were conducted in a manner that, in the circumstances, was inconsistent with an intent to bring the person concerned to justice.

A. Summary of Findings

Principle 26 deals with bars to extradition and the principle *ne bis in idem*. It provides for the non-application of some traditional arguments against extradition (political offence objection, non-extradition of nationals); yet it also confirms that in circumstances where the person concerned would be in danger of being subjected to gross violations of human rights, extradition shall not be granted. In this case the refusal to extradite shall result in a prosecution in the requested state. As for *ne bis in idem*, which protects any person against the risk to be prosecuted twice for the same facts, Principle 26 takes over the restriction adopted in the Rome Statute of the International Criminal Court (ICC)[1] vis-à-vis the so-called 'sham or shield trials' aimed at hampering a prosecution in a country willing to lead a fair and efficient prosecution for serious crimes; it also provides for the non-recognition of a previous prosecution or trial which has proved unfair. Principle 26 tries to balance all the aspects of the protection of human rights, including the rights of the person accused of serious crimes, and in this sense it does not limit itself to the fight against impunity, but also contributes to the foundation of a fair system of criminal justice.

[1] Rome Statute of the International Criminal Court (17 July 1998) 2187 UNTS 3 (hereinafter 'Rome Statute'), Arts 17 and 20.

B. Contextual and Historical Introduction

1 In its original version, the relevant provision of the Joinet Principles[2] was far more limited and synthetic than the present version of Principle 26. The Principles contained nothing on the *ne bis in idem* rule's barring any new prosecution or a new trial for facts which have already been judged.[3] The revised version of 1997[4] was still addressing only limitations to extradition, without reference to *ne bis in idem*. Although much more succinct, its Principle 30 was close to the present version of the first paragraph of Principle 26, except for the last sentence concerning the obligation to prosecute in case of refusal to extradite. It introduced an important nuance to the exception regarding the death penalty, which was at the core of the original version (no extradition to countries where the extraditee could be subjected to the death penalty), by distinguishing between abolitionist and non-abolitionist countries.[5]

2 The new 2005 version of the Principles substantially enriched Principle 26. On the one hand, bars to extradition, according to the first paragraph of the Principle, have been extended to a series of 'gross violations' of human rights; on the other, a second paragraph has been added, on 'another significant development' in substantive law: 'the principle of non bis in idem,[6] which generally prohibits a second trial of defendants for the same offence'.[7]

3 Principle 26 is part of a section (Principles 22–30) dealing with *restrictions on rules of law* ('*certaines* règles de droit') justified by the combat against impunity. The systematics of the whole of the section, however, raise a difficult question of vocabulary. According to Principle 22, the objective of the Principles that follow is to combat 'abuse' of the rules; yet the refusal of 'abuses' (of law, of process) pertains to the core principles of any reasonable legal system, and the Principles would be unnecessary if all the situations addressed by the provisions were to be labelled as abusive. In reality, Principle 26 addresses a series of controversial issues, from the denial of extradition to countries enforcing the death penalty to the so-called 'shield trials', and, rather than (or in addition to) preventing abuses, tries to strike a balance between the fight against impunity and the enhancement of individual rights for persons facing trials, even for 'serious crimes under international law'.[8]

[2] *Report of the Special Rapporteur on the question of the impunity of perpetrators of violations of human rights (civil and political rights)*, UN Doc E/CN.4/Sub.2/1996/18 (29 June 1996) Principle 31.

[3] It shall anyhow been noted that former Principle 27 (in the present version, Principle 22), which covered the limitations to 'restrictive measures' deemed to favour impunity, targeted 'in particular' the institutions addressed in the following Principles (including Principle 31). *Ne bis in idem* could have thus been included in the list of 'restrictive measures', but at a high price regarding the principle of legality.

[4] See Set of Principles for the protection and promotion of human rights through action to combat impunity, UN Doc E/CN.4/Sub.2/1997/20/ Rev.1 (2 October 1997) Principle 30.

[5] See a comment on this point at para 24 of this commentary.

[6] The correct Latin expression is *ne bis in idem* (injunction not to retry for the same facts). The equivalent in Anglo-Saxon law (with some non-minor differences as to the content, which cannot be addressed here) is 'double jeopardy'.

[7] Special Rapporteur Diane Orentlicher, *Independent study on best practices, including recommendations, to assist states in strengthening their domestic capacity to combat all aspects of impunity*, UN Doc E/CN.4/2004/88 (27 February 2004) (hereinafter '*Independent study on best practices*') paras 36–37. See *Report of Diane Orentlicher, independent expert to update the Set of principles to combat impunity*, UN Doc E/CN.4/2005/102 (18 February 2005) 14; and *Report of Diane Orentlicher, independent expert to update the Set of principles to combat impunity—Updated Set of principles for the protection and promotion of human rights through action to combat impunity*, UN Doc E/CN.4/2005/102/Add. 1 (8 February 2005) (hereinafter '*Report of the independent expert*') 15.

[8] This notion is defined in the 'Definitions' section of the Updated Principles, UN Doc E/CN.4/2005/102/Add. 1, n 7, 6.

Principle 26 is divided into two paragraphs, which in appearance address two entirely separate topics: (a) obstacles to extradition; and (b) double jeopardy (*ne bis in idem*). Both place restrictions on the exercise of criminal jurisdiction, rather than prohibitions or interdictions on asserting jurisdiction.[9] They raise similar questions of principle,[10] and they may be interlinked, since one of the reasons not to extradite is the risk of double jeopardy.[11] 4

The drafting of Principle 26(a) is quite tortuous. First, the provision aims at *neutralizing* the two main *obstacles* to extradition: the political offence objection and the rule of non-extradition of nationals. Then in turn it provides support for the *non-extradition* of persons facing the death penalty or other infringements of fundamental rights. Lastly, an *aut dedere aut prosequi* clause[12] lays down an obligation for the state that denies extradition to 'submit the case to its competent authority'. 5

Principle 26(b) is less original in its structure, since it has been 'adapted' from the text of Article 20(3) of the Rome Statute.[13] It endorses two exceptions that are based on the same idea, namely, that the *ne bis* protection shall not be *abused*. The existence of two discrete exceptions may lead to misinterpretations, since the provision distinguishes between, on the one hand, shield or shame trials[14] and, on the other, 'partisan justice'.[15] Both amount to the same idea: *ne bis* shall apply only if the first trial has been led in good faith and with the purpose, already, to fight impunity. The additional conditions, in the second limb of Principle 26(b), referring to infringements of the guarantees of fair trial as an exception to the *ne bis in idem* rule, are misleading, since they create the impression that the second judge or jurisdiction would be the guarantor of the human rights of the accused vis-à-vis the state of the first judgment.[16] This is not the case.[17] 6

[9] See YQ Naqvi, *Impediments to Exercising Jurisdiction over International crimes* (Asser 2010) 9 et seq.

[10] See in particular paras 9 and 22 of this commentary.

[11] Cf R Maison, '*Ne bis in idem* et cooperation judiciare internationale' (2013) 117 *Revue générale de droit international public* 663–75, 672; *Independent study on best practices*, n 7, 14. See, eg, in treaty law, European Convention on Extradition (1957) CETS no 024, Art 9; Additional Protocol to the European Convention on Extradition (1975) CETS no 086, Art 2. Yet this very situation is not addressed by Principle 26.

[12] '*Aut dedere aut judicare/prosequi*' means that the requested state shall prosecute (*prosequi*) or try (*judicare*) the person it detains in the event that it does not grant extradition to the requesting state. The classical version was '*aut dedere aut judicare*' (or even '*aut dedere aut punire*' in more ancient versions—either you extradite or you punish). Many scholars have recently insisted on the necessity to respect constitutional or legal domestic provisions on the principle of prosecutorial discretion; therefore the most correct and contemporary version is '*aut dedere aut prosequi*'. See M Henzelin, *Le principe de l'universalité en droit pénal international* (Helbing/Bruylant 2000) 239.

[13] *Independent study on best practices*, n 7, fn 57 and para 45. The exception draws its origin from Art 4(2) of Protocol no 7 to the (European) Convention for the Protection of Human Rights and Fundamental Freedoms (22 November 1984), which provides for an exception to the *ne bis* principle (at a purely domestic level), 'if there has been a fundamental defect in the previous proceeding, which could affect the outcome of the case'. See also the American Convention on Human Rights, Art 8 § 4 of the Inter-American Convention, as summarized by Naqvi, n 9, at 316–317.

[14] For an elaborated definition, see para 16 of this commentary.

[15] C van den Wyngaert and T Ongena, '*Ne bis in idem* Principle, including the Issue of Amnesty' in A Cassese, P Gaeta, and J Jones (eds), *The Rome Statute of the International Criminal Court. A Commentary*, vol I (OUP 2002) 725.

[16] Ibid; and see I Tallgren and A Reisinger Coracini, 'Article 20' in O Triffterer (ed), *Commentary on the Rome Statute* (2nd edn, Nomos 2008) MN 13.

[17] See D Bernard, '*Ne bis in idem*—Protector of Defendants' Rights or Jurisdictional Pointsman?' (2011) 9 Journal of International Criminal Justice 863–80, 878, who observes, with a reference to the Preparatory Works of the International Law Commission (ILC), that the first procedure would at first sight have been considered as deficient only when the sentence had been too lenient.

C. Theoretical Framework

7 What does international law say about the principles enshrined in Principle 26? The answer is fairly clear for some of its components: *ne bis in idem* shall (still) not be considered as a general principle of international law,[18] so that at least exceptions such as the ones provided by Principle 26(b) are perfectly acceptable under international law; the rule of non-extradition of nationals has progressively lost support in many national laws;[19] as will be seen, refusal to extradite based on the risk of death penalty or of being ill-treated is now part of the core extradition case law of regional courts, as well as of national courts; it is generally accepted that the political offence objection to extradition requests should be repealed for the most serious crimes.[20]

8 The stakes are higher when it comes to the *aut dedere aut prosequi* rule (Principle 26(a) *in fine*). First, the status of this rule as part of customary international law is still disputed after the Decision of the International Court of Justice (ICJ) in *Belgium v Senegal*,[21] and the 2014 *Final Report* of the ILC[22] has been, to say the least, inconclusive on this issue. Secondly, and more importantly with respect to the very meaning of Principle 26 (a), under the condition that *aut dedere* is customary under international law, 'when the crime was allegedly committed abroad with no nexus to the forum State, the obligation to extradite or prosecute would *necessarily reflect* an exercise of universal jurisdiction'.[23] This would mean that respect for Principle 26(a) *in fine* would oblige states to anticipate the need for a jurisdictional basis and provide for universal jurisdiction based (only) on the application of *aut dedere*. This conclusion is still heavily discussed in the literature.[24]

9 The principle *ne bis in idem* and extradition law have experienced a series of *paradigm shifts* over the last decades. These evolutions are partially similar. Both domains have experienced a shift from a 'state-oriented' approach towards an 'individual-oriented approach'. Initially conceived for the benefit of states,[25] *ne bis in idem* has been more and more widely recognized as a right of the individual, as precisely illustrated by the norm borrowed by Principle 26(b) from the Rome Statute.[26] Lately, in the wake of the institution

[18] See already the assertive negative position of the Trial Chamber of the International Criminal Tribunal for the former Yugoslavia (ICTY) in *The Prosecutor v Duško Tadić*, Trial Chamber Decision on the Defence Motion on the Principle *Non-Bis-in-Idem*, IT-94-1-T (15 November 1995) para. 9; further the German Constitutional Court (31 March 1987), as quoted by C Safferling, *Towards an International Criminal Procedure* (OUP 2001) 324. Further Naqvi, n 9, 310–15.

[19] Cf Z Deen-Racsmany and R Blekxtoon, 'The Decline of the Nationality Exception in European Extradition?' (2005) 13 European Journal of Crime, Criminal Law and Criminal Justice 317–64.

[20] See G Gilbert, *Aspects of Extradition Law* (Nijhoff 1991)145; G Gilbert, *Responding to International Crime* (Nijhoff, 2006) 271.

[21] *Obligation to prosecute or extradite (Belgium v Senegal)* (Judgment) (ICJ, 20 July 2012).

[22] *Final Report of the International Law Commission on the obligation to extradite or prosecute (aut dedere aut judicare)*, 2014, in Report of the International Law Commission, Sixty-sixth Session, UN Doc A/69/10, ch VI para 65 notes 49–55. See also the comprehensive discussion in R Van Steenberghe, 'The Obligation to Extradite or Prosecute. Clarifying its Nature' (2011) 9 Journal of International Criminal Justice 1089–1116, who pleads at length for recognition of a rule under customary law.

[23] *Final Report of the ILC*, n 22, note 18 (emphasis added).

[24] Even the seminal book by MC Bassiouni and EM Wise, *Aut Dedere Aut Judicare: The Duty to Extradite or Prosecute in International Law* (Nijhoff 1995), who take a strong standing in favour of the customary character of *aut dedere*, is fairly cautious: 'It is harder to be sure that there currently exists a customary obligation imposed on all states ... to exercise "universal jurisdiction" whenever they possibly can.' One should, however, distinguish between a duty to *establish* universal jurisdiction and a duty to *exercise* it.

[25] I borrow this expression from M O'Boyle, '"Ne bis in idem" for the Benefit of States' in L Caflisch et al (eds), *Liber Amicorum Luzius Wildhaber* (Engel 2007) 329–46.

[26] Cf van den Wyngaert and Ongena, n 15, 708; Bernard, n 17, 878.

of the ICC, it has been aptly described as a '*structuring rule*' governing the prosecution of serious crimes.[27] For its part, extradition has long been exclusively an inter-state practice, judges and prosecutors acting only as 'executive agents' of the state. This has changed in recent times, in Europe in particular, with the elaboration of legal tools allowing for direct cooperation between magistrates.[28] This phenomenon has in turn increased the possibilities of invoking individual (human) rights in the processes, and has also opened up a (limited) possibility of bringing the grievances concerning infringements of these rights before the judge of the requested state. The extensive practice of human rights regional bodies illustrates this evolution.

D. Practice

I. Bars to extradition

Principle 26(a), second and third sentences impose on states an *extraterritorial responsibility* with respect to the prevention of torture and ill-treatment in line with current international law standards.[29] 10

Principle 26 *does not directly address* the argument under which the extraditee would have to face '*unfair justice*',[30] but limits itself to referring to bars to extradition based on the risk of the extraditee's being subject to the death penalty or major infringements of Article 7 of the International Covenant on Civil and Political Rights (ICCPR)[31] (Article 3 of the European Convention on Human Rights (ECHR)[32]). Still, the case law of the European Court of Human Rights (ECtHR) has demonstrated that a link exists between both arguments: in its *Othman* Decision of early 2012, the Court barred extradition on the ground that the applicant would be at risk[33] of a conviction based on declarations obtained under torture. It was thus a combination of the rejection of torture and the guarantees of a fair trial that led to the decision not to allow extradition. The protection against unfair justice is therefore not absent from Principle 26(a). The breach of the principles of a fair trial must yet be 'so fundamental as to amount *to a nullification, or destruction* of the very essence of (this right).'[34] 11

[27] Cf D Bernard, *Juger et juger encore les crimes internationaux. Etude du principe ne bis in idem* (Bruylant 2014) 8 et seq; Y Shany, *Regulating Jurisdictional Relations between national and international courts* (OUP 2007) 159; Maison, n 11, 669, who aptly speaks of a 'principe de distribution'.

[28] Cf the EU Mutual Assistance Convention in criminal matters between Member States [2000] OJ C197/1, 12 July 2000, especially Art 6.

[29] Human Rights Committee, General Comment no 20, Article 7 (Prohibition of torture, or other cruel, inhuman or degrading treatment or punishment), UN Doc HRI/GEN/1/Rev.9-Vol-1 (27 May 2008) 30, MN 9.

[30] Whereas the emergence of the protection against 'unfair justice' can be held as 'one of the main developments in extradition law during the past two decades', B Swart, 'Arrest and Surrender' in Cassese, Gaeta, and Jones (eds), n 15, vol II, 1652.

[31] International Covenant on Civil and Political Rights (1966) (16 December 1966) 999 UNTS 171.

[32] European Convention for the Protection of Human Rughts and Fundamental Freedoms (1950) (4 November 1950) ETS no 5.

[33] 'Only a real risk' (*Othman v United Kingdom* App no 8139/09 (Judgment) (ECtHR, 12 January 2012) para 273), which must be 'foreseeable and personal'; see also *Wong Ho Wing v Peru* (Judgment) IACtHR Series C no 297 (30 June 2015) paras 157 and 160 et seq, and para 163 on the specific obligations of the state party when confronted with allegations of real risks of torture: it 'must assess this possibility (the risk) *effectively*' (emphasis added).

[34] *Ahorugeze v Sweden* App no 37075/09 (Judgment) (ECtHR, 27 October 2011) para 115 (emphasis added). The ECtHR applies, in its own words, a 'flagrant denial of justice' test. See the cases quoted in this section.

12 When 'unfair justice' is at stake, the protection against serious mistreatment is indirect. Principle 26(a) also directly protects persons who would be in danger of being subjected to the death penalty (second sentence)[35] or other 'gross violations of human rights' (third sentence). There is little doubt about the 'absolute prohibition'[36] of torture, and consequently of any cooperation that would expose the extraditee to a 'real risk'[37] of being tortured. The same applies to the other gross violations of human rights, such as enforced disappearance or extrajudicial execution. The situation is far less clear and consistent when it comes to the death penalty and long-term imprisonment, qualified as a 'lesser form of ill-treatment'.[38] Here 'the absolute nature of Article 3 ECHR does not mean that any form of ill-treatment will act as a bar to removal from a Contracting State'.[39]

13 On the exposure to risk of being subjected to the death penalty, the ECtHR has taken the lead since its *Soering* judgment of 1989,[40] and the bar is now absolute.[41] Other human rights bodies are less assertive and consider the mode of inflicting the sentence rather than the sentence itself.[42]

14 On life imprisonment and long-term imprisonment, the ECtHR has developed over the last years quite an elaborated case law, in dialogue with national jurisdictions and other supreme courts. Even if ill-treatment may not be interpreted differently according to the contexts, supranational and foreign jurisdictions will apply self-restraint when asserting that extradition would result in violations of Article 7 ICCPR or Article 3 ECHR. Respect for foreign sovereignty and difficulties in evidencing such violations concur in this self-restricting attitude. Within this context, and having admitted that as a matter of principle a risk of being subjected to long-term or life imprisonment is not deemed sufficient to bar extradition, the ECtHR adopts a two-step approach of exceptional cases, shared with other jurisdictions. First it applies a '*gross disproportionality test*', which will be met only on 'rare and unique occasions'.[43] In the event that the test is not met, the applicant must prove '(i) that his or her continued imprisonment can no longer be justified on any legitimate penological grounds; and (ii) that the sentence is irreducible de facto and de iure'.[44] The methodological difficulty, which concurs with the sovereignty issue in imposing self-restraint, is that the Court must anticipate either the severity of the sentence—so that it would be disproportionate vis-à-vis '*any of the other types* [or long-term] of life [or long-term] sentence'[45]—or the concrete treatment imposed on the extraditee. Therefore ill-treatment may only be anticipated in special cases—such as a long period of detention, which would be incompatible with the mental health condition of the prisoner.[46] With respect to all these constraints and the dense case law of

[35] In this case, 'especially abolitionist countries' are concerned. On this odd double standard approach, see paras 23–24 of this commentary.

[36] *Trabelsi v Belgium*, App no 140/10 (Judgment) (ECtHR, 7 October 2014) paras 116–20.

[37] Cf *mutatis mutandis*, *Othman*, n 33, para 273.

[38] *Harkins and Edwards v UK* App nos 9146/07 and 3326507 (Judgment) (ECtHR, 17 January 2012) quoting in para 37 the House of Lords (and endorsing its approach) on this very sensitive issue.

[39] Ibid, para 129.

[40] ECtHR, *Soering v United Kingdom* (1989) Series A no 161.

[41] *Al Saadoon and Mufdih v United Kingdom* App no 61498/08 (Judgment) (ECtHR, 2 March 2010) paras 115 et seq.

[42] For instance, *AS v Sweden*, Communication no 149/1999 (2000), CAT/C/25/D/149/1999.

[43] *Harkins and Edwards*, n 38, para 133, quoting the Supreme Court of Canada in *R v Latimer* [2001] 1 SCR 3. The gradation between rare and unique escapes this author's understanding. The Court adds that this test would be met only in 'very exceptional cases', see *Harkins and Edwards*, n 38, para 134.

[44] *Harkins and Edwards*, n 38, para 138.

[45] Ibid (original emphasis).

[46] *Aswat v United Kingdom* App no 17299/12 (Judgment) (ECtHR, 16 April 2013) paras 48 et seq.

these last years, the protection provided by the third sentence of Principle 26(a) is a *fairly narrow* one.[47]

II. Limitations to *ne bis in idem*

At the international level, the principles drawn from the Rome Statute and incorporated into Principle 26(b) have thus far not given rise to much case law. There has hardly been more national case law, in the countries which have adopted similar provisions.[48] 15

The exception to the application of the *ne bis in idem* principle based on the fact that the previous proceedings had the purpose to shield the person concerned ('*shield or sham trials*') directly refers to Article 17(2)(a) of the Rome Statute, which allows the ICC to hold a case admissible even when proceedings take place in a state which has jurisdiction, when these proceedings 'were or are being undertaken … for the purpose of shielding the person concerned from criminal responsibility for crimes within the jurisdiction of the Court'. This provision has been interpreted fairly broadly by the Court, for instance when Kenya challenged its jurisdiction on this basis.[49] As demonstrated by the majority of the Court and the dissenting judge, respect for the sovereignty of the state is the major issue here.[50] 16

This has also been recognized by national courts when they have had to apply similar provisions. In the terms of the Spanish Constitutional Court, 'basing [a] decision on either real or apparent inactivity on the part of the courts of another sovereign State implies judgment by one sovereign State on the judicial capacity of similar judicial bodies in another sovereign State'.[51] As rightly pointed out by the minority in the same Spanish decision, this involves 'proving something that is practically impossible, and determining the necessity of an extremely sensitive evaluation at an early procedural stage'.[52] This assessment is far easier to make for a court within the same jurisdictional system, as demonstrated by a decision of the Constitutional Court of Colombia, holding the state in breach of its obligations after an acquittal based on an 'ineffective' investigation.[53] 17

The 'restrictions' relating to amnesty are extensively dealt with by Principle 24.[54] It is nonetheless worth mentioning here the effect on the *ne bis* principle of the 'growing tendency in international law to see such amnesties as unacceptable because they are incompatible with the unanimously recognised obligation of States to prosecute and punish grave breaches of fundamental human rights'[55]: in the words of the IACtHR, 'a judgment 18

[47] Cf the critics in (2012) 18 EHRLR 466 to another landmark judgment of the ECtHR, *Babar Ahmad v United Kingdom* App nos 24027/07 and others (Judgment) (ECtHR, 10 April 2012).

[48] See, eg, Canadian law as summarized by Naqvi, n 9, 316; or Art 7, s 4 of the Swiss Criminal Code <www.admin.ch/opc/en/classified-compilation/19370083/201501010000/311.0.pdf> accessed 10 August 2015.

[49] *The Prosecutor v William Samoei Ruto and others*, Appeals Chamber Judgment on the appeal of the republic of Kenya against the decision of Pre-Trial Chamber II of 30 May 2011 (ICC, 30 August 2011).

[50] See the Dissenting Opinion of Judge Anita Usacka, 20 September 2011, paras 28 et seq., where the dissenting judge blamed the Trial Chamber, and thus the Appeals Chamber which had upheld the Trial Chamber's decision, because it 'did not give sufficient weight to the sovereign rights of Kenya'.

[51] Spanish Supreme Court Decision concerning the Guatemala Genocide Case, 25 February 2003, (2003) 42 ILM 683.

[52] Ibid.

[53] Quoted from Naqvi, n 9, 316. Unlike other important decisions, this one is not translated on the precious English website of the Constitutional Court of Colombia <english.corteconstitucional.gov.co/>; it may be found in Spanish in the database of the International Committee of the Red Cross <www.icrc.org/applic/ihl/ihl-nat.nsf/caseLaw.xsp> accessed 4 August 2015.

[54] See the commentary to Principle 24 in this volume.

[55] *Margus v Croatia* App no 4455/10 (Judgment) (ECtHR, Grand Chamber, 27 May 2014) para 139.

rendered in the foregoing circumstances [following an amnesty] produces an "apparent" or "fraudulent" *res judicata* case'.[56] Even if the words are not exactly the same, the approximation with the exception to the *ne bis* principle as provided by Article 4(2) of Protocol 7 to the ECHR,[57] ancestor to our Principle 26, is striking.[58]

19 The exception to the *ne bis in idem* principle based on the unfairness of the first proceedings ('due process clause') raises the same sort of problems relating to infringements of sovereignty and difficulty in assessing the quality of a foreign proceeding.[59] The paradox of denying human rights protection to somebody who has presumably been already convicted, and has perhaps served his or her sentence, after a flawed trial has already been identified.[60]

20 Upon the revision of the Joinet Principles, the provision on *in absentia* proceedings (successively Principles 32, 31, and 28 in the first versions)[61] has been removed, probably for the purpose of ensuring that the Principles 'are readily adapted to diverse legal systems'.[62] Since the spirit of the said provision has not been abandoned,[63] the possibility for states not to recognize *in absentia* judgments, which have been one of the major sources of inter-state tensions in the field of cooperation in criminal matters,[64] must

[56] *Almancid-Arellano v Chile* (Judgment), IACtHR Series C no 154 (26 September 2006) para 154. See also *La Cantuta v Peru* (Judgment), IACtHR Series C no 162 (29 November 2006) para 153: 'A judgment issued in the circumstances described above only provides "fictitious" or "fraudulent" grounds for double jeopardy.'

[57] Whereas the wording of Art 8(4) ACHR does not provide exceptions to the *ne bis in idem* principle, the case law of the IACtHR has stated that 'it is not an absolute right, and therefore, is not applicable where: i) the intervention of the court that heard the case and decided to dismiss it or to acquit a person responsible for violating human rights or international law, was intended to shield the accused party from criminal responsibility; ii) the proceedings were not conducted independently or impartially in accordance with due procedural guarantees; or iii) there was no real intent to bring those responsible to justice' (*Almancid-Arellano v Chile*, n 56, para 154).

[58] See also *Margus v Croatia*, n 55, where the Grand Chamber of the ECtHR does not yet base its decision to ignore the amnesty granted at the time by the Croatian authorities directly on Art 4(2) of Protocol 7 but on more technical arguments, about the quality of the decision based on this amnesty (and supposedly barring a fresh prosecution for the same facts).

[59] Normally, and except for radical regime changes, it should not apply in the same state. See Naqvi, n 9, 317 et seq, who develops the example of Cambodia, where the Extraordinary Chambers in the Court of Cambodia did not apply the *ne bis* protection to Ieng Sary, who had been previously tried and convicted for genocide in a trial *in absentia* in 1979.

[60] See para 7 of this commentary.

[61] In the revised final report prepared by Mr Joinet pursuant to Sub Commission decision 1996/119 (2 October 1997), Principle 28 reads: 'In order to avoid establishing a guarantee of impunity, non-recognition of *in absentia* procedure by a legal system should be limited to the judgment stage, so that the necessary investigations, including the hearing of witnesses and victims, may be carried out and charges may be preferred, followed by wanted notices and arrest warrants, if necessary international, executed according to the procedures laid down in the Constitution of the International Criminal Police Organization (ICPO—Interpol).' Cf UN Doc E/CN.4/Sub.2/1997/20/Rev.1.

[62] *Report of the independent expert*, n 7, para 10: 'The last change in no way implies, however, that States may abuse the absence of in absentia procedures in their own legal systems in ways that foster or contribute to impunity.'

[63] Ibid, para 46.

[64] For instance, Art 3 of the 1978 Second Protocol to the European Convention on Extradition (n 11) leaves it open for the requested state to refuse to extradite in order to allow for the enforcement of an *in absentia* sentence. An exception to the exception is provided, however, 'if the requesting Party gives an assurance considered sufficient to guarantee to the person claimed the right to a retrial which safeguards the rights of defence'. In this case, however, the requesting state will have the choice between enforcing the judgment or, if the extraditee makes an opposition, 'to take proceedings against him or her'. The question of recognition of *in absentia* sentences is particularly sensitive within the European Union, see the Council Framework Decision 2009/299/JHA of 26 February 2009, fostering the application of mutual recognition to decisions rendered in the absence of the person concerned at the trial [2009]OJ L 81/24, 27 March 2009.

be limited. The 'due process clause' shall not be abused. In line with the present text of Principle 26(b), there is yet still room for a refusal to give a *ne bis* effect to decisions which have infringed the minimal standards set up by the international courts of human rights.[65] The issues are very similar to those previously discussed[66] concerning shield or shame trials (sovereignty, different conceptions of justice).

E. Critical Assessment

Part of the content of Principle 26 may surprise in its context: the drafters of the Principle have reaffirmed and reinforced impediments to the exercise of (adjudicatory) jurisdiction over international crimes, and therefore the fight against impunity may seem weakened rather than strengthened. Addressing this criticism in general terms, Naqvi submits that the assertion that impediments to the exercise of (adjudicatory) jurisdiction over international crimes are contributing or would contribute to the culture of impunity is '*incomplete, inaccurate and simplistic*'.[67] A call for just 'more repression, more prosecution' would indeed be far too mechanical. Leaving aside the cases where prosecution may not be desirable, which are not directly addressed by Principle 26, the reminder of some essential procedural guarantees of the accused displays a respectable desire to pinpoint the fight against impunity in the broader context of enhancing *all the aspects* of the promotion of human rights. 21

The developments discussed have also reminded us of the importance of sovereignty issues in this debate. International and supranational courts exercise self-restraint when it comes to concretely promoting human rights, by denying extradition to a country whose criminal system is not stainless or refusing to recognize a judgment issued in disputable conditions. In both cases the fight against impunity may be slowed down, if not stopped. 22

The controversy between British superior court judges and the ECtHR regarding the limits of judicial intervention in the processes of extradition, based on human rights concerns such as those discussed, has revealed an important aspect of the backdrop of Principle 26: it is admissible to *balance the interests* between extradition on the one hand and alleged violations of human rights on the other hand. The majority of the House of Lords, in one of the cases where the superior court expressed some defiance towards the too 'interventionist' case law of the ECtHR, found that 'the desirability of extradition is a factor to be taken into account in deciding whether the punishment likely to be imposed in the receiving state attains the "minimum level of severity" which would make it inhuman and degrading'.[68] This *functionalist approach* to extradition[69] has been rejected by the ECtHR, which considered that the opportunity to extradite—based on 'the concepts of risk and dangerousness'—and the risk of ill-treatment of the would-be extraditee were 'notions that [could] only be assessed independently of each other'.[70] This issue is fundamental for the future of criminal justice, and especially of cooperation in 23

[65] See, even if the argument was non *ne bis in idem* but the enforcement of a foreign (and allegedly flawed) foreign sentence, *Krombach v France* App no 29731/96 (Judgment) (ECtHR, 13 February 2001) at paras 82–91.

[66] See paras 16–17. [67] Naqvi, n 9, 367 et seq.

[68] Quoted in *Harkins and Edwards*, n 38, para 38.

[69] The judges concerned themselves spoke of a 'relativist approach to the scope of Article 3', which they considered 'essential' in order to allow extradition to 'continue its function': ibid.

[70] Ibid, para 139.

criminal matters, but also for the weight that considerations of human rights will have in the debate on the fight against impunity.

24 This fight shall be universal. In this respect the words 'especially by abolitionist countries', in the second sentence of Principle 26(a), is worrisome. It is certainly unrealistic to advise countries that practise the death penalty—some of them on a very broad scale—not to extradite accused people to other non-abolitionist countries.[71] Yet, in the context of fairness through promotion of human rights for *all* protagonists—including the major offenders—and the fight against impunity, this two-tier provision looks inappropriate.

Bibliography

Bernard, D, 'Ne bis in idem—Protector of Defendants' Rights or Jurisdictional Pointsman?' (2011) 9 Journal of International Criminal Justice 863–80.

Cassese, A, *International Criminal Law* (3rd edn, OUP 2013) ch 17.

Dugard, J and Van den Wyngaert, C, 'Reconciling Extradition with Human Rights' (1988) 92 American Journal of International Law 187–212.

Naqvi, YQ, I*mpediments to Exercising Jurisdiction over International crimes* (Asser 2010).

Shany, Y, *Regulating Jurisdictional Relations between National and International Courts* (OUP 2007).

[71] Even if this was the case in the original version of the Joinet Principles, cf n 2.

Principle 27. Restrictions on Justifications Related to Due Obedience, Superior Responsibility, and Official Status

Max du Plessis

(a) The fact that the perpetrator of violations acted on the orders of his or her Government or of a superior does not exempt him or her from responsibility, in particular criminal, but may be regarded as grounds for reducing the sentence, in conformity with principles of justice;
(b) The fact that violations have been committed by a subordinate does not exempt that subordinate's superiors from responsibility, in particular criminal, if they knew or had at the time reason to know that the subordinate was committing or about to commit such a crime and they did not take all the necessary measures within their power to prevent or punish the crime;
(c) The official status of the perpetrator of a crime under international law—even if acting as head of State or Government—does not exempt him or her from criminal or other responsibility and is not grounds for a reduction of sentence.

A. Summary of Findings

I. Due obedience (superior orders)

The order to commit an international crime does not, in principle, absolve the accused of criminal responsibility. A perpetrator will be presumed to know that orders to commit genocide, crimes against humanity, or war crimes are manifestly illegal. While it remains unclear whether it is conceivable under customary international law for an order to commit an international crime not to be manifestly illegal, it remains theoretically possible, particularly for war crimes, for a perpetrator to show—as a species of mistake of law—that he or she did not appreciate the manifest illegality of the order.

II. Superior responsibility

Under the doctrine of superior responsibility, political and military leaders can be held criminally responsible for international crimes committed by their subordinates. The superior's responsibility arises from his or her dereliction of duty to prevent or punish crimes committed by subordinates. It is a liability separate from the superior's responsibility for his or her direct participation in the commission of the crime, either as a perpetrator or as an accomplice. In practice, the doctrine is increasingly limited to holding military commanders responsible for a failure of their supervisory duty in typical military contexts, and regarded as less appropriate for dealing with political or military leaders who are more remote from, and do not have direct participation in, international crimes.

III. Official status

The current state of international law regarding the availability of international immunities in respect to international crimes may be summarized as follows: immunity *ratione materiae* (or functional immunity) does not apply to criminal prosecutions, regardless of the forum (ie international or domestic). Immunity *ratione personae* (or personal immunity) does not apply before international criminal tribunals but does apply before domestic courts, unless there is a waiver from the state which the officeholder represents.

B. Contextual and Historical Introduction

I. Due obedience (superior orders)

1 The defence of due obedience (or superior orders) is born of military tradition. The defence is premised on the notion that orders must be obeyed, which has long been considered necessary to ensure an orderly and effective military force[1] and recognizes that subordinates often have little or no discretion to refuse to abide by orders of superiors.

2 In the present context, the question is whether subordinates may avail themselves of this defence when they have committed a 'serious crime' under international law pursuant to a superior's orders, and which oftentimes is lawful from the point of view of the domestic legal order, such as the Führer's orders during the Third Reich.[2]

3 There is some debate as to the extent to which an accused might rely on the defence as a ground for excluding responsibility for the commission of an international crime. That difference of opinion is reflected at the international level: at Nuremberg[3] and the International Military Tribunal for the Far East (Tokyo Tribunal),[4] and today before the ad hoc International Criminal Tribunal for the former Yugoslavia (ICTY) and the International Criminal Tribunal for Rwanda (ITCR),[5] the Special Court for Sierra Leone (SCSL), and the East Timor Special Panels,[6] a claim to have been following superior orders was/is not an available defence, although it may be considered in mitigation of punishment.[7] However, the Statute of the International Criminal Court (ICC) allows for the defence, although it is available only in respect of war crimes and the recently adopted

[1] See Y Dinstein, *The Defence of 'obedience to superior orders' in International Law* (OUP 2012).

[2] Nuremberg Trial, *Closing Speech for the Defence (by Jahrreis), International Military Tribunal*, vol 17, 491, quoted ibid, 141 <http://avalon.law.yale.edu/imt/07-26-46.asp> accessed 30 November 2017.

[3] Art 8 of the Charter of the International Military Tribunal reads, 'the fact that the defendant acted pursuant to an order of his government or of a superior shall not free him from responsibility, but may be considered in mitigation of punishment if the Tribunal determines that justice so requires'.

[4] Art 6 of the International Military Tribunal for the Far East Charter Special proclamation by the Supreme Commander for the Allied Powers at Tokyo, 19 January 1946; charter dated 19 January 1946, reads, 'Neither the official position, at any time, of an accused, nor the fact that an accused acted pursuant to order of his government or of a superior shall, of itself, be sufficient to free such accused from responsibility for any crime with which he is charged, but such circumstances may be considered in mitigation of punishment if the Tribunal determines that justice so requires.'

[5] Art 7(4) of the Statute of the International Tribunal for the Prosecution of Persons Responsible for Serious Violations of International Humanitarian Law Committed in the Territory of the Former Yugoslavia since 1991, UN Doc S/25704, annex (1993) and S/25704/Add.1 (1993), adopted by Security Council on 25 May 1993; UN Doc S/RES/827 (1993) and Art 6(4) of the Statute of the International Criminal Tribunal for the Prosecution of Persons Responsible for Genocide and Other Serious Violations of International Humanitarian Law Committed in the Territory of Rwanda and Rwandan Citizens Responsible for Genocide, Security Council resolution 955 (1994), 8 November 1994, S/RES/955 (1994).

[6] Art 6(4) of the Statute of the Special Court for Sierra Leone and United Nations Transitional Administration in East Timor, Section 21 of Regulation 2000/15, UN Doc UNTAET/REG/2000/15 (6 June 2000).

[7] See A Zahar, 'Superior Orders' in A Cassese (ed), *The Oxford Companion to International Criminal Justice* (OUP 2009) 525–27, 525.

crime of aggression, and only to an accused who can show, inter alia, that the order was not manifestly unlawful.[8]

II. Superior responsibility

The doctrine of command responsibility (or superior criminal responsibility) is a creation of international criminal law and has no equivalent application in national legal systems.[9] Under the doctrine the superior is criminally liable for the failure to prevent or punish the crimes committed by the subordinates, as distinct from the responsibility arising from ordering or instigating the principal crime, or aiding or abetting it.[10] 4

Neither the Nuremberg nor the Tokyo Charters referred to this doctrine, which was subsequently developed by military courts in the aftermath of the Second World War to hold military commanders criminally liable. The decision of the US Supreme Court in 1946 in *Yamashita*[11] is regarded as the modern birth of the doctrine of command responsibility,[12] in which the Supreme Court enounced the principles that commanders have a clear responsibility to control subordinates and to ensure that they respected international humanitarian law, and that a failure by the commander to do so is itself a violation of international humanitarian law. 5

The principle of command responsibility was subsequently enshrined in Articles 7(3) and 6(3) of the Statutes of the ICTY and ICTR, Article 28 of the ICC Statute,[13] Article 87 of Additional Protocol I to the Geneva Conventions[14] and Article 3(2) of the Statute of the Special Tribunal for Lebanon.[15] 6

III. Official status

Immunities have long been considered a legitimate and necessary feature of international law. As Cryer et al note,[16] the law of immunities has its ancient roots in, and is a corollary to, the fundamental idea of sovereignty and equality of states. Immunity, as an exemption from judicial interference, is linked to the customary rule of state immunity, which itself is linked to the idea of the sovereign equality of states. 7

[8] Art 33(1) of the Rome Statute of the International Criminal Court A/CONF.183/9 of 17 July 1998—the accused must show additionally that he was under a lawful obligation to obey orders of the government or the superior in question, and that he did not know that the order was unlawful. Art 33(2) of the Statute provides that orders to commit genocide or crimes against humanity are manifestly unlawful.

[9] See G Werle, *Principles of International Criminal Law* (TMC Asser Press 2005) 128.

[10] There are similarities between the modes of liability of instigation and aiding and abetting and that of superior responsibility, in that both are derivative of principal crimes committed by direct perpetrators. The difference between the two, however, is that in order for an accused to be convicted of aiding and abetting, there must be some specific contribution to the crime on the part of the accused, whereas superior criminal responsibility is characterized by the mere omission to prevent or punish crimes committed others.

[11] *In Re Yamashita*, no 61, Misc Supreme Court of the United States, 327 US 1; 66 S Ct 340; 90 L Ed 499; 1946 US LEXIS 3090.

[12] G Mettraux, *The Law of Command Responsibility* (OUP 2009).

[13] See Werle, n 9, 128. The nature and elements of superior responsibility are now regarded as well established under customary international law; see *The Prosecutor v Delalić et al* ('*Celebici*') (Trial Chamber Judgment) ICTY-96-21-T (16 November 1998) para 333.

[14] Protocol Additional to the Geneva Conventions of 12 August 1949, and relating to the Protection of Victims of International Armed Conflicts (Protocol I) (8 June 1977).

[15] Statute of the Special Tribunal for Lebanon S/RES/1757 (2007) (30 May 2007).

[16] R Cryer et al, *An Introduction to International Criminal Law and Procedure* (CUP 2010) 531.

8 Historically, the law of immunities developed in order to maintain channels of communication, and thereby prevent and resolve conflicts. Societies needed to have confidence that their envoys could have safe passage, particularly in times when emotions and distrust were at their highest, ensuring the smooth conduct of international relations necessary for the maintenance of a system of peaceful cooperation and coexistence among states. Domestic and international law developed to provide both inviolability for the person and premises of a foreign state's representatives, and immunities from the exercise of jurisdiction over state representatives.

C. Theoretical Framework

I. Due obedience (superior orders)

9 Principle 27(a)'s exclusion of an accused who committed a 'serious crime' under international law is an expression of the presumption that an order to commit 'serious crimes under international law' is always manifestly illegal.[17] For this reason, the ICC Statute presumes that the illegality of orders to commit genocide and crimes against humanity will be (or will be regarded as being) obvious to the subordinate.[18]

10 The relationship between the defence of superior orders and the defences of duress and mistake of fact should also be noted. If a soldier commits an international crime (eg bombing a hospital) by virtue of following an order whose factual underpinnings are wrong (to bomb an arms cache at coordinates that turn out to be those of a hospital) then the soldier has followed a manifestly illegal order, but his defence will be that he had no *mens rea* to commit the crime because of a mistake of fact. Similarly, duress may override the defence of superior orders.

11 As Judge Cassese pointed out in *Erdemović*:

> Superior orders may be issued without being accompanied by threats to life or limb. In these circumstances, if the superior order is manifestly illegal under international law, the subordinate is under a duty to refuse to obey the order. If following such a refusal, the order is reiterated under a threat of life or limb, then the defence of duress may be raised, and superior orders lose any legal relevance.[19]

In the *Einsatzgruppen* case, a plea of duress succeeded, even in case of unlawful killings, as the threat was imminent, real, and inevitable.[20]

12 Lastly, it must be recalled that even if the defence of due obedience is not available to an accused, principle 27(a) affirms the customary international law position that obeying an order to commit an international crime may nevertheless be taken into account in mitigation of punishment, if the court determines that justice so requires.[21]

[17] See, on the absolute liability principle, or the manifest illegality principle, Werle, n 9, 155.

[18] Recalling that Art 33(2) of the ICC Statute provides that orders to commit genocide or crimes against humanity are manifestly unlawful.

[19] *Prosecutor v Erdemović* (Appeals Chamber) (Judgment) ICTY IT-96-22-A (7 October 1997) Separate and Dissenting Opinion of Judge Cassese, para 15.

[20] *United States of America vs Otto Ohlendorf, et al* ('*Einsatzgruppen*' case) in *Trials of War Criminals before the Nuernberg Military Tribunals under Control Council Law No 10*, vol IV (US Govt Printing Office, Washington DC 1950) 471 and 480–81: '[I]t is stated that in military law even if the subordinate realises that the act he is called upon to perform is a crime, he may not refuse its execution without incurring serious consequences, and that this, therefore, constitutes duress.'

[21] See further J-M Henckaerts and L Doswald-Beck, *Customary International Humanitarian Law*, vol I: *Rules* (ICRC 2009) 567.

Under customary international law, the fact that a person is acting under orders does not absolve that person from liability for committing international crimes. As the Nuremberg Tribunal explained, 'That a soldier was ordered to kill or torture in violation of the international law of war has never been recognized as a defence to such acts of brutality, though . . . the order may be urged in mitigation of punishment'.[22] 13

Accordingly, the position is that if the superior order is manifestly illegal, obedience thereto is not due. On the contrary—as President Cassese held in *Erdemović*—'if the superior order is manifestly illegal under international law, the subordinate is under a duty to refuse to obey the order'.[23] The statement by President Cassese highlights abiding difficulties in the application of the principle[24]—one of which is whether the order to commit an international crime is always manifestly illegal, given the severity of these crimes. 14

II. Superior responsibility

The doctrine exists to hold superiors—of both military and civilian status[25] —accountable for international crimes committed by their subordinates. 15

It is generally accepted that three elements must exist for such responsibility to arise:[26] (i) there existed a superior–subordinate relationship between the accused and the principal perpetrator(s) (*superior–subordinate relationship*); (ii) the accused, as a superior, knew or had reasons to know that the subordinate was about to commit such crimes or had done so (*actual or constructive knowledge*); and (iii) the accused failed to take necessary and reasonable measures to prevent such crimes or punish the perpetrator(s) (*failure to prevent or punish*). 16

i. Superior–subordinate relationship

Traditionally, the superior–subordinate relationship was narrowly defined as a *de jure* military relationship. However, a number of recent instruments have interpreted the doctrine more broadly to include not only 'military commanders within its scope of liability, but also political leaders and other civilian superiors in possession of authority'.[27] Superior authority exists where the superior has effective control over the subordinate, manifested in the superior's 'material ability to prevent and punish commission of the offences'.[28] 17

[22] *Judgment of the Nuremberg International Military Tribunal 1946* (1947) 41 AJIL 172, 221.

[23] *Prosecutor v Erdemović*, Separate and Dissenting Opinion of Judge Cassese, n 19, para 15.

[24] It has been noted, however, that this rejection of the superior defence was a 'novelty and went far beyond the existing international law at the time'. See K Ambos, *Treatise on International Criminal Law*, vol 1 (OUP 2013) 378.

[25] Hence the idea of 'superior' responsibility is preferable to the original conception of 'command' responsibility—and Art 28 of the ICC Statute accordingly speaks of the 'Responsibility of Commanders and Others Superiors'.

[26] *Prosecutor v Orić* (Trial Chamber Judgment) ICTY-03-68 (30 June 2006) para 29F4. See further C Gevers and M du Plessis, 'Prosecutor v Oric' in A Klip and G Sluiter (eds), *Annotated Leading Cases of International Criminal Tribunals, The International Criminal Tribunal for the Former Yugoslavia 2003–2004*, vol 19 (Intersentia 2010).

[27] See *Prosecutor v Orić*, n 26, para 308. The Tribunal further held (ibid, para 310): '[R]egardless of which chain of command or position of authority the superior subordinate relationship may be based, it is immaterial whether the subordination of the perpetrator to the accused as superior is direct or indirect, and formal or factual. In the same vein, the mere ad hoc or temporary nature of a military unit or an armed group does not per se exclude a relationship of subordination between the member of the unit or group and its commander or leader.'

[28] *Prosecutor v Mucić et al* (Trial Chamber Judgment) ICTY-96-21 (16 November 1998) para 378; and *Prosecutor v Mucić et al* (Appeals Chamber Judgment) ICTY-96-21 (20 February 2001).

ii. Actual or constructive knowledge

18 There are two types of mens rea for superior responsibility: actual knowledge and imputed knowledge. The first requires proof of actual knowledge, and can be proved by way of either direct or circumstantial evidence.[29] The second 'requires proof only of some grounds which would have enabled the superior to become aware of the relevant crimes of his or her subordinates'.[30] Knowledge will be imputed where the superior had information 'which would have put him on notice of offences committed by subordinates';[31] and 'as soon as the superior has been put on notice of the risk of illegal acts by subordinates, he or she is expected to stay vigilant and to inquire about additional information, rather than doing nothing or remaining "wilfully blind" '.[32]

iii. Failure to prevent or punish

19 The failure to prevent the commission of crimes by subordinates and the failure to punish subordinates who have already committed crimes are two distinct duties, and in respect of which the superior's liability arises separately. In both cases, the superior's obligation is limited to those measures that are necessary and reasonable in the circumstances.

a. The duty to prevent

20 The duty to prevent requires necessary and reasonable measures to prevent crimes being committed to be taken by a superior.[33]

b. The duty to punish

21 Once the crime has been committed by the subordinate, it is no longer possible to prevent its commission. A superior must nevertheless take necessary and reasonable measures to punish such crimes or be liable under superior responsibility. The ICTY has held that in order to be found to have failed in his or her duty to punish a crime by subordinates, it must be shown that the superior had 'effective control of the relevant subordinate at the time when measures of investigation and punishment are to be taken against them'.[34]

III. Official status

22 Immunities are divided into functional immunity (immunity *ratione materiae*) and personal immunity (immunity *ratione personae*).

23 Immunity *ratione materiae* relates to *conduct* carried out on behalf of a state. This form of immunity is based on the notion that 'a State may not sit in judgment on the policies and actions of another State, since they are both sovereign and equal'.[35] For this reason,

[29] This circumstantial evidence includes the type and scope of illegal acts, the time during which they took place, the number of troops involved, the geographic location of the acts, whether they were widespread, and so on and so forth.

[30] *Prosecutor v Orić*, n 26, para 317.

[31] *Prosecutor v Mucić et al* (Appeals Chamber Judgment), n 28, paras 238 and 241.

[32] *Prosecutor v Orić*, n 26, para 322.

[33] See, eg, ICC Statute, Art 28(a)(ii), (b); and *Prosecutor v Kamuhanda* (Trial Chamber Judgment) ICTR-99-54A (22 January 2004) para 601.

[34] *Prosecutor v Orić*, n 26, 335.

[35] Cryer et al, n 16, 422. The ICTY Appeals Chamber explained the rationale for functional immunity as follows: 'State officials acting in their official capacity ... are mere instruments of a State and their official actions can only be attributed to the State. They cannot be the subject of sanctions and penalties for conduct that is

functional immunity does not attach to *all conduct* performed by state officials, but only to conduct carried out in a state official's official capacity.

24 Immunity *ratione personae* 'provides complete immunity of the person of certain officeholders while they carry out important representative functions'.[36] In contrast to functional immunity, personal immunity is absolute (ie it covers both private and public acts committed by officials) but temporary (ie it only applies in so far as the person holds the office in question), and it can be waived by the state the office holder represents.

25 These two types of immunities seek to achieve different objectives, even if the distinction is a fine one: in respect of immunity *ratione material* the motivation is to protect official acts and sovereign equality; in respect of immunity *ratione personae* the motivation is to facilitate international relations.

26 That said, the rise of international criminal law has produced a competing good: prosecuting those most responsible for international crimes. As a result, there is a tension between these two imperatives; and although there is some movement towards resolving this tension in favour of combating impunity, immunities continue to be an absolute (if temporary) bar to prosecution in certain instances[37]—including, for instance, arguments advanced against immunity based on the concept of *ius cogens*.[38]

D. Practice

I. Due obedience (superior orders)

27 This Principle has meant that obeying orders has not been accepted as a defence, to any of the international crimes charged, in the practice of the international Tribunals,[39] nor before the Nuremberg Tribunal.[40]

not private but undertaken on behalf of a State. In other words, State officials cannot suffer the consequences of wrongful acts which are not attributable to them personally but to the State on whose behalf they act: they enjoy so-called "functional immunity".' *Prosecutor v Blaskić* (Appeals Chamber Judgment on the request of the Republic of Croatia for review of the Decision of Trial Chamber II of 18 July 1997) ICTY-95-14 (29 October 1997) para 38. Akande adds to this that 'the immunity of state officials in foreign courts prevents circumvention of the immunity of the state through proceedings brought against those acting on behalf of the state. In this sense, this immunity operates as a jurisdictional or procedural bar and prevents courts from indirectly exercising control over acts of the foreign state through proceedings against the official who carried out the act': D Akande, 'International Law Immunities and the International Criminal Court' (2004) 98(3) AJIL, 409–15, 413. See further the study on the topic by the International Law Commission: Kolodkin, *Second Report on immunity of State officials from foreign criminal jurisdiction*, UN Doc A/CN.4/631 (3 May–4 June and 5 July–6 August 2010) 56. See also *Report on the work of the sixty-third session of the International Law Commission* 2011, UN Doc A/66/10 (26 April–3 June and 4 July–12 August 2011) ch VII.

[36] Cryer et al, n 16, 422.

[37] *Jurisdictional Immunities of the State (Germany v Italy: Greece Intervening)*, (Judgment) [2012] ICJ Rep 139. For further discussion, see S Talmon '*Jus Cogens* after *Germany* v *Italy*: Substantive and Procedural Rules Distinguished' (2012) 25 Leiden Journal of International Law 979–1002, 979.

[38] In *Jurisdictional Immunities of the State (Germany v Italy: Greece Intervening)*, n 37, the International Court of Justice (ICJ) held that rules of *jus cogens* did not automatically displace the hierarchically lower rules of state immunity as, it reasoned, there was no conflict between these rules, the former being substantive rules while the latter were procedural in character.

[39] See, generally, Dinstein n 1.

[40] The Nuremberg Tribunal stated, 'Superior Orders, even to a soldier, cannot be considered in mitigation where crimes as shocking and extensive have been committed consciously, ruthlessly and without military excuse or justification'. See *France and ors v Göring (Hermann) and ors* (Judgment and Sentence) (1946) 41 AJIL 172, pt 22, 493, cited in Werle, n 9, 155, fn 367.

28 The defence has, however, had some practical importance, particularly at the national level.[41] In *R v Finta*,[42] the Supreme Court of Canada opined that a defence of superior orders could be raised in certain circumstances, even where an order was manifestly illegal, if the subordinate had no moral choice about obeying the order: 'There can be no moral choice where there was such an air of compulsion and threat to the accused that he or she had no alternative but to obey the orders.'

29 Given the growing consensus in the international community on the need to prioritize or limit the prosecution of core international crimes to those perceived to bear the greatest responsibility (superiors and commanders),[43] the practical importance of the Principle could well be limited.

II. Superior responsibility

30 Superior responsibility has proved to be a vital tool for prosecutors to bring to trial heads of government, ministers, and other civilian superiors who played substantial roles in committing violations of international humanitarian law.[44] Although the defence is conceptually different from liability for positively ordering the commission of crimes, case law of the ad hoc tribunals has not clearly delimited the two, and there has been a tendency to use the superior responsibility doctrine as a kind of fall-back liability for cases in which a positive act cannot be proved.[45]

III. Official status

31 As far as international criminal law is concerned, there is near universal acceptance of the principle that international crimes cannot be covered by immunity *ratione materiae* before international or domestic tribunals.[46]

32 While the law is clear, [47] the practice has been often contradictory. The ICJ muddied the waters in the *Arrest Warrant Case*,[48] where it found that immunities prevail for serving

[41] For example, see the judgment considering the rule in Supreme Court of Argentina, 22 June 1987, 'Causa no 547incoada en virtud del Decreto no 280/84 del Poder Ejectivo Nacional', 1987-D Revista La Ley 194–266. For an English translation, see AM Garro and E Dahl, 'Legal accountability for Human Rights violations in Argentina: One step forwards and two steps backwards' (1987) 8 Human Rights Law Journal 283–344, 283.

[42] *R v Finta* [1994] 1 SCR 701.

[43] XA Aranburu, 'Prosecuting the Most Responsible for International Crimes: Dilemmas of Definition and Prosecutorial Discretion' in J Gonzalez (ed) *Protección Internacional de Derechos Humanos y Estado de Derecho* (Grupo Editorial Ibáñez 2009) 381–404.

[44] JA Williamson, 'Some considerations on command responsibility and criminal liability' (2008) 90:870 International Review of the Red Cross 303–17, 303.

[45] K Ambos, 'Current Issues in International Criminal Law' (2003) 14 Criminal Law Forum 225–60. See *Prosecutor v Kayishema & Ruzindana* (Judgment) ICTR 95-1-T (21 May 1999); *Prosecutor v Kordic & Cerkez* (Judgment) IT-95-14/2-T (26 February 2001); and *Prosecutor v Krstic* (Judgment) IT-98-33/T (2 August 2001).

[46] In *Re Goering and others* (1946) 13 ILR 203, 221. See further *Case Concerning the Arrest Warrant of 11 April 2000 (Democratic Republic of the Congo v Belgium)* (International Court of Justice (ICJ), 14 February 2002), Dissenting Opinion of Judge Van den Wyngaert, para 36 (hereinafter '*Arrest Warrant case*').

[47] Art 7(2) of the ICTY Statute and Art 6(2) of the ICTR Statute. The International Military Tribunal at Nuremberg held that such immunity does not apply to 'acts condemned as criminal by international law'. Similarly, the Statutes of both the ICTY and the ICTR contain a provision stating that '[t]he official position of any accused person, whether as Head of State or Government or as a responsible Government official, shall not relieve such person of criminal responsibility nor mitigate punishment'. The Rome Statute, in Art 27(2), similarly provides that immunities which may attach to the official capacity of a person, whether under national or international law, shall not bar the ICC from exercising its jurisdiction over such a person.

[48] See *Arrest Warrant case*, n 46.

heads of state and foreign ministers for the effective performance of their functions on behalf of their respective states; and when abroad that they enjoy full immunity from arrest in another state on a criminal charges, including charges of war crimes or crimes against humanity.

Much of domestic jurisprudence on immunity *ratione materiae* reflects the principle that international crimes cannot be covered by functional immunity. In the leading domestic decision on the irrelevance of functional immunity in the *Pinochet* case, the majority of the UK House of Lords[49] found that General Pinochet could not rely on functional immunity in order to avoid being extradited for allegations of torture[50]—since 'international law does not protect the same acts that it prohibits and condemns'.[51] 33

The relevance of immunity *ratione personae* in the prosecution of international crimes is more complex. One must separate proceedings before international tribunals and those before domestic courts. 34

Support for the proposition that customary international law immunity *rationae personae* does not apply to individuals in proceedings before international criminal courts can be found in the jurisprudence of a number of such courts, as well as in academic writings. International tribunals have, either expressly or by implication, considered such immunities to be irrelevant for their purposes. The Statute of the Nuremburg Tribunal stated that '[l]eaders, organizers, instigators and accomplices participating in the formulation or execution of a common plan or conspiracy to commit any of the foregoing crimes are responsible for all acts performed by any persons in execution of such plan'.[52] 35

Although the Statutes of the ad hoc UN Tribunals of the 1990s did not contain a specific provision addressing immunity *ratione personae*, the ICTY issued an arrest warrant for Slobodan Milosevic while he was a still a sitting head of state. Similarly, the *hybrid* SCSL held that 'the principle seems now established that the sovereign equality of states does not prevent a Head of State from being prosecuted before an international criminal tribunal or court'.[53] Finally, in the *Arrest Warrant* case, the ICJ stated that[54] 36

> an incumbent or former Minister for Foreign Affairs may be subject to criminal proceedings before certain international criminal courts, where they have jurisdiction. Examples include the International Criminal Tribunal for the former Yugoslavia, and the International Criminal Tribunal for Rwanda, established pursuant to Security Council resolutions under Chapter VII of the United Nations Charter, and the future International Criminal Court created by the 1998 Rome Convention.

State practice thus consistently confirms that the rules on personal immunities are made to yield in prosecutions before international criminal tribunals: such tribunals may indict and charge and issue arrest warrants against the most senior officials of a 37

[49] *R v Bow Street Metropolitan Stipendiary Magistrate and others, ex p Pinochet Ugarte (No 3)* [1999] 2 All ER 97, HL, Lord Nicholls, with whose Opinion Lord Hoffman concurred, and Lord Steyn.

[50] Ibid.

[51] Cryer et al, n 16, 430. See further C Chinkin, 'Regina v Bow Street Stipendiary Magistrate, *Ex Parte* Pinochet Ugarte (No 3)' (2003) 93 American Journal of International Law 703, 703–04. See, however, Akande, n 35, 414–15.

[52] Art 6, United Nations Charter of the International Military Tribunal—Annex to the Agreement for the prosecution and punishment of the major war criminals of the European Axis ('London Agreement'), 8 August 1945 (1946).

[53] *Prosecutor v Charles Ghankay Taylor* (Decision on Immunity from Jurisdiction) (Appeals Chamber) SCSL-2003-01-1 (31 May 2004) para 52.

[54] See ICJ, *Arrest Warrant case*, n 46, para 61.

state, including heads of state, suspected of crimes under their jurisdiction, even if those officials are still in power.

38 Conversely, there is considerable authority for the opposite proposition in so far as domestic prosecutions are concerned: *customary international law* immunity *ratione personae* continues to apply in such proceedings.[55] As Cryer et al note, 'while inroads have been made into functional immunity, State practice and jurisprudence have consistently upheld personal immunity, *regardless of the nature of the charges*'.[56] In the *Arrest Warrant* case, the ICJ held that Belgium had 'failed to respect the immunity from criminal jurisdiction and the inviolability which the incumbent Minister for Foreign Affairs of the Democratic Republic of Congo enjoyed under international law' when it issued an arrest warrant for him for crimes against humanity and war crimes.[57] This has been confirmed by a number of domestic courts in subsequent decisions in the UK (in respect of General Pinochet,[58] albeit obiter), Belgium, France, Spain, and the United States, amongst others.[59] Therefore, under customary international law, heads of state and certain other officials enjoy absolute personal immunity, even for international crimes, before the domestic courts of other states.

39 There has been considerable debate concerning President Omar Al Bashir and the scope of Article 98(1) of the ICC Statute, particularly in the context of Security Council Resolution 1593 by which the situation in Sudan was referred to the ICC.[60] In the *Decision on the Cooperation of the Democratic Republic of the Congo regarding Omar Al Bashir's arrest and Surrender to the Court*,[61] the ICC Pre-Trial Chamber dismissed the DRC's reasons for failing to arrest President Al Bashir. More recently, Pre-Trial Chamber II further clarified that South Africa is under an obligation to immediately arrest and surrender Al Bashir to the ICC.[62]

40 At the domestic level, the South African High Court has now had occasion to hold that the South African Government's failure to arrest President Al Bashir contravened both international law and South Africa's domestic legislation implementing the ICC Statute. It held:

[55] Akande, n 35, at 411, notes: 'Judicial opinion and state practice on this point are unanimous and no case can be found in which it was held that a state official possessing immunity ratione personae is subject to the criminal jurisdiction of a foreign state when it is alleged that he or she has committed an international crime.'

[56] Cryer et al, n 16, 425.

[57] ICJ, *Arrest Warrant case*, n 46, para 75.

[58] For instance, Lord Nicholls in the first *Pinochet* case held that 'there can be no doubt that if Senator Pinochet had still been the head of the Chilean state, he would have been entitled to immunity' (see *R v Bow St Magistrate, ex p Pinochet Ugarte* [1998] 4 All ER 897, 938). Lord Millett in the third *Pinochet* case said that 'Senator Pinochet is not a serving head of state. If he were, he could not be extradited. It would be an intolerable affront to the Republic of Chile to arrest him or detain him' (see *R v Bow St Magistrate, ex p Pinochet (No 3)* [1999] 2 WLR 824, 905 H).

[59] See, eg: *Ghaddafi case*, no 1414 (Cass crim 2001) (France), 125 ILR 456; *Castro case*, no 1999/2723, Order (Audiencia nacional 4 March 1999) (Spain); *HSA et al v SA*, Cass 2e civ, 12 February 2003, no P.02.1139.F (Belgium), translated in (2003) 42 ILM 596; *R v Bow Street Stipendiary Magistrate, ex p Pinochet (No 3)* [1999] 2 All ER 97, 126–27, 149,179, 189 (HL) (per Goff, Hope, Millett, Phillips, LJJ); *Plaintiffs A, B, C, D, E, F v Jiang Zemin*, 282 F Supp.2d 875 (ND Ill 2003); *Tachiona v Mugabe*, 169 F Supp.2d 259 (SDNY 2001); *Arrest Warrant Against General Shaul Mofaz* (2004) 53 International & Comparative Law Quarterly 769, 771.

[60] Resolution 1593 adopted by the Security Council at its 5158th meeting, on 31 March 2005 (2005)S/RES/1593 (2005). See further D Akande, 'The Legal Nature of Security Council Referrals to the ICC and its Impact on Al Bahir's Immunities' (2009) 7 Journal of International Criminal Justice 333–52, 334; and P Gaeta, 'Does President Al Bashir Enjoy Immunity from Arrest?' (2009) 7 Journal of International Criminal Justice 315–32, 318.

[61] See *Decision on the Cooperation of the Democratic Republic of the Congo Regarding Omar Al Bashir's Arrest and Surrender to the Court*, ICC-02/05-01/09-195 (9 April 2014) (see in particular paras 28–31).

[62] ICC Pre-Trial Chamber II, ICC-02/05-01/02 (13 June 2015) (per Judge Tarfusser) (see in particular paras 8 and 9).

> [T]he Rome Statute expressly provides that heads of state do not enjoy immunity under its terms ... It means that the immunity that might otherwise have attached to President Bashir based on customary international law as head of state, is excluded or waived in respect of crimes and obligations under the Rome Statute.[63]

On appeal, the Supreme Court of Appeal[64] confirmed the High Court's findings, concluding that

> when South Africa decided to implement its obligations under the Rome Statute by passing the Implementation Act it did so on the basis that all forms of immunity, including head of state immunity, would not constitute a bar to the prosecution of international crimes in this country or to South Africa cooperating with the ICC by way of the arrest and surrender of persons charged with such crimes before the ICC, where an arrest warrant had been issued and a request for cooperation made.[65]

Pre-Trial Chamber II of the ICC decided on 6 July 2017 in Prosecutor v Omar Hassan Ahmad Al-Bashir Judgment No ICC-02/05-01/09 that immunity of Al Bashir as Head of State did not bar state parties to the Rome Statute from executing the Court's request to arrest and surrender Al Bashir.

E. Critical Assessment

I. Due obedience (superior orders)

What remains is the difficult practical question of whether an accused is entitled to the benefit of the defence when he is subjectively mistaken as to the manifest illegality of the offence. That may arise, most realistically, in respect of war crimes, given their varied forms and differing levels of severity.[66] It may also—despite the Rome Statute's insistence to the contrary—arise notionally in relation to orders to commit genocide or crimes against humanity. The exclusion of the defence in respect of genocide and crimes against humanity was a political compromise at Rome that has no legal foundation.[67] Crimes against humanity or genocide are oftentimes complex crimes that entail a number of different elements in order to meet the required level of reprehensibility necessary for a conviction.[68] As Zahar points out, '[t]he idea that a crime against humanity or genocide are necessarily constituted of acts which the "reasonable soldier" would always perceive as manifestly criminal is questionable'.[69] 41

Related, then, to the defence of superior orders is the defence of mistake of law. Under Principle 27(a), an accused may be excused—as Schabas puts it—'for ignorance of the illegality of the order but not for ignorance of the manifest illegality of the order'.[70] But 42

[63] *Southern Africa Litigation Centre v Minister of Justice And Constitutional Development and Others* (27740/2015) [2015] ZAGPPHC 402 (24 June 2015), 2015 (5) SA 1 (GP).

[64] *Minister of Justice and Constitutional Development and Others v Southern African Litigation Centre and Others* (867/15) [2016] ZASCA 17, 2016 (4) BCLR 487 (SCA).

[65] Ibid, para 103.

[66] The precise legal limits on conduct in times of war have been (and remain) contentious. For instance, as Zahar points out (n 7, 526), 'The desire to shield combat troops from criminal responsibility in connection with debatable laws of war is a reflection of the many aspects of that law which are (still) uncertain. In *Llandovery Castle* (Dithmar and Boldt case), which is considered a landmark in the history of the superior orders defence, reference was made to the "ambiguity of many of the rules of International Law".'

[67] P Gaeta, 'The Defence of Superior Orders: The Statute of the International Criminal Court versus Customary International Law' (1999) 10 European Journal of International Law 172–90, 189.

[68] I Bantekas, 'Defences in International Law' in D McGoldrick et al (eds), *The Permanent Court* (Hart Publishing 2004) 263–85, 273.

[69] Zahar, n 7, 527.

[70] W Schabas, *An Introduction to the International Criminal Court* (3rd edn, CUP 2007) 231.

that does not answer the question: when is an order manifestly illegal? That is, when will an accused person be excused for making a mistake of law as to the illegality of an order to commit an international crime? This was considered by the District Court of Jerusalem in *Israel v Eichmann*:[71]

> The identifying mark of a 'manifestly unlawful' order must wave like a black flag above the order given, as a warning saying: 'forbidden'. It is … not unlawfulness that is detectable only by legal experts … but an overt and salient violation, a certain and obvious unlawfulness that stems from the order itself, … an unlawfulness that pierces the eye and agitates the heart, if the eye be not blind nor the heart closed or corrupt.

43 Accordingly, where the illegality of the order was manifest, the subordinate must have known—or, at least, should have known.[72]

II. Superior responsibility

44 While superior responsibility has been an important means of holding military commanders responsible for a failure of their supervision duty in typical military contexts, it is less appropriate to deal with political or military leaders who are more remote from the direct perpetrators and hence perpetration of international crimes. That is particularly so because of the difficulty of establishing the superior–subordinate nexus, in respect of which the ad hoc Tribunals, in particular, have adopted a rigorous and fact-specific approach.[73] Accordingly, there has been a gradual preference emerging for 'direct' liability as opposed to superior responsibility:[74] and accordingly a number of superiors charged with superior responsibility have been convicted only (where the evidence has been available) for their direct responsibility in the commission of crimes, either as accomplices or as participants in a joint criminal enterprise.[75]

45 Interestingly, the ICC Statute, in Article 28, advances two separate standards for military commanders and non-military commanders: for military commanders the test is whether the commander knew or, owing to the circumstances at the time, should have known; whereas for non-military commanders the test is whether the commander knew of, or consciously disregarded, information that clearly indicated that the subordinates were committing or about to commit such crimes.

46 However, some concerns have been raised with the doctrine of joint criminal enterprise, as well as with aspects of the principle of superior responsibility, as being inconsistent with the fundamental principle that culpability is the foundation of criminal responsibility, as 'a person may be convicted for a serious international crime without the commission, participation, contribution, or subjective *mens rea* that would normally be required for such crimes'.[76]

47 Tribunals have thus rightly remained alive to the risk of expecting more than was within the capacity of a superior at the time of the violations. As the ICTY stated in *Celebici*,[77] it must 'be recognised that international law cannot oblige a superior to perform the

[71] *Israel v Eichmann* (District Court, 12 December 1961). [72] Zahar, n 7, 526–27.

[73] See B Bonafe, 'Finding a proper role for Command Responsibility' (2007) 5 International Court of Justice 270–73, quoted in Cassese (ed), n 7, 273.

[74] See, eg, ICTY, *Prosecutor v Orić*, n 26, paras 342 and 343. [75] See Bonafe, n 73, 272.

[76] Robinson, 'The Identity crisis of International Criminal Law' (2008) 21 Leiden Journal of International Law 925–63, 944.

[77] See ICTY, *The Prosecutor v Delalić et al*, n 13.

impossible. Hence, a superior may only be held criminally responsible for failing to take such measures within his powers'.[78]

III. Official status

As to the scope of personal immunity, while it clearly applies to heads of state and (according to the ICJ in the *Arrest Warrant case*) a Foreign Minister, it remains to be determined which other officials enjoy this form of immunity whilst in office. However, the Court's finding that 'diplomatic and consular agents, [and] certain holders of high ranking office in a State, such as the Head of State, Head of Government and Minister for Foreign Affairs' enjoy immunity *ratione personae* suggests that more officials might be added to this list.[79] In the *Arrest Warrant case*, the ICJ suggested that considerations include the function performed by the official and the duties he or she would otherwise be hindered in performing:[80] 48

> [T]he functions of a Minister for Foreign Affairs are such that, throughout the duration of his or her office, he or she when abroad enjoys full immunity from criminal jurisdiction and inviolability. That immunity and that inviolability protect the individual concerned against any act of authority of another State which would hinder him or her in the performance of his or her duties.

Some national courts recently have considered immune from their jurisdiction foreign Defence Ministers and Ministers of the Interior.[81] The trend to extend immunities beyond heads of state and Foreign Ministers is not yet established as a rule of customary international law.[82] It is suggested by Frulli that such extension of immunity 'risks the enlargement indefinitely of the categories of state officials who benefit from personal immunities' and 'does not express an adequate balance between the need to preserve the stability of international relations and the fight against impunity for the most serious international crimes'.[83] 49

Lastly, the Al Bashir saga has highlighted the potential for competing obligations between African states parties to the Rome Statute, who are expected on the one hand to cooperate with the ICC in the arrest and surrender of senior officials despite the immunities that are accorded to them under customary international law, and who on the other are obliged by their membership of the African Union to respect those selfsame immunities.[84] The question is in need of clarification, as Akande says, probably best through a decision by the ICJ.[85] 50

[78] Ibid, para 935. [79] ICJ, *Arrest Warrant case*, n 46, para 51.

[80] Ibid, para 45.

[81] See the decision by the German Federal Prosecutor General on the complaint against Rumsfeldet et al of 10 February 2005, Juristenzeitung (2005), 311. 976; and Mofaz (*Application for Arrest Warrant against General Shaul Mofaz* (Bow Street Magistrates' Court, London, 12 February 2004)), and Bo Xilai (*Re Bo Xilai* (2005) 128 ILR 713 (8 November 2005)) in the UK.

[82] M Frulli, 'Immunities of Persons from Jurisdiction' in Cassese (ed), n 7, 369.

[83] Ibid.

[84] See further M du Plessis and C Gevers, 'Balancing competing obligations: The Rome Statute and AU decisions', ISS Paper 225, October 2011.

[85] See D Akande, quoted in 'Move Presidential Immunity Debate On, Says Former AU Advisor' (16 June 2015) <www.justiceinfo.net/en/analysis/745-move-presidential-immunity-debate-on,-says-former-au-advisor.html> accessed 30 November 2017.

Bibliography

Akande, D, 'International Law Immunities and the International Criminal Court' (2004) 98(3) American Journal of International Law 407.

Cryer et al, R, *An Introduction to International Criminal Law and Procedure* (CUP 2010.

Dinstein, Y, *The Defence of 'obedience to superior orders' in International Law* (OUP 2012).

Gaeta, P, 'The Defence of Superior Orders: The Statute of the International Criminal Court versus Customary International Law' (1999) 10 European Journal of International Law 172–90, 172.

Mettraux, G, *The Law of Command Responsibility* (OUP 2009).

Report on the work of the sixty-third session of the International Law Commission 2011, UN Doc A/66/10 (26 April–3 June and 4 July–12 August 2011) ch VII.

Werle, G, *Principles of International Criminal Law* (TMC Asser Press 2005).

Zahar, A, 'Superior Orders' in A Cassese (ed), *The Oxford Companion to International Criminal Justice* (OUP 2009) 525–27, 525.

Principle 28. Restrictions on the Effects of Legislation on Disclosure or Repentance

Christopher Gosnell

The fact that a perpetrator discloses the violations that he, she or others have committed in order to benefit from the favourable provisions of legislation on disclosure or repentance cannot exempt him or her from criminal or other responsibility. The disclosure may only provide grounds for a reduction of sentence in order to encourage revelation of the truth.

When disclosures may subject a perpetrator to persecution, principle 25 notwithstanding, the person making the disclosure may be granted asylum—not refugee status—in order to facilitate revelation of the truth.

A. Summary of Findings

Principle 28 declares that confession of a crime may, pursuant to 'provisions of legislation on disclosure or repentance', justify a 'reduction of sentence' but not 'exempt[ion]' from 'criminal or other responsibility'. Confession also allows a person to receive asylum, but not refugee status, in another state where a confession 'may subject the perpetrator to persecution'.

Principle 28 addresses the permissible scope of amnesties. An amnesty, according to Principle 28, may grant a reduction of sentence in return for a confession, but not an exemption from legal responsibility. The prohibition on exemption from responsibility is hard to reconcile with the South African truth and reconciliation process, which included exempting from penal measures those who made a full and individual confession before a specialized judicial body. The South African experience, far from being considered illegal or a deviation from international norms, has been widely praised by states and international actors. The recently negotiated Colombia peace agreements, which have been emphatically endorsed by the UN, go almost as far in limiting the punishments that can be imposed in exchange for a full and individual confession.

These examples suggest that the imposition of a non-custodial sentence for serious crimes is not categorically prohibited under international law. This does not mean, however, that amnesties are categorically permitted. State and international practice has, on the contrary, consistently condemned 'blanket' amnesties for past crimes that are not accompanied by full, individual, and formal confessions. The circumstances of an amnesty's adoption are also relevant. A 'self-amnesty' granted by the party leaving power is very different from a democratically approved effort at reconciliation, whose genuine purpose is reconciliation and the repression of future serious crimes. The international legality of amnesties depends more on these factors than the purported distinction between reduction of sentence and exemption from responsibility.

The international legality of a national amnesty does not mean that it is binding on an international court. On the contrary, international prosecutors are duty-bound to prosecute crimes within their jurisdiction, regardless of purported national exemptions. Yet Kofi Annan, speaking about the South African amnesty programme, has rightly observed that '[i]t is inconceivable … the [International Criminal Court (ICC)] would seek to substitute its judgment for that of a whole nation which is seeking the best way to put a traumatic past behind it and build a better future'.[1] This is a political judgement that requires political legitimation at the international level. A formal ratification mechanism is necessary to preserve the judicial nature of the ICC, and to avoid placing judges and prosecutors in the inappropriate position of refraining from exercising their jurisdiction based on a national amnesty.

B. Contextual and Historical Introduction

1 The Treaty of Versailles placed criminal responsibility on the international agenda by calling for prosecution of the German Kaiser 'for a supreme offence against international morality and the sanctity of treaties'.[2] The international prosecution of war crimes and crimes against humanity became a practical reality with the extensive prosecution of those crimes by international and occupation authorities at the end of the Second World War. The international law-making that followed—including the criminalization of 'grave breaches' of the Geneva Conventions and the crime of genocide, as well as the adoption of numerous human rights instruments—has seen criminal law evolve from a matter of purely national concern and national jurisdiction to concurrent international concern and international jurisdiction.

2 The UN, after having been involved in the negotiation of many unconditional national amnesty agreements that encompassed crimes that could be characterized as international crimes, signalled a disorderly policy shift in respect of such agreements in 1999. At the signing of the peace settlement concluding years of civil war in Sierra Leone, which included a particularly unconditional and unqualified amnesty provision, the Secretary-General's special representative scribbled a hand-written note on his copy of the agreement, stating that 'The UN holds the understanding that the amnesty provisions of the Agreement shall not apply to the international crimes of genocide, crimes against humanity, war crimes and other serious violations of international humanitarian law.'[3] A subsequent report by the Secretary-General explained that this notation had been inserted to reflect the concrete possibility, in light of the creation of the International Criminal Tribunal for the former Yugoslavia (ICTY) and International Criminal Tribunal for Rwanda (ICTR), of international adjudication of such crimes.[4] This shift brought the UN Secretariat into line with the long-standing hostility of the UN Human Rights Committee (UNHRC) towards amnesties in general.[5] However, the ensuing Security Council debate on the report reflected no consensus concerning the permissible scope of national amnesties.[6]

[1] M Freeman, *Necessary Evils: Amnesties and the Search for Justice* (CUP 2009) 88–89.

[2] Treaty of Peace between the Allied and Associated Powers and Germany (entered into force 28 June 1919) (Treaty of Versailles) Art 227. A O'Shea, *Amnesty for Crime in International Law and Practice* (Kluwer Law International 2002) 15.

[3] P Hayner, *Negotiating Peace in Sierra Leone: Confronting the Justice Challenge*, Report (Henry Dunant Centre for Humanitarian Dialogue, December 2007) 5.

[4] Report of the Secretary-General, *The rule of law and transitional justice in conflict and post-conflict societies*, UN Doc S/2004/616 (23 August 2004) <www.refworld.org/docid/45069c434.html> accessed 4 December 2017.

[5] See UNHRC 'General Comment No 20: Article 7 (Prohibition of Torture, or Other Cruel, Inhuman or Degrading Treatment or Punishment)' in Compilation of General Recommendations adopted by Human Rights Treaty Bodies, UN Doc HRI/GEN/1/Rev.9 (10 March 1992).

[6] See MP Scharf, 'From the eXile Files: An Essay on Trading Justice for Peace' (2006) 63 Washington & Lee Law Review 339–79, 363.

States have continued to make use of amnesties since 1999,[7] although their terms and conditions vary dramatically. At one end of the spectrum are those that are unqualified in scope (ie encompassing all crimes, regardless of gravity or degree of responsibility), unconditional in application (ie imposing no pre-conditions for a perpetrator to benefit), and 'self-granted' (ie by the perpetrators themselves). At the other end are those that are narrowly tailored in application, conditional upon the satisfaction of specific and personal conditions and approved by a formal process of adjudication, and which appear to have been adopted democratically as part of a broader reconciliation programme.[8] The UN has demonstrated its willingness to endorse these narrowly-tailored, conditional, and democratically-negotiated amnesties. For example, the first Colombia peace accord in 2016, which was strongly endorsed by the UN, promised almost no penal sanction for those making full 'acknowledgment' of their crimes, including international crimes. 3

As a matter of state and international practice, the propriety and legal effect of national amnesties for serious crimes, including international crimes, remains a contingent and contested issue. Few subjects in international justice have generated sharper disagreements amongst commentators and academics. The text of Principle 28, rather than declarative of a settled international legal norm, adopts a particular position within this debate. 4

C. Theoretical Framework

The first paragraph of Principle 28 provides: 5

> The fact that a perpetrator discloses the violations that he, she or others have committed in order to benefit from the favourable provisions of legislation on disclosure or repentance cannot exempt him or her from criminal or other responsibility. The disclosure may only provide grounds for a reduction of sentence in order to encourage revelation of the truth.

Principle 28 expressly presupposes the existence of amnesty agreements of some sort, whereas Principle 19 implies that amnesties should not be employed as a transitional justice device, and Principle 24 purports to impose additional restrictions or conditions on amnesties. Principle 28 asserts that confessions made pursuant to such amnesty 'legislation' may provide only for a reduction of sentence, not an exemption from 'criminal or other responsibility'. 6

Most criminal justice systems, even without any amnesty legislation, treat confession as a mitigating factor in sentencing, but not as justifying any exemption of responsibility. Principle 28, in effect, declares that this general principle applies regardless of amnesty legislation. Nothing is said, however, about the extent of sentence reduction that is permitted, or whether it can be automatic. The amnesty provisions of the Colombian peace accords, 7

[7] See Freeman, n1; M Freeman and M Pensky, 'The Amnesty Controversy in International Law' in F Lessa and LA Payne (eds), *Amnesty in the Age of Human Rights Accountability* (CUP 2012) 42–68, pinpoint; L Mallinder 'Amnesties' Challenge to the Global Accountability Norm? Interpreting Regional and International Trends in Amnesty Enactment' in F Lessa and LA Payne (eds), *Amnesty in the Age of Human Rights Accountability* (CUP 2012) 79–95, pinpoint; L Mallinder, 'Amnesties' in W Schabas and N Bernaz (eds), *Routledge Handbook of International Criminal Law* (Routledge 2011) 419–34, pinpoint.

[8] R Jeffrey, *Amnesties, Accountability, and Human Rights* (University of Pennsylvania Press 2014) 51–53; K Ambos, 'The Legal Framework of Transitional Justice: A Systematic Study with a Special Focus on the Role of the ICC' in K Ambos et al (eds), *Building a Future on Peace and Justice: Studies on Transitional Justice, Peace and Development* (Springer 2009) 19–103, 55.

for example, prescribe a mandatory maximum of eight years for 'very serious offences'.[9] The original 2016 peace accord, which was supported by the UN, did not even require imprisonment during this term, allowing instead for vague restrictions on 'freedom of residency and movement'. The final peace accord still permits excusal from imprisonment, but specifies a geographic restriction of residency and movement.[10] The UN's position, accordingly, seems to be that national amnesties may go as far as exempting a person from imprisonment even for 'very serious offences', in exchange for a full acknowledgement of guilt.

8 Principle 28 does not define the 'criminal or other responsibility' from which no exemption may be granted. It is not clear, for example, whether a formal confession of guilt before a judicial authority that imposes no sentence at all constitutes an exemption from criminal responsibility. The South African Truth and Reconciliation Commission (TRC), for example, was a 'juristic person' under the Promotion of National Unity and Reconciliation Act no 34 of 1995. This removed the TRC from the definition of 'truth commission', defined in the Principles as a 'non-judicial' body.[11] This 'juristic person' was empowered to 'facilitat[e] the granting of amnesty to persons who make full disclosure of all the relevant facts relating to acts associated with a political objective and comply with the requirements of this Act'. Applications to the Commission were then subject to an individual decision, turning primarily on whether there had been 'full disclosure', after a full public hearing.[12] The procedure closely resembled a formal confession, which included an acknowledgement of culpability. Any granting of 'amnesty' was therefore accompanied by a quasi-judicial declaration of culpability similar to a formal finding of guilt.

9 The position of the International Committee of the Red Cross (ICRC) on the South African example is illustrative of the potential compatibility of an amnesty with the duty to investigate and prosecute international crimes. The ICRC has asserted that amnesties issued by 'a number of States' have 'often been found to be unlawful by their own courts or by regional courts and were criticized by the international community'.[13] This ignores, however, the extent and variety of amnesties to be found in state practice, including many that have been promulgated with the support of the UN.[14] And, importantly, the ICRC itself accepts that the South African reconciliation process did not offend against 'the rule obliging States to investigate and prosecute persons suspected of having committed war crimes in non-international armed conflicts', because 'it did not involve the granting of blanket amnesties [and] it required full disclosure of the relevant facts'.[15] The ICRC's position suggests that the non-application of penal measures

[9] Final Agreement to End the Armed Conflict and Build a Stable and Lasting Peace (signed 24 November 2016) pp 174–75, para 60 <especiales.presidencia.gov.co/Documents/20170620-dejacion-armas/acuerdos/acuerdo-final-ingles.pdf> accessed 4 December 2017.

[10] Ibid (see reference to 'Transitional Local Zones for Normalisation'). See also Washington Office on Latin America, 'Key Changes to the New Peace Accord' *Colombia Peace* (15 November 2016) <Colombiapeace.org/2016/11/15/key-changes-to-the-new-peace-accord/> accessed 4 December 2017; and 'Colombia and the FARC strike a new peace agreement' *The Economist* (13 November 2016).

[11] Updated Principles, Definitions, 'D. Truth commissions'.

[12] A du Bois-Pedain, 'Accountability through Conditional Amnesty: The Case of South Africa' in Lessa and Payne (eds), n 7, 241–51, pinpoint.

[13] ICRC, *Customary IHL*, Rule 158. Prosecution of War Crimes <ihl-databases.icrc.org/customary-ihl/eng/docs/v1_rul_rule158> accessed 4 December 2017.

[14] Freeman, n 1, 138–80; Mallinder, 'Amnesties' Challenge to the Global Accountability Norm? Interpreting Regional and International Trends in Amnesty Enactment' in Lessa and Payne (eds), n 7, pinpoint.

[15] ICRC, *Customary IHL*, Rule 159. Amnesty <ihl-databases.icrc.org/customary-ihl/eng/docs/v1_rul_rule159> accessed 4 December 2017.

conditional upon full disclosure of the relevant facts and acknowledgement of responsibility does not necessarily offend against the duty to investigate and prosecute international crimes.

The legality of an amnesty does not track neatly onto the binary distinction posited by Principle 28. Legality depends instead on a range of factors, including: the requirement of a full and unequivocal confession of the facts; that the confession be subject to some form of acceptance by a judicial body that has the capacity to verify its veracity through investigation; that the confession and determination of acceptance be individual, and not collective; that the confession be public; and, preferably, complementary procedures to make sure that the acknowledgement means something for victims, in particular through restorative justice policies such as compensation. A mechanism with these attributes does not fit into a traditional model of criminal responsibility, and transcends the distinction between 'exemption from responsibility' and 'reduction of sentence'. **10**

The second aspect of Principle 28 concerns the availability of asylum to those offering confessions under an amnesty programme. **11**

Asylum can be defined as the protection a state affords to a foreign national against the exercise of jurisdiction by another state. Asylum is typically, as in Article 14 of the International Covenant on Civil and Political Rights,[16] associated with flight from persecution in another country. Article 1(2) of the UN General Assembly's Declaration on Territorial Asylum,[17] which is specifically mentioned in Principle 25, declares that the **12**

> right to seek and to enjoy asylum may not be invoked by any person with respect to whom there are serious reasons for considering that he has committed a crime against peace, a war crime or a crime against humanity, as defined in the international instruments drawn up to make provision in respect of such crimes.

The second paragraph of Principle 28 carves out an exception from this prohibition where confession of such crimes 'may' cause the asylum claimant to be 'subject ... to persecution'. Principle 28 addresses only asylum, not just because the rights conferred are 'typically fewer and more limited than those granted under the Refugee Convention',[18] but also because the Principles could not contradict the same prohibition that appears in Article 1(F) of the Refugee Convention.[19] Principle 28 therefore has the salutary purpose of ensuring that the General Assembly's Declaration on Territorial Asylum does not condemn individuals to persecution as a result of the confession of their crimes. Incidentally, the state granting asylum would still be required to consider whether it has an obligation to prosecute any crimes of universal jurisdiction to which the person had confessed, and which would potentially be amenable to transfer to an international court. The second paragraph of Principle 28 should, accordingly, not be misread as legalizing or **13**

[16] UN General Assembly, International Covenant on Civil and Political Rights (adopted 16 December 1966, entered into force 23 March 1976) 999 UNTS 171 (ICCPR).

[17] UN General Assembly, Declaration on Territorial Asylum (14 December 1967) A/RES/2312(XXII).

[18] J Rikhof, *The Criminal Refugee: The Treatment of Asylum Seekers With A Criminal Background in International and Domestic Law* (Republic of Letters Publishing 2012) 12.

[19] UN General Assembly, Convention Relating to the Status of Refugees (adopted 28 July 1951, entered into force 22 April 1954) 189 UNTS 137.

encouraging exile of international criminals, as was the case in respect of Idi Amin and other notorious dictators.[20]

D. Practice

14 The most prominent example of exemption from criminal responsibility in return for confession comes from the practice of the South Africa TRC. Perpetrators were entitled to a full exemption from penal sanction if they provided a full and frank confession of their crimes, if the veracity and completeness of that confession was accepted by a quasi-judicial panel, and if those crimes were committed within the framework of the goals of the organization to which the person belonged. Further, the amnesty process was part of a broader procedure involving public hearings at which confessions were heard; participation of, and reparations for, victims; and a report by the TRC making findings as to the nature of the crimes committed. These measures were enacted by the new South African parliament as part of a political settlement that was democratic and peaceful.

15 The settlement was also found to comply with domestic constitutional requirements. The South African Constitutional Court acknowledged its

> grave discomfort in living with a consequence which might allow the perpetrators of evil acts to walk the streets of this land with impunity, protected in their freedom by an amnesty immune from constitutional attack, but the circumstances in support of this course require carefully to be appreciated. Most of the acts of brutality and torture which have taken place have occurred during an era in which neither the laws which permitted the incarceration of persons or the investigation of crimes, nor the methods and the culture which informed such investigations, were easily open to public investigation, verification and correction. … The Act seeks to address this massive problem … crucially, to help [the victims] to discover what did in truth happen to their loved ones, where and under what circumstances it did happen, and who was responsible. That truth, which the victims of repression seek so desperately to know is, in the circumstances, much more likely to be forthcoming if those responsible for such monstrous misdeeds are encouraged to disclose the whole truth with the incentive that they will not receive the punishment which they undoubtedly deserve if they do. Without that incentive there is nothing to encourage such persons to make the disclosures and to reveal the truth which persons in the positions of the applicants so desperately desire.[21]

16 The Court also expressed the view that Article 6(5) of Additional Protocol II to the Geneva Conventions was meant to encourage amnesties, even for international war crimes, because of the specific circumstances of non-international conflicts:

> The erstwhile adversaries of such a conflict inhabit the same sovereign territory. They have to live with each other and work with each other and the state concerned is best equipped to determine what measures may be most conducive for the facilitation of such reconciliation and reconstruction. That is a difficult exercise which the nation within such a state has to perform by having regard to its own peculiar history, its complexities, even its contradictions and its emotional and institutional traditions. What role punishment should play in respect of erstwhile acts of criminality in such a situation is part of the complexity.[22]

[20] Freeman, n 1, 120–21.

[21] *Azanian People's Organisation (AZAPO) and others v Truth and Reconciliation Commission and others*, Constitutional Court of South Africa, Case CCT 17/96 (25 July 1996) para 17.

[22] Ibid, para 31.

Few would suggest that the South African truth and reconciliation experience violated international law, or even that it was bad policy. Numerous states and the Secretary-General of the United Nations applauded the process. From an international justice perspective, the prevailing view is that the process as a whole, particularly the requirement for full and candid confession, discharged South Africa's obligation to investigate and prosecute international crimes, and upheld victims' rights.[23] Recent amnesties in Portugal, Poland, and Algeria likewise exempted criminal liability for international crimes based on full and frank confession of the crimes, without having attracted any significant international disapproval.[24] **17**

The amnesty provisions of the 2016 Colombia peace agreements have been justified at length on the basis of the need to balance the obligation to punish human rights violations with the obligation to prevent future human rights violations, and to preserve peace.[25] A good faith assessment of that obligation, particularly in conjunction with the fullest possible conditions on amnesty, is a delicate balancing of obligations and rights in which international law, for the reasons expressed by the South African Constitutional Court, should not lightly interfere. **18**

The Inter-American Court of Human Rights (IACtHR) has adopted a hostile approach towards amnesties that are neither conditional nor limited, or are not adopted as part of a democratic or open process. One such amnesty 'was not publicly announced or discussed, but was adopted as soon as it was submitted, in the early hours of June 14, 1995'.[26] The IACtHR went beyond the particularities of the case to broadly condemn amnesties: **19**

> This Court considers that all amnesty provisions, provisions on prescription and the establishment of measures designed to eliminate responsibility are inadmissible, because they are intended to prevent the investigation and punishment of those responsible for serious human rights violations such as torture, extrajudicial, summary or arbitrary execution and forced disappearance, all of them prohibited because they violate non-derogable rights recognized by international human rights law.[27]

This has been described as 'the most assertive of all the international courts' decisions on point',[28] and other courts have not followed suit. A bench of the Special Court for Sierra Leone (SCSL) Appeals Chamber—which was assessing the extremely broad and unconditional amnesty that had been the object of the Secretary-General's hand-written reservation in 1999—found that an international legal norm prohibiting amnesties for serious international crimes was 'developing' but had not yet 'crystallized'.[29] Recent state practice casts doubt on whether there actually is any trend towards 'crystallization', let alone what norm exactly is being crystallized. **20**

[23] G Meringues and J Mendez, 'Reconciling Amnesties with Universal Jurisdiction' (2000) 2 International Law Forum 76–97, 90; Scharf, n 6, 346.

[24] Freeman, n 1, 166–67.

[25] See Final Agreement to End the Armed Conflict and Build a Stable and Lasting Peace, n 9, 153, para 3 ('with the aim of defending the rights of future generations'), 156, para 13 ('guarantees of non-repetition are realised').

[26] *Barrios Altos (Chumbipuma Aguierre et al v Peru)* (Judgment) IACtHR Series C no 75 (14 March 2001) para 2(i).

[27] Ibid, para 41.

[28] R Cryer et al, *An Introduction to International Criminal Law and Procedure* (CUP 2010) 565.

[29] SCSL, *Prosecutor v Morris Kallon and Brima Bazzy Kamara* (Decision on Challenge to Jurisdiction: Lomé Accord Amnesty) (Appeals Chamber) SCSL-2004-15-AR72-(E)-2004-16-AR72(E) (13 March 2004) para 82.

21 An entirely different question from that of the legal validity of national amnesties under international law is whether international courts can be, or should be, constrained by such national legislation at all. International courts have so far never given effect to a national amnesty. The Extraordinary Chambers in the Courts of Cambodia (ECCC) declined to give 'weight' to what was, in effect, a royal pardon granted directly to an individual without any conditions.[30] The Trial Chamber deprecated what it described as 'blanket amnesties', while observing that 'conditional amnesties such as those providing for some form of accountability have also met with widespread approval, such as in the case of South Africa, where amnesties were granted as part of the reconciliation process'.[31] The Trial Chamber noted that these conditional amnesties have been 'applied on a case-by-case' basis, but cited only a Ugandan judicial decision in respect of a Ugandan amnesty.[32] In the absence of any 'conditions' imposed on the royal pardon, the Trial Chamber decided that it would not exercise its discretion, 'contrary to the direction in which customary international law is developing'.[33]

22 The SCSL Appeals Chamber found that it was not bound by the 1999 national amnesty law because it was institutionally autonomous from, and could not be bound by, acts of the Sierra Leone Government.[34]

23 The ICTY did not find that the amnesty agreement that had been negotiated by Richard Holbrooke with Radovan Karadžić was, in substance, unlawful under international law, but rather that only the Security Council 'could, through statutory amendments, limit or expand the Tribunal jurisdiction, including *jurisdiction personae*, if it deemed it appropriate'.[35] The Appeals Chamber expressed no disagreement with this proposition, although it insisted that a variation to jurisdiction could not be accomplished by a negotiator with 'apparent authority' to act on behalf of the Security Council; only a formal Security Council resolution would suffice to modify or curtail the ICTY's jurisdiction, which was itself conferred by way of Security Council resolution.[36]

24 There is no known state practice concerning the granting of asylum to individuals who claim that their confession of crimes under an amnesty programme would subject them to persecution.

E. Critical Assessment

25 Amnesties are inherently anathema to the integrity and continuity of a legal order. By their nature, they disrupt the equal application of the law to perpetrators; yet they are a common feature of transitional justice and are perceived as a useful tool in the process of reconciliation.

26 Amnesties raise issues of international law not only in respect of the international obligations of states to suppress human rights violations, but also the enforceability of any national amnesty in respect of international jurisdictions that might wish to prosecute certain

[30] ECCC, *The Prosecutor v Ieng Sary* (Decision on Ieng Sary's Rule 89 Preliminary Objections (*Ne bis in idem* and Amnesty and Pardon)) (Trial Chamber) 002/19-09-2007/ECCC/TC (3 November 2011) para 54.

[31] Ibid, paras 51–52. [32] Ibid, para 52. [33] Ibid, para 54. [34] Ibid, paras 88, 90.

[35] *The Prosecutor v Karadžić* (Decision on the Accused's Holbrooke Agreement Motion) (Trial Chamber) IT-95-5/18-PT (8 July 2009) para 57.

[36] *The Prosecutor v Karadžić* (Decision on Karadžić's appeal of Trial Chamber's decision on alleged Holbrooke Agreement) (Appeals Chamber) IT-95-5/18-AR73.4 (12 October 2009) paras 35–39.

acts as international crimes. There appears to be no categorical prohibition on adopting amnesty provisions that provide for limited or no incarceration, such as those employed in South Africa or Colombia. Whether such provisions comply with states' obligations to investigate and prosecute international crimes depends on the specific provisions adopted, including the existence of a judicial mechanism before which confessions may be heard, the completeness of such confessions, the individual nature of such confessions, and the democratic nature of the process by which such provisions are adopted.[37]

No judicial institution, including the ICC, should curtail prosecutions on the basis of a national amnesty. An amnesty, by definition, is a political incursion on the rule of law. The incursion may be justified but is not amenable to judicial analysis, and it is not the function of judges and prosecutors to make that determination. Article 17 of the Rome Statute, referring only to whether a state is investigating and prosecuting a particular offence, does not incorporate criteria by which the merits of an amnesty can be evaluated.[38] Expecting the ICC prosecutor and judges to make those decisions risks undermining their integrity and legitimacy by requiring them to make decisions about whether or not to prosecute crimes within their jurisdiction based on non-judicial criteria. 27

The ideal solution is for the ICC Assembly of State Parties or the Security Council to develop a mechanism by which it may ratify or approve national amnesties that impact the jurisdiction of courts of their creation. This is necessary to ensure both the integrity of the amnesty itself and the integrity of any decision by the ICC not to prosecute crimes for reasons falling outside of Article 17 of the Rome Statute. The Colombia peace agreements, which grant almost as much leniency for confessions as was accorded under the South African truth and reconciliation process, may or may not be viewed as satisfying the requirements of a 'prosecution' under Article 17. The existence of doubt undermines the certainty that can be accorded to the Colombian peace agreements, and risks drawing the ICC's judicial organs into applying criteria that are not to be found in Article 17. In the event of an ICC arrest warrant, a State Party also risks being placed in the position of choosing between breaking its obligations under the Rome Statute, or breaking its commitments under a transitional peace agreement. 28

The Security Council has previously legislated to curtail the ICC's jurisdiction, exempting non-nationals in Libya from prosecution under Resolution 1970.[39] A Security Council resolution recognizing a national amnesty in the case of a mandate conferred by the Security Council would probably suffice to ensure recognition of a national amnesty by the ICC, but in other cases the formal authority of the Assembly of States Parties to curtail the Court's jurisdiction short of an amendment to the Rome Statute is doubtful. This raises the question, given the high threshold imposed for amending the Rome Statute, as to which political authority is, or should be, competent to ratify or recognize *bona fide* amnesties that curtail the ICC's jurisdiction—yet another example of the problems that can arise from creating a judicial jurisdiction without a cognate legislative body. The Assembly of States Parties should, notwithstanding this formal difficulty, take 29

[37] See Transitional Justice Institute, *The Belfast Guidelines on Amnesty and Accountability* (University of Ulster 2013) <peacemaker.un.org/sites/peacemaker.un.org/files/BelfastGuidelines_TJI2014.pdf.pdf> accessed 4 December 2017.

[38] UN General Assembly, Rome Statute of the International Criminal Court, A/CONF. 183/9, 17 July 1998.

[39] UNSC Res 1970, UN Doc S/RES/1970 (26 February 2011) <www.icc-cpi.int/NR/rdonlyres/2B57BBA2-07D9-4C35-B45E-EED275080E87/0/N1124558.pdf> accessed 4 December 2017.

active measures to recognize legitimate national amnesties, thus alleviating the need for the judicial and prosecutorial organs to make judgments that are intrinsically unsuited to their functions and statutory framework.

Bibliography

Ambos, K, et al (eds), *Building a Future on Peace and Justice: Studies on Transitional Justice, Peace and Development* (Springer 2009).

Cryer, R et al, *An Introduction to International Criminal Law and Procedure*' (CUP 2010).

du Bois-Pedain, A, *Transitional Justice in South Africa* (CUP 2007).

Freeman, M, *Necessary Evils: Amnesties and the Search for Justice* (CUP 2009).

Goodwin-Gill, GS and McAdam, J, *The Refugee in International Law* (OUP 2007).

Hayner, P, 'Negotiating Peace in Sierra Leone: Confronting the Justice Challenge', Report (Henry Dunant Centre for Humanitarian Dialogue, December 2007).

Jeffrey, R, *Amnesties, Accountability, and Human Rights* (University of Pennsylvania Press 2014).

Lessa, F and Payne, LA (eds), *Amnesty in the Age of Human Rights Accountability* (CUP 2012).

Meisenberg, SM, 'Legality of amnesties in international humanitarian law—The Lomé Amnesty Decision of the Special Court for Sierra Leone', 86 International Review of the Red Cross 856 (31 December 2004) 837–51 <www.icrc.org/eng/assets/files/other/irrc_856_meisenberg.pdf> accessed 4 December 2017.

Meringues, G and Mendez, J, 'Reconciling Amnesties with Universal Jurisdiction' (2000) 2 International Law Forum 76–97.

Orentlicher, D, 'Settling Accounts, The Duty to Prosecute Human Rights Violations of a Former Regime' (1991) 100 Yale Law Journal 2537–615.

O'Shea, A, *Amnesty for Crime in International Law and Practice* (Kluwer Law International 2002).

Rikhof, J, *The Criminal Refugee: The Treatment of Asylum Seekers With A Criminal Background in International and Domestic Law* (Republic of Letters Publishing 2012).

Schabas, W and Bernaz, N (eds), *Routledge Handbook of International Criminal Law* (Routledge 2011).

Scharf, MP, 'From the eXile Files: An Essay on Trading Justice for Peace' (2006) 63 Washington & Lee Law Review 339–79.

Transitional Justice Institute, *The Belfast Guidelines on Amnesty and Accountability* (University of Ulster 2013).

Principle 29. Restrictions on the Jurisdiction of Military Courts

Fionnuala Ní Aoláin

The jurisdiction of military tribunals must be restricted solely to specifically military offences committed by military personnel, to the exclusion of human rights violations, which shall come under the jurisdiction of the ordinary domestic courts or, where appropriate, in the case of serious crimes under international law, of an international or internationalized criminal court.

A. Summary of Findings

International human rights and international humanitarian law broadly agree on the framework principles applicable to the administration of justice, including military jurisdiction. Among these general principles are included the notion of equality before courts; the right of every person to be neutrally judged by competent, independent, and impartial courts; the requirement of legality; and the right to an effective and fair trial. Principle 29 broadly affirms the exceptionality of military courts, but not their complete ouster. Principle 29 explicitly excludes the adjudication of human rights' violations by military courts, mandating ordinary domestic courts as the only appropriate venue of judicial oversight. Nonetheless, military courts remain functionally important for the routine and uncontroversial deployment of military law consistent with international law. Contemporary challenges emerge in determining whether military courts have any legal authority to judge civilians (functionality principle), whether new wars and the increasingly legalized exceptionality of military jurisdiction are rewriting hitherto accepted practice on restrictive and exceptional competence for such bodies, and the obstacles that military tribunals pose for victims seeking justice for human rights and humanitarian law violations. Incompatibility may be more pronounced in fragile, transitional, and conflict-affected states, where prior histories of human rights violations create greater sensitivity to the use of exceptional procedure and exceptional courts. Normative development in international law, as well as the jurisprudence of international courts and tribunals, has increasingly stymied the operation of military courts, and affirmed that such courts must be human-rights and specifically fair-trial compliant.

B. Contextual and Historical Introduction

The precise role and scope of military jurisdiction has long been tackled by international law. The Universal Declaration and International Covenant on Civil and Political Rights address public trial (Articles 8, 10, 2.3(a), and 14 respectively);[1] legality of procedure is emphasized by all regional human rights treaties; and Article IX of the Inter-American 1

[1] Universal Declaration of Human Rights, UN Doc A/RES/217(III) (10 December 1948) (UDHR); International Covenant on Civil and Political Rights, UN Doc A/RES/2200(A) (23 March 1976) (ICCPR).

Convention on Forced Disappearance of Persons (1994)[2] excludes military courts from exercising jurisdiction over this category of cases. Numerous soft law standards have addressed independence of military jurisdiction, including: the Report to the General Assembly (2006);[3] the Project of Principles on the Administration of Justice by Military Tribunals (2006);[4] the multiple Reports of the United Nations Special Rapporteurs on Torture and Extrajudicial, Summary or Arbitrary Executions[5] as well as the Resolution on the Right to a Fair Trial and Legal Aid in Africa (1999).[6] All of these soft and hard law standards have been consistently supplemented by a reservoir of contentious jurisprudence from the Inter-American and European human rights systems.

2 The Sub-Commission's engagement with amnesty, impunity, and accountability stretches back to its thirty-eighth session in August 1985, when Special Rapporteur Joinet presented his *Study on amnesty laws and their role in the safeguard and promotion of human rights*.[7] Military courts are only mentioned in passing in this early study, as sites in which amnesty may be enabled.[8] The first fulsome reflection on the intersection between impunity came in the Joinet Principles (1997), which substantively addressed military courts in Principle 38. The phrasing of Principle 38 is somewhat more tenuous than its revised form in the Orentlicher 2005 Updated Set of Principles. In the 1997 version, the provision qualifies the exclusion of military courts exclusively because they 'do not have sufficient statutory independence'. By 2005, the ouster is definitive and without qualification: 'The jurisdiction of military tribunals must be restricted solely to specifically military offences committed by military personnel'. The other notable difference between the two texts is that in 1997, Special Rapporteur Joinet affirmed only that adjudication of human rights violation could only come 'within the jurisdiction of the ordinary courts'. By 2005, that narrow jurisdiction for human rights violations had been updated to allow for the jurisdiction of 'an international or internationalized criminal court', a pragmatic acknowledgement of the reach of international accountability for systematic human rights and humanitarian law violations. The tightening of the language between 1997 and 2005 also reflects an intention to be compliant with a wide range of special mechanisms created by the Commission on Human Rights, the Declaration on Enforced Disappearances,[9] resolutions of the Commission and Sub-Commission, the practice of human rights treaty bodies, and state practice.

3 The most notorious contemporary military commissions are those established by President George W Bush on 13 November 2001.[10] Their creation focused significant

[2] Inter-American Convention on Forced Disappearance of Persons (entered into force 28 March 1996) (1994) 33 International Legal Materials 1429.

[3] UN Secretary-General, *Civil and Political Rights, Including Questions of Independence of the Judiciary, Administration of Justice, Impunity*, UN Doc A/61/384 (12 September 2006).

[4] UN Commission on Human Rights, Draft Principles Governing the Administration of Justice Through Military Tribunals, UN Doc E/CN.4/2006/58 (13 January 2006).

[5] See, eg, Joint Report of the Special Rapporteur on the question of torture and the Special Rapporteur on extrajudicial, summary or arbitrary executions, UN Doc E/CN.4/1995/111 (4 August 1994) IV(B); Report of the Special Rapporteur on extrajudicial, summary or arbitrary executions, Mission to Mexico, UN Doc A/HRC/26/36/Add.1 (28 April 2014) paras 27–29, 90.

[6] African Commission on Human and Peoples' Rights, Resolution on the Right to Fair Trial and Legal Aid in Africa (15 November 1999) 41.

[7] UN Doc E/CN.4/Sub.2/1985/16/Rev.1 (21 June 1985).

[8] Ibid, para 48(c).

[9] Declaration on the Protection of All Persons from Enforced Disappearances, UN Doc A/RES/47/133 (18 December 1992) Art 16.

[10] Military Order of 13 November 2001, 66 Fed Reg 57, 833.

global attention on the use of military courts as a mechanism to process and try individuals suspected of involvement in statute-defined (terrorist) acts or offences committed during armed conflict. The Guantanamo Commissions have re-energized global conversations about the abuse of military jurisdiction, as well shining a light on the lack of meaningful control over their day-to-day operations in situations of conflict and extremity. With much less publicity than one finds for the Guantanamo Military Commissions, multiple states have long used military courts as means to manage and address exceptional threats and challenges,[11] and they have long pedigrees of operation in multiple parts of the world, as well as on the international plane.[12] A challenge for the contemporary relevance of Principle 29, is the extent to which it adequately balances a necessary reliance on military commissions and courts to discharge an important justice role for states with restraint on the abuses that can be exercised by such bodies.

A number of early definitional matters present and require elucidation. First, as to the distinctions between civilian and military courts, including the operational and jurisdictional patterns that have historically framed their respective spheres of influence. This means addressing the extent to which the presumed rigidity of differences between ordinary courts and military courts holds up to scrutiny. Is it always necessarily true that military commissions will be prejudicial to human rights protections? While there may be an early temptation to view military courts and commissions as de facto exceptional and incompatible with accepted notions of the rule of law, we should avoid this easy presumption. As Gary D Solis observes, 'in many democracies, military courts in the form of courts-martial also have uncontroversial ordinary functions in implementing military codes of justice and regulating and enforcing military discipline'.[13] 'Military tribunal' is the unifying term for all military proceedings of a judicial nature. Courts-martial, employed in virtually all military legal systems, constitute a form of military tribunal, as do courts of inquiry, which investigate serious military incidents such as the loss of ships at sea. Provost courts,[14] another form of military tribunal, convene in occupied territory to try offences alleged against civilians. Military government courts and Provisional Courts are additional specific forms of military tribunal. Military commissions should not be (but often are) confused with courts-martial. Courts-martial try offences committed by members of the armed forces against the state's military criminal code.[15] 4

The Principles are most relevant when military courts are deployed as a means to process ordinary crimes and regular defendants deemed unsuitable by executive or legislative regulation for the ordinary courts. In this guise, such bodies are prima facie non-compliant with the Principle. Understanding when and if a military court/commission contravenes the Principle requires paying attention to the following elements: 5

[11] See, eg, S Enright, *The Trial of Civilians by Military Courts: Ireland, 1921* (Irish Academic Press 2012).

[12] F Ní Aoláin and O Gross (eds), *Guantanamo and Beyond: Exceptional Courts and Military Commissions in Comparative Perspective* (CUP 2013).

[13] G Solis, 'Contemporary Law of War and Military Commissions' in Ní Aoláin and Gross (eds), n 12, 73–94.

[14] WA Gabrielson, 'Martial Law and Crime' (1943) 33 Journal of Criminal Law and Criminology 381–84.

[15] Manual for Courts-Martial (MCM), I-1, II-1, II-10, United States (2008 edn), 'the jurisdiction of courts-martial is entirely penal or disciplinary'; Uniform Code of Military Justice, 816.30, 822.22; Manual for Military Commissions (MMC), I-1, II-3; United States (2010 edn); Military Commissions Act of 2009, Title XVIII, HR 2647—385 §948b ('establishes procedures governing the use of military commissions to try alien unprivileged enemy belligerents for violations of the law of war and other offenses triable by military commission').

- The authorization basis and context of a court's establishment, whether exceptional or regularly constituted.
- The limits articulated to such courts in their operation (time limited, geographical and jurisdictional limits) and the extent to which different standards of justice are applied breaching the norm of equality for all before law.
- The range of offences over which the courts have jurisdiction, and whether such offences include jurisdiction over human rights violations or recharacterize generally understood civilian crime as military offences. These issues were directly addressed in the *Incal, Gerger, Karatas*, and *Çiraklar v Turkey* cases.[16] The European Court of Human Rights (ECtHR) has consistently held that the principles of competence, independence, and impartiality were compromised by extending the range of (ordinary) crimes subject to military jurisdiction.
- Permissibility and/or limitations in the range of evidence that can be brought before the military courts, and whether manipulation of evidence enables greater power to the state, thereby enabling de facto impunity.
- The judicial appointment mechanisms to such courts, and specifically adherence to norms of judicial independence and impartiality (perceived and actual). The African Commission on Human and Peoples' Rights (AComHPR) has adjudicated a series of cases addressing independence and impartiality of courts consisting of army officers, and found them wanting.[17]
- The perceived neutrality and impartiality of such courts from the executive, and the extent to which restrictions and/or operation impedes open justice.
- The limitations on due process rights ascribed to those subject to the court's authority, including right of access to legal counsel and conditions of detention.[18] Numerous cases from the Inter-American Court of Human Rights (IACtHR) underscore the extent to which military courts were synonymous with systemic and wide-ranging violations of due process rights.[19]

6 It is the totality of these concerns that underpins the reluctance to cede to military commissions the right to review human rights violations. The procedural faultlines previously identified, including legality, formal, and informal inequality before law, the flaws of prosecutorial charging accompanying military justice, judicial independence, and due process weaknesses are particularly fatal to the adjudication of human rights violations. Human rights violations committed by state actors have heightened stakes in adjudication and outcome. These proceedings are rarely judged on their narrow merits alone, but rather attest to rule-of-law adherence and the capacity of the state to self-correct. Military justice fails to provide reassurance and legitimacy when the state and the military are invariably and inextricably bound to one another.

[16] *Incal v Turkey* (Judgment) (ECtHR, 9 June 1998); *Gerger v Turkey* (Judgment) (ECtHR, 8 July 1999); *Karatas v Turkey* (Judgment) (ECtHR, 8 July 1999); *Ciraklar v Turkey* (Judgment) (ECtHR, 28 October 1998).

[17] *Constitutional Rights Project v Nigeria (in respect of Wahab Akamu and Others)*, report no 60/91 (AComHPR, 22 March 1995); *Annette Pagnoulle (on behalf of Abdoulaye Mazou) v Cameroon*, report no 39/90 (AComHPR, 24 April 1997); *Civil Liberties Organisation, Legal Defence Centre, Legal Defence and Assistance Project v Nigeria*, report no 218/98 (AComHPR, 7 May 2001); *Forums of Conscience v Sierra Leone*, report no 223/98 (AComHPR, 6 November 2000).

[18] See F Ní Aoláin and O Gross, 'The Trial of Terrorism' in C Walker and G Lennon (eds), *Routledge Handbook of Law and Terrorism* (Taylor & Francis 2015) 206–21.

[19] *Rosendo Radilla Pacheco v Mexico* (Judgment) IACtHR Series C no 209 (23 November 2009).

C. Theoretical Framework

One of the basic human rights is the right to a fair trial.[20] The right to a fair trial ensures that no person is deprived of liberty without due process of the law.[21] Constraints on military courts are the natural outworking of an entrenched value given to fair trial within human rights and humanitarian law regimes. Rule-of-law and fair trial provisions take on a particular cogency in situations of transition, in part because prior conflict and/or repression generally mean that the rule of law is degraded, and lacks legitimacy and confidence for a sizeable portion of the transitioning polity. In crude terms, the 'rule of law' is an assertion of law's pre-eminence—its autonomy from and superiority to fallible politics. However, while variously lauded as the 'signal virtue of civilized societies'[22] and 'an unqualified human good',[23] rule of law can be difficult to pin down in practice. At its most basic, the rule of law is seen as a means to stymie the worst excesses of arbitrary power, and in societies that have experienced military rule, military imprints on civilian politics and/or the engagement of military forces in systematic human rights abuses underscore why the emphasis on civilian trials is a symbolic short-cut to emphasize a new kind of rule-of-law primacy. 7

While military courts may operate in violation of the Principle, arguably military commissions may fall into a singular category of perceived exceptionalism when they are utilized by democratic states, and when they try civilians. Exceptionalism is defined as the recourse by states to exceptional legal measures, whether by derogation, limitation, reservation, or de facto emergency practice, to enable greater latitude, flexibility, and power to the executive.[24] Exceptionalism is often revealed when the state moves outside the regular legal system to military, emergency, or ad hoc justice systems. 8

Despite jurisprudence that military courts do not inherently violate the fair trial provisions of international law,[25] many scholars underscore the resistance by international courts and other review mechanisms to accepting the legitimacy of civilian trial before military commissions. Such resistance follows organically from the Principle, and echoes discomfort with the normalization of regime exception. The disquiet at military jurisdiction opposes the political move (and motivation) to constrained rules that limit full transparency in legal process and outcomes, allied with a sense that military and civilian life ought rightly to function in separate spheres and that legal amalgamation between the two is undesirable. There are narrow formal exceptions to this bar: for example, accepting that in extreme exigencies, where regular trials before civilian courts are impossible, limited military jurisdiction might be undertaken. A paradox emerges in core resistance to the seepage of military justice beyond a narrowly defined remit, and in practice a fairly reliable usage by both democratic and non-democratic states on military courts. Increasingly there are also less clear demarcation lines between civilian and military jurisdiction. 9

[20] See, eg, UDHR, n 1, Art 10; Geneva Convention Relative to the Treatment of Prisoners of War, 75 UNTS 135 (12 August 1949) Art 3.

[21] ICCPR, n 1, Art 9(1).

[22] N MacCormick, *Rhetoric and the Rule of Law: A Theory of Legal Reasoning* (OUP 2005) 12.

[23] EP Thompson, *Whigs and Hunters: The Origins of the Black Act* (Pantheon Books 1975) 266.

[24] F Ní Aoláin and O Gross, *Law in Times of Crisis: Emergency Powers in Theory and Practice* (CUP 2006).

[25] See *contra*, *Ergin v Turkey (No 6)* App no 47533/99 (ECtHR, 4 May 2006) at para 45, regarding military courts in Turkey. The Court found that criminal jurisdiction of military courts over civilians requires particularly careful scrutiny, and can only be justified in very exceptional circumstances, demanding compelling justifications in addition to a clear and foreseeable legal basis that must be substantiated in each case.

10 The rehabilitation of law in many transitional settings gives a particular cogency to this idea of judicial restraint and judicial limits, and Principle 29 inherently absorbs that concept of limit and constraint. Importantly, many commentators have linked the exceptionalism and unacceptability of military courts to practices that occur long before civilian defendants appear before the courts. In particular, concerns about military jurisdiction have to be placed in a broader context of modified arrest and detention practices that invariably precede trial before military officers and have equal (if not greater) effects on fair trial outcomes. Scholars and practitioners have ably argued that there is a continuum of exceptionalism pervading the preventive detention paradigm in which military courts are an essential and not auxiliary element, hazardously infected with a sweeping view of security threats, posing a fundamental threat to due process rights and fair trial.[26]

D. Practice

11 Ireland and Turkey offer two prominent European examples of the use of military courts.[27] In both cases military courts operated as jurisdictional 'gap fillers' for two states looking to short-circuit the usage of the ordinary courts in situations of emergency and low-intensity internal armed conflict.[28] Criminal trials of civilians by military courts staffed by military personnel, or a mixture of military and non-military judges, effectively existed only in Turkey until the practice was abolished at the beginning of the twenty-first century.[29] Turkey was also effectively the only state in Europe to conduct trials of civilians for terrorist and non-terrorist offences by mixed National (or state) Security Courts (NSCs), staffed by a military and two non-military judges. The basis for the Special Criminal Court in Ireland was laid down in the Irish Constitution, which enabled the establishment of 'special courts' with wide-ranging powers when the 'ordinary courts are inadequate to secure the effective administration of justice'. The Court was established by parliamentary legislation in 1939 and was originally staffed by military officers; it remains operative to the present day. It has consistently processed terrorist-related offences, but its use was extended to allow organized crimes cases to be processed by three-judge panels with no jury. It has been subject to sustained critique on grounds of fairness and independence.

12 Turkey has been subject to sustained challenge on its use of military courts. In *Ergin*, the applicant argued that his fair trial rights under Article 6 ECHR were violated because his trial court had not been independent or impartial.[30] While the ECtHR was not prepared to absolutely prohibit military courts in all circumstances, it affirmed a trend towards the exclusion of criminal jurisdiction by military judges over civilians. It argued cogently that the constitutional position of the military in democratic states

[26] F de Londras, *Detention in the 'War on Terror': Can Human Rights Fight Back?* (CUP 2011); F De Londras, 'Prevention, Detention, and Extraordinariness' in Ní Aoláin and Gross (eds), n 12, 117–36.

[27] See FF Davis, *The History and Development of the Special Criminal Court—1921–2005* (Four Courts Press 2007) on the Irish Special Criminal Court. See A Mowbray, 'Military Judges and the Right to a Fair Trial' (2006) 6 Human Rights Law Review 176–83, 176, on Turkey.

[28] M Robinson, *The Special Criminal Court* (Dublin University Press 1974).

[29] See also *Martin v United Kingdom* (Judgment) (ECtHR, 24 January 2007), where the Court condemned as a violation of Art 6 of the European Convention on Human Rights (ECHR) the trial for murder of a civilian in a military court. At the material time, the accused had been living in Germany with his family—including his father, a solider serving with the British Army. In accordance with the NATO Status of Forces Agreement 1951, he was subject to Army jurisdiction rather than that of the German courts.

[30] *Ergin v Turkey (No 6)*, n 25, para 12.

should be limited to national security matters, on the basis that judicial power is normally an attribute of civil institutions. In 1999, following constitutional and legislative amendments, the military judge was replaced by a civilian judge in these courts, and in 2004 NSCs were abolished entirely.[31]

Core concepts of a fair trial, namely independence and impartiality, seem inherently compromised when civilians find themselves within the jurisdiction of military courts. For example, reviewing courts in Turkey and Peru, the Human Rights Committee determined that the special courts in those states were not structurally independent and, consequently, that the accused had been denied a fair trial.[32] The AComHPR determined that Nigeria had breached fair trial protections in its military tribunals by denying access to counsel, conducting the trial in camera, and allowing an appeal only to a military council that exercised the various roles of complainant, prosecutor, and judge.[33] International human rights courts and mandated human rights bodies have carefully scrutinized the conduct of military and police officers selected to serve as judges or lawyers in extraordinary courts.[34] Indeed, even in a structurally independent tribunal system, the simple presence of such judges will inevitably raise valid concerns over their objective impartiality.[35] Hence, while military courts' trying civilians and other extraordinary courts are not violations per se, they rarely pass muster, because they fail to achieve the independence, impartiality, and judicial guarantees required by human rights and humanitarian law. 13

In a striking analysis of the difficulties of ensuring fair trials in military courts, the IACtHR found that convictions by 'faceless' Peruvian military courts of civilians accused of terrorist activities violated the right to a fair trial.[36] Peru defended its military courts, arguing that the courts were legitimately established, that their independence and impartiality were guaranteed under the national Constitution, and that, given the danger of terrorism, it was necessary to try the civilians in a military court. The IACtHR rejected Peru's arguments, stating that 'military tribunals are not the tribunals previously established by law for civilians'.[37] According to the Court, 'a basic principle of the independence of the judiciary is that every person has the right to be heard by regular courts', and the very act of trying a civilian in an extraordinary military court for a matter that a regular court should hear violated the individual's right to an independent tribunal.[38] Moreover, the Court concluded that the military judges were not independent or impartial, and that the military courts also violated various other fair trial protections. 14

The case is notable because despite Peru's undisputed claim that it had 'scrupulously complied with the procedural guarantees established in Peruvian law',[39] the Court found 15

[31] *Incal v Turkey* (Judgment) (ECtHR, 9 June 1998). Here, the ECtHR considered the compatibility of pre-1999 arrangements with the ECHR and found them non-Convention compliant.

[32] See generally R Wilson, 'Can the US Courts Learn from Failed Terrorist Trials by Military Commission in Turkey and Peru?' (2003) 11 Human Rights Brief 12–14.

[33] See DM Amann, 'Guantánamo' (2004) 42 Columbia Journal of Transnational Law 263–348, 331–32.

[34] See, eg, UN Working Group on Arbitrary Detention, Decision no 40/1995 (Turkey), UN Doc E/CN.4/1997/4/Add.1 (29 October 1996) 14.

[35] Courts considering violations of the right to an independent and impartial tribunal in the context of extraordinary courts have generally found such courts to be both non-independent and partial. The AComHPR, without analysing independence (Art 7(1) of the African Charter only ensures trial by an impartial court), has found that the presence of military and police officers as judges in special tribunals by 'its composition alone creates the appearance, if not actual lack of impartiality'. See, *Constitutional Rights Project v Nigeria*, report no 87/93 (AComHPR, 22 March 1995) at paras 5, 14.

[36] *Castillo Petruzzi v Peru* (Judgment) IACtHR Series C no 52 (30 May 1999).

[37] Ibid, para 128. [38] Ibid, para 129. [39] Ibid, para 171.

that the procedures established under national law nonetheless violated the basic right to a fair trial as provided under the American Convention. Consequently, the Court extended the protections of independence beyond separation of powers and judicial conditions of service, by declaring that trying a civilian in an extraordinary court—even one with formal, constitutionally-ensured independence—for a matter that should be heard by a regular court facially violated the right to an independent tribunal.[40] Following 9/11, the Inter-American Commission on Human Rights (IAComHR) produced a report consistent with this holding, stating that the right to a fair trial 'generally prohibits the use of ad hoc, special, or military tribunals or commissions to try civilians for terrorist-related or any other crimes'.[41]

E. Critical Assessment

16 In conclusion, military courts, while assuredly serving important functions within the military forces of states, remain wholly within the purview of human rights and humanitarian law compliance. Military courts are not outside the boundaries of human rights norms but subject to overview on the same basis as any other court or tribunal. The use and abuse of military courts to achieve objectives of speed, seclusion, and security for states, when applied to civilian crimes and persons who do not belong to military forces, clearly falls outside the bounds of acceptable practice within existing norms. Military courts are consistently deemed inappropriate venues to adjudicate human rights violations. Nonetheless, as the use of military commissions by the US post 9/11 reveals, states continue to flirt with the use of such exceptional bodies, notwithstanding the increased international and domestic scrutiny they bring. In part, the resort may be as much symbolic as practical, messaging some notion about the status of conflict and the political positioning of the state with regard to certain groups and individuals, as it is efficiency or security driven. When military courts are deployed in fragile, transitional, and post-conflict states there is a clear and present danger that the modality of trial may compound rather than address serious human rights violations and the deficiencies of the rule of law. This is because the symbolism and practice of open, transparent, and civilian-run trials are an integral component of institutional reform in states where legal legitimacy is compromised, and courts suffer from a deficit of public trust. Principle 29 cautions states clearly that military courts cannot entrench or enable impunity, and that overreach will result in palpable condemnation and inspection for the state.

Bibliography

Amann, DM, 'Guantánamo' (2004) 42 Columbia Journal of Transnational Law 263–348, 331–32.

Davis, F, *The History and Development of the Special Criminal Court—1921–2005* (Four Courts Press 2007).

de Londras, F, *Detention in the 'War on Terror': Can Human Rights Fight Back?* (CUP 2011).

Enright, S, *The Trial of Civilians by Military Courts: Ireland, 1921* (Irish Academic Press 2012).

[40] See DS Weissbrodt and JC Hansen, 'The Right to Fair Trial in an Extraordinary Court' in Ní Aoláin and Gross (eds), n 12, 305–20.

[41] IAComHR, *Report on Terrorism and Human Rights*, OEA/Ser.L/V/II.116 (22 October 2002) Doc 5 rev 1 corr, para 18.

Gibson, MR, 'International Human Rights Law and the Administration of Justice through Military Tribunals: Preserving Utility while Precluding Impunity' (2008) 4 Journal of International Law and International Relations 1–48.

Gutierrez, JC and Cantu, S, 'The Restriction of Military Jurisdiction in International Human Rights Protection Systems' (2010) 13 International Journal on Human Rights 74–97.

Andreu-Guzman, F, *Military Jurisdiction and International Law*, vol 1: *Military Courts and Gross Human Rights Violations* (International Commission of Jurists 2004).

Mowbray, A, 'Military Judges and the Right to a Fair Trial' (2006) 6 Human Rights Law Review 176–83.

Ní Aoláin, F and Gross, O (eds), *Guantanamo and Beyond: Exceptional Courts and Military Commissions in Comparative Perspective* (CUP 2013).

Ní Aoláin, F and Gross, O, 'The Trial of Terrorism' in C Walker and G Lennon (eds), *Routledge Handbook of Law and Terrorism* (Taylor & Francis 2015) 206–21.

Wilson, R, 'Can the US Courts Learn from Failed Terrorist Trials by Military Commission in Turkey and Peru?' (2003) 11 Human Rights Brief 12–14.

Principle 30. Restrictions on the Principle of the Irremovability of Judges

Christopher Gosnell

The principle of irremovability, as the basic guarantee of the independence of judges, must be observed in respect of judges who have been appointed in conformity with the requirements of the rule of law. Conversely, judges unlawfully appointed or who derive their judicial power from an act of allegiance may be relieved of their functions by law in accordance with the principle of parallelism. They must be provided an opportunity to challenge their dismissal in proceedings that meet the criteria of independence and impartiality with a view toward seeking reinstatement.

A. Summary of Findings

Judicial independence, both institutional and individual, is a condition of any justice system. Respecting this principle in a trans-regime setting, while at the same time ensuring that the judiciary adjudicates the crimes of a past regime with adequate vigour, can present a genuine dilemma between continuity and reform. Principle 30 addresses this paradox, affirming that judges may not be removed if they were appointed 'in conformity with the requirements of the rule of law', but not if they were 'unlawfully appointed' or 'derive their judicial power from an act of allegiance'. Judges in the latter category 'must be provided an opportunity to challenge their dismissal', but only with a view to subsequent reinstatement and not as a pre-condition to removal.

The distinction is a helpful starting point, but fails to incorporate the well-established international criteria for assessing judicial independence and impartiality. Further, Principle 30 fails to offer adequate criteria for assessing institutional independence, which will seldom be particular to the circumstances of appointment of any individual judge.

Just because an office-holder's appointment does not satisfy the minimum conditions for security of tenure does not mean, on the other hand, that removal is always good policy. Other considerations, including public confidence and expertise, may weigh in favour of retaining independent and competent judges from the old regime, even if their offices lack the minimum attributes of judicial independence.

B. Contextual and Historical Introduction

1 One of the most fundamental human rights is that 'everyone shall be entitled to a fair and public hearing by a competent, independent and impartial tribunal established by law'.[1] Fairness depends on adjudicators who are, and reasonably perceived to be, independent

[1] International Covenant on Civil and Political Rights, 16 December 1966, United Nations, Treaty Series, v. 999, p 171, Art 14(1).

and impartial in assessing the law and the facts of a case.[2] The appearance of legitimacy is vital and precious in societies fractured by socio-economic, ethnic, religious, or racial divisions. The adjudicators, charged with the 'ultimate decision over life, freedoms, rights, duties and property of citizens',[3] must appear to the well-informed citizenry to be fully independent of any influence by the state—especially in respect of criminal prosecutions, which typically place the state and the individual at odds. The legitimacy and integrity of the entire system of governance, in a broad sense, depend on independent adjudicators.

Judges, in order to be impartial between the government and individuals, must have 2 guarantees that they cannot be removed merely because they displease the government of the day. Likewise, it must not be within the gift of a new government to simply replace the judiciary at will. A system with these attributes would not sufficiently ensure the reality, or the perception, of independence of judges.

This principle creates challenges in a transitional justice setting. First, the formal 3 guarantees of judicial independence—that is, security of tenure and freedom from any control or instruction from other organs of the state—mean that members of the judiciary cannot be dismissed in the same way as politicians, police, prosecutors, and other civil servants. Second, the wholesale or even selective removal of judges by a new regime risks, in itself, undermining the rule of law and the legitimacy of the new judiciary. Indeed, given the type of contested claims that can arise in a transitional environment, this is an original sin that can undermine the fight against impunity by creating a perception that the new judiciary is, itself, tainted by a lack of judicial independence.

Germany in the first half of the twentieth century presents a striking example of a trans- 4 regime judiciary. The political revolutions of the Weimar Republic, the Third Reich, and the Federal Republic of Germany were not accompanied by the wholesale replacement of the judiciary.[4] The post-Second World War occupying powers initially considered 'closing all German courts for ten years and replacing them with a "colonial" system', but in the end almost all Nazi-era judges retained their posts.[5] The need for root-and-branch reform was undoubtedly reduced by the occupation legal system that adjudicated a large number of Nazi crimes, thus decreasing the impetus for abolition of regular German courts or the wholesale removal of its judges.[6]

[2] ICTY, *The Prosecutor v Furundzija* (Judgment) (Appeals Chamber) IT-95-17/1-A (21 July 2000) para 177: 'The fundamental human right of an accused to be tried before an independent and impartial tribunal is generally recognized as being an integral component of the requirement that an accused should have a fair trial'; Bangalore Principles of Judicial Conduct, Value 1: 'Judicial independence is a prerequisite to the rule of law and a fundamental guarantee of a fair trial.'

[3] Preamble, UN Basic Principles on the Independence of the Judiciary, Adopted by the Seventh United Nations Congress on the Prevention of Crime and the Treatment of Offenders held at Milan from 26 August to 6 September 1985 and endorsed by General Assembly Resolutions 40/32 of 29 November 1985 and 40/146 of 13 December 1985 <www.ohchr.org/EN/ProfessionalInterest/Pages/IndependenceJudiciary.aspx> accessed 22 January 2018. (hereinafter 'UN Basic Principles').

[4] A notorious exception was the *Volksgerichtshof*, created outside of the existing constitutional framework by order of Adolf Hitler in 1934.

[5] E Posner and A Vermeule, 'Transitional Justice as Ordinary Justice' (2004) 117 Harvard Law Review 761–825, 778; I Markovitz, 'Children of a Lesser God: GDR Lawyers in Post-Socialist Germany' (1996) 94 Michigan Law Review 2270–2308, 2273.

[6] D Cohen, *Transitional Justice in Divided Germany After 1945* <www.ocf.berkeley.edu/~changmin/Papers/cohen-trans-justice-germany.pdf> accessed 6 December 2017, at 3 ('American military tribunals convicted 1814 German war criminals (450 received death sentences), British tribunals 1085 (240 death sentences), French 2107 (104 death sentences) ... the Soviet Union tried and convicted as many as 45,000 Germans for war crimes, though some other figures are lower and caution is required.')

C. Theoretical Framework

5 Principle 30 appears in the section of the Principles entitled 'Restrictions on rules of law justified by action to combat impunity'. The implication is that Principle 30 is defining an exception to the principle of 'irremovability' of judges.

6 The first draft of Principle 30 provided little practical guidance as to how to distinguish a judicial office entitled to irremovability from those that were not:

> Irremovability, though vital as a safeguard of the independence of judges, must not benefit impunity. Judges appointed in conformity with an earlier legal regime may be confirmed in their positions. Conversely, judges appointed unlawfully may be relieved of their functions in accordance with the principle of parallelism, subject to appropriate safeguards.[7]

7 No description is provided of the attributes that a judge must possess to be worthy of the title and, hence, privileged from removal. Further, this first iteration of the rule has little consequence, since it merely says that judges in either category 'may be confirmed', or 'may be relieved'.

8 The current version of Principle 30 is a substantial improvement. It prohibits the removal of judges who were 'appointed in conformity with the requirements of the rule of law' but allows, subject to challenge, the removal of those who were 'unlawfully appointed or who derive their judicial power from an act of allegiance'. The criteria for distinguishing between judges who may not, and those who may, be removed are not defined.

9 This lack of definition is surprising in light of the wealth of international instruments, as well as a widespread consensus, concerning the three essential characteristics of a judicial office: (i) a degree of security of tenure;[8] (ii) institutional independence, including the manner of selection and remuneration of the judiciary;[9] and (iii) lack of interference from the executive by way of instructions, pressures, or inducement to decide cases in particular ways.[10]

10 The requirement of security of tenure does not require absolute 'irremovability'. Judges need not be appointed for life or until a set retirement age, but the minimum term should at least be several years in respect of courts of general jurisdiction.[11] If the position is subject to renewal then such renewal must be decided in accordance with some

[7] UN Doc E/CN.4/Sub.2/1997/20/Rev.1 (2 October 1997), para 39.

[8] UN Basic Principles, Arts 11 and 12; Bejing Statement of Principles of the Independence of the Judiciary in the Lawasia Region (1995) <www.hurights.or.jp/archives/other_documents/section1/1995/08/beijing-statement-of-principles-of-the-independence-of-the-judiciary-in-the-lawasia-region-beijing-1.html> accessed 6 December 2017 (hereinafter 'Beijing Statement'), Principles 19 and 20: 'It is recognised that, in some countries, the tenure of judges is subject to confirmation from time to time by vote of the people or other formal procedures. However, it is recommended that all judges exercising the same jurisdiction be appointed for a period to expire upon the attainment of a particular age.'

[9] Principles and Guidelines on the Right to a Fair Trial and Legal Assistance in Africa <hrlibrary.umn.edu/research/ZIM%20Principles_And_G.pdf> accessed 6 December 2017 (hereinafter 'African Principles') A(4)(i): 'The sole criteria [sic] for appointment to judicial office shall be the suitability of a candidate for such office by reason of integrity, appropriate training or learning and ability'; Council of Europe, Recommendation no R (94) 12 of the Committee of Ministers of the Council of Europe (1994) (hereinafter 'Council of Europe Recommendation'), Principle I(2)(c); Bejing Statement, Principles 11, 12, and 15; UN Basic Principles, Art 10.

[10] UN Basic Principles, Arts 1, 4; Council of Europe Recommendation, Principle I(2)(c): 'In the decision-making process, judges should be independent and be able to act without any restriction, improper influence, inducements, pressures, threats or interferences, direct or indirect, from any quarter or for any reason.'

[11] UN Basic Principles, Art 12: 'Judges, whether appointed or elected, shall have guaranteed tenure until a mandatory retirement age *or the expiry of their term of office*, where such exists' (emphasis added).

'formal procedure' that, in particular, ensures independence from the executive branch.[12] Disciplinary removal of judges should be restricted to 'incapacity or behaviour that renders them unfit to discharge their duties',[13] or for 'commission of criminal offences or serious infringements of disciplinary rules'. [14] Suspension or removal of a judge on these grounds should, in principle, be decided by the judiciary itself, or by some other body independent of the legislative and executive branches.[15] The need for such a control is not to benefit the individual judge, but rather to ensure that disciplinary proceedings are not used by the executive as a means of exercising control over the judiciary.

The second criterion, institutional independence, requires that judges be appointed based on merit rather than political favouritism, and that the remuneration and management of the judiciary be secured from arbitrary interference by the other branches of government. 11

The third criterion, non-interference by political actors, requires that judicial independence be observed in practice. Evidence of actual interference or exertion of pressure by the executive, or a trend of decisions so one-sided as to be indicative of judicial partiality, may be enough to deprive an office of its apparently judicial character. 12

Principle 30 also says very little as to how this evaluation must be made to avoid infringing the requirement of irremovability. The only procedure specifically required by Principle 30 is that, subsequent to dismissal, judges 'must be provided an opportunity to challenge their dismissal in proceedings that meet the criteria of independence with a view toward seeking reinstatement'. This approach appears to be derived from the international standards concerning the removal of judges for misconduct, which require that judges facing removal 'shall have the right to a fair hearing' 'subject to an independent review'.[16] This disciplinary context, however, addresses a very different problem than that typically arising in the transitional justice setting, namely, the independence of the judiciary as an institution. 13

If the judiciary as a whole has sufficient attributes of independence then most of its members will presumptively also be immune from removal within their terms; if the judiciary as a whole does not have those attributes then most of its members will presumptively be removable. Principle 30, however, prescribes only an individual procedure apparently modelled on the international standards for dealing with judicial misconduct. Not only is this procedure unsuitable for addressing the systematic issues involved, but it also allows the removal of judges subject only to *post facto* review. 14

D. Practice

The treatment of judges in a trans-regime setting has varied from situation to situation. South Africa retained its entire corps of judges without requiring them to re-apply for 15

[12] Beijing Statement, Principle 19; African Principles, A(4)(g); UN Human Rights Commission (UNHRC), General Comment no 32, UN Doc CCPR/C/GC/32 (23 August 2007).

[13] UN Basic Principles, Art 18.

[14] Council of Europe Recommendation, Principle VI(2).

[15] Beijing Statement, Principle 24 ('Where parliamentary procedures or procedures for the removal of a judge by vote of the people do not apply, procedures for the removal of judges must be under the control of the judiciary'); UNHRC, Consideration of Reports Submitted By States Parties Under Article 40 of the Covenant, CCPR/CO/79/LKA (11 December 2003) para 16, encouraging Sri Lanka to strengthen judicial independence by 'providing for judicial, rather than parliamentary, supervision and discipline of judicial conduct'; The German Judiciary Act, Arts 61, 62.

[16] UN Basic Principles, n 3, Arts 17, 19.

their positions or undergo any other vetting. The apartheid-era judiciary was criticized not so much for its lack of independence as for being profoundly unrepresentative of the race and gender of the general population, and conservative and positivistic in respect of iniquitous laws.[17] It is important to remember, however, that judges are no more shielded from international criminal responsibility by invoking the 'evil but valid' defence than are soldiers by the superior orders defence. Judges could, for example, arguably incur liability for persecution as a crime against humanity merely by applying a persecutory law, regardless of the validity of the law or even their own personal opposition to a law the implementation of which they facilitate. The extent to which South African judges could have thus been disqualified from office—or even put on trial—was never put to the test. Reform efforts, in accord with international sentiment, were directed instead towards the promulgation of constitutional rights, a new constitutional court, and a new system of judicial appointments to promote a judiciary more representative of the population.[18] The potential impact of this incrementalist approach on the judiciary's willingness and ability to tackle impunity will never be known, since responsibility for past crimes was addressed in South Africa mainly through a non-judicial truth and reconciliation process.

16 At the other end of the spectrum is East Germany.[19] The judicial system of the German Democratic Republic (GDR) was essentially abolished and replaced with that of the Federal Republic of Germany. On 3 October 1990, for example, almost all of East Berlin's judges were suspended and replaced by West German judges pending a review of their political affiliations and professional qualifications. After this review, only about 17 per cent of East German judges in Berlin were reinstated; the numbers in other Eastern German States was higher, varying from 41 per cent to 63 per cent.[20] The West German authorities considered the GDR judicary to be part of 'an exercise in political authority' in which '[j]udges were functionaries rather than watchmen, aligned with and dependent upon the state rather than charged to supervise its activities'.[21] Judges performed much the same role as other civil servants and, in terms of removability, were treated accordingly. Like civil servants, judges were sometimes retained in the interests of continuity, but not in order to preserve judicial independence. The obvious lack of independence of the GDR judiciary meant that most of its office-holders had to be removed in order to instill the principle of judicial independence, and any crimes committed by GDR state officials were prosecuted by this new judiciary.

17 The UN Mission in Bosnia and Herzegovina, after a vetting process that required every judge to re-apply for his or her position, reinstated 70 per cent of the incumbent

[17] E Cameron, D Davis, and GJ Marcus, 'The Administration of Justice, Law Reform and Jurisprudence' 1993 Annual Survey of South African Law 791–828, 795; M Wesson and Max Du Plessis, 'Fifteen Years On: Central Issues Relating to the Transformation of the South African Judiciary' (2008) 24 South African Journal on Human Rights 187–213, 190–91.

[18] International Bar Association, *Beyond Polokwane: Safeguarding South Africa's Judicial Independence* (International Bar Association 2008) <www.ibanet.org/Article/Detail.aspx?ArticleUid=B2397A56-9D7C-4990-9B57-2749409604A5> accessed 6 December 2017, 18; J Klaaren, 'Institutional Transformation and the Choice Against Vetting in South Africa's Transition' in A Mayer-Rieck and P de Greiff (eds), *Justice as Prevention: Vetting Public Employees in Transitional Societies* (SSRC 2007) 159 ('Both [the apartheid government] and international opinion were thus strongly committed to maintaining rather than modifying the existing institutional independence of the South African judiciary.')

[19] Markovitz, n 5, 2273.

[20] D Kommers, 'Transitional Justice in Eastern Germany' (1997) 22 Law and Social Inquiry 829–48, 838.

[21] Markovitz, n 5, 2278.

judges. The review was conducted by regional panels consisting of national and international officials. Rather than respecting the principle of security of tenure, the UN actually engineered an amendment of the constitutions of all three constituent entities of Bosnia to abrogate the otherwise constitutionally protected independence of judges.[22] The need to attack impunity cannot be relied on as a justification for this frontal violation of the principle of judicial independence, especially in light of the robust activity of the International Criminal Tribunal for the former Yugoslavia (ICTY) and the hybrid panels of the War Crimes Chamber of Bosnia that were vigorously adjudicating the crimes of previous regimes.

The Greek administration following the Junta period from 1967 to 1974 consciously attempted to respect the independence of the judiciary, while also targeting high-level judicial promotions or appointments that had been made by the Junta. Judges who had been removed by the Junta were reinstated, and those promoted above a relatively high threshold were referred to an independent 'Higher Disciplinary Council', which was independent of the executive. The presiding judges of the three main courts, who had been hand-picked by the Junta, were immediately removed, and in the end, twelve judges were removed from office out of a total of twenty-three whose appointments or promotions during the Junta period were reviewed.[23] This approach contrasted with the vetting of the civil service and para-statal sector, in which a wider range of officials who had supported or collaborated with the Junta was removed without recourse to judicial or independent review. The respect accorded to the judiciary may have been attributable to the judiciary's perceived independence and contributions to the rule of law in the period prior to the Junta's assuming power. 18

Judicial independence was abolished in Iraq in 1977 when the Judicial Council was in practice placed under Cabinet control.[24] The Coalition Provisional Authority accordingly treated judges much like any other civil servants, tending to leave them in place but subject to removal in accordance with 'de-Baathification' criteria. This approach was similar to the 'lustration' criteria applied in many East European states, where the judges could be removed for close associations with the Communist Party or the security apparatus of those states. The criteria of judicial independence assist in understanding why an unduly close affiliation to the ruling party or security apparatus would vitiate judicial independence. Nevertheless, the Coalition Provisional Authority, as in Bosnia and in post-Second World War Germany, removed the fight against impunity from the realm of 'regular' courts and conferred it on a newly appointed 'Iraqi High Tribunal'. The creation of such a supplemental 'special' court with this specific jurisdiction reflects a potential compromise between preserving the incumbent judiciary while at the same time ensuring that specific types of crimes will be robustly addressed. Unfortunately, the creation of 'special courts'—whether it be the Iraqi High Tribunal, the infamous *Volksgerichtshof*, or the English medieval Star Chamber—is not infrequently associated with partiality and politicization. Indeed, the UN Basic Principles on the Independence of the Judiciary 19

[22] United Nations Development Programme, Bureau for Crisis Prevention and Recovery, Justice and Security Sector Reform, *Vetting Public Employees in Post-conflict Settings* (UNDP 2006) 39.

[23] D Sotiropolous, 'Swift Gradualism and Variable Outcomes: Vetting in Post-Authoritarian Greece' in Mayer-Rieck and de Greiff (eds), n 18, 120–45, 131–33.

[24] C Bassiouni, 'Post-Conflict Justice in Iraq: An Appraisal of the Iraq Special Tribunal' (2005) 38 Cornell International Law Journal 327–90, 367.

prohibits the creation of such courts,[25] despite international and state practice to the contrary in transitional justice settings.[26]

E. Critical Assessment

20 A new judicial order built at the expense of judicial independence may generate grievances and divisions that undermine even the most impartial and professional judiciary. Principle 30, when interpreted in light of the broader principles of judicial independence, reminds states that a new judicial order must build on, not destroy, any sound foundations that remain from the past. A commitment to judicial independence requires preserving those judges whose office possessed the essential attributes of judicial independence, and whose conduct reflected those attributes.

21 Principle 30 could, however, be formulated to better reflect the international standards of judicial independence, the typically systemic nature of the issue, and the type of procedure that would be suited to this assessment. A revised Principle 30, for example, could provide as follows:

> The security of tenure of judges must be respected. Judges who hold offices lacking the essential attributes of judicial independence may be removed. The determination whether a judiciary or judge possesses the attributes of independence must be made by an independent and impartial judicial body. States should consider, in appropriate cases, requesting international or regional organizations to assist in assessing whether a judiciary, or individual judge, possesses those attributes.

22 This revision would remedy several weaknesses in the current text. First, 'irremovability' is replaced with the broader notion of security of tenure. Second, the central criterion of removability becomes 'judicial independence' as a whole, rather than only the manner of 'appointment'. Not only is this concept well-established in international instruments, but it provides the criteria for a holistic assessment of a judge's appointment, performance, and status. Third, lack of independence becomes a condition precedent for removal, rather than merely a *post facto* review. Fourth, the reference to 'judiciary' invites a systemic, rather than individual, assessment in appropriate cases. Fifth, the body making the decision must itself possess the attributes of independence and impartiality. This may be considered controversial to the extent that it purports to remove issues of judicial independence from the realm of politics. The minimum guarantees of judicial independence are, however, a subject that has, in many countries, been treated as a justiciable issue. Lastly, the momentous consequences of any decision, combined with the

[25] UN Basic Principles, n 3, Art 5: 'Everyone shall have the right to be tried by ordinary courts or tribunals ... Tribunals that do not use the duly established procedures of the legal process shall not be created to displace the jurisdiction belonging to the ordinary courts.'

[26] In addition to the courts with special jurisdiction that were created with the assistance of the international community in Bosnia and Iraq, the ICTY and International Criminal Tribunal for Rwanda are themselves examples of courts of special jurisdiction that expressly displaced the 'jurisdiction belonging to the ordinary courts'. This practice suggests that there is, in fact, no prohibition on the creation of such courts. On the other hand, the legitimacy—and even of the legality—of such courts depends on scrupulous and transparent adherence to the principles of judicial independence and impartiality. The model presented by the Bosnia War Crimes Chamber, with the direct involvement of international judges and other international institutions, seems to offer a better model than that presented by the Iraqi High Tribunal.

stringent standards of impartiality and independence, will often require international assistance and involvement in order to be conducted in a genuinely independent manner.

An additional question, probably best left to the purview of Principle 36, is whether the jurisdiction of regular courts can be displaced by the creation of courts of special jurisdiction. Such a measure may constitute a less disruptive alternative to rooting out the existing judiciary because of a possibility that specific crimes might not be tackled. Any such special court, given its potential implications for the principle of judicial independence as a whole, would have to be created in accordance with the highest standards of transparency, impartiality, and independence. **23**

Bibliography

Bassiouni, C, 'Post-Conflict Justice in Iraq: An Appraisal of the Iraq Special Tribunal' (2005) 38 Cornell International Law Journal 327–90.

Cohen, D, *Transitional Justice in Divided Germany After 1945* <www.ocf.berkeley.edu/~changmin/Papers/cohen-trans-justice-germany.pdf>.

Markovitz, I, 'Children of a Lesser God: GDR Lawyers in Post-Socialist Germany' (1996) 94 Michigan Law Review 2270–2308.

Mayer-Rieck, A and de Greiff, P (eds), *Justice as Prevention: Vetting Public Employees in Transitional Societies* (SSRC 2007).

Posner, E and Vermeule, A, 'Transitional Justice as Ordinary Justice' (2004) 117 Harvard Law Review 761–825.

Stahn, C, 'Justice Under Transitional Administration: Contours and Critique of a Paradigm' (2005) 27 Houston Journal of International Law 311–44.

UN Office on Drugs and Crime (UN ODC), *Commentary on The Bangalore Principles of Judicial Conduct* (UN ODC, 2007) <www.unodc.org/documents/corruption/publications_unodc_commentary-e.pdf>.

Wesson, M and Du Plessis, M, 'Fifteen Years On: Central Issues Relating to the Transformation of the South African Judiciary' (2008) 24 South African Journal on Human Rights 187–213.

PART IV

THE RIGHT TO REPARATION/ GUARANTEES OF NON-RECURRENCE

—

A.

THE RIGHT TO REPARATION

Principle 31. Rights and Duties Arising Out of the Obligation to Make Reparation

Frank Haldemann

Any human rights violation gives rise to a right to reparation on the part of the victim or his or her beneficiaries, implying a duty on the part of the State to make reparation and the possibility for the victim to seek redress from the perpetrator.

A. Summary of Findings

Inspired by a cosmopolitan vision of global justice, Principle 31 conceives of 'reparation' as an individual right owed to any person whose human rights have been violated. Cast in categorical language, the Principle is meant to reflect *existing* international law rather than a desideratum of legal policy. The claim as it stands has a strong moral appeal, and recent years have seen an increasing recognition of a right for individuals to claim reparation under international law. However, as discussed in this commentary, the idea of a general individual right, as 'codified' in Principle 31, arguably rests on rather weak legal foundations. Moreover, even if one admits the existence of such a right as a matter of international law, its strict application to contexts of large-scale atrocities and political transitions is likely to prove a daunting undertaking. While the call for 'reparation' is nowhere more needed than in such contexts of unspeakable cruelty and suffering, the inescapable truth about mass atrocity is that it is irreparable: nothing can ever 'wipe out' the wrong done as if it had never occurred. With this in mind, this commentary concludes with the observation that the right to reparation is both 'necessary' and 'impossible'.

B. Contextual and Historical Introduction

Principle 31 reflects a significant trend in recent international affairs: the call for 1 'reparations' as a means of 'correcting' legacies of serious and widespread human rights abuses. Since the end of the Second World War, and especially over the course of the 1990s, reparation claims have been presented for a variety of historical injustices, including the Holocaust; forced and slave labour in Nazi-dominated Europe; Japanese abuse of the 'comfort women' in Korea and the Philippines; 'state terrorism' and other authoritarian practices in Latin America, Eastern Central Europe, and South Africa; the oppression of indigenous peoples in Australia, New Zealand, and the United States; and the enduring legacy of slavery and institutional racism in the United States.[1]

[1] On the recent spread of reparations politics, see J Torpey, *Making Whole What Has Been Smashed: On Reparations Politics* (Harvard University Press 2006); R Ludi, *Reparations for Nazi Victims in Post-War Europe* (CUP 2014).

2 Reflecting this change in the *Zeitgeist*, the 1990s and early 2000s saw a range of normative developments pointing to an increased international recognition of aggrieved individuals as holders of legitimate claims to reparation. Among these *fin-de-siècle* developments was the adoption in 1998 of the Rome Statute of the International Criminal Court (ICC),[2] which established a permanent system of international criminal justice with the power to provide redress in respect to the harm suffered by victims of genocide, crimes against humanity, and other 'core' crimes under the jurisdiction of the Court. One should mention, too, the progressive elaboration of the Basic Principles and Guidelines on the Right to a Remedy and Reparation for Victims of Gross Violations of International Human Rights Law and Serious Violations of International Humanitarian Law, which were finally adopted by the United Nations General Assembly in 2005.[3]

3 To be sure, the concept of 'reparation' is anything but new in international law. As early as 1927, the Permanent Court of International Justice (PCIJ) famously stated, in the oft-cited *Factory at Chorzów case*, that 'it is a principle of international law, and even a general conception of law, that any breach of an engagement involves an obligation to make reparation'.[4] Undisputed ever since, this principle has been laid down in the 2001 International Law Commission (ILC) Articles on the Responsibility of States for Internationally Wrongful Acts.[5] And yet the perspective adopted by Principle 31 differs significantly from such 'ordinary' cases of state responsibility. Firmly embedded in cosmopolitan discourses of human rights, this Principle marks a shift from an exclusive concern with disputes among sovereign states to the protection of the basic rights of *individual* human beings, regardless of nationality, creed, gender, age, or any other status.

4 Principle 31 figures prominently in section IV of the Updated Principles, entitled 'The Right to Reparations/Guarantees of Non-Recurrence'. In the course of the revision of the Principles by independent expert Diane Orentlicher, the title of this section was changed from 'Right to Reparation', thus giving expression to the common idea that reparation and non-repetition, while separate issues, are both essential aspects of the repair and continuation of a legal relationship affected by a breach of international obligations.[6] The wording of Principle 31, however, is identical to that of Principle 33 in the original 1997 version of the Principles drafted by UN Special Rapporteur Louis Joinet. Both Joinet and Orentlicher devoted little, if any, space to commenting on these principles in their respective reports.[7] One notes, here, a certain disproportion between the complexity and scope of the problem addressed and its laconic treatment.

[2] *Rome Statute of the International Criminal Court* (17 July 1998) (entry into force 1 July 2002) 2187 UNTS 90 (hereinafter 'Rome Statute').

[3] UN Doc A/RES/60/147 (16 December 2005) Annexe (hereinafter 'Basic Principles on Reparation').

[4] PCIJ, *Factory at Chorzów* (Judgment of 26 July 1927) (1927) PCIJ Series A no 9, 21.

[5] See Articles on the Responsibility of States for Internationally Wrongful Acts (hereinafter 'ARSIWA') 2001/II(2) International Law Commission Yearbook, Art 31(1).

[6] See J Crawford, *The International Law Commission's Articles on State Responsibility: Introduction, Text and Commentary* (CUP 2002) 199.

[7] See, respectively, *Question of the impunity of perpetrators of human rights violations (civil and political), Revised final report prepared by Mr Joinet pursuant to Sub-Commission decision 1996/119*, UN Doc E/CN.4/Sub. 2/1997/20/Rev. 1 (2 October 1997) (hereinafter 'Joinet Report'); *Report of the independent expert to update the Set of Principles to combat Impunity, Diane Orentlicher*, UN Doc E/CN.4/2005/102 (18 February 2005) (hereinafter 'Orentlicher Report').

C. Theoretical Framework

Principle 31 opens with a strong normative claim: 'Any human rights violation', it states, 'gives rise to a right to reparation'. The claim, as it stands, may appear to many so intuitively appealing, so deeply ingrained in current legal thinking and social moralities, as not to require further explanation. However, far from being self-explanatory, the claim raises a variety of questions about its meaning and foundations—including, to begin with, the question of what it is to have a *right* to reparation. 5

I. Reparation as a right

In the context of Principle 31, the relevant notion of 'right' is arguably that of a 'claim right'. To have a claim right, as commonly defined, means that one holds a claim *to* something *against* others.[8] A claim right, so understood, imposes corresponding duties on others, duties that can be negative (requiring non-interference) or positive (demanding the provision of some good or service). Viewed in these terms, the right stated in Principle 31 can be understood as a *positive claim right*, which correlates with a duty to make reparation to anyone whose human rights were violated. 6

A further common distinction is that between moral and legal rights. While legal rights are those rights we have in consequence of the existence of some legal system, moral rights are grounded in morality and are said to exist regardless of whether they are recognized by the law. That distinction is significant. Holding legal—rather than 'merely' moral—claim rights is an essential part of what it means to be *recognized* as full members of the political community.[9] As Joel Feinberg argues, a world without legal claim rights would be one in which human beings 'would no longer hope for decent treatment from others on the ground of desert or rightful claim'.[10] 7

What kind of right, then, is the right stipulated by Principle 31—moral, legal, or both? In the eyes of many, if not most people, victims of serious wrongdoing have a morally justified claim to reparation.[11] But does this claim also amount to a legal right—a claim actually recognized and protected by *law*? 8

II. Reparation in human rights treaties

While not legally binding in themselves, the Principles are intended to 'reflect recent developments in international law and practice, including international jurisprudence and State practice'.[12] This idea of a 'codification' of the law as it *is* (as distinct from what it ought to be) appears clearly in Principle 31, cast as it is in categorical language that leaves no room for ambiguity. The question, however, remains whether Principle 31 is an *accurate* reflection of the present state of international law. To assess whether this is so, 9

[8] For an influential modern analysis, see WN Hohfeld, 'Fundamental Legal Conceptions as Applied in Legal Reasoning' (1917) 26:8 The Yale Law Journal 710–70.

[9] On the relationship between rights and recognition, see A Honneth, *The Struggle for Recognition: The Moral Grammar of Social Conflicts* (MIT Press 1995) 92–130. See also F Haldemann, 'Another Kind of Justice: Transitional Justice as Recognition' (2008) 41:3 Cornell International Law Journal 675–737.

[10] J Feinberg, *Social Philosophy* (Prentice-Hall, Inc 1973) 58.

[11] On moral dimension of repairing wrongdoing, see MU Walker, *Moral Repair: Reconstructing Relations after Wrongdoing* (CUP 2006).

[12] UN Commission on Human Rights Res 2004/72: Impunity, UN Doc E/CN.4/RES/2004/72 (21 April 2004) para 20.

it is necessary to examine the existing normative framework, and especially the relevant provisions of international human rights treaties. This section will provide a general, necessarily brief and sketchy, overview of those provisions.[13]

10 It bears noting, at the outset, that there is no human rights treaty explicitly affirming a right to reparation in terms as general as those employed by Principle 31. Where treaties do make explicit reference to the duty to provide reparations, they tend to do so in a limited and specific manner. The International Covenant on Civil and Political Rights (ICCPR),[14] for instance, recognizes in Articles 9(5) and 14(6) a right to compensation for persons subjected to unlawful arrest or detention or to miscarriages of justice. Other conventions, while focused on specific types of violations, adopt a more comprehensive notion of reparation, extending beyond 'mere' financial compensation.[15]

11 At the regional level, Article 41 of the European Convention for the Protection of Human Rights (ECHR)[16] empowers the Strasbourg Court to provide, 'if necessary', for 'just satisfaction to the injured party' in the event that domestic law provides only for 'partial reparation' of the harm suffered as a result of a violation of the Convention. As the phrase 'if necessary' indicates, a considerable measure of discretion is given to the Court as to how to exercise that power. Something similar can be said about the American Convention on Human Rights (ACHR),[17] Article 63(1) of which enjoins the Inter-American Court on Human Rights (IACtHR) 'to rule, if appropriate, that the consequences of the measure or situation that constituted the breach of... [a] right or freedom [protected by this Convention] be remedied and that fair compensation be paid to the injured party'.

12 The foregoing suggests, if anything, that human rights treaties offer a rather weak foundation upon which to build a general right to reparation as envisaged by Principle 31. It could be objected, however, that one crucial element of virtually all human rights instruments has been overlooked so far: the obligation to provide 'effective remedy' in the event of a human rights violation.[18] It has been argued that 'effective remedy' has both a procedural and substantive meaning: a remedy is only effective, so the argument goes, if it entails access to *remedial procedures* and *adequate redress* for the harm suffered by victims of human rights violation.[19] While not uncontroversial, this interpretation has been influential in the recent practice of human rights bodies and courts.[20]

[13] For a more extensive analysis, see in particular D Shelton, *Remedies in International Human Rights Law* (3rd edn, OUP 2015).

[14] International Covenant on Civil and Political Rights (ICCPR) (adopted December 16 1966, entered into force March 23 1976) 999 UNTS 171.

[15] See, eg, Convention against Torture and Other Cruel, Inhuman or Degrading Treatment or Punishment (CAT) (opened for signature 10 December 1984, entered into force 26 June 1986) 1465 UNTS 85, Art 14(1); International Convention for the Protection of All Persons from Enforced Disappearance (ICPPED) (adopted 20 December 2006, entered into force 23 December 2010) 2716 UNTS 3, Art 24(4) and (5).

[16] European Convention for the Protection of Human Rights and Fundamental Freedoms (ECHR) (signed 4 November 1950, entered into force 3 September 1953) 213 UNTS 221, ETS 5.

[17] American Convention on Hman Rights (ACHR) (opened for signature 22 November 1969, entered into force 18 July 1978) 1144 UNTS 123.

[18] See, eg, Art 2(3a) ICCPR, which states that 'any person whose rights or freedoms as herein recognised are violated shall have effective remedy'.

[19] See H Rombouts, P Sardaro, and S Vandenginste, 'The Right to Reparation for Victims of Gross and Systematic Violations of Human Rights' in K de Feyter et al (eds), *Out of the Ashes: Reparations for Victims of Gross and Systematic Human Rights Violations* (Intersentia 2005) 345–503, 367–69.

[20] Illustrative of this trend is the practice of the Human Rights Committee (HRC). See, eg, HRC, *Il Khwildy v Libya*, case 1804/2008 (1 November 2012) para 9. For a critical assessment of this practice, see C

Lastly, the 'respect-and-ensure' provision in human rights treaties may offer yet another, though perhaps rather thin, basis from which to derive a right to reparation. The requirement that state parties 'respect and ensure' (or 'secure') rights to all individuals has become a standard formula for describing human rights obligations.[21] The idea that victim redress is required to effectively 'ensure' human rights whenever they are violated has been widely endorsed by leading human rights institutions, and it is also reflected in the UN Basic Principles on the Right to Reparation.[22] This view is not uncontested, however, and has been criticized for being conceptually problematic, if not flawed.[23] 13

III. A customary right to reparation?

A further question to be asked, at this stage, is whether there is a *customary* international right for individuals to receive reparations for human rights violations. The question matters, of course: if recognized as part of international customary law, an individual right to reparation may be opposable to a state even if it is not party to a relevant human rights treaty, or if it has made a reservation to a relevant human rights provision. [24] 14

Proponents of a customary right to reparation often refer to the above-mentioned ILC Articles on State Responsibility to support their argument.[25] This may seem plausible enough: these Articles, after all, reflect well-established, customary rules on the state's responsibility under international law—including the principle, stated in Article 31(1), that the responsible state is under an obligation to make 'full reparation' for the injury caused by internationally wrongful acts. Moreover, while designed to regulate legal relations between states, these Articles are—as stated in the 'savings clause' of Article 33(2)—'without prejudice' to the possibility that individuals may be entitled to invoke state responsibility on their own account. And yet it is open to debate whether it is legally sound, or even desirable, to simply transpose the remedial logic inherent in the ILC Articles to the relationship between the state and its citizens.[26] 15

IV. Why reparation?

Any serious discussion of the topic at hand cannot fail to ask detailed questions about the precise meanings, scope, and purposes of reparation. Such questions are, indeed, variously addressed by the different Principles within section IV. While Principles 32 16

Tomuschat, *Human Rights: Between Idealism and Realism* (3rd edn, OUP 2014) 404 (speaking of a 'flawed literal construction' of Art 2(3) ICCPR).

[21] See Art 2(3) ICCPR; Art 1(1) ACHR; Art 1 ECHR.

[22] See HRC, General Comment no 31 [80], The Nature of the General Legal Obligations Imposed on State Parties to the Covenant (29 March 2004), CCPR/C/21/Rev.1/Add.13, para 15; *Velásquez Rodríguez v Honduras* (Judgment) IACtHR Series C no 4 (29 July 1988) para 176; Basic Principles on Reparation, n 3, Principle 3(d).

[23] See, eg, A Gattini, 'Reparations to Victims' in A Cassese (ed), *The Oxford Companion to International Criminal Justice* (OUP 2009) 487–89, 487.

[24] For an argument in support of an 'emerging customary right to reparation', see, eg, C Evans, *The Right to Reparation in International Law for Victims of Armed Conflict* (CUP 2012) 39–42 (with further references). *Contra*: Tomuschat, n 20, 415.

[25] ARSIWA, n 5. See, eg, E Schwager, 'Reparation for individual victims of armed conflict' in R Kolb and G Gaggioli (eds), *Research Handbook on Human Rights and Humanitarian Law* (Edward Elgar 2013) 628–59, 634–37. On the relevant practice of the IACtHR, see para 30 of this commentary.

[26] See A Nollkaemper, *National Courts and the international Rule of Law* (OUP 2011) 184; Tomuschat, n 20, 416.

and 33 address the question of *how* to provide reparation, through which procedures and forums, Principle 34 deals with the *substance* of reparation, its scope and modalities. As for Principle 31, it specifically focuses on three questions: Why are reparations owed? To whom are they owed? And by whom?

17 With respect to the first question, Principle 31's opening phrase implies a simple answer: the reason why reparation is owed is it that a human right has been violated. Given the 'universalist' outlook of the Principles, it seems safe to assume that the focus here is on *internationally* guaranteed human rights—minimum guarantees the source of which is international law and which, therefore, are not dependent at all on any domestic legal system.[27] Interestingly, and in contrast with the UN Basic Principles on Reparation, Principle 31 does not limit its scope to particularly grave instances of human rights violations. Nor does the Principle make any distinctions between different categories or 'generations' of human rights, as if stressing the indivisibility and interdependence of human rights.[28]

V. Whose rights? Whose duties?

18 If there is an individual right to reparation, *who may claim it*? The question is given only passing treatment by Principle 31, which broadly refers to 'the victim or his or her beneficiaries' as holders of a right to reparation. One will also look in vain for further clarification of these terms in the relevant Reports by Joinet and Orentlicher, both of which are conspicuously silent on the matter.

19 While powerful and evocative, the notion of 'victim' is not uncontested.[29] Nor is its meaning settled under international law. As has been noted, international human rights law lacks a consistent and shared definition of 'victim', and the meaning of the word 'continues to be disputed terrain'.[30] And yet some efforts have been made in the direction of clarifying the notion of 'victim' as relevant to the arena of human rights. An influential definition can be found in the Declaration of Basic Principles of Justice for Victims of Crime and Abuse of Power. The Declaration defines victims broadly as 'individuals who have individually or collectively suffered harm', and allows, 'where appropriate', for the extension of the victim status to individuals other than the direct victim (including 'direct family members' and 'dependents of the direct victim').[31] The specific reference in Principle 31 to the victim's 'beneficiaries' may be taken as evidence of such a large understanding of the victims' status.

20 If victims of human rights violations have a right to reparation then there is a correlative *duty to repair* the harm caused by the violation. That duty is the other side of the coin, so to speak. So whose duty is it? Principle 31's concern is mainly with states as primary bearers of human rights obligations. It does not venture into controversial debates

[27] See R Higgins, *Problems & Process: International Law and How We Use It* (OUP 1994) 96.

[28] See Vienna Declaration and Programme of Action (25 June 1993) (1993) 32 ILM 1663.

[29] See T Govier, *Victims and Victimhood* (Broadview Press 2015) 30–31 (stressing the term's connotation of passivity and vulnerability).

[30] C Sandoval, 'The Concept of "Injured Party" and "Victim" of Gross Human Rights Violations in the Jurisprudence of the Inter-American Court of Human Rights: A Commentary on their Implications for Reparations' in C Ferstman, M Goetz and A Stephens (eds), *Reparations for Victims of Genocide, War Crimes and Crimes against Humanity: Systems in Place and Systems in the Making* (Martinus Nijhoff 2009) 243–82, 249.

[31] Declaration of Basic Principles of Justice for Victims of Crime and Abuse of Power, UN Doc A/RES/40/34 (29 November 1985) Annex, paras 1 and 2. For a similar definition, see Basic Principles on Reparation, n 3, Principle 8.

about human rights obligations of non-state actors, such as transnational corporations and other business enterprises.[32]

Moreover, Principle 31 links the right to reparation to 'the possibility for the victim to seek redress from the perpetrator'. Within domestic legal systems around the world, persons unlawfully harmed by others are entitled to obtain reparation through criminal or civil proceedings, or, where the system exists, a combination thereof.[33] Some domestic legal systems go even so far as to enable victims of human rights violations to claim reparation from perpetrators in respect to human rights abuses committed *abroad*. The best-known example is the Alien Tort Statute (ATS), a prominent human rights tool in the United States that gives federal district courts 'original jurisdiction of any civil action by an alien for a tort only, committed in violation of the law of nations or a treaty of the United States'.[34] 21

At the level of international law, the Rome Statute of the ICC provides an innovative framework through which the harm suffered by victims of egregious conduct may be redressed.[35] As part of this framework, Article 75(2) empowers the Court to 'make an order directly against the convicted person specifying appropriate reparation'. In addition, Article 79 provides for the establishment of a Trust Fund, which has the power to render assistance to victims outside the context of Court-ordered reparations.[36] 22

V. Reparation and mass violations

As noted, Principle 31 does *not* require a human rights violation to have a systematic or serious character before it gives rise to a right to reparation. Nonetheless, the combat against impunity as envisaged in the set of Updated Principles can hardly be disconnected from contexts of gross human rights violations and transitions from authoritarianism or armed conflict to a more just, peaceful, and decent political order. It is surely no coincidence, after all, that the Principles' definitional part proposes clarifications of what both the phrases 'serious crimes under international law' and 'restoration of or transition to democracy and/or peace' mean. 23

It is precisely in contexts of mass violations and political transition that the challenges in terms of repairing harm tend to be most daunting. In such situations, the victims number in the thousands, if not millions, as a result of which the burden placed on the judiciary may become overwhelming, especially when actions are filed in a short period. Moreover, many of the substantive criteria or procedural rules applicable to traditional judicial proceedings—in matters of evidence or of statute of limitations, for instance—seem ill fitted to the reality of collective violence and may, therefore, turn out to be fatal for the victims as plaintiffs.[37] 24

[32] See Shelton, n 13, at 55–58 (noting the lack of order and precision in the area of international legal obligations on corporations and other businesses).

[33] See J Sarkin, 'Reparations for Gross Human Rights Violations as an Outcome of Criminal Versus Civil Court Proceedings' in K De Feyter et al (eds), *Out of the Ashes: Reparation for Victims of Gross and Systematic Human Rights Violations* (Intersentia 2005) 151–88.

[34] Alien Tort Statute, 28 USC § 1350.

[35] For an in-depth study of the ICC's regime of reparations and victim support, see C McCarthy, *Reparations and Victim Support in the International Criminal Court* (CUP 2012).

[36] This role of the Trust Fund is laid down the Fund's Regulations, especially Rule 98(5).

[37] On this issue, see JE Malamud-Goti and LS Grosman, 'Reparations and Civil Litigation: Compensation for Human Rights Violations in Transitional Democracies' in P de Greiff (ed), *The Handbook of Reparations* (OUP 2006) 539–59.

25 Principle 31 is silent on these issues, just as it is silent on the general question of *how* a right to reparation may be realized. As mentioned, the matter of 'how' is left to subsequent principles—especially Principle 32, which, in its updated version, refers to 'reparations programmes' as alternative (and seemingly 'second-best') avenues for providing reparations. The question of how to translate the language of an individual 'right to reparation' into the context of gross and systematic human rights violations poses, however, major challenges for human rights courts and treaty bodies—an issue to which the next section will return.

D. Practice

26 This section reviews some of the legal and predominantly international practices relevant to Principle 31. In doing so, the focus of attention is on how regional human rights courts and UN treaty bodies have addressed the three basic questions that, as suggested earlier, lie at the very heart of Principle 31—the questions of why reparations are owed, to whom, and by whom. The section closes with a tentative overview of approaches that regional human rights courts have adopted to deal with the challenge of affording reparation in cases of large-scale human rights violations.

I. The right to reparation in international human rights practice

27 In practice, the right to reparation is typically read into and derived from the general duty to provide 'effective remedy', which, as noted, is explicitly stated in virtually all human rights conventions. Illustrative of this approach is the relevant practice of the UN HRC. In its General Comment no 31, the HRC takes great pains to establish an intrinsic link between reparations and the 'effective remedy' requirement as stated in Article 2(3) ICCPR.[38] Ever since, the HRC has routinely reiterated this approach, in spite of some occasionally severe criticism from scholars.[39] A similar perspective, albeit expressed in somewhat differing terms, is adopted by the Committee against Torture. In its General Comment no 3, issued in 2012, the Committee considers that the term 'redress' used in Article 14 CAT should be understood broadly as encompassing both 'effective remedies' and 'reparation'.[40]

28 At the level of regional courts, the European Court of Human Rights (ECtHR) has for a long time taken a rather restrictive approach in awarding 'just satisfaction' under Article 41 ECHR. In its early jurisprudence, the Court regularly confined itself to noting that the finding of a breach of the Convention in itself constitutes sufficient satisfaction.[41] More recently, however, the Court has increasingly awarded financial redress in respect to damage, either pecuniary or non-pecuniary, shown to be caused by violations of the Convention.[42]

[38] HRC, General Comment no 31, The Nature of the General Legal Obligation Imposed on States Parties to the Covenant, CCPR/C/21/Rev.1/Add. 13 (26 May 2004) at para 16.

[39] See Tomuschat, n 20, 404 (speaking of a 'flawed literal construction').

[40] Committee against Torture, General Comment no 3, Implementation of Article 14 by State Parties, CAT/C/GC/3 (19 November 2012) para 2.

[41] See, eg, *Golder v United Kingdom* App no 4451/70 (Judgment) (ECtHR, 21 February 1975) para 46.

[42] See, eg, *Selmouni v France* App no 25803/94 (Judgment) (ECtHR, 28 July 1999) para 123; *Scordino v Italy (No 1)* App no 36813/97 (Judgment) (ECtHR, 29 March 2006) paras 267–73; *Oyal v Turkey* App no 4864/05 (ECtHR, 23 March 2010) paras 98–107; *Cyprus v Turkey* App no 25781/94 (Judgment) (ECtHR, 12 May 2014) para 58.

At any rate, as already noted, there is no 'automatic' right to 'just satisfaction' under the ECHR. Even if an applicant meets all the requirements laid down in Article 41 ECHR, it is left to the discretion of the Court to assess whether compensation, or any other measure of satisfaction, is 'necessary'. It is against this background that the Court considers that 'the awarding of sums of money to the applicants by way of just satisfaction is not one of the Court's main duties but is incidental to the task of ensuring the observance by States of their obligations under the Convention'.[43] Given this strong discretionary dimension, it seems difficult to speak here properly of a 'right' to reparation; and even more so if one considers that the Court's remedial jurisprudence has attracted a good deal of criticism for its lack of coherence and predictability.[44] 29

Of all regional human rights courts, it is the IACtHR that has been the most innovative in its approach to reparations. Equipped with comparatively broad remedial powers, the Court has ordered a remarkably broad range of non-monetary reparative measures in tandem with compensation.[45] Since its first contentious case, the San José Court has consistently (though not uncontroversially) interpreted Article 63(1) ACHR as codifying, and transposing into the human rights context, a long-established principle under the law of state responsibility: that 'every violation of an international obligation which results in harm creates a duty to make adequate reparation'.[46] As for the duty's scope, the Court has vigorously endorsed the so-called 'principle of full reparation', insisting that the responsible state must undo, as far as possible, all the harmful effects resulting from the violation.[47] In the Court's recent jurisprudence, however, there has been a certain retreat from—or at least qualification of—this principle in relation to domestic reparations programmes in contexts of political transition.[48] 30

II. Who is a victim?

As previously noted, the notion of 'victim' lacks clear contours in international human rights law. All the more important is the role of human rights courts and bodies in clarifying and substantiating it. Once again, the Inter-American jurisprudence is of particular relevance here. In interpreting the term 'injured party', as employed in Article 64(1) ACHR, the IACtHR subscribes to a remarkably broad understanding of victimhood, expanding well beyond the strict definition of 'direct victims' (ie individuals directly harmed as a result of a human rights violation).[49] Particularly in cases involving death or disappearance, the Court is willing to recognize the victim's next of kin as 'injured parties', and hence as 31

[43] *Salah v the Netherlands* App no 8196/02 (Judgment) (ECtHR, 6 July 2006) para 70.

[44] For a recent critique along these lines, see, eg, O Ichim, *Just Satisfaction under the European Convention on Human Rights* (CUP 2015). See also Tomuschat, n 20, 408.

[45] For a useful overview of the Court's remedial jurisprudence, see TM Antkowiak, 'Remedial Approaches to Human Rights Violations: The Inter-American Court of Human Rights and Beyond' (2008) 46 Columbia Journal of Transnational Law 351–419.

[46] *Velásquez Rodríguez v Honduras* (Reparations and Costs) IACtHR Series C no 7 (21 July 1989) para 25 (citing PCIJ, *Factory at Chorzów*, n 4, 29).

[47] See, eg, *Mendoza et al v Argentina* (Judgment) (Preliminary objections, merits, and reparations) IACtHR Series C no 247 (14 May 2013) para 307; *Gonzales Lluy et al v Ecuador* (Judgment) (Preliminary objections, merits, reparations, and costs) IACtHR Series C no 298 (1 September 2015) para 342.

[48] *Afro-Descendant Communities Displaced from the Carica River Bassin (Operation Genesis) v Colombia*, (Judgment) (Preliminary objections, merits, reparations and costs), IACtHR Series C no 270 (20 November 2013) para 470.

[49] For a careful analysis of the Court's relevant jurisprudence, see Sandoval, n 30.

eligible for reparations, even if they are not direct victims of any violation of the ACHR.[50] The San José Court, one should note, interprets the notion of 'next to kin' so broadly as to include half-siblings, aunts, stepmothers, and stepfathers, even partners, with close ties to the victim.[51]

32 The ECtHR, by contrast, has adopted a much more restrictive interpretation of the term 'injured party'. Since the entry into force of Protocol no 14 in 2010, that term is essentially synonymous with the notion of 'victim' as a requirement for lodging an individual petition;[52] and the Court has only reluctantly subsumed family members under the category of 'victim'. In cases involving forced disappearance, the Strasbourg Court has held that the victim status of a family member will depend upon 'the existence of special factors' beyond the 'emotional distress which may be regarded as inevitably caused to relatives of a victim of serious human rights violations'.[53]

33 Among the UN treaty bodies, the Committee against Torture has defined 'victims' as 'persons who individually or collectively suffered harm', and has, furthermore, insisted that the term also applies to 'affected immediate family or dependents of the victim as well as persons who have suffered harm in intervening to assist victims or to prevent victimization'.[54] As to the HRC, it has stated, referring to the mother of a disappeared daughter, that 'she too is a victim of the violations of the Covenant suffered by her daughter'.[55]

III. Seeking redress from the perpetrator

34 If Principle 31 links the right to reparation to 'the possibility for the victim to seek redress from the perpetrator', the Rome Statute's redress regime provides an important example of such a possibility at the international level. The reparations jurisprudence of the ICC is still in its early days, however. The first reparation decision was handed down by Trial Chamber I on 7 August 2012, in connection with the conviction of Thomas Lubanga.[56] In August 2015, the Appeals Chamber of the Court reversed the Trial Chamber's decision in a long-awaited judgment. While the Trial Chamber had refrained from issuing a reparation order against Lubanga because of his indigence, the Appeals Chamber insisted that 'indigence is of no relevance to the imposition of liability for reparations'.[57] Moreover, it took pains to stress that reparations orders are 'intrinsically linked to the *individual* whose criminal liability is established in a conviction and whose culpability for those criminal acts is determined in a sentence'.[58] Reactions to the appeal judgment have been positive

[50] See, eg, *Trujillo Oraza v Bolivia* (Reparations and Costs) IACtHR Series C no 92 (27 February 2002) paras 54–57.

[51] See, eg, *Juan Humberto Sanchez v Honduras* (Preliminary Objections, Merits, Reparations and Costs) IACtHR Series C no 99 (7 June 2003) paras 173–75.

[52] Protocol no 14 to the European Convention for the Protection of Human Rights and Fundamental Freedoms, amending the control system of the Convention, ETS 194, Art 12 (establishing the requirement of a 'significant disadvantage' as an additional admissibility condition). See Ichim, n 44, 70–72.

[53] *Çakici v Turkey* App no 23657/94 (Judgment) (ECtHR, 8 July 1999) para 98. See also *Janowiec and Others v Russia* App nos 55508/07 and 29520/09 (Judgment) (ECtHR, 21 October 2013) paras 177–78 (mentioning factors such as the proximity of the family tie and the dismissive response of authorities).

[54] Committee against Torture, n 40, para 3.

[55] Human Rights Committee, Communication no 107/198 (17 September 1981) para 14.

[56] ICC,Trial Chamber I, *Lubanga* (Decision establishing the principles and procedures to be applied to reparations) ICC-01/04-01/06 (7 August 2012).

[57] ICC Appeals Chamber, *Lubanga* (Order for Reparations) ICC-01/04-01/06 A A 2 A 3 (3 March 2015) para 105. For a detailed analysis, see C Stahn, 'Reparative Justice after the Lubanga Appeals Judgement' (2015) 13:4 Journal of International Criminal Justice 1–13.

[58] ICC Appeals Chamber, *Lubanga*, n 57, para 65 (original emphasis).

overall, with some commentators going so far as to herald it as a 'turning point for further practice'.[59]

35 The US ATS is another prominent example of a legal framework through which victims of serious human rights abuse may seek redress from perpetrators of abuse if they are unable to obtain an effective remedy in their own domestic legal system. In a series of cases starting with the famous 1980 decision in *Filártiga v Peña-Irala*, [60] this statute has served as a basis for US courts to hear human rights claims against serious violators of international law, despite the absence of any connection in most cases between the parties and conduct at issue and the US.[61] More recently, and more controversially, plaintiffs have increasingly invoked the ATS to sue multinational corporations alleged to have aided and abetted states outside the US in violating international law, or to have directly committed such violations themselves.[62] The US Supreme Court's decision in *Kiobel v Royal Dutch Petroleum* in 2013 marked, however, a significant change of direction in judicial interpretation, by introducing the presumption that the ATS does not generally apply to claims arising from conduct outside the US.[63] Unsurprisingly, the ruling has sparked a great deal of controversy, with some commenters reading it as 'a giant setback for human rights' and others as 'a blessing in disguise'.[64]

IV. Mass violations as a challenge to human rights complaints systems

36 The practice of human rights treaty bodies and courts revolves essentially around a model of individualized, case-by-case adjudication. This model is reflective of a 'day-in-court ideal' deeply influential in western legal thought.[65] However, as already noted, such a case-by-case mode of adjudication appears in many ways ill-suited to dealing with legacies of widespread and systemic human rights violations. Not only does it tend to be too time-consuming and costly to deal efficiently with large numbers of claims; it may also—as has been forcefully argued by Pablo de Greiff—'disaggregate' victims and the various efforts undertaken to achieve reparative justice.[66]

37 In response to such challenges posed to 'individualized' complaints procedures, regional human rights courts in Europe and the Americas have explored ways in which human rights systems can be interpreted anew so as to deal more efficiently with mass violations. Noteworthy in this context is the so-called 'pilot judgment procedure' of the ECtHR. The Strasbourg Court introduced this special procedure in 2004, and has since applied it in more than 20 cases, mostly dealing with property rights issues involving large numbers of applications similar in substance.[67] The aim of this procedure is essentially

[59] Stahn, n 57, 6. [60] *Filártiga v Peña-Irala*, 630 F 2d 876 (2d Cir 1980).

[61] On the development and history of ATS litigation, see B Stephens, 'The Curious History of the Alien Tort Statute' (2014) 89:4 Notre Dame Law Review 1467–1543.

[62] See, eg, *Khulumani v Barclay National Bank Ltd*, 509 F 3d 148 (2nd Cir 2007); *Abdullahi v Pfizer, Inc*, 562 F 3d 163 (2nd Cir 2009).

[63] *Kiobel v Royal Dutch Petroleum Co*, 133 S Ct 1659 (2013).

[64] See respectively, Editorial Board, 'A Giant Setback for Human Rights' *New York Times* (18 April 2013) A26; S Moyn, 'Why the Court Was Right About the Tort Claim Statute' *Foreign Affairs* (2 May 2013).

[65] See Justice Sourter in *Ortiz v Fibreboard Corp*, 527 US 818 (1999), 846.

[66] P de Greiff, 'Justice and Reparations' in de Greiff (ed), n 37, 451–77, 458.

[67] See, eg, *Broniowski v Poland* App no 31443/96 (Judgment) (ECtHR, 22 June 2004); *Broniowski v Poland* App no 31443/96 (Judgment) (ECtHR, 28 September 2005); *Hutten-Czapska v Poland* App no 35014/97 (Judgment) (ECtHR, 19 June 2006); *Maria Atanasiu and others v Romania* App nos 30767/05 and 33800/06 (Judgment) (ECtHR, 12 October 2010).

two-fold: to identify a *general structural* problem underlying a specific case at hand; and to indicate measures which a respondent state must take to remedy that problem.[68] As for the IACtHR, it too has developed a number of strategies for responding to large-scale human rights violations.[69] Among these, there is the Court's practice of easing the burden of proof laid on complainants, namely through the use of presumptions and circumstantial evidence.[70] Other strategies involve, for instance, the application of standardized compensation amounts to particular categories of harm,[71] as well as the award of collective reparations to entire communities.[72]

E. Critical Assessment

38 While central to Principle 31, the idea of a general *individual* right to reparation rests on 'fairly weak foundations'.[73] As the discussion in this commentary shows, it is doubtful whether current international law provides for a such a general right to reparation for individual victims of serious human rights violations. To say this, however, is not to deny that recent decades have seen a trend, especially at the UN level, toward an increased recognition of victims and their rights to remedy and reparation. In line with a 'constructivist' approach to international law, we may see in these developments the emergence of a 'reparations ethos' with the potential to 'shape perceptions as to the evolving character of "the law" '.[74]

39 'Where there is a right, there is a remedy' (*ubi ius, ibi remedium*)—this old legal adage, much quoted by scholars and practitioners alike, emphasizes the importance of appropriate procedures for enforcing rights. It is some such thought that lies behind the claim that the notion of an 'individual right' lacks real content and significance without the availability of legal avenues for effectively enforcing it.[75] In both international law scholarship and jurisprudence, however, it has been held that a right under international law exists *regardless* of whether the holder of the right has the capacity to exercise it through adequate enforcement mechanisms at the international level.[76] Wherever we stand in this unresolved debate, this issue is relevant for understanding the limits of international law in granting reparation to individual victims of state-sponsored atrocities. One should recall, after all, that there exists so far no general international forum for individuals to

[68] See Rule 61 of the Court's Rules as of 14 November 2016. See generally A Buyse, 'The Pilot Judgment Procedure at the European Court of Human Rights: Possibilities and Challenges' (2009) 57 Nomiko Vima [The Greek Law Journal] 78–90.

[69] See generally L Oette, 'Bringing Justice to Victims? Responses of Regional and International Human Rights Courts and Treaty Bodies to Mass Violations' in C Ferstman, M Goetz, and A Stephens (eds), *Reparations for Victims of Genocide, War Crimes and Crimes against Humanity: Systems in Place and Systems in the Making* (Martinus Nijhoff 2009) 217–42.

[70] For a general statement of this approach, see *Blake v Guatemala* (Judgment) (Merits) IACtHR Series C no 36 (24 January 1998) para 49.

[71] An example is *Massacre v Colombia* (Judgment) (Merits, Reparations and Costs) IACtHR Series C no 163 (11 May 2007) para 273.

[72] See, eg, *Plan de Sánchez Massacre v Guatemala* (Judgment) (Reparations) IACtHR Series C no 116 (19 November 2004) paras 86 and 101.

[73] Tomuschat, n 20, 419.

[74] R Falk, 'Reparations, International Law, and Global Justice: A New Frontier' in de Greiff (ed), n 37, 478–503, 485 and 490–91.

[75] See R Geuss, *Philosophy and Real Politics* (Princeton University Press 2008) 62.

[76] For such argument, see Schwager, n 25, 629, citing in support the ruling of the ICJ in *La Grande (Germany v United States)* [2001] ICJ Rep 466, 494, para 77.

file civil claims against governments responsible for human rights violations; and it is unlikely, if not inconceivable, that such a forum will emerge in the near future. It is a 'hard fact', as Thomas Tomuschat puts it, that the so-called 'international community' has not yet consolidated into something like 'a community of solidarity' sharing jointly the burdens caused by episodes of political upheaval and violence, and it is doubtful that it ever will.[77]

But even if we were to admit the existence of an 'international' right to reparation, its actual realization in contexts of mass violations will prove a daunting, if not impossible, task. In such contexts, the capacity of transitional governments to provide anything approaching 'full' and 'prompt' reparation will be severely tested by the overwhelming number of claims and other 'factual' obstacles (lack of resources, institutional decay, etc). Moreover, claims for 'reparation' will tend to conflict with other, perhaps equally weighty, considerations, including claims for a more just distribution of social goods.[78] Lastly, and more fundamentally, it is difficult to see what 'reparation' might possibly mean, and how it might be achieved, in the face of evils so outrageous in scope and nature as to defy computation and comprehension.[79] 40

The ambivalence at work here is, in a sense, unsurprising. As has been argued, law may aptly be thought of as a mediation between the ideal and the real, between what should be and what is actually done.[80] However, while built into law, this gap between declaring a norm and realizing it is further exacerbated in the aftermath of mass atrocity. Nowhere more than here does the concrete implementation of an abstract political ideal or imperative depend on the particularity of each situation and require what Isaiah Berlin called 'a sense of reality'.[81] Now international law, apart from showing the general direction in which to proceed, has little guidance to offer in terms of how to realize—make 'real'—the right to reparation in such extraordinary circumstances. As Richard Falk suggests, it therefore seems appropriate to view reparations arrangements in transitional contexts 'as primarily an expression of moral and political forces in particular contexts'.[82] 41

This account, to be sure, will not satisfy those who believe that international law should play a more direct role in guiding reparations processes in the aftermath of large-scale human rights violations. It is not clear, however, what this role would be. After all, even those who advocate the existence of a right to reparation under current international law are ready to concede not only that such a right is surrounded by a 'significant degree of discretion and flexibility', but also that it can be subject to limitations, if 'fair' and 'appropriate'.[83] 42

But if, as it appears, the discourse of a right to reparation is imbued with ambivalences and unfulfillable expectations, what is the point of holding on to it? Why should the idea of a right to reparation, as codified in Principle 31, matter in contexts of collective evildoing and political transformation? It matters primarily, it seems, as a projection of 43

[77] Tomuschat, n 20, 400.

[78] A good illustration of such tensions is provided by the South African Constitutional Court's decision in *Richtersveld Community and Others v Alexkor Ltd and Another* 2001 (3) SA 1293 (LCC). For a helpful analysis, see J Webber, 'Forms of Transitional Justice', in MS Williams, R Nagy and J Elster (eds), *Transitional Justice: Nomos LI* (New York University Press 2012) 98–128, 106–08.

[79] See M Minow, *Between Vengeance and Forgiveness* (Beacon Press 1999) especially 104.

[80] See P Gewirtz, 'Remedies and Resistance' (1983) 92:4 *The Yale Law Journal* 587–681, 587.

[81] See I Berlin, *The Sense of Reality: Studies in Ideas and Their History* (Farrar, Straus and Giroux 1996).

[82] Falk, n 74, 485 (emphasis in the original).

[83] See Rombouts, Sardaro, and Vendegiste, n 19, 452–53.

what *should* be: as a standard, an ideal, towards which to aspire and against which to critically judge given transitional policies. At the same time, however, Principle 31 serves as a critical reminder of what is inevitably *lost* after mass atrocity. The uncomfortable truth about radical political evil is that it is irreparable: no response can ever undo the harm done, make the victims 'whole', or bring back what was lost. The slate cannot be wiped clean. To suggest otherwise is not only excessively naive; it is deeply offensive to those at the receiving end of such evils.[84] And yet the call for a right to reparation seems nowhere more necessary than in a political landscape transfigured by atrocity.

44 Here, somewhat paradoxically, one might end up saying—borrowing from Martti Koskenniemi—that the right to reparation is 'both necessary and impossible'.[85]

Bibliography

Antkowiak, TM, 'Remedial Approaches to Human Rights Violations: The Inter-American Court of Human Rights and Beyond' (2008) 46 Columbia Journal of Transnational Law 351–419.

Buyse, A 'The Pilot Judgment Procedure at the European Court of Human Rights: Possibilities and Challenges' (2009) 57 Nomiko Vima [The Greek Law Journal] 78–90.

Falk, R, 'Reparations, International Law, and Global Justice: A New Frontier' in P de Greiff (ed), *The Handbook of Reparations* (OUP 2006) 478–503.

Malamud-Goti, JE and Grosman, LS, 'Reparations and Civil Litigation: Compensation for Human Rights Violations in Transitional Democracies' in P De Greiff (ed), *The Handbook of Reparations* (OUP 2006) 539–59.

McCarthy, C, *Reparations and Victim Support in the International Criminal Court* (CUP 2012).

Oette, L, 'Bringing Justice to Victims? Responses of Regional and International Human Rights Courts and Treaty Bodies to Mass Violations' in C Ferstman, M Goetz, and A Stephens (eds), *Reparations for Victims of Genocide, War Crimes and Crimes against Humanity: Systems in Place and Systems in the Making* (Martinus Nijhoff 2009) 217–42.

Rombouts, H, Sardaro, P, and Vandenginste, S, 'The Right to Reparation for Victims of Gross and Systematic Violations of Human Rights' in K de Feyter et al (eds), *Out of the Ashes: Reparations for Victims of Gross and Systematic Human Rights Violations* (Intersentia 2005) 345–503.

Sandoval, C, 'The Concept of "Injured Party" and "Victim" of Gross Human Rights Violations in the Jurisprudence of the Inter-American Court of Human Rights: A Commentary on their Implications for Reparations' in C Ferstman, M Goetz, and A Stephens (eds), *Reparations for Victims of Genocide, War Crimes and Crimes against Humanity: Systems in Place and Systems in the Making* (Martinus Nijhoff 2009) 243–82.

Schwager, E, 'Reparation for individual victims of armed conflict' in R Kolb and G Gaggioli (eds), *Research Handbook on Human Rights and Humanitarian Law* (Edward Elgar 2013) 628–59.

Shelton, D, *Remedies in International Human Rights Law* (3rd edn, OUP 2015).

Tomuschat, C, *Human Rights: Between Idealism and Realism* (3rd edn, OUP 2014) ch 13.

Walker, MU, *Moral Repair: Reconstructing Relations after Wrongdoing* (CUP 2006).

[84] See Minow, n 79, 93.

[85] M Koskenniemi, *The Politics of International Law* (Hart Publishing 2011) 153.

Principle 32. Reparation Procedures

Pierre d'Argent and Isabelle de Ghellinck

All victims shall have access to a readily available, prompt and effective remedy in the form of criminal, civil, administrative or disciplinary proceedings subject to the restrictions on prescription set forth in principle 23. In exercising this right, they shall be afforded protection against intimidation and reprisals.

Reparations may also be provided through programmes, based upon legislative or administrative measures, funded by national or international sources, addressed to individuals and to communities. Victims and other sectors of civil society should play a meaningful role in the design and implementation of such programmes. Concerted efforts should be made to ensure that women and minority groups participate in public consultations aimed at developing, implementing, and assessing reparations programmes.

Exercise of the right to reparation includes access to applicable international and regional procedures.

A. Summary of Findings

Entitled 'Reparation Procedures', Principle 32 addresses the procedural aspect of the right to reparation, that is, the right for victims of human right violations to access remedial procedures. While the obligation of states to provide effective remedies is enshrined in most of, if not all, the key international human rights treaties, this Principle provides for a right to all victims to access remedies. The distinction between 'reparation' and 'remedies', both envisaged as victims' rights, is not always clear-cut and is somehow blurred: while, under the Basic Principles and Guidelines on the Right to a Remedy and Reparation for Victims of Gross Violations of International Human Rights Law and Serious Violations of International Humanitarian Law,[1] the 'victims' right to remedies' is said to 'include' '*a*) Equal and effective access to justice; (*b*) Adequate, effective and prompt reparation for harm suffered; and (*c*) Access to relevant information concerning violations and reparation mechanisms',[2] the Principles envisage that rights and duties arise out of the obligation to make reparation,[3] and that, among those rights, is the right to seek redress by accessing remedial procedures.

The content of the right to access remedies has been defined through national and international practice. It entails that alleged violations must be examined by competent and independent authorities in an effective, timely, and thorough manner.

In the aftermath of gross or systematic human rights violations, states may choose to provide reparations to victims through a variety of means detailed by Principle 32. While various standards applicable to remedial programmes have developed, such as

[1] Adopted and proclaimed by General Assembly Resolution (Res) 60/147 of 16 December 2005, UN Doc A/RES/60/147 (16 December 2005) (hereinafter 'Basic Principles and Guidelines on Reparation').

[2] Ibid, Principle 11.

[3] Principle 31, 'Rights and duties arising out of the obligation to make reparation'.

the effective and meaningful participation of all victims and particularly of vulnerable groups, some uncertainties remain. It is indeed unclear when a state can be considered as having fully complied with its obligations to provide effective remedies to victims. In such circumstances, when assessing whether remedies have effectively been provided, not only the nature of the obligation at stake, but also the specific context of transitional justice, together with the transformative role of reparations, must be taken into account.

B. Contextual and Historical Introduction

1 In 2004,[4] the Commission on Human Rights[5] tasked Diane Orentlicher with updating the Principles on impunity, as drafted by Louis Joinet in 1997.[6] The update of the Principles to combat impunity have particularly benefitted from the study on the right to a remedy and reparation undertaken by Theo van Boven and Cherif Bassiouni,[7] which led to the adoption in 2005 of the Basic Principles and Guidelines on Reparation.[8]

2 Principle 32, included under the general heading 'A. The right to reparation', provides for the right for 'all victims' of human rights to access remedial procedures. This represents a significant conceptual change compared to the classical international law understanding, which considered individuals as objects, rather than subjects, of international law.[9] While accepting that a state could suffer an injury through the wrongs committed against its nationals, and that it could therefore claim reparation through diplomatic protection, classical international law did not envisage that the individual victims of internationally wrongful acts could be the direct beneficiaries of a right to reparation under international law. Therefore, the idea that international law needed to assert the right of individuals to access remedial procedures was alien to that classical understanding.

3 This new Updated Principle is nearly identical to the one drafted by Joinet, but for the inclusion of specific modalities regarding national reparation programmes, which can be 'addressed to individuals and to communities'. Reparation programmes have flourished since the late 1980s–early 1990s in 'transition' countries following authoritarian regimes or internal conflicts that have been marked by wide-scale human rights violations. While

[4] UN Commission on Human Rights, Commission on Human Rights Resolution 2004/72: Impunity, 21 April 2004, E/CN.4/RES/2004/72.

[5] The Commission on Human Rights was replaced in 2006 by the Human Rights Council.

[6] *Question of the impunity of perpetrators of human rights violations (civil and political). Revised final report prepared by Joinet pursuant to Sub-Commission decision 1996/119*, E/CN.4/Sub.2/1997/20/Rev.1 (2 October 1997).

[7] Diane Orentlicher notes in her independent study that 'In view of the in-depth work on reparations undertaken by M Cherif Bassiouni and Theo van Boven, principles 33–42 have not received the independent attention in this study that would be merited by their importance alone.' *Independent Study on best practices, including recommendations, to assist states in strengthening their domestic capacity to combat all aspects of impunity, by Professor Diane Orentlicher*, UN Doc E/CN.4/2004/88 (27 February 2004) para 7.

[8] See n 1.

[9] The international law of state responsibility provides that the commission of an internationally wrongful act entails the obligation of the responsible State to make full reparation to the injured party. See *Factory at Chorzów* (Judgment no 8) (Jurisdiction) (1927) PCIJ Series A no 9, 21; and the commentary on Article 31 of the Draft Articles on Responsibility of States for Internationally Wrongful Acts, Report of the International Law Commission on the work of its fifty-third session, UN Doc A/56/10 (2001), 91–94. On this paradigmatic change, see P d'Argent, 'Le droit de la responsabilité internationale complété? Examen des "Principes fondamentaux et directives concernant le droit à un recours et à réparation des victimes de violations flagrantes du droit international des droits de l'homme et de violations graves du droit international humanitaire"' (2005) 51 Annuaire français de droit international 27–55.

initial procedures and mechanisms have been very heterogeneous, recent practice has drawn from past experiences. Best practices have emerged from this diversity, resulting in procedural standards with which these programmes ought to comply.

The right to access remedial procedures as included in Principle 32 is provided for 4
victims of all human rights breaches, regardless of the nature of the rights, the gravity or egregious character of the violations, or even the identity of the perpetrator (according to Principle 31 '*[a]ny* human rights violation gives rise to a right to reparation on the part of the victim'). While it thus primarily covers remedies for violations of civil and political rights, breaches of social, economic, and cultural right are not excluded. Its scope of application is hence wider than the initial Principles (which covered only civil and political rights)[10] and the Basic Principles and Guidelines on Reparation (which focus on gross violations of international human rights law and serious violations of international humanitarian law). Another question concerning the scope of Principle 32 is whether it is limited to human rights enshrined in international instruments having a self-executing character, or whether it also applies to fundamental rights under domestic (often constitutional) law. That issue was not addressed in the preparatory work leading to the adoption of the Principles, nor in the way they were drafted, but the context from which they stem makes clear that their main concern relates to international human rights.

C. Theoretical Framework

The right to reparation provided under Principle 31 entails two aspects: a substantive 5
one and a procedural one. The substantive aspect concerns the various forms that reparation may take (restitution, compensation, satisfaction, or rehabilitation); those forms are addressed in Principle 34. The procedural aspect, covered under Principle 32, concerns access afforded to victims to 'prompt and effective' remedial procedures. In other words, Principle 32 governs the duty to provide remedial procedures in order to vindicate and make effective the substantive right to reparation. In that sense, the right to reparation and the right to access remedial procedures are distinct from each other and complement each other because the latter is the means to vindicate the former. However, because the remedial process is also, in and of itself, a remedy, it contains a substantive aspect that must not be underestimated. Therefore, the right to access remedial procedures is not only a means to an end; it is also an end in itself, as it allows victims to bring to light, through a public procedure, their grievances and see them addressed by state authorities.[11]

Principle 32 is divided into three subparagraphs. The first subparagraph enunciates and 6
details the right to access remedial procedures. The second subparagraph covers procedural requirements of national reparation programmes. The third subparagraph relates to regional and international procedures. While the first and last subparagraphs use verbs in prescriptive tenses ('shall', 'includes'), similar to the language used by Joinet in the 1997

[10] Revised final report prepared by Joinet, n 6. In 1994, the Sub-Commission on Prevention of Discrimination and Protection of Minorities decided by its Res 1994/34 to disjoin the study on civil and political rights (entrusted to Louis Joinet) from the one on economic, social, and cultural rights: see Report of the Sub-Commission on prevention of discrimination and protection of minorities on its 46th session, E/CN.4/Sub.2/1994/56, p 81.

[11] See B Hamber, 'The Dilemnas of Reparations: In Search of a Process-Driven Approach' in K De Feyter, S Parmentier, M Bossuyt, and P Lemmens (eds), *Out of the Ashes, Reparation for Victims of Gross and Systemic Human Rights Violations* (Intersentia 2005) 135–49.

Principles, the second subparagraph, inserted by Orentlicher, is drafted in the conditional ('may' and 'should'), attesting to its developing nature.

I. The right to access remedial procedures

7 The right for victims of alleged human rights violations to access remedial procedures is central to any human rights system. Absent any guaranteed remedy in case of an alleged violation, the obligation to respect human rights would indeed be at risk of remaining rather ineffective. Yet the right to access remedial procedures has developed to encompass a double function. It has a complementary function, as it primarily aims at ensuring respect for all human rights through legal oversight. But it has also gained an autonomous meaning, as the procedural right to an effective remedy has developed as a free-standing right. Such right for the victims of human rights violations entails a corresponding state obligation to establish and offer remedial procedures. Despite being drafted using a 'rights' language, Principle 32 is—at least in the first and second subparagraphs—very much about the content and scope of corresponding state obligations.

8 According to Principle 32, remedial procedures ought not to be judicial in nature;[12] they may take the 'form of criminal, civil, administrative or disciplinary proceedings'. Such diversity is not endorsed by all international human rights instruments, which tend to favour procedures of a judicial nature for the procedural guarantees they offer.[13] Moreover, administrative or disciplinary procedures have sometimes been deemed insufficient or inadequate in the event of grave human rights violations.[14]

9 If the remedial authority is not judicial, the guarantees concerning its independence and impartiality—both features usually associated with judicial procedures—are relevant in order to assess the effectiveness of the remedy. The authority should also have the power to take binding decisions and grant appropriate relief. Moreover, non-judicial procedures should be subject to judicial review.

10 The right to access remedial procedures exists only in so far as the claim is plausible and arguable. In other words, if the case is manifestly ill-founded or without merit, there could be no wrongful deprivation of the right to access remedial procedures if such procedures do not exist. Different types of remedy may be appropriate to redress violations, and states have a discretionary right as to how they wish to implement their obligation.[15]

[12] Some instruments refer to informal proceedings *where appropriate*, such as mediation, arbitration, and customary justice: see Art 7 of the Declaration of Basic Principles of Justice for Victims of Crime and Abuse of Power, adopted by the General Assembly through A/RES/40/34 on 29 November 1985 (hereinafter 'the 1985 Principles').

[13] See, eg, Art 8 of the Universal Declaration of Human Rights ('competent national tribunals'), Art 25 of the American Convention on Human Rights ('a competent court or tribunal'), and Art 47 of the Charter of Fundamental Rights of the European Union ('tribunal'). *Contra*, see, eg, Art 3 of the International Covenant on Civil and Political Rights ('competent judicial, administrative or legislative authorities') and Art 13 of the Convention for the Protection of Human Rights and Fundamental Freedoms (the European Convention on Human Rights (ECHR)) ('national authority').

[14] 'Purely disciplinary and administrative remedies cannot be deemed to constitute adequate and effective remedies within the meaning of article 2, paragraph 3, of the Covenant, in the event of particularly serious violations of human rights, notably in the event of an alleged violation of the right to life', *Bautista de Arellana v Colombia*, Communication no 563/1993, UN Doc CCPR/C/55/D/563/1993 (27 October 1995) para 8.2. See also Art 12 of the Basic Principles and Guidelines on Reparation, n 1, which provides that 'A victim of a gross violation of international human rights law or of a serious violation of international humanitarian law shall have equal access to an effective judicial remedy as provided for under international law.'

[15] See, eg, *Kudła v Poland* App no 30210/96 (ECtHR Grand Chamber, 26 October 2000) paras 154–55, and *Scordino v Italy (No 1)* App no 36813/97 (ECtHR Grand Chamber, 29 March 2006) paras 186–88.

Furthermore, if a single remedy does not by itself entirely satisfy the requirements of effective remedies, the aggregate of remedies provided for under domestic law might do so.

Under the first paragraph of Principle 32, the remedies must be 'readily available, prompt and effective'. Effectivity must exist in practice and not only in law. This implies, notably, the obligation to afford protection to victims against intimidation and reprisals. While intimidation of victims may occur in order to discourage the use of remedial procedures, it may also be used during those procedures. Victims must also be protected against reprisals occurring after the remedial procedures have been completed. State obligations furthermore include taking positive measures to ensure the participation of victims, minimizing inconveniences, ensuring protection against unlawful interference with their privacy as appropriate, and taking into account the special vulnerability of certain categories of persons (such as children, women, the elderly, or disabled persons). These measures must be guaranteed before, during, and after the proceedings.[16] Specific obligations may also arise from particular circumstances.[17] **11**

The right to access a court is not absolute and may be subject to limitations. These limitations must not, however, restrict or reduce the access left to the individual in such a way or to such an extent that the very essence of the right is impaired.[18] Principle 32 refers to Principle 23 in that regard. **12**

II. National reparation programmes

The second component of Principle 32 relates to the procedural requirements of national reparation programmes. While Orentlicher remained somehow laconic on the two previously existing aspects of the Principle, she elaborated on this third aspect in her independent study on best practices[19] and in her report as Independent Expert.[20] **13**

National reparation programmes are usually administrative, out-of-court processes designed to provide reparations to a large number of victims in the aftermath of mass violations of human rights. Like some international reparation processes,[21] they allow for the processing of a large number of cases following a standardized procedure, while using standards of proof that are much lower than in judicial proceedings. Prior to their **14**

[16] See, eg, Art 12(b) of the Principles on Remedy and Reparation and Human Rights Committee, General Comment no 31, Nature of the general legal obligation on states parties to the Covenant, UN Doc CCPR/C/21/Rev.1/Add.13 (26 May 2004), para 15; General Comment no 3 of the Committee Against Torture, paras 29–36, Art 6 of the 1985 Principles, n 12; Committee on Economic, Social and Cultural Rights, General Comment no 9, The domestic application of the Covenant (nineteenth session, 1998), UN Doc E/C.12/1998/24 (28 December 1998) para 9; *Prosecutor v Thomas Lubanga Dyilo* (Decision establishing the principles and procedures to be applied to reparations) ICC-01/04-01/06 (7 August 2012), as amended on appeal on 3 March 2015 (ICC-01/04-01/06 A A 2 A 3).

[17] For example, while remedies with suspensive effect are normally not required, the ECtHR has declared that whenever a person is facing the risk of an expulsion that would expose him/her to a real risk of suffering treatment contrary to Art 3 of the ECHR, effectiveness requires that he/she should have access to a remedy with automatic suspensive effect. See *De Souza Ribeiro v France* App no 22689/07 (ECtHR Grand Chamber, 13 December 2012) para 82.

[18] See *Waite and Kennedy v Germany* App no 26083/94 (ECtHR Grand Chamber, 18 February 1999) para 59, and *Al-Adsani v the United Kingdom* App no 35763/97 (ECtHR Grand Chamber, 21 November 2001) para 53, ECHR 2001-XI for considerations on immunity. These considerations were made with regard to the right to a fair trial (Art 6 ECHR) and not the right to an effective remedy (Art 13 ECHR).

[19] *Independent Study on best practices*, n 7.

[20] *Report of the independent expert to update the Set of Principles to combat impunity, Diane Orentlicher*, UN Doc E/CN.4/2005/102 (18 February 2005).

[21] Notably, the United Nations Compensation Commission or the Ethiopia-Eritrea Claims Commission.

implementation, such programmes usually identify the categories of victims, the human rights violations that can be redressed, and set out the various forms of reparations that will be provided along with the applicable procedure to seek redress.[22] Such programmes can eventually be funded by international donors, a practice which may raise some concerns in certain situations, and are 'addressed to individuals and to communities'. By this, Principle 32 reflects on the fact that abuses are sometimes directed at communities and that, as a consequence, remedies ought to be designed in order to meet the collective character of the injury. While communities may be recipient of reparations, their form should not include basic services owed to every person.[23]

15 When setting up reparation programmes, the question of their relation with other remedies (especially judicial)[24] must be determined. Reparations provided administratively may indeed be exclusive and final, in the sense that they waive the possibility for the victim to seek redress by judicial means for the same violations for which he/she has been compensated. The exclusive character of redress means that it can be questioned when the conditions of the waiver are themselves legally doubtful. Reparation programmes may also be complementary—subject to some conditions—to judicially administered reparations. The question of the suitability of exclusive administrative reparations is debated.[25] It is difficult to opine *in abstracto* in that regard, while it must be kept in mind that equality between victims is essential. Such equality may be jeopardized if some are able to receive additional reparation because they can afford judicial procedures, while others cannot. Furthermore, when large-scale breaches are addressed, the financial resources of the state should not be monopolized or diverted to the benefit of some victims, leaving others with limited reparation.

16 Contrary to judicial processes, for which clear procedural standards have been articulated, criteria applicable to administrative reparation programmes are still in the making.[26] These mechanisms are intrinsically context dependent, which renders their

[22] See *Report by the Special Rapporteur on the promotion of truth, justice, reparation and guarantees of non-recurrence, Pablo de Greiff*, UN Doc A/69/518 (14 October 2014).

[23] Ibid, 11.

[24] See JE Malamud-Goti and LS Grosman, 'Reparations and Civil Litigation: Compensation for Human Rights Violations in Transitional Democracies' in P de Greiff (ed), *The Handbook of Reparations* (OUP 2006) 539–59.

[25] Pablo de Greiff considers that it is difficult to determine in the abstract whether final reparation are desirable (P de Greiff, '*Reparations Programs: Patterns, Tendencies, and Challenges*' *Politorbis* Nr 50-3/2010, 59–60); Rombouts, Sardaro, and Vandeginste also seem to opt for a contextual determination based on the actual "'fairness and appropriateness" of the reparation' (H Rombouts, P Sardaro, and S Vandeginste, 'The Right to Reparation for Victims of Gross and Systematic Violations of Human Rights' in K De Keyter, S Parmentier, M Bossuyt, and P Lemmens (eds), *Out of the Ashes: Reparation for Victims of Gross and Systematic Human Rights Violations* (Intersentia 2005) 4491–92). Diane Orentlicher supports the exclusivity of the Peruvian programme (*Independent Study on best practices*, n 7, para 60), while some (especially civil society) claim that administrative reparations should never preclude individuals from seeking redress through judicial means (*Articulating Minimum Standards on Reparations Programmes in Response to Mass Violations Submission to the Special Rapporteur on the Promotion of Truth, Justice, Reparation and Guarantees of Non-Recurrence* (Redress, July 2014) para 43; *Guidance note of the Secretary-General. Reparations for conflict-related sexual violence* (June 2014) 6).

[26] National reparation programmes have been the subject of various studies (see UN Office of the High Commissioner for Human Rights, *Rule of Law Tools for Post-Conflict States: Reparations Programmes*, 2008, HR/PUB/08/1; and de Greiff (ed), n 24. More recently, procedural standards of reparation programmes have specifically been examined by international fora and non-governmental organizations. See, eg, the *Procedural Principles for Reparation Mechanisms*, adopted by the International Law Association at the seventy-sixth ILA Conference (Washington, Res 1/2014); *Articulating Minimum Standards on Reparations Programmes*, n 25; *Nairobi Declaration on Women's and Girls' Right to a Remedy and Reparation*, adopted at the International Meeting on Women's and Girls' Right to a Remedy and Reparation, held in Nairobi from 19–21 March 2007; *Guidance note of the Secretary-General*, n 25.

standardization uneasy.[27] Nevertheless, various guidelines and best practices have clearly emerged. The meaningful involvement of victims and civil society, and the effective participation of women and minority groups, is a key component in setting up such programmes. The need to actively and meaningfully involve them is affirmed in virtually all the recent instruments dealing with transitional justice issues.[28] It includes creating occasions for victims to speak up, but more specifically opportunities to participate to the furthest extent possible[29] in the conceptualization, design, implementation, and assessment of the programme. It also embraces the need to reach out to, communicate with, and provide adequate information to the victims.[30]

III. Access to international and regional procedures

In addition to the right to access domestic remedial procedures, Principle 32 also provides for the right to access international and regional procedures. It is clearly established that international and regional[31] mechanisms are subsidiary to the primary obligation of states to offer remedial procedures at the domestic level, and the exhaustion of local remedies rule gives effect to the subsidiary character of international protection. 17

One must bear in mind, however, that the scope of protection differs from one mechanism to the other, each allowing for the protection of a clearly defined set of substantive rights, namely the ones that are specifically included in the international instrument they were designed to monitor. The right to access international and regional mechanisms is therefore narrower than the general right to access remedial procedures at the domestic level. 18

If the right to access remedial procedures is considered to have an autonomous status and has allegedly been breached, the scope of the substantive rights for which redress is sought may differ. Some international entities consider that the violation of the right to an effective remedy may be invoked only in so far as redress is sought for the violation of a right conventionally protected.[32] Other international bodies accept to hear complaints 19

[27] Falk argues that in 'postauthoritarian political settings, where there is an impulse to achieve redress, the magnitude of the challenge requires some categorization of the victims as well as a recognition of severe limits on the capacity of the new government to provide anything approaching "adequate compensation". In this sense, the contribution of international law at this stage must be mainly viewed as indirect, and the actual dynamics of reparations arrangements reflect a variety of specific circumstances that exist in particular states. These arrangements have an ad hoc character that makes it impossible to draw any firm conclusions about *legal* expectations, much less frame this practice in the form of *legal doctrine*': R Falk, 'Reparations, International Law, and Global Justice: A New Frontier' in de Greiff (ed), n 24, 428–503, 485.

[28] 'The most successful transitional justice experiences owe a large part of their success to the quantity and the quality of public and victim consultation carried out.' *The rule of law and transitional justice in conflict and post-conflict societies. Report of the Secretary-General*, UN Doc S/2004/616 (23 August 2004) para 16. See also Art 6(b) of the 1985 Principles, n 12; *Guidance note of the Secretary-General*, n 25, 10–12; B Hamber, 'The dilemmas of Reparations: In search of a Process-Driven Approach' in De Feyter et al (eds), n 11, 135–49.

[29] Victim participation must indeed be carefully crafted and adapted to each stage of the proceedings. See C Correa, J Guillerot, and L Magarrell, 'Reparations and Victim Participation: A Look at the Truth Commission Experience' in C Ferstman, M Goetz, and A Stephens (eds), *Reparations for Victims of Genocide, War Crimes and Crimes Against Humanity* (Brill-Nijhoff 2009).

[30] See Principle 33.

[31] This latter element ('regional') is a new inclusion in the Updated Principle.

[32] See the wording of Art 3(a) ICCPR and Art 13 ECHR. The ECtHR has held that the right to an effective remedy does not apply whenever redress is sought for a right that is not protected by the convention. *Ärtze für das Leben v Austria* App no 10126/82 (ECtHR, 21 June 1988).

concerning the alleged violation of the right to an effective remedy whenever redress is sought for the violation of any (fundamental) right, be it protected under domestic law or international law.[33]

20 So far, only a limited number of instances of gross human rights violations have been addressed by international and regional mechanisms.[34]

D. Practice

21 No reparation procedure, judicial or administrative, dealing with gross violations of human rights at national or international level has so far reached the objective of achieving completeness (reach all victims of violations) and comprehensiveness (redress all violations), and none probably ever will due to inherent practical and financial limitations.[35] This can result from the chosen definition of 'victim',[36] 'beneficiaries',[37] or even perpetrator, although some mechanisms, while not formally excluding some categories of victims, do so in practice as a consequence of being ill-designed.[38] Moreover, reparation programmes must select violations that can be redressed, as it is virtually impossible to address all violations.[39]

22 Regarding the goal of completeness, the IACtHR has probably developed the most progressive case law at the international level. It has dealt with various cases involving large groups of victims, being either members of indigenous groups or victims of gross human rights violations. The Court has adopted a very inclusive definition of 'victim' throughout its case law,[40] which has allowed it to grant reparation to communities as a whole, without considering whether each member of the community could individually be considered as a victim.[41] The IACtHR has in that vein ordered the state to

[33] See Art 25(1) of the ACHR and Art 7(1)(a) of the African Charter on Human and Peoples' Rights.

[34] See De Feyter et al (eds), n 11, 155–57.

[35] Surveys of practice can be found ibid, 5 (on the Inter-American Court of Human Rights (IACtHR), the International Criminal Court (ICC), the Human Rights Chamber for Bosnia and Herzegovina, the Truth and Reconciliation Commission for Sierra Leone) and also in de Greiff (ed), n 24 (on Argentina, Chile, Brazil, El Salvador and Haiti, South Africa, Malawi).

[36] Some exclusions stem from deliberate policy choices (in Peru, members of subversive groups were excluded from the definition of 'victim' (Art 4 Law 28592)).

[37] In South Africa, access to reparations was provided only to victims who participated in the works of the Truth and Reconciliation Commission. In Colombia, beneficiaries must seek redress for violations that occurred after 1985 (Art 3(4) Law 1448). This was declared constitutional by the Constitutional Court. In Malawi, claimants must come with 'clean hands', ie not be human rights perpetrators themselves.

[38] In Sierra Leone, the National Commission for Social Action had one year to establish a victims' registry. As a consequence of these hasty proceedings, many victims were not reached out to and ultimately not taken into account.

[39] Most of the reparations programmes provide redress solely for some pre-listed violations. While most of the addressed violations are gross violations of civil and political rights (torture, death, enforced disappearance, arbitrary detention, and sexual violence), social rights are sometimes addressed. The 'Chega Report' of the Timor-Leste Commission for Reception, Truth and Reconciliation (CAVR—the Portuguese acronym), contains a specific chapter on abuses of economic and social rights. However, education and health are still rarely addressed as violations that ought to be redressed, but rather as forms of reparations (usually collective reparations) or as means to better articulate transitional justice and development. On reparation programmes, see the 2014 evaluation by P de Greiff, *Report on the promotion of truth, justice, reparation and guarantees of non-recurrence*, UN Doc A/69/518 (14 October 2014).

[40] The Rules of Procedures of the IACtHR provide for a much narrower definition of 'victim' ('a person whose rights have been violated, according to a judgment emitted by the Court').

[41] In *Plan de Sánchez Massacre v Guatemala*, the IACtHR has stated, eg, that 'Given that the victims in this case are members of the Mayan people, this Court considers that an important component of the individual

re-open a village school and staff it with personnel,[42] implement educational and cultural programmes,[43] or repeal laws.[44] On the other hand, the Appeals Chamber of the ICC, due to the criminal nature of the Court, adopted a very distinct position toward collective reparation measures. Collective reparations might only be awarded when *all* the members of the community met the eligibility criteria of 'victim'.[45] However, the Appeals Chamber stated that other members of the affected communities may still benefit from activities undertaken by the Trust Fund in relation to its assistance mandate (to the exclusion of its reparation mandate).[46]

From a procedural perspective, recent reparation programmes could draw from previous experiences, where a lack of outreach, communication to, and participation of victims has led to negative perceptions regarding certain reparation programmes. The Peruvian experience is in that sense recognized as being a compilation of best practices regarding its perception of reparation as a process,[47] where the participation of the population, and especially the victims, is an essential component in the decision-making process regarding the general objectives and applicable proceedings.[48] Besides, the Peruvian Comprehensive Reparation Programme (PIR) is especially attentive to pre-existing structural patterns of discrimination, marginalization, or vulnerability of some parts of the population (women,[49] rural or indigenous communities, the elderly, etc).[50] 23

Regarding the interrelation between administrative and judicial remedies, distinct choices have been made. Some programmes, such as in Brazil, Chile, and Slovenia, have opted for a complementary approach. Under the Slovenian Compensation Act,[51] adopted following the *Kurić and others v Slovenia* judgment,[52] victims may lodge a civil complaint 24

reparation is the reparation that the Court will now grant to the members of the community as a whole': *Plan de Sánchez Massacre v Guatemala (Reparations)* (Judgment) IACtHR Series C no 116 (19 November 2004), para 86 <http://www.corteidh.or.cr/docs/casos/articulos/seriec_116_ing.pdf>.

[42] *Aloeboetoe v Suriname (Reparations and Costs)* (Judgment) IACtHR Series C no 15 (10 September 1993) operative paragraphs <http://www.corteidh.or.cr/docs/casos/articulos/seriec_15_ing.pdf>.

[43] *Plan de Sánchez Massacre v Guatemala (Reparations)*, para 86, n 41.

[44] *Castillo-Pertruzzi v Peru (Merits, Reparations and Costs)* (Judgment) IACtHR Series C no 52 (30 May 1999) operative paragraphs <http://www.corteidh.or.cr/docs.casos/articulos/seriec_52_ing.pdf>.

[45] The Appeals Chamber declared that the Trial Chamber erred in 'grant[ing] an award for reparations to communities without setting out any criteria for distinction between those members of the communities who meet the above-mentioned eligibility criteria and other members of the communities'. ICC, *Judgment on the appeals against the 'Decision establishing the principles and procedures to be applied to reparations' of 7 August 2012*, ICC-01/04-01/06 (3 March 2015) para 214.

[46] Ibid, para 215.

[47] Art 4 of the *Reglamento de la Ley* N° 28592.

[48] Comisión de la verdad y Reconciliación, Final Report, 'Tomo IX – Cuarta Parte: Recomendaciones de la CVR, Hacia Un Compromiso Nacional por la Reconciliación' (hereinafter 'CVR, Final Report') <www.cverdad.org.pe/ifinal/> accessed 16 January 2018, 114.

[49] Procedures should be established to ensure that women have effective access to benefits, especially where women have traditionally little access to resources. In South Africa, many women had no access to the benefits, as compensatory sums were transferred to the bank accounts of male family members whenever women had no private bank accounts of their own. In Colombia, the Victims and Land Restitution Law contains specific measures ensuring that women heads of households are privileged in the various processes, eg that registration of property should be made in the name of both spouses. Consequently, in 2009, 87% of the beneficiaries were women, while 92% of direct recognized victims were men. In Peru, an amendment to the law creating the PIR inserted a new Art 7 g), affirming that the differences between men and women in the access to resources as well as in the decision-making processes should be taken into account, and that affirmative steps ought to be taken in order to promote the effective participation of women during decision making.

[50] Art 7 of the *Reglamento de la Ley* N° 28592; and CVR, Final Report, n 48, 113–15.

[51] Act Regulating Compensation for Damage to Persons Erased from the Permanent Population Register, which entered into force 18 December 2013 and become effective on 18 June 2014.

[52] *Kurić and others v Slovenia* (ECtHR Grand Chamber 26 June 2012).

seeking damages alternatively or in addition to an administrative procedure. The total amount of the damages granted by court is limited to a maximum of three times the (flat-rate) amount the victim is entitled to through administrative procedures.

25 Programmes that have opted for exclusivity may also draw a distinction between judicial claims against the state and proceedings against private perpetrators. In that vein, the report of the Peruvian Truth and Reconciliation Commission recommended that beneficiaries of the PIR would be barred from seeking damages from the state through civil claims, but could still seek damages from the perpetrator through civil claims. In that scenario, compensation obtained through the PIR should be returned to the state to avoid double compensation.[53]

26 The Colombian Victims and Land Restitution Law of 2011 established a hybrid mechanism: administratively granted reparations are complementary to judicial remedies, except if victims choose to consider the administrative compensation as a civil-based transactional settlement. The Law specified that accepting the transaction was without prejudice to the perpetrator's obligation to provide reparation to the victims, but barred all pending or future judicial proceedings against the state. In the event of acceptance, the victim therefore received a higher damage award.[54] However, the Colombian Constitutional Court, while endorsing the constitutionality of transactions, ruled transactions to be unconstitutional if they relate to crimes against humanity attributable to the state and result in exonerating the latter's responsibility.[55] The transaction clause was ultimately abrogated by Law 1753 of 9 June 2015 establishing the National Development Plan 2014–2018.[56]

E. Critical Assessment

27 Procedural guarantees are essential when providing remedies, in particular in transitional justice contexts. Principle 32 offers helpful guidance in that regard. However, over the years, it seems that there has been a paradigmatic shift from reparation through process to process *as* reparation. This shift leaves two issues unaddressed by the Principles.

28 The first issue relates to the bearer of the obligation to afford remedial mechanisms to victims. Despite the Principles' silence on the issue, it is clear from their object and purpose, together with the practice on which they are based, that the obligation to offer remedial procedures is only owed by the state under whose jurisdiction the victims or the perpetrators were at the time of the violations. It would therefore be questionable to use the Principles in order to allocate an obligation to offer remedial procedures to states other than the state responsible for the violations, the state where the violations occurred, or the state having jurisdiction over the perpetrators, in the event that the state apparatus did not carry them out. It is not because the substantive obligations breached are owed *erga omnes* that the obligation to provide means of redress would be owed universally. To derive from the *erga omnes* character of the substantive obligation breached a positive

[53] CVR, Final Report, n 48, 156 ('Relación con la vía judicial'); and Art 52 of the *Reglamento de la Ley* N° 28592.

[54] Art 132, Victims and Land Restitution Law (Law 1448) of 2011.

[55] Colombian Constitutional Court, Judgment C-099/13 (27 February 2013).

[56] Art 132, Law 1753. Law 1753 has been much criticized by human rights organizations, as it was said, amongst other things, to hamper the effectivity of land restitution. The Colombian Constitutional Court has followed their arguments by declaring several provisions of Law 1753 unconstitutional. Colombian Constitutional Court, Judgment C-035/16 (8 February 2016).

duty of solidarity bearing on all states to provide access to justice for victims is very questionable, both as a matter of *lex lata* and a matter of *lex ferenda*.[57] This is of course without prejudice to the duty to prosecute those responsible for international crimes, in accordance with the relevant international obligations to do so.

The second issue concerns the actual performance of the obligation to offer remedial procedures. When can one be certain that a state has duly discharged its obligation to provide remedies? This question relates to the exclusive or complementary nature of administrative procedures (an issue already addressed), but also to the comprehensiveness and completeness of the various mechanisms. While procedural requirements have been relatively well circumscribed for individual proceedings, they are much more blurred for large-scale mechanisms. International standards or best practices have unquestionably emerged, but these are still developing and their nature remains fairly nebulous: best practices are at the high end of a spectrum, and not meeting those does not necessarily entail being in breach of an obligation to provide access to effective remedies. It is clear that these standards are not binding on states as such, yet it seems difficult to claim that a state can nowadays fulfil its obligation, and thus extinguish its debt towards the victims, by implementing a reparation programme that does not follow them. Furthermore, the specific context of transitional justice must be borne in mind when assessing such procedures. Reparations, next to their primary function of redressing harm, strive for national reconciliation and to overcome pre-existing patterns of structural discrimination, and in that sense are transformative.[58] Judicial proceedings lead to 'patent inequalities'[59] between the victims, and full reparation for all victims is, in practice, impossible. This reinforces the importance of adopting a 'political and humanitarian' view on reparations,[60] and of finding an equilibrium between the individual right to remedies and the right of all to achieve peace and reconciliation. This should also lead to the consideration that the obligation to provide victims with remedial mechanisms combines an obligation of result and an obligation of conduct. It is an obligation of result in so far as states have a duty to address reparation claims, but it is an obligation of conduct because the adequacy of the means designed for that purpose very much depends on all the relevant circumstances, so that due diligence, rather than full reparation in all its forms to all victims of any type of breach, will inevitably be the yardstick against which to assess the correct performance—*hic et nunc*—of the obligation to provide an effective remedy to the fullest extent. 29

Bibiliography

Antkowiak, T, 'Remedial Approaches to Human Rights Violations: The Inter-American Court of Human Rights and Beyond' (2008) 46/2 Columbia Journal of Transnational Law 351–419.

[57] See in that regard the report by A Bucher, 'La compétence universelle civile en matière de réparation pour crimes internationaux' (Institut de droit international, Tallinn Session (2015)) 56–59. The corresponding draft resolution read, 'A State *shall* accept that its courts have universal civil jurisdiction over claims for relief by victims as referred to ...'. The final resolution tuned down the 'shall' to a 'should', and was still only adopted by thirteen votes in favour, six against, and eight abstentions.

[58] 'What the Constitution seeks to do is to facilitate the transition to a new democratic order, committed to "reconciliation between the people of South Africa and the reconstruction of society". The question is how this can be done effectively with the limitations of our resources and the legacy of the past.' *The Azanian Peoples Organization (AZAPO) et al v The President of the Republic of South Africa et al* (Judgment) Case no CCT 17/96 (Constitutional Court of South Africa, 25 July 1996) para 42.

[59] See CVR, Final Report, n 48, 105. [60] Ibid, 107.

d'Argent, P, 'Le droit de la responsabilité internationale complété? Examen des "Principes fondamentaux et directives concernant le droit à un recours et à réparation des victimes de violations flagrantes du droit international des droits de l'homme et de violations graves du droit international humanitaire" '(2005) 51 Annuaire français de droit international 27–55.

De Feyter, K, Parmentier, S, Bossuyt, M, and Lemmens, P (eds), *Out of the Ashes, Reparation for Victims of Gross and Systemic Human Rights Violations* (Intersentia 2005).

de Greiff, P (ed), *The Handbook of Reparations* (OUP 2006).

Evans, C, *The Right to Reparation in International Law for Victims of Armed Conflict* (CUP 2012).

Ferstman, C, Goetz, M, and Stephens, A (eds), *Reparations for Victims of Genocide, War Crimes and Crimes Against Humanity* (Brill-Nijhoff 2009).

Principle 33. Publicizing Reparation Procedures

Lisa J Laplante[1]

Ad hoc procedures enabling victims to exercise their right to reparation should be given the widest possible publicity by private as well as public communication media. Such dissemination should take place both within and outside the country, including through consular services, particularly in countries to which large numbers of victims have been forced into exile.

A. Summary of Findings

Principle 33 highlights the obligation of states to publicize 'ad hoc procedures' set up to distribute reparations. For example, a government might establish an administrative reparation programme following the work of a truth commission, as a non-judicial mechanism to distribute a range of measures, including compensation, restitution, and non-material and symbolic reparations. The 'publicity principle' assures the right to these remedies and places the onus on policymakers to design outreach campaigns to inform victims of these rights and how to access them.[2] Otherwise, 'a reparation mechanism has little practical value if potentially eligible victims are not aware of the opportunity to make claims or are not given timely information on how to do so in a language they can understand'.[3]

B. Contextual and Historical Introduction

1 The publicity principle appeared in early versions of Special Rapporteur Louis Joinet's reports on impunity with very little textual change.[4] Special expert Diane Orentlicher retained the same text, although renamed as Principle 33, and explained in the commentary that the phrase 'widest possible publicity' should be understood 'to include other appropriate measures for identifying potential beneficiaries of reparations programmes that may, under some circumstances, be more effective than dissemination through public media'.[5]

[1] The author would like to acknowledge the research assistance of Brian Flaherty, Joyell Johnson, Matthew Burns, and Jacob Edmister.

[2] Outreach, as a technical term, refers to a set of materials and activities that builds *direct* channels of communication with affected communities in order to raise awareness of the justice process. See C Ramírez-Barat, *Guidelines on Designing and Implementing Outreach Programs for Transitional Justice* (Center for Transitional Justice 2011) 7.

[3] International Committee on Reparations for Victims of Armed Conflict, *Commentary to Principle 5, Draft Procedural Principles for Reparation Mechanisms* (International Law Association 2014).

[4] Principle 39, *Question of the impunity of perpetrators of human rights violations (civil and political), Revised final report prepared by Mr Joinet pursuant to Sub-Commission decision 1996/119*, UN Doc E/CN.4/Sub.2/1997/20/Rev.1 (2 October 1997).

[5] D Orentlincher, *Report of the independent expert to update the Set of Principles to combat impunity*, UN Doc E/CN.4/2005/102 (18 February 2005) para 60.

C. Theoretical Framework

2 In her 2005 report, Special Expert Orentlicher explains that publicity assures effective implementation of reparations programmes, as well as advancing two core aims of reparations programmes: 'providing recognition to victims as citizens who bear equal rights vis-à-vis other citizens and facilitating their trust in State institutions'.[6]

3 Principle 33 plays a fundamental role in assuring the protection of the substantive right to a remedy and reparation. When governments develop administrative programmes to distribute reparations, policymakers must ensure that they design proper and adequate outreach campaigns to assure that victims are informed of their right to a remedy and how to access it. This information assures the 'accessibility' of a remedy and is a due process right, since access to information ensures 'equality of arms' and procedural fairness.[7]

D. Practice

4 Normative justifications for the publicity principle arises out of human rights law, which recognizes the right to 'impart and receive' information. Interpreting Article 19 of the International Covenant on Civil and Political Rights,[8] the United Nations Special Rapporteur on the Promotion and Protection of the Right to Freedom of Opinion and Expression indicates that the freedom of information implies that 'public bodies publish and widely disseminate documents of significant public interest'.[9] The right to information includes certain 'procedural characteristics', such as maximum disclosure and the presumed public nature of meetings and key documents.[10]

5 The Organization of American States General Assembly 'urge[d] the States to respect and promote respect for everyone's access to public information and to promote the adoption of any necessary legislative or other types of provisions to ensure its recognition and effective application'.[11] The Declaration of Principles on Freedom of Expression (2000) in which '[a]ccess to information held by the state' is considered a fundamental right of every individual and 'States have the obligation to guarantee the full exercise of this right.[12]

[6] Ibid.

[7] Due Process of Law Foundation (DPLF), *Disclosing Justice: A Study on Access to Judicial Information in Latin America* (DPLF with the support of Open Society Justice Initiative 2007) <www.dplf.org/en/resources/disclosing-justice-study-access-judicial-information-latin-america> accessed 13 January 2018. See M Freeman, *Truth Commissions and Procedural Fairness* (CUP 2006) 162–68 (writing that publicity and outreach assures 'procedural fairness' and victims' right to participation); Inter-American Commission on Human Rights (IAComHR), *Principal Guidelines for a Comprehensive Reparations Policy*, OEA/SER/L/V/II.131 Doc. 1 (19 February 2008) paras 9–11 (writing that reparation procedures must be respectful of the rights and due process guarantees established by Arts 8 and 25 of the Organization of American States, American Convention on Human Rights (ACHR) (22 November 1969) 1144 UNTS 123.

[8] International Covenant on Civil and Political Rights (ICCPR) (16 December 1966) 999 UNTS 171.

[9] Economic and Social Council, *Report of the Special Rapporteur on the promotion and protection of the right to freedom of opinion and expression, submitted in accordance with Commission resolution 1999/36*, UN Doc E/CN.4/2000/63 (18 January 2000) para 44.

[10] Human Rights Council, *Report of the Special Rapporteur on the promotion and protection of the right to freedom of opinion and expression*, UN DocA/HRC/14/23 (20 April 2010) para 32.

[11] Cf Resolution (Res) AG/RES. 2252 (XXXVI-O/06) on Access to public information: strengthening democracy (6 June 2006) second operative paragraph.

[12] Art 4, Declaration of Principles on Freedom of Expression (2000) <www.oas.org/en/iachr/expression/showarticle.asp?artID=26> accessed 24 November 2017.

I. United Nations guidelines and principles

The Office of the United Nations High Commissioner for Human Rights (OHCHR) remarks, '[e]ven a well-designed reparation programme will fail to distribute benefits to every potential beneficiary if it is not accompanied by effective outreach efforts once it is set in place'.[13] 6

Principle 12(a) of the Basic Principles and Guidelines on the Right to a Remedy and Reparation for Victims of Gross Violations of International Human Rights Law and Serious Violations of International Humanitarian Law directs states to 'Disseminate, through public and private mechanisms, information about all available remedies for gross violations of international human rights law and serious violations of international humanitarian law'.[14] 7

The United Nations Declaration on Justice for Victims of Crime and Abuse of Power directs that '[v]ictims should be informed of their right in seeking redress through [judicial and administrative] mechanisms'.[15] Other principles elaborated under the aegis of the UN similarly include the publicity principle.[16] 8

The Special Rapporteur on the promotion of truth, justice, reparation and guarantees of non-recurrence has recognized that 'Victim participation in reparation programmes is not possible without effective outreach, information and access.'[17] He recommends that 'Strategies need to be designed in order to overcome cleavages related to differences between urban and rural populations, indigenous and other cultural and ethnic groups, linguistic factors and literacy rates.' 9

In 2015, the European Union recommended that Transitional Justice Policy include 'appropriate outreach and communication activities', especially with affected populations.[18] 10

II. International mass claims processes

Despite the importance of publicizing reparations, it is an often overlooked detail in the design of such programmes. However, there exists growing practice that lends guidance on how the publicity principle works in the field.[19] 11

[13] OHCHR, *Rule-of-Law Tools for Post-Conflict States: Reparations programmes* (United Nations 2008) 16.

[14] Adopted and proclaimed by General Assembly Res 60/147 of 16 December 2005, UN Doc A/RES/60/147 (21 March 2006).

[15] Declaration of Basic Principles of Justice for Victims of Crime and Abuse of Power, UN Doc A/RES/40/34 (29 November 1985) paras 4 and 5.

[16] See, eg, the UN Secretary-General's set of operational guidelines for working with victims of conflict-related sexual violence, which calls for supporting '[m]eaningful participation and consultation of victims in the mapping, design, implementation, monitoring and evaluation of reparations'. United Nations General Secretary, *Guidance Note of the Secretary-General: Reparations for conflict-related sexual violence* (June 2014) 10. See also Protocol to Prevent, Suppress and Punish Trafficking in Persons especially Women and Children, supplementing the United Nations Convention against Transnational Organized Crime (25 December 2003) 2237 UNTS 319; United Nations Convention against Transnational Organized Crime, Art 6 (29 September 2003) 2225 UNTS 209; Nairobi Declaration on Women's and Girls' Right to a Remedy and Reparation: Basic Principles Relating to Women's and Girls' Right to a Remedy and Reparation (March 2007) Principle 2.

[17] Report of the Special Rapporteur on the promotion of truth, justice, reparation and guarantees of non-recurrence, UN Doc A/69/518 (14 October 2014) para 76 <ap.ohchr.org/documents/dpage_e.aspx?m=193> accessed 13 January 2018.

[18] The EU's Policy Framework on support to transitional justice (2015) <eeas.europa.eu/archives/docs/top_stories/pdf/the_eus_policy_framework_on_support_to_transitional_justice.pdf> accessed 13 January 2018.

[19] Ramírez-Barat, n 2, 6: 'Reparations programs, finally, have rarely engaged in comprehensive outreach efforts, despite the fact that they need not only to reach as large a number of potential beneficiaries as possible,

12 Based on the experience of mass claims processes, the Committee on Reparation for Victims of Armed Conflict of the International Law Association drafted the 'Draft Procedural Principles for Reparation Mechanisms' in 2014, which advise that outreach may vary due to particular circumstances but should address:

(a) where most of the eligible victims live and whether publicity should be directed to a limited geographical area;
(b) whether victims speak various languages;
(c) whether victims have a basic educational level; and
(d) whether claims arise from recent events or from events that date back a long time.[20]

13 The Commission for Real Property Claims of Displaced Persons and Refugees, established to redress victims of the 1992–95 war in Bosnia and Herzegovina, ensured potential claimants would receive oral and written instructions through the media, via pamphlets and by direct communication from government officials on radio, television, and at community meetings.[21] Likewise, the United Nations Compensation Commission established in 1991 considered its extensive outreach and publicity as essential to the success of its large-scale victims' compensation programme.[22]

14 Similarly, a class action settlement agreement for Holocaust victims in the US led to the Claims Resolution Tribunal's including direct mail and worldwide publication through the Internet, the grassroots community, newspapers, and direct mailing.[23]

III. International courts, commissions, and committees

15 Rule 96 of the International Criminal Court (ICC)'s Rules of Procedure and Evidence requires the Prosecutor to 'take all the necessary measures to give adequate publicity of the reparation proceedings before the Court, to the extent possible, to other victims, interested persons and interested States'.[24] The Registrar is obligated to consider the 'specific context, such as languages or dialects spoken, local customs and traditions, literacy rates and access to the media'.[25]

16 In 2012, the ICC declared that 'any reparation proceedings before the Court should be publicized by all necessary means, including by outreach activities with the national

but also to promote a broad message of recognition among the rest of the population (not to mention the mobilization of public resources on behalf of groups of people who are rarely popular). As a consequence, outreach has not been widely systematized.'

[20] Declaration of International Law Principles on Reparation for Victims of Armed Conflict, adopted on 20 August 2010 at the ILA Hague Conference, Art 6, Res 2/2010, International Law Association, *Report of the Seventy-Fourth Conference held in The Hague* (15–19 August 2010) (discussing fifteen mass claims commissions). See also AJ Carrillo and JS Palmer, 'Transnational Mass Claims Processes International Law and Practice' (2010) 28(2) Berkeley Journal of International Law 343–430.

[21] HM Holtzmann and E Kristjánsdóttir (eds), *International Mass Claims Processes: Legal and Practical Perspectives* (OUP 2007) 143–44.

[22] LA Taylor, 'The United Nations Compensation Commission' in C Ferstman, M Goetz, and A Stephens (eds), *Reparations for Victims of Genocide, War Crimes and Crimes Against Humanity* (Martinus Nijjhoff 2009) 197–214, 203–04; HM Holtzmann and E Kristjánsdóttir (eds), n 21, 144–47 (writing that publicity occurs in many forms, including public service announcements, posters, brochures, press releases, newspapers advertisements, radio and television spots, websites, hotlines, and special campaigns targeting particularly disadvantaged victim communities).

[23] Holtzmann and Kristjánsdóttir (eds), n 21, 144–45.

[24] ICC Rules of Procedure and Evidence, Rule 96, ICC-PIDS-LT-02-002/13 (2013).

[25] See Regulation 103 of ICC, Regulations of the Registry, ICC-BD/03/01/06 (6 March 2006).

authorities, local communities and the affected populations'.[26] Transparency requires timely notice of these proceedings and access to awards.[27]

The Inter-American Court of Human Rights (IACtHR) recognized the right to 'seek, receive and impart information' in its landmark judgment in *Claude Reyes et al v Chile* in 2006.[28] Interpreting Article 13 of the ACHR, the Court held that the state has a positive obligation to protect 'the right of all individuals to request access to State-held information'.[29] 17

Specific to reparations, the IACtHR has also recognized the importance of publicizing reparations, in *The Street Children* and *White Van* cases brought against Guatemala. The Court ordered the State to publicize these cases in national newspapers, and on radio and television, to ensure that the relatives of victims could participate in the reparation proceedings.[30] 18

The IAComHR has issued guidelines for administrative reparation programmes in transitional justice settings, which call upon the state to 'pursue an active strategy of disseminating information and reaching victims', which might include broad information campaigns and administrative decentralization.[31] 19

In its guidelines on reparation programmes, the IAComHR recognizes that the procedures designed to implement comprehensive reparation programmes must be respectful of the rights and due process guarantees established by Articles 8 and 25 of the ACHR, which include the principle of transparency.[32] Ultimately, publicity and outreach assure a type of 'procedural fairness', especially within the larger context of transitional justice processes.[33] 20

Within the United Nations, the Human Rights Committee noted that General Comment no 31 on the nature of the general legal obligation imposed on the parties to the ICCPR states that persons should, pursuant to Article 2 of the Covenant, be in receipt of information regarding their Covenant rights in general.[34] The Committee has recognized the general right 'seek' and 'receive' information contained in Article 19(2) included the right of individuals to receive state-held information, subject to the exceptions provided for in the Covenant.[35] Moreover, the Committee has recognized that accessing positive rights depends on receiving information.[36] 21

[26] ICC, *Prosecutor v Thomas Lubanga Dyilo* (Decision establishing the principles and procedures to be applied to reparations) ICC-01/04-01/06 (7 August 2012) para 258.

[27] Ibid, para 259.

[28] *Claude Reyes et al v Chile* (Judgment) (Merits, Reparations and Costs) IACtHR Series C no 151 (19 September 2006) para 76.

[29] Ibid, para 77.

[30] *Paniagua Morales et al v Guatemala (The White Van Case)* (Judgment) (Reparations) IACtHR Series C no 37 (25 May 2001) para 13; *Villagrán Morales et al v Guatemala (The Street Children Case)* (Judgment) IACtHR Series C no 77 (26 May 2001) para 17.

[31] IAComHR, *Principal Guidelines*, n 7, para 12.

[32] Ibid, paras 9–11.

[33] See M Freeman, *Truth Commissions and Procedural Fairness* (CUP 2006) 166 (referring to outreach and publicity mandates of truth commissions and how they ensure victims' right to participation and access to reparations).

[34] Human Rights Committee, General Comment no 31, Nature of the general legal obligation imposed on States Parties to the Covenant, CCPR/C/21/Rev.1 (26 May 2004), (2004) 11 IHRR 905.

[35] *Toktakunov v Kyrgyzstan* App no 1470/2006 (Merits) CCPR/C/101/D/1470/2006 (21 April 2011), (2011) 18 IHRR 1039.

[36] UN Committee on Economic, Social and Cultural Rights, General Comment no 19, The right to social security (Art 9) UN Doc E/C.12/GC/19 (4 February 2008), (2008) 15 IHRR 605 (determining that the

22 The European Court of Human Rights (ECtHR) has generally recognized the right to receive information through Article 10 of the European Convention on Human Rights,[37] but it has been more conservative in its approach to the right to impart information, limiting the 'positive information dissemination obligations' of the state and viewing the role of the state as being merely not to interfere with the dissemination of information.[38] However, the ECtHR does recognize procedural obligations to information under other articles of the ECHR that protect fundamental rights.[39] It has also held that the lack of information about a violation and the availability of redress may violate the right to remedy as recognized in Article 13 of the ECHR.[40] The Court has held that 'the remedy required by Article 13 must be "effective" in practice as well as in law, in particular in the sense that its exercise must not be unjustifiably hindered by acts or omissions of the authorities of the respondent State'.[41]

IV. Country-specific practice

23 The International Organization for Migration (IOM) currently assists governments with reparation programmes in the aftermath of conflict. For example, it helped the National Commission for Social Action in Sierra Leone to include outreach campaigns to inform victims of the conflict, including amputees, the severely war-wounded, victims of sexual violence, and other vulnerable groups, about reparations. Messages in newspapers and posters included general information on why reparations were being implemented, the eligibility criteria, and how to submit a claim and what to expect. Given that 90 per cent of the victims reside within national borders, the campaign did not include outreach in other countries where refugees might be found. The publicity helped to manage the expectations of the victims, while increasing the programme's legitimacy overall.[42]

24 Similarly, the IOM works with local partners in Colombia to provide reparations for victims of that country's internal armed conflict between the Government, FARC, and paramilitary groups. As a part of its transitional justice process, the country passed the 'Victims Law' in 2011. The Law includes provisions specific to the rights of victims to information, requiring the Colombian Government to promote effective publicity mechanisms to inform victims of the administrative and judicial avenues for exercising their right to reparation, including information on how to file a claim.[43]

ability to access positive rights requires the state to 'ensure the right of individuals and organizations to seek, receive and impart information on all social security entitlements in a clear and transparent manner').

[37] European Convention for the Protection of Human Rights and Fundamental Freedoms (ECHR) (4 November 1950) 213 UNTS 221.

[38] M McDonagh, 'The Right to Information in International Human Rights Law' (2013) 13 Human Rights Law Review 25–55, 35, 37.

[39] *Pereira Henriques v Luxembourg* [2006] ECHR 60255/00 (Fourth Section, 9 May 2006) (finding the right to information is essential for protecting the right to life under Art 2 ECHR); *Roche v United Kingdom* (2006) 42 EHRR 30 (finding a breach of Art 8 ECHR because the state failed to operate an effective and accessible procedure allowing the applicant access to all relevant and appropriate information about the impact of chemical weapons).

[40] *Case of Association for European Integration and Human Rights and Ekimdzhiev v Bulgaria* App no 62540/00 (ECtHR, 28 June 2007) paras 95, 103.

[41] *Case of Kolyadenko and others v Russia* (Judgment) Application nos 17423/05, 20534/05, 20678/05, 23263/05, 24283/05, and 35673/05 (ECtHR, 28 February 2012) para 225.

[42] Author's interview with Igor Cvetkovski, Land, Property, and Reparations Specialist for the Land, Property, and Reparations Division (LPR), Department of Operations and Emergencies (DOE) at the IOM (3 March 2014).

[43] Congreso de la República, Ley 1448 de 2011, *Por la cual se dictan medidas de atención, asistencia y reparación integral a las víctimas del conflicto armado interno y se dictan otras disposiciones*, Diario Oficial no

The Law also required the Colombian Government to reach victims residing outside of the country through various embassies for six months. It targeted Ecuador and Chile, on the understanding that most refugees lived there. It also employed different communication strategies, using the mass media to inform Colombian citizens of the law and its implications.[44] 25

E. Critical Assessment

Despite the importance of outreach and publicity, there are practical hurdles that obstruct their full implementation. There are particular challenges with reaching vulnerable groups, such as women, children, the illiterate, and rural populations. The means by which a government disseminates information must be capable of reaching every sector of the population, regardless of language, gender, age, socioeconomic status, and other demographic characteristics. Victims often present a diversified population that may require a comprehensive outreach strategy, which may exhaust local resources and capacity. 26

There are special challenges with reaching victims in exile, especially if they are refugees. Despite the fact that the OHCHR has reinforced the need to reach people forced into exile, this group tends to be considered less in country outreach campaigns, with some exceptions.[45] 27

Historically few countries have formalized an approach to publicity and outreach.[46] Yet it is most often the lack of information that explains why a significant number of victims never receive the relief to which they are entitled.[47] 28

Bibliography

Freeman, M, *Truth Commissions and Procedural Fairness* (CUP 2006).

Holtzmann, HM and Kristjánsdóttir, E (eds), *International Mass Claims Processes: Legal and Practical Perspectives* (OUP 2007).

Magarrell, L, *Outreach to and Engagement of Victims on Reparations-Lessons Learned from Truth and Reconciliation Processes* (Center for Transitional Justice 2007).

McDonagh, M, 'The Right to Information in International Human Rights Law' (2013) 13(1) Human Rights Law Review 25–55.

Ramírez-Barat, C, *Guidelines on Designing and Implementing Outreach Programs for Transitional Justice* (Center for Transitional Justice 2011).

Ramírez-Barat, C (ed), *Transitional Justice, Culture and Society: Beyond Outreach* (Social Science Research Council 2014).

Schulz, P, 'Justice seen is Justice done? Assessing the Impact of Outreach Activities by the International Criminal Tribunal for Rwanda (ICTR)' (2015) 21:74 Croatian International Relations Review 63–93.

Suchkova, M, 'The Importance of a Participatory Reparations Process and its Relationship to the Principles of Reparation' Transitional Justice Network Briefing Paper, no 5 (2011).

48.096 (10 June 2011), Arts 28, 30, and 35 <www.secretariasenado.gov.co/senado/basedoc/ley_1448_2011.html> accessed 13 January 2018.

[44] Interview with Felipe Cortes, Advisor to the IOM (5 March 2014).

[45] OHCHR, n 13, 16–17.

[46] Personal interview with Ruben Carranza, Director, Reparative Justice Program, International Center for Transitional Justice (19 June 2014).

[47] See, eg, International Center for Transitional Justice, *From Relief to Reparations: Listening to the Voices of Victims* (2012) <ictj.org/publication/relief-reparations-listening-voices-victims> accessed 13 January 2018.

Taylor, LA, 'The United Nations Compensation Commission' in C Ferstman, M Goetz, and A Stephens (eds), *Reparations for Victims of Genocide, War Crimes and Crimes Against Humanity* (Martinus Nijjhoff 2009) 197–214.

Vinck, P and Pham, PN, 'Outreach Evaluation: The International Criminal Court in the Central African Republic' (2010) 4(1) The International Journal of Transitional Justice 421–42.

Principle 34. Scope of the Right to Reparation

Lucas S Grosman[1]

The right to reparation shall cover all injuries suffered by victims; it shall include measures of restitution, compensation, rehabilitation, and satisfaction as provided by international law.

In the case of forced disappearance, the family of the direct victim has an imprescriptible right to be informed of the fate and/or whereabouts of the disappeared person and, in the event of decease, that person's body must be returned to the family as soon as it has been identified, regardless of whether the perpetrators have been identified or prosecuted.

A. Summary of Findings

The right to reparation includes restitution, compensation, rehabilitation, and satisfaction. To understand what each of such measures entails, reference to the UN Reparation Principles is crucial. Furthermore, there is robust state practice providing examples of how such measures have been implemented, despite the difficulties encountered in transitional situations. This practice and the opinion of experts reaffirm the idea that the right to reparation must be analysed realistically and with flexibility to adapt to particular contexts, and highlight the importance of conceiving of reparations as part of a comprehensive programme, rather than as a collection of isolated measures.

In addition, Principle 34, second paragraph, spells out the content of certain rights owed to families of victims of forced disappearance: first, the right to be informed of the fate or whereabouts of the disappeared; and, second, the right to obtain the body of the victim, once it has been identified. These rights have a substantial as well as a remedial dimension, and therefore contribute to the reparation of the harm.

B. Contextual and Historical Introduction

Reparation efforts have become a central aspect of the fight against impunity as a means of restoring the victims' dignity and their sense of belonging to the community as full members. Accordingly, the section on reparations occupies a central place in the Impunity Principles, although there is a separate and contemporaneous United Nations (UN) document specifically devoted to this topic, the Basic Principles and Guidelines on the Right to a Remedy and Reparation for Victims of Gross Violations of International Human Rights Law and Serious Violations of International Humanitarian Law.[2] 1

[1] The author would like to thank Catalina Fuentes Benitez and Juan Agustín Otero for their excellent research assistance.

[2] UN General Assembly, Basic Principles and Guidelines on the Right to a Remedy and Reparation for Victims of Gross Violations of International Human Rights Law and Serious Violations of International Humanitarian Law: resolution adopted by the General Assembly, UN Doc A/RES/60/147 (21 March 2006) (hereinafter 'Reperation Principles') <www.refworld.org/docid/4721cb942.html> accessed 28 April 2016.

2 The state's obligation to provide reparation for violations of international law is now firmly established. It can be traced back to a famous dictum by the Permanent Court of International Justice (PCIJ) in the *Chorzów Factory* case,[3] and figures prominently in a number of international and regional human rights treaties. Furthermore, the obligation to provide adequate reparation in cases of human rights violation is generally considered part of customary law,[4] and has been recognized by the International Court of Justice (ICJ) as well.[5] Widespread use of reparations programmes, UN documents such as the Reparation Principles, and the decisions of regional human rights courts, which will be discussed throughout this commentary, speak to the emergence of such customary rule. The Impunity Principles must be analysed as a decisive step along that road.

3 However, and despite the fact that individuals are now considered subjects of international law, the extent to which the state's obligation to provide adequate reparation gives rise to a universal individual right to obtain it is still the subject of debate.[6] Furthermore, it has been argued that, even when such right is expressly granted, its content might be limited to a procedural right to access courts.[7] There is certainly a gap between aspirations to full reparation as reflected in international documents, on the one hand, and practice, on the other.

C. Theoretical Framework

I. The right to reparation

4 Principle 34 establishes that reparation should include measures of restitution, compensation, rehabilitation, and satisfaction. In order to determine what each of such measures entails, the Impunity Principles should be read in conjunction with the Reparation Principles, adopted and proclaimed by General Assembly Resolution 60/147 of 16 December 2005. Although the former have not yet been adopted by the UN while the latter have, both sets of principles have been understood as complementary.[8] In fact, the independent expert Diane Orentlichter makes several references to the Reparation Principles when she discusses articles of the Updated Principles on reparations.[9] Moreover, human rights tribunals, especially the Inter-American Court of Human Rights (IACtHR), have often used the Reparation Principles as a reference.[10] It is therefore quite

[3] PCIJ, *Factory at Chorzów (Germany v Poland)* (Jurisdiction) (1927) Series A no 17, 67, 80, 86, 99, 121.

[4] See D Shelton, *Remedies in International Human Rights Law* (2nd edn, OUP 2006) 238; C Bassiouni, 'International Recognition of Victims' Rights' (2006) 6(2) Human Rights Law Review 203–79, 217.

[5] See *Armed Activities on the Territory of the Congo (Democratic Republic of the Congo v. Uganda)* (Judgment) [2005] ICJ Rep 168; and *Legal Consequences of the Construction of a Wall in the Occupied Palestinian Territory* (Advisory Opinion) [2004] ICJ Rep 136.

[6] See H Rombouts, *Victim Organisations and the Politics of Reparation: A Case-study on Rwanda* (Intersentia 2004) 19; see also H Rombouts et al, 'The Right to Reparation for Victims of Gross and Systematic Violations of Human Rights' in K Feyter et al (eds), *Out of the Ashes* (Intersentia 2005) 345–502.

[7] See Rombouts, *Victim Organisations*, n 6, 19–20.

[8] See T van Boven, 'Victims' Rights to a Remedy and Reparation: The New United Nations Principles and Guidelines' in C Ferstman, M Goetz, and A Stephens (eds), *Reparations for Victims of Genocide, War Crimes and Crimes against Humanity: Systems in Place and Systems in the Making* (Martinus Nijhoff Online 2009) 19–40, 37.

[9] See *Report of the independent expert to update the Set of Principles to combat impunity*, UN Doc E/CN.4/2005/102 (18 February 2005) especially para 61, note 76, and note 88.

[10] See, eg, cases discussed in section D, and van Boven, n 8, 5. Van Boven emphasizes that several Latin American countries based their reparation programmes on the Reparation Principles when designing those

pertinent to turn to those Principles to understand the content of each measure of reparation included in Principle 34 of the Impunity Principles.

i. Restitution

According to the Reparation Principles: 5

Restitution should, whenever possible, restore the victim to the original situation before the gross violations of international human rights law or serious violations of international humanitarian law occurred. Restitution includes, as appropriate: restoration of liberty, enjoyment of human rights, identity, family life and citizenship, return to one's place of residence, restoration of employment and return of property.[11]

The Reparation Principles thus place returning the victim to the *statu quo ante* as the primary goal. This is in line with the statement of the PCIJ in the *Chorzów Factory* case that, if restitution is not possible, compensation is owed.[12] 6

Restitution is an aspiration that can rarely be fulfilled in cases of gross human rights violations, given the nature of the loss involved. However, there are certain deprivations that can, indeed, be addressed through restitution. Thus, while the harm caused by illegal imprisonment cannot be undone, restitution of liberty—that is, release of persons illegally detained—can stop the harm and is, therefore, of the utmost importance. In the face of on-going violations of human rights, restitution of such rights means that violations should cease.[13] To that extent, restitution of rights overlaps with other measures of reparation.[14] 7

The Reparation Principles refer explicitly to the right to restitution of employment. If persons have been dismissed from their jobs or public positions because of their ideology, this right means that they should be re-employed. This can be seen as a complement of 'vetting', a formal procedure for the identification and removal of individuals responsible for abuses, especially from the police, prison services, the army, and the judiciary.[15] Restitution of identity, in turn, is particularly relevant in the context of appropriation of children born in captivity.[16] 8

ii. Compensation

Compensation is a central aspect of reparations efforts, to the point that reparation and compensation are frequently treated as synonymous. In the Impunity Principles and Reparation Principles, however, reparation is the gender and compensation the species. 9

According to the Reparation Principles, '*[c]ompensation* should be provided for any economically assessable damage, as appropriate and proportional to the gravity of the violation and the circumstances of each case'.[17] Compensation is a form of material 10

programmes, and that the Rome Statute of the International Criminal Court, UN Doc A/CONF.183/9; (1998) 37 ILM 1002; 2187 UNTS 90 follows their wording in its Art 75.

[11] Reparation Principles, n 2, Principle 19.

[12] See *Chorzów Factory*, n 3, 67, 80, 86, 99, 121.

[13] See A Buyse, 'Lost and Regained? Restitution as a Remedy for Human Rights Violations in the Context of International Law' (2008) 68 Heidelberg Journal of International Law 129–53, 132–38.

[14] Thus, restitution may overlap with cessation, which, as will be explained, is part of satisfaction as a form of reparation. See C Droege, *The Right to a Remedy and to Reparation for Gross Human Rights Violations—A Practitioners' Guide* (International Commission of Jurists 2006) 96.

[15] See UN, *The rule of law and transitional justice in conflict and post-conflict societies. Report of the Secretary-General*, UN Doc S/2004/616 (23 August 2004) para 52.

[16] The UN General Assembly has dealt specifically with this issue in its Declaration on the Protection of All Persons from Enforced Disappearance (Res GA 47/133) Art 20.

[17] Reparation Principles, n 2, Principle 20.

reparation. Since nothing can truly erase the effects of severe human rights violations, it is an open question what amount of money is appropriate.

11 The language of the Reparation Principles suggests that such determination should take into account the specificities of the situation of each particular victim. However, reparation programmes actually implemented in the context of transitional democracies and mass violations often have not focused on the individual dimension of the harm and the specificities of particular situations, but rather on their common or collective features. Pablo de Greiff, UN Special Rapporteur on the promotion of truth, justice, reparation and guarantees of non-recurrence, argues that 'the proper metric for assessing the size of the compensation owed in fairness to the victims stems directly from the very violation of rights held in common by human beings and particularly by citizens, and not from each individual's particular position prior to the violation'.[18] He understands that the phrase 'circumstances of each case', used in Article 18 of the Reparation Principles, 'provides room for departures from the criterion of full compensation'.[19] Professors van Boven and Letschert also understand this language as an invitation to determine the amount and mode (collective or individual) of compensation with certain latitude.[20]

12 Thus, authorities on the matter accept, or even advocate for, general compensation programmes in which differences among victims are not necessarily taken into account. This is consistent both with programmes that provide compensation to individual victims without making distinctions among them except at the most basic level through very broad categories *and* with programmes that provide compensation to victims collectively. This more flexible approach, which is sensitive to the structural scarcity of resources typical of transitional situations in the aftermath of mass atrocity, and therefore to the inevitable constraints reparations face in practice, may seem in tension with the more ambitious aspiration conveyed by the language of the Reparation Principles.

13 These two alternative approaches, in turn, relate to the mechanism chosen to implement compensation programmes. Thus, a basic distinction can be drawn between judicial and administrative approaches to compensation. Judicial approaches tend to account for differences among individuals, whereas administrative programmes do not. Moreover, some administrative programmes entail judicial closure and are therefore final, whereas others leave open the possibility of opting out of the administrative scheme and resorting to judicial compensation.[21]

14 This potential tension between the ambitious language of the Reparation Principles and the more flexible approach that, as will be discussed, tends to be followed in practice, will be critically assessed in section E of this commentary.

[18] Office of the United Nations High Commissioner for Human Rights (OHCHR), *Rule-of-Law Tools for Post-Conflict States. Reparations Programmes* (United Nations 2008) 30 (hereinafter '*Rule-of-Law Tools*'). Pablo de Greiff was primarily responsible for this document (see 'Acknowledgements', ibid, vi).

[19] Ibid, 28.

[20] RM Letschert and T van Boven, 'Providing reparation in situations of mass victimization. Key challenges involved' in RM Letschert, R Haveman, A De Brouwer, and A Pemberton (eds), *Victimological Approaches to International Crimes* (Intersentia 2011) 153–84.

[21] See JE Malamud-Goti and LS Grosman, 'Reparations and Civil Litigation: Compensation for Human Rights Violations in Transitional Democracies' in P de Greiff (ed), *The Handbook of Reparations* (OUP 2006) 539–59; and *Rule-of-Law Tools*, n 18, 35–36.

iii. Rehabilitation and satisfaction

The Reparation Principles state that *rehabilitation* should include medical and psychological care, as well as legal and social services.[22] The goal of reinserting the victim as a full member of society appears most clearly in this component of reparation. Accordingly, 'restoring the good name of the victim' has been considered a form of rehabilitation.[23] 15

Provision of medical and related services is crucial in these contexts. It has been shown that victims of human rights abuse seem more prone to disease, and therefore such services are an effective means of improving their quality of life.[24] 16

In turn, in the case of satisfaction, diverse measures are enumerated, including the cessation of continuing violations, disclosure of truth, recovery of bodies, an official declaration to restore dignity, public apology, sanctions to perpetrators, commemorations, and inclusion of an account of the violations in educational material.[25] 17

In its original formulation, current Principle 34 referred to measures of rehabilitation (as well as restitution and compensation) as *individual*, whereas measures of satisfaction were preceded by the adjective *general*. Both qualifications have been deleted in the revised version. This revision expresses the belief that all four measures could, in principle, be understood from both an individual and a collective perspective. This approach is more flexible, and therefore can better accommodate the requirements of different transitional situations. 18

II. Right to know and to recover mortal remains in cases of forced disappearance

Principle 34, second paragraph, establishes rights owed to families of victims of forced disappearance: first, the right to be informed of the fate or whereabouts of the disappeared; second, the right to obtain the body of the victim, once it has been identified. This is in line with the International Convention against Enforced Disappearance.[26] 19

In her report, the independent expert Diane Orentlicher emphasizes that these rights are unqualified, hence her decision to eliminate the provision establishing that the rights become operative 'when the fate of the disappeared person has become known'. She also explains why these rights are included as part of the right to reparation: there is not only a substantial but also a remedial dimension to the right to know. Therefore, knowing the fate of the disappeared persons, as well as having a chance to bury their bodies, contributes to the reparation of the harm. 20

D. Practice

I. Restitution

i. Rights

To the extent that restitution of a right means stopping its ongoing violation, instances of this practice are widespread. Just to mention a couple of examples, the African Commission on Human and Peoples' Rights (AComHPR), in *Article 19 v Eritrea*, urged 21

[22] Reparation Principles, n 2, Principle 21. [23] See *Rule-of-Law Tools*, n 18, 22.
[24] Ibid, 24. [25] Reparation Principles, n 2, Principle 22.
[26] 2716 UNTS 3. Adopted by GA Res 61/177 on 12 January 2007. See Arts 15, 17(3), 18.

the state of Eritrea 'to release or to bring to a speedy and fair trial the 18 journalists detained since September 2001, and to lift the ban on the press'.[27] The IACtHR, in turn, in *Lori Berenson Mejía v Peru*, ordered, inter alia, the improvement of prison conditions in the Yanamayo Prison to meet international standards, and the transfer of inmates whose personal circumstances so required.[28]

ii. Assets

22 Although German reparation efforts are best known for their compensation aspect, restitution of assets has played a role as well.[29] Since 1947, laws mandating restitution of goods illegally taken by the Nazi regime to their original owners or their successors were passed in the three Allied Occupation zones. On the basis of such laws, the Federal Restitution Law of 1957 was passed in order to restore or replace identifiable items seized by the Nazis.[30]

iii. Children

23 In Argentina, between 1976 and 1982, many children were born in captivity from mothers illegally detained, tortured, and eventually murdered by the military government. Several of those children were, soon after birth, adopted by members of the military and security forces or families related to them. Since their family name was changed and they were never told who their biological parents were, they were denied their true identity.[31] 'Restitution of identity', in these cases, entails making such information available to them; 'restitution of family life', in turn, entails the right to meet what remains of their original family.[32] The Argentine state and civil society took concrete steps to facilitate this form of restitution[33] and, to date, 125 children (now adults) have recovered their identities.[34]

iv. Employment

24 Instances of restitution of employment ordered by the IACtHR as a form of reparation can be found in *Baena v Panama*[35] and in *Loayza-Tamayo v Peru*, in which the state was enjoined to reinstate 270 workers.[36]

[27] AComHPR, *Article 19 v Eritrea*, Communication no 275/03 (30 May 2007).

[28] *Lori Berenson Mejía v Peru* (Judgment on the Merits, Reparations and Costs) IACtHR Series C no 119 (25 November 2004) para 248.

[29] See A Colonomos and A Armstrong, 'German Reparations to the Jews after World War II: A Turning Point in the History of Reparations' in de Greiff (ed), n 21, 390–419.

[30] Ibid.

[31] See MJ Guembe, 'Economic Reparations for Grave Human Rights Violations; The Argentinean Experience' in de Greiff (ed), n 21, ch 1, fn 92.

[32] The Inter-American Commission of Human Rights recognized those rights in the case *Reggiardo Tolosa v Argentina* (Provisional Measures), Resolutions of 19 November 1993 and 19 January 1994. The Commission requested the IACtHR to rule on certain measures related to this right. However, the issue became moot, since the Argentine Government took satisfactory steps, as reflected by the Court in its 19 January 1994 decision on the matter.

[33] Thus, Law 23511 of 1987 created the Bank of Genetic Data to facilitate the process of identification of biological ties. Organizations from civil society, especially the non-governmental organization Abuelas de Plaza de Mayo, played a crucial role.

[34] The figure corresponds to November 2017.

[35] *Baena et al v Panama* (Judgment) IACtHR Series C no 72 (2 February 2001).

[36] *Case of Loayza-Tamayo v Peru* (Merits) (Judgment) IACtHR Series C no 33 (17 September 1997).

II. Compensation

Human rights courts and commissions around the world often establish the obligation to compensate in response to human rights violations. For example, the AComHPR, in *Article 19 v Eritrea*, '[r]ecommends that the government of Eritrea takes appropriate measures to ensure payment of compensation to the detainees'.[37] However, it has been observed that the efficacy of the African system in bringing justice to the victims is to be doubted, given the lack of state implementation of the Commission's rulings.[38] 25

In several cases, the European Court of Human Rights (ECtHR) has construed the obligation to provide 'just satisfaction' established in Article 41 of the European Convention of Human Rights as covering pecuniary compensation. That was the case, for example, in *Ribitsch v Austria*,[39] *Mikheyev v Russia*,[40] and *Aksoy v Turkey*.[41] 26

In cases of mass violations, state practice has favoured administrative approaches, and generally compensation has been provided to individual victims by establishing broad categories, rather than by identifying the specific harm suffered by each individual. As the examples following illustrate, the amounts paid in each country vary significantly, and it is difficult to attribute such differences to the seriousness of the violation or the wealth of the country, although the influence of the latter factor and of the political context is undeniable. 27

In South Africa, a single payment of less than $4,000[42] was made to victims of apartheid, although the Truth and Reconciliation Commission had suggested a larger sum. In the US, Japanese Americans whose rights were violated during the Second World War received $20,000. In Brazil, a minimum of $100,000 was paid as compensation for the violations perpetrated by the military dictatorship. In Argentina, the amount paid in each case was of $224,000. In Chile, victims received a monthly pension of $537.[43] 28

After the first Gulf War, the UN Compensation Commission processed more than 2.5 million claims, paying out more than $18 billion to victims of Iraq's unlawful invasion and occupation of Kuwait.[44] Transnational mass claims processes such as this one possess features of their own, which, it has been argued, distinguish them from transitional justice claims processes.[45] 29

In some cases compensation has been granted collectively to groups or nations. Thus, Germany's reparation programme benefited both individual victims of the Holocaust and the State of Israel.[46] In turn, the IACtHR, in *Aloeboetoe*,[47] ordered the opening and staffing of a school and a hospital, which can be considered a form of collective compensation. 30

[37] *Article 19 v Eritrea*, n 27, para 108.

[38] See F Viljoen and L Louw, 'State Compliance with the recommendations of the African Commission on Human and Peoples' Rights, 1994–2004' (2007) 101(1) American Journal of International Law 1–34.

[39] *Ribitsch v Austria* (Judgment) (ECtHR, 4 December 1995).

[40] *Mikheyev v Russia* (Judgment) (ECtHR, 26 January 2006).

[41] *Aksoy v Turkey* (Judgment) (ECtHR, 26 November 1996).

[42] All amounts are expressed in US dollars, unless otherwise indicated.

[43] See *Rule-of-Law Tools*, n 18.

[44] See UN Security Council, *The rule of law and transitional justice in conflict and post-conflict societies*, UN Doc S/2004/616 (23 August 2004) para 54.

[45] For a discussion of similarities and differences between these two types of processes, see A Carrillo and J Palmer, 'Transnational Mass Claim Processes (TMCPs) in International Law and Practice' (2010) 28 Berkeley Journal of International Law 343–430.

[46] It has been estimated that German reparations for different violations amount to approximately US$ 61.5 billion. See 'German reparations', Colonomos and Armstrong, n 29, 408.

[47] *Aloeboetoe et al v Suriname* (Reparations and Costs) IACtHRSeries C No 15 (10 September 1993).

Similarly, in *Comunidad Mayagna*,[48] it decided that the state had to invest $50,000 in facilities and services for the benefit of the victimized community.

31 As already mentioned, it is beyond dispute that state practice regarding compensation, especially in the face of mass violations, falls short of the aspiration to full compensation enshrined in international conventions and other documents.

III. Rehabilitation

32 Medical services, including psychiatric and psychological treatment, have been included as part of reparation programmes in Chile, Peru, and Morocco.[49] Furthermore, the case law of the IACtHR is rich in examples of measures of rehabilitation.[50] For example, in *Cepeda Vargas*[51] and *Barrios Altos*,[52] free provision of psychological treatment was ordered as a form of reparation that can be regarded as rehabilitation. In *Cepeda Vargas*, it was considered that psychological treatment could be individual or collective, depending on the victims' needs.[53] Similar considerations can be found in *19 Merchants*; [54] *'Las Dos Erres' Massacre*;[55] and *Kawas Fernández*.[56]

33 The Commission of Human Rights, in its 2004 Resolution on Torture and Other Cruel, Inhuman or Degrading Treatment or Punishment,[57] encouraged the development of rehabilitation centers for victims of torture. The UN Special Rapporteur on Torture Manfred Nowak, in his report to the General Assembly in August 2010, argued that the Convention against Torture[58] demands that torture rehabilitation centers are established and that such centers must provide holistic treatment for survivors.[59]

IV. Satisfaction

34 In several cases, the IACtHR has also enjoined states to provide forms of reparation that qualify as satisfaction. Thus, in *Molina Theissen*,[60] it ordered the state to search for the bodies, investigate, publicly report the decision and acknowledge responsibility, and name a school, making reference to the disappeared children; in *Benavides Ceballos*,[61] the

[48] *Comunidad Mayagna (Sumo) Awas Tingni v Nicaragua* (Merits, Reparations and Costs) IACtHR Series C no 79 (31 August 2001).

[49] See *Rule-of-Law Tools*, n 18, 24.

[50] For a discussion of this Court's 'remedial' approach, see T Antkowiak, 'Remedial Approaches to Human Rights Violations: The Inter-American Court of Human Rights and Beyond' (2008) 46(2) Columbia Journal of Transnational Law 351–419.

[51] *Manuel Cepeda Vargas v Colombia* (Preliminary Objections, Merits, Reparations and Costs) (Judgment) IACtHR Series C no 213 (26 May 2010).

[52] *Case of Barrios Altos v Peru* (Merits) (Judgment) IACtHR Series C No 75 (14 March 2001).

[53] *Manuel Cepeda Vargas v Colombia*, n 51, para 235.

[54] *Case of the 19 Merchants v Colombia* (Merits, Reparations and Costs) (Judgment) IACtHR Series C no 109 (5 July 2004).

[55] *Case of the 'Las Dos Erres' Massacre v Guatemala* (Preliminary Objection, Merits, Reparations and Costs) (Judgment) IACtHR (4 November 2009).

[56] *Case of Kawas-Fernández v Honduras* (Merits, Reparations and Costs) (Judgment) IACtHR (3 April 2009).

[57] HRC/2004/41 (19 April 2004).

[58] Convention against Torture and Other Cruel, Inhuman or Degrading Treatment or Punishment, 1465 UNTS 85.

[59] UN General Assembly, *Interim report of the Special Rapporteur of the Human Rights Council on torture and other cruel, inhuman or degrading treatment or punishment*, UN Doc A/65/273 (10 August 2010).

[60] *Case of Molina-Theissen v Guatemala* (Reparations and Costs) (Judgment) IACtHR Series C no 108 (3 July 2004).

[61] *Case of Benavides Cevallos v Ecuador* (Merits, Reparations and Costs) (Judgment) IACtHR Series C no 38 (19 June 1998).

Court ordered Ecuador to proceed with the investigation of the human rights violations; in *Trujillo Oroza*[62] and *Barrios Altos*,[63] it ordered certain conduct to be criminalized. In *Loayza-Tamayo*,[64] Peru was enjoined to adapt its domestic laws to abide by the American Convention on Human Rights. In *Girls Yean*,[65] the IACtHR ordered the Dominican Republic to issue a public apology as a form of satisfaction; the same order was issued against Peru in *Castro-Castro Prison*.[66]

In *El Masri v Former Yugoslav Republic of Macedonia*,[67] the ECtHR recognized the right to access concrete information about gross violations of human rights, which can be regarded a form of satisfaction under Principle 22(b) of the Reparation Principles. 35

V. Mortal remains

The case law of the IACtHR provides examples of enforcement of rights included in the second paragraph of Principle 34. In *Juan Humberto Sanchez*,[68] the Court ordered the state to search for the bodies of persons illegally killed, as it did in *Molina Thiessen*. In *Trujillo-Oroza*, the Court ordered the state to devote all available means to locating the body of the victim and delivering it to the family for adequate burial.[69] 36

E. Critical Assessment

In the preceding sections, different elements of the right to reparation were analysed separately; it is important, however, to emphasize the interconnection that exists between them, and the importance of understanding and presenting them as part of a comprehensive programme rather than in isolation. No single element may seem sufficient or adequate on its own, but all or several of them together may allow a state to approach as much as possible to the demands of justice in transitional contexts.[70] 37

Interdependence affects the way in which each measure of reparation may be read, whether by the victims or by other relevant actors.[71] Thus, for example, if compensation to the victims is not part of a more general reparations programme that includes criminal prosecutions and truth-telling, it could be 'counterproductive and be perceived more like a payment in exchange for the silence or acquiescence of victims and their families'.[72] 38

[62] *Case of Trujillo-Oroza v Bolivia* (Reparations and Costs) (Judgment) IACtHR Series C no 92 (27 February 2002).

[63] *Case of Barrios Altos v Peru*, n 52. [64] *Case of Loayza-Tamayo v Peru*, n 36.

[65] *Case of the Girls Yean and Bosico v The Dominican Republic* (Preliminary Objections, Merits, Reparations and Costs) (Judgment) IACtHR Series C no 130 (8 September 2005).

[66] *Case of the Castro-Castro Prison v Peru* (Merits, Reparations and Costs) (Judgment) IACtHR Series C no 160 (25 November 2006).

[67] *El Masri v Former Yugoslav Republic of Macedonia* (Judgment) (ECtHR, 13 December 2012).

[68] *Case of Juan Humberto Sánchez v Honduras* (Preliminary Objections, Merits, Reparations and Costs) (Judgment) IACtHR Series C no 102 (7 June 2003).

[69] *Case of Trujillo-Oroza v Bolivia*, n 62, para 115.

[70] See UN Security Council, *The rule of law and transitional justice in conflict and post-conflict societies*, UN Doc S/2004/616 (23 August 2004) para 55.

[71] For empirical evidence on the importance of considering individual reparation as 'an organic part of a broader policy of social reconstruction', see R David and SYP Choi, 'Victims on Transitional Justice: Lessons from the Reparation of Human Rights Abuses in the Czech Republic' (2005) 27(2) Human Rights Quarterly 392–435.

[72] *Rule-of-Law Tools*, n 18, 30. See also UN General Assembly, *Report of the Special Rapporteur on the promotion of truth, justice, reparation and guarantees of non-recurrence, Pablo de Greiff*, UN Doc A/HRC/21/46 (9 August 2012). As an illustration of these dynamics, compensation granted to victims of the military

39 Comprehensiveness may therefore be more important than munificence, which should lead us to re-evaluate the extent to which the ideal of full compensation should be reflected in international law. As noted, there is a gap between legal standards regarding compensation and practical application. This gap has, according to Special Rapporteur de Greiff, reached 'scandalous proportions'.[73] As was mentioned, de Greiff and other authorities on the matter advocate for a more flexible approach to compensation, and emphasize its collective dimension. Principle 18 of the Reparation Principles, however, urges account to be taken of individual circumstances and the provision of full reparation, with a focus on what has been labelled 'Reparation as right'.[74] To that extent, the Reparation Principles do not accommodate this more flexible approach easily.[75]

40 Adjusting legal standards to what is feasible in transitional contexts seems desirable, since creating the impression that reparation efforts systematically fall short of legal demands may only compound the victims' suffering and hamper the effort to restore their dignity. To that extent, it might be advisable to emphasize the need of a holistic approach, and to explicitly acknowledge that sufficiently comprehensive reparation programmes may meet the demands of justice even when full and individual compensation is not provided.

Bibliography

Antkowiak, T, 'Remedial Approaches to Human Rights Violations: The Inter-American Court of Human Rights and Beyond' (2008) 46(2) Columbia Journal of Transnational Law 351–419.

Bassiouni, C, 'International Recognition of Victims' Rights' (2006) 6(2) Human Rights Law Review 203–79.

Buyse, A, 'Lost and Regained? Restitution as a Remedy for Human Rights Violations in the Context of International Law' (2008) 68 Heidelberg Journal of International Law 129–53.

Carrillo, A, and Palmer, J, 'Transnational Mass Claim Processes (TMCPs) in International Law and Practice' (2010) 28 Berkeley Journal of International Law 343–430.

David, R, and Choi, SYP, 'Victims on Transitional Justice: Lessons from the Reparation of Human Rights Abuses in the Czech Republic' (2005) 27(2) Human Rights Quarterly 392–435.

de Greiff, P (ed), *The Handbook of Reparations* (OUP 2006).

Droege, C, *The Right to a Remedy and to Reparation for Gross Human Rights Violations—A Practitioners' Guide* (International Commission of Jurists 2006) 96.

Evans, C, *The right to reparation in international law for victims of armed conflict* (CUP 2012).

Letschert, RM and van Boven, T, 'Providing reparation in situations of mass victimization. Key challenges involved' in RM Letschert, R Haveman, A De Brouwer, and A Pemberton (eds), *Victimological Approaches to International Crimes* (Intersentia 2011) 153–84.

Rombouts, H, *Victim Organisations and the Politics of Reparation: A Case-study on Rwanda* (Intersentia 2004).

dictatorship in Argentina was regarded by many victims and their relatives with scepticism or hostility because, in spite of being a munificent reparation programme, it was implemented soon after a presidential pardon to the perpetrators, who had been convicted only a few years earlier for the most serious of crimes. See Malamud-Goti and Grosman, n 21, 552–53.

[73] See UN General Assembly, *Report of the Special Rapporteur on the promotion of truth, justice, reparation and guarantees of non-recurrence, Pablo de Greiff*, UN Doc A/69/518 (8 October 2014), para 6.

[74] See Letschert and van Boven, n 20, 160–61.

[75] The argument according to which reference to the 'circumstances of each case', in the Reparation Principles, opens the door to this more flexible approach might not be quite persuasive; that language rather seems to emphasize the singularity of each victim.

Rombouts, H, et al, 'The Right to Reparation for Victims of Gross and Systematic Violations of Human Rights' in K Feyter et al (eds), *Out of the Ashes* (Intersentia 2005) 345–502.

Shelton, D, *Remedies in International Human Rights Law* (2nd edn, OUP 2006).

Tomuschat, C, 'Darfur—Compensation for the Victims' (2005) 3(3) Journal of International Criminal Justice 579–89.

Van Boven, T, 'Victims' Rights to a Remedy and Reparation: The New United Nations Principles and Guidelines' in C Ferstman, M Goetz, and A Stephens (eds), *Reparations for Victims of Genocide, War Crimes and Crimes against Humanity: Systems in Place and Systems in the Making* (Martinus Nijhoff Online 2009).

Van Boven, T, *The United Nations Basic Principles and Guidelines on the Right to a Remedy and Reparation for Victims of Gross Violations of International Human Rights Law and Serious Violations of International Humanitarian Law* (United Nations Audiovisual Library of International Law 2010) <legal.un.org/avl/ha/ga_60-147/ga_60-147.html> accessed 22 November 2017.

B.

GUARANTEES OF NON-RECURRENCE OF VIOLATIONS

Principle 35. General Principles

Alexander Mayer-Rieckh and Roger Duthie

States shall ensure that victims do not again have to endure violations of their rights. To this end, States must undertake institutional reforms and other measures necessary to ensure respect for the rule of law, foster and sustain a culture of respect for human rights, and restore or establish public trust in government institutions. Adequate representation of women and minority groups in public institutions is essential to the achievement of these aims. Institutional reforms aimed at preventing a recurrence of violations should be developed through a process of broad public consultations, including the participation of victims and other sectors of civil society.

Such reforms should advance the following objectives:

(a) Consistent adherence by public institutions to the rule of law;
(b) The repeal of laws that contribute to or authorize violations of human rights and/or humanitarian law and enactment of legislative and other measures necessary to ensure respect for human rights and humanitarian law, including measures that safeguard democratic institutions and processes;
(c) Civilian control of military and security forces and intelligence services and disbandment of parastatal armed forces;
(d) Reintegration of children involved in armed conflict into society.

A. Summary of Findings

Principle 35 introduces guarantees of non-recurrence of human rights violations, along with some general principles and objectives. This commentary offers an overview of the contextual and historical background, theoretical framework, and critical assessment of the notion of guarantees of non-recurrence itself. The specific measures mentioned in Principle 35 are elaborated in Principles 36–38, and hence are discussed in the subsequent commentaries on these Principles.

The notion of guarantees of non-recurrence developed out of the international legal obligation to ensure human rights as well as the right to reparation. Guarantees of non-recurrence are the least developed category of measures to combat impunity: while the human rights community agrees on the importance of preventing the recurrence, it has limited understanding of what that entails and how it is done. This commentary argues that the specific measures discussed in the Principles are insufficiently contextualized and transformative, and could be grouped under broader goals, such as corrective justice and distributive justice.

B. Contextual and Historical Introduction

In the preparatory reports drafted by Louis Joinet up to 1995, the concept of guarantees of non-recurrence was not discussed. This changed with the 1996 version and then the 1 revised 1997 version of the Principles to combat impunity, which included a section on reparation that incorporated a subsection on guarantees of non-recurrence. This report structure was based on the 1996 version of the Basic Principles and Guidelines on Reparation.[1]

2 The specific prevention measures included in the subsection on guarantees of non-recurrence, such as disbanding paramilitary groups, abolishing emergency courts, or removing abusive officials, were not drawn from the Basic Principles and Guidelines on Reparation, however, but from Joinet's preparatory reports—although not under the heading of guarantees of non-recurrence—and were seen to be particularly relevant to combating impunity at the time, especially in Latin American transitions.

3 The 2005 Updated Principles to combat impunity kept, but revised, the subsection on guarantees of non-recurrence included in the 1997 Principles, and added further measures aimed at ensuring non-recurrence. These revisions reflected recent developments in law and practice, and took into consideration concerns that had arisen in regions other than those reflected in the 1997 version. For instance, a new measure introduced the need to establish effective institutions of civilian oversight over security institutions, echoing a growing understanding in the development and security communities that the provision of security should be responsive to the needs of the people and governed by the rule of law, and that security institutions should be accountable to multiple external mechanisms.[2]

C. Theoretical Framework

4 The 1996 version of the Principles refers to 'guarantees of non-repetition', whereas the 1997 and 2005 Updated Principles refer to 'guarantees of non-recurrence of violations'. These terms are, however, used interchangeably without variation in meaning. When describing the scope and content of guarantees of non-recurrence, the different versions do not use the verb 'to guarantee' but rather 'to ensure'.[3] In fact, hardly any measure taken by a state can be a definitive guarantee that a violation does not recur. Hence a state does not have obligations 'of results' but 'of means'. A state's obligation is to make good faith efforts and do all that is 'reasonably within its means' to ensure the non-recurrence of a violation.[4]

5 International law knows an obligation not only to respect, but also to ensure human rights. This duty to ensure includes a general duty to prevent future violations of human rights,[5] as well as a specific obligation to prevent the recurrence of violations that have

[1] United Nations, *Basic Principles and Guidelines on the Right to a Remedy and Reparation for the Victims of Gross Violations of International Human Rights Law and Serious Violations of International Humanitarian Law*, UN Doc A/RES/60/147 (21 March 2006) (hereinafter 'Basic Principles and Guidelines on Reparation').

[2] The importance of governance and oversight in the security sector was developed, in particular, in the context of security sector reform. See UN, *Securing peace and development: The role of the United Nations in supporting security sector reform. Report of the Secretary-General*, UN Doc A/62/659-S/2008/39 (23 January 2008) para 15; OECD DAC, *OECD DAC Handbook on Security System Reform (SSR): Supporting Security and Justice* (OECD 2007) 21.

[3] Updated Principles to combat impunity, Principle 35.

[4] JE Méndez, 'Accountability for Past Abuses' (1997) 19 Human Rights Quarterly 255–82, 264.

[5] See, eg, International Covenant on Civil and Political Rights (ICCPR), Art 2(1) 999 UNTS I-14668. The Inter-American Court of Human Rights (IACtHR) described the duty to prevent in the context of the general duty to ensure; see *Velásquez Rodríguez v Honduras* (Judgment) IACtHR Series C no 4 (29 July 1988) para 166.

taken place.[6] This obligation is part of the overall obligation to conform to a norm of international law. Once a norm has been violated, the overall commitment to conform to the norm implies making efforts to ensure that the violation is not repeated.[7]

The obligation to prevent recurrence can also be understood as one of several forms of reparation for a violation.[8] Along these lines, Principle 35 of the 2005 Updated Principles introduces the notion of guarantees of non-recurrence of violations as a state obligation to 'ensure that victims do not again have to endure violations of their rights'. This understanding of guarantees of non-recurrence was largely developed in the context of jurisprudence exploring the scope of reparations owed to victims of human rights violations, particularly in the inter-American human rights system.[9] According to the Basic Principles and Guidelines on Reparation, five forms of reparation have to be provided if it is to be full and effective: restitution, compensation, rehabilitation, satisfaction, and guarantees of non-repetition.[10] 6

The 1997 Principles to combat impunity follow the structure of the Basic Principles and Guidelines on Reparation, and present guarantees of non-recurrence of violations as a sub-category of the right to reparation.[11] The 2005 Updated Principles separate the guarantees of non-recurrence more clearly from the right to reparation. Guarantees of non-recurrence are more accurately understood as a distinct obligation rather than as a subset of reparations. States have an obligation to cease a violation and prevent its repetition not just because they have to provide reparations to victims, but also because they have a general obligation to conform to the norms of international law.[12] The UN Committee against Torture has stated that by undertaking guarantees of non-repetition, states may not only be providing one form of reparation, but 'may also be fulfilling their obligations to prevent acts of torture under Article 2 of the Convention'.[13] At the same time, the justiciability of guarantees of non-recurrence presupposes the existence 7

[6] UN Human Rights Committee, General Comment no 31 [80]. The nature of the general obligation imposed on state parties to the Covenant, UN Doc CCPR/C/21/Rev.1/Add.13 (26 May 2004) para 17.

[7] International Law Commission, 'Draft articles on Responsibility of States for Internationally Wrongful Acts, with commentaries' UN Doc A/CN.4/SER.A//2001/Add.1 (Part 2) (2001) vol II International Law Commission Ybk, Part Two, 88–91.

[8] Basic Principles and Guidelines on Reparation, n 1, para 23. See also UN Committee against Torture, General Comment no 3, Implementation of Article 14 by state parties, UN Doc CAT/C/GC/3 (13 December 2012).

[9] United Nations, *Study Concerning the Right to Restitution, Compensation and Rehabilitation for Victims of Gross Violations of Human Rights and Fundamental Freedoms. Final Report Submitted by Mr Theo van Boven*, UN Doc E./CN.4/1993/8 (2 July 1993) paras 40–130.

[10] Basic Principles and Guidelines on Reparation, n 1, paras 18–23. The 2006 International Convention for the Protection of All Persons from Enforced Disappearance 2716 UNTS I-48088, explicitly states in Art 24 that guarantees of non-repetition are one form of reparation.

[11] 1997 Principles to combat impunity, Principles 37–42. However, when discussing the scope of the right to reparation in Principle 36, Joinet seems to imply that reparation covers restitution, compensation, rehabilitation, and satisfaction, but not guarantees of non-recurrence. In the revised final report that is part of the same UN document, Joinet clearly separates guarantees of non-recurrence from the right to reparation. See UN, *The administration of justice and the human rights of detainees: Question of the impunity of perpetrators of human rights violations (civil and political). Revised final report prepared by Mr Joinet*, UN Doc E/CN.4/Sub.2/1997/20/rev.1 (2 October 1997) paras 16, 43.

[12] The inclusion of cessation within the concept of reparation 'seems to imply that in the absence of a victim there is no cessation. It undermines the rule of law which is the basis of the obligation to cease any conduct that is not in conformity with an international duty.' (D Shelton, 'The United Nations Principles and Guidelines on Reparations: Context and Contents' in K De Feyter, S Parmentier, M Bossuyt, and P Lemmens (eds), *Out of the Ashes: Reparation for Victims of Gross and Systematic Human Rights Violations* (Intersentia 2005) 11–34.

[13] UN Committee against Torture, General Comment no 3, n 8, para 18.

of a victim whose rights have been violated. Both understandings of guarantees of non-recurrence have their merits, and should be understood to complement rather than contradict each other.

8 The first paragraph of Principle 35 highlights 'institutional reforms and other measures' as the means of achieving prevention through their contribution to the rule of law, respect for human rights, and public trust in government institutions, and emphasizes the importance of adequate representation of women and minority groups as well as broad public consultation in the process. The second paragraph then lists four 'objectives', the first of which repeats the notion of the rule of law, while the next three refer to specific measures, which are among those included in Principles 36–38.

9 The first UN Special Rapporteur on the promotion of truth, justice, reparation and guarantees of non-recurrence, Pablo de Greiff, in 2015 released a report developing the notion of guarantees of non-recurrence. It presents the main elements of a framework for policies on guarantees of non-recurrence, including: (i) institutional interventions, such as the ratification of treaties concerning gross human rights violations and serious violations of international humanitarian law, as well as legal, judicial, and constitutional reforms; (ii) societal interventions, such as legal empowerment and strengthening of civil society; and (iii) interventions in the cultural and individual spheres, such as education, arts and culture, archives, and trauma counselling and psychological support (which we discuss in more detail in the commentary on Principle 36).[14]

D. Practice

10 Principle 35 focuses on the institutional reforms and other measures that states must undertake to prevent human rights violations from recurring, highlighting institutional adherence to the rule of law, repeal of laws that facilitated violations and enactment of new legislation to protect rights, civilian control of the military, disbandment of parastatal armed groups, and reintegration of children involved in armed conflict.

11 Institutional reform measures aimed at ensuring respect for the rule of law are proposed in more detail in Principle 36, but it is worth emphasizing here that truth-telling initiatives often examine the role of the judiciary in past abuses and make recommendations for its reform,[15] as in Chile, El Salvador, Guatemala, and Sierra Leone.[16] Furthermore, reforms are often not limited to the judicial system but include the police, military, and other public institutions, illustrated by vetting processes in Greece after 1974, El Salvador after 1992, central and eastern Europe after 1989, Bosnia and Herzegovina after 1995, Liberia from 2004 to 2006, and Kenya after 2012. Measures to increase civilian control and oversight, a key feature of security sector reform, also help to ensure that security and intelligence agencies operate in accordance with the rule of law.[17]

[14] UN, *Report of the Special Rapporteur on the promotion of truth, justice, reparation and guarantees of non-recurrence, Pablo de Greiff,* UN Doc A/HRC/30/42 (7 September 2015) (hereinafter '*Report of the Special Rapporteur*').

[15] PB Hayner, *Unspeakable Truths: Facing the Challenge of Truth Commissions* (Routledge 2002) 102–06; P de Greiff, 'Truth Telling and the Rule of Law' in TA Borer (ed), *Telling the Truths: Truth Telling and Peace Building in Post-Conflict Societies* (University of Notre Dame Press 2006) 181–206.

[16] *Report of the Special Rapporteur,* n 14, 14.

[17] *Report of the Secretary-General,* n 2, 12.

Numerous countries emerging from conflict and repression also reform legislation, with some, such as Kenya in 2010 and Tunisia in 2014, adopting new constitutions,[18] and others enacting narrower legislative reforms aimed at specific issues, as with Northern Ireland's review of emergency legislation after the 1998 peace agreement.[19] Legislative reform is also often recommended by truth commissions, as in Guatemala in 1999, Sierra Leone in 2004, and Morocco in 2005. 12

Attempts to disband unofficial armed groups have faced significant challenges, as in Afghanistan in 2005,[20] in Côte d'Ivoire between 2006 and 2009,[21] and in Colombia after 2003, where, as is common with disarmament, demobilization, and reintegration (DDR) efforts, limited progress has been made in fostering trust between former paramilitaries and others.[22] Programmes aimed in particular at the reintegration of children associated with conflict have been enacted in many countries, often as part of larger DDR processes.[23] In countries such as Mozambique, Liberia, Sierra Leone, and Uganda, research has shown that former child combatants face a range of difficulties, but also that many of them do experience successful reintegration.[24] 13

E. Critical Assessment

The obligation to guarantee non-recurrence is the least developed category of the measures to combat impunity. The 2005 Updated Principles devote only four out of thirty-eight principles to this obligation, and little systematic attention has been paid to the topic. While the literature on prosecution, truth-seeking, and reparation abounds, guarantees of non-recurrence remain under-explored. The human rights community broadly agrees on the importance of preventing recurrence, but has limited understanding of what it entails and how it is done. 14

At the same time, the development and peacebuilding communities are heavily engaged in many of the activities listed under the category of guarantees of non-recurrence. While the term 'guarantees of non-recurrence' is not used, and its implications are not considered by such actors, activities such as the ones listed in the 15

[18] *Report of the Special Rapporteur*, n 14, 15–18.

[19] M O'Rawe, 'Security System Reform and Identity in Divided Societies: Lessons from Northern Ireland' in P Arthur (ed), *Identities in Transition: Challenges for Transitional Justice in Divided Societies* (CUP 2011) 89.

[20] UN Department of Peacekeeping Operations, *Integrated Disarmament, Demobilization and Reintegration Standards (IDDRS)* (United Nations 2006) s 6.10, at 8.

[21] Ibid, 47–48.

[22] M Derks, H Rouw, and I Briscoe, 'A Community Dilemma: DDR and the Changing Face of Violence in Colombia' (Peace and Security Development Network, no 30, July 2011) 4. See also S Jaramillo, Y Giha, and P Torres, 'Transitional Justice and DDR: The Case of Colombia' (ICTJ Research Unit, June 2009).

[23] I Derluyn, S Vindevogel, and L de Haene, 'Toward a Relational Understanding of the Reintegration and Rehabilitation Processes of Former Child Soldiers' (2013) 22(8) Journal of Aggression, Maltreatment & Trauma 869–86, 872.

[24] C Blattman and J Annan, 'The Consequences of Child Soldiering', Households in Conflict Network (HICN) Working Paper no 22 (August 2007); N Boothby, J Crawford, and J Halperin, 'Mozambique Child Soldier Life Outcome Study: Lessons Learned in Rehabilitation and Reintegration Efforts' *Global Public Health* (February 2006); J Weinstein and M Humphries, 'Disentangling the Determinants of Successful Demobilization, and Reintegration', Center for Global Development, Working Paper no 69 (September 2005); I Specht and H Tefferi, 'Impact Evaluation of the Reintegration Programme of Children Associated with Fighting Forces (CAFF) in Liberia' (UNICEF, April 2007).

Principles, including reform of public institutions, the establishment of civilian oversight over security forces, the disbandment of unofficial armed groups, or the demobilization and reintegration of child combatants, fall within their areas of expertise and are familiar terrain to them.

16 Guarantees of non-recurrence can be thought to include the entire range of measures—in addition to prosecution, truth-telling, and reparation—that are necessary to ensure justice in the aftermath of atrocity and to prevent its recurrence. They encompass the transitional justice measures most directly aimed at prevention. The term 'guarantees of non-recurrence' is somewhat misleading, however, in that non-recurrence can never be fully guaranteed by any set of measures. The terms 'preventing recurrence' or 'measures to prevent recurrence' more adequately express what these measures aim to do.

17 Guarantees of non-recurrence have to vary considerably depending on the context in which the violations occurred. Measures such as those listed in Principles 35–38 aim at preventing the recurrence of *specific* violations that happened for *certain* reasons in a *concrete* context. Nevertheless, the approach adopted in the 2005 Updated Principles elevates to the level of principle or goal certain measures that were relevant in particular historical circumstances—such as disbanding paramilitary groups in Latin American transitions—but which do not apply universally or are not a priority in other circumstances. Rather than adopting an approach that is insufficiently contextualized, specific measures could be grouped according to the broader goals to whose achievement they aim to contribute.

18 Effective prevention of recurrence cannot just deal with the individual circumstances of violations but must address their causes. The measures listed in Principle 35–38 focus on relatively immediate structural causes of violations, such as inadequate civilian oversight of the security sector. Usually, such immediate structural causes are not the root causes of a situation that resulted in serious violations. More often than not, these immediate structural causes of abuse are symptoms of underlying root causes that are related to economic, social, or cultural factors, such as controversies over access to land and resources, deprivation and marginalization of certain social groups, or other situations of oppression and exploitation. Eliminating immediate structural causes without addressing the root causes may not be sufficient to quell future abuse. A deeper socio-economic transformation of society may be needed to prevent a relapse into conflict and a recurrence of violations. Effective efforts to prevent future abuse therefore need to adopt a 'unitary approach in tackling impunity'.[25] In order to emphasize the contextual and transformative nature of guarantees of non-recurrence, different measures could be grouped within a more comprehensive framework of prevention according to the following goals:

- Disabling abusive capacities: removing opportunities to commit future wrongs of the same kind.
- Enabling integrity capacities: establishing conditions to correct future wrongs of the same kind.

[25] The United Nations Updated Set of Principles for the Protection and Promotion of Human Rights through Action to Combat Impunity: Drafting History, 2nd Working Draft, at 16. See also L Arbour, 'Economic and Social Justice for Societies in Transition', Centre for Human Rights and Global Justice, Working Paper no 10 (2006).

- Disavowing the abusive past: verbally or symbolically signalling a turning away from the abusive past and a commitment to norms.
- Redistributing opportunities: providing equal opportunities to victims and perpetrators, ensuring equal provision of service, and encompassing efforts to include victims in the reform process itself.
- Addressing socio-economic deficits: establishing conditions of equality that render conflict over resources and opportunities less likely.

Guarantees of non-recurrence must stress the links between the specific violations in the past and the measures aimed at preventing violations in the future. If corrective justice, on the one hand, refers to the repair of specific harms to individuals or groups, while distributive justice, on the other hand, refers to the distribution of goods and opportunities and to equitable outcomes, guarantees of non-recurrence can encompass both, as long as the link with the specific violations in the past is maintained.[26] The measures listed in Principles 35–38 may lean more toward the corrective side of justice, but in order to effectively prevent the recurrence of violations these measures must be part of a broader effort to address the root causes of violations. 19

The extent to which transitional justice measures including guarantees of non-recurrence should focus on economic and social crimes and injustices, as opposed to a more narrow set of civil and political ones, is debated.[27] These different injustices are connected, which means it is often impossible to provide accountability or truth about the most serious human rights violations without addressing in some way their economic and social elements and underlying causes. Corrective measures can certainly face significant political, legal, and practical constraints in dealing with such issues directly, however, and should maintain realistic expectations about their potential impact on structural problems such as poverty and inequality. The arguments against using transitional justice measures to address economic and social injustices include the risk of overburdening the measures, the potential for provoking greater political resistance, and the 'overarching structural limitation' that national and international law is much less developed for economic crimes than for atrocities.[28] Corrective and distributive justice should not be thought of as strictly separate spheres, however, but rather as two dimensions of justice that condition and reinforce each other. While guarantees of non-recurrence are always designed in response to specific past atrocities, in order to prevent their recurrence they are situated at the interface between corrective and distributive justice. 20

[26] P Kalmanovitz, 'Corrective Justice versus Social Justice in the Aftermath of War' in M Bergsmo, C Rodriguez-Garavito, P Kalmanovitz, and MP Saffon (eds), *Distributive Justice in Transitions* (Torkel Opsahl Academic Publisher 2010) 71–96, 85; R Williams, 'Protection in the Past Tense: Restitution at the Juncture of Humanitarian Response to Displacement and Transitional Justice' in R Duthie (ed), *Transitional Justice and Displacement* (Social Science Research Council 2012) 85–138, 102.

[27] On the question of whether transitional justice measures should address economic and social injustice, see DN Sharp (ed), *Justice and Economic Violence in Transition* (Springer 2014); P de Greiff, 'Articulating the Links Between Transitional Justice and Development: Justice and Social Integration' in P de Greiff and R Duthie (eds), *Transitional Justice and Development* (SSRC 2009) 28–75; P Kalmanovitz, 'Corrective Justice versus Social Justice' (2008) 2:3 International Journal of Transitional Justice, Special Issue on Transitional Justice and Development.

[28] de Greiff, n 27, 40. R Duthie, 'Transitional Justice, Development, and Economic Violence' in Sharp (ed), n 27, 189–95.

21 Prevention is a concern that guarantees of non-recurrence share with other fields, such as genocide prevention and the responsibility to protect (R2P).[29] At the 2005 World Summit, all UN member states endorsed the responsibility to protect populations from genocide, war crimes, ethnic cleansing, and crimes against humanity (the so-called atrocity crimes).[30] As described in the World Summit Outcome document, R2P covers two types of responsibilities: states have primary responsibility to protect their populations and prevent atrocity crimes; the international community has the responsibility, should peaceful means be inadequate and states 'manifestly fail' to protect their populations, to take collective action in a timely and decisive manner in response to imminent or ongoing atrocity crimes. In his 2015 report on the responsibility to protect, the Secretary-General added another dimension of prevention to R2P: efforts to prevent recurrence of atrocities in societies recovering from these horrifying forms of violence.[31] Attention to the aftermath of atrocities links R2P more clearly to transitional justice, particularly to guarantees of non-recurrence.

Bibliography

Arbour, L, 'Economic and Social Justice for Societies in Transition', Centre for Human Rights and Global Justice, Working Paper no 10 (2006).

Bergsmo, M, Rodriguez-Garavito, C, Kalmanovitz, P, and Saffon, MP (eds), *Distributive Justice in Transitions* (Torkel Opsahl Academic Publisher 2010).

Blattman, C and Annan, J, 'The Consequences of Child Soldiering', Households in Conflict Network (HICN) Working Paper no 22, August 2007.

Boothby, N, Crawford, J, and Halperin, J, 'Mozambique Child Soldier Life Outcome Study: Lessons Learned in Rehabilitation and Reintegration Efforts' *Global Public Health* (February 2006).

de Greiff, P, 'Articulating the Links Between Transitional Justice and Development: Justice and Social Integration' in P de Greiff and R Duthie (eds), *Transitional Justice and Development* (SSRC 2009) 28–75.

de Greiff, P, 'Truth Telling and the Rule of Law' in TA Borer (ed), *Telling the Truths: Truth Telling and Peace Building in Post-Conflict Societies* (University of Notre Dame Press 2006) 181–206.

Derks, M, Rouw, H, and Briscoe, I, 'A Community Dilemma: DDR and the Changing Face of Violence in Colombia' (Peace and Security Development Network, no 30, July 2011).

Federal Department of Foreign Affairs, 'Genocide Prevention' *Politorbis* 47 (2/2009).

Hayner, PB, *Unspeakable Truths: Facing the Challenge of Truth Commissions* (Routledge, 2002).

(2008) 2:3 International Journal of Transitional Justice, Special Issue on Transitional Justice and Development.

Jaramillo, S, Giha, Y, and Torres, P, 'Transitional Justice and DDR: The Case of Colombia' (ICTJ Research Unit, June 2009).

Méndez, JE, 'Accountability for Past Abuses' (1997) 19 Human Rights Quarterly 255–82.

OECD DAC, *OECD DAC Handbook on Security System Reform (SSR): Supporting Security and Justice* (OECD 2007).

[29] See, eg, UN, *Responsibility to protect: state responsibility and prevention. Report of the Secretary-General,* UN Doc A/67/929-S/2013/399 (9 July 2013).

[30] UN General Assembly Res 60/1, 2005 World Summit Outcome, UN Doc A/RES/60/1 (24 October 2005).

[31] UN General Assembly, *Report of the Secretary-General on a vital and enduring commitment: implementing the responsibility to protect,* UN Doc A/69/981-S/2015/500 (13 July 2015), paras 65–67.

O'Rawe, M, 'Security System Reform and Identity in Divided Societies: Lessons from Northern Ireland' in P Arthur (ed), *Identities in Transition: Challenges for Transitional Justice in Divided Societies* (CUP 2011).

Sharp, DN (ed), *Justice and Economic Violence in Transition* (Springer 2014).

Shelton, D, 'The United Nations Principles and Guidelines on Reparations: Context and Contents' in K De Feyter, S Parmentier, M Bossuyt, and P Lemmens (eds), *Out of the Ashes: Reparation for Victims of Gross and Systematic Human Rights Violations* (Intersentia 2005) 11–34.

Specht, I and Tefferi, H, 'Impact Evaluation of the Reintegration Programme of Children Associated with Fighting Forces (CAFF) in Liberia' (UNICEF, April 2007).

Weinstein, J and Humphries, M, 'Disentangling the Determinants of Successful Demobilization, and Reintegration', Center for Global Development, Working Paper no 69, September 2005.

Williams, R, 'Protection in the Past Tense: Restitution at the Juncture of Humanitarian Response to Displacement and Transitional Justice' in R Duthie (ed), *Transitional Justice and Displacement* (Social Science Research Council 2012) 85–138.

Principle 36. Reform of State Institutions

Alexander Mayer-Rieckh and Roger Duthie

States must take all necessary measures, including legislative and administrative reforms, to ensure that public institutions are organized in a manner that ensures respect for the rule of law and protection of human rights. At a minimum, States should undertake the following measures:

(a) Public officials and employees who are personally responsible for gross violations of human rights, in particular those involved in military, security, police, intelligence and judicial sectors, shall not continue to serve in State institutions. Their removal shall comply with the requirements of due process of law and the principle of non-discrimination. Persons formally charged with individual responsibility for serious crimes under international law shall be suspended from official duties during the criminal or disciplinary proceedings;

(b) With respect to the judiciary, States must undertake all other measures necessary to assure the independent, impartial and effective operation of courts in accordance with international standards of due process. Habeas corpus, by whatever name it may be known, must be considered a non-derogable right;

(c) Civilian control of military and security forces as well as of intelligence agencies must be ensured and, where necessary, established or restored. To this end, States should establish effective institutions of civilian oversight over military and security forces and intelligence agencies, including legislative oversight bodies;

(d) Civil complaint procedures should be established and their effective operation assured;

(e) Public officials and employees, in particular those involved in military, security, police, intelligence and judicial sectors, should receive comprehensive and ongoing training in human rights and, where applicable, humanitarian law standards and in implementation of those standards.

A. Summary of Findings

This commentary examines Principle 36 of the 2005 Updated Principles to combat impunity on measures of institutional reform in the aftermath of human rights violations. It tracks the discussion of reform measures in the relevant documents, depicting the shift in focus from purges, to vetting, to broader institutional reform; the influence of historical context in Latin America and Eastern Europe, in particular on the articulation of the measures; and the emphasis on the preventive function of the measures. All the measures in Principle 36 focus on state institutions that were responsible for violations, and aim to address the causes of the violations. The measures aim to reform structures and systems that allowed, facilitated, or promoted violations. With processes such as vetting, however, states must balance broad institutional reform goals with respect for the basic rights of individuals. The measures in Principle 36 also have the potential to act as an enabling condition for other transitional justice mechanisms by weakening or removing institutional sources of opposition. Nevertheless, the commentary argues that prevention can be achieved more effectively if measures target not just the institutional sphere, but also the societal, cultural and personal spheres.

B. Contextual and Historical Introduction

While the notion of guarantees of non-recurrence relates to a function that can be achieved, in principle, by an open-ended variety of measures, Principle 36 focuses on the reform of state institutions, with the aim of preventing the recurrence of human rights violations. According to Principle 36, 'States must take all necessary measures, including legislative and administrative reforms, to ensure that public institutions are organized in a manner that ensures respect for the rule of law and protection of human rights'. 1

The development of Principle 36 goes back to the preparatory reports drafted by Louis Joinet. These reports do not discuss the concept of guarantees of non-recurrence, but they do deal repeatedly with 'purges', an issue eventually taken up in the section on guarantees of non-recurrence in the 1997 Principles to Combat Impunity, and which made its way into Principle 36 in the Updated Principles.[1] 2

Principle 36 in the 2005 Updated Principles corresponds to Principles 40–42 in the 1997 Principles. In his 1997 Report, Joinet uses the phrase 'removal from office' rather than the controversial term 'purge'[2] to describe the 'administrative measures' discussed in these Principles, highlighting their preventive character and the importance of safeguarding the rights of state officials. Principle 40 of the 1997 Principles refers to measures relating to state officials implicated in gross human rights violations; Principle 41 to the implementation of such measures, giving priority to 'positions of responsibility in the army, the police and the judiciary', and consideration to a state official's human rights record among other factors, and noting certain due process requirements; and Principle 42 to possible sanctions for an official, including suspension. 3

Principles 40–42 in the 1997 Principles focus on measures discussed in Joinet's preparatory reports that were seen to be particularly relevant to combating impunity at the time the Principles were drafted. For instance, the measures on removal of state officials draw heavily on the provisions on purges in the 1992 El Salvador peace agreement[3] and, to some extent, on experiences with lustration processes in former communist countries in Central and Eastern Europe.[4] 4

In the 2005 Updated Principles, the focus of Principle 36 is broadened from measures targeting individual state officials to the reform of state institutions. The 2005 Report explains that experience since 1997 has demonstrated the 'need to consider comprehensive institutional reform as a foundation for sustainable justice during periods of democratic transition', as well as the continued importance of vetting in particular.[5] 5

[1] United Nations, *Progress report on the question of the impunity of perpetrators of violations of human rights (civil and political rights), prepared by Mr Joinet, pursuant to Subcommission resolution 1994/34*, UN Doc E/CN.4/Sub.2/1995/18 (28 June 1995) 8; United Nations, *The Administration of Justice and the Human Rights of Detainees: The Question of Human Rights of Persons Subjected to any Form of Detention or Imprisonment. Progress Report on the Question of the Impunity of Perpetrators of Human Rights Violations, Prepared by Mr Guissé and Mr Joinet*, UN Doc E/CN.4/Sub.2/1993/6 (19 July 1993) (hereinafter 'Joinet 1993') 33–35.

[2] The term 'purge' is generally used to refer to massive dismissals on the basis, for example, of mere membership in a party or organization. Such informal exercises violate basic human rights standards. See para 10 of this commentary.

[3] *Peace Agreement signed at Mexico City on 16 January 1992 between the Government of El Salvador and the Frente Farabundo Martí para la Liberación Naciona*l (the so-called 'Chapultepec Peace Agreement'), UN Doc A/46/864-S/23501 (30 January 1992) annex I.3.A.

[4] Joinet 1993, n 1, 33–35.

[5] United Nations, *Report of the independent expert to update the Set of Principles to combat impunity, Diane Orentlicher*, UN Doc E.CN.4/2005/102 (18 February 2005) (hereinafter 'Orentlicher Report') 12, 19–20.

Administrative vetting measures are now condensed into Principle 36(a), while Principle 36(b) calls for an independent, impartial, and effective judiciary; Principle 36(c) for civilian control of military and security forces and intelligence agencies, as well as civilian oversight; Principle 36(d) for civilian complaint procedures; and Principle 36(e) for comprehensive and ongoing training of public officials and employees in human rights and humanitarian law. In broadening the focus to institutional reform, the 2005 Updated Principles introduce some of the measures that originally appeared in the Basic Principles and Guidelines on Reparation,[6] in the section on guarantees of non-repetition, but which were not included in the 1997 Impunity Principles.

6 The different versions of the Impunity Principles and their accompanying reports, as well as the Basic Principles, all emphasize the preventive character of the measures included in Principle 36 of the Updated Principles. The Basic Principles explicitly state that guarantees of non-repetition in general 'contribute to prevention'.[7] The 1997 Principles emphasize that measures relating to abusive officials 'should be of a preventive, not punitive character'.[8] The 2005 Report states that 'human rights treaty bodies have recognized the role of vetting in fulfilling States' general obligation to prevent violations of human rights'.[9] Principle 35 also notes the preventive function of the reforms described in Principle 36. In addition, Principle 36 emphasizes the process and rights of officials,[10] which is consistent with previous reference documents.

C. Theoretical Framework

7 All the measures listed in Principle 36 focus on state institutions that were responsible for violations, and aim to address the causes of violations. Largely, the measures aim to reform structures and systems that allowed, facilitated, or promoted violations. The measures focus on strengthening in various ways the accountability of institutions that are prone to committing serious violations, such as security institutions, because they possess the means to use force and have a mandate to do so. These measures meet with the agenda of security sector reform, for which the establishment of effective accountability, governance, and oversight of the security and justice sectors are central goals.[11]

8 Institutional reform measures also have implications for individuals. Vetting, for example, is defined by the UN Secretary-General as 'a formal process for the identification and removal of individuals responsible for abuses, especially from police, prison services, the army and the judiciary'.[12] In any vetting process, states have to ensure that the basic

[6] United Nations, *Basic Principles and Guidelines on the Right to a Remedy and Reparation for the Victims of Gross Violations of International Human Rights Law and Serious Violations of International Humanitarian Law*, UN Doc A/RES/60/147 (21 March 2006) (hereinafter 'Basic Principles and Guidelines on Reparation').

[7] Ibid, para 23.

[8] United Nations, *The Administration of Justice and the Human Rights of Detainees: Question of the Impunity of Perpetrators of Human Rights Violations (Civil and Political). Revised Final Report Prepared by Mr Joinet*, E/CN.4/Sub.2/1997/20/rev.1 (2 October 1997) Principle 40.

[9] Orentlicher Report, n 5, 19. [10] Ibid, 20.

[11] United Nations, *Securing Peace and Development: The Role of the United Nations in Supporting Security Sector Reform. Report of the Secretary-General,* UN Doc A/62/659- S/2008/39 (23 January 2008) 6; OECD DAC, *OECD DAC Handbook on Security System Reform (SSR): Supporting Security and Justice* (OECD 2007) 21.

[12] United Nations, *The rule of law and transitional justice in conflict and post-conflict societies. Report of the Secretary-General,* UN Doc S/2004/616 (3 August 2004) para 52. See also Office of the United Nations High Commissioner for Human Rights (OHCHR), *Rule-of-Law-Tools for Post-Conflict States. Vetting: an Operational*

rights of those subject to the process are respected. In particular, a vetting process ought to comply with the principle of non-discrimination, the right of equal access to public service, and with minimum requirements of due process.[13] A failure to respect these fundamental rights opens the door to political manipulation of a vetting process, and may lead to politically motivated purges.[14]

In his 2004 Report on the rule of law and transitional justice in conflict and post- 9
conflict societies, the UN Secretary-General did not broadly elaborate on guarantees of non-recurrence but instead focused his discussion of preventive measures on vetting.[15]

It is important, the 2005 Orentlicher Report suggests, that the different transitional jus- 10
tice measures, including institutional reform, are coherent and complement each other.[16] Vetting, for instance, can contribute to addressing the 'impunity gap' between the large number of perpetrators of violations and the limited capacity and political constraints of justice systems to prosecute those responsible,[17] providing a form of non-criminal sanction by ensuring that those responsible for past violations at least do not continue to enjoy or are prevented from gaining access to the rewards and privileges of public office.[18] More importantly, however, in disabling structures that allowed individuals to commit criminal acts, vetting and other measures in Principle 36 not only contribute to institutional reform, but also have the potential to act as an enabling condition for other transitional justice measures—criminal prosecutions, truth-telling, and reparations—by weakening or removing institutional sources of opposition, and by contributing to the goals of a holistic transitional justice policy—recognition and trust.[19]

D. Practice

Vetting (Principle 36(a)) is a recurring phenomenon in transitional settings, but its scope 11
and shape vary considerably from one context to another. Vetting can target a range of institutions, but commonly it is applied in the security and justice sectors. Vetting can target the entire personnel of an institution, or just certain categories of personnel. The criteria used can be limited to very specific conditions, such as respect for human rights, or they can deal with a broad range of suitability requirements. Contextual factors affect what form of vetting is both desirable and feasible. Political resistance against or support for a vetting process, as well as operational factors such as institutional capacities and the

Framework (United Nations 2006); A Mayer-Rieckh and P de Greiff (eds), *Justice as Prevention: Vetting Public Employees in Transitional Societies* (Social Science Research Council 2007).

[13] Updated Principles to Combat Impunity, Principle 36(a).

[14] However, judges and other public officials who were unlawfully appointed—in violation of procedural and qualification requirements—may be relieved of their functions by law without establishing other reasons for their removal. See Principle 30 of the Updated Principles.

[15] *Report of the Secretary-General*, n 12, 17.

[16] Orentlicher Report, n 5, 17. See also OHCHR, *Rule-of-Law-Tools for Post-Conflict States. Prosecution Initiatives* (United Nations 2006) 9.

[17] Orentlicher Report, n 5, 19.

[18] OHCHR, n 16, 9. See also GL Naarden, 'Non-Prosecutorial Sanctions for Grave Violations of International Humanitarian Law: Wartime Conduct of Bosnian Police Officials' (2003) 97 American Journal of International Law 342–52.

[19] P De Greiff, 'Vetting and Transitional Justice' in P de Greiff and A Mayer-Rieckh (eds), n 12, 522–37, 531.

level of know-how, the availability of resources, and cost implications, will determine the design and implementation of vetting.

12 Examples of vetting processes include 'dejuntification' in Greece after 1974; 'purification' in El Salvador after 1992; 'lustration' in the former communist countries in central and eastern Europe after 1989; certification of police and reappointment of judges in Bosnia and Herzegovina after 1995; vetting of the national police in Liberia from 2004 to 2006; and the vetting of judges, magistrates, and police officers in Kenya after 2012. In some transitional contexts, such as Nepal, the Democratic Republic of the Congo, and Burundi, efforts to establish a vetting process were effectively resisted and/or the institutional conditions for it were absent.

13 Experience shows that vetting processes often fail to meet their stated objectives because their design was overly ambitious and the resource and operational requirements to implement the process were underestimated. A failed or badly designed vetting process can further erode public trust in the institution, undermine confidence in the transition, and increase insecurity. Arguably, the purge-like 'debaathification' process in Iraq, and the disbanding of its military and other security institutions by the Coalition Provisional Authority from 2003 onwards, contributed to the subsequent insurgency in the country.

14 Judicial reform (Principle 36(b)) measures aimed at building the independence, impartiality, and effectiveness of courts and their adherence to international standards of due process are particularly important from a prevention standpoint, where the judiciary collaborated with or failed to stop abuses under the previous regime.[20] Judicial reform can play a role in enabling other justice measures, particularly criminal prosecutions. At the same time, truth-telling initiatives, particularly commissions of inquiry, can examine the role of the judiciary in past abuses and make recommendations for its reform,[21] as in countries such as Chile, El Salvador, Guatemala, and Sierra Leone.[22]

15 Civilian oversight (Principle 36(c)) helps to ensure that security and intelligence agencies operate in accordance with international human rights standards. Establishing civilian oversight of the security sector is one of the key features of any effective security sector reform process.[23] Civilian oversight can be provided formally and informally. Formal oversight mechanisms include parliamentary oversight, executive oversight, and judicial review, as well as independent mechanisms such as national human rights commissions and offices of ombudspersons. Commonly, such independent mechanisms give the public an opportunity to submit complaints (Principle 36(d)). Informal oversight of security actors can be provided by civil society groups, the media, and research institutions.

16 Experience suggests that oversight and internal discipline complement each other. Internal discipline mechanisms alone run the risk of giving in to internal pressures and an inappropriate *esprit de corps* that is commonly found in security institutions, and may not enjoy the people's trust. External oversight, on the other hand, can act more

[20] United Nations, *Report of the Special Rapporteur on the promotion of truth, justice, reparation and guarantees of non-recurrence, Pablo de Greiff*, UN Doc A/HRC/30/42 (7 September 2015) 13 (hereinafter '*Report of the Special Rapporteur*').

[21] PB Hayner, *Unspeakable Truths: Facing the Challenge of Truth Commissions* (Routledge 2002) 102–06; P de Greiff, 'Truth Telling and the Rule of Law' in TA Borer (ed), *Telling the Truths: Truth Telling and Peace Building in Post-Conflict Societies* (University of Notre Dame Press 2006).

[22] *Report of the Special Rapporteur*, n 20, 14.

[23] *Report of the Secretary-General*, n 9, 12.

independently and put pressure on the institution it monitors, but it cannot substitute for effective internal accountability mechanisms that have more direct access to information and can intervene more quickly and systematically. Accountability is provided more effectively, particularly in the aftermath of violations, if security institutions are answerable 'to multiple audiences through multiple mechanisms'.[24]

Training public employees in human rights and humanitarian law standards (Principle 36(e)) is easily implemented and a welcome initial reform measure. However, the efficacy of such training is limited if it is not accompanied by broader institutional reforms that ensure holding individuals accountable if they fail to adhere to the behavioural change conveyed in the training. In the police, for example, studies have emphasized the difficulty in attaining lasting change in culture and performance through training.[25] 17

E. Critical Assessment

The measures discussed in Principle 36 target state institutions, importantly focusing on the structures that facilitated violations. The institutional approach represents just one sphere of intervention, however. Prevention can be achieved more effectively if measures target not just the institutional sphere, but also civil society and the cultural and personal spheres.[26] 18

Interventions in civil society can include efforts to stop the persecution, intimidation, and harassment of civil society actors, the removal of restrictive measures, and legal empowerment.[27] 19

Interventions in the cultural sphere can include education programmes; publications in the press and activities by other media; social mobilization using new social media; advocacy by civil society organizations; and works of art such as novels, movies, paintings, or plays; and access to archives.[28] Interventions in the personal sphere can include efforts to empower victims as citizens,[29] efforts to provide access to justice,[30] or counselling of victims to overcome trauma.[31] Cultural and personal interventions are well suited to identifying and redressing long-term effects and the complex nature of abuses, but are less appropriate to tackle rights-based claims. 20

[24] DH Bayley, 'The Contemporary Practices of Policing: A Comparative View', paper presented at Center for Strategic and International Studies and Police Executive Research Forum (6 October 1997), quoted in CE Stone and HH Ward, 'Democratic Policing: A Framework for Action' (2000) 10(15) Policing and Society 11–45, 15.

[25] Independent Commission for Aid Impact, *Review of UK Development Assistance for Security and Justice*, Report 42 (March 2015) 13 and 25; citing RN Haarr, 'The Making of a Community Policing Officer: The Impact of Basic Training and Occupational Socialization on Police Recruits' (2001) 4(4) Police Quarterly 402–33.

[26] *Report of the Special Rapporteur*, n 20, 18–22.

[27] Ibid, 18–19; On legal empowerment, see S Golub, 'Legal Empowerment's Approaches and Importance' in Open Society Justice Initiative, *Justice Initiatives. Legal Empowerment* (Open Society Justice Initiative 2013) 5–14.

[28] *Report of the Special Rapporteur*, n 20, 21–22.

[29] A Mayer-Rieckh, *Dealing with the Past in Security Sector Reform*. DCAF SSR Paper no 10 (DCAF 2013) 26–27.

[30] On access to justice, see, eg, Avocats sans Frontières, *Access to Justice*, at <www.asf.be/action/asf-programmes/access-to-justice> accessed 20 November 2017.

[31] *Report of the Special Rapporteur*, n 20, 21.

21 State authorities can support or create space for intervention in these spheres but cannot intervene directly. Culture and personality structures are more resistant to intervention. Change in these spheres is, therefore, more difficult and takes longer to achieve, but it is more resilient once it has been obtained. Interventions in the cultural and personal spheres can also provide entry points in environments in which interventions in the societal sphere are not possible due to political or institutional resistance to change.

Bibliography

Bayley, DH, 'The Contemporary Practices of Policing: A Comparative View', paper presented at Center for Strategic and International Studies and Police Executive Research Forum (6 October 1997).

de Greiff, P, 'On Making the Invisible Visible: The Role of Cultural Interventions in Transitional Justice Processes' in C Ramírez-Barat (ed), *Transitional Justice, Culture, and Society. Beyond Outreach* (Social Science Research Council 2014).

Golub, S, 'Legal Empowerment's Approaches and Importance' in Open Society Justice Initiative, *Justice Initiatives. Legal Empowerment* (Open Society Justice Initiative 2013).

Mayer-Rieckh, A, *Dealing with the Past in Security Sector Reform.* DCAF SSR Paper no 10 (DCAF 2013).

Naarden, GL, 'Non-Prosecutorial Sanctions for Grave Violations of International Humanitarian Law: Wartime Conduct of Bosnian Police Officials' (2003) 97 American Journal of International Law 342–52.

OECD DAC, *OECD DAC Handbook on Security System Reform (SSR): Supporting Security and Justice* (OECD 2007).

OHCHR, *Rule-of-Law-Tools for Post-Conflict States. Prosecution Initiatives* (United Nations 2006).

Principle 37. Disbandment of Parastatal Armed Forces/Demobilization and Social Reintegration of Children

Roger Duthie and Alexander Mayer-Rieckh

Parastatal or unofficial armed groups shall be demobilized and disbanded. Their position in or links with State institutions, including in particular the army, police, intelligence and security forces, should be thoroughly investigated and the information thus acquired made public. States should draw up a reconversion plan to ensure the social reintegration of the members of such groups.

Measures should be taken to secure the cooperation of third countries that might have contributed to the creation and development of such groups, particularly through financial or logistical support.

Children who have been recruited or used in hostilities shall be demobilized or otherwise released from service. States shall, when necessary, accord these children all appropriate assistance for their physical and psychological recovery and their social integration.

A. Summary of Findings

Principle 37 of the Updated Impunity Principles focuses on the disbandment of parastatal armed groups and the demobilization and reintegration of children involved in the armed conflict. This commentary reviews how the discussion in the preparatory reports and different versions of the Principles expanded from a focus on purges of unofficial armed groups to one of demobilization and reintegration of such groups, as well as children. It points out the relevance of measures for dealing with these groups from an impunity standpoint, as well as the efforts of disarmament, demobilization, and reintegration (DDR) programmes to address them. The importance of reintegration processes is highlighted, along with how transitional justice measures can affect them, and the implications for former child combatants. The articulation of measures for demobilization and reintegration in Principle 37 is problematic because it is too specific and contextual, failing to extend the discussion to other groups of combatants and not considering the gender dimensions of reintegration for children. The measures in Principle 37 could be cited as examples of types of measures that could fall under broader principles: preventing the transformation of conflict violence to criminal violence through the dismantling and reintegration of all armed groups engaged in abuses; and comprehensive responses to the injustices experienced by children during armed conflict.

B. Contextual and Historical Introduction

The preparatory reports drafted by Louis Joinet prior to 1995 address the disbandment of 'parastatal groups'. For example, making explicit reference to the experience of El Salvador, the 1993 preparatory report includes a section on 'purges of paramilitary 1 forces', but noting that these are different from purges applied to the armed forces or police because they are 'concerned with the elimination or eradication of shadowy units such as death squads, paramilitary or mercenary groups and private militias, which are characterized by their secret links with State structures and the private sector (large landowners, entrepreneurs)'.[1]

2 In his 1997 report accompanying the Impunity Principles, Joinet introduced the notion of 'reintegration' as a mechanism for preventing the recurrence of abuses and/or the transformation of unofficial armed groups. Principle 38 of the 1997 Impunity Principles calls for the 'disbandment' of 'unofficial armed groups directly or indirectly linked to the state' and 'private groups benefitting from the state's passivity'.[2] Referring to the context of a restoration of or transition to democracy and/or peace, Principle 38 recommends measures to: retrace and make public the organizational structures of such groups by identifying agents and their position in the army or police, and by determining their covert links with intelligence and security services; investigate intelligence and security services; secure the cooperation of third countries that provide financial or logistical support; and develop 'a reconversion plan to ensure that members of such groups are not tempted to join the ranks of organized crime'.[3] An effort to specifically prevent such groups from turning to criminal activities is now made part of the recommended measures themselves.

3 Principle 37 of the 2005 Updated Impunity Principles refers to 'parastatal' and 'unofficial' armed groups, calls for them to be 'demobilized' and 'disbanded' and their position in or links to state institutions (army, police, intelligence, and security) to be investigated and made public, and advocates for the creation of a reconversion plan with the specific aim of 'social reintegration' of their members, while securing the cooperation of third countries. The main addition to the 2005 Principles is the concern with children who were recruited or used in hostilities, whom the state now needs to demobilize and accord 'all appropriate assistance for their physical and psychological recovery and their social integration'.[4]

C. Theoretical Framework

4 Principle 37 of the Updated Impunity Principles uses the terms 'parastatal' and 'unofficial' armed groups, but as we have seen in section B, the broader discussion includes terms such as 'paramilitary' and 'private' armed groups to refer to the actors in question.

[1] United Nations Economic and Social Council, *The Administration of Justice and the Human Rights of Detainees. The Question of Human Rights of Persons Subjected to Any Form of Detention or Imprisonment: Progress Report on the Question of the Impunity of Perpetrators of Human Rights Violations*, UN Doc E/CN.4/Sub.2/1993/6 (19 July 1993) 34.

[2] United Nations, *The Administration of Justice and the Human Rights of Detainees: Question of the Impunity of Perpetrators of Human Rights Violations (Civil and Political). Revised Final Report prepared by Mr L. Joinet*, E/CN.4/Sub.2/1997/20/rev.1, 2 October 1997, 10.

[3] Ibid.

[4] United Nations, *Impunity. Report of the independent expert to update the Set of Principles to combat impunity, Diane Orentlicher. Addendum: Updated Set of Principles for the protection and promotion of human rights through action to combat impunity*, UN Doc E.CN.4/2005/102/Add.1 (8 February 2005) Principle 37. Orentlicher notes in her accompanying report that the text of Principle 37 on children derives from the Optional Protocol to the Convention on the Rights of the Child on the Involvement of Children in Armed Conflict, 2173 UNTS A-27531. UN, *Impunity. Report of the independent expert to update the Set of Principles to combat impunity, Diane Orentlicher*, UN Doc E.CN.4/2005/102 (18 February 2005) 19, fn 94.

For a definition of such terms, it is useful to start with Article 5 of the Draft Articles on Responsibility of States for Internationally Wrongful Acts, which refers to states' responsibility for the conduct of 'a person or entity which is not an organ of the State ... but which is empowered by the law of that State to exercise elements of the governmental authority'.[5] The literature on 'parastatal' armed groups contains several terms to refer to such actors, including 'paramilitary groups', 'pro-government militias', and 'civil defense groups', which share the characteristics of being armed and outside of, yet established, supported, used, or tolerated by, state institutions or factions within them.[6]

Parastatal armed groups can be significant actors from an impunity perspective. 5 Research suggests that pro-government militias, for example, increase the risk of certain human rights violations against civilians, as states have difficulty controlling groups that have different goals and lower standards of recruitment, training, and codes of conduct.[7] Importantly, governments often use such actors specifically to maintain impunity—that is, 'to opportunistically use agents that are, or appear to be, difficult to control in order to evade accountability to state and non-state actors and international organizations'.[8]

Disarmament, demobilization, and reintegration (DDR) programmes, commonly 6 implemented in post-conflict situations, have not focused on parastatal or unofficial armed groups. The UN's Integrated DDR Standards, for example, mention such actors only briefly, calling for a framework to be set up to address groups, such as informal militias, that are not included in political processes and DDR programmes.[9] More recently, the UN has acknowledged the diffuse nature of violence against civilians, which is 'often perpetrated by undisciplined armed elements, such as militia and gangs, operating at the sub-national level',[10] and has begun to develop what it calls 'second generation' DDR measures 'targeting specific groups with different approaches and incentives', including through the disarmament and dismantlement of militias (DDM), which is 'aimed at addressing such groups which might otherwise be left out of more traditional DDR processes'.[11] Generally, DDR practice and literature is, however, concerned more with state and non-state armed groups than parastatal ones, as these represent the primary security and prevention challenge in most environments. The 2005 Updated Principles

[5] International Law Commission, 'Draft articles on Responsibility of States for Internationally Wrongful Acts, with commentaries' (2001) II International Law Commission YBk, Part Two, 42.

[6] J Mazzei, *Death Squads or Self-Defense Forces? How Paramilitary Groups Emerge and Challenge Democracy* (University of North Carolina Press 2009) 4, 5, 22; SC Carey, NJ Mitchell, and W Lowe, 'States, the Security Sector, and the Monopoly of Violence: A New Database on Pro-Government Militias' (2013) 50 Journal of Peace Research 249–58; B Oswald, 'Civil Defense Groups: Developing Accountability', US Institute of Peace Special Report 350 (Washington, DC, August 2014) 2; 'The Montreux Document: On pertinent international legal obligations and good practices for States related to operations of private military and security companies during armed conflict' (International Committee of the Red Cross, Swiss Federal Department of Foreign Affairs, September 2008).

[7] NJ Mitchell, SC Carey, and CK Butler, 'The Impact of Pro-Government Militias on Human Rights Violations' (2014) 40 International Interactions 812–36, 830–31.

[8] Ibid; see also Oswald, n 6, 4; United Nations General Assembly, *Report of the Special Rapporteur on Extrajudicial, Summary or Arbitrary Executions, Philip Alston*, UN Doc A/HRC/14/24 (20 May 2010) 18.

[9] United Nations Inter-Agency Working Group (IAWG) on DDR, *Integrated Disarmament, Demobilization and Reintegration Standards* (DPKO 2006) (hereinafter 'IAWG, *IDDRS*') Module 2.30, 8.

[10] UN Department of Peacekeeping Operations, *Second Generation Disarmament, Demobilization and Reintegration (DDR) Practices in Peace Operations: A Contribution to the New Horizon Discussion on Challenges and Opportunities for UN Peacekeeping* (United Nations 2010) 7.

[11] Ibid, 22, 24–25.

remain here largely within the framework of the 1997 Principles, neglecting a broader focus on the demobilization and reintegration of all types of combatants.

7 Principle 37 of the 2005 Updated Impunity Principles introduces the issue of children associated with armed conflict into its concern with reintegration. Unlike with parastatal groups, the reintegration of former child combatants is a goal of many DDR programmes and other child-focused peacebuilding initiatives. According to the UN's Integrated DDR Standards, for instance, child-specific reintegration should allow a child to access education, a livelihood, life skills, and a meaningful role in society.[12] Furthermore, in order to be sustainable, child-specific reintegration 'must be based on broader community development processes'.[13]

8 The Updated Principles do not explain why reintegration constitutes a measure to prevent the recurrence of violations. Rationales for reintegration assistance elsewhere generally include humanitarian ones and development ones, but most important from a preventive standpoint are the security concerns that ex-combatants, including former child combatants, can become sources of insecurity and spoilers in peace processes.[14] As a response to past abuses, reintegration measures importantly have a social (in addition to an economic and a political) dimension, and it is here that other measures aimed at increasing trust may contribute to the promotion of reintegration. For example, giving ex-combatants public spaces to tell the truth about their actions and apologize may reduce hostility among receiving communities; providing reparations to victims may reduce resentment towards ex-combatants because of the assistance they receive; and assuring victims and communities that the worst perpetrators among ex-combatants will be punished may reduce feelings of insecurity. Transitional justice 'may help reduce reprisal, stigmatization, or discrimination against ex-combatants—something that will obviously benefit DDR'.[15]

9 This applies to children involved in conflict as well,[16] although in practice DDR processes tend to focus more on demobilization and individual rehabilitation than on children's social relationships with their communities.[17] Because children recruited into armed groups are the victims of an international crime, reintegration itself can be considered as a form of justice: 'measures that aim to prevent their recruitment, or that attempt to reintegrate them into their communities, should not be viewed as a routine component of peacemaking, but as an attempt to prevent or redress a violation of children's

[12] IAWG, *IDDRS*, n 9, Section 5.30, 2.

[13] Ibid. Similarly, the 2007 strategic review of Graça Machel's 1996 study on the 'Impact of Armed Conflict on Children' describes reintegration for children as a process requiring programming beyond DDR programmes, one with 'wide-ranging aims, different for each boy and girl involved, including building emotional trust and reconciling with family and community, providing access to education and developing a means of livelihood'. UN, *Report of the Special Representative of the Secretary-General for Children and Armed Conflict*, UN Doc A/62/228 (13 August 2007) 31. See also M Wessells, *Child Soldiers: From Violence to Protection* (Harvard University Press 2006) 182.

[14] L Waldorf, 'Introduction: Linking DDR and Transitional Justice' in A Cutter Patel, P de Greiff, and L Waldorf (eds), *Disarming the Past: Transitional Justice and Ex-Combatants* (Social Science Research Council 2009) 14–35.

[15] Ibid.

[16] R Duthie and I Specht, 'DDR, Transitional Justice, and the Reintegration of Former Child Combatants' in Cutter Patel, de Greiff, and Waldorf (eds), n 14, 190–227.

[17] I Derluyn, S Vindevogel, and L De Haene, 'Toward a Relational Understanding of the Reintegration and Rehabilitation Processes of Former Child Soldiers' (2013) 22(8) Journal of Aggression, Maltreatment and Trauma 869–86, 877; M Drumbl, *Reimagining Child Soldiers in International Law and Policy* (OUP 2012) 1–25.

human rights'.[18] In terms of children who are also perpetrators of crimes, the Convention on the Rights of the Child requires that state responses must take into account the 'desirability of promoting the child's reintegration and the child's assuming a constructive role in society'.[19] While DDR discourse tends to treat former child combatants as victims alone, however, some experts argue that acknowledging the potential of child combatants to perpetrate abuses and their subsequent exposure to accountability measures other than criminal trials may facilitate reintegration by treating children as agents with both claims to rights and obligations, rather than as merely passive victims.[20]

D. Practice

Like DDR programmes that have focused on armed groups, attempts to disband unofficial armed groups have faced significant challenges. In Afghanistan, for example, the Disbandment of Illegal Armed Groups Programme was set up in 2005 primarily for semi-formal militias, but faced capacity and management challenges as well as the slow delivery of projects in exchange for disarmament, and complications created by the ongoing insurgency throughout the country.[21] In Côte d'Ivoire, multiple attempts to profile, disarm, and demobilize militias between 2006 and 2009 encountered difficulties with the collection of weapons.[22] In Colombia, DDR programmes since 2003 demobilized and provided reintegration assistance to more than 30,000 paramilitaries but, as with most DDR efforts, made limited progress towards fostering trust between them and citizens and victims of human rights violations, or toward community security more generally. With 'the political, economic and criminal roots of the paramilitary phenomenon' unaddressed, many former paramilitaries joined new illegal armed groups, known as *bandas criminales*.[23] 10

Programmes aimed at supporting the rehabilitation and reintegration of children formerly associated with armed conflict have been enacted in many countries, often as part of larger DDR processes, and often through non-governmental organizations.[24] According to one expert, 'the postconflict landscape is littered with questionable DDR processes offering inadequate assistance to children', while many former child combatants avoid formal programmes and self-demobilize.[25] In countries such as Mozambique, Liberia, Sierra Leone, and Uganda, research has shown not only that former child combatants face a range of difficulties, but also that many of them do experience successful reintegration processes.[26] 11

[18] IAWG, *IDDRS*, n 9, Section 5.30, 1.

[19] Convention on the Rights of the Child (20 November 1989) 1577 UNTS I-27531, Art 39.

[20] MA Drumbl, *Reimagining Child Soldiers in International Law and Policy* (OUP 2012).

[21] IAWG, *IDDRS*, n 9, Section 6.10, at 8. [22] Ibid, 47–48.

[23] M Derks, H Rouw, and I Briscoe, 'A Community Dilemma: DDR and the Changing Face of Violence in Colombia' (Peace and Security Development Network no 30, July 2011) 4. See also S Jaramillo, Y Giha, and P Torres, 'Transitional Justice and DDR: The Case of Colombia' (ICTJ Research Unit, June 2009).

[24] I Derluyn, S Vindevogel, and L de Haene, 'Toward a Relational Understanding of the Reintegration and Rehabilitation Processes of Former Child Soldiers' (2013) 22(8) Journal of Aggression, Maltreatment & Trauma 869–86, 872.

[25] M Wessells, *Child Soldiers: From Violence to Protection* (Harvard University Press 2006) 155.

[26] C Blattman and J Annan, 'The Consequences of Child Soldiering', Households in Conflict Network (HICN) Working Paper no 22 (August 2007); N Boothby, J Crawford, and J Halperin, 'Mozambique Child Soldier Life Outcome Study: Lessons Learned in Rehabilitation and Reintegration Efforts' *Global Public Health* (February 2006); J Weinstein and M Humphries, 'Disentangling the Determinants of Successful Demobilization, and Reintegration', Center for Global Development, Working Paper no 69, September 2005;

E. Critical Assessment

12 The demobilization/disbandment of parastatal armed groups and the reintegration of their members, as well as children involved in armed conflict, are the primary measures called for in Principle 37. These are often critical measures in transitions to peace and democracy, demonstrated by the frequency with which the significant presence of parastatal groups and child combatants characterize current and recent armed conflicts and repression. The articulation of these measures as a principle of guarantees of non-recurrence, however, is problematic for a number of reasons. Similarly to Principle 36, the measures listed in Principle 37 may be too specific and contextual. As Joinet acknowledged, the focus on parastatal groups drew from the experiences of Latin America and El Salvador in particular, where state auxiliaries were among the main perpetrators of abuses. The Principle contains no mention, however, of the demobilization and reintegration of members of state armed forces or non-state armed forces, which are usually the actors most responsible for human rights violations in armed conflicts. The reference to children seems to be to children generally, not specifically to those involved with parastatal armed groups, which highlights further the absence of a more general principle on demobilization and reintegration of all groups.

13 While the measures listed are important, the Principle does not articulate their rationale (why they are critical to preventing the recurrence of abuses and combating impunity), and insufficiently links them to each other (why they are included in the same Principle). The inclusion in the Updated Principles of measures aimed at the reintegration of children also makes no mention of the specific reintegration needs of other groups involved in demobilization. There is, for example, no discussion of gender, despite the fact that women and girls often have very different experiences in their involvement with armed groups, and often have different reintegration needs as well. Children, it may be argued, warrant special mention because they are often victims of illegal recruitment, and their victimhood bears upon their reintegration prospects, but they are certainly not alone in having specific reintegration needs. At the same time, it can also be argued that in the long-term interest of preventing the recurrence of abuses, a focus on children and youth within the Principles should not be limited to reintegration measures for those engaged in hostilities. The measures in Principle 37 could therefore be cited as examples of specific types of measures that would fall under broader principles, in this case perhaps of: (i) preventing the transformation of violence through the dismantling and reintegration of all armed groups engaged in abuses; and (ii) comprehensive responses to the injustices experienced by children and youth during armed conflict, including through transitional justice and broader measures such as education reform.

Bibliography

Blattman, C and Annan, J, 'The Consequences of Child Soldiering', Households in Conflict Network (HICN) Working Paper no 22 (August 2007).

Boothby, N, Crawford, J, and Halperin, J, 'Mozambique Child Soldier Life Outcome Study: Lessons Learned in Rehabilitation and Reintegration Efforts' *Global Public Health* (February 2006).

I Specht and H Tefferi, 'Impact Evaluation of the Reintegration Programme of Children Associated with Fighting Forces (CAFF) in Liberia' (UNICEF, April 2007).

Carey, SC, Mitchell, NJ, and Lowe, WW, 'States, the Security Sector, and the Monopoly of Violence: A New Database on Pro-Government Militias' (2013) 50 Journal of Peace Research 249–58.

Cutter Patel, A, de Greiff, P, and Waldorf, L (eds), *Disarming the Past: Transitional Justice and Ex-Combatants* (Social Science Research Council 2009).

Derks, M, Rouw, H, and Briscoe, I, 'A Community Dilemma: DDR and the Changing Face of Violence in Colombia' (Peace and Security Development Network no 30, July 2011).

Derluyn, I, Vindevogel, S, and De Haene, L, 'Toward a Relational Understanding of the Reintegration and Rehabilitation Processes of Former Child Soldiers' (2013) 22(8) Journal of Aggression, Maltreatment & Trauma 869–86.

Drumbl, M, *Reimagining Child Soldiers in International Law and Policy* (OUP 2012).

International Committee of the Red Cross, Swiss Federal Department of Foreign Affairs, *The Montreux Document: On pertinent international legal obligations and good practices for States related to operations of private military and security companies during armed conflict* (September 2008).

International Law Commission, 'Draft articles on Responsibility of States for Internationally Wrongful Acts, with commentaries' (2001) II International Law Commission YBk.

Mazzei, J, *Death Squads or Self-Defense Forces? How Paramilitary Groups Emerge and Challenge Democracy* (University of North Carolina Press 2009).

Mitchell, NNJ, Carey, SSC, and Butler, CK, 'The Impact of Pro-Government Militias on Human Rights Violations' (2014) 40 International Interactions 812–36.

Oswald, B, 'Civil Defense Groups: Developing Accountability', US Institute of Peace Special Report 350 (Washington, DC, August 2014).

Specht, I and Tefferi, H, 'Impact Evaluation of the Reintegration Programme of Children Associated with Fighting Forces (CAFF) in Liberia' (UNICEF, April 2007).

UN Department of Peacekeeping Operations, *Second Generation Disarmament, Demobilization and Reintegration (DDR) Practices in Peace Operations: A Contribution to the New Horizon Discussion on Challenges and Opportunities for UN Peacekeeping* (United Nations, 2010).

United Nations Inter-Agency Working Group (IAWG) on DDR, *Integrated Disarmament, Demobilization and Reintegration Standards* (DPKO 2006).

Weinstein, J and Humphries, M, 'Disentangling the Determinants of Successful Demobilization, and Reintegration', Center for Global Development, Working Paper no 69 (September 2005).

Wessells, M, *Child Soldiers: From Violence to Protection* (Harvard University Press 2006).

Principle 38. Reform of Laws and Institutions Contributing to Impunity

Roger Duthie and Alexander Mayer-Rieckh

Legislation and administrative regulations and institutions that contribute to or legitimize human rights violations must be repealed or abolished. In particular, emergency legislation and courts of any kind must be repealed or abolished insofar as they infringe the fundamental rights and freedoms guaranteed in the Universal Declaration of Human Rights and the International Covenant on Civil and Political Rights. Legislative measures necessary to ensure protection of human rights and to safeguard democratic institutions and processes must be enacted.

As a basis for such reforms, during periods of restoration of or transition to democracy and/or peace States should undertake a comprehensive review of legislation and administrative regulations.

A. Summary of Findings

Principle 38 of the Updated Impunity Principles focuses on the reform of laws and institutions that contribute to impunity for human rights violations. This commentary summarizes the development of this Principle, from an initial narrower focus only on emergency legislation and courts in preparatory reports and prior versions, to a broader focus on legislative and institutional reform to combat impunity. It then reviews the theoretical framework for such legislative reform, and explains how it can both facilitate and be facilitated by other transitional justice measures, as well as how such reform can include a range of measures and address a range of issues, including gender justice. The commentary reviews examples of legislative reform in cases such as Northern Ireland, Sierra Leone, Morocco, Guatemala, and Uganda, particularly where truth commission recommendations have addressed the matter. It is argued that legislative change is not an end in itself but requires further efforts to ensure its implementation. Principle 38 is a good example of moving from a narrow focus on specific measures to a broader focus on legislative reform, but a lack of clarity blurs the distinction between the institutional reforms being proposed here and those being proposed in Principle 36. In addition, a Principle focused on legislative reform needs to cover not just constitutional reform, but also peace agreements as frameworks for future reform in post-conflict contexts. Lastly, we emphasize the complementary nature of legislative and institutional reform.

B. Contextual and Historical Introduction

1 Principle 38 of the 2005 Updated Principles calls for the repeal or abolition of laws and institutions that contribute to impunity for human rights violations. In a 1993 preparatory report, Louis Joinet pointed to the 'pernicious role' that courts of

special jurisdiction, especially military courts, play in encouraging impunity under government-declared states of emergency. As part of the military hierarchy, these courts tend 'to justify or even legitimize violations in the name of a higher interest or the performance of a mission ... with which the armed forces have supposedly been vested', and 'to make "national security" the rule rather than the exception, which provides a means of concealing evidence and preserving the anonymity of the perpetrators of violations'.[1] A first step towards correcting this situation is to abrogate these laws and courts, 'which have been instrumental in or sanctioned the violations suffered by those expressing their need for justice'.[2] The 1993 report here cites the final document of the 1993 World Conference on Human Rights, which says that 'States should abrogate legislation leading to impunity for those responsible for grave violations of human rights such as torture and prosecute such violations, thereby providing a firm basis for the rule of law'.[3]

In the 1997 Impunity Principles, this topic is addressed in Principle 39, which calls 2
for 'emergency legislation and courts of any kind' that infringe on the rights guaranteed in the Universal Declaration of Human Rights[4] and the International Covenant on Civil and Political Rights[5] to be repealed or abolished. Principle 39 also declares habeas corpus to be a fundamental and non-derogable individual right. The Basic Principles and Guidelines on Reparation, in their suggested measures to guarantee non-repetition, include the review and reform of laws that contribute to or allow serious violations of international human rights and humanitarian law.[6]

In the 2005 Updated Impunity Principles, these issues are addressed in Principle 38, 3
but the focus has been expanded to include not just emergency legislation, but also any '[l]egislation and administrative regulations and institutions that contribute to or legitimize human rights violations'. Furthermore, Principle 38 calls for the enactment of '[l]egislative measures necessary to ensure protection of human rights and to safeguard democratic institutions and processes', and, drawing on the Basic Principles, 'comprehensive review of legislation and administrative regulations'. As the accompanying report to the 2005 Updated Principles explains, the focus of Principle 38 was 'broadened in light of recent experience' to recognize 'the importance of broader legislative reform'.[7] As with other principles on guarantees of non-recurrence, these preventive measures include but go beyond those—such as abolishing emergency courts—that were particularly relevant when the 1997 Principles were drafted, especially in Latin American transitions in the early 1990s.

[1] United Nations, *The Administration of Justice and the Human Rights of Detainees: The Question of Human Rights of Persons Subjected to Any Form of Detention or Imprisonment: Progress Report on the Question of the Impunity of Perpetrators of Human Rights Violations, prepared by Mr Guissé and Mr Joinet, pursuant to Sub-Commission Resolution 1992/23*, E/CN.4/Sub.2/1993/6 (19 July 1993) 11–12.

[2] Ibid, 20.

[3] UN, Vienna Declaration and Programme of Action, A/CONF.157/23 (25 June 1993) para 60.

[4] UNGA Resolution (Res) 217 A, 'Universal Declaration of Human Rights', 10 December 1948.

[5] International Covenant on Civil and Political Rights (ICCPR) 999 UNTS I-14668.

[6] UN, *Basic Principles and Guidelines on the Right to a Remedy and Reparation for the Victims of Gross Violations of International Human Rights Law and Serious Violations of International Humanitarian Law*, UN Doc A/RES/60/147 (21 March 2006) 9 (hereinafter 'Basic Principles').

[7] UN, *Report of the independent expert to update the Set of Principles to combat impunity, Diane Orentlicher*, UN Doc E.CN.4/2005/102 (18 February 2005) 19.

C. Theoretical Framework

4 The need for reform of laws and institutions to prevent the recurrence of human rights violations is developed through the preparatory reports and different versions of the Basic Principles and the Impunity Principles, but these documents also draw on or are complemented by other sources and thinking. For example, as the UN Special Rapporteur on the promotion of truth, justice, reparation and guarantees of non-recurrence pointed out, regional human rights courts have often issued orders relating to guarantees of non-recurrence such as legislative reform. The Inter-American Court of Human Rights (IACtHR), for one, has ordered states to change laws that put civilians under military court jurisdiction because they violate the American Convention on Human Rights,[8] as for example in its 1988 *Velásquez Rodríguez* decision.[9]

5 In 2004, the UN Secretary-General's report on transitional justice and the rule of law also drew attention to the need for legislative reform in post-conflict settings, where 'legislative frameworks often show the accumulated signs of neglect and political distortion, contain discriminatory elements and rarely reflect the requirements of international human rights and criminal law standards. Emergency laws and executive decrees are often the order of the day'. Where there are adequate laws, it observed, they are often unknown to the public and not implemented because of capacity constraints, thus connecting the need for legislative reform with broader institutional reform.[10]

6 In a 2015 report, the Special Rapporteur on the promotion of truth, justice, reparation and guarantees of non-recurrence argues that legal reforms aimed at incorporating international legal obligations—covering issues like criminal types, statutes of limitations and retroactivity questions, and the de-incentivizing of violations—can enable transitional justice measures. Such reforms can highlight states' obligations according to international law, address legal problems that have 'increasingly become an excuse for inaction', and help to guarantee respect both for principles such as due process and for the rights of victims.[11] He raises the need for reform of 'emergency, anti-terrorism or other security-related legislation' such that it is 'fully compatible with human rights standards, so that it does not incentivize violations of rights'.[12]

7 In addition, constitutional reforms aimed at non-recurrence should include the removal of 'provisions that may fuel discrimination' and the introduction of 'mechanisms of inclusion'; the introduction of a bill of fundamental rights, including guarantees for minorities; the separation of powers in order to limit executive branches; limiting the scope of military courts to military crimes and not human rights violations; the establishment of a constitutional court; and the adoption of a new constitution.[13] Particular attention here should be paid to enacting legislation meant to establish accountability in

[8] UN, *Report of the Special Rapporteur on the promotion of truth, justice, reparation and guarantees of non-recurrence, Pablo de Greiff*, UN Doc A/HRC/30/42 (7 September 2015) 6 (hereinafter '*Report of the Special Rapporteur*'), citing AJ Carrillo, *Justice in Context: The Relevance of Inter-American Human Rights Law and Practice to Repairing the Past* (OUP 2008).

[9] *Velásquez Rodríguez v Honduras* (Judgment) IACtHR Series C no 4 (29 July 1988) para 166.

[10] UN, *The rule of law and transitional justice in conflict and post-conflict societies. Report of the Secretary-General*, UN Doc S/2004/616 (23 August 2004) 10.

[11] *Report of the Special Rapporteur*, n 8, 12.

[12] Ibid, 13.

[13] Ibid, 15–18. See also M O'Rawe, 'Security System Reform and Identity in Divided Societies: Lessons from Northern Ireland' in P Arthur (ed), *Identities in Transition: Challenges for Transitional Justice in Divided Societies* (CUP 2011) 87–117, 113.

its various forms within security sector institutions, such as vetting, internal discipline, and all relevant oversight mechanisms.[14] As with other types of institutional reform, however, while legislative reform can facilitate transitional justice measures, the reverse is also true: truth-seeking mechanisms and other transitional justice measures can help to trigger legislative and constitutional and reforms by drawing attention to the institutional and legal structures that facilitated or allowed violations to occur.[15]

Within the broad focus on the reform of laws, measures aimed at preventing the recurrence of human rights violations often focus on particular impunity issues such as gender justice. The UN Secretary-General's 2011 report on transitional justice and the rule of law, for example, observes an increase in 8

> efforts to reform discriminatory legislation, to enhance access to justice and end impunity for crimes of sexual and gender-based violence, and to ensure women's participation in institutions and peacebuilding forums as part of a comprehensive response to create transformational change in the lives of women and girls.[16]

Civil society and transitional justice processes can help in 'spurring' such legislative changes—truth commission findings and recommendations, for instance, can highlight the need for change and 'generate momentum' for new legislation.[17]

D. Practice

There are numerous examples of countries emerging from violent conflict or repression reforming legislation and institutions in the manner called for by Principle 38. Some countries, such as Kenya in 2010 and Tunisia in 2014, have adopted new constitutions.[18] It is more common, however, for countries to enact narrower legislative reforms aimed at specific issues. In Northern Ireland, for example, the peace process and reform of security institutions following the 1998 peace agreement included a review of the 'operation of emergency legislation in a postceasefire context', the 'establishment of a Human Rights Commission charged, inter alia, with providing advice to parliament on the drafting of a Bill of Rights specific to Northern Ireland', and the 'passing of strong equality legislation'.[19] 9

Legislative reform in particular is often recommended by truth commissions, based on their examination of and findings relating to the institutional and legal frameworks that facilitated or allowed human rights violations to occur. In Uganda, for example, the 1986 Commission of Inquiry into Violations of Human Rights may have helped to incorporate a Bill of Rights in the national constitution and to establish the Uganda Human Rights Commission.[20] 10

In Guatemala, the Commission on Historical Clarification in 1999 recommended that the government incorporate the standards of international humanitarian law into 11

[14] A Mayer-Rieckh, 'Dealing with the Past in Security Sector Reform', Geneva Centre for the Democratic Control of Armed Forces (DCAF), SSR Paper 10 (2013).

[15] V Arnould and C Lekha Sriram, 'Pathways of Impact: How Transitional Justice Affects Democratic Institution-Building', Impact of Transitional Justice on Democratic Institution-building (TJDI) Policy Paper 1 (October 2014) 6.

[16] UN, *The rule of law and transitional justice in conflict and post-conflict societies. Report of the Secretary-General*, UN Doc S/2011/634* (12 October 2011) 12 (hereinafter '2011 Report').

[17] Ibid, 12. [18] *Report of the Special Rapporteur*, n 8, 15–18. [19] O'Rawe, n 13, 89.

[20] Arnould and Lekha Sriram, n 15, 6.

national legislation and provide instruction on this law to personnel of state institutions, particularly the military. Moreover, the Commission recommended that the government use legislative measures to 'establish the fundamental bases for the correct relationship between the Army and civil society within a democratic system, and the necessary subordination of the Army to civilian rule', by reforming military legislation (eg, a new military code in accordance with the constitution) and creating new legislation on the state intelligence apparatus (eg, establishing parliamentary control).[21] It also 'elaborated recommendations on inclusion and the protection of indigenous rights, calling for modes of governance that enable individual and collective rights of the indigenous population and encourage their social and political participation'.[22]

12 The Sierra Leone Truth and Reconciliation Commission recommended in 2004 the removal of racist and sexist provisions from the Sierra Leone Citizenship Act of 1973 and the establishment of equitable citizenship in the Constitution—that citizenship be acquired by birth, descent, or naturalization.[23] As the Secretary-General's 2011 report on transitional justice claims, the truth commission process in Sierra Leone 'helped generate momentum for subsequent legislation that enhanced rights and security for women, including by criminalizing domestic violence'.[24]

13 Morocco's Equity and Reconciliation Commission in 2005 recommended consolidating constitutional guarantees of human rights by, among other reforms aimed at preventing the recurrence of abuses, ascribing the primacy of international over domestic law, clarifying basic freedoms and rights, and prohibiting crimes such as forced disappearance, arbitrary detention, genocide, and torture, as well as internationally prohibited discrimination and incitement of racism, hatred, or violence.[25] It also called for legislative reform for 'developing a clear and precise definition of violence against women, in conformity with international law'.[26]

14 The impact of various transitional justice measures on legislative reform is difficult to discern and always debatable. At the same time, legislative change should not be considered an end in itself. As the UN Secretary-General put it:

> Successful legislative reform [*sic*] addressing sexual and gender-based violence, family, property and land tenure issues in Colombia, Nepal, Rwanda and Uganda are potent symbols of national commitment to end violence against women and girls. However, too often the passage of legislation is not followed by implementation. Implementation is more likely when accompanied by a comprehensive policy framework which includes dedicated funding modalities and a national action plan or strategy.[27]

Implementation of legislative reform depends in many ways on both the reform of state institutions, such as those called for in Principle 36, and 'societal interventions',

[21] *Guatemala: Memory of Silence*, Report of the Commission for Historical Clarification, Conclusions and Recommendations (1999) 57, 59–61.

[22] *Report of the Special Rapporteur*, n 8, 16; *Guatemala: Memory of Silence*, n 21, 66.

[23] *Witness to Truth: Final Report of the Sierra Leone Truth and Reconciliation Commission* (2004), vol 2, ch 3: 'Recommendations', paras 82–87; *Report of the Special Rapporteur*, n 8, 15.

[24] 2011 Report, n 16, 12.

[25] Equity and Reconciliation Commission, English Summary of Final Report, 35 <http://www.cndh.org.ma/sites/default/files/documents/rapport_final_mar_eng-3.pdf> accessed 20 January 2018.

[26] Equity and Reconciliation Commission, Final Report, quoted in 'A Window of Opportunity: Making Transitional Justice Work for Women' *UN Women* (October 2012) 14.

[27] 2011 Report, n 16, 12–13.

such as measures of legal empowerment, which seek to help excluded or disadvantaged citizens engage with and make claims on the law and to have access to justice.[28]

E. Critical Assessment

Principle 38 is a good example of moving from a narrow focus on specific measures, such as emergency courts and legislation, to a broader focus on legislative reform to combat impunity. However, because it retains an emphasis on institutions such as emergency courts, there is some lack of clarity about the distinction between the institutional reforms being proposed here and the institutional reforms being discussed in Principle 36. We would argue that the issue of legislative and constitutional reform, broadly speaking, should be the subject of Principle 38, and that it should highlight the importance of such reform from the standpoint of preventing the recurrence of violations and facilitating measures of redress. Constitutions provide the framework within which further legislative reforms and transitional justice measures can be enacted in a context-specific manner. Constitutions can include an explicit mandate to conduct transitional justice, incorporate international legal obligations regarding addressing past abuses, and impose constraints on their implementation such as due process requirements.[29] Constitutions remain, however, an under-examined instrument of transitional justice and guarantees of non-recurrence. 15

Furthermore, despite the appropriate broadening of Principle 38, it still remains more focused on post-authoritarian contexts than post-conflict ones. We have argued that constitutional reform should be included here, but in addition, the Principle should make explicit reference to peace negotiations and agreements. Similarly to constitutions, peace agreements can provide the framework within which the parties to a conflict resolve to manage conflict without violence and reach consensus on fundamental constitutional and institutional matters, and can mandate the establishment of transitional justice mechanisms. 16

Despite the fact, as noted in section C, that legislative reform often addresses gender justice issues such as sexual and gender-based violence and discrimination in land and property arrangements, Principle 38 does not address the gender dimension. When gender is addressed as part of guarantees of non-recurrence, it is reduced to a matter of increasing representation of women, as in Principle 35. In practice, post-conflict and transitional processes often reinforce rather than reduce gender inequalities.[30] 17

Lastly, it needs to be emphasized that legislative reform is not enough in itself, and that the implementation of legislative reforms aimed at preventing the recurrence of violations will depend on the institutional reforms proposed in Principle 36, particularly those to do with accountability in its various forms, such as vetting, impartiality, and oversight. Both 18

[28] See *Report of the Special Rapporteur*, n 8, 19; J O'Connell, 'Empowering the Disadvantaged After Dictatorship and Conflict: Legal Empowerment, Transitions and Transitional Justice' Legal Empowerment Working Papers, Paper no 8, International Development Law Organization (1 November 2009); S Golub, 'What is Legal Empowerment? An Introduction' in S Golub (ed), *Legal Empowerment: Practitioners' Perspectives* (International Development Law Organization 2010) 9–18.

[29] J Mendez, 'Constitutionalism and Transitional Justice' in M Rosenfeld and A Sajo (eds), *The Oxford Handbook of Comparative Constitutional Law* (OUP 2012) 1270–86.

[30] See F Ní Aoláin, D Francesca Haynes, and N Cahn, *On the Frontlines: Gender, War, and the Post-Conflict Process* (OUP 2011) ch 9.

Principle 36 and 38 concern legislative and administrative reforms that seek the protection of human rights and the prevention of the recurrence of violations, and we would argue that it might make sense to merge the two into one focused on state institutional and legislative reform more broadly.

Bibliography

Arnould, V and Lekha Sriram, C, 'Pathways of Impact: How Transitional Justice Affects Democratic Institution-Building', Impact of Transitional Justice on Democratic Institution-building (TJDI) Policy Paper 1 (October 2014).

Golub, S, 'What is Legal Empowerment? An Introduction' in S Golub (ed), *Legal Empowerment: Practitioners' Perspectives* (International Development Law Organization 2010) 9–18.

Mayer-Rieckh, A, 'Dealing with the Past in Security Sector Reform', Geneva Centre for the Democratic Control of Armed Forces (DCAF), SSR Paper 10 (2013).

Mendez, J, 'Constitutionalism and Transitional Justice' in M Rosenfeld and A Sajo (eds), *The Oxford Handbook of Comparative Constitutional Law* (OUP 2012).

Ní Aoláin, F, Francesca Haynes, D, and Cahn, N, *On the Frontlines: Gender, War, and the Post-Conflict Process* (OUP 2011).

O'Connell, J, 'Empowering the Disadvantaged After Dictatorship and Conflict: Legal Empowerment, Transitions and Transitional Justice', Legal Empowerment Working Papers, Paper no 8, International Development Law Organization (1 November 2009).

O'Rawe, M, 'Security System Reform and Identity in Divided Societies: Lessons from Northern Ireland' in P Arthur (ed), *Identities in Transition: Challenges for Transitional Justice in Divided Societies* (CUP 2011).

Index

Note: please see tables of legislation for references to legislation, including conventions.

absolutism 22
accountability
  age of accountability 4, 5, 25
  archives 168, 181, 182, 196, 198, 199
  balance between accountability and other considerations 248
  Belfast Guidelines (2013) 260, 262 n.23, 268, 313 n.37
  conditional amnesties 259, 264, 268, 312
  fairness and accountability 248
  global accountability 4, 5, 19, 20
  impunity as opposite 36
  Individual criminal accountability 36, 44, 89, 90, 210,
  Institutional Reform 394, 397, 408, 411
  non-criminal accountability 27, 33, 99, 124, 127, 148, 151, 168, 181, 182, 207, 248, 394, 403
  obstacles to accountability 249, 271, 272, 279
  state obligations and fair accountability 17
  truth seeking, 124, 127, 148, 151, 153, 154, 158
  victim-oriented perspective 9, 30
  victims' participation 9, 206,
  violations of economic, social and cultural rights 389
ACHR *see* **American Convention on Human Rights (ACHR)**
ACHPR (African Charter on Human and Peoples' Rights) 64, 68, 83–4, 274
ACJHR (African Court of Justice and Human Rights) 206
acknowledgment 29, 33, 73, 84, 93, 103-4, 124, 259, 307-9, 316
ACLU (American Civil Liberties Union) 179
AComHPR (African Commission on Human and Peoples' Rights) 68, 52, 316, 321, 365, 373–4
Additional Protocol I to Geneva Conventions of 1949 59, 63, 208
Additional Protocol II to Geneva Conventions of 1949 210, 261, 310
administration of justice, duties of states with regard to 18, 205–15
Afghanistan
  amnesties 266
  disbanding unofficial armed groups 387, 403
  Disbandment of Illegal Armed Groups Programme 403
Africa *see* **African Union (AU)**
  African Charter on Human and Peoples' Rights (ACHPR) 64, 68, 83–4, 274
  African Commission on Human and Peoples' Rights (AComHPR) 68, 52, 316, 318, 321, 365, 373–4
  African Court of Justice and Human Rights (ACJHR) 206
  family life, right to 84
  Organization of African Unity (OAU) 274
  restitution 373–4
  Specific Aspects of Refugee Problems in Africa Convention 1969 274
  truth, right to the 68
African Union (AU)
  immunity of senior officials 303
  South Sudan, release of report on 157
  regional transitional justice policy 51
  universal jurisdiction 237
aggression, crime of 253, 292–3
Akande, Dapo 303
Algeria
  amnesties 267 n.65, 311
  enforced disappearances, unpublished report of commission on 156
  independence, impartiality, and competence of commissions of inquiry, guarantees of 109
Alston, Philip 139, 141
American Civil Liberties Union (ACLU) 179
American Convention on Human Rights (ACHR) *see also* **Inter-American Court of Human Rights (IACtHR)**
  administration of justice, duties of states with regard to 212
  fair trial, right to a 322
  impunity, definition of 36–7, 39
  justice, access to 83–4
  know, right to 83–4
  life, right to 83–4
  non bis in idem 288 n.57
  prescription, restrictions on 254
  reform of laws and institutions 408
  reparations 338, 343–4, 365, 377
  truth, right to the 64, 66
  victim, definition of 343–4
Amin, Idi 310
amnesties, restrictions and other measures relating to 7, 258–69
  acknowledgment of crimes 259
  Additional Protocol II to Geneva Conventions 310
  alternatives 269
  amnesty, definition of 259
  asylum 309

amnesties, restrictions and other measures relating to (*cont.*):
Belfast Guidelines on Amnesty and Accountability 2013 260, 268–9
blanket or unconditional amnesties 259–63, 267, 306, 308–9, 312
confessions 307
customary international law 262
democratically endorsed amnesties 267
dictatorships, ending 268
disclosure or repentance, restrictions on the effects of 305–12
effective remedy, right to an 262–3
ending of conflicts 259, 266, 268
enforced disappearances 261–2
extradite or prosecute, duty to 262–3
Geneva Conventions of 1949 261, 310
genocide 258, 266
international courts 312–13
international criminal law 264–5
international criminal tribunals 264–5
international humanitarian law 266
investigate, duty to conduct 263–4, 268
Joinet Principles 260
know, right to 263
life, right to 268
limited or conditional amnesties 259, 264, 268–9, 312
Lomé Amnesty of 1999 259, 306–7
national amnesties 305–6, 311–13
national courts 266
pseudo or *de facto* amnesties 259, 262
refuse amnesty, right to 265–6
self-amnesties 259, 266–8, 305
torture 261–2, 264
Amnesty International 28, 158
Annan, Kofi 305–6
anti-impunity agenda 4, 11–13, 20–9
1990s 4, 11
campaign against impunity 27, 28–9
core assumptions 20–1
cosmopolitan ethics 12, 24–5
criticism 20–4
definition 6, 21
disconnectedness critique 21–2, 23
holistic approach 16–17
international law 13–17
legalism critique 6, 21, 22, 23
neglect of economic, social and cultural rights critique 22, 23
apologies
as a form of reparation 17, 373
reintegration 402
memorial practice 73
Arab League Commission, unpublished report on Darfur by 157
Arab Spring 196
Arbour, Louise 60–1, 268
archives 35, 43–4
commissions of inquiry, cooperation with 181–7
cooperation 44, 181–7
definition of 35, 43–4
fact-finding or inquiry missions 43–4
immunity 43
Updated (Orentlicher) Principles 43
archives, measures for facilitating access to 172–9
archives, definition of 163, 165
Basic Principles on the Role of Archivists and Records Managers 173, 174 n.6
best practices 172, 175
code of ethics 173
confidentiality 43–4
courts, cooperation with 181–7
declassification of military and intelligence records 177, 178–9
description of archives, international standard for 175
electronic records 178
historical research, for purposes of 172–3, 175–6
inalienability, archival principle of 199
International Council of Archives (ICA) 173, 175
international organizations 43
Joinet Principles 43
names, specific measures relating to 188–95
non-disclosure, privilege of 43
old regime, specific measures to 196–202
preservation, measures for 163–70
private sector 43
security 172–3, 175–7, 179
special categories of archives 177
truth commissions 43, 69, 84
truth, right to the 59, 61, 65, 69
voluntary disclosure 201
Argentina
amnesties 258–9, 263
archives 181, 200
children born in captivity 371, 374
compensation 375
enforced disappearances 104
identification/naming 124
National Archive of Memory 200
records of military junta, discovery of 177
reporting role of commissions 127–8
resources for commissions, adequacy of 141
third wave transitions 20
truth commissions, establishment of 100–1
Armenian genocide 175
asylum, restrictions on the right to 270–9
accountability 270, 272, 279
amnesties 309
confessions 312
crimes against humanity 270, 273–4, 276–7, 279
crimes against peace 273
criminal justice 270
disclosure or repentance, restrictions on the effects of 305, 309–10, 312

exclusion clauses of refugee law 271, 273–9
extradition 271, 272, 275, 277–8
fair hearing, right to a 275, 277
holistic approach 270
Human Rights Committee (UN) 278
justice, right to 271, 274
non-refoulement 271, 273–5, 279
proportionality 270
Qualification Directive 274
Refugee Convention 1951 270–1, 273–4, 278–9, 309
return 272–3, 278
state sovereignty 271
terrorism 275–7
torture
evidence obtained by torture 278 n.50
Torture Convention 1984 275
treaty-monitoring bodies (UN) 275
UN Declaration on Territorial Asylum 1967 273
universal jurisdiction 309–10
war crimes 270, 273–4, 277, 279
well-founded fear of persecution 273
AU *see* **African Union (AU)**
Auschwitz concentration camp 71
Australia, reparations in 335
***aut dedere aut judicare* principle** *see* **extradite or prosecute, duty to**
authoritarianism 28–9
Al Bashir, Omar 300, 303

Basic Principles and Guidelines on the Right to a Remedy and Reparation *see* **UN Basic Principles and Guidelines on the Right to a Remedy and Reparation**
Bassiouni, Cherif 10, 49, 350
Bay of Pigs incident 176
Belgium 50, 228–9, 238
beneficiaries critique 22–3
Berlin, Isaiah 347
bias *see* **independence and impartiality of judges; independence, impartiality, and competence of commissions of inquiry, guarantees of**
Bloody Sunday Inquiry (Saville), costs of 139
Bodies, recovery of 73, 373, 376, 377
Bolivia 101
Bosnia and Herzegovina
archives, access to 178
Commission for Real Property Claims of Displaced Persons and Refugees 364
Human Rights Chamber (HRCBiH) 66–8, 81
Human Rights Ombudsman 184
judiciary
independence 329
reappointment 396
police, certification of 396
reparations 364
security of tenure 329
UN Mission in Bosnia and Herzegovina 329
vetting 396
war crimes 178
Brazil
amnesties 266
archives, access to 185
Brasil: Nunca Mais report 181
Cold War-era crimes, investigation of 185
compensation 375
enforced disappearances 185
freedom of information 184
military regime 181, 375
reparations 357
burials 75–7, 105, 377
Burundi
fabrication of memories 77
Hutu and Tutsi memories 77
truth and reconciliation commission 77, 102
vetting 396
Bush, George W 316–17

Cambodia
amnesties 211, 262, 312
archives 181, 184–5, 197, 200
crimes against humanity 256
Documentation Center 202
Extraordinary Chambers in the Courts of Cambodia (ECCC) 184–5
amnesties 211, 262, 312
jurisdiction 220
prescription, restrictions on 256
victim participation 211
Khmer Rouge
records 202
secret prison 200
non bis in idem 288 n.59
Tuol Seng Archives 200
victim participation 211
war crimes 256
Campisi, Maria Chiara 74
Canada
archives, access to 185
asylum 276
due obedience 298
indigenous people 101
Truth and Reconciliation Commission 101, 185
Cassese, Antonio 252, 294, 295
CAVR *see* **East Timor Commission for Reception, Truth, and Reconciliation (CAVR)**
Central African Republic (CAR) 92
Central and Eastern Europe
archives 168
authoritarian practices, reparations for 335
European Convention on Human Rights (ECHR) 16
judicial independence 329
lustration 329, 396
non-recurrence, guarantees of 386
state institutions, reform of 392

Central and Eastern Europe (*cont.*):
- state terrorism, reparations for 335
- transitional justice 18
- vetting 396

Chad
- Commission of Inquiry into Ex-President Habré, costs of 139
- identification/naming 123–4
- terms of reference of inquiries 119
- truth commissions 101, 114

Charter of UN 29, 236, 274
Chechnya, enforced disappearances in 184
Child soldiers, reintegration of 54, 383, 386, 387, 388, 399, 400-404
Children, born in captivity 371, 374
Chile
- amnesties 258, 263
- archives 201
- compensation 375
- General Assembly resolution 60
- judiciary 386, 396
- medical and psychological care 376
- Ministry of Foreign Affairs 175
- National Commission for Truth and Reconciliation
  - budget 139, 141
  - establishment 100–1
  - persons implicated, guarantees for 128
  - resources for commissions, adequacy of 141
- reparations 357
- secret police, access to information on 175
- terms of reference, definition of commissions of inquiry's 119
- universal criminal jurisdiction 228

Chomsky, Noam 178
civil and political rights 7–8, 38 *see also* **International Covenant on Civil and Political Rights (ICCPR)**
civil law jurisdictions
- *parties civiles* 205, 210
- victims, interests of 205, 210

civil society
- access to archives
  - Global Principles on National Security and the Right to Information 185
  - Freedom of Information (FOI) Laws 200, 201
- identity of children born in captivity 374
- absence of 92
- consultation 97, 101, 383
- institutional reform, informal oversight 383, 396, 409
- memorialization 72
- participatory involvement in fighting impunity 27, 33
- prevention measures targeted at 397
- reparations procedures, design and implementation 349, 355
- role in shaping UN anti-impunity agenda 7
- security/military sector 410
- truth commissions
  - monitoring of government's implementation of recommendations 148, 150
  - Report Brasil: Nunca Mais 181
  - role in establishment 100, 101
  - role in urging publication of reports 156, 159

Cold War 4, 9, 173
Colombia
- administrative compensation 358
- amnesties 21, 269, 307–8, 311, 313
- Constitutional Court 358
- crimes against humanity 358
- disarmament, demobilization, and reintegration (DDR) efforts 403
- disbanding unofficial armed groups 387, 403
- human rights obligations 70, 90
- FARC 54, 70, 168–9, 269, 366
- General Archives of the Nation Documentary Management Protocol 169
- Havana peace process 269
- holistic approach 92
- imprisonment, mandatory terms of 308
- information, right to 366
- institutions 92
- Justice and Peace Law (975) 269
- know, right to 90
- National Centre of Historical Memory 169
- National Development Plan 358
- *non bis in idem*, restrictions on 287
- paramilitaries 54, 269
- peace agreements 90, 307–8, 311, 313
- pragmatic approach 90
- prioritization of cases according to responsibility 269
- punishment, limits on 305
- reparations 358, 366–7
- sentencing scheme, reduced 54, 269
- truth, right to the 60–1
- Victims and Land Restitution Law 2011 358, 366–7

colonies, cancellation of debt for ex 8
comfort women, reparations for abuse of 335
common law jurisdictions 207, 210
compensation
- administrative programmes 372, 375
- amount 372
- collective compensation 375–6
- judicial approaches 372
- just satisfaction 375
- mass violations 375
- rights and duties arising out of obligation to make reparations 338, 343
- silence or acquiescence, in exchange for 377
- transitional justice 372
- UN Compensation Commission 364, 375
- victims, interests of 212

complementarity principle 206–7, 219, 222, 224
confessions 305, 307–10, 312–13

confidentiality 132, 183
ICRC archiving policies for confidential documents 44
confidentiality guaranteed by truth commissions 129, 132-135, 152-158, 186
access to archives 178, 181, 183
access to files of truth commissions 188, 190
Consultation, public
importance in shaping anti-impunity measures 22
institutional reform 383, 386
memorials 75
reparations procedures 349
truth commissions 42, 97, 98, 99, 101, 102
core rights, trilogy of 26, 29–30, 33 *see also* **justice, right to, know, guarantees to give effect to right to; non-recurrence, general principles on**
corruption 54, 138–9, 148, 175
cosmopolitan ethics 11–17
anti-impunity agenda 12, 24–5
deontological (duty-based) moral theories 12
moral cosmopolitanism 11–12
teleological (goal-based) moral theories 12
universal human rights standards 11–12
Côte d'Ivoire
disarmament, demobilization, and reintegration (DDR) efforts 403
disbanding unofficial armed groups 387, 403
gender equality 102
Security Council commission, unpublished report by 157
truth commissions, establishment of 101–2
Council of Europe Convention on Access to Official Documents 183
courts *see* **jurisdiction of international and internationalized criminal tribunals; military courts, restrictions on the jurisdiction of**
Covarrubias y Leyva, Diego 231–2
Cox, Robert W 23
criminal justice
as a core dimension of the fight against impunity 6, 37, 87, 221
as a means to implement the right to know 33, 89, 90, 92
relationship to truth commissions 111, 120
duty to prosecute 210, 215
interests of justice, ICC 265
asylum 270
confession as a mitigating factor 307
crimes against humanity
customary international law 253 n.18
statutory limitations 254, 255
European Convention on the Non- Applicability of Statutory Limitations to War Crimes and Crime against Humanity 1974 (Council of Europe) 253–4
reparations 336
UN Convention on the Non- Applicability of Statutory Limitations to War Crimes and
universal and international jurisdiction 239
widespread or systematic attack 253 n.18
Croatia, amnesties in 288 n.58
Cruvellier, Thierry 141
Cryer, Robert 293, 300
Cuba 176
culture of impunity, **4, 33, 117, 289**
customary international law
crimes against humanity 253 n.18
enforced disappearances 63
erga omnes obligations 209
extradite or prosecute, duty to 284
general principles of law 62–3
jus cogens 209, 256, 264, 297
opinio juris 62–3, 201, 208–9
sources of law 14
state immunity 293
state practice 14, 62–3
truth, right to the 63
Cyprus
Greek-Cypriots, rights of 68 n.56, 83
missing persons 83
peaceful enjoyment of possessions 68 n.56
private and family life, right to respect for 68 n.56
Turkey 68 n.56, 83

Dachau concentration camp 73
Darfur, Sudan 157
data protection 178, 190, 193
de Greiff, Pablo 2, 183, 187, 345, 372, 378, 386
de Klerk, FW 156
demobilisation *see* **disbandment of parastatal armed forces/demobilization and social reintegration of children**
Democratic Republic of Congo (DRC)
asylum 276
Belgium 228–9
crimes against humanity 300
peace process, political allegiances in 102
ratione personae immunity 300
Truth and Reconciliation Commission 101–2
universal criminal jurisdiction 228–9
vetting 396
war crimes 300
deontological (duty-based) moral theories 12
detention
children born in captivity, identity of 371, 374
incommunicado, persons held 83
long-term/life imprisonment 286–7
mandatory minimum terms of imprisonment 308
prisoners of war and civilian detainees 82
restitution 371, 374
disarmament, demobilization, and reintegration (DDR) efforts 18, 53, 387, 399–405

disbandment of parastatal armed forces/ demobilization and social reintegration of children 399–404
child combatants 399–400, 403–4
Convention on the Rights of the Child 1989 403
definitions 400–1
disarmament, demobilization, and reintegration (DDR) efforts 399, 401–4
Joinet Principles 399–400, 404
non-recurrence, guarantees of 18, 387, 388, 399–404
organized crime 400
paramilitaries 399–403
persons implicated, guarantees for 11
reparations 54
secret links with state structures 400
transitional justice 399–400, 402, 404
women and girls 404
discrimination 395 *see also* **Sub-Commission on Prevention of Discrimination and Protection of Minorities (UN)**
domestic violence 148
Dominican Republic 377
double jeopardy *see* ***non bis in idem*****, restrictions on**
drafting UN Principles to Combat Impunity, history of 6–11
1996 version 10–11
1997 version 10–11
dual track approach 8
endorsement of Principles 9–10
experts on human rights 1, 7–8
four pillar structure of transitional justice 9, 11
hybrid courts 9
Joinet Principles 1, 8–11, 20, 24, 38, 40–1
DRC *see* **Democratic Republic of Congo (DRC)**
Duch (Kang Kek Iew) 200
due obedience (superior orders)
aggression, crime of 292–3
crimes against humanity 291, 298, 301
customary international law 291, 295–6
duress 295
genocide 291, 298, 301
illegality 291, 294–5, 298, 301–2
international crimes 291, 292, 294–5, 298
mistake of fact 295
mistake of law 291, 301–2
war crimes 291, 292–3, 298, 301

East Timor *see* **East Timor Commission for Reception, Truth, and Reconciliation (CAVR)**
crimes against humanity 256
exclusive jurisdiction 256
genocide 256
self-incrimination 120
Special Panels of the Dili District Court 211, 220–1, 292
terms of reference, definition of commissions of inquiry's 117, 121
traditional, customary, or informal mechanisms 53
UN Transitional Administration in East Timor 255–6
war crimes 256
witness protection 132
East Timor Commission for Reception, Truth, and Reconciliation (CAVR)
advisory function 148
Community Reconciliation Processes 53 n.26
confidentiality 132–3
domestic violence 148
establishment 101–2
gender equality 102
reparations 53 n.26
reply, right to 127
resources for commissions, adequacy of 141
traditional local and religious authorities 53 n.26
unpublished reports 156
Victim Support Division 134
Eastern Europe *see* **Central and Eastern Europe**
ECHR *see* **European Convention on Human Rights (ECHR)**
economic, social and cultural rights 7–9
civil and political rights 22, 23, 38
drafting history 22
interpretation 23
Joinet Principles 38
neglect critique 22, 23
truth commissions 66, 142
violations as international crimes 8
ECtHR *see* **European Court of Human Rights (ECtHR)**
Ecuador 101
effective remedy
access to justice 131
amnesty 260, 262, 263, 268
archives 166, 190, 192
commissions of inquiry 136, 137
duty to prosecute 212, 215
fight against impunity 26, 30
Human rights obligations 17, 37
Identification and punishment of those responsible 213, 214
prescription 250-257
publicity 361-368e (Principle 3)
remedial procedures 349-360
right to reparation 49, 338, 342
Egypt
archives 197, 200
National Library and Archives 200
State Security Police HQ, destruction of files at 197
El Salvador
amnesties 263
Commission on the Truth 76, 141, 147
evidence, categories of 126
foreign nationals, appointment of 113
identification/naming 123–4
judiciary 147, 386, 396

non-recurrence, guarantees of 386
paramilitaries, purges of 399–400
parastatal groups 404
peace agreements 393
purification 396
removal from office 393
resources for commissions, adequacy of 141
vetting 396

employment, restitution of 371, 374

enforced disappearances
access to documents 183
administration of justice, duties of states with regard to 208
amnesties 261–2
customary international law 63
Declaration on Enforced Disappearances (UN) 137, 316
definition of 63
Inter-American Convention on Forced Disappearance of Persons 1994 253
International Convention for the Protection of All Persons from Enforced Disappearance 2006 (ICPPED)
access to documents 183
administration of justice, duties of states with regard to 208
amnesties 261–2
know, right to 81–2, 89, 373
military courts, jurisdiction of 316
ratifications and accessions 63
truth, right to the 59, 63
mortal remains 373, 377
prescription, restrictions on 253
prosecute and punish, duty to 209
reparations 373, 377
truth commissions 66, 88

Eritrea
compensation 375
restitution 373–4
witness interviews, confidentiality of 155

ethics *see* **cosmopolitan ethics**

European Convention on Human Rights (ECHR) *see also* **European Court of Human Rights (ECtHR)**
administration of justice, duties of states with regard to 213–14
amnesties 268
effective remedy, right to an 213
equal protection of the law 67
fair hearing, right to a 320–1
inhuman or degrading treatment 67
justice, access to 67
military courts, jurisdiction of 316, 320–1
non bis in idem 283 n.13
non bis in idem, restrictions on 288
private and family life, right to respect for 67
respect and ensure, obligation to 213–14
truth, right to the 67
victims, rights of 213–14

European Court of Human Rights (ECtHR)
administration of justice, duties of states with regard to 213
amnesties 263–4, 268
archives 166, 174–6, 183, 192
asylum 275, 277–8
Chechnya, enforced disappearances in 184
commissions of inquiry 183
extradition 285–6, 289–90
four human rights obligations 16
information, right to 366
inhuman or degrading treatment 286, 289–90
investigate and prosecute, duty to 213–214, 222
know, right to 81, 83
long-term/life imprisonment 286
prescription, restrictions on 254
private and family life, right to respect for 192
rehabilitation 377
reparations, right to 342–342, 366, 375, 377
secrecy claims in Russia 184
truth, right to the 66

European Union
administration of justice, duties of states with regard to 211–12
anti-impunity policy 51
Council of EU 51
crimes against humanity 239
declassification of military and intelligence records 177
European Commission 193
forced migration 239
forgotten, right to be 193
General Data Protection Regulation 193
genocide 239
minimum standards for victims 212
private and family life, right to respect for 67–8
Qualification Directive 274
transitional justice 363
universal and international jurisdiction 237, 239
victim participation 211–12
war crimes 239

exhumations 77

exile 310

extradite or prosecute, duty to 226–7, 231–5
administration of justice, duties of states with regard to 209
customary international law 232–3
Geneva Conventions, grave breaches of 233–5
Hague formula 232
natural law 231–2
presence of suspect on territory 233, 235
refusal of extradition 233
representation principle 232
Torture Convention 232
treaties and conventions 232
universal and international jurisdiction 226–7, 231–5, 236

extradition *see* **extradite or prosecute, duty to; extradition, restrictions on**
extradition, restrictions on 281–90
alternatives 227
bars to extradition 285–7
death penalty 282–4, 285–6, 290
enforced disappearances 286
extrajudicial executions 286
extraterritoriality 285
fair hearing, right to a 285
functionalist approach 289
gross disproportionality test 286
individual-oriented approach 284–5
inhuman or degrading treatment 285–6, 289–90
long-term/life imprisonment 286–7
nationals, non-extradition of 281, 283
non bis in idem 283, 288 n.57
political offence objection 281, 283–4
prosecute, duty to 281, 282–3
refusal to extradite 226, 281, 282, 284
torture and ill-treatment, real risk of 285–6, 299
universal and international jurisdiction 226–7, 229, 231–5, 236
extrajudicial executions 103, 111, 138, 209
extraordinary rendition 199

fact-finding
applicable international standards 111
as a measure for implementing anti-impunity obligations 17, 33
principles of publicity 152, 154
removal of members of fact-finding missions 112
right to truth 65
truth commissions 42, 88
fair trial, right to a
access to archives 173, 182
amnesty 260, 265-266
as a condition for extradition 275, 277, 285
delays in criminal action 251
infringement as an exception to ne bis in idem rule 283
military courts 319-320
fairness, procedural
emergency laws 408, 411
institutional reform 392, 393, 395, 396
military courts 320
ne bis in idem 281-290
reparation procedures 362, 365
truth commissions 114, 123-128, 138, 147, 155, 158
Falk, Richard 347
families
enforced disappearances 60
know, right to 59, 83–4
right to family life 67–8, 83–4, 192
torture or ill-treatment 174 n.10
truth, right to the 67, 174
Federation of Associations of Relatives of Disappeared Detainees (FEDEFAM) 28
Feinberg, Joel 337
First World War 220
forced labour 335
former Yugoslavia *see* **International Criminal Tribunal for the former Yugoslavia (ICTY)**
genocide 6
missing persons 82–3
Srebrenica massacre 229
France
French Revolution 172
information, access to 172
Republic of the Congo 237
universal jurisdiction 237
Franco, Francisco 200, 266
freedom of expression or opinion
amnesties 260, 265
archives 174 n.10
Special Rapporteur 362
freedom of information *see* **information, access to**
Freeman, Mark 124, 127
Frulli, Micaela 303
Fujimori, Alberto 52, 179

Garzón, Baltasar 266
gender
demilitarisation, demobilization, reintegration 404
gender equality 100, 114
gender justice 406, 409, 411
gender representivity in commissions of inquiry 108, 114
gender-based sexual violence 102, 409
gender-sensitive approach 145, 148
Human rights obligations 11, 12, 336
outreach 367
General Assembly (UN)
adoption of UN Principles to Combat Impunity 10
archives 177
asylum, declaration on territorial 309
drafting UN Principles to Combat Impunity 9
enforced disappearances, declaration on 60, 137
know, right to 89–90
prescription, restrictions on 255–6
general obligations of states to take action to combat impunity 36, 47–54
ambiguities and weaknesses 47, 52, 54
amnesties 48, 52
attribution 49
due process 54
expert treaty bodies 48
fair trials 54
four human rights obligations 6, 49, 51–2
gross violations 51–2
holistic approach 50
international humanitarian law (IHL) 49
investigations 48, 50–3
Joinet Principles 47–8
justice, right to 47
national law 47

non-recurrence, guarantees of 50, 53–4
non-state actors 53
private sector 52
prosecute and punish, obligation to 48, 50–4
ratione temporis limitations 50
regional human rights courts 47–8
reparations 48–9, 53
rule of law 48
soft law 47, 52, 54
torture 48, 50
trials 52, 54
truth commissions 52
truth, right to 48, 50, 52
victims, interests of 48, 52
Vienna Declaration 48

general principles of international law 14, 62–3, 205, 215

Geneva Conventions *see* **Additional Protocol I to Geneva Conventions**
administration of justice, duties of states with regard to 208, 210
amnesties 210
families, assistance to 82
grave breaches 235–6, 306
information bureaus, establishment of 82
jurisdiction of international and internationalized criminal tribunals 221, 223
national military manuals 82
Pictet Commentary 235
prescription, restrictions on 254
prisoners of war and civilian detainees 82
transfer of suspects to international or internationalized tribunals 235

genocide
administration of justice, duties of states with regard to 207
Armenian genocide 175
Genocide Convention 220, 221, 223, 237 n.55
Holocaust 71–2, 335, 364, 375
jurisdiction of international and internationalized criminal tribunals 220, 221, 223
reparations 336
universal and international jurisdiction 229 n.13, 237, 239–40

Germany
Allied Occupation zones 374
commissions of inquiry 112, 181
East Germany 168–9, 181, 185–6, 199–200
destruction of documents 197
judiciary 328–9
Stasi archives 168–9, 185–6, 190, 199–200
Federal Restitution Law of 1957 374
forced and slave labour, reparations for 335
Holocaust 71–2, 335, 364, 375
Judiciary, post-World War II
independence of 330
replacement 325
Weimar Republic, judges during 325

Ghana
commissions of inquiry, irremovability of 109
Diaspora Project 134
emotional and psychological support 133

Global Principles on National Security and Right to Information (Tshwane Principles) 185, 186–7

González, Eduardo 139

González Quintana, Antonio 198

Greece
declassification of military and intelligence records 177
dejuntification 396
destruction of records 193
judicial independence 329
Junta period 329, 396
non-recurrence, guarantees of 386
Society of Greek Archivists 193
vetting processes 386, 396

Grotius, Hugo 231

Guantanamo Military Commissions 317, 322

Guarantees of non-recurrence
archival practice 167
disarmament, demobilization and reintegration (DDR) 404
institutional reform 393-397, 406-412
notion of guarantees of non-recurrence, 383-390
relation to reparation 336
truth commissions, 103, 104, 146

Guatemala *see* **Guatemalan Commission for Historical Clarification**
amnesties 263
archives 178, 179, 181, 197, 201–2
death squads, identification of persons seized by 179
Diario Militar 179
enforced disappearances 178
foreign nationals, appointment of 113
Historical Archive of the National Police 202
Human Rights Ombudsman (PDH) 169
judiciary 386, 396
Mayan civilians, massacres of 179
national archives 169
non-recurrence, guarantees of 386
Operation Sofia 179
police archives 169
reform of laws and institutions 387, 406
reparations, publicity for 365
terms of reference, definition of commissions of inquiry

Guatemalan Commission for Historical Clarification 74–6
advisory functions 148
archives, access to 185
confidentiality 132
freedom of information 184
governance 410
indigenous rights 410

Guatemalan Commission for Historical Clarification (*cont.*):
international humanitarian law 409–10
legislative reform 409–10
memory, duty to preserve 74–5
Plan Sanchez Massacre 75
Recovery of Historical Memory Project 66
reparations 74
resources 140–1
training and instruction 409–10
Guissé, El Hadji 7–9, 38

Habré, Hisséne 50, 139, 239
Hague Convention for the Protection of Cultural Property in the Event of Armed Conflict 1954 198–9
Haiti
commission of inquiry reports, publication of copies 157–8
confidentiality 124
gender equality 102
truth commissions, establishment of 101
United States, return of documents by 201
Hall, Christopher Keith 2
Hayner, Priscilla 2, 127
heads of state 4–5, 105, 222, 239, 299, 303
heard, right to be 212
Higgins, Rosalyn 14
High Commissioner of Human Rights *see* **Office of the High Commissioner for Human Rights (OHCHR) (UN)**
historical background *see* **drafting UN Principles to Combat Impunity, history of**
holistic approach 16–17, 87, 92–3, 330, 395
Holocaust 71–2, 335, 364, 375
Holy See 80
HRC *see* **UN Human Rights Council (HRC)**
human remains 69 n.67, 75–7, 105, 373, 377
Human Rights Watch (HRW) 157
Hungary
destruction of archives 193
Historical Archives of the Hungarian State Security 200
security 176
Stasi files 186

IACs *see* **international armed conflicts (IACs)**
IAComHR *see* **Inter-American Commission on Human Rights (IAComHR)**
IACtHR *see* **Inter-American Court of Human Rights (IACtHR)**
ICC *see* **International Criminal Court (ICC)**
ICCPR *see* **International Covenant on Civil and Political Rights (ICCPR)**
ICJ *see* **International Court of Justice (ICJ)**
ICTR *see* **International Criminal Tribunal for Rwanda (ICTR)**
ICTY *see* **International Criminal Tribunal for the former Yugoslavia (ICTY)**
identity
children born in captivity 371, 374
identification techniques 83
restitution 371, 374
ILC *see* **International Law Commission (ILC)**
immunity
heads of state 222
national courts 303
official status 291–4, 298–301, 303
ratione materiae (functional immunity) 291–2, 296–9
ratione personae (personal immunity) 292, 296–7, 299–300, 303
senior officials 222, 303
state immunity 228–9, 240, 293
truth commissions 113–14
impartiality *see* **independence and impartiality of judges; independence, impartiality, and competence of commissions of inquiry, guarantees of**
implicated persons *see* **persons implicated, guarantees for**
impunity, definition of 6, 35–9, 44
consequences of impunity 36
Council of Europe Guidelines 2011 37–8, 39
de facto impunity 36
drafting 36, 38
investigate, obligation to 6, 15, 36–7, 39
Joinet Principles 36, 38–9
opposite of accountability 36
partial impunity 36
reasons for fighting impunity 36
total impunity 36
impunity gap 10, 227, 395
Impunity Watch 52, 77
***in absentia* proceedings** 246
independence *see* **independence and impartiality of judges; independence, impartiality, and competence of commissions of inquiry, guarantees of**
independence and impartiality of judges
appointments 318, 324–6, 330–1
criteria for assessment 324
fair hearing, right to a 320–1
individual independence 324
institutional independence 324, 326
irremovability of judges, principle of 247, 324–6, 329–31
military courts, jurisdiction of 316, 318, 320–1
reform 394, 396
restrictive measures in national legal systems, nature of 247
standards 330
independence, impartiality, and competence of commissions of inquiry, guarantees of 107–15
appointments 109–11, 113–14
composition 108–10
conflicts of interest 108–9

context 108–10
equal representation 113
ethnic bias 114
expertise 108, 114
financial interests 109, 110, 113
foreign nationals, appointment of 113
grades of independence 109
historical context 108–10
individual commissioners, bias of 113
irremovability 108–9, 112
Joinet Principles 107–10, 112
judicial review 114
oaths 113
penalties for misbehaviour 110
practice 112–14
privileges and immunities 110
procedural fairness 114
recusal 113
regional balance 114
removal of commissioners 108–9, 112
retired judges, appointment of 113
indigenous people
reparations 335
transitional justice 53–4
truth commissions, establishment of 101
individual criminal responsibility 36–7, 90, 206
information, access to *see* **archives**
Convention on Access to Official Documents 183
information bureaus, establishment of 82
reparation procedures, publicizing 366
inhuman or degrading treatment 67, 81 n.19, 286, 289–90
Inter-American Court of Human Rights (IACtHR)
administration of justice, duties of states with regard to 212–13
amnesties 263, 311
anti-impunity agenda 16
archives 165–6, 173–4, 176, 183, 184–5
commissions of inquiry 173–4, 176
cosmopolitan ethics 13
employment, restitution of 374
enforced disappearances 83, 212–13
extrajudicial executions 212–13
four human rights obligations 16–17
general obligations of states 48, 51–2
impunity, definition of 16
investigate, duty to 83
jurisdiction 222
mortal remains 377
non bis in idem 287–8
non-recurrence, guarantees of 16
prescription, restrictions on 254
prosecute and punish, right to 16
reform of laws and institutions 408
rehabilitation 376–7
reparations 338, 343, 346, 356–7, 365, 376–7
restitution 374
torture 212–13
truth commissions 68
victim, definition of 343
International Center for Transitional Justice (ICTJ) 93, 154
Inter-American Commission on Human Rights (IAComHR)
fair hearing, right to a 322
reparation procedures, publicizing 365
International Commission of Jurists (ICJ) 28
International Commission on Missing Persons (ICMP) 82–3
International Conference of the Round Table on Archives 198
International Council on Archives (ICA) 164, 173–5
Basic Principles on the Role of Archivists and Records Managers 167, 173, 174 n.6, 191
code of ethics 173
description of archives, international standard for 175
names, specific measures relating to 191, 193
national archives law, principles for 173
open source software for description 175
Principles of Access to Archives 173–4
Technical Guidance on Managing Archives with Restrictions 173, 193
UNESCO-funded study on archives of security service 173
International Court of Justice (ICJ)
administration of justice, duties of states with regard to 207, 208–9
anti-impunity 13–14
extradite or prosecute, duty to 284
general obligations of states 47, 50
general principles of law 62
head of state immunity 222
immunity 222, 246
jurisdiction 220, 222
official status 298–300
opinio juris 62
reparations 370
restrictive measures in national legal systems, nature of 246
state practice 62
Statute 13–14, 62, 207, 208–9
universal and international jurisdiction 228–9, 237
International Covenant on Civil and Political Rights (ICCPR)
archives 174 n.10, 181, 183
asylum 278, 309
compensation, right to 338
duty to investigate 263
disclosure exemptions 181
effective remedy, right to an 137
extradition, bars to 285
justice, access to 67
know, right to 64, 83
military jurisdiction, 315
ne bis in idem 222
prescription, restrictions on 254

International Covenant on Civil and Political Rights (ICCPR) (*cont.*):
public information, access to 362, 365
reform of laws and institutions 407
reparations 338, 342, 362, 365
truth, right to the 64, 66–7
International Covenant on Economic, Social and Cultural Rights (ICESCR) 8, 66 n.49 see **economic, social and cultural rights**
international crimes *see* **crimes against humanity; genocide; war crimes**
core international crimes 207, 215
jurisdiction of international and internationalized criminal tribunals 219–23
serious crimes under international law, list of 206
victims, interests of 205
International Criminal Court (ICC)
administration of justice, duties of states with regard to 205–7, 210–11, 215
aggression, crime of 292–3
amnesties 258, 264–6, 267, 306, 313
Assembly of States Parties 211, 313
complementarity principle 206–7, 222, 224
core crimes 336
cosmopolitanism 12
ne bis in idem 283
duty to prosecute 207, 208, 209
fight against impunity 206,
immunity 300, 301
jurisdiction 220–4, 287
national security 184, 206–10, 215
statute of limitations, restrictions on 253–6
reparations 341, 344–5, 357
due obedience 292–3, 295, 301
Rules of Procedure and Evidence (RPE) 184, 206, 364
superior responsibility 293, 302
Trust Fund for Victims 211, 341, 357
Truth commissions, coordination with 121, 132
universal and international jurisdiction 235
victims' rights to participation 69, 85, 205, 210
war crimes 40, 292–3, 336
witness protection 131, 132–3
International Criminal Tribunal for Rwanda (ICTR)
amnesties, prohibition of 306
archival materials, access 69, 184
documentary evidence 69
due obedience 292
guilty plea 69
head of state immunity 222
jurisdiction 220, 222–4
national courts, transfer to 224
obligation to judge or surrender, 236
primacy 222
superior responsibility 293
transfer of suspects to international or internationalized tribunals 236
universal and international jurisdiction 236, 239
victim participation 206, 211
International Criminal Tribunal for the former Yugoslavia (ICTY)
administration of justice, duties of states with regard to 206
amnesties 306, 312
cooperation by states 229
documentary evidence 69, 184
due obedience 292
immunity 299
national courts, transfer to 224
national security 184
primacy 222
prescription, restrictions on 256
Security Council resolution 312
superior responsibility 293, 296, 302–3
torture, jus cogens character of 256
transfer of suspects to international or internationalized tribunals 236
universal and international jurisdiction 229, 236, 239
victims, role of 69, 206
international humanitarian law *see* **Geneva Conventions**
individual criminal responsibility 39–40
know, right to 59, 63
serious violations 39–40
International Labour Organization (ILO) Commission of Inquiry 111
international law *see* **customary international law; serious crimes under international law**
anti-impunity agenda 13–17
codification 15
cosmopolitan ethics 13
existing international law, extent UN Principles reflect 15
general principles of international law 14, 62–3, 205, 215
interpretation 14–15
lex lata 14
policy-science approach 14
process-based view 14–15
respecting and ensuring human rights guarantees 16
social and political considerations 14
soft law 1, 14–15
sources of law 13–14
International Law Commission (ILC)
Articles on State Responsibility 48, 336, 339, 401
Draft Code of Crimes against the Peace and Security of Mankind 1996 254
transfer of suspects to international or internationalized tribunals 235
International Organization of Migration (IOM) 366
international organizations, definition of 35, 44
International Tracing Service (ITC) 182, 200–1
Internationalized or hybrid courts
amnesty 258, 264,
as an alternative for states to implement their duty to prosecute or extradite 227, 229, 235

emergence 9
Notion 220-221
victims' rights 211
Internet 186
intimidation of witnesses 154
investigate, duty to
effectiveness, definition of 263
enforced disappearances 60, 83
investigative mechanisms, definition of 35, 44
Iran 64 n.39
Iraq
Ba'athist records taken by United States, return of 201
Coalition Provisional Authority 330, 396
de-Baathification 329, 396
insurgency 396
judiciary
de-Baathification criteria 329
independence, abolition of 329–30
Kuwait, invasion of 364, 375
National Library and Archives 197, 201
UN Compensation Commission 364, 375
United States-led invasion 197, 201
Ireland
Constitution 320
Special Criminal Court 320
terrorism 320
irremovability of judges, restrictions on principle of 324–31
Israel 365
Ivory Coast *see* **Côte d'Ivoire**

Japan
comfort women, reparations for abuse of 335
Korea, abuse of comfort women in 335
Philippines, abuse of comfort women in 335
Japanese Americans, internment of 375
Joinet Principles 1, 5, 7–11, 24
definition of 34, 35, 44
judiciary *see* **independence and impartiality of judges**
compensation 372
irremovability, restrictions on principle of 324–31
reform 147, 394, 396
jurisdiction *see* **jurisdiction of international and internationalized criminal tribunals; military courts, restrictions on the jurisdiction of; universal and international jurisdiction, measures for strengthening effectiveness of**
jurisdiction of international and internationalized criminal tribunals 219–24
jus cogens 209, 256, 264, 297
justice *see* **administration of justice, duties of states with regard to; justice, right to**
justice, right to 8, 18
Declaration of Basic Principles of Justice for Victims of Crime and Abuse of Power (UN) 340
know, right to 83–4
missing persons 83–4
prosecute and punish, obligation to 12
reparations 30
truth, right to the 67
victims, interests of 210
Justinian Code 239

Kant, Immanuel 4, 11
Karadžić, Radovan 229, 312
Kenya
confidentiality 132
constitution 387, 409
gender equality 102
ICC, jurisdiction of 287
judges, magistrates, and police, vetting of 396
non-recurrence, guarantees of 386
Truth, Justice and Reconciliation Commission (TJRC) 101, 113–14, 127, 132
establishment 101
expertise 114
notification 127
vetting 396
women 114
King Jr, Martin Luther 189
know, guarantees to give effect to right to 87–93
know, victims' right to 18, 30, 79–85
Additional Protocol I to Geneva Conventions 79–80
archives 18, 163–171, 190
Catholic priests, children fathered by 85
children 81, 85
commissions of inquiry 18
customary status 63
dead persons 80
detainees 79–80, 83
guarantees to give effect to 87–94
enforced disappearances 81–3
families 79–81, 83–5
Geneva Conventions 82
human rights mechanisms 82
information, access to 84
international criminal justice mechanisms 82, 85
international organization 82–3, 85
ICRC 82
Joinet Principles 80–1
justice, right to 81, 83–4
memory, duty to preserve 71, 74
missing persons 80–5
non-recurrence, guarantees of 81
privacy, protection 191
scope 81
truth commissions 84
truth, right to the 79–81, 83, 85
Kohl, Helmut 185–6
Kok, Ruth A 255
Korea
comfort women, reparations for abuse of 335
South Korea 102, 109, 197

Koskenniemi, Martti 348
Kundera, Milan 188
Kuwait, Iraq's invasion of 364, 375
Kwoyelo, Thomas 267
Kyrgyzstan, national commission in 158

Latin America
archives 173, 176–7, 186
authoritarianism 28, 335
commissions of inquiry 173, 176–7
Communist era 255
disbanding unofficial armed groups 388
enforced disappearances 117
four human rights obligations 52
habeas data 190
Inter-American Convention on Forced Disappearance of Persons 1994 253
military juntas 255
national courts 176–7
national security 176–7
NGOs 28
Operation Condor 199
parastatal groups 404
prosecute and punish, duty to 54
reparations 335
Second World War 255
state institutions, reform of 392
terrorism, reparations for state 335
transitional justice 11, 18, 91
truth commissions 88
Latvia 200
Lebanon 109, 211, 293
legal services 373
legalism critique 6, 21, 22, 23
legality, principle of 62, 251, 254–5, 315
legislation *see* **reform of laws and institutions contributing to impunity**
Letschert, Rianne 372
Liberia
advisory functions of the truth commission 145
child combatants 387, 403
emotional and psychological support 134
gender equality 102
identification/naming 123–4
non-recurrence, guarantees of 386
police, vetting of 396
resources for commissions, adequacy of 141
truth commissions 101–2, 133–4
vetting 396
Libya
amnesties 266, 313
archives 200
life, right to 83–4, 222, 268
Lillich, Richard 62–3
limitation periods *see* **prescription, restrictions on**
Local ownership
informal processes 87, 93
justice from above critique 21
limits of local discretion 3, 25
localizing transitional justice 100
project of Communal reckoning 2, 24
reparations 149, 364, 365, 366
truth commissions 141, 148, 154
Lubanga, Thomas 344

Macedonia 377
Malaysian Airlines flight MH 370, disappearance of 85
Mallinder, Louise 266
Mamdani, Mahmood 22–3
Manning, Bradley (Chelsea) 179
mass claims
compensation 375
international processes 363–4
reparations 372, 375
Mauritius 109, 113–14
media 105, 397
medical and psychological care 373, 376
medieval Italian and German cities 239
memorialization see **memory, duty to preserve**
memory, duty to preserve 71–7
apologies and acknowledgment of facts 73
archives 71
best practices 77
bodies, recovery of 73
case law 74–5
collective dimension of memory 71–2, 75, 76–7
commemorations and tributes to victim 73, 76–7
complexity 71
enforced disappearances 73
ethnic division 77
fabrication of memories 77
global rush to commemorate 71–2
history textbooks, development of 73
Holocaust 71–2
identities, shaping 77
international crimes 71
international law 72
internet 186
Joinet Principles 72
judicial processes 75
know, right to 12, 71
memorials, construction of 73, 74–5, 76
non-recurrence, guarantees of 73
ranking of legitimacy amongst victims 76
recognition, acts of 72–3, 75
reparations 71–7
satisfaction 48–9, 71–7, 373, 377
symbolism 73–4, 75–7
truth and reconciliation commissions 73–4, 75–7
UN Reparation Principles 73
victims, interests of 72–3, 75–6
Méndez, Juan 49
Merkel, Angela 71
Meron, Theodor 62
Mexico
archives 200

freedom of information 184
Zetas drug cartel, files relating to massacre by 184
military courts, restrictions on the jurisdiction of 315–22
amnesties 316
arrest and detention 320
breach of Principle, list of matters amounting to 318
civilian courts distinguished 317
commissions 316–19
criminal offences 315–22
courts-martial 317
definitions 317
due process 318, 319–20
enforced disappearances 315–16
equality before the law 315, 318
fair hearing, right to a 315, 319–22
functionality principle 315
independence and impartiality 315–16, 318, 320–1
Joinet Principles 316
judiciary 320–1
appointments mechanism 318
independence and impartiality 320–1
military and non-military judges 320–1
jurisdiction 315–16, 318–20
legality, principle of 315
military government courts 317
national security 320–1
provisional courts 317
provost courts 317
rule of law 317–19
state practice 316
symbolism, as part of institutional reform 322
terrorism 320–2
treaty bodies 316
military manuals 82
Milošević, Slobodan 4–5, 299
minorities *see* **Sub-Commission on Prevention of Discrimination and Protection of Minorities (UN)**
missing persons 80–5, 91, 104
identification techniques 83
justice, access to 83–4
national governments, work of 83
natural disasters 83
notification requirements 84
Mladić, Ratko 229
Morocco
CCDH (national human rights commission) 149
Community Reparation Program 149
discrimination 410
domestic violence 410
emotional and psychological support 133–4
Equity and Reconciliation Commission 105, 133–4, 149, 410
gender equality 102
medical and psychological care 376
reform of laws and institutions 387, 406, 410
mortal remains 69 n.67, 75–7, 105, 373, 377
Mothers and Grandmothers of the Plaza de Mayo 28
Moyn, Samuel 4
Mozambique
child combatants 387, 403
peace agreement between Felimo and Renamo 266
multinational corporations (MNCs) 23, 345
mutual legal assistance treaties (MLATs) 199

naming and shaming 12–13
national security
archives, withholding files from 199
civil society 185, 186–7
confidentiality 152–4, 156
identification/naming 124
Open Society Justice Initiative 185, 186–7
Tshwane Principles 185, 186–7
vetting 394, 395
Naqvi, Yasmin Q 289
Nepal 101–2, 396
Netherlands 52
New Zealand, reparations in 335
next of kin, definition of 344
NIACs *see* **non-international armed conflicts (NIACs)**
Nicaragua 376
Nigeria
military courts, jurisdiction of 321
truth commission, report of 156
***non bis in idem*, restrictions on** 281–5
amnesties 287–8
due process 288
extradition 283
fair hearing, right to a 283
in absentia proceedings 288–9
individual-oriented approach 284–5
Joinet Principles 282, 288–9
jurisdiction 287
limitations 287–9
non bis in idem 288
partisan justice 283
prosecute and punish, duty to 287–8
rule of law 282
sham or shield trials 281, 282–3, 287–8
state sovereignty 287, 288–9
non-governmental organisations (NGOs)
anti-impunity campaign 28
archives 43
definition 35, 44
guidance 35
non-international armed conflicts (NIACs)
know, right to 80, 82
military courts, jurisdiction of 319
war crimes 39–40, 310
non-recurrence, general principles on 9, 383–90 *see* **guarantees of non-recurrence**
non-state actors 23, 39, 53

Northern Ireland
emergency legislation, review of 387, 409
equality legislation, passing of 409
Human Rights Commission, establishment of 409
non-recurrence, guarantees of 387
peace agreement 1998 387, 409
reform of laws and institutions 406
Saville Inquiry (Bloody Sunday), costs of 139
security institutions, reform of 409
Nowak, Manfred 376
Nuremberg Military Tribunal (NMT)
archives 181
Charter 293
due obedience 292, 295, 297
jurisdiction 220
superior responsibility 293

OAS (Organization of American States) 61, 166, 362
OAU (Organization of African Unity) 274
Office of the High Commissioner for Human Rights (OHCHR) (UN)
archives 166–7, 177, 183, 197, 198
asylum 276
good practices, collection of information on 177
reparation procedures, publicizing 363, 367
Rule-of-Law Tool for Post-Conflict States 166–7, 174–5
truth commissions, establishment of 100
truth, right to the 64
official status, restrictions on justifications related to
ad hoc tribunals 299
customary international law 299–300, 303
immunity 291–4, 298–301, 303
jus cogens 297
punish, duty to 296
senior officials 299–300, 303
sovereign equality of states 293, 296–7
state immunity 293
state practice 299–300
state sovereignty 293
officials *see* **state officials**
Open Society Justice Initiative 185, 186–7
open source software 175
opinio juris 62–3, 201, 208–9
Orentlicher, Diane 1, 5, 9–11, 20, 21–2, 24–5, 28
Organization of African Unity (OAU) 274
Organization of American States (OAS) 61, 166, 362
outreach, public see also **publicizing the commissions' reports**
truth commissions 104, 140, 145, 152-159
reparation programmes 357, 361-368

Palestine, Wall in the Occupied Territory 220
Panama 201, 374
Paraguay, archives in 165–6, 182, 200
paramilitary groups, disbanding 11
parastatal armed forces see **disbandment of parastatal armed forces/demobilization and social reintegration of children**
peace
amnesty 21, 259, 266, 268
Kant, Immanuel 4, 11
fight against impunity 21
ICC, interests of justice 265
justice and peace 21, 206, 209, 267, 311
peace agreements and negotiations 51, 52, 157, 258, 406, 411
peacebuilding 51, 87, 93, 146, 387, 402
relation to fight against impunity 245, 248
relation to individual right to remedies 359
restoration of or transition to peace 28-29, 40-41, 196-202
spoilers 402
transition from armed conflict 17, 18
Peace Agreements
Central African Republic 92
Colombia 90, 169, 269, 305, 307, 308, 311, 313
El Salvador 393
Mozambique 266
Northern Ireland 387
Sierra Leone 266, 306
Permanent Court of International Justice (PCIJ) 220, 336, 370, 371
personal immunity 292, 296–7, 299–300, 303
persons implicated, guarantees for 123–8
Peru *see* **Peruvian Truth and Reconciliation Commission**
amnesties 264
apologies 377
archives, access to 178–9, 185
classified information 184
Comprehensive Reparation Programme (PIR) 357
confidentiality 124
Constitution 321–2
damages 358
discrimination, marginalization, or vulnerability, structural patterns of 357
employment, restitution of 374
enforced disappearances 52
extrajudicial killings 52
fair hearing, right to a 321–2
freedom of information 184
general obligations of states 52
Human Rights Ombudsman 184
medical and psychological care 376
military courts, jurisdiction of 321–2
persons implicated, guarantees for 128
prison standards 374
rehabilitation 377
reparations 357, 377
terrorism 321
United States archives, access to declassified 179
Peruvian Truth and Reconciliation Commission
burial sites, discovery of 105
corruption, funds derived from 141
establishment 101–2
funding 141–2
gender equality 102

persons implicated, guarantees for 128
public hearings 105
reparations 358
staff salaries, disclosure of 142
transparency 142
witness protection 132
Philippines, abuse of comfort women in 335
Pinochet, Augusto 4–5, 228, 238, 266–7, 299
Pol Pot 197
Poland 311
Portugal, amnesties in 311
prescription, restrictions on 250–7
abuse of process 255
accused, rights of 256–7
civil law countries 250–1, 255
common law countries 255
continuing crimes 250
crimes against humanity 250–6
customary international law 250–1, 253, 256
definitions 251
effective remedy, right to an 252
enforced disappearances 253–4
European Convention on the Non- Applicability of Statutory Limitations to War Crimes and Crime against Humanity 1974 (Council of Europe) 253–4
Inter-American Convention on Forced Disappearance of Persons 1994 253
Joinet Principles 251
legality, principle of 251, 254–5
purpose 251
reparations 250, 252
serious international crimes, definition of 251
torture 254, 256
UN Convention on the Non- Applicability of Statutory Limitations to War Crimes and
prisoners of war 82
privacy
archive departments and the courts and non-judicial commissions of inquiry, cooperation between 181–3, 185–7
confidentiality 183
definition 186–7
right to respect for family and private life 67–8, 192
truth, right to the 185–6
victims 186
witnesses 186
proportionality, principle of 209, 213, 286
prosecute and punish, duty to
administration of justice, duties of states with regard to 206, 207–9, 215
decisions not to prosecute, review of 212
flexibility, degree of 54
general obligations of states 48, 50–4
justice, right to 12
national laws 206
political approval or authorization 223
prosecution *see* **extradite or prosecute, duty to; prosecute and punish, duty to**
protected persons, identification of 80 n.6
psychological and medical care 133–4, 373, 376
public officials *see* **state officials**
publicity *see* **publicizing the commissions' reports; reparation procedures, publicizing**
publicizing the commissions' reports 152–9
accountability 152, 153, 158
anonymity 155
censorship 152, 158
civil society 156, 159
commissioners, interference with 152
confidentiality 152–6, 158
culture 152, 154
final reports
access 152
fact-finding guidelines 154
full publication and wide dissemination 154, 156–8
investigations 153
Joinet Principles 152
know, right to 153
language 154, 158
mandating authorities, responsibility of 154, 156, 159
media 154
memory, duty to preserve 153
methods of dissemination 154, 157
national security 154, 156, 158
online publication 158
procedural fairness 158
recommendations, implementation of 154
security reasons for confidentiality 152–4, 156, 158
terms of reference 155
transparency 158
punishment *see* **prosecute and punish, duty to; sentencing**

rape, definition of 62
reconciliation
amnesty 41, 264, 305, 307, 310, 312
archives 198
community-based, local approaches 53, 90
forgiveness 28, 29
memorialization 73, 74, 75, 77
relation to fight against impunity 10, 12, 24, 29, 33, 246, 248
reparations 359
truth commissions 74, 75, 76, 77, 103, 104, 105, 146, 152, 153
recurrence *see* **non-recurrence, general principles on; guarantees of non-recurrence**
Red Cross, Committee of the
amnesties 261, 262 n.22, 308–9
confidentiality 43
customary international law 262 n.22
know, right to 82

Red Cross, Committee of the (*cont.*):
missing persons 82
transfer of suspects to international or internationalized tribunals 235
redaction of court documents 185–6, 191
reform *see* **reform of laws and institutions contributing to impunity; state institutions,**
reform of laws and institutions contributing to impunity 17–18, 36, 406–12
accountability 23, 408–9, 411
civil society 409
complementary nature 406
constitutional reforms 408–9, 411
criminal law 408
discrimination 409, 411
emergency courts 411
emergency laws 408
gender justice 409, 411
governance 410
habeas corpus 407
Joinet Principles 406–7
military court jurisdiction 408
national security 407
non-recurrence, guarantees of 406–12
preparatory reports 408
rule of law 407
security sector 409
societal interventions 410–11
special courts 406–7
truth commissions 406, 409
vetting 17, 409
World Conference on Human Right 407
Refugee Convention 1951 270–1, 273–4, 278–9
Protocol 1967 273
reservations 273
rehabilitation
apologies 377
centres 376
collective psychological care 376
legal services 373
medical and psychological care 133–4, 373, 376
social services 373
torture 376
reintegration *see* **disbandment of parastatal armed forces/demobilization and social reintegration of children**
remembrance *see* **memory, duty to preserve**
reparation, right to
access remedial procedures, right to 352–3
access to international and regional procedures 351, 355–6
administrative measures 352, 354, 357–9
best practices 355, 357, 359
claim rights 337
collective reparation 357
compensation/damages 357–8
complementary programmes 354, 357–9
disciplinary measures 352
discrimination, structural 359
effective remedy, right to an 349–50, 352–6, 359
equality between victims 354
erga omnes obligations 358–9
exhaustion of local remedies 355
funding 354
general obligations of states 48–9, 53
human right treaties 337–9
Joinet Principles 350–2
judicial proceedings 352–4, 356–9
mass violations 353–4
national programmes 351, 353–5
objects of international law, individuals as 350
perpetrator, seeking redress from 344–5
prompt and effective procedures 349, 351
regional procedures 351, 355–6
reprisals 353
respect-and-ensure provisions in treaties 339
solidarity, positive duty of 358–9
standard of proof 353
standards 349–50, 353–4, 359
Trust Fund (ICC) 357
whose rights and duties 340–1
reparation procedures, publicizing 361–7
outreach campaigns 361–7
procedural fairness 362, 365
state-held information, right to receive 365
transitional justice 363
transparency 365
truth commissions 361
UN guidelines and principles 363
reparation, rights and duties arising out of obligation to make 9, 335–48 *see also* **reparation, right to; reparation, scope of right to**
reparation, scope of right to 369–78
compensation 369, 371–2, 375–7
comprehensiveness 369, 378
customary international law 370
rehabilitation and satisfaction 369, 373, 376
restitution 369, 371, 373–4
satisfaction 373, 376–7
UN Basic Principles and Guidelines 369–73
reparations *see* **reparation procedure and programmes; reparation, rights and duties arising out of obligation to make; UN Basic Principles and Guidelines on the Right to a Remedy and Reparation repentance** *see* **disclosure or repentance, restrictions on the effects of reprisals**155
Republic of the Congo 237
resources for commissions, adequacy of 136–42
autonomy 137
best practice 136
budget 136, 138–41
corruption 138–9
funding from donors 136
funding principles 138
impact of inadequate resources 140–1
independence 137–8
international assistance 141

investigations 136, 140
salaries 140, 142
sources of funding 141–2
state funding 141–2
transparency 142
UN Manual on the Effective Prevention and Investigation of Extra- Legal, Arbitrary and Summary Executions 138
Responsibility to Protect (RP2) 390
restitution of assets 259, 369, 371, 373–4
restitution of identity 374
restoration of or transition to democracy and/or peace, definition of 40–1, 44
restorative justice 27, 33, 69, 309
restrictive measures in national legal systems, nature of 36, 245–57
amnesties 245, 247, 248
asylum, right to 245, 247, 248
civil proceedings 247
criminal proceedings 245–7
due obedience 245
extradition 245, 247
immunity 247
in absentia proceedings 246
jurisdictional immunities 247
military courts, jurisdiction of 245, 247, 248
mitigation 247
non bis in idem 245–6, 247
official immunities 245–6
prescription 245, 247, 248
reconciliation 245
repentance 245, 247
superior orders 247
Rikhof, Joseph 276
Romania
confiscation, compensation for property 175
Property Restitution Agency 175
Revolution 1990, deaths during 192 n.14
Roth, Ken 266–7
rule of law see also fairness, procedural
amnesty 313
fight against impunity 7, 18, 48
institutional reforms 383, 384, 386, 387, 392, 393, 407
Judicial independence 324, 326, 329
justice, right to 18
military courts 317, 318, 319,
notion 319, 322
reparations 30
Rule-of-Law Tool for Post-Conflict States. OHCHR 166–7, 174–5
transitional justice 89
rules and principles, difference between 24 n.102
Russia
archives 200
Katyn massacre 183
Second World War 201
security 176
trophy archives, return of 201
Rwanda *see* **International Criminal Tribunal for Rwanda (ICTR)**
Gacaca courts 53 n.26
genocide 6, 278
traditional, customary, or informal mechanisms 53

Sandoz, Yves 80
Sarajevo, siege of 229
satisfaction 48–9, 71–7, 373, 377
Saville Inquiry (Bloody Sunday), costs of 139
Schabas, William A 301
scholarships, establishment of 74
SCSL *see* **Special Court for Sierra Leone (SCSL)**
Second World War
amnesties 260
archives 164
disclosure or repentance, restrictions on the effects of 306
jurisdiction of international and internationalized criminal tribunals 220
judges, irremovability of 325
prescription, restrictions on 251, 255
trophy archives, return of 201
Secretary-General (UN)
non-judicial processes 89
transitional justice 27–8, 408–10
truth commissions, establishment of 99–100
Security Council (UN)
amnesties 265–6
asylum 276
disclosure or repentance, restrictions on the effects of 306
jurisdiction of international and internationalized criminal tribunals 220, 222
Right to Truth Day (24 March 2011) 61
transfer of suspects to international or internationalized tribunals 236
universal and international jurisdiction 239
Security Sector
civilian oversight 388, 394, 396
reform 17, 387
Senegal 50, 239
senior officials 65, 228, 299–300, 303
sentencing
proportionality 213
prosecute and punish, duty to 54
reduction 305, 307–9
serious crimes under international law 34–5, 39–40, 44
crimes against humanity 40
criminalization 40
definitions 18, 34–5, 39–40, 44, 221, 251
developments in international law 35, 40
enforced disappearances 40
extrajudicial executions 40
genocide 40

serious crimes under international law (*cont.*):
individual criminal responsibility 39–40
investigate, prosecute, and punish, obligation to 39
Joinet Principles 39–40
list of serious crimes 206
servitude 40
slavery 40
torture 40
war crimes 39–40
sexual violence 62, 132
Shaheed, Farida 77
Shklar, Judith 6, 22
Sierra Leone *see* **Sierra Leone Truth and Reconciliation Commission (TRC); Special Court for Sierra Leone (SCSL)**
amnesties 306
child combatants 387, 403
foreign nationals, appointment of 113
judiciary 386, 396
legislative reform 387
National Commission for Social Action 366
non-recurrence, guarantees of 386
outreach 366
pre-listed violations 356 n.38
reform of laws and institutions 406
reparations 366
terms of reference, definition of commissions of inquiry's 117, 119, 121
victims' register 356 n.38
Sierra Leone Truth and Reconciliation Commission (TRC)
advisory functions 148, 150
amnesties 305–6, 308–9, 312–13
budget 140–1
children, rights of 148
citizenship law, reform of 410
civil society 148
confessions 305, 308, 310–11
confidentiality 132–3
Constitutional Court 310
corroboration 126
corruption prosecutions 148–9
disclosure or repentance, restrictions on the effects of 308–13
domestic violence, criminalizing 410
enforced disappearances 104
establishment 101–2
gender equality 102, 410
Human Rights Commission (HRC), recommendation for establishment of 148
legislative reform 410
memory, duty to preserve 74, 75–6
monitoring mechanisms, matrix for 148
National Reconciliation Day 75
National War Memorial 75
persons implicated, guarantees for 128
public participation 101
racism 410
recommendations 145, 150
Red Cross 308–9
resources 140–1
SCSL 132
staff 141
symbolic reparations 75–6
UN Integrated Office in Sierra Leone (UNIOSIL) 148
victims, interests of 75–6, 311
war crimes 308–9
witnesses, anonymity of 155
women 148
slavery 208–9, 335
Slovakia, Stasi files in 186
Slovenia
administrative procedure for reparations 357–8
Compensation Act 357–8
Human Rights Ombudsman 184
Snowden, Edward 179, 194
social media 397
social reintegration *see* **disbandment of parastatal armed forces/demobilization and social reintegration of children**
social services 373
socio-economic justice 53–4
soft law
legal nature of UN Principles to Combat Impunity 1, 14, 15, 52
administration of justice, duties of states with regard to 209–10
archives 167, 191
independence of military jurisdiction 316
opinio juris 209
Solis, Gary D 317
Solomon Islands Truth and Reconciliation Commission
budget 140
foreign nationals 140
gender-based and sexual violence 102–3
immunity 113–14
unpublished reports 156
South Africa *see* **South African Truth and Reconciliation Commission (TRC)**
amnesties 258, 265
archives 197
authoritarian practices, reparations for 335
commissions of inquiry, irremovability of 109
ICC
amnesties 265
implementation of Rome Statute of 300–1
judiciary
apartheid-era judiciary 328
conservativeness and positivism 328
representativeness 328
official status 300–1
state terrorism, reparations for 335
women, access to resources of 357 n.49

South African Truth and Reconciliation Commission (TRC)
advisory functions 149
amnesties 259
archives 185, 200
audit commission 139
beneficiaries critique 22–3
budget 139, 142
civil society 101
compensation 375
culturally appropriate ceremonies 76
emotional and psychological support 133
enforced disappearances 149
gender equality 102
injunctions to prevent publication of reports 156
juristic person, as 308
legislation, establishment by 101
media coverage 105
memory, duty to preserve 74, 76
national days of remembrance 76
persons implicated, guarantees for 126–7
priorities 66 n.50
public hearings 105
public participation 101
recommendations, implementation of 149
reparations 149
reply, right to 126
report, expenses of 158
resources 134, 139–41
symbolic reparations 76
television, broadcasting live hearings on 157
terms of reference, definition of 117, 119, 121
transparency on funding 140
ubuntu 76
witness protection 132
South Korea 102, 109, 197
South Sudan 157
sovereign immunity 228–9, 240, 293
Soviet Union 16, 197
Spain
amnesties 266–7
Historical Memory Law 168 n.23
national courts 176, 287
National Historical Archive 200
Spanish Civil War 176
universal criminal jurisdiction 228, 238, 266
Special Court for Sierra Leone (SCSL)
amnesties 262, 264, 266, 311–12
archives 184–5
closure 224
confidentiality 132
detainees, interviewing 120
jurisdiction 220, 224
jus cogens 264
terms of reference, definition of commissions of inquiry's 120–1
Truth and Reconciliation Commission (TRC) 132
universal jurisdiction 264
special courts 224, 247, 248, 320, 330, 406–7
Special Panels of the Dili District Court (East Timor) 211, 220–1, 292
Special Tribunal for Lebanon (STL) 211, 293
Special Rapporteurs (UN)
archives 167, 177, 183, 187
drafting UN Principles, history of 10
Freedom of Opinion and Expression 362
know, right to 89, 91
non-recurrence, guarantees of 30
reform of laws and institutions 408
reparation procedures, publicizing 363
Torture and Extrajudicial, Summary or Arbitrary Executions, reports of 316
Truth, Justice, Reparation and Guarantees of Non-recurrence 10, 29–30, 51, 53, 89
archives 167, 177, 183, 187
reform of laws and institutions 408
reparations 363
right to the truth 61, 66
Srebrenica massacre 229
Sri Lanka
International Independent Group of Eminent Persons (IIGEP) 140–1
truth commissions 101, 140–1, 155
witness intimidation 140–1, 155
standing 207, 248
Stasi archives 168–9, 185–6, 190, 199–200
state immunity 228–9, 240, 293
state institutions, reform of 392–8 *see also* **reform of laws and institutions contributing to impunity**
accountability 394, 397
civil society 397–8
civilian complaint procedures 394
civilian oversight 396
culture 392, 397–8
discipline 396–7
due process 393, 395–6
employment 394
governance 394
holistic approach 395
Joinet Principles 393–4
judiciary, independent and impartial 147, 394, 396
non-recurrence, guarantees of 18, 392–8
ombudsman 396
oversight 394, 395–7
personal sphere 392, 397–8
public officials 394
removal from office 393
rule of law 393, 395
security and justice sectors 394, 395–7
training in public employees 397
vetting 392–6
state obligations, arising from human rights violations 6, 16–18, 49, 51–2

state officials
abusive officials, purging 11
immunity 303
senior officials 65, 228, 299–300, 303
training 397
universal and international jurisdiction 226, 228, 240
war crimes 65
state security *see* **national security**
statutory limitations *see* **prescription, restrictions on**
STL (Special Tribunal for Lebanon) 211, 293
Stroessner, Alfredo 165–6
Sub-Commission on Prevention of Discrimination and Protection of Minorities (UN)
amnesties 7
civil and political rights 7–8
economic, social and political rights 7–9
experts 7–8
NGOs 7
recommendations 8
reparations 11
reports 7–9
transitional justice 28–9
Sudan 300
superior orders *see* **due obedience (superior orders)**
superior responsibility
accomplices 302
accountability 295
actual or constructive knowledge 295, 296
ad hoc tribunals 293, 296, 298
Additional Protocol I to Geneva Conventions 293
aiding and abetting 293 n.10
direct liability 302
instigation 293 n.10
joint criminal enterprise 302
mens rea 302
Nuremberg Military Tribunal, Charter of 293
prevent or punish crimes, failure to 291, 295, 296
superior-subordinate relationship 295, 302
suspects *see* **persons implicated, guarantees for**
Sweden, Freedom of the Press Act of 1766 in 172
Switzerland
archives 170
Law on the Protection of Cultural Property 170
symbolism 73–4, 75–7

technology
archives 163–5, 173, 191
open source software for description 175
publicizing commission's reports 152, 158
terms of reference, definition of commissions of inquiry's 116–21
amnesties 117
confidentiality 155
conflicts of jurisdiction 116–17, 120
coordination 116–17, 120
criminal justice, alternative to 117, 120
enforced disappearances 117, 119
fair hearing, right to a 121
final reports 119
information, access to 118, 120–1
institutions 118
international corporations 119
investigations 117–21
Joinet Principles 117
judicial proceedings 116–17, 118–21
legitimacy 121
mandates 119–21
non-recurrence, guarantees of 118
overlapping mandates 116–17
Principle 6, overlap with 97
privacy 118
quasi-judicial powers 117
reputation 118
resources 119–20
self-incrimination 118, 120
transitional justice 119–21
truth commissions 117, 119–20
truth, right to the 118
victims 117–18
terrorism
Latin America 335
military courts, jurisdiction of 320, 322
September 11, 2001, attacks on United States 322
state terrorism, reparations for 335
time limits *see* **prescription, restrictions on**
Timerman, Jacobo 188
Timor-Leste *see* **East Timor**
Togo 101
Tokyo Military Tribunal 220, 293
Tomuschat, Thomas 347
torture
Committee against Torture (CAT) (UN) 342, 344, 385–6
extradite or prosecute, duty to 50
extraterritoriality 285
jus cogens 256
non-recurrence, general principles on 385–6
prescription, restrictions on 256
prosecute and punish, duty to 209
rehabilitation 376
reparations 342, 344
resources, adequacy of 138
Torture Convention 50, 208, 221, 228, 254, 261–2, 275, 376
training in human rights and humanitarian law standards 397
transformative justice 27, 33, 53
transitional justice
amnesty 307, 312
conception of transitional justice as compromise 87
definition 27, 40–1, 44
European Union 51
flexible approach 210, 215
Four- pillar conception structure of transitional justice 9, 11, 18, 30, 72
holistic approach 50, 92, 395

localizing transitional justice 20-1, 100
Preamble 30
relation to fight against impunity 20-1, 47
reparation procedures, publicizing 366
rigidity critique 21
root causes of violations, lack of focus on 21
trauma recovery 134,
tribunals *see* jurisdiction of international and internationalized criminal tribunals
Trust Fund for Victims (ICC) 211, 341, 357
truth commissions
archives 69, 84
amnesties 265
composition 98, 100–1
consultation 97–102
definition 35, 41–2, 44
delay 98, 102
economic, social and cultural rights 66
establish a commission, preliminary decision to 98
establishment 97–102
gender equality 98, 100, 102
independence and impartiality 100
independent and impartiality 88
indigenous victims, consultation with 101
Joinet Principles 98
legislation, establishment by 101
legitimacy 97, 98, 100, 102
know, right to 82, 84, 87–92
mandates 66, 87–102, 117, 186
nominations 100
objectives 104
presidential decrees, establishment by 98, 100–1
public hearings 104, 105
public participation 97–101
publicizing reports 152–9
report for children 157
resources, adequacy of 136–4
statements, taking 104
terms of reference 98, 100
title of commissions 14
witnesses and victims, guarantees for 88, 129–35
women 98, 100, 101–2
truth, inalienable right to 15–16, 59–70
ad hoc tribunals 62, 69
Additional Protocol I to Geneva Conventions 59, 63
archives 59, 61, 65, 69
codification 61
collective dimension 59–60, 65, 68–9
customary international law 59, 61–5
definitions 59–62, 70
effective mechanisms, provision of 61
enforced disappearances 60, 63–4, 66
equal protection of the laws 61, 67
exhumation work 69
fact-finding commissions 65
families 60–1, 64–8, 75, 174
family life, right to 61, 67
forgiveness 29
general principles of law 62–3
grave violations of human rights 59, 70
guarantee of right to truth 59
human rights commissions 59, 64
human rights instruments 16, 66–9
individual dimension 59–60, 65, 68–9
information, right of access to 59, 61, 64, 70
international courts 59, 65
investigate, corresponding duty to 12, 65, 67–8
Joinet Principles 60
justice, right to 61, 67–8
know, right to 59, 61, 63, 68, 70
mechanisms, establishment of 59
meta-right, as 61, 66
national courts 59, 65
normative status 64, 70
opinio juris 62–3
privacy 185–6
reconciliation 29
regional courts 67–9
regional human rights conventions 65, 67
reparations 61
Right to Truth Day (24 March 2011) 61
state-held information 59, 61
state practice 61–3
truth commissions 59, 64, 65–6
universalism 59, 54, 70
victims, rights of 65, 69
war crimes 65
Tshwane Principles 185, 186–7
Tunisia
constitution 387, 409
gender equality 102
non-recurrence, guarantees of 387
transitional justice 92
Truth and Dignity Commission 76, 102, 114
Turkey
Armenian genocide, in 175
Cypher Office records 175
fair hearing, right to a 320–1
Greek-Cypriots 68 n.56, 83
military courts, jurisdiction of 320–1
National Security Courts (NSCs) 320–1
terrorist trials 320

Uganda
amnesties 266, 312
child combatants 387, 403
Constitution, Bill of Rights in 409
Human Rights Commission 409
reform of laws and institutions 406
traditional, customary, or informal mechanisms 53
truth commission, establishment of 101
Ukraine 200
UN Basic Principles and Guidelines on the Right to a Remedy and Reparation 369–73
accountability 30
adequate, effective and prompt reparation 349
adoption 370

UN Basic Principles and Guidelines on the Right to a Remedy and Reparation (*cont.*):
coexistence with UN Principles to Combat Impunity 10
compensation 371–2
defence, as 370
equal and effective access to justice 349
experts 10
General Assembly, adoption by 336
grave breaches of human rights 340
information, access to 349
interrelated obligations 32
justice, right to 30
memory, duty to preserve 73
object and purpose 30
Preamble 26, 30, 31–2
prescription, restrictions on 252
procedure 349
publicity 363
rehabilitation 373, 377
reparations 10–11, 370–3, 378
reports 10
respect-and-ensure provisions in treaties 339
rule of law 30
standard-setting 32
state obligations 5
structure 31
victims, interests of 5, 30, 31
UN Commission on Human Rights (UNCHR)
anti-impunity agenda 19–20
drafting 1, 7, 9
endorsement of UN Principles 30–1
general obligations of states 48
Joinet Principles 27
Project on Principles on the Administration of Justice by Military Tribunals 316
rehabilitation 376
reparations 32, 376
torture 376
Vienna World Conference on Human Rights 28
UN Compensation Commission (UNCC) 364, 375
UN Human Rights Committee (UNHRC)
archives 174
asylum 278
disclosure or repentance, restrictions on the effects of 306
know, right to 83
UN Human Rights Council (HRC)
archives 183, 198
commissions of inquiry 198
know, right to 89–90
soft law 89–90
Special Rapporteur on truth, justice, reparation, and guarantees of non-repetition 51, 89
UN Manual on the Effective Prevention and Investigation of Extra- Legal, Arbitrary and Summary Executions 138
UN Office of the High Commissioner of Human Rights *see* **Office of the High Commissioner of Human Rights (OHCHR) (UN)**
UN Principles on the Prevention and Investigation of Summary Executions and those on the Investigation of Torture 138
United Nations (UN) Principles to Combat Impunity
drafting history 6–11
nature 24
preamble 26–33
structure and organization 17–18
UN Sub-Commission on Prevention of Discrimination and Protection of Minorities
Joinet Report 27–8, 31
military courts, jurisdiction of 316
reparations 32
UNCC (UN Compensation Commission) 364, 375
UNCHR *see* **UN Commission on Human Rights (UNCHR)**
UNESCO 164, 196–9
UNHRC (UN Human Rights Committee) 16, 222
United Kingdom
asylum 276–7
ECtHR 289
freedom of information 64 n.39
Inquiries Act 2005 113
military courts, right to a fair hearing in 320 n.29
war crimes 231 n.22
United States
Alien Tort Statute (ATS) 228, 341, 345
extraterritoriality 345
multinationals 345
universal jurisdiction clause 228
archives, access to 176, 178–9, 199
Bay of Pigs incident 176
CIA, access to information of 176, 178
civil rights movement 189
Claims Resolution Tribunal 364
effective remedy, right to an 345
extraordinary rendition 199
extraterritoriality 345
fair hearing, right to a 322
FBI, access to information of 178, 189
freedom of information 176, 178, 189
Greensboro, North Carolina, truth commission in 66
Guantanamo Military Commissions 317, 322
Haiti 201
Holocaust 364
ICC, Rome Statute of 265
Iraq
Ba'athist records, return of 201
invasion 197, 201
Japanese Americans, internment of 375
KKK, deaths of demonstrators against 66
leaks of military and State Department records 179

mass call-tracking programme, constitutionality of NSA's 179
military commissions 317, 322
multinationals 345
National Security Archive 199
Panama, intervention in 201
racism, reparations for institutional 335
reparations 341, 345
September 11, 2001, attacks 322
slavery, reparations for 335
terrorism 322
transitional justice 199
universal and international jurisdiction 228

universal jurisdiction
active nationality principle 230–1
amnesties 264
amnesty 264
criminal jurisdiction 226–40
crimes against humanity 229 n.13, 237, 239–40
customary international law 227, 230–1, 237–8
duty to provide for universal jurisdiction 284
European Union 237, 239
extradition 226–7, 229, 231–5, 236, 284
extraterritoriality 226–7
forced migration 239
Geneva Conventions, grave breaches of 235–6
genocide 229 n.13, 237, 239–40
immunity 226, 228–9, 240
international law 227, 237–8
international organizations 237
Joinet Principles 226–7
local agency 25
low-cost defendants 239, 240
measures for strengthening effectiveness of 226–40
nationality 230–1
passive nationality principle 230
Pinochet case 266
piracy 229 n.13, 237, 240
practice 236–9
presence of suspects on territory 226, 233, 235–8
pure or absolute jurisdiction 226, 231, 236, 238
scope 230–1, 237
senior state officials 228
sovereign immunity 228–9, 240
standards 11–12
state officials 226, 228, 240
territoriality principle 230
theoretical framework 230–6
torture 228, 237
transfer of suspects to international or internationalized tribunals 223, 229, 235–6
treaties and conventions 226–8, 231, 235–8, 240
universal criminal jurisdiction, definition of 226, 230–1
war crimes 229 n.13, 237, 239–40

Universal Declaration of Human Rights (UDHR) 29, 30, 137, 315

Uruguay
amnesties 263
enforced disappearances 104
freedom of information 184
general obligations of states 52

van Boven, Theo 10–11, 49, 247, 350, 372
Varney, Howard 139
Vattel, Emir de 231
Verbalpraxis 208–9
vetting
commissions of inquiry 33
definition 394–5
due process 395
employment, restitution of 371
equal access to public service, right of 395
institutional reform 17, 392–6
non-discrimination, principle of 395
operational factors 396
political factors 395–6
rights of those subject to process 394–5
security and justice sectors 394, 395
transitional justice 392–3, 395–6
truth commissions 33

victims and witnesses testifying on their behalf, guarantees for 129–35
ad hoc tribunals 131
anonymity 130, 133
commissions of inquiry 129–35
compulsion, powers of 130
confessions 309
confidentiality 129–30, 132–5
criminal justice 134
disclosure 129, 134–5
emotional and psychological support 133–4
freedom of information 129, 133
information, access to 132–3
Joinet Principles 130
privacy 133, 134–5
resources 132, 134
sexual violence 132
social stigma 130
temporal mandates 134
transitional justice 134
truth commissions 129–35
vulnerable witnesses 133
witness protection 131–2

victims, interests of *see* know, victims' right to; reparation procedure; reparation, rights and duties arising out of obligation to make; UN Basic Principles and Guidelines on the Right to a Remedy and Reparation; victims and witnesses, testifying on their behalf, guarantees for; women
administration of justice, duties of states with regard to 205–7, 210–12, 215
civil law jurisdictions 205, 210
common law jurisdictions 207, 210
compensation, decisions on 212
confidentiality 43
fair hearing, right to a 215

victims, interests of (*cont.*):
forgiveness 29
heard, right to be 212
international crimes 205
justice, right to 210
legal standing 207
participation 38, 30–1, 33, 85, 205–7, 210–12, 215
Preamble 30
privacy 186
soft law 210
tracing victims 88, 91
Trust Fund for Victims (ICC) 211, 341, 357
truth commissions 88, 92, 98
victim, definition of 343–4
Victims' Participation
advisory functions of truth commissions 148
design and implementation of transitional justice 92, 98
designing policies for fighting impunity 28, 30
establishment of truth commissions 99
European Union Directive 2012/29 EU 211
Institutional reform 383
international Criminal Court 9, 69, 85, 205, 206, 210, 215
Reparations Procedures 350, 353, 355, 357, 363
truth-seeking processes 129, 134, 310
Vienna World Conference on Human Rights (1993) 28
vulnerable persons, protection of 2–3, 33, 108, 112, 118, 133, 158, 159, 350, 366, 367

war crimes
amnesties 310
European Convention on the Non- Applicability of Statutory Limitations to War Crimes and Crime against Humanity 1974 (Council of Europe) 253–4
IACs 39–40
NIACs 39–40, 310
reparations 336
UN Convention on the Non- Applicability of Statutory Limitations to War Crimes and Crimes against Humanity 251, 252–3
universal and international jurisdiction 239
war, law of *see* **international humanitarian law**
Wiebelhaus-Brahm, Eric 156
Wilhelm II, German Emperor 306
witnesses *see* **victims and witnesses, testifying on their behalf, guarantees for**
interference with 152, 154
intimidation 154
privacy 186–7, 190
protection 119, 153–6, 131-2, 134, 183
reprisals 155
truth commissions 88
women
advisory functions of commissions 147–8
commissions of inquiry, irremovability of 108, 110
domestic violence 148
reparations 148
transformative justice 53–4
truth commissions, establishment of 98, 100, 101–2
World Summit Outcome 390

Yugoslavia *see* **former Yugoslavia; International Criminal Tribunal for the former Yugoslavia (ICTY)**

Zahar, Alexander 301
Zimbabwe 156